Debating
Archaeology

Debating
Archaeology

Lewis R. Binford

Department of Anthropology
University of New Mexico
Albuquerque, New Mexico

ACADEMIC PRESS, INC.
Harcourt Brace Jovanovich, Publishers
San Diego   New York   Berkeley   Boston
London   Sydney   Tokyo   Toronto

ACADEMIC PRESS, INC.
San Diego, California 92101

United Kingdom Edition published by
ACADEMIC PRESS LIMITED
24-28 Oval Road, London NW1 7DX

Library of Congress Cataloging-in-Publication Data

Binford, Lewis Roberts, Date
  Debating archaeology.

  1. Archaeology. I. Title.
CC173.B56 1989   930.1   88-8098
ISBN 0-12-100045-1 (alk. paper)

PRINTED IN THE UNITED STATES OF AMERICA
89 90 91 92   9 8 7 6 5 4 3 2 1

Contents

I. Introduction

II. Much Ado About Nothing

III. Empiricism and Other Problems in Contemporary Archaeology

IV. Models and Accommodating Arguments versus Pattern Recognition: What Drives Research Best?

List of Figures

List of Tables

Acknowledgments

This book is a product of my recent research investments, which in turn reflect both my long-term research interests and the ongoing intellectual developments within archaeology. As such, I strongly acknowledge the contributions of my colleagues and debate partners who are active participants in contemporary archaeology.

The issues of the 1960s revolved around the accuracy and utility of the interpretive principles to which traditional archaeologists appealed when giving meaning to archaeological observations. The debates of the 1970s shifted to the issue of how we put in place useful and accurate knowledge to serve the important task of inference from archaeological observations to past dynamics. The 1980s have seen the growth of skepticism with regard to our ability to learn and/or use our experience either as an arbiter for the accuracy and utility of our ideas or as a source of knowledge and inspiration for new ideas about how the world works. Debate has been hard and heavy on all these issues, yet the growing skeptical and reactionary literature has certainly had a dampening effect on the growth of knowledge within archaeological science in general. There are several very bright spots, however—particularly Paleolithic studies and large archaeological landscape studies—where our science is quite healthy. In addition, the rapid growth of evolutionary biology and biological anthropology is certain to impact our literature in the next decade in a most constructive manner. Archaeologists have tended to steer clear of such major issues as evolution and the principles of community ecology as germane to their views as to how the world works. I suspect that this reluctance will be overcome in the next decade. In the meantime, I strongly acknowledge all the intellectual "players" who introduce the issues and argue their positions, and in so doing enhance the intellectual content of our field.

As the intensity of debate grows in any field, so does the content for those students seeking to know and understand the field in which they seek to be contributors. Similarly, the problem of how to make contributions certainly appears more confused when intellectual activity is high and publication rates are rapid. I am primarily a teacher, one who seeks to guide the brave student into a disputatious field of great diversity and enormous breadth. The student's dedication to learning continually forces the teacher to re-evaluate postures, positions, paradigms, arguments, and, importantly, debates. It is to these dedicated learners that my most heartfelt acknowledgments are given. In fact, the very issue of addressing debate directly, as I have attempted in this book, was a consequence of students seeking to learn how to evaluate arguments when their knowledge bases were admittedly less "deep" than those of many of the authors whose works they were regularly assigned in class.

If one accepts that the task of science is the evaluation of our ideas about the world (our culture), then teachers who misguide students into thinking that our contemporary ideas are "true," accurate, and adequate are simply not doing their job. Students get their earliest opportunities to evaluate our ideas in the record of our debates—the literature. Unfortunately, there have been few guides to this activity; most teachers treat students as potential converts to their particular beliefs about our field. I offer no acknowledgment to such teachers, because they distort the purpose of science and render the students partisans of the self-satisfied, uninquisitive intellectual "ethnic groups" that still persist within archaeology.

At a more proximate level I acknowledge with great joy the collaborators who appear as joint authors, as well as those who aided the research reported here. Particularly important is James O'Connell, with whom I shared extraordinary experiences in Australia and to whom I continually turn for good ideas, thoughtful considerations of argument, and stimulating observations on the world. Nancy Stone has made my life richer in many ways. I first knew her as an extraordinary student, later as a friend, now as my wife. During this progression she engaged our field with great enthusiasm and now enriches my life as a stimulating colleague as well. Guz and Margie Mills are extraordinary people and scientists whom I first met in the Kalahari in 1981. Since then they have been keenly interested in how archaeologists use knowledge from the study of wildlife to unravel the past. The work on hyenas reported here was made possible by their interest in our field and by their willingness to let us into their research world with our particular research concerns. I have learned much from Guz and look forward to future collaborative efforts.

During much of the time that these articles were written Jeremy Sabloff and I were team-teaching beginning graduate students at the University of New Mexico. Jeremy was a constant source of knowledge, showing dedication to students and thoughtful concern for issues. Jeremy once pointed out to me that even archaeologists who were not empiricists frequently debated as though they were! It was this observation that later served as a basis for the organization of this book. For our years together I am most grateful.

My department and college at the University of New Mexico have supported my efforts both in research and in teaching and have graciously provided me with a full-time research assistant. June-el Piper is that assistant. She has changed my life both as a teacher and as a researcher. She has invested long hours in the preparation of the materials published here; her skills as an editor, organizer, and logical reader of literature are certain to be recognized by the readers of this book. June-el is a new kind of colleague for me, and one that has truly enriched my professional life and its products.

It is time to make an important point. A casual glance at the frequency of citations and at the arguments presented here may not make it easy to infer the strength of friendships. I consider F. Clark Howell, Mike Schiffer, James Sackett, and Les Freeman to be personal friends of long standing. Clearly we have our intellectual disagreements, as the reader will discover, yet all are dedicated and important "players" in our exciting field. I respect these authors and do not consider our debates to be ad hominem statements in any way; all are valued friends and colleagues.

In looking backward, there has been one teacher who has continually inspired me and enriched me with his sound thought, reasoning, and perspective. This most valuable teacher is Albert C. Spaulding. Others have certainly been important, but in the context of the subject matter of this book Spaulding stands out as an intellectual rock of constructive thought and keen insight.

I cannot thank you too much, Albert.

Part I

Introduction

Chapter 1

"Culture" and Social Roles in Archaeology

Long ago Albert Spaulding observed, correctly in my opinion, that the science of archaeology could be properly described in terms of (a) its subject matter and (b) the dimensions in terms of which this subject matter is studied (Spaulding 1960). The subject matter that we as archaeological scientists study is simply artifacts. We observe all of those modifications of natural materials and, secondarily, of artifacts themselves that humans and hominids produce as a result of their lifeways. We do not study human behavior, as Schiffer advocates, we do not study symbolic codes (cf. Hodder, Patrik), we do not study social systems (cf. Redman), we do not study ancient cultures, we do not study ancient settlements, nor do we study the past. We study artifacts.

In addition, archaeologists study artifacts with respect to three broad dimensions: form, space, and the inferred dimension of time. Any arguments that we might make about the past in any form—for instance, this was an ancient camping place, ancient peoples were hunters and gatherers, these ancients were organized into egalitarian societies, the producers of the artifacts had certain religious beliefs—are all inferences made from our study of artifacts. This means quite directly that all statements we make about the past as a result of our archaeological endeavors are only as good as the justifications we offer for the inferences that we make. The single most important aspect of any approach to the past through the study of artifacts attributed to the past concerns the methods of inference justification used by the archaeologist so bold as to make assertive statements about the past from the study of artifacts here in the present.

A survey of the contemporary discipline of archaeology reveals a bewildering array of individuals who call themselves archaeologists yet in many cases neglect the most important aspect of the challenge of being one, that is, the development of reliable means for inference justification. There are the advocates of contextual archaeology, behavioral archaeology, social archaeology, Marxist archaeology, historical archaeology, demographic archaeology, Southwest archaeology, Paleolithic archaeology, nationalist archaeology, humanist archaeology, classical archaeology, and realist archaeology. Many of these labels betray the kinds of pasts that have been targeted as desirable to explore through archaeological endeavor. Since we cannot address the entire past, we carve up what we would like to know about in different ways, which is, of course, perfectly legitimate.

There are other ways in which the advocates of different kinds of archaeology seek to partition our challenge. These are in terms of (a) what they think is most important to know about, given their contemporary values and their cultural as well as scientific biases, and more important, (b) how to go about the difficult job of inferring any kind of past. In the latter case the divisions represent differing views on how to do archaeology and how to justify statements about the past through the use of contemporary inferential tools. In the former we enter the domain of contemporary values and are strictly speaking not talking about archaeology at all. Instead, we are identifying the intellectual products of archaeologists as either "good" or "bad" postures, depending upon the critic's values and the popularity of such postures with other archaeological writers.

In the contemporary era there is much confusion in the archaeological literature as many authors shift back and forth among these very different concerns, apparently assuming that there is some regular and self-evident relationship among the different domains that they address. For instance, it is not uncommon to hear the following argument: (1) I believe that symbolic codes are the fundamental explanatory phenomena underlying the meanings we should be giving to archaeological observations on artifacts. (2) I believe that those who do not agree with me are wrong. (3) Those who disagree with me ignore symbolic codes. (4) This proves that their approaches are worthless. Such an argument is, of course, nonsense. One is only led to such a conclusion if one is operating as an ideologue and not as a scientist.

Another common argument of this type is sometimes found in the feminist literature and takes the following form: (1) Understanding gender relationships is fundamental to understanding past social systems. (2) Examination of the archaeological literature reveals that archaeologists either have not addressed this important issue or, when gender is discussed, have dealt with it in terms of the "common knowledge" biases of the author. The conclusion is that we are all culture-bound, and it is suggested that the only way to overcome this situation is to become "self aware."

Once again, this is nonsense. If the goal of a science is to know something about the past that is dependent upon inference, then one must develop a reliable methodology that permits reliable inferences to the phenomena of interest. In the absence of such methodology, the only possible treatment of the subject of interest will be in terms of unevaluated "common knowledge" or ideas about the subject available to any writer.

How do we put into place a reliable inferential procedure for learning? It is not a matter of "clearing one's mind of cultural biases," as Sir Francis Bacon suggested more than 300 years ago. And responding to the exhortations to seek "awareness" only results in the trivial replacement in our prose of offensive words ("mankind") with neutral ones ("humankind") but not necessarily with any growth in knowledge. Similarly, the substitution of one set of cultural biases, those being criticized, for another, those being advocated, does not lead to learning. At best our contemporary culture is updated; at worst it is totally misguided, and hindsight, a perspective only accessible to the next generation, becomes the only arbiter. This is negligence, not epistemology.

Clearly, I have criticized two points of view in the examples above. Have I also criticized two persons, two debate participants? The answer must, I think, be yes. Were these personal attacks or were they arguments of the kind that logicians term *ad hominem*? By asking this question I introduce another major source of confusion and perplexity for the inexperienced reader of archaeological literature. Any serious student probably knows something about logic and knows that *ad hominem* argument means literally "argument against the man." These can take the form of insinuations or allegations of bad character or low intelligence in the author of any argument (to cite only two common tactics) and are followed by the recommendation that the argument of such a person should obviously be dismissed. Logicians and those who observe logical conventions reject as invalid an approach that focuses on personal characteristics of the argument maker rather than on any reasoned criticism of the properties of the argument itself.

If, however, the construction of an argument is a personal activity, and if one points out what are considered to be deficiencies in the construction of the argument, is this not also a comment on the skill and thoughtfulness of the author of the argument? It is certainly likely to be perceived as such by the person whose argument is being criticized. Is this, however, an *ad hominem* argument? The answer must be a resounding no. It is a critical assessment of flaws in an argument that the author may or may not interpret as a commentary on his or her skills and scholarship. The ego sensitivity and perception of the criticized persons do not in any way determine whether the debate has any *ad hominem* properties whatsoever.

Frequently the sensitive subject of criticism responds by accusing the critic of *ad hominem* argument, clearly suggesting that the critic's views should be dismissed since they violate rules of logic and, by implication, scientific ethics. Ironically, this classic form of *ad hominem* argument becomes a major debate tactic by the very person who claims that it is unacceptable. No wonder the discussion of issues in the archaeological literature is confusing to students. What I hope to show as we review several contemporary controversies is that even this ironic response is intellectually conditioned and is not simply a character flaw in those who use such tactics.

A TAXONOMY OF ARCHAEOLOGISTS

As I suggested, there is a strange, mushy mixing in the contemporary literature of (a) interest preferences, (b) subject performances, and (c) the crucial issue of inference justification. The mushiness is attributable to the debate that centers on how we learn and how we evaluate ideas, and the themes and postures associated with this issue will be outlined for the reader of the debate literature in the following epistemological field guide and intellectual species list. For instance, there is the Yippie, who is responsible for what I call Yippie archaeology, which is, of course, inseparable from its ideological underpinnings. Fundamental to Yippie archaeology is the assumption previously alluded to that disciplinary progress results from awareness, from self-examination, from the adoption of a heavily value-laden, humanistic approach to improving ourselves. It is therefore somewhat surprising that, in their less humanistic moments, Yippies indulge in name calling: non-Yippie archaeologists are intellectual imperialists, knowledge colonialists, chauvinistic dehumanizers of mankind. These claims are generally made in the context of rejecting science. Scientists are said to make "absolutist" knowledge claims that are then imperialistically imposed on other eras, peoples, places, genders, and persuasions. Scientists are called dupes of the establishment, which is a windmill constructed during their 1960s past with which Yippies are still tilting. Of course, they are unaware that they might be guilty of blindness to their own particular ideological commitment, and they demonstrate by their own behavior that they are not free, aware, outside observers capable of direct perception of truth.

Archaeological Yippies depend exclusively upon the strict empiricist assumptions of Baconian science, except in one respect: self-evident truth is not revealed through an examination of the external world. Instead, the Freudian approach of introverted self-examination is adopted. We look within ourselves individually or collectively, and if the questions we ask ourselves about the past are good ones, then we will simply know the appropriate meaning to be given to archaeological phenomena.

Religions are philosophies that consider their fundamental assumptions to be intrinsically true and therefore beyond debate, and all argument is of necessity absolutist in character. We are right, say the believers, and thus the rules of logic and reason are suspended and conversion to the "true" way is the only alternative. Discussion presented from such a perspective frequently adopts any argument that supports one's belief. Arguments from authority predominate, although these arguments themselves remain unevaluated as to accuracy, logical validity, or even relevance to the context into which they are inserted. Archaeological issues are presented in these terms in much of the contemporary Yippie literature.

A contemporary and sympatric species, although only distantly related to Yippie archaeologists, are the Yuppies, those gadget-oriented, technologically dependent experts who look to instrumentation of all kinds as the way to advance archaeological knowledge and understanding. As in the case of the Yippies, I agree with some of their interests and concerns. Nevertheless I disagree on the fundamental question of how we learn. Like many practicing traditional archaeologists, Yuppies are examples of that intellectual dinosaur, the true empiricist. They share the Yippie's fundamental belief in self-evident truth, although they differ over where and how to look for it. The Yippie looks inside himself, the Yuppie looks into a microscope, at a report of a specialist, through an EDM (electronic distance measuring device), or at a class of things not previously examined. The annual meetings of archaeological societies are increasingly dominated by Yuppie symposia with such titles as zooarchaeology, microwear studies, reduction sequences, ceramic technology, phytoliths and man, fish remains and culture, palynology and context, debitage and progress, chi-squares I have known and loved, a *K*-means analysis and nonconclusions, using LSA (LANDSAT aids) for PM (predictive modeling) in CRM studies on BM (Black Mesa), and the SEM (scanning electron microscope) and hominid evolution. If there are stylistic markers, isochrestic perhaps, of the Yuppie versus the Yippie, it is the Yuppie's use of acronyms for everything and the Yippie's endless citations to philosophical literature that most readers mistakenly interpret as a knowledge of that literature's contents.

Yuppies do not normally engage in fundamental debate regarding how to gain knowledge of the past. For them it is simple: we look hard at the world, we look at as many different things as we can think of, in as many different ways as we can imagine, and what we see is truth as a function of the sophistication of our aids to observation.

The greater the variety of such formal aids, the more truth we will see. There have been many Yuppie arguments in the recent literature: the SEM as the only true way of seeing cutmarks; the chi-square as the only true way of recognizing patterning; micro-wear (as evaluated at a stated microscopic power) as the only true way to recognize function, to cite only a few examples.

Because of Yuppies' commitment to strict empiricism, they have rough, competitive lives. A successful Yuppie is one who is the first to use a new device, an SEM, for instance, and then make the claim that he can see truth denied to others not using such equipment. For a while, the Yuppie rides high with his monopoly on truth. But, alas, soon other empiricists gain access to such equipment and they frequently see Different Things! Different Truth! But how can this be, since the empiricist believes that there is only one truth and it can be known directly? The problem must therefore arise from the inability of the observer to see what the successful Yuppie has seen. The observer must be stupid, sloppy, blind, untruthful, misguided, using old equipment, or self-serving. Thus, as in case of the Yippie, we return by a very different route to essentially the same epistemological position: truth is established by the personal credentials of the claimant. The Yippie asks: does the claimant have acceptable moral, ethical, and political views? For the Yuppie, debate descends to a less abstract level at which one must defend one's own position by slandering those who have different views: they see a different "truth" only because they are deficient in character, intel-ligence, honesty, and so on.

There is another group of archaeologists called Guppies. Guppies are either older than the mean age of contributors to the literature of contemporary debate or they are Canadian. Elder Guppies were frequently the renaissance men and women of their time, since none of the Yuppie specialties proliferating today were developed when Guppies began their careers. Like the Yuppies, however, they were and are strict empiricists. They write books in which the word "evidence" is featured prominently in the title. Unlike their role for Yuppies, technical aids are adjuncts to the pursuit of the archaeologist's quintessential goal—knowing the material. Technical aids may be useful, but there is no substitute for having seen the artifacts, dug up the artifacts, gotten to know the material. In short, a Guppie is an empiricist, but the credentials for Guppie knowledge claims are not, like the Yuppie's, based on the sophistication of the equipment one uses. Instead, the Guppie claims that he knows truth directly because he has spent more time with the data and has seen more of or worked more diligently with the data than others. Like the species that they resemble, Guppies have enormous appetites and are prodigious data consumers. No one could possibly see a different reality unless perhaps he can claim to have seen more artifacts, logged more field time, or spent longer periods of time in intimate association with the artifacts. If alternative views are proposed by other researchers, it is not because they are stupid, dishonest, or manipulative persons. Their error simply lies in their inexperience. Male Guppies see themselves as gentlemen. Opposing views come from upstarts who speak out of turn in a world of truth judged by virtue of "time in grade."

The professional life of the Guppie is more dignified than that of the Yuppie. The Yuppie seeks a monopoly on a way of looking at the world, but the accelerated pace and accessibility of technological change makes preeminence difficult to maintain.

The Guppie gains a monopoly on empirically justified truth by accumulating a greater quantity of observations, normally with the naked eye, which is an instrument that is unlikely to become passé. A Guppie's credentials include numbers of filled-up passports, years of fieldwork, and particularly, years of dedication to a specific region or time period. Given the generational reality in archaeology, this kind of monopoly is rarely challenged during one's career.

As one might imagine, such an advantage over the Yuppie strategy is clearly recognized by some promising students; hence we have another class of archaeologist, the Puppies. Puppies are aspiring Guppies whose claim for credibility as a young person is their association with and support from an acknowledged Guppie. Puppies are assured an audience for their views because of their privileged access to and support from an acknowledged Guppie.

Guppies can defend their monopolies much more successfully than can Yuppies. They create networks to ensure that unwanted challengers are denied access to the all-important data, which for the Guppie is the means to Guppie status. When at last Guppies retire in glory to contemplate their "Golden Marshalltown awards," they are replaced by their Puppies rather than by thoughtful challengers, since succession is determined by the Puppie's access to "the evidence" controlled by a skillful Guppie.

Like the other fauna thus far discussed in this field guide, there is a manner of discourse distinctive to the Guppie. I have already mentioned that the Guppie is a gentleman or gentlewoman. Challengers or those who offer new or different ideas are "taken seriously," although they are dismissed in other ways. Their failure to cite an obscure reference, or their lack of familiarity with the data, or their less than journeyman investment of energy in the relevant region or time period is certain to be pointed out. Discretion is advised because the challenger or innovator is not a Guppie, although perhaps there is some Guppie potential, but for now the Guppie's judgment must prevail, and the ideas of the non-Guppie should be viewed as evidence of youthful enthusiasm. Puppies, however, should be taken seriously because they are Guppie protegees, and Guppies frequently use their Puppies in debate with colleagues. This is a subtle form of insult.

Guppies are susceptible to a disease inherent in all empiricist approaches, the tendency to deceive oneself. The true Guppie is a strict empiricist who believes in self-evident truth. Similarly, the true Guppie believes that the Guppie Way is the only valid procedure or reliable set of tactics that result in the ability to see nature truly. Guppies can frequently be heard bewailing the "theoretical," the "speculative," the "provocative," the "philosophical" discussions of non-Guppies. They deny any such unfounded nonsense in their own thought since they reason only "from the evidence." Because they have invested heavily in the process of acquiring the evidence, their ideas of the past must be untouched by theory, speculation, and all the other tainted intellectual shortcuts employed by the disadvantaged as compensation for their inability to follow the Guppie Way. Herein lies their self-deceit. There is, in fact, an antidote. Guppies need take seriously the non-Guppie-generated debates in archaeology, since most such debates at least acknowledge the role that our own ideas play in conditioning the conclusions we draw from experience. In fact, most controversies involve attacks on strict empiricism and come from many different species in our archaeological bestiary.

The Guppie, like the Yippie, Yuppie, and particularly the Puppie, ultimately relies on arguments that are *ad hominem* in character, although the form of such argument varies with each of these empiricist subspecies. Yippies use moral, ethical, and political criteria, whereas Yuppies commonly are more personal and attack the character, reliability, and honesty of their adversaries. The Guppie dismisses adversaries by weighing the "time and investment" criteria relative to the Guppie Way. Puppies, however, are more eclectic in their choice of *ad hominem* argument. After all, their perspective is constantly being upgraded by the addition of new data. These are interfertile subspecies, and one can sometimes find hybrids.

There are other species in our midst. Distantly related to the Yuppies and the Puppies, the Lollies are a suite of subspecies that share the ancestral trait of hyper-ambitiousness. They deviate significantly, however, from Guppies, who deny the role that their own ideas play in structuring their conclusions. Carefree Lollies deny that the problem of epistemology and method has any relevance whatsoever to what they do as archaeologists, while at the same time boasting of the importance of their ideas to their conclusions. Lollies are the "model fitters and builders," the voices who claim that the albatross around archaeologists' necks is methodology and a concern with epistemology. The Lollie is musically oriented. His methodological prescription for archaeologists is derived from an old partytime song: "Hey Lollie, lollie, lollie/Hey lollie, lollie-oh." This lighthearted refrain instructs us how to proceed: we are to make up the words as we go along. The winning Lollie, then, is the one who makes up the best words to accommodate the most widely known and appreciated human situations. In archaeology these are frequently identified as the origins of the state, the origins of agriculture, the appearance of stratification, the appearance of sedentism, the peopling of the New World, the appearance of trade—human situations about which any party-goer is likely to have some familiarity. The successful Lollie is one who is able to fit his new words in a clever way to as much previously appreciated experience as possible. An unsuccessful Lollie is one who requires that you appreciate his song by denying previously shared and accepted "knowledge." This means that in the absence of methodology such a Lollie has to sing many songs at different scales and with respect to many different domains of previous observation to keep the party going long enough to get to the really big rendition. Given the "make up the words as you go along" procedure, the preliminary songs rarely hang together and the final rendition frequently falls on its face.

The fate of the overly ambitious Lollie is really no big loss to archaeology. The skillful Lollie, however, may be charming, even convincing some that he offers to the field more than just fun at a party. Eating *R*-selected species may be taken as a serious replacement for other lyrics involving diet breadth, package size, and other concepts developed in the thoughtful context of ecological studies. Songs that tell of great redistributive agents and impressive chiefs in Chaco Canyon can serve as the basis for convening still other parties at our national meetings.

This intellectual safari is meant to be fun, so don't take it too seriously. It is my own Jollie approach to the introduction of a few examples of the species that participate in archaeological debates. If my little excursion into Jollie-ism has been successful, it is only because I allude to a descriptive taxonomy that is widely recognized within the field. My Jollie-esque generalizations are one way of encouraging the reader to realize that the participants in archaeological debates are comparable to different species, only on an intellectual plane. The reader of debates in archaeology, like spectators at any other scientific combat, must become skilled in recognizing different types of archaeologists and must become knowledgeable with regard to their intellectual clades and phylogenetic interrelationships. Each different species takes certain forms of behavior for granted, has different values, and frequently makes very different ontological assumptions about the world. The reader of debates needs to appreciate such things.

CURRENT DEBATES IN THE LITERATURE

I have long been associated with what critics have called the "new archaeology" of the 1960s. This was a label given to us, and not advocated by us, during the days of debate, primarily in American archaeology, over the degree to which the methods commonly in use by archaeologists at the time could in fact lead to a realistic accomplishment of their goals. The issues were epistemological: fundamentally, how do we have confidence in or render secure the inferences and descriptions of the past offered by virtue of our study of artifacts? This question unites all archaeology, regardless of what one might think is appropriate to know about the past or what regional or temporal segments of the past one addresses.

There was a past. It had properties unto itself. The goals of science are to understand the external world in terms of itself. An archaeological scientist must accept the challenge to understand the past in its own terms. If we can suspect that the past was different from the present, then it should be obvious that we cannot simply project in any simple form our knowledge of the present onto the past. When we do this, we prevent the past from being known in its own terms! At the same time, our complete dependence upon prior knowledge ensures that we do not recognize or even acknowledge phenomena about which we know nothing. The intellectual tightrope that archaeologists must dextrously walk requires that we use our knowledge, knowledge available in the contemporary world, in such a way as to expose new knowledge about pasts previously unknown. At the end of this tightrope is the demand that we work accurately so that the past is described in its own terms. We seek to know a past in terms that do not distort its own characteristics, yet we must accomplish this in our terms, through the use of our available knowledge. Given such challenges, it is not surprising that there are many "points of view" and many approaches. Is each view equally valid and worth investigating simply because the variants represent cultural variety in the contemporary world? I think the answer must be no. The serious archaeologist must accept the intellectual challenge to address the epistemological and methodological problems we all face in our attempts to gain knowledge of the past. We must evaluate and criticize our own work, as well as the proposals of our colleagues of different persuasions, in order to know how we might proceed and what are realistic goals toward which our research efforts should be aimed. An active, serious, and progressive scientific discipline is by nature disputatious.

From the perspective of the serious student who faces the mounds of literature currently available in archaeology, it might appear that in terms of the "disputatious" criterion archaeology is an "active, serious, and progressive" discipline. Would such a judgment be accurate? I would have to say that perhaps the literature is misleading on this score. Much of the disputatious character of the literature arises from the bruised egos of participants and not from substantive discussion of the issues in the field. In fact, in many of the more visible disputes, one or more participants may be unaware of or deny the validity of the issues upon which their adversaries base their challenge. This situation results in many assertions and rebuttals but no clarification of the argument, much less progress toward its resolution. From time to time a Yippie-like article will appear (sometimes written by a Guppie) pointing out that archaeologists are endlessly calling one another "slimy green frogs" and that such childish behavior is inappropriate in a serious discipline. Nevertheless it continues. Why? Is this a reflection of the character of archaeologists?

I will adopt a non-Yippie position and try to argue throughout this book that such behavior is the only logical outcome of the initial, and to my mind inappropriate, epistemological position of most practicing archaeologists. The species that I have poked fun at share an uncritical acceptance of empiricist principles, and at the same time they behave in ways that contradict those principles. I have been selective in my choice of debates in which to participate, areas of research interest to use as a debate arena, and levels of detail at which I should become involved. These choices have directly influenced my judgments about where and how to criticize what I consider to be intellectual straightjackets that divert productive archaeological investigations and interfere with recognition of important domains in need of serious attention. I will argue that Albert Spaulding's description of archaeology with which I began this introduction is appropriate and, as such, has far-reaching implications for archaeological research and intellectual speciation.

Chapter 2

The New Archaeology, Then and Now

A review of the arguments and developments that characterized American archaeology during the late 1950s and early 1960s shows that several basic positions were being advocated, and, as a result, subsequent archaeological work has pursued several different directions. Central to the arguments advanced by so-called new archaeologists in America was the issue of *how to accurately give meaning* to archaeological observations. This concern, at least during the 1960s, was embedded within arguments that addressed how archaeologists had traditionally given meaning to the archaeological record. The early years of this discussion, which opponents called the "new archaeology" (generally said with scathing sarcasm), were characterized by attempts to evaluate the validity or accuracy of the propositions that had guided the interpretation of (and the assignment of meaning to) archaeological remains by the leading archaeologists who had been our teachers. The ideas that the new archaeologists criticized might be thought of as basic aspects of the culture-history view of culture, which dominated the writings of archaeologists during the 1930s, 1940s, and 1950s.

Culture history is first and foremost an idealistic approach to understanding. By *idealism* I mean "any system or doctrine whose fundamental interpretative principle is ideal" (Runes 1979:136–137). Most anthropologists and archaeologists were not mentalists, in that they acknowledged a reality (e.g., historical or environmental) outside of their own minds, but they were idealists in the sense that culture was considered to be a product of the workings of individual minds as those individuals reacted to the events of cultural and natural history. If any order in culture history could be demonstrated or any predictive knowledge could be gained about culture, it was thought that a greater understanding of individual psychology was the key.

> It is not possible to predict the behavior resulting from historical events that made the people what they are. The problem is essentially a psychological one and beset with all the difficulties inherent in the investigation of complex mental phenomena of the lives of individuals. (Boas 1938:5–6)

At the same time that culture was seen as being understandable in idealistic terms there was a tendency to distrust the methods of the natural sciences as they had been

To appear in *Aspects of Method and Theory in American Archaeology,* edited by C. C. Lamberg-Karlovsky and P. L. Kohl, published by Cambridge University Press, Cambridge, in press.

developed by the end of the nineteenth century. Part of this distrust lay in the reaction against "analogies," or the selective study of similarities (in modern parlance, the use of etic categories). This Boasian shaping of American anthropology and its subfield, archaeology, has been summarized as follows:

> The second issue on which historians and physicists differed was the legitimacy of the study of phenomena having "a merely subjective" as opposed to an "objective" unity. Physicists would grant the legitimacy of certain types of historical studies. But even here, the physicist does not study "the whole phenomenon" as it represents itself to the human mind, but resolves it into its elements, which he investigates separately; and insofar as he was interested in the history of these elements, it was in order to create a "systematical arrangement" whose order was "objective." On the other hand, the historian insisted on equal scientific validity of the study of more complex phenomena whose elements "seem to be connected only in the mind of the observer"; and in studying them, he was interested not in elements but in the "whole phenomenon." (Stocking 1974:10)

Searching for similarities—analogies, as they were commonly labeled—violated an important tenet of the idealistic philosophy with which Boas-influenced culture historians worked. Things that to us appear to be similar may have been dissimilar by virtue of the idealistic integration achieved for those phenomena in the minds of the ancients. Understanding this integration was viewed as the only correct way to understand varying cultural responses to environmental and historical stimuli. One had to uncover the underlying cultural context that conditioned the way past individuals reacted to external events and stimuli.

In such an environment of thought, archaeology was in a very paradoxical position. The materials remaining from the past were seen as the only sources of potential knowledge about the past, yet the causes of those remains, the way the world had worked, was a knowledge inaccessible to the archaeologist using only those material remains. Past dynamics were seen as the consequences of unique interactions achieved in ancient holistic cultural contexts operating in conjunction with the "laws of the human mind," which together conditioned how individuals reacted to events in their social and natural environments. Since the causes were said to be idealistic, the archaeologist saw only material by-products as they had been structured by ancient idealistic forces. Because no further understanding seemed possible, archaeologists did not search for theories to explicate the actual workings of those dynamics. There was no way to anticipate relationships between the character of the alleged causes and the character of material remains that might have been idealistically structured in the past. There was no apparent way to recover the intellectual contexts or to formulate laws of the human mind, since it was essentially denied that these "variables" would condition in regular ways properties of artifacts and other material remains archaeologists might find. Archaeologists operated with a theory that basically claimed its irrelevance to the things that archaeologists studied!

> An archaeologist may recover material but not the substance of aboriginal artifacts. The exact meanings of any particular object for the living group or individual is forever lost, and the real significance or lack of importance of any object in an

ethnological sense has disappeared by the time it becomes a part of an archaeologist's catalogue of finds. (Griffin 1943:340)

Traditional archaeology could not address itself to the testing of theory, since relevant
information on assumed seats of causation was not preserved. In addition, the results
of the operation of causal forces could only be described and systematized but could
not be investigated, since there were thought to be no regular relationships between
similar material things and the meanings—the cultural contexts—in terms of which
they were integrated in the minds of past humans. The paradox of adopting a strict
empiricist's view of science while at the same time adopting an idealist's theory of
causation, where the "black box"—the minds of the ancients—was not available for
investigation, placed archaeology in a strange position indeed.

Strict empiricism argued against inference and interpretation, yet the past was gone
and could only be known through inference from the remnants surviving in the
present. The position adopted by traditional archaeologists publicly assumed that
similarities did not necessarily imply similar causal conditions. Inference was therefore only justifiable when continuity and stability could be assumed between the past
and the present. Under these conditions, the modern contexts could be used to guide
interpretation. Such beliefs by the archaeologists left the remote past, for which no
"historical" connection could be demonstrated between the archaeological remains
and contemporary peoples, seemingly beyond the pale of archaeological illumination.
Nevertheless, archaeologists studying the remote past did offer inferences and interpretations. When they did so they appealed to "the other half" of the traditionalist's
view of cultural causality—the concept of human nature as elaborated by an assumed
understanding of "culture" viewed as a unique by-product of that underlying human
nature. This particular approach to archaeological interpretation was suspected by the
new archaeologists as being a sterile and misleading convention.

First and foremost, traditional archaeologists sidestepped the problems of inference
by adopting a set of conventions for assigning meanings to their data. They committed
what in any science would be considered a basic error: they stipulated the meaning to
be given to generalizations made from their data. They did not seek to know the world
in its terms; they assumed they knew what the world of culture was like, and they
proceeded to order the world of archaeological experience in these a priori terms. In
a productive science the aim is to learn something of the limitations and inadequacies
of one's received knowledge. The tactics of traditional archaeology prevented the
archaeologists from availing themselves of this possibility.

Perhaps the most explicit and understandable exposition of the strategy of traditional archaeology has been given by Robert Dunnell (1971). He provides one of the
best discussions that I have been able to find of what traditional archaeologists did and
also what they thought they were doing. Dunnell correctly suggests that a very simple
argument permitted traditional archaeologists to link their observations of phenomena (their data) to the a priori ideas they held about that data.

The field is that encompassed by the concept *artifact,* objects which owe some of
their attributes to human activity. The problem similarly is to provide categories for
these data that are cultural, for the ultimate purpose of explaining the products of

> human behavior and with them the behavior that created them in terms of ideas
> held in common by the makers and users. (Dunnell 1971:130)

At the root of this argument is the idealistic assumption that the causes of the archaeological record, and any derivative information obtained therefrom, were the ideas
held in the minds of past people.

> Prehistory assumes that attributes which are the products of human activity and
> which recur over a series of artifacts . . . can be treated as manifestations of ideas
> held in common by makers and users of those artifacts. (Dunnell 1971:132)

In other words, traditional archaeologists forged an analytical linkage, by stipulation,
between the generalizations archaeologists might make from their data, commonly
called patterns, and the alleged causes, the shared ideas held by past peoples.

> If the attributes considered are only those which are the products of human
> endeavor, it follows that any explanation of these attributes is necessarily done in
> human rather than natural terms. If their distinctiveness lies in their humanness,
> then so does their explanation. Further, given our assumptions about the unique-
> ness of the phenomenological world, recurrence or sharing necessitates an idea-
> tional element in the explanation. (Dunnell 1971:133)

> If several objects hold features in common, and those features are of human origin,
> there is but a single plausible account. Intentionally or unintentionally, consciously
> or unconsciously, the objects were made to look alike by people who can be
> treated as possessing similar ideas about them and who have the same categories
> of features and ways of articulating the features into whole artifacts. In short, the
> objects can be treated as expressions of the same mental template. (Dunnell
> 1971:132)

> The definition of culture not only stipulates the element of human involvement
> (ideas) but restricts this general field to that set of ideas which can be assumed to
> be shared. This is a most crucial point, for it is here that the articulation of
> phenomena with concepts is made. This connection necessarily must be made by
> means of assumptions. . . . Prehistory assumes that attributes which are the prod-
> ucts of human activity and which recur over a series of artifacts . . . can be treated
> as manifestations of ideas held in common by makers and users of those artifacts.
> Thus the link is made between the phenomenological and the ideational. (Dunnell
> 1971:133)

In fact, the archaeologists were not linking the archaeological record with the *ancients'* ideational milieu but with *their own*. In addition, this link between the phenomenological (the world of experience) and the ideational (the ideas about that
world) was made, as Dunnell noted, by assumption. The world of experience was
assimilated directly with the archaeologists' prior beliefs about the world, and thus
experience could never be used to expose limitations in our beliefs and ideas, nor
could it be used to guide evaluations of their utility or accuracy. The goals of science
as a learning process were effectively cut off, closed to participation by archaeologists.
    Under the above solution to the "archaeologists' paradox"—namely, working with
a contemporary world of material phenomena and believing that it was to be under-

stood in terms of an idealist past—the practice of archaeology became essentially a game. Just as one plays a game within the framework of stipulated rules for participation, so did the traditional archaeologists. Their energies were directed toward competing, using their personal skill linked with their knowledge of archaeological data, within the framework of the prescribed rules of the game. Little puzzles were recognized during the course of playing the game, and much energy was directed toward their solution. In reality this activity took the form of an endless and energetic search for new observations on the archaeological record, since only the generalizations made directly from the data could change the views of the past proposed by archaeologists. Their interpretive procedures were a closed system of stipulations not subject to evaluation from experience, that is, not subject to tests using the data. The understanding of the past was changed by archaeologists as a simple function of changes in the amount and quality of data available for generalization. New discoveries were the means to fame and recognition, not critically designed research aimed at evaluating ideas (theories) used in interpreting such discoveries. This was an intellectual climate in which archaic empiricists' ideas thrived. The good archaeologist was the one who could synthesize observations and generate defensible generalizations seemingly directly from the phenomenological world of artifacts. Once done, the interpretation appeared to flow self-evidently from the facts. Truth about the past seemingly came directly from the remains of the past; the role of all those stipulated meanings used in interpretation was largely not acknowledged by archaeologists who were "playing the game." Those who were sarcastically referred to as new archaeologists questioned the utility of the game for gaining a knowledge of the past by questioning the accuracy and adequacy of the stipulations used in assigning meanings to archaeological observations.

The situation in traditional archaeology was a classic example of history as described by Bruce Trigger:

> History differs from the generalizing social sciences only in that its primary aim is to explain individual situations in all their complexity rather than to formulate general laws for indefinitely repeatable events and processes. That is what is meant by saying that history is ideographic, the social sciences monothetic. . . . This does not mean that historians deny the existence of general rules; rather they seek to employ them to gain an understanding of individual (i.e., unique and non-recurrent) situations. The generalizing social sciences, on the other hand, extract recurrent variables from their socio-cultural matrix so that relationships of general validity can be established between them. (1978:26–27)

Traditional archaeology was a "law-using" (rather than law-formulating) field addressing itself to the interpretation and elucidation of unique events and conditions of the past. To the new archaeologists, the problems seemed to be clear: where did these laws used for historical interpretations come from, and were they valid? Another problem might be recognized by asking whether archaeology was "historical" by virtue of its law-using posture or by virtue of its desire to know about the past. Did the latter interest limit our methods for learning to the law-using posture? Oddly enough, a historical discipline like geology did not seem to be so limited. To many of the new archaeologists the answer to this question was a resounding no.

> The use of general rules to explain a concrete situation is no less an act of creative skill than is the formulation of such rules to explain repeated correlations. Because the aim is to explain a particular situation in all its complexity, the application of such rules serves as a test of theory, and because a variety of different bodies of theory may have to be applied in conjunction with one another, historical interpretation serves as an interdisciplinary arena in which the explanatory power of different theoretical approaches may be ascertained. (Trigger 1978:27)

The situation in traditional archaeology did not seem conducive even to the demands of valid inductive argument, which as suggested above are basic to the study of history. Archaeological laws were stipulations about the meaning of properties of the archaeological record in general, and they never seemed to lead to the explanation of "a particular situation in all its complexity." Inferential assessments, such as whether people were culturally similar or different, whether a migration or invasion of culturally distinct peoples occurred, or whether one ethnically distinct people differentially "influenced" surrounding peoples as judged from measures of similarity viewed through time, did not seem to measure up to the goal of explaining particular situations in all their complexity. As traditional archaeology was practiced, its historical orientation never led to the testing of theories, which a stated above is a component of "good" history. All archaeologists' interpretations were either theory-dependent or ad hoc inferences, and in both cases the world of experience was accommodated to the theory through the stipulations or accommodative arguments offered as to the meanings of observations. It seemed quite possible, and even necessary, for archaeology to maintain its goals for the growth of historical knowledge, but the methods advocated by culture historians did not seem to be appropriate given those interests; there had to be better ways of learning about the past.

Because our criticisms of traditional archaeology were so strong, the challenge facing the new archaeology appeared overwhelming to many of us. We began in obvious ways. First, it was recognized that *generalization* was the basic source of new views of the past arising from traditional approaches. We began to explore the methods of generalization, emphasizing sampling strategies and more sophisticated methods for pattern recognition. At the same time, we wanted to know if the stipulated links between archaeological experience and interpretation were accurate and valid. We had to know how to interpret patterns once valid generalizations could be made. This problem seemed to demand a testing program aimed at evaluating the utility and accuracy of ideas. This procedure was science. The scientific method was never a component of traditional archaeology; only the fit between generalization and the data was commonly evaluated under the older procedures. It was in this context of problem recognition that we began to explore the epistemological procedures available to us for evaluating ideas. Emphasis was placed on deductive forms of reasoning, since the problem as it was perceived in the 1960s was one of evaluating the utility of ideas already in existence. There was never a claim for the absolute priority of deduction over induction, as many critics have asserted. We fully acknowledged the crucial role of induction, while at the same time we realized that inductive arguments were not verifiable by simple reference back to the manner in which they may have been constructed in the first place.

What is argued here is that the generation of inferences regarding the past should not be the end-product of the archaeologist's work. . . . The main point of our argument is that independent means of testing propositions about the past must be developed. Such means must be considerably more rigorous than evaluating an author's proposition by judging his professional competence or intellectual honesty (Binford 1968:17)

Given the situation as it was perceived in the 1960s, it was the propositions basic to traditional archaeology that were in need of validation independent of the seeming "strength" with which they had been presented by authorities. Deductive argument seemed an important avenue to explore.

Second, it was argued that the acknowledged "law"-dependent status of history was inappropriate to archaeology. Historians are said to draw upon the "sciences" for their theories utilized in interpreting historical documents. Our "historical documents" were archaeological remains, and we could find no scientists who were already studying such phenomena. We could find no rules being produced by other scientists that informed us about what our phenomena, pottery sherds, house remains, garbage, and so on, might mean in either historical or processual terms. We concluded that archaeologists themselves had to accept the challenge of theory development; we had to develop and evaluate the rules used for interpreting our data. Archaeology had to become a science concerned with understanding the significance of patterning observed in the archaeological record. More important, it also had to evaluate the ideas it used when interpreting observations and patterning. No other science was addressing our phenomena or our problems.

Finally, it was argued that, insofar as the past was an inference from contemporary observations made on the archaeological record, the archaeologists had to decide which past should be the target of their inferential constructions. In any concrete archaeological situation the archaeologist faced some segment of the archaeological record, some "site" or collection of archaeological materials from a region. The situation represented the potentially unique, discrete characteristics of past dynamics. These dynamics could be manifest at different levels or scales (e.g., varying but cyclical phenomena, or variable but internally differentiated phenomena not indicative of organizational change, or variability between systems). Thus, before archaeologists could cite formal variability in the archaeological record as indicative of large-scale processes, evolution, systems change, ethnicity, or even such historical events as migrations, we had to be able to diagnose the archaeological record at differing organizational scales. Variability in the archaeological record did not necessarily have reference to a single scale of dynamics. Variability was not directly referable to modifying processes; it may equally and ambiguously refer to stable but internally complex processes. Variability in the archaeological record may have reference to multiple and differing causes and conditioning phenomena. The archaeologists not only had to diagnose the statics of the archaeological record in dynamic terms, but in addition they had to diagnose the relevance of those dynamics with respect to different goals of knowledge seeking. These three general points of view conditioned and guided the development of research by new archaeologists.

During the 1960s, research and argument was begun on two of these points. The factors that might be internal to a system and yet condition variability among archaeological sites with reference to pottery styles were explored (Longacre 1963; Hill 1965). At roughly the same time arguments were initiated regarding the "meaning" of seemingly anomalous patterning (with respect to traditional assumptions) in lithic materials documented within the Mousterian sequences of the Old World (Binford and Binford 1966). These early researchers were working from the perspective of the third approach described above, but the presentation was commonly made as if we were "testing" the validity of the stipulated meanings traditionally used by earlier archaeologists and the propositions that made possible alternative arguments. Unfortunately this posture was adopted by some who focused on the testing aspects (Fritz and Plog 1970; Watson et al. 1971) that new archaeologists saw as a necessary component of archaeological activity. It was clear that if we were to succeed in confronting the issue of the accurate linkage between our observations and our ideas, testing had to be accomplished. Ironically, most of this early research did not succeed in testing traditional arguments but instead dissolved into what I have called "arguments of relevance" (Binford 1983a:3–20). The validity of propositions was not being evaluated directly—only the relevance of those propositions to certain specific cases.

This was an important learning experience for most of us. It brought home forcefully the need to directly confront the second point listed above, namely, to be directly engaged in theory building and to accept the scientific responsibility for the growth of our understanding of the archaeological record itself. The attempts by some to propose and test theory simultaneously were clearly misleading (see my discussion of Plog's work: Binford 1983a:14–17). Rather than testing the traditional propositions, the tempo of the field shifted very quickly to a demand for new theory and finished historical models. Clearly, in this posture the idea of testing the traditional propositions appeared to be a waste of time. Given this shift in emphasis from the early testing attempts to the more ambitious need to develop our own science aimed at understanding the archaeological record itself, both testing and the growth of knowledge were linked in a new and fascinating manner.

When I went north to study the Nunamiut, I sallied forth as a beneficiary of the learning that the early days of the new archaeology had provided. My Nunamiut research was certainly a testing of the traditional archaeologists' stipulations as to the significance of variability in the archaeological record, but it was more. It was an attempt to develop a methodology for evaluating from archaeological remains the relevance and meaning of variability in the archaeological record, which could then be used in evaluating or rendering judgments of relevance for the organizational knowledge gained from the Nunamiut experience. I emphasized these aspects of the research because I felt that the discussion on testing had at that time become extremely confused. My research rested on the recognition of what any good designer of scientific experiments already knows: a general theory cannot be tested on the assumption that all cases (or experiments) are equally relevant to the testing. The scientist engaged in testing theories must be able to unambiguously isolate critical and relevant experiences—any experience per se is not necessarily relevant.

From my perspective, a good example of the use of irrelevant arguments (in this case propositions rather than experiences) is provided by Ian Hodder. Although

Hodder maintains that ideas cannot be tested or evaluated by scientific means, he ironically claims that he has tested (and discounted) the general approaches of the new archaeology by virtue of having demonstrated that humans act intentionally! Was denial of the ability of humans to act intentionally ever a proposition critical to the positions advocated by the new archaeology? No. The only related argument advanced by the new archaeologists of which I am aware was that apparent free will and volitional action by individuals was not the explanation for long-term historical processes. Intentional action was never denied; it was only suggested that human actions could be explained as manifestations of other causal forces, and it was maintained that intentional acts were not *the* causal force standing behind history.

The problem of relevance for the archaeologist is central and crucial. This arises from the fact that all interpretations of archaeological observations are inductive arguments of some kind. The successive introduction of propositions into an inductive argument requires that two features be sustainable: (a) the propositions must be accurate, and (b) they must be relevant to the materials being interpreted. A proposition may be accurate but irrelevant, inaccurate and irrelevant, inaccurate but relevant, or accurate and relevant. Evaluations must be made with regard to the above possibilities before the strength of an inductive argument can be judged. It is the strength of such arguments that determines the accuracy of the past we infer from our observations. Such judgments cannot be made simply from evaluations of how well the argument fits the facts. The accuracy of component propositions must be evaluated independently of the accommodative argument made to advocate their relevance and link them to a conclusion. In turn, the relevance must be judged independently of arguments offered as to the accuracy of components introduced into argument. The demonstration of the accuracy of the proposition that humans act intentionally does not establish the relevance of this fact to the explanation of a given body of humanly produced materials; intentionality may well be conditioned. In fact, one could argue that I demonstrated this in my Nunamiut study.

It was in this context of appreciation for the problem of interpretation facing archaeologists that I advocated the conscious investment in *middle-range research* as being basic to the development of archaeology (Binford 1977a, 1981a). This is not the place to discuss this suggestion at length; it should be noted, however, that all inductive argument draws upon "source-side" knowledge (Watson 1979) in building arguments about its subject. Archaeologists have not pursued the study of source-side knowledge, even though it is crucial to interpretations of their subject matter. Most inductive arguments are forged by archaeologists from propositions having differing referents to domains of knowledge and areas of phenomena extant in the archaeological record. The claims to knowledge and the meanings given to observations are not all justified by reference to a given theory or paradigm; instead, these archaeologists commonly appeal to many different theories and interpretive principles. The claim of many that all inferences are "paradigm-dependent" and hence tautological is not sustained by most concrete examples in inductive argument. Middle-range research is proposed as a means of developing secure and intellectually independent interpretive principles and of expanding our knowledge of phenomena of relevance to our interpretive task.

Let me see if I can illustrate the importance of this research with some concrete examples. An examination of some of the propositions basic to traditional archaeology renders the activities of the new archaeologists quite understandable.

> If the attributes considered are only those which are the products of human endeavor, it follows that any explanation of these attributes is necessarily done in human rather than natural terms. (Dunnell 1971:133)

This proposition has certainly been basic to the interpretations that traditional archaeologists have offered regarding our past. It sounds very clear and unambiguous to the traditional believer. Let us see what happens to this basic proposition in scientific practice. "If the attributes considered are only those which are the products of human endeavor" is a stipulation of relevance as discussed above. How have archaeologists traditionally dealt with this stipulation? Certainly it is defensible to generalize that archaeologists developed "rules of thumb" for meeting this criterion of relevance. For instance, until quite recently animal bones were considered to be attributes of the natural world. They were not artifacts and were therefore not analyzed except as potential sources of information regarding past environments or climates or at best as clues to food preferences conceived as idealistically guided customs of past peoples. One can search in vain for any type of analysis other than species lists appearing as appendices to traditional archaeological reports. In short, a categorical approach was taken; animals were natural, and thus their bones were not "products of human endeavor." The archaeologist needed a "natural scientist" to deal with these aspects of the archaeological record. If a similar approach had been taken to stones, clearly a "natural" phenomena, our field might never have developed! What was needed was not a judgment of relevance, but instead concrete investigations aimed at uncovering the *attributes* of relevance for our science. This was my middle-range approach to the study of animal bones documented in the Nunamiut book (Binford 1978a). I sought to investigate the linkages between natural elements incorporated within a cultural system and attributes thereof, which could carry significant and relevant information for the archaeologist seeking to understand how a cultural system was organized.

The other side of this coin is illustrated in *Bones: Ancient Men and Modern Myths* (Binford 1981a). There I explored the willingness of archaeologists to accept categorically animal bones in the archaeological record as "products of human endeavor." In the *Bones* book I argued that there are many situations and contexts in which patterned associations may exist in nature that in no way implicate human endeavor. It is interesting that, while my Nunamiut research, the positive side of the coin, largely fell on deaf ears, the response to the *Bones* book was loud and outraged. There, of course, I had been arguing that archaeologists had made poor and inaccurate judgments of relevance, while in the Nunamiut book I was suggesting how we might make new and potentially informative arguments of relevance. In both books I was strongly advocating the fact that advances in archaeology are dependent upon archaeologists accepting the responsibility for developing their own criteria of relevance and, by extension, their own theories for meanings that could be reliably assigned to observations. I think it is sad that the most productive consequences for the field have stemmed from the *Bones* book. Many archaeologists began middle-range research not because they considered it basic to the field but because they wanted to defend their personal positions.

Let us explore another aspect of this same proposition: "if the attributes considered are only those which are the products of human endeavor," what is human? Is it the behavior considered unique to our species? If so, and if one can demonstrate in the behavior of our ancestors some property previously considered unique to our species, does it follow that the ancient actors who were *not* members of our species were also human? Of course I am referring here to the problem that traditional archaeology dictated for the archaeologist of the Middle and Lower Paleolithic. As outlined by Dunnell, "it follows that any explanation of these attributes is necessarily done in human rather than natural terms." As I suggested above, traditional archaeologists interested in the very ancient past could only appeal to laws of human nature when interpreting their observations. These laws nearly always took the same form as those used by any other archaeologist—interpretations of culture history in terms of the stipulations or meanings referable to culture. If we as archaeologists accept conventions of relevance, such as "man the tool maker," or arguments to the effect that the archaeological record is necessarily a *cultural* record, we are creating a past stipulated in cultural terms that may not have a historical reality. Archaeologists must accept the middle-range research challenge of investigating the unambiguous indicators for culture rather than simply accepting the old convention of equating patterned behavior, which is clearly also a product of the animal world, with cultural behavior.

If we acknowledge the possibility that our ancient ancestors, who were demonstrably different species, may well have left an archaeological record but may not have been culture bearers, then all the conventions for the interpretation of the ancient archaeological record in culture-historical terms quickly become irrelevant. Even if we accepted traditional conventions as accurate for "humans," the archaeologist of the Lower Paleolithic would be at best investigating *when* these conventions may have become relevant. Traditional archaeology provided no guidelines on this issue.

An additional problem that the fundamental principles of traditional archaeology dictated for the Lower Paleolithic archaeologist is seen in the second phrase of Dunnell's fundamental statement: "explanation . . . is necessarily done in human rather than natural terms." Of course, what the traditional archaeologists had in mind was that *culture* was the "human terms" within which explanation was to be sought. By virtue of accepting these basic tenets, Paleolithic archaeologists were in the interesting position of never being able to investigate the origins of or the conditions for the emergence of culture itself. As suggested above, if we can imagine a time when hominids produced an archaeological record yet did not yet possess the capacity for culture, then it would be both possible and important to seek an understanding of the very appearance of culture itself. Could we expect the appearance of culture to be explicable in cultural terms? Of course not. Since we cannot rule out the possibility that hominids produced artifacts but not cultural records, then clearly the basic arguments of relevance establishing the boundary conditions for traditional archaeological explanation are false, misleading, and if accepted uncritically, certain to produce conventionalism rather than research.

Many more propositions of traditional archaeology require discussion and investigation at the middle range. Investigations in contemporary archaeology of the accuracy, utility, and relevance of basic propositions introduced in inferential argument are leading to a growth in our understanding of the archaeological record. This was the goal of the new archaeology, and this goal is being pursued with productive results in contemporary archaeology.

Unfortunately, not all contemporary archaeology is productive. There are many reactionary movements advocating the use of propositions and beliefs of traditional archaeology whose limited utility has already been demonstrated. We see Richard Gould (1980a) advocating the "law"-dependent status for archaeology and at the same time advocating an idealist philosophy of culture. We see James Sackett (1977, 1982, 1986a, 1986b) seeking to subsume functional variability into his unique characterization of style, thus limiting the possibility of explaining cultural variability to the traditional view that people behave the way they do because their grandfathers behaved that way. We see Ian Hodder (1982a) and the "coggies" rediscovering traditional archaeology as if it were new and innovative. We see a new skepticism linked to the Frankfurt school of philosophy, which essentially claims that we cannot learn about a past reality—we can only create a past in "our own image," so we should shift our concerns to social criticism (Saitta 1983). Finally, we have been introduced to the wonders of the "power motive" as the driving force of human nature, dictating a dialectical history and serving as the basis for appreciating our past as a guide to contemporary political truths (Miller and Tilley 1984).

As Gellner (1985:8) has said, the theoretical "barrel" is never empty. Removing bad apples does not ensure against further decay occurring in similar ways or in new and innovative ways. Throwing ideas out of the barrel, or clutching them to one's heart, does not permit evaluation—only judgment. Science is a learning process. Scientists pursue knowledge through the evaluation of ideas. Unfortunately, as we should know by now, the simple accumulation of knowledge is not sufficient to explain the cultural process. Our contemporary culture of archaeology goes on in terms frequently quite independent of science and its goals. Students of contemporary archaeology must concern themselves with much more than seeking an understanding of the archaeological record. Nevertheless, archaeology will progress as a simple function of increases in our understanding. This growth can be enhanced by the scientific evaluation of ideas, as I have illustrated here, whether or not the original ideas were true, accurate, or ultimately proven useful. Learning goes on when we seriously investigate the properties of our own ideas as they condition the way we treat our experiences. This investigation can only be accomplished in the context of intellectual independence between our tools for experiencing and our tools for explaining. Not only is this procedure possible; it is done all the time in science. Much of contemporary archaeology appears to be engaged in a search for truth judged in terms of extrascientific criteria and not in the serious job of doing scientific archaeology. This smacks of religion to me, but regardless of its connotations, it will not advance the field of archaeology. The new archaeology was dedicated to the scientific growth of knowledge; this goes on today in spite of much opposition.

Much Ado about Nothing

Part II

Much Ado about Nothing

Chapter 3

Science to Seance, or Processual to "Post-Processual" Archaeology

If I were to assert that investigation of the nature of life after death was an area for which any increase in knowledge would be important, enriching as regards age-old debates, and certainly timely in the modern world, few would disagree. If I were to suggest further that contemporary science (a) has not really addressed this issue and (b) has generally failed even when it has tried, and if I were to observe that a knowledge of life after death might not be germane to a growth of knowledge regarding how our world of experience, the natural world, actually works (i.e., we can learn about our world without a prior knowledge of the question of life after death), would it be logical to conclude from this discussion that science has failed, that science is worthless, and that one should accordingly abandon science as a learning strategy as far as the world of experience is concerned? Should we really kick over the traces of an allegedly failed science in favor of another learning strategy that is said to make possible a knowledge of life after death? We may query still further, has science really failed in terms of its goals, the accumulation of knowledge and understanding of the world as we know it? Such a claim would certainly be difficult to defend. Faced with this type of logical situation, what is the form that debate over this issue is likely to take?

Advocates of the "life after death" goal of knowledge seeking have only two alternatives to pursue in this type of debate. They can endlessly reiterate the fact that scientists have not pursued a knowledge of life after death (there would be little basis for debate here, so why spend much time talking about it?), or they must present compelling reasons as to why a prior knowledge about life after death is necessary for the achievement of a meaningful understanding of the world of experience as we know it. The advocates of the "life after death" goal for research are making an ontological assertion about this world, the world of experience (at least of experiences to which we have thus far been exposed). They must claim (a) that in reality there is life after death and, most important, (b) that it is a major determinant in the dynamics of life in the here and now. Thus any attempt to understand life in the here and now that does not consider this adjudged important determinant is said to be unrealistic, misguided, and clearly on the wrong track.

Such an ontological claim should be amenable to investigation. Is our world organized as implied by the ontological claim? An ontological claim about this world must be just that—a claim about this world. Life after death is a claim about the interaction of this world with another not available to investigation. How may such a claim be addressed? It was just this type of problem that stood as the basis for the development of science. Each science must treat the experiences of this world in such a way that ontological claims are capable of being evaluated in this world.

Strictly speaking, what is the world of experience for the archaeologist? As suggested in Chapter 1, that world is the world of the archaeological record, the world of artifacts—modifications of nature effected by hominids/humans. What we can see are artifacts in the broadest sense of the word and relationships among those artifacts as well as with associated indicators of the environment and other natural conditions that existed when the artifacts were produced, used, and discarded. Archaeologists study the relationships among artifacts (conceived in the broadest manner—i.e., the archaeological record) in terms of the dimensions of form and space and the inferred dimension of time (it is acknowledged that both time and space have dynamic characteristics). An archaeologist listening to the above argument about the importance of a knowledge regarding the issue of life after death as a prerequisite to his or her performing as an archaeologist would certainly raise several issues not made clear by the "life after death" advocates. Where is the evidence in the archaeologist's domain of experience for the operation of this important "cause"? If this "cause" is truly otherworldly, then how can we "see" it in this world? The answer—by its effects on this world. How do we know these effects when we see them? By virtue of a knowledge of the effects of one world upon the other. How do we gain such knowledge? Investigate the other world. If the other world is truly different, how do we know of its effects on the world we can experience? A true knowledge of the world of life after death will permit us to know its impact on the world of experience as we know it. Given such a knowledge, we can "read" our world using decoding devices invented in terms of our knowledge of the other world. I will not continue further with this metaphor. I suggest that many debates, particularly those by the Yippie subpopulation of archaeologists, bear a striking resemblance in form to the above.

The papers that follow were either delivered in large public gatherings or appear in publications that do not provide opportunities for replies. This is not because I am unwilling to debate. I do not take the arguments seriously, yet regrettably I find that many students and colleagues have strangely found the otherworldly arguments appealing. The advocates of "post-processual archaeology" are clearly not guilty of advocating life after death as an active cause of variability in the archaeological record (except perhaps as this concept might be "negotiated" by the living). Why have I chosen such a seemingly inappropriate metaphor? In order to clarify things I must recognize four worlds: (a) our contemporary world of participation—the social milieu in which we live, (b) the contemporary static world of the archaeological record, (c) the vanished past—the social milieu of participation by ancient peoples, and (d) the vanished formation processes that brought into being the patterned remains we see today as the archaeological record. The post-processualists have set up their arguments in order to convince the rest of us that they can accurately and productively move at will among these worlds.

THREE PROBLEMS WITH LINKAGES

Problem 1. Articulating our contemporary world of participation or the social milieu in which we live with the vanished past, the social milieu of participation experienced by ancient peoples

The central position or claim made by the post-processualists is simply that the ancient world was exactly like the present world. Both the ancient world and the present world are fundamentally to be understood by recognizing the individual person as the causal actor. As Tilley (1982:27) puts it,

> The results of individual actions form society which, in turn, reacts back and shapes individual actions. . . . This dialectical process is comprised of three synchronous moments: externalization, objectification, and internalization. . . . The individual internalizes features that are given to him from outside and these become contents of his own consciousness which he externalizes again as he continues to live and act in society. . . . People act in terms of intentions, motivations and choices between different courses of action. As a consequence of these actions society exists; it is not consciously produced by individuals any more than these individuals are predetermined in their actions or "programmed" by society.

For purposes of discussion let us accept this description of what most people believe about themselves and others. I have free will and can act on my world; others might also add that some persons are less inventive and thus behave like cultural sheep, programmed by their culture. Either or both are "real" and accommodating statements about the way participants in our sociocultural world see themselves. The post-processualists present this egocentric view of the world as self-evident truth and claim that archaeologists must accept this egocentric, participant view of the world as reality if they are to be successful in decoding the remnants of past realities. Thus, in treating the problem of articulating the present and the past, it is assumed that this way of viewing the present is the only accurate one and that this understanding can be assumed to apply to the past as well (a uniformitarian assumption).

Problem 2. Articulating the world of the contemporary production of material remains (ethnoarchaeology) with the world of the contemporary participant in a social system

The linkage between statics and dynamics in the modern world is made by the post-processualist in much the same way that traditional archaeologists solved this problem—assumptively. The common convention of traditional archaeology was simply stated as follows: culture is patterned, therefore patterning is cultural. For the traditional archaeologist, "culture" referred to the ideas and values, codes and rules that guided or at least provided a framework for individuals who then "negotiated" their behavior. The rules and codes were therefore the causes of redundancy or patterning as might be demonstrated by an archaeologist through the study of the archaeological record. Post-processualists tell us:

> I wish to distinguish between system and structure . . . by defining structure not as
> system, pattern or style, but as the codes and rules according to which observed
> systems of interrelations are produced. (Hodder 1982c:7)

Structure, then, is the causal context for the production of interrelationships that
archaeologists might cite, and this causal context comprises the "codes and rules"
extant in the sociocultural world of the individual participant, which when mediated
through individual actions are the formation processes of the archaeological record.
On this point there is little difference between post-processualists and traditional
archaeologists except for a greater emphasis on individual action and variability arising from negotiated conditions in the former.

Post-processualists differ from traditional archaeologists, however, in the imagined
process whereby rules and codes are imprinted onto the archaeological record.
Traditional archaeologists recognized that all patterning is not necessarily a direct
translation of culture into static form in spite of their very broad convention linking
the world of dynamics to the world of statics. They also recognized that, while patterning might have reference to culturally embedded behaviors, the resulting archaeological patterning might not have any directly readable meaning with reference to
the specific norms and values, codes and rules in the sociocultural domain (the idea of
isomorphism between idea and pattern is dealt with in Chapter 15).

No such caution stands behind the works of post-processualists. Patterning or even
lack of patterning demonstrable in the material "residues" of action are "textual" in
character. The analogy is to a language, and archaeological remains in all forms are
considered to be the direct consequences of continually changing symbolic codes
remaining from the active negotiations of individuals manipulating their symbolic
worlds to their own advantage. Thus the causes of archaeological phenomena derive
from the "unity of meaning and action" in the past.

> It is not possible to divorce process from culture, to study one without the other,
> because the emphasis on action rather than behavior states a unity of idea (inten-
> tionality) and material event, and the challenge is to develop theories that specify
> integration and allow both for general principles of human action and for the
> particularity of cultural constructions. (Hodder 1985:9)

In short, there is no difference between the static and the dynamic worlds, contrary to
what most who have seriously addressed the problem of formation processes for the
archaeological record have clearly suggested. Archaeologists do not see a different
world; instead, they see the same world that a participant sees and even designs
through the participant's acts of intentionality. Archaeologists have been misled into
thinking of their world as a static world of artifacts; instead, it is a world of immediate
social reality.

*Problem 3. Articulating the static world of the present with the dynamic world of the
past*

The post-processualist vehemently argues for the independence of the static world
of the present and the dynamic world of the past. We are also told that one cannot
know one world in terms of the other; we can only meaningfully know the past in

terms of the past. We are told that the problem with most non-post-processual archaeology is that it creates a "timeless past" by virtue of its assimilation of the past to the present through scientific approaches that employ uniformitarian assumptions. "Oh dear. How do I know the past if it is gone?" This question becomes even more serious when it is placed in the context of post-processual argument. Since the underlying causal or formational structure of an archaeological "document" is said to be unique to the time and place, "artefacts and their organisation come to have specific cultural meanings as a result of their use in particular historical contexts" (Hodder 1982c:101).

The search for an answer to our question regarding how we get to know the past is further complicated by the "contextual" qualifiers—we must know a unique, historically particular past. What suggestions are offered to the potential follower of the post-processual way? Adopt the strategies of "contextual archaeology." What are they?

> A more precise definition for the context of an archaeological attribute is the totality of the relevant environment, where "relevant" refers to a significant relationship to an object—that is a relationship necessary for discerning the object's meaning. (Hodder 1986:139)

What Hodder is telling us here is that in order to understand the meaning of archaeological remains we must be able to see significant relationships—those things necessary to knowing its meaning. What are significant relationships? They are the relevant environment, which is of course the ancient cultural context of thought and action as molded together by the ancients' cultural rules and codes. At any point in time those rules and codes are a function of the history of that time and place as modified by individual causal actors behaving volitionally. In short, we must know the past first— then we can understand the archaeological record. This is a complete reversal of what I think most archaeologists have thought they were doing. I do not think it is unfair to suggest that most archaeologists have generally thought that they were studying the archaeological record in order to learn about the past. Hodder tells us we must know the past in order to understand the archaeological record. Clearly we are in trouble here. We are in exactly the position of those who advocate life after death as a causal determinant of life here in the present.

If we demand that we know the other world first, and we have no access to that other world, what do we do? Hodder tells us two things. On the one hand, follow the methods of "empathetic understanding" as advocated by Collingwood (1956). One "immerses oneself in the contextual data," says Hodder (1986:94). On the other hand, Hodder tells us that "an object [here in the present, for instance?] out of context is not readable. . . . So everything depends on everything else, and the definition of attributes depends on the definition of context, which depends on the definition of attributes" (Hodder 1986:141). What does this mean? It means that there are no appeals to "outside knowledge." There are no data from which inferences can be made; data and knowledge are created simultaneously! How do we do this? We follow Collingwood's advice. We relive the past in our minds. This is to be achieved by "the method of question and answer" (Hodder 1986:94). The mind is said to be able "to imagine and criticize other subjectivities, the inside of other historical events" (Hodder 1986:95). In short, we carry on a dialogue with ourselves; we ask such questions as

"Why should anyone want to erect a building like that?" (Hodder 1986:94). Ego creates the past in its own image. The inner subjective thoughts of the individual archaeologist become the source of knowledge and understanding for others in all times and places. The arbiter of the past is not the archaeological record, it is not the past as was, it is the past as imagined by the individual archaeologist.

Thus we have a massive contradiction. We do not have two worlds, as claimed by others. We do not seek ways of knowing the past in its own terms. We do not need to know the past reality before interpreting the archaeological record. All we need to believe is simply that a modern individual can see through all the cultural variability into the core of "humanness" standing behind the epiphenomenal archaeological variability. I am human; they were human; therefore I can directly empathize with them and know their motives. (This belief refers back to the descriptions of human behavior summarized in the Tilley quote given above.)

> Although each context is unique, in that it derives from a particular historical circumstance, we can have an identity or common feeling with it; each event, though unique, has a universality in that it possesses a significance which can be comprehended by all people at all times. (Hodder 1986:95, paraphrasing Collingwood)

Hodder continues, "Since, 'properly speaking,' the data do not exist, all one can do is identify a reconstruction that makes sense, in terms of the archaeologist's picture of the world." In short, all the interpretive products of archaeologists following the "Hodder way" are massive post hoc accommodative arguments. As Hodder notes, "Archaeology uses accommodative arguments: it has no other viable options" (Hodder 1986:96). Ironically, after all Hodder's ranting and raving about "scientists" creating a timeless past, and their demands that we know the past in its own terms, we are finally told that we are to assume enormous amounts of self knowledge as the means to reconstructing a past in our own image!

Earlier I mentioned that Hodder had two pieces of advice for us. That is true. In addition to using the method of intuitive empathy we may also fall back on the argument that the archaeological record is a text. Recall that the methods of contextual archaeology demand that we somehow recognize or, more accurately, invent what was significant in the past as our way of prescribing the meanings given by the ancients to their actions, thereby providing us with an understanding of the archaeological legacies remaining from the past. We are told that we can accomplish this astonishing feat by virtue of "some very simple rules underlying all languages—or at least underlying the ways in which *Homo sapiens sapiens* at all times and in all places gives meaning to things" (Hodder 1986:123). Thus Hodder again denies the existence of the two worlds, past and present. But does this knowledge not come from our world? Is this not the hated uniformitarian assumption? Is this not creating a "timeless past?" Does this not deny the freedom of individuals to negotiate and change the way they assign meanings? Are we not biologically determined or at least constrained by virtue of our "essential" characteristics as *Homo sapiens*? I conclude from all this that illogical argument is very difficult to follow.

ACCOUNTABILITY IN ARCHAEOLOGY

There is more than regrettable logic to these arguments. It is clearly suggested that there is nothing within the archaeological record that we do not already know about as a result of our massive egotism, our inherent ability to understand mankind in our own image whenever and wherever they may present themselves. This is why I do not take the Yippie papers and publications seriously. I must know the past in its own terms. How do I know those terms? I use a contextual approach. What is that? One isolates the totality of the relevant environment—relevant to the ancients, that is. How do I know what was relevant? Relevance is known by significance; significance is what one must know to know its meaning. How do I know that? I look inside myself. I become the arbiter of the past.

There is no methodological challenge; there is in fact no need for methodological discussions. In turn, there is nothing to be learned of processes. The patterns already demonstrated by archaeologists are delusions arising from a misguided cross-cultural approach. The remarkable parallels in sequence and even form among archaeological remains from many different places and eras hold no potential for further learning; patterning is simply that—oneness of intentionality conditioned by "history" and leading to uniqueness, not to something in need of explanation. If archaeologists "see" large-scale patterns, which are normally taken to indicate the operation of determinant causal processes, they should not pursue further knowledge of processes operative at scales clearly beyond the scope of individuals. We know such processes do not exist, since our tiny, egocentric views of process are judged complete. The archaeologist is not a scientist with a legitimate domain to learn from; in fact, we do not need science. Archaeology is a "literary" field concerned with developing those personal skills sufficient to permit the past to be read from the text remaining to us from the past. We are to become translators, or perhaps cultural critics in the sense of literary criticism. All this post-processual wonder is held out to us as desirable not because it might enhance knowledge and learning; instead it is seen as a way of moving toward a better life and a more "human," Hodder imagined, world to enjoy in the present.

> I have tried in this essay to sketch out an alternative approach. By emphasizing the meaningful construction of social acts and the historical particularity of human culture I seek to dissolve the timeless past both in its role as the ultimate legitimation of the modern technocratic West and in its function as the prop of the professional theoretician. (Hodder 1985:22)

Here the Yippie speaks. Our goal is not knowledge of the past, since that knowledge is only subject to abuse in the present. We need to cut away the "false" supports for the false world in which we live, dissolve the timeless past, and presumably restore ourselves to the Utopian condition in which individuals engage in the negotiation of power (Hodder 1985:15) and "create meaningful acts." One wonders how this new order would be different from the present; is not all the alleged understanding generalized from the present? I guess the only difference might be the identity of those successful in the power negotiation game.

How does Hodder think himself into such positions? Basic to all the above is one big red herring. Revolving around this red herring is the undiscussed question of accountability. Clearly what Hodder is suggesting is simply that archaeologists are not accountable to a real past, nor to a body of experience; they are accountable to the moral and ethical challenges of their time and place. "An open relativism appears at first to be the only solution, whereby 'anything goes'" (Hodder 1986:169). Hodder moves beyond this suggestion, however, by repeated reference back to the position that "any reconstruction of the past is a social statement in the present. It orders experience and creates social positions. The past is used as an effective structuring principle in many walks of contemporary life" (Hodder 1985:18–19). Thus, for Hodder, reconstructions of the past must be accountable to the contemporary "moral order," not to the world of observation and experience. He believes that what we see in the archaeological record is what we want to see; we are all paradigm-dependent. Accountability must be not to observations and the world of experience but instead to critical discussion of "social theory"—in short, debate over the morality of the modern world.

I suggest that archaeology, like any other science, can develop two major contexts of accountability. Debate is one, but to be fruitful it must be purged of the underpinnings of empiricism. Rendering our arguments accountable to experience is the other. Before many contemporary readers will even listen to the latter suggestion we must deal with the red herring of much contemporary thought. The common argument goes something like this:

> Given the close formative relation between fact and theory . . . observation is constituted as fact and facts acquire significance as relevant evidence only within a theoretical framework, generally the one which is under test. (Wylie 1982a:44)

The recognition of this condition was the very basis for criticisms of traditional archaeological practice by the new archaeologists. This position has now been expanded to suggest that science in general is playing a giant joke on itself. That this is a general or inevitable condition is accepted by Hodder and many others. Science is said to be engaged in a giant accommodative argument. Scientists' behavior is tautological, and we can never expect experience already filtered by our beliefs to be an arbiter of the accuracy of our ideas. Our ideas dictate what we see; thus we see what we want to see. As is common to many intellectual red herrings, the components of the above statement are essentially all correct; the implications drawn from these statements are, however, unjustified (see my discussion of data production in Chapter 5).

THE RED HERRING OF PARADIGM DEPENDENCE

As seen above, the argument of paradigm dependence begins with the observation that we choose to look at what we think is potentially informative. This is accurate. Of course, such a judgment cannot be made except by reference to what we think in an a priori sense; our paradigm, if you will, guides our judgment. Again the claim appears accurate. But may we not ask what actions of scientists are impacted by these observations or claims? I suggest very few indeed, if the methods of science as opposed to the guidelines of outdated empiricism are followed. Modern scientists rarely attempt to evaluate ideas or seek guides as to the nature of our ignorance from first-order observations. *First-order observations* are all the properties or characteristics that the scientist chooses to observe in the partitive or particular acts of observation. Archaeologists may make first-order observations in the field—what they record in their notebooks—or in the laboratory—what they tabulate regarding chosen properties observed, for instance on a projectile point or pottery shard. At this level it is true that the intellectual currency may be paradigm-dependent—that is, the *choice* of properties or, more often, classes of properties to be observed is justified by virtue of being potentially germane with reference to what one thinks one knows about the world. At this stage, the next step most commonly is to generalize one's observations: for example, there were 243 blue glazed pottery shards and 109 brown ones in excavation unit B3. These generalized data are *not* in any sense paradigm-dependent. If the procedures used to make the observations, the procedures used to isolate excavation unit B3, and the methods used for recovering pottery shards are all described so that others can "look at the world through the same pair of glasses," then these generalizations are objective statements about those segments of nature being observed (to my knowledge the first archaeologist to make this powerful argument was Albert Spaulding in the course of his debates with James Ford; see Spaulding 1953a, 1953b, 1954a, 1954b).

Similarly, the magnitude of a measurement is not determined by the measuring device used. The weight of a pumpkin is not determined by my having chosen to weigh it with a scale. The accuracy and utility of my observations on weight may be judged contingent upon my making public the character of the scale, its level of accuracy, and so forth. Nevertheless, the objectivity of my observation that the pumpkin weighs 21 lbs. is not determined by my paradigm.

If we go beyond simple enumerations and generalizations of first-order observations, we approach the situation in which "nature gets a chance to talk back" to our ideas. This is what I generally refer to as *pattern-recognition work,* the pursuit of what I sometimes refer to as second-order derivative patterns or second-order observations. It is the study of these relationships that I stress throughout this book: the study of how one set of observations or properties appears when viewed interactively with another set of observations that were produced by different recording procedures. A simple Cartesian graph of the relationships among, say, frequencies of pottery shards plotted on one axis and frequencies of burned rocks plotted on the other is one example of second-order observation. Both could be independently justified observations made on, for example, the contents of excavated grids across an excavation unit. The pattern that might emerge as the paired values of excavation units are plotted is not determined by our paradigm. The pattern made visible in this manner is a descriptive statement about the relationships between the chosen two variables in that segment of nature being studied. The pattern is a property of nature, not a fiction derived from an inevitable paradigmatic filter shutting us off from nature. It is true that the currency, or the type of glasses we have chosen to look through, conditions what aspects of nature we might see as well as the terms in which we can make generalizations and pursue pattern-recognition work, but this currency does not determine what we see when pattern-recognition work is conducted. What we see are properties of nature viewed through glasses we are capable of using and, more important, instructing others to use (the latter is what renders our observations objective).

Since theories treat the world of dynamics, the world of interactive causation, they are concerned with why the world is the way it appears to be, and they are almost inevitably about relationships between characteristics or states of nature. Theories enable predictions to be made about the relationships between causal and conditioning variables, which, it is argued, necessarily result in certain states or conditions of nature. These predictions refer to the relationships that one expects to characterize the dynamic states of nature prior to, during, and following observable changes in natural states. In short, they are about how the world works.

Testing theories is dependent upon anticipating patterned relationships between variables. As we have seen in the above examples, we can monitor nature and make observations that are justified as being germane to a theoretical argument (here one must establish convincing arguments that what one chooses to observe—first-order observations—are uniquely germane to a theoretical argument, then go out into the world of experience and make these paradigmatically or, more important, theoretically germane observations). This essential link between theory and observation in no way ensures that relationships among these "germane" observations, when studied at the second or third or other derivative level, will be those that are predicted by the theory. Nature gets to speak back through pattern-recognition studies. To be productive, theories must be directed toward anticipating relationships among variables, and such relationships may be monitored by scientists. Perceived relationships are not determined by one's paradigm or theory when one is making reasoned predictions to second- and third-order patterns. Theories do not address the unique first-order observations; they are concerned with how the world works, with dynamics, and in turn predictive statements are made about relationships between variables, something not determined or rendered tautological by the choice of variables. There is no truth to the claim that we cannot appeal to experience as an arbiter of ideas about nature.

Casual, polemic-filled discussion regarding the alleged general truth of the claim of paradigm dependence for science even affects those who are commonly less susceptible to false claims. The red herring about paradigm dependence is frequently cited in dark and threatening terms. For instance, in her review of "Working," Watson says,

> the two papers following his commentary (on paradigms and on middle-range research respectively) are simultaneously fascinating and disturbing because here one finds Binford entrapping himself in the serious sceptical crisis. . . . By immersing himself in living societies in order to study cultural processes relevant to formation of the archaeological record, Binford seems to have completely lost his faith in the archaeological record itself as the chief guide and final arbiter on the past. . . . Binford goes on to conclude that the archaeological record cannot be used in any direct way to test ideas about the meaning of archaeological observa-

tions. He believes that such testing is possible only in actualistic (middle-range) research, or in the context of checking general theories about causation in history. Alison Wylie . . . makes the point that actualistic studies are just as "paradigm-bound" as are interpretations of archaeological remains so there is no logical difference between conclusions drawn from observations on living societies and interpretations based on observations of the archaeological record. (Watson 1986:266)

In the above statement we see the red herring of paradigm dependence and additional confusion between an epistemological issue and a learning strategy. My discussions of actualistic research were in no way an attempt to escape from the bogeyman of the "paradigm dependence" claim. That particular issue never bothered me, and it still does not seem to be a general or necessary problem for scientists. Although many examples of tautological arguments and complete circularity in reasoning appear in the literature, these are abuses and are not symptomatic of a crisis for science, if one understands how to conduct science. Nor do my suggestions call up the dark spector of skepticism, which is frequently claimed to result from acknowledging even a widespread presence of such abuses. We have working procedures that ensure against tautology. This problem is not a general or necessary consequence of research; it is, however, regrettable that it is common in our literature.

The other claim in the above quote is to the effect that by suggesting a very important role for actualistic research I had therefore "completely lost [my] faith in the archaeological record . . . as the chief guide and final arbiter on the past." This is nonsense. It should be clear from the brief description of pattern recognition given above that the major productive activity of the archaeologist is the study of relationships among objectively defined properties of the archaeological record. That is the only way we can gain any description of archaeological remains that may be relevant to the past. Given that we seek to learn in an accurate manner about the past, it is only through pattern-recognition work that we can place ourselves on the threshold of learning. Pattern-recognition work drives our field and is the object of our curiosity. Gaining some understanding of what the patterns might mean is the only way of saying anything about the past.

The failure of traditional archaeology was simply that it stipulated what meanings were to be given to patterns (certain kinds of patterns) that we might see (see Binford 1983a:157–209; Binford and Sabloff 1982; as well as Part IV of this volume). I have consistently taken the position that the justifications for such stipulations were ill-founded and generally wrong. This brings us to the second point in Watson's comments. Where do we get the knowledge necessary to interpret accurately the patterning that may be demonstrated as a result of the study of relationships? When the question is put this way, it is clear that archaeologists study the archaeological record and that an accurate understanding of these phenomena makes possible accurate statements about the past. How can we claim, as Hodder does, that a prior knowledge of the past is the only proper basis for interpreting the archaeological record? Do we not study the archaeological record as a means to enlightenment of the past? We would not be studying the archaeological record if we did not acknowledge that our knowledge of the past is inadequate, inaccurate, or even nonexistent. The bogeyman is not paradigm dependence per se; it is the unthinking solution to the question of what prior knowledge we can reliably draw upon to aid in our search for understanding that produces the abuses that unfortunately abound in archaeology.

One cannot clear one's mind, one cannot create knowledge from nothing, one cannot just accept contemporary alleged knowledge as adequate. The scientist must accept the responsibility for testing both the accuracy and the relevance of the prior knowledge used to infuse meaning into the patterning documented in the archaeological record. Since our prior knowledge is not of the past but is in fact of contemporary phenomena, and in most cases is an alleged knowledge (a received knowledge) gained culturally, not through research in the strict sense of the word, we must accept the responsibility for its use. Is it accurate, is it germane, is it incomplete, is it false? How can I learn such things and make such judgments? I certainly cannot learn about the quality of my prior knowledge by studying the archaeological record, where meaning is infused through the use of such alleged knowledge. If I do that, then the bogeyman of paradigm dependence is real, and citing it points to an abuse of scientific learning procedures.

Archaeological science must accept responsibility for the accuracy of the intellectual tools used to infer a past from the contemporary archaeological record. It must study contemporary dynamics considered germane to understanding the formation dynamics standing behind archaeological remains. Through actualistic studies we put in place the intellectual tools germane to our activities as archaeologists. We seek thoughtful understanding of dynamics as a basis for using uniformitarian assumptions. In addition we seek to build up a body of useful knowledge with an underlying history of reliability testing to use in interpreting the archaeological record. It is important that the building of such a baseline of knowledge must be pursued independently—that is, the knowledge claims for different observations must be developed independently or adopted from other research domains where the justifications for the knowledge claims are independent of the researcher's interests—as in the case of radiocarbon dating, which I have discussed previously (Binford 1981a:290).

As I have previously suggested, no other science seeks to understand the archaeological record, so we must accept the responsibility for putting into place a robust body of understanding through middle-range research, thus providing ourselves with a wide variety of independently justified propositions about the causes of archaeologically observable properties. Seeking middle-range research opportunities does not address itself to the bogeyman of paradigm dependence; to the contrary, it addresses the need for useful, germane knowledge regarding the various properties of the archaeological record that we can observe. We need to know something of the conditions, the dynamics, that stand behind the different properties we can observe (see Binford 1981a:29). Interpretation must proceed by reference to our accumulated knowledge regarding these independent properties. Interpretation that can appeal to many independently justified inferences is a robust argument.

Archaeologists must spend much research time trying to understand the "parts," the different observational domains available to them in the archaeological record, before convincing interpretations of the past will be forthcoming. I have seen no other source of prior knowledge and understanding to bring to the task of interpreting the archaeological record except through our own dedicated and time-consuming research directed toward the properties and attributes that we observe in the archaeological record. This is not an indication that I have "lost faith" in the archaeological record. That is what we study, and pattern recognition guides us in the search for and recognition of what we want to know about formation conditions. But I see no way of obtaining from the archaeological record the prior knowledge necessary to the development of inferential techniques to be used in interpreting the archaeological record; those must be justified in a nontautological and mutually independent fashion.

Empiricists are blindly willing to interpret observations as having self-evident meaning to the past, as in the case of Hodder's proposals about empathy. No knowledge of the world of patterning is available, and no theory has been proposed, much less tested, that could justify such empathetic inferences. What is a scientist to do when faced on the one hand with the empiricists' "quick fix" notion of understanding and on the other with their willingness to interpret the past when only ignorance and lack of research stand behind their "bright ideas"? Under these conditions, debate can be used to suggest that there might be more to the world than the empiricist is considering (my strategy on cutmarks in Chapter 23 or the "embedded" procurement suggestions made in Chapters 9–11) and thus it might be prudent to think twice before accepting the empiricists' knowledge claims. Such a conservative posture is sure to infuriate empiricists, since they think they can simply see the world truly. In their eyes, advances in the field should proceed rapidly as a result of blinding flashes of insight. Science actually must proceed slowly, deliberately, and with great care if it is to be successful. It can only succeed if there is a hardheaded consideration of where knowledge comes from coupled with great care in the use of alleged prior knowledge. Citing patterning in the archaeological record as the justification for the devices used for interpreting the patterning seems to me to be the ultimate accommodative argument (see Binford and Sabloff 1982 for examples, particularly the Kriegerian approach). That this has been done is not questioned; that it is inevitable is, however, not true. That I seek prior knowledge where it is accessible, in the present, seems to me the only option available; that this indicates a loss of faith in the archaeological record as our guide to the past is nonsense.

THE CHALLENGE FOR ARCHAEOLOGY

Archaeology is the science of the archaeological record. The first problem we face is simply how to conduct our studies so we are not led to construct a false past. Seeking meaning directly from the archaeological record is what Hodder is telling us to do, and ironically this can only be accomplished by infusing meaning into the archaeological record. The crucial question then becomes, Where do we obtain this prior knowledge and how do we evaluate its accuracy and relevance to what we see in the archaeological record? Second, there is the issue of accountability. Hodder suggests that we must be accountable to the moral and ethical debates of our times. I suggest that we must be accountable to the world of experience for the ideas we employ in interpreting the archaeological record.

In the following essays, I address Hodder's views but I also address what I call "reconstructionist" goals. I do this because I consider the prior decision as to what kind of past I seek to be a judgment a good archaeologist is incapable of making. Just as Hodder has adopted the quick-time actions, motives, and thoughts of individuals as the only true causes of the past and hence of the archaeological record, I consider the desire to reconstruct little ethnographic pictures of the past an imposition on the archaeological record. If we admit that we do not know the causes of patterning or really understand the scales at which dynamics operate to produce the patterning we might see, the prior assumption that it is simply the accumulation of little quick-time ethnographic pictures is premature. Our challenge is to understand the patterning we can recognize within the archaeological record. The enormous potential provided by this challenge is the possibility of monitoring dynamics that remain unseen to the quick-time view of a participant within a cultural system. In short, there are potentially very important things remaining for us to see and learn. Assuming a priori that we already know the processes that operate in history brings us back to Hodder's view that we have nothing to learn, that the only problem facing us is how to use our knowledge to further contemporary moral, ethical, or political goals. We *do* have things to learn—the nature of the past and the causes of its trajectories. The central issue in archaeology is simply how we learn, and fundamental to this issue is how we use our prior knowledge and how we enhance our prior knowledge when we seek to make inferences to the past from the patterning demonstrable in the archaeological record.

Chapter 4

In Pursuit of the Future

BACKGROUND

In the late 1950s and early 1960s a number of us advocated some fundamental changes in the way archaeologists viewed the archaeological record and particularly in the conventions then current for assigning meaning to archaeological facts. Subsequently, there have been major changes in the ways archaeologists approach the archaeological record and, in turn, in the ways in which we seek to justify the meanings we assign to archaeological observations. What I wish to discuss is not what we have done—that is a matter of record and should perhaps more appropriately be discussed by others. Instead, I want to discuss what needs to be done.

Science is a field that is dedicated to addressing our ignorance and, as such, should have built-in tactics designed to guide us to the recognition of ignorance in need of investigation. For the generation of those who were my teachers, recognized ignorance consisted largely of the sites we had not dug or the places and time periods we had not investigated. Ignorance was recognized as primarily arising from a lack of observations or discoveries. I tried to challenge this view of ignorance by pointing out that ignorance must also be recognized in the character of the knowledge and belief base that we use when interpreting our observations.

This challenge arose directly from the implications that the findings of general anthropology have for archaeology. It was difficult to ignore the teachings of anthropology, especially the demonstration that culture, the received knowledge and beliefs that we use in viewing the world, (1) is different among diverse sociocultural systems, and (2) is characterized by different stages during the historical trajectory of a given cultural system. It had to be acknowledged that scientists are not exempt from culture; they, like all other humans, are participants in culture. This means that for science to be truly successful it not only has to acknowledge ignorance about the external world but also to view its task as recognizing ignorance of a particular type, ignorance relative to the culture, the received "knowledge" and beliefs, of the scientists themselves. This is a very different view of science than that which characterized the earlier phases in the development of scientific methods. Under early, strict empiricists' views it was thought that the dedicated scientist could clear his mind of

Originally appeared in *American Archaeology Past and Future,* edited by David J. Meltzer et al., published by Smithsonian Institution Press, Washington, D.C., pp. 459–479, © 1986.

cultural bias and see reality "objectively." Anyone familiar with anthropology cannot accept such a position. We cannot operate as humans outside our cultural milieu.

The task of science is not only to sharpen and hone our culturally conditioned ideas about the external world but, in addition, to investigate the limitations of our received knowledge and beliefs about the external world. In short, the task of science is not the objective approximation of "truth" but just the opposite: the investigation of our culturally guided ignorance about reality. If we accept this goal, and the view that culture is learned, then it is clear that the enhancement of knowledge could modify our culture. If as anthropologically informed scientists we are successful in approaching our goal, then our refinement of knowledge (and thus of culture itself) will enrich our ability for dealing with reality.

How well does our received knowledge allow us to deal with the world of experience? How accurate is our alleged knowledge of the world? If one adopts other perspectives or contrastive means of observation, how different does the world of experience appear? These are the questions and tactics I used in my early papers to question the utility of the traditional archaeological paradigm. I tried to demonstrate that using the normative culture concept as an exclusive explanation for archaeologically observed differences and similarities was inadequate and misleading. I tried to demonstrate that processes and forces other than the mental templates of the ancients conditioned the archaeological record as seen by archaeologists. Once this is recognized, it becomes clear that the archaeological record contains information of relevance to the interesting problem of understanding cultural differences themselves. This was an attempt to enrich our archaeological knowledge. At the same time it was a critical evaluation of the inadequacy of traditional archaeological concept of culture to guide us to an understanding of the past and, more importantly, of cultural processes themselves.

TWO RESPONSES TO THE NEW ARCHAEOLOGY

The shift from believing in culture as the exclusive explanation for the archaeological record to recognizing that the deposits contain information that will potentially enlighten us as to the very nature of culture itself is described by David Clarke (1973) as our loss of innocence. For many, the state of innocence was a secure one. With the loss of innocence and security, they found themselves in a sea of uncertainty. What do we do? How do we proceed? What is a productive strategy? In this situation many archaeologists began to seek guidance from other fields of investigation; in many cases, this has had enriching consequences. On the other hand, there has grown up within archaeology a number of misguided arguments that many claim are gaining converts among those who will replace the current generation. It is these arguments that I feel are in need of review. If they are not treated seriously, they could well lead archaeology into still another backward and nonproductive era. I will refer to these arguments as (1) reconstructionism and (2) contextual-structuralism. There are many points of disagreement between these two approaches, and while I treat them as intellectually unique, their proponents will surely be offended by my failure to acknowledge many of their detailed claims to distinctiveness.

I consider reconstructionism to be an intellectual legacy of archaic science or strict empiricism. It is an approach with which traditionalists would be quite comfortable. It advocates the position that the growth of knowledge and understanding is exclusively dependent upon building an accurate structure of knowledge about external reality brick by brick. While in a strict sense this is not completely wrong, it is tragically limiting. Its practitioners may acknowledge that we are the ones who think about the world of experience, yet it operationally assumes (as did the archaic scientists) that truth resides in the external world. It assumes that by gaining an accurate understanding of archaeological formation processes—processes that should be clear to the "objective" observer—we can, by force of will, see the archaeological record objectively. Thus, criticism from this point of view frequently takes the form of attempting to point out, by remonstration and cautionary tales, the biases of "this world" that keep the archaeologist from seeing the "true" nature of the archaeological record (see Binford 1983b for a previous statement on this issue).

In addition, reconstructionism tends to be anti-intellectual, in that advocates fail to appreciate the importance of both conceptual growth and change. New ideas that are not perceived as simple, self-evident extensions of "direct-empirical" experience are disparaged (e.g., Schiffer's 1985:192 concept of personal gear and Gould's 1985:640–641 discussion of the same issue). In such discussions the demand is made that the warrant for an idea of potentially great importance must rest with the empirical credentials out of which the reconstructionists expect it to have arisen. Here we see the old, discredited notion that theory and concepts *must* be directly generalized from experience! If one is evaluating and seeking a more useful set of intellectual tools and one demands that all new tools be justified with respect to experiences cognized in a manner consistent with the old tools, then one never changes the paradigm; one only elaborates the old one. New approaches come from new ideas. Their utility must be tested in the future, not by reference to old ideas or to the credentials of their origins.

Nevertheless, at the observational level reconstructionists admonish us to build brick by brick a solid structure of knowledge and understanding about the processes of archaeological formational dynamics, without addressing the important issue of evaluating our archaeological culture or seeking to understand what we want to know in new ways. We are only reminded of alleged biases that could prevent us from seeing "reality" clearly. According to reconstructionist literature, if we would only open our eyes to the lessons of nature through the use of more detailed and rigorous observational strategies, we could empirically understand archaeological formation processes and, therefore, archaeological truth.

I recently read a paper by two behavioral archaeologists who list all the "distorting" events that might stand between the archaeological record as observed and the systemic context as it might have existed in a past system. The paper is supposed to be an object lesson to archaeologists who would seek to make statements about past systems before they had recognized and correctively "transformed" all the behavioral events that intervened to render the organization of the archaeological record different from the organization of on-going life as it existed in the past. The old empiricists' argument regarding the limitations of the archaeological record is central to these positions. The distortions, and the reality that all events are not equally visible archaeologically, are boringly repeated to caution archaeologists not to think beyond their data (Gould 1980a:1–28, 1985; Schiffer 1985:192). The message is clear. We must build up generalizations about past systemic contexts by the laborious "transformation" of contemporary data in its archaeological context into descriptive statements about past behavior. This reconstructionist process assumes that the inferential target is the on-going behavioral events of the once-living individuals who participated in the community responsible for the archaeological remains. Presumably, if we could accomplish this we could then participate as peers with ethnologists in their discussions of behavioral variability.

In the early days of the new archaeology a number of arguments were mounted to demonstrate that cultural systems were internally differentiated and, as such, could be expected to result in the differential spatial partitioning of distinctive cultural remains within and among sites. If true, this ontological assertion about the world would devastate the ways in which traditional archaeologists sampled the archaeological record and would successfully challenge the basic assumptions underlying their interpretive arguments. If these new arguments were accurate, it would no longer be possible to consider measured differences among casually collected archaeological samples as direct measures of cultural differentiation at the ethnic level of organization. These arguments called for a restudy of the nature of archaeological reality in order to demonstrate that the archaeological concept of culture was inadequate and thus had a distorting effect on our views of the past.

In this context, it became important to demonstrate that cultural systems were in fact internally differentiated organizationally so that a difference in cultural content could not necessarily be taken as a simple measure of ethnic difference. (This position has been sustained by every major piece of research designed to evaluate it, e.g., Binford 1976, 1978a, 1979, 1980a, 1982a; Hodder 1982b; Longacre 1981; Wiessner 1983.) The focus in this intellectual context was to demonstrate that organizational conditions within cultural systems could produce different forms of archaeological remains without implying different cultures at the pansystemic level. There was discussion of the meaning of interassemblage variability, study of the internal differentiation of sites into activity areas, and exploration of social differentiation from the standpoint of status and social groupings within societies that might affect variability in the archaeological record.

This was a testing period, an exploration of the external world for the purpose of evaluating the utility of the assumptions made about that world by traditional archaeologists. It exposed and criticized the degree to which certain conventional interpretive devices were unrealistic or simply wrong. It focused on the world of experience but was guided by new ideas about that world. Instead of viewing this situation as a tactical phase in the growth of a science, the reconstructionists seem to have tossed out the "testing of ideas" aspects and focused on the external world as the direct source of knowledge. They saw knowledge as flowing to us from "discoveries" in the world of experience (Gould 1985). Our ideas were tacitly seen as potential "distortions" of the true reality, a reality that could be known directly through insightful, observational "purification" and accurate measurement. This purification has been extended to include skepticism regarding the "borrowing" of ideas from other fields (Schiffer 1981:901–904), a failure to see value in concept and theory development (Schiffer 1981:905), and, recently, the open advocacy of a return to empiricism (Gould 1985).

The tactical research focus on behavior by new archaeologists, which occurred in the context of idea evaluation, has been strangely misinterpreted as a denial of the importance of culture itself. Some have even advocated the scrapping of the culture concept in favor of a focus on behavior (see Flannery 1982 for a reaction to this trend). For them, the goal of archaeology should be the accurate reconstruction of past dynamics in the proximate or behavioral sense, which will eventually lead to an "ethnographic" picture of the past. The final goal is seen as uncovering, in the empiricist's sense, laws of human behavior. The challenge offered by new archaeologists and the tactics appropriate to that challenge were proposed as an evaluation of the intellectual tools of archaeology and paradigmatic growth. Reconstructionists, however, were led to redirect the goals of archaeological inference (i.e., describing past behaviors particularistically rather than past cultures organizationally) and adopted a reactionary idea of science.

At the same time that reconstructionism was building in the literature, another important and very different reaction to the new archaeology was taking place. This response was guided not from an attempt to return to outdated methods of science, but from what was thought to be a "new" view that challenged the very utility of science itself. I refer to this reaction as contextual-structuralism.

The recognition that we cannot achieve "objectivity" in the manner conceived by archaic scientists became a popular point for endless reiteration. The recognition of the importance of culture, standing as a filter between us and "reality," was emphasized. During the era of the growth of the new archaeology the writings of Thomas Kuhn (1970) were read widely by the new generation of archaeologists. Kuhn makes important points regarding objectivity that are directed toward philosophers of science. When read from a nonscientific perspective, however, these arguments appear to cripple the approach to learning that many readers naively believe to be the scientific method: the archaic view of science. The result has been exactly the opposite of the response by the reconstructionists. Where the reconstrutionists have adopted a "reactionary" view of science by returning to a strict empiricism, the contextual-structuralists have largely rejected all science. Where some reconstructionists essentially reject the concept of culture, the contextual-structuralists embrace it not only as the explanation for the archaeological record (Hodder 1982a) but the explanation for the behavior of scientists (Landau 1981, Perper and Schrire 1977). They espouse the view that science is incapable of producing knowledge; instead, it is thought to be capable only of projecting subjective, culture-bound views onto the external world. From this perspective the new archaeologists are labeled out-of-date archaic scientist/empiricists or "dirty" positivists, while at the same time the demand is made for a return to the traditional "cultural" approach for the interpretation of archaeological remains. This posture leads to crippling skepticism. It denies that we can evaluate the utility of our own ideas and that we can analytically understand culture; in short, it denies that science can help us to learn.

> We might be able to see the past more clearly if we could distinguish between our misinterpretations and what actually occurred. But realistically, there is no suitable method. (Leone and Palkovich 1985:430)

What can we do? Advocates of this position have only nihilistic answers. We should abandon the "tyranny" of scientific methodology in favor of "important" issues of relevance in our own society, since "our research is a result of our social context" (Moore and Keene 1983:4–11). For those of us who are convinced that we can learn from our interaction with experience, these appear to be silly, chauvinistic suggestions. In contending with contextual-structuralism and reconstructionism, archaeology is clearly in an intellectual "double bind."

A THEORETICAL RESPONSE TO THE ISSUES

As in many conflicts there are nuggets of truth mixed with misguided thought. For instance, it is quite true that I cannot use knowledge I do not have. It is equally true that I cannot think with ideas I do not have. Thus, the contextual-structuralist argument that we are limited by received knowledge and by the conceptual tools available in our time is demonstrably correct. Demonstrating that the ideas with which we work are consistent with the culture of which we are a part is trivial. Do we really expect scientists to be "outside" their culture? That, of course, is impossible. Pointing such things out, however, does not mean that we are intellectually determined. Just because scientists are culture-bearing animals does not mean that they are intellectually shackled by culture and doomed to the ignorance and subjectivity of their time. Similarly, demonstrating a consistency between what we think at any one time and the broader cultural matrix in which we participate does not provide an evaluation of the utility and accuracy of those ideas, regardless of their origin.

The reconstructionist position contains equally limiting ideas. The most restricting, in my opinion, is the strict empiricist approach to learning. The reconstructionist tendency is to view empirical generalizations as the primary goal of research; to attempt the inductive elevation of such descriptive statements to "lawlike" status; and in turn to believe that this empirically grounded description of the world will somehow allow us to gain an understanding of the world (Raab and Goodyear 1984; Salmon 1982a; Schiffer 1976:4; Smith 1982). The positive aspects of this "empirically grounded" posture are that a focus on description can lead to more accurate recording, to the recognition of complexity (such as many of the so-called distortions that may stand between the static record and the dynamics of the past), and to a greater appreciation for the character of the empirical domain that we study: the archaeological record. Accurate description and justified inference are crucial to science, but as Hugh Mellor (1982:60) has pointed out:

> Explanation is not a kind of inference. Just because the phenomenon to be explained would be more safely predictable if it were more probable doesn't mean it would therefore also be better explained.

When the strict empiricist approach to understanding is followed there is a disdain for the use of imagination and for inventive thought, and a cry for grounded empirical relevance for every idea introduced (Gould 1985:641). But the search for understanding—explanation—is an intellectual activity and not strictly a synthesis of observations. Thus, the empiricist approach ensures that understanding will not be forthcoming, only that we will have a more accurate description of the world as it appears when we are guided by our particular cognitive framework. If one accepts this damning criticism of empiricism, then the consequence will be that empiricists in fact only describe the world "subjectively," and the growth of knowledge will be tragically curtailed.

The defenders of empiricism could note with justification that "discoveries" are possible, that we can encounter experiences for which we have no prior cognitive devices for accommodation, and that we can thereby expose the limitations of our ideas. Although this is certainly correct, the presence of anomalies does not ensure their recognition. As most cultural anthropologists would be quick to point out, we have the remarkable capacity to accommodate the world of experience to what we already believe about that world. I would argue that discoveries are not simply the intrusion of the external world on our cognitive framework. Instead, they come about largely from a skeptical posture on the part of the scientists, who search for the inadequacies in their received wisdom and thereby prompt their most valuable asset (their imaginations) to develop and invent new and more appropriate cognitive devices and theories. Such things come from us, not from experience.

The empiricist approach seeks to ground empirically our experiences in conventionally made and synthesized observations. This ensures that we will never see challenges to our conventions. A strict empirical approach tends to reinforce the false view that our contemporary cognitive tools and knowledge are adequate and at the same time suppresses our most valuable asset, our imaginations. The important point here is to have a clear understanding of how we use our experiences. An approach that seeks empirical generalizations demands description in conventional terms. On the other hand, the correct approach to learning is dependent upon the use of experience to expose the limitations of our conventions. As a learning strategy, empiricism is clearly limited.

Although the contextual or structuralist approaches may appear to challenge science itself, many of these positions can be argued in ways that could well contribute to the growth of our science. For instance, strong dedication to the position that we cannot think thoughts that we do not have or use knowledge that is unavailable to us is crucial. Acceptance of this position validates the goals of science as I have presented them, namely, the skeptical mistrust of our own cognitive and theoretical tools and hence the scientists' dedication to the exposure of their limitations. The continuous demonstration of our own culture-bound perspectives clearly falsifies the old claim of "free will" and "objectivity" that plagued both archaic science and traditional attempts to explain human behavior. The limitations of the contextual-structuralist position appear when there is a failure to acknowledge that the enhancement of scientifically guided learning strategies can result in the growth of knowledge.

The anti-science posture derives not from recognizing the role of culture in our daily lives but from the acceptance of "generative" model of culture change, which is characteristic of the contextual-structuralist position. A generative view assumes that an inner core serves as the organizing feature for surficial behavior or action. This organizing feature is manifest by the actions of participant/actors who are programmed to this core of belief, meaning, or symbolic structure (for a clear example of this view, see Glassie 1975 and Deetz 1982).

As Ernest Gellner (1982:116) has insightfully argued, however,

> the point about the symbol tokens used by systems such as language is that they are cheap. . . . Sounds, marks on the paper, symbolic gestures, all cost virtually nothing. . . . Because this is so, but only because this is so . . . we can expect symbolic systems to play out their full inner potential.

Unfortunately, as Gellner (1982:116) also points out, adherents to this "generative" view fail to appreciate a fundamental point, namely, that

> there are extensive aspects of human life, alas including those that seem essential to survival, whose actual sequence of events is determined not merely by the free play of some underlying core mechanism (if it indeed exists at all), but by the blind constraints and shortages and competitions and pressures of the real extraneous environment.

Generative approaches fail to explain cultural systems because of their stubborn denial that we are dealing with thermodynamic systems, not simply with cost-free symbolic codes. Cultural systems are organizations with essential dynamics that are dependent upon the flow of energy through them. Energy is captured by such systems in nature, not by human participants thinking or codifying costless symbolic dreams about this very concrete materialist process. In turn, the trajectory of a culturally organized thermodynamic system is not determined by what the bearers think about the process. Instead, it is determined by the behavioral and organizational ways in which the system articulates with energy sources and with internal and external competitors. Understanding patterning in the history of past cultural systems derives from an understanding of these processes, not from some imaginative characterization of a stable and internally closed symbolic system capable only of "acceptable" rearrangement of its finite components. The structuralist position is inappropriate to sociocultural systems, and more importantly, it is wrong.

The falsity of this posture is demonstrable by the fact that a paradox is inherent in its arguments. For instance, we acknowledge, as contextual-structuralists have, that we cannot use ideas we do not have or reason with information we do not possess. The paradox arises when this proposition is linked with the false generative idea of sociocultural dynamics described above. When this is done, it is commonly suggested that we cannot know the past except by seeking to understand the particular symbolic codes or systems of thought held by ancient peoples. We might reasonably ask, how would this aid us if those ancient peoples, like us, could neither think ideas they did not have nor accumulate knowledge relevant to questions they never asked? For example, from my retrospective viewpoint as an archaeologist I might reasonably ask, what caused the transition from Middle to Upper Paleolithic? If I could magically go back in time for an ethnographic interview with a population of late Neanderthals, I would most certainly find that (1) they would not know that they were living during such a transition, and (2) they would have little if any awareness that major processes both condition their lives and at the same time move the trajectory of their culture history in the direction of a way of life unknown or unimaginable to them.

How can the thoughts, beliefs, or opinions of the participants in ancient cultural systems aid me in solving a problem that arises from a totally different perspective—a perspective that the ancients could neither experience nor reason about with knowledge they did not have? No Neanderthal would or could provide realistic solutions to problems posed by me, problems arising in the context of my vastly different perspective, knowledge base, and temporal viewpoint. As a modern archaeologist I have the wonderful opportunity to know something of the past on a temporal scale virtually invisible to participants in any intellectually unspecialized cultural system. Similarly, from the perspective of past participants I can know something of their future in ways unimaginable to them. I can quite literally gain insights into an order of reality that was unknown to participants in ancient cultural systems. Demanding that I adopt a participant's perspective (see Binford and Sabloff 1982 for a discussion of this issue) as the only reality makes about as much sense as demanding that we not look through microscopes, since the "true" reality is that which is available only to the naked eye! Archaeology is not served by acceptance of a false ontological assumption.

We cannot understand the past through the eyes of the ancients. Similarly, we cannot know the past or the present by simply accepting one form of subjective view as correct on the basis of asserted privileged insight (e.g., binary oppositions). We must seek to know the past accurately through, and not in spite of, the use of our perspective. It follows that we must accept responsibility for the character of the intellectual tools we use, and we must continuously seek to improve and modify them in terms of the knowledge available to us and the opportunities for learning open to us. At the same time we accept this responsibility, we must realize that both our knowledge base and the conceptual tools with which we approach the archaeological record may be limited and/or inappropriate. As suggested earlier, our job is quite literally the evaluation of our own cultural tools—the tools that we use in seeking to describe and understand the external world, which for us is simply the archaeological record.

Most contemporary archaeologists, except the strict empiricists, acknowledge that we cannot know reality in terms of itself, but only through the cognitive and explanatory devices that we use. We further acknowledge that these devices may be wrong and are part of a broader tradition of received "knowledge" within which we participate (in other words, our own culture). Many may reasonably ask, how can we know the past? Frequently, the answer is that we cannot. We should, therefore, abandon our self-deceiving exercises and address ourselves to a critical understanding of our own culture-bound ideas from the perspective of internal criticism, since the external world is thought to be denied us by virtue of our subjectivity (see Hodder 1984a).

This position has been well stated by Mary Hesse. She concludes that we must adopt a position denying "that there is a fundamental distinction between theoretical and observation predicates and statements" (Hesse 1974:33). The nature of the external world is denied to us by virtue of the assumed fact that our cognitive system molds experience so that the external world is not permitted to intrude on its internal integrity. At first blush this sounds reasonable; it even appears consistent with many of the points I have advocated here. In addition, on one level it is good advice. Certainly, the more aware we are of the context of our ideas, the less likely we would be to accept such received ideas as "true" (Leone 1982). In denying a scientific method for evaluating ideas, however, the position moves so as to transform archaeology into moral philosophy.

We can accept the fact that we can neither reason with knowledge we do not have nor think with cognitive devices unknown to us, and we can also acknowledge the fact that we commonly accommodate the world of experience to our own belief system of the moment. We can support the view that an awareness of how our ideas of the moment came into being could constructively sharpen our skepticism. We can subscribe to the position that we should be both moral and ethical in our search for knowledge. We may subscribe to the view that our choices of research problems should be sensitive to the needs for knowledge within our own society. None of these positions, however, demands that we deny our ability to learn and in turn to modify the limiting effects that our culture places on our understanding of external reality.

A PRACTICAL RESPONSE TO THE ISSUES

Science is a strategy for learning. What scientists hope to accomplish is to perfect ways of seeking experiences in the external world so that they will implicate inadequacies in our alleged knowledge. Put another way, scientists study the accuracy and reliability of their alleged knowledge by seeking experiences designed to expose limitations in the body of ideas and beliefs with which they begin their quest. They seek to put their ideas in jeopardy, not to make them more secure, as a creationist might be prone to do. Science is not dedicated to the discovery of "truth" or to the demonstration that a given body of ideas is "right."

These ideas constituted the central thrust of the new archaeology. It advocated attention to the procedure that seeks to transform ignorance into knowledge. The important issues to be addressed are whether we can learn and, if we can, how we learn. We do not learn by falsely deceiving ourselves into thinking that we can purge ourselves of ignorance and "objectively" approach nature for instruction. Similarly, we do not learn by denying that learning is possible. Finally, we do not learn by editing an alleged past to serve as justification for adopting a particular value-laden political or moral posture in the present. We learn by exploring learning strategies, by experimenting with scientific methods that continuously place our ideas in jeopardy relative to the world of experience.

There was a past, and there is an archaeological record that was created in the past. Although we may be capable of fooling ourselves for a time about both of these realities, a learning procedure that continuously compares our ideas with our experiences cannot help but reveal situations in which our ideas are inadequate. In short, ambiguities deriving from inadequacies in our cognitive and intellectual tools will be exposed. I am suggesting that, like sociocultural systems, intellectual systems can also be open systems, although at times they may appear to be closed and internally "generative." This is particularly true for archaeologists, since the target of our search for knowledge no longer exists. The past cannot speak back or object; in short, there is little cost and hence little risk of being wrong that does not derive from our own competitive social matrix. The openness of our intellectual structure must be provided by our methods and procedures. We must ensure that the past "gets a say," that it can object and guide our growth toward understanding.

The opportunity that opens this important door, that gives the past a chance to object, occurs when ambiguity arises in our own thoughts relative to external experiences we have had. Ambiguity exists relative to some experience when two or more lines of reasoning would lead us to two or more incompatible conclusions. In this situation we are in a deductive posture aimed at evaluating our ideas. (This is quite different from Gould's 1985 demand for inductive justification for ideas.) In such a situation we can be sure that there are inadequacies in one or more of our lines of reasoning. This is the flag, the signal, that we must examine in detail. When this signal is given we must research both our intellectual tools and the cognitive tools with which we assimilate experiences (Binford 1987a). At the same time we must use our most powerful tool, our imagination, to generate new cognitive devices and intellectual tools that will resolve the ambiguity. This is how we learn and how we grow: by placing our intellectual tools in interaction with one another in the context of experience.

Given such a posture, what realities do we address? Where do we seek experience? I have already suggested that archaeology is the science of the archaeological record. Pessimists, and particularly empiricists, endlessly point to aspects of the past about which we cannot learn, even given our increasing ability to understand the archaeological record and the conditions in the past that brought it into being. This pessimistic attitude is incorrect; we will not know what these limitations on understanding the past might be until we completely understand all facets of the archaeological record, a condition that we have not yet achieved. On the other hand, optimists commonly identify goals for learning that do not derive from an understanding of the archaeological record but arise instead from their limited experiences and from the political/moral biases of our contemporary world.

Pessimists decry attempts to develop learning strategies regarding aspects of the past for which they see no concrete, "empirical" remnants in the archaeological record, but they fail to realize that all statements about the past are inferences. On the other hand, optimists seek to learn things for which there are no understood methods for knowing. The pessimistic situation results in dull description of the archaeological record in contemporary terms, while the overly optimistic situation results in wild, speculative, just-so stories. Archaeologists must face the fact that they do not study the past, they create it. What they study is the archaeological record. The created past is only as correct as the understanding of the properties of the archaeological record, and the processes that brought those properties into being. The development of theoretically guided middle-range research is the key to the inferential problem.

Another problem concerns the distinction between the aspects of the past we seek to know and the aspects of past reality that the archaeological record indicates. Some would say that the archaeological record is the simple result of human actions, that is, human behavior as we understand it, given our perspective as participants in a cultural system. Others, as discussed above, assert that the archaeological record is a manifestation of a core ideational structure insulated from the energetic world of life and changing only through the free, creative actions of individuals (Leaf 1979:336). Still others suggest that it is a distorted, fragmented, limited record of *the* past, as if there had been only one past reality. From an ontological standpoint I would like to suggest that all these views are inaccurate. I have already suggested that the archaeologist can know something of both the past and the future of a past cultural manifestation, knowledge that was denied the participants. Clearly, then, the archaeological record presents us with information vastly different from that which was available to the participants within past systems. In turn, the type of information that is available must guide what we seek to know of the past.

The archaeological record also demonstrates temporal durations or a tempo of chronological change that is very different from that perceived by persons who participated in it. The rates of culture change for most archaeologically known eras are much slower than the rates of generational replacement for participants in those systems. This fact must be appreciated in two ways. First, the beliefs and perceptions of the past participants could not have been germane to a reality of which they could not have been aware, the macrotemporal scale of systems change and the factors that were conditioning it. Second, the observations by ethnographers and historical figures, while perhaps documenting something of the internal dynamics of cultural systems, cannot be expected to be necessarily germane to an understanding of a much slower and larger-scale process of change and modification. Thus, the reality with which we deal is one that living, breathing persons have in fact never directly experienced. It is true that their cumulative participation provides the energy base upon which the macroforces of change operate; yet they never experienced such impersonal forces. The archaeologist, seated in the present, is outside history in the participant sense. We have a chance to understand humankind in a way that no participant, or no social scientist addressing the quick-time events of direct social experience, could ever imagine. To fail to recognize this potential, to fail to grasp a new understanding of humankind from this different perspective—the perspective of the macroforces that condition and modify lifeways in contexts unappreciated by the participants within complex thermodynamic systems—is quite literally to "abandon our birthright."

It is true that archaeology is anthropology in that it seeks to understand humankind. Yet it is simply wrong to attempt to force our unique data and our ability to appreciate dynamics on a macroscale, in the organizational sense of the term, into the limiting experiences and frameworks developed for treating the quick-time events of the human participants in history. We are not ethnographers of the past, we are not sociologists, we are not historians in the humanistic sense of the term; we are scientists dedicated to an understanding of the archaeological record. Its patterning and character strongly suggests that the common social science perspectives on humankind are inappropriate to our archaeological view of humanity. Although we may, in Pompeii-like situations, sometimes reconstruct quick-time events and situations, it is equally true that we have the opportunity to view these human-scale events simultaneously in terms of other observational properties indicative of the organizational contexts in which they were conducted. In this opportunity we can learn something of the properties of the systems within which past persons participated but did not necessarily cognize.

For a long time archaeologists have had an inferiority complex relative to ethnologists and cultural anthropologists. We were convinced that the participant perspective and its personalized scale of experience was the only reality. The archaeological record was viewed as a poor, distorted reflection of this assumed unitary reality. Surely we need to develop links between the varying scales of perception suggested above; but more importantly we must realize that we have the opportunity to study scales of reality that are experientially denied to the ethnographer. The appropriate action for us is not to lament the "limitations" of the archaeological record but to appreciate the limitations of the ethnographic experience and the records and ideas that arise in the ethnographer's brief touch with a circumscribed reality. The archaeological record documents a broader and potentially more fascinating reality.

CONCLUSION

My message in pursuit of the future has been made up of several components. First, I have argued that cultural systems are not closed ideological structures. They are thermodynamic systems open to influence and even determinancy from the broader thermodynamic forces with which they must articulate. Second, I have suggested that since there is an external world our scientific culture need not be viewed as a closed system that is subject only to internal generative types of change. We as scientists have the opportunity to learn by placing our received and subjective views of the world in jeopardy, by seeking experiences in the external world that are designed to expose the limitations of our ideas. Finally, I have suggested that the particular experiential domain that archaeologists study, the archaeological record, documents a scale and domain of process that was operative in the past and undoubtedly continues to operate today, but because of our limited life span and knowledge this process is generally not appreciated by participants.

Archaeologists are faced with the challenging task of seeking to understand at least two kinds of phenomena that none of us have ever experienced directly: the past itself and, more important, the long-term macroprocesses that the archaeological record documents. Archaeologists have the opportunity to gain an understanding of humankind and its transformations not previously appreciated by most social scientists.

I think it is fair to say that most practicing archaeologists see themselves as strict empiricists at the level of "dirt archaeology" and relegate the fundamental debates regarding methods for inference to an independent domain of theoretical discussion that is considered to be largely irrelevant to their day-to-day activities. This response stems from the fact that at least one of the messages central to the "new archaeology" has not been received: namely, the view that our ideas directly condition how we meaningfully organize and assimilate experience at the very point of observation. On the other hand, unquestioning acceptance of this same proposition has led to the belief that we cannot learn from experience; hence, nihilism and skepticism permeate many "theoretical discussions." In turn, the "dirt archaeologists," correctly convinced that they can learn from experience, relegate such discussions to the stratosphere of speculative, irrelevant side issues. Many return to the sterile posture of particularism, as exemplified by traditional culture-historical approaches, even though this posture has long since been demonstrated to be inadequate. Our success in the future depends upon our thoughtful attention to this impasse.

I suggest that there are solutions. I also believe that our future depends not only upon our successful response to the "dirt archaeologist's" view of the problem but upon a shift in the character of archaeological education as well. If the young persons entering our field are not educated to the character of the very real intellectual issues that archaeologists must solve, and if education continues to be in the hands of "dirt archaeologists" who largely do not understand the nature of our intellectual problems, archaeology will stagnate in the dead end of strict empiricism and particularism. On the other hand, if theoretical discussion remains in the hands of those who are skeptical about our abilities to learn, "dirt archaeologists" are correct in rejecting theory as being irrelevant.

In my opinion, many of our problems stem from adopting the arguments of ethnologists as if they somehow had a more "direct" understanding of reality. Similarly, the skeptical attitude of many "dirt archaeologists" regarding theory is probably rooted in a realistic appreciation of what the archaeological record is. It is not the same reality that ethnologists study. We need to devote our energies to the development of archaeological science, which means the building of theory appropriate to our world of experience as guided by scientifically rooted learning strategies.

In the future we must pursue increased sophistication in scientific learning strategies, increased dedication to understanding the archaeological record, and importantly, the development of knowledge regarding the operation of processes that transcend the quick-time events and experiences of participants in systems. Pursuit of these goals will realize for us a potential understanding of humankind that is uniquely offered to archaeologists.

Chapter 5

Data, Relativism, and Archaeological Science

Contemporary archaeology is coping with some of the fundamental philosophical issues of our time through argumental posturing and polemics. Today I will suggest that many of these arguments and postures stem from a poor understanding of the philosophical issues themselves, but more importantly, many are metaphysical issues that are not really appropriate to science in fundamental ways. Thus, when introduced, these issues become distractions and lead to unproductive argument. This is not a new situation. Thomas Huxley spent much of his intellectual life coping with just such issues. Even when solved, these issues would never lead to greater learning, only to a kind of intellectual comfort or discomfort with the act of seeking knowledge itself and the methods proposed for doing so. I will seek to elaborate these introductory remarks with what I consider to be some fundamental issues around which current controversy swirls.

WHERE DO DATA COME FROM?

It has been said that any science can be operationally defined with respect to the way it interacts with its empirical domain or subject to study. Albert Spaulding (1960) has cogently argued that archaeology may be productively considered as that science which studies artefacts (I would say the archaeological record) with respect to the dimensions of form, time (inferred), and space. This statement sounds neat and concise, but when it actually comes down to doing archaeology we need a better understanding of process—of how we actually go about learning from archaeological observations.

Crucial to the process of learning is a clear understanding of what a fact is for a scientist. Within science the term *fact* refers to aspects of the actual occurrence of an event. More importantly, scientists generally attribute factual status to "recognisable'," singular events that occur at given times. While a *fact* exists in an event or part thereof that occurs once and is then gone forever, *data* are the representations of facts by some relatively permanent convention of documentation. The astute person will recognise that this conventionally used definition of a fact signals for archaeologists

The Huxley Memorial Lecture 1986. Originally published in *Man* (N.S.) 22:391–404, © 1987.

some interesting methodological problems that the very nature of their experience with the archaeological record prescribes. For instance, if we accept the equation of facts with events, we must conclude that archaeologists can never work with facts of the past. Nevertheless, archaeologists produce many data as a result of their study and observation of the archaeological record. These studies may result in relatively permanent records of their observations. What then are the events that archaeologists describe so as to produce data? They record the events of observation in which they participate. These observational events, occurring in the present, may be recorded in notes and laboratory attribute tabulations. These observational records, reported as the data of archaeology, refer to contemporary facts—contemporary observational events. No historical facts (past events) are available for archaeologists to observe. Archaeologists produce data from facts of contemporary observations on artefacts. This important point is given further importance when we consider the criteria commonly employed in science for judging the admissibility of data for scientific treatment.

1. *The event that is accepted as a scientific fact must be singular. Data are representations of singular events.*

This idea has been introduced above, and it can be accepted as a given. The rationale for it will become more clear when we consider the operations that scientists perform with their data.

2. *The event must, in principle, be available for public scrutiny. That is, it must be an event that could be sensed by more than one person.*

Another way of stating this criterion is that the fact must be objectively observable. In modern science the word *objective* has a very specific meaning. It simply means that the rules for observation are made explicit so that another observer using the same rules for looking it would see the same fact if given the opportunity.

3. *The description of the event should be such that different individuals can know, as specifically as is reasonable, the nature of the event that is being described.*

This additional criterion of objectivity implies that the rules for seeing an event are also specified by the investigator so that another person would be able to isolate an event in the same way as the scientist reporting factual events as data. In the case of archaeologists, the context of observation is most unambiguously seen as the observation of an entity by an archaeological observer. Archaeologists do this all the time, with the result that observations on one pottery sherd or projectile point are treated as single events and hence sources of facts. This criterion can become somewhat confusing when the archaeologist speaks of observations on other types of units considered to be unitary phenomena, such as archaeological features, pits, house remains, burials, or sites or regions. I suggest that a bounded phenomenon, where the bounds are visible to the observer at the time of observation, may legitimately be treated as an observational unit for purposes of the production of archaeological data. Phenomena that can be seen at the time of observation by virtue of visible and specifiable boundaries, such as pits, postmolds and hearths, may for purposes of data production be considered units of observation. It is the rules for the recognition of unitary phenomena that provide the archaeologist with the ability to identify units of observation objectively for purposes of the production of data from observational events.

Since all relevant archaeological facts are inherent in events of observation, the archaeologist has many advantages over other social scientists who report facts of social interaction, facts of events from on-going dynamic experiences, facts that are uncontrolled or constrained in ways that render their data inadmissible for scientific research. Quite literally the archaeologist seeks to render his factual observations admissible for scientific use by developing and explicating operational definitions, or descriptions of how one documents a fact. These definitions describe the operations the observer performs in order to produce data, the records of facts.

The domain of archaeological investigation is the archaeological record. When archaeological phenomena are recovered from a static context—a buried surface, a surface of the earth not currently used by man, or one on which man currently lives but does not use any previously deposited artefacts—it seems probable that the artefacts must relate to past events. This is the reasoning that renders it rational for archaeologists to seek knowledge of the past through the study of artefacts. Nevertheless, we cannot confuse implications with facts. The artefacts so discovered may have had their origin in the past, but the past events in which they participated are gone—not available for observation—and hence there are no historical facts remaining for us to see or record.

Archaeologists study contemporary data, data generated by them in the act of observing the archaeological record. This means that the possible observational events in which the archaeologist might participate are the result of the archaeologist's judgements as to what might be profitable to observe—that is, what properties might implicate the past in reliable ways. Putting this situation very bluntly, all archaeological data are generated by us in *our* terms. We are responsible both for the production of data and, as we will see later, for what we have to say about it in so far as we use it to implicate the past. All responsibility for accuracy and reliability rests with us.

During the early days of science this was not the manner in which data production was conceived. Strict empiricists believed that data were derived from nature and experience itself. Put another way, data were handed over to the astute observer as "natural" packages residing in nature. As Francis Bacon said,

> I am of the opinion that if men had ready at hand a just history of nature and experience, and labored diligently thereon; and if they could bind themselves to two rules,—the first, to lay aside received opinions; and the second, to refrain the mind for a time from the highest generalizations, and those next to them,—they would be able by the native and genuine force of the mind, without any other art, to fall into my form of interpretation. For interpretation is the true and natural work of the mind when freed from impediments. (in Commins and Linscott 1947:154)

Bacon saw the weakness of poor theories as guides to the interpretation of nature and suggested that all theories should be abandoned in favour of the gift of conclusions arising from the "natural work of the mind." Similarly, archaeologists viewing the frequently racist products of theoretically guided interpretation produced by the nineteenth-century evolutionists adopted the strict empiricism of Bacon's thought and rejected theory as a useful component of scientific procedure. Not only did they reject the particular theories of the nineteenth century, they concluded that all theory must therefore be misleading. They operated with the naive belief that they could clear their minds of "received opinions and notions" and be guided to understanding through simple observation and the natural "discoveries" that might result from such procedures. Data were thought to reside in natural units of nature, awaiting our discovery.

HOW DO WE EVALUATE OUR DATA?

If one adopts a strict empiricist's view of the growth of knowledge and believes that "interpretation is the true and natural work of the mind when freed from impediments," then clearly the best way to evaluate knowledge claims is to evaluate something of the "quality" of the mind at work and the degree to which it has been truly "freed of impediments." In short, the way to judge the validity of inferences offered by archaeologists would be to evaluate the archaeologists and their states of mind. It is interesting that serious epistemological discussion during the heyday of traditional archaeology stressed only the subjective element as crucial in the evaluation of archaeological interpretations.

> The final judgment of any archaeologist's cultural reconstruction must therefore be
> based on an appraisal of his professional competence, and particularly the quality
> of the subjective contribution to that competence. (Thompson 1956:331–332)

This was a total endorsement of ad hominem *argument,* sanctioning the introduction of character and personality into archaeological debate (see Binford 1983b for a response to this type of evaluative discussion).

I think most people acknowledge that the strict empiricist's view of fact and data is faulty. Anthropology has demonstrated again and again that the facts of culturally guided cognition render naive the empiricist's claim of a privileged ability to see nature and experience "truly." In the past, however, many archaeologists purporting to adopt the posture of empiricism nonetheless operated with "received opinions and notions" and were quick to generalise, while in the same breath they advertised that their claims for knowledge flowed self-evidently from nature and experience.

It was in the context of strict empiricism that one such knowledge claim was made, and it has debilitated archaeology even into the current era. This is the claim of relativism. I am quite aware of the experiences that have propelled researchers to this viewpoint and will suggest that it is the naive psychology of certain types of ethnographic and social research that has led to relativist conclusions. I will further suggest that a careful examination of the locus of responsibility for the production of data in a science will negate the claims of utility made for the relativist viewpoint in the science of archaeology.

Let me present a story of ethnographers and their experiences. Typically ethnographers are trained in "their" culture; they are schooled in the culture of their particular research specialisation. As students they learn all the "received knowledge and opinion" of their predecessors in their research field. If lucky, they are given the opportunity to go out to a "group" or "society" to do fieldwork. I have done this several times and can attest to the fact that this experience is generally traumatic. In fact, I tell my students that no more unnatural position exists for any person. All our culturally conditioned expectations for behaviour and belief are challenged. The people the fieldworker is with behave differently, express different concerns, and express themselves and their motives in terms unfamiliar to the observer. In this context the fieldworker becomes increasingly dependent upon informants to provide him or her with *information* regarding their knowledge and beliefs in terms of which the local people operate. This needed understanding must come from the informants, the local experts, who it is hoped can enculturate the fieldworker sufficiently to be able to see the world from their perspective.

We may ask the interesting question: if the field observer is a scientist, who is creating the data? In this situation the answer is always that the local people provide the fieldworker with information regarding what they consider to be "data," in response to the researcher's request that the informants provide an understanding of their own behaviour. In so far as ethnographers are successful in understanding a different cultural system from the perspective of "participant observers", they will do so in the terms of the people being studied. The circumstances of the ethnographic situation reinforce the researchers' convictions that their approach is purely empirical, for they have successfully laid aside "received opinions and notions," and understanding has flowed directly from experience.

Even though ethnographers are successful in communicating their new-found cultural experiences to readers in their own culture, they are still not operating in a scientific role. Instead, they have adopted the role of intercultural translators; they provide an intellectual Rosetta Stone–the monograph–so that the alien cultural behaviour of one group can be appreciated by an outsider. Throughout this experience field researchers are continuously bombarded by the recognition that their own cultural guides to understanding appear to be inadequate: they find that their ways of thinking about their experiences may not anticipate the responses of the informants. In short, their conventional codes for thinking do not work very well in the face of an unknown and different way of thinking about and interpreting experience.

As Clifford Geertz has said:

> The whole point . . . is . . . to aid us in gaining access to the conceptual world in which our subjects live so that we can, in some extended sense of the term, converse with them. (Geertz 1973:24)

> The essential vocation of interpretive anthropology is not to answer our deepest questions, but to make available to us answers that others, guarding other sheep in other valleys, have given, and thus to include them in the consultable record of what man has said. (Geertz 1973:30)

I suggest that these goals, coupled with baffling experiences in the ethnographic world, have compelled many social researchers to rely on their informants to create their data. In turn, these same informants guide the interpretation and ultimately mediate the understanding of the data. What ethnographers report is not data but information, the intellectualised expression of experience. If the ethnographer is successful in capturing the character of others "guarding other sheep in other valleys," the act of intellectualising is done by the informants. It is no wonder that from this context each culture appears unique, each culture has a logic all its own, and each culture must be understood in its own terms. Ironically, this relativistic conclusion appears to be consistent with the archaic assumptions of strict empiricism. The ethnographers had to clear their minds of received knowledge and beliefs in order to experience a different cultural reality.

This ethnographic procedure has had important and confusing impacts "at home," in the centres of social science research. To begin with, although it affirmed one basic principle of empiricism (that we must clear our minds of preconceived ideas and received knowledge), it demonstrated the inapplicability of another: ethnographers were capable of comprehending nature directly when dealing with the intellectualising of others. The social scientist was dependent upon an informant, an expert guide to alien cultural realities. In an ethnographic setting, understanding was not the consequence of mental liberation as much as it was the result of fortuitous collaboration.

If this was the only "world," the only way to study man and his works, then (alas!) archaeology was cut off. All such potential sources of information regarding the alien cultural materials that had been dug up were long since dead and gone! From this perspective, the pessimistic viewpoint of Edmund Leach (1973) was correct. He said, "The contents of the Black Box, social organization as the social anthropologist understands that term, must forever remain a mystery." Strangely, archaeologists accepted the participant-observer perspective and committed themselves to the frustrating goal of seeking understanding in terms that, as Leach points out, "must forever remain a mystery." They persisted in seeking to understand the past in seemingly unobtainable terms. As Robert Dunnell has said,

> the field is . . . encompassed by the concept artifact, objects which owe some of their attributes to human activity. The problem similarly is to provide categories for these data that are cultural, for the ultimate purpose of explaining the products of human behavior and with them in the behavior that created them *in terms of ideas held in common by the makers and users.* (Dunnell 1971:130; emphasis added)

Crucial to this view of archaeology is the belief that we do not study the archaeological record; rather, we seek to organise the remnants of the past into cultural categories that were significant in the past. In turn, culture itself is considered to be a mental phenomenon held in the heads of persons now gone.

As Walter Taylor has said:

> culture is a mental construct consisting of ideas . . . attitudes, meanings, sentiments, feelings, values, goals, purposes, interests, knowledge, beliefs, relationships, associations. . . . For example, there is present in an Indian's mind the idea of a dance. This is a trait of culture. This idea influences his body so that he behaves in a certain way. The result of this behavioral activity is the pattern of the dance. . . . Both the behavior itself and the resulting patterns are observable, but for this very reason they are fleeting. The culture idea is not observable but endures in the Indian's mind to be repeated again. (Taylor 1948:101–102)

As Leach (1973) has pointed out, there is no way the archaeologist can study culture when it is conceived of in these terms. This was acknowledged by ethnologists and traditional archaeologists alike. For instance, James Griffin has said,

> An archaeologist may recover material but not the substance of aboriginal artifacts. The exact meaning of any particular object for the living group or individual is forever lost, and the real significance or lack of importance of any object in an ethnological sense has disappeared by the time it becomes a part of an archaeologist's catalogue of finds. (Griffin 1943:340)

In spite of these misgivings, archaeologists continued to delude themselves into believing they could achieve the improbable. This was accomplished by assuming that culture, when conceived of in a mentalist fashion, was the explanation for certain selected manifestations remaining from the past. They assumed a conventionalist posture in which meaning was assigned to archaeological observations chosen by us, made in the contemporary world by us, yet presented not as data but as *information* reflecting the ideas held in the minds of long dead persons.

> Artifacts are concrete objects. Types and modes, on the contrary, are conceptual patterns set up by the archaeologist to represent ideas possibly held by the artisan. . . . Artifacts have little historical significance. Types and modes, however, are well suited for historical study. (Chang 1967a:91)

Stated another way, archaeologists presented their own observations as "pre-intellectualised" understandings, just as the ethnographer presents his intercultural experiences "pre-intellectualised" by his informants' understandings. *The great problem with this approach was that the archaeologist had no informant from whom to receive understanding,* yet he behaved as if he were capable of penetrating the minds of past men and rendering his observations into information about the past in cultural terms. This was and continues to be a great self-deception. We are surrounded today by arrogant intellectual inventions that claim to make possible a discussion of the past in the intellectual terms of the past. Accepting a mentalist definition of culture, James Deetz notes:

> Culture is patterned . . . (therefore) the patterning which the archaeologist perceives in his materials is a reflection of the patterning in the culture which produced it. (Deetz 1967:7)

This approach is also emphasized by Ian Hodder:

> Excavated artifacts are immediately cultural, not social, and they can inform on society only through an adequate understanding of cultural context. (Hodder 1982c:10)

In Hodder's view, *cultural context* refers to the received knowledge, beliefs, and "codes" for conceptualisation held in the minds of past men. Both these conventionalist approaches share the belief that artefacts directly implicate the mental codes held in the minds of past men. The first approach represents the view of traditional archaeology, in which it was acknowledged that not all artefacts directly implicate past ideas, only those that are patterned in certain ways (Dunnell 1971; Ford 1962; Krieger 1944; Spaulding 1960). The more recent view, championed by those adopting a "textual" approach, assumes that all artefacts are symbols and are direct semiotic evidence or, in a more structuralist posture, present themselves as clues to the intellectual determinants of the ancients' behaviour.

It is interesting that archaeologists who adopt culture as an explanation for their observations do so by virtue of the ethnographer's experience with the domain of intercultural experience. In the manner in which it has been predominantly championed by anthropology, this experience ensures that the discipline is not a science. In this experience the researcher does not generate his data, and he does not intellectualise it except in an intercultural, translator fashion. Since "explanations" of cultural phenomena are always in terms of information *received from informants,* from a scientific perspective the anthropologist never, in fact, seeks explanations—only understanding in others' terms.

This is not to say that anthropologists have not attempted to treat the understandings so generated as data to be explained. In some cross-cultural studies, advocates of behavioural observation have sought to move anthropology in the direction of science. Nevertheless, there are those who are convinced that their experience (viewed from a strict empiricist perspective) is the only "true" one, and they preach the "conclusion" that their ability to communicate with others renders the domain of human experience inaccessible to the methods of science. This claim for "truth" is made in the context of empiricism. Ironically, it is cited as the justification for rejecting science as a learning procedure appropriate to man and his works. Since archaeological remains are said to be derived from this human domain, then in the view of the textualists a scientific approach applied to these remains is a violation of the ethnographic truths of nature that they enjoy by virtue of their actions as empiricists. At the same time they behave as believers in the "received knowledge" obtained from their communicative, information-passing informants—the relativist posture—to claim that since scientists create their data they violate the great "truth" discovered by them in empiricist terms: that each culture, including that of the scientist, is unique and therefore the scientist operates as an *intellectual imperialist,* and his perspective is therefore unacceptable.

The fact nevertheless remains: archaeologists have no informants. We cannot see the past from the ancients' cultural perspective because they cannot tell us what that might have been. We have no access to truth by authority emanating from the past. For those impressed by the cultural relativist's experience, such authority is the source of the only "true" reality regarding the human domain. What is such an archaeologist to do? There are two suggestions currently in vogue: adopt a universalistic interpretive approach and/or give up and exploit the past for contemporary purposes, disregarding the search for an understanding of the past in its own terms. The justification for knowledge claims is abandoned in favour of moral justifications for one's own interpretive scenarios.

ADOPTING A UNIVERSALISTIC INTERPRETIVE APPROACH

This is the most highly recommended approach. We search the historical literature or our own human experience, seeking to abstract universals, particularly regarding "human nature," and then we use these universals as premisses in a deductively reasoned interpretation of the archaeological remains. As Hodder suggests,

> Theories basic to archaeological knowledge must be concerned with the principles according to which individuals construct their social worlds. (Hodder 1985:13)

Where do we obtain such principles? We obtain these principles by reasoned recognition of certain "truths of humanity," a procedure only made rational if one accepts the empiricists' doctrine of archaic science.

The situation is interesting. We do not compare properties cross-culturally that appear similar or different and seek to understand their distributions, since such formal characteristics chosen by us are illusions conditioned by our judgements as to what we should look for and how we should view the world—in short, by our production of data. This relativistic posture was outlined long ago by Boas:

> research which compares similar cultural phenomena from various parts of the world . . . makes the assumption that the same ethnological phenomenon has everywhere developed in the same manner. Here lies the flaw . . . , for no such proof can be given. Even the most cursory review shows that the same phenomena may develop in a multitude of ways. (Boas 1943:273)

It is quite clear that Boas, who viewed the ethnological world from the participant perspective, saw that different informants from different culture-historical backgrounds viewed phenomena judged similar by us as carrying highly variable meanings. Since he believed that causes had reference to culturally variable ways of thinking about experience (the relativist view), then comparing phenomena considered similar by us is said to violate the cultural contexts of the informants. They thought about these things differently, thus their cultural causes were said to be different. Boas also states,

> it is not possible to predict the behavior resulting from the historical events that made the people what they are. This problem is essentially a psychological one and beset with all the difficulties inherent in the investigation of complex mental phenomena of the lives of individuals. (Boas 1938:5–6)

To a scientist this is an intellectually strange conclusion to draw. The ethnologist generally depends on his informants to create his data and, importantly, to give it meaning in the informants' terms. When this is accomplished, the investigator discovers that he could not have anticipated his informants' different perspective because of his own ethnocentric cultural perspective. He concludes that the only reliable commonality between himself and his informants is the fact that all possess a symboling capacity and a common human nature. If we are to go beyond simple appreciation and respect for cultural differences, this extension must be made through the medium of the properties that all individuals share, their "human nature," which is believed to flow "self evidently" from the "human" experience, an empiricist doctrine.

Is this view correct? The answer must be no. The simple fact is that the methods of science have never been attempted or implemented. The above conclusions derive from the research posture and the particular social articulation of the observer with his or her subject matter, not from some inherently self-evident truth of nature or privileged insight regarding the human condition. This fact is not appreciated by its advocates. Nevertheless, the conclusion is drawn that because we can communicate our inner thoughts, we are thus removed from nature and can be understood only in these "inside" terms.

The historian Collingwood summarised this perspective nicely when he noted,

> I shall contend that the work which was to be done by the science of human nature is actually done, and can only be done, by history; that history is what the science of human nature professed to be. (Collingwood 1956:209)

> The historian, investigating any event in the past, makes a distinction between what may be called the outside and the inside of an event. By the outside of the event I mean everything belonging to it which can be described in terms of bodies and their movements; the passage of Caesar, accompanied by certain men, across the river called the Rubicon at one date, or the spilling of his blood on the floor of the senate-house at another. By the inside of the event I mean that in it which can only be described in terms of thought: Caesar's defiance of Republican law, or the clash of constitutional policy between himself and his assassins. The historian is never concerned with either of these to the exclusion of the other. He is investigating not mere events (where by a mere event I mean one which has only an outside and no inside) but actions, and an action is the unity of the outside and inside of an event. . . . His work may begin by discovering the outside of an event, but it can never end there; he must always remember that the event was an action, and that his main task is to think himself into this action, to discern the thought of its agent. (Collingwood 1956:213)

> The cause of the event . . . means the thought in the mind of the person by whose agency the event came about: and this is not something other than the event, it is the inside of the event itself. (Collingwood 1956:214–15)

In short, Collingwood is arguing that in order to understand human action we must adopt the "human" perspective, the "inside humanity" view of humanity's experience. This is a value judgement offered by Collingwood to explain what gives history meaning for some humans; we want to view ourselves in terms that we all intuitively appreciate. On the other hand, when these same ideas are adopted by Marxist, "textual," or "contextual" archaeologists, a very different claim is being made—namely, that the recognition of our perspective as a cognitive filter to experience justifies the claim for an independent ontological realm of "reality." The human or "inside" perspective is said to prove the existence of a new and independent domain of phenomena that must be understood only in terms of itself, in human terms.

In this approach, man is raised above nature, capable of self-generative, self-guided, or self-determined action such that only a "deep" understanding of human nature can render human actions, history and contemporary events understandable. Scientific study of the "outside" of events is irrelevant; the inside view of humanistic history is seen as the only "proper" perspective. The emphasis on the term *event* is not accidental here. It will be recalled that in science the objective specification of an "event," as well as the facts of events to be described, was a fundamental act leading to data production. It was also emphasised that no events remain from the past for archaeological observation. All observations and hence all "data" generated by archaeologists have reference to observational events in the present and represent facts selected by us for systematic observation. The attempt to use history as the model for archaeological investigations is therefore totally inappropriate. At least the historian begins with some "outside" description of "events" in the past and then proceeds to try to insinuate himself into the actor's roles in those events, to see them from the actor's "inside" viewpoint. The archaeologist sees no past events, only contemporary phenomena. To play the historian's game (as understood by the textual-contextualists) archaeologists must infer past events and then insinuate themselves into these inferred events so as to produce for contemporary readers a "you were there" inside view of the past.

What happened to cultural relativism? Where is the claim that there are many different "inside views"? How do the contemporary "contextualists" create past events from contemporary static phenomena and then proceed to insinuate themselves into these created events so as to see them from *the* perspective of past humans? How did we move from the posture of cultural relativism, which recognised many different human worlds, to that of cultural universalism, which proposes the existence of a common, unique and distinctive human experience that transcends cultural differences and renders intercultural understanding possible even across the "barriers of time"? The answer is simple: just accept the intuitive, subjective insight implicit in the principles of empiricism, which of course dictates these conclusions.

The result for the thinking person is a paradox that leads to the second posture common today. The argument is outlined here by Ian Hodder:

> whether I accept any test of my theory as valid or relevant, depends on my theory (or paradigm). (Hodder 1984b:66)

This relativist claim is elaborated upon as follows:

> The past exists for us through our perceptions of it. And the process of perception is not passive—we do not just receive patterns from the world out there. We seek for pattern. To perceive is to create pattern and meaning. (Hodder 1984b:67)

Here we see the relativist position. There are many cultural worlds; all are subjective and represent particular "inside" views. We perceive or create pattern for the past in terms of our "theories" (or paradigm) in the present. All history becomes myth produced to serve a contemporary hunger for justifying a past consistent with what one wants to believe as viewed from the "inside" world of the present. At the same time, however, those persons wedded to the "truth" of relativism (an argument that a true relativist position ensures cannot be made!) step out even further on the small, fragile branches of a convoluted logical tree and make the claim that a knowledge of the universal properties of humanity or human action will make possible the "translation," the understanding, not only of the past but of the different cultural worlds of contemporary men. How do we escape the relativist's dilemma and obtain a universalistic view of man?

It was appreciated long ago that attempts to understand such properties as redness were not advanced by postulating inherent red tendencies underlying the surface manifestations of redness. Redness, in fact, became understandable only through the recognition of natural properties that were not "red" in themselves but interacted in ways so as to appear red to us. This lesson has been repeated over and over again as our knowledge of the world around us has grown and accumulated. Is it unreasonable to explore the possibility that when we demand an understanding from the "inside view," we prevent and ensure against learning and a more reliable basis for understanding?

EXPLOITING THE PAST FOR CONTEMPORARY PURPOSES

Another basic assumption of science is that we cannot assume we possess a sufficient knowledge of the subject matter of study. We must assume there is something to learn. If we adopt the procedures advocated by the "textual-contextualists," interpretation of the archaeological record is dependent upon adequate and sufficient knowledge of human nature linked to an interpretative art in order to recreate the "codes" or "masked expressions" of ancient power negotiations as played out by ancient men! Strangely, I thought that it was culture and man that we sought to investigate, yet in the hands of the "textual-contextualists" these are not the subjects of investigation at all. Rather, it is human history, the variable actions in which past men participated, that is to be understood in terms of a priori knowledge of culture and man. In short, we simply translate the inferred past into our contemporary view of ourselves. We accommodate the phenomonological world of the past to what we believe about ourselves and the present. This is the very act that leads to claims that science is inappropriate as a learning procedure. "Textual-contextualists" assert that scientists cannot escape "theory-laden" or paradigm-dependent thoughts, while at the same time they argue that men are "free" to negotiate their own cultural worlds! The implication seems to be that scientists are not human!

This suggestion is not simply a smart remark. Scientists are viewed with contempt by the advocates of the "textual-contextual" approach. Scientists are viewed as having been duped, as having sold their birthright of "free will," and as masking their true motives. We are told that

> perhaps the clearest attempts to hide the political in reconstruction of the past is found in the embrace of the hypothetico-deductive method, independent tests and "middle range theory", prediction, and objective measurement. (Hodder 1984b:67)

We see further moralising by Ian Hodder in the following statement:

> The ideology of science, and the control of nature through knowledge, are [also] linked to strategies of social dominance. . . . The culture of science and modernism is linked . . . to the control of men through the control of knowledge and machines. (Hodder 1984b:68)

This type of approach—truth as rendered up by socio-political moralising—becomes the justification for using the past to suit our contemporary ends.

> From the standpoint of dialectical materialism the knowledge claims delivered by any theory . . . can only be considered "true" insofar as their own validity criteria are concerned; that is, they are relative truths. . . . By rejecting the notion . . . that theories can be evaluated and rank ordered using some standard measure of validity, the dialectical materialist does not mean to imply a relativist indifference toward alternative theoretical or epistemological frameworks. Rather, dialectical materialism specifies a form of critique . . . [to] determine the consequences of competing theoretical approaches for those other aspects of the [contemporary] social totality . . . Since, from the standpoint of dialectical materialism, theories end only when their social conditions of existence end, pursuit of these tasks is seen to serve the purposes of radical social criticism. (Saitta 1983:301)

Here we have laid bare the programme of those who advocate the "critical" approach of the Frankfurt school, the ideological dialectic of much modern Marxist archaeology, and the extreme view of the "textual-contextualists." The past does not matter. The framework for evaluating the accuracy of any inferred past is not the record remaining from the past and our tentative knowledge thereof, but instead it is the present intellectual world. This intellectual world consists of values placed on knowledge and ideas in our contemporary setting. Here the second component of an empiricist's view is implemented by the most vocal critics of empiricism: namely, one must evaluate the quality of the mind at work. Instead of the old, tiresome, personalised, *ad hominem* argument we are now given the same form of argument on a larger scale. Ideas must be rejected or accepted in terms of their sociopolitical affinities. Empiricism reclothed in Marxist contextual clothes is still an intellectual failure.

CONCLUSION: WHERE DO WE GO WITH OUR DATA?

Science works responsibly. We create our data in the present. We seek through pattern recognition studies to gain an insight into how the past was organised. We propose ideas as to the nature of past organisations and how they changed. At this juncture the scientist is responsible for seeking out experiences as widely as possible in order to provide reality checks on the accuracy and utility of his ideas. Responsible learning is dependent upon the degree to which research is designed so as to expose ambiguity, inadequacy and inaccuracy in our ideas guiding both the production of data and our attempts to understand it. The backboard for achieving this is the world of experience. The external world exists in its own right, and that includes the properties of the archaeological record. This external reality must be used in skilful ways to inform us about our ideas concerning that reality. The claim that our cognitive devices insulate us from the external world is false. The claim that we may accommodate properties of the external world wrongly through our cognitive devices may be correct. It is the availability of the external world, regardless of the character of our cognitive devices, that makes it possible for science to work. We can learn the limitations of our own ideas, as science has demonstrated over and over again, through skilful interaction with the world of experience, the external world.

This is the view that Thomas Huxley so eloquently adopted. Today, however, we must combat the self-appointed authorities who proclaim what we are like and then use such alleged knowledge to create pasts consistent with their beliefs. As in the past, a natural science, in this case the study of the archaeological record, is the only way to expose the current crop of archaeological theologians and move us in an orderly manner, through learning, to an accurate appreciation of the past.

Chapter 6

Review of Hodder, *Reading the Past: Current Approaches to Interpretation in Archaeology*

This is a little book with a little message being blown through a large horn with a loud noise. Hodder works from three basic premises: (a) the archaeological record is to be explained by reference to the culture of the persons responsible for the production of the remains; (b) culture is conceived of primarily as idealistic, ideational, and ideological; and (c) culture is to be understood in terms of the volitionally negotiated actions of individual persons. In spite of much ranting and raving about the fallacy of accepting self-evident truth, these propositions are simply stated as self-evident and only violated by such duped or culturally misguided persons as positivists, processualists, Marxists, materialists, etc., etc. Post-processual archaeologists are considered to be enlightened individuals who clearly see the truth of such propositions and who have abandoned such false approaches to learning as science. These are some of this book's tiny messages.

The loud noise relates to the last point. Science is depicted to the assumedly naive reader as committed to a belief in "laws" and "determinancy," said to deny humankind's "humanity" and the reality that individuals act volitionally and negotiate their own worlds. It is said to "deny people their freedom" (Hodder 1986:102). The science that I know about is very different from Hodder's characterization. Science simply assumes that the external world is knowable, and knowable in terms of itself. The scientist fully recognizes that in acting on these assumptions, in the sense of seeking knowledge about the external world, we use our minds, imaginations, knowledge, alleged knowledge, and unrecognized assumptive knowledge. The task of science therefore is to evaluate the utility and accuracy of our own ideas so as to bring our ideas about the external world increasingly into concordance with the way the external world works. In short, it is a continuously contentious and self-evaluative learning process.

How does this (the process of science) demean humanity? It does not. But what about laws and the concept of determinancy? In science these terms come into play when we begin to consider the methods that scientists employ for learning. In seeking to know something about the external world (in our case, the past), we know full well that it is gone and therefore inaccessible in any direct sense. Thus any knowledge (accurate statements about the past) gained is going to be made in the form of inferences from observations on the contemporary archaeological record.

Originally published in *American Antiquity*, © 1989

And how do we know when an inference is accurate? Singing one tune, Hodder claims with the Frankfurt school that we cannot answer this question, because all of our observations are theory-dependent and hence are subjective from the perspective of the investigator. At the same time, Hodder sings another tune when he claims that this question is simply and easily resolved by following Collingwood's advice and "reading the past" by immersing ourselves in the data and "re-enacting past thought through [our] own knowledge."

Where is the other Frankfurt tune, the concern about relativism, the belief that each culture is unique and the unique product of the participants negotiating the meanings given to experiences played out within the repertoire of options provided as a result of one's "culture history"? How can I simply read the past by reenacting past thoughts derived from my own subjective knowledge? Paradoxically, given the latter position one would have to have *prior knowledge* of the very features that one seeks to investigate in order to make meaningful statements about the past. Even Hodder acknowledges this paradox when he says over and over again that archaeologists cannot interpret the archaeological remains of a past culture without prior knowledge of that culture.

Alleged violations of the above principle are the basis for much loud noise about violations of cultural context in cross-cultural comparisons. How can we have prior knowledge about that for which we admit our ignorance and are seeking to explore through research? Hodder answers:

> historical meanings, however "other" and coherent to themselves, are nevertheless real, producing real effects in the material world, and they are coherent, and thereby structured and systematic. In relation to the real, structured system of data, archaeologists critically evaluate their theories. (1986:154)

Holy-moley, Hodder, you have just discovered science through Collingwood! This is a real accomplishment. We can evaluate our ideas about the past by reference to the "reality" remaining from the past. I wonder how many people have said that before? What about those inferences, those troubling propositions about meaning put forth by us? Hodder has an answer:

> I wish to argue that there are some very simple rules underlying all languages or at least underlying the ways in which *Homo sapiens sapiens* at all times and in all places give meaning to things.

In short, there are laws—determinancies operating to ensure cross-culturally valid interpretations of cultural materials. Material culture is, however, a language, but simpler than a spoken language, making it "simpler to decipher than those written documents for which we do not know the language."

Here we see Hodder singing two songs at once. He can interpret the past culturally because there are laws of cultural production. One wonders if this scientific position does not deny freedom and demean humanity. These were the very issues that processual archaeologists sought to learn about—those basic laws. Unlike processualists, however, Hodder does not think we need to learn; we seemingly already know these things and can thus proceed like Collingwood.

As the reader has probably gathered, this book is packed with contradictions, misrepresentations, and distortions, and the author totally misunderstands the challenges facing archaeologists. There is much less here than meets the eye. What is all the noise about, and why are two different songs being sung at the same time? It becomes clear in the final chapters (see Hodder 1986:164). We are not seeking to see the past as past participants saw it, in spite of claims to this effect. We are not trying to understand the external world in terms of itself—a real past. Instead we should be using our work as archaeologists in the context of "critical theory."

> That there are dichotomies between the pasts produced by different interest groups and that archaeology does not appear to have been successful in encouraging alternative perceptions and experiences of the past may be linked to the role of archaeology and archaeologies in power strategies in Western society. . . . It is of particular relevance to archaeology as it is involved in class domination." (1986:164)

Hodder is involved in a power play, seeking domination for his value-laden ideas. It is difficult to take seriously his suggestions about how we should deal with the real issues of archaeology when, after the loud parade passes by, what we do with the past is to be tempered and guided not by what the past was like but how it should be used today. More important, for Hodder the question is, Who should be the broker of the past for contemporary investors?

This is a book about politics negotiated by Hodder, not about archaeology.

Part III

Empiricism and Other Problems
in Contemporary Archaeology

Chapter 7

Coping with Debate Tactics

In the previous section of this book there was little debate. I was more engaged in stating my position on some postures that are "topical" in the literature. Some of the articles reprinted here are getting down to cases. In my response to Freeman (Chapter 8) I address some of the effects of empiricists' assumptions and suggest some of their consequences for debate. This is also true in my exchanges with Gould (Chapters 9–11); however, in the latter exchanges as well as those with Sackett (e.g., Chapters 14 and 16) other devices of argument not previously discussed raise their heads:

> *Argumentum ad Ignorantiam*: an argument purporting to demonstrate a point or to persuade people, which avails itself of facts and reasons the falsity or inadequacy of which is not readily discerned, a misleading argument used in reliance on people's ignorance. (Runes 1979:19)

Use of this form of argument is perhaps best described as a strategy ready-made for the Guppie. It will be recalled from the introduction to this volume that the Guppie is the data gobbler and the tactician who seeks to gain lifetime monopolies on data. If successful, the Guppie is very capable of presenting arguments that draw upon accumulated experience and therefore depend for their acceptance upon others not having the needed knowledge to pass judgment on them. It must be admitted, however, that this is a difficult device to diagnose, since it presupposes a design rather than an oversight on the part of the author. Similarly, recognition is at least partially dependent upon the knowledge of reader, but this is of course the very power of this form of argument. A beginning reader of archaeological debate or a foreign author directing his words to a local audience regarding debates or developments in other countries or published in "foreign" languages frequently cannot resist the persuasive power of such arguments. Puppies sometimes try this strategy, hoping that they will not be called to task by those who can see through such arguments.

The critical reader, and particularly the student, is advised to read from the hardheaded perspective of his or her own knowledge base and remain skeptical of arguments "beyond his depth." In turn, the good student, having recognized his limitations, proceeds to correct the deficiency so as to make possible his own independent judgments. If all students did this, the success of *argumentum ad ignorantiam* in our literature would decline.

Perhaps the most common fallacious device used in much archaeological debate is technically referred to as *ignoratio elenchi.* This is the fallacy committed when one seeks to discredit an opponent's position by disproving an assertion that the opponent has not actually made. In a subtle way this is also *argumentum ad ignorantiam* in that the success of this tactic presupposes that the listeners do not know the arguments of the opponent being unjustly discredited. There are some astonishing examples of this fallacy in the archaeological literature. Perhaps one of the most frequently repeated fallacies of *ignoratio elenchi* was Schiffer's claim that

> The early years of the new archaeology witnessed the frequent and unquestioning repetition of major methodological principles. One such principle was enunciated by Binford (1964:425) in perhaps its most explicit form:
>
> > The loss, breakage, and abandonment of implements and facilities at different locations, where groups of variable structure performed different tasks, leaves a "fossil" record of the actual operation of an extinct society.
>
> . . . Under the aegis of this principle, new archaeologists have approached the remains of the past in bold and exciting ways, seeking with sophisticated techniques assorted patterns in artifact distributions and interpreting them directly in terms of past behavior and social organization. As often happens in times of normal science, few investigators have noticed that the principle is false. It is false because archaeological remains are not in any sense a fossilized cultural system. (Schiffer 1976:1–2)

Schiffer has since attempted to build a career on his discovery of this "false" principle said to have been fundamental to the new archaeology. This classic case of *ignoratio elenchi* serves as the basis of a series of unfounded criticisms and a misleading series of discussions in the literature. Only an empiricist could read the literature of the 1960s and conclude that a principle, ontological in character, was being enunciated regarding the nature of the archaeological record as discovered or "seen" by the archaeologist. What was being discussed was the nature of the link between the dynamics of the past and the production of entropy resulting in the formation of material remains or static by-products of the system's operation. It was offered as an alternative to the view that the archaeological record had reference to the ideas in the minds of the ancients as to how to make artifacts and organize their material world. It was not a discussion of the archaeological record as it might be "seen" in any direct sense by an archaeologist. The literature of the 1960s is explicit on this issue.

> The position being taken here is that different kinds of phenomena are never remote: they are either accessible or they are not. "Non-material" aspects of culture are accessible in direct measure with the testability of propositions being advanced about them. Propositions concerning any realm of culture—technology, social organization, psychology, philosophy, etc.—for which arguments of relevance and empirically testable hypotheses can be offered are as sound as the history of hypothesis confirmation. The practical limitations on our knowledge of the past are not inherent in the nature of the archaeological record; the limitations lie in our methodological naivete, in our lack of development for principles determining the relevance of archaeological remains to propositions regarding processes and events of the past. (Binford 1968:23)

I think it should be clear that I was not an empiricist advocating that one could go out and dust off a fossil record that had complete, direct, and intuitively clear reference to a past cultural system. The fundamental call of the new archaeology was to address the central issue of inference justification, and it was clearly argued that all statements about the past were inferences. Thus the arguments regarding the nature of dynamics standing behind patterning that might be demonstrable in the archaeological record are all inferential, and they are only as good as the justifications presented for those inferences. I know of no so-called new archaeologists who believed that such inference justification was to be found in a "false principle" asserting any ontological or essential characteristic inherent in the archaeological record. That was the very position we were arguing against. Only to an empiricist could my statements be read as offering an essentialist proposition in substitution for the essentialist propositions of traditional archaeology in order to justify discussion of social organization. We took the opposite view, namely, that both the practical justifications for and the limitations on inference did not lie with the essential properties of the archaeological record but instead with our methodology. If Schiffer recognized "formation processes" as relevant considerations, good for Schiffer, but such a recognition in no way challenged the principles upon which the new archaeologists argued. It simply represented a contribution to the very goals of the new archaeology—to reduce our "methodological naivete." I should point out, however, that I know of no archaeologists operating in the 1960s and worth their salt who did not know that the archaeological record as observed by the archaeologist was apt to have been modified by "time's arrow" (see Asher 1968 and Binford 1975a for comments on the great revelations of the Arizona group).

There are many other examples of pervasive empiricism within archaeology conditioning how archaeologists read the literature of the new archaeology. Read the early discussions in the literature about site structure (originally presented in the context of arguments against normative assumptions about internally undifferentiated, "homogeneous" cultures). Traditionalists assumed such internally homogeneous cultures; we were arguing that systems could be expected to be internally differentiated and that variability in this property could well inform us about organizational characteristics of the past. Yellen understood these arguments like a traditional archaeologist and saw them as simply seeking to replace one set of conventions for another. If you are an empiricist, you believe it is the only way; empiricists translate the words of others into their own monolithic way of thinking. Yellen states that

> one may evaluate models of archaeologists often use to examine activity patterning within an excavated site. What underlies many of these is the a priori assumption that most activities are performed by special-purpose, job specific groups, and that individual tasks are spatially segregated from one another. (Yellen 1977a:97)

No such a priori assumption guided those of us working on site structure from the perspective of new archaeology, past or present (see Binford 1978b).

Empiricists die hard. For instance, Kent, writing about activity areas, says

> my research was designed to test the assumptions made by archaeologists attempting to delineate activity areas. These usually implicit assumptions include the

presumption . . . that the activities performed at such areas are generally both sex specific and monofunctional. (Kent 1984:1–2)

This is hard to understand. What is going on? It appears that the tactics of the new archaeologists were not seen by readers as timely, issue-oriented debates but instead as attempts at simple substitution of one set of interpretive conventions by another with no fundamental implications regarding the central issue, namely, how we learn and how we justify inferences. Traditional archaeologists viewed the literature as suggesting that different conventions simply be substituted for the old ones. The tactics I had pursued relative to the conventions of traditional archaeology were then adopted and turned on the alleged conventions offered by us! The only problem was that no such conventions were being set forward. *Ignoratio elenchi* reigns.

This type of "paradigm translation" has been pervasive in the modern literature of archaeology. For instance, I was once jumped upon by Hodder and his students from this same perspective. Hodder claimed that I was arguing in my mortuary paper (Binford 1971) for a law to be used in the interpretation of archaeological mortuary data. In fact, what I had done was seek to determine using a miserable sample of cases if it was reasonable to pursue further the possibility of relationships existing between mortuary practice and the status structure of societies. I concluded that my results were "provocative and indicative of the postulated positive relationships between the structure of mortuary ceremonialism and the status structure characteristic of any given sociocultural system" (Binford 1972a:231). I did not say that this was the only possible relationship; I did not say that a mechanical isomorphism was operating; essentially all I said was that this line of research was worth pursuing and that the traditional conventions used in discussing mortuary data were inadequate.

Some of the Yippie admonitions to become aware should be adopted by the Yippies themselves. For instance, one of the patterns I observed and mentioned in the mortuary study was that "the specific dimensions of the social persona commonly given recognition in mortuary ritual varies significantly with the organizational complexity of the society" (Binford 1972a:235). Later the "masking argument," justified primarily by studies of modern British mortuary practices, appears in the Yippie literature (Pearson 1982), where it is accepted as a functional law applicable to all societies. The Yippie then behaves like a Lollie and accommodates by convention all the variability in prehistoric mortuary data from Europe! Traditional archaeology and empiricism reigns even in Yippiedom.

Another tactic common in debate is a modification of the use of *ignoratio elenchi* tactics referred to here as the "straw man" argument. This is a Lollie style of use for *ignoratio elenchi*. One does not argue with an argument or a specific point therein but with a false model of an opponent's position. Of course the false model is constructed to serve the goals of the person whose position is being advocated (the old "have you stopped beating your wife?" tactic). Faced with this type of argument, the respondent is forced into the position of saying over and over that he never did beat his wife. The defender is forced to deny the characterization in the model constructed by the opponent rather than dealing with issues. This is the position I am arguing from in many of the reprinted essays to follow. It is the position I would have been forced to adopt if I had chosen to reply to Hodder's (1982c) remarkable article. Righteous empiricists can use this situation in many secondary ways. Being righteous, they can say that the denials by the accused are feeble attempts to save face in light of the revelations forced on them by the "straw man" model (this was Schiffer's 1985 strategy in his review of *Working at Archaeology*). They can claim that their interpretation of the works of others is the only true (self-evident) interpretation and that, if their model misrepresents the thoughts of another, then the problem rests with the writing skills of the person characterized. Is this a form of *ad hominem* argument?

As mentioned at the beginning of this chapter, the following articles are my views in recent debates. Clearly, the reply to Freeman (Chapter 8), the Gould articles (Chapters 9–11), as well as the Sackett piece (Chapter 16) are all debate-oriented. The "Alyawara Day" articles included here represent a continuation of my earlier style of debate wherein I test certain assumptions (e.g., in Chapter 13 the common assumption that observation in the modern world is accurate and unambiguous). This latter assumption (empirical in character) has opened up a new route to Guppiehood, namely, gaining a monopoly on observations in the modern world. Since the empiricist assumes that these observations are self-evidently true, a monopoly on such knowledge is certainly a desirable posture from which to seek Guppie status. In Chapter 13 I point out that even in the ethnoarchaeological world "facts do not speak for themselves." In the article authored with O'Connell (Chapter 12) my concerns were less with argument and more with the rare opportunity we had to observe phenomena about which many archaeologists have a great interest but for which few opportunities to observe have ever been available. I could not resist taking advantage of this rare opportunity to comment on some assumptions currently standing behind some experimental work as well as controversies over typologies. The "Men's Knives" article (Chapter 14) is the one that got Sackett all upset and hence led to another debate. The final chapter in this section, "Researching Ambiguity" (Chapter 17), is argumentative but is primarily substantive in that it offers certain tactical research suggestions that I feel are useful and productive. It also represents the last of my "Australian experience" papers, unless I have the opportunity to work there in the future.

Chapter 8

Reply to "More on the Mousterian: Flaked Bone from Cueva Morín," by L. Freeman

Many books on early man, the history of archaeological research, etc., begin with a recitation of the "obviously" faulty views advanced by our predecessors. A delightful book of this type is Wendt's (1956) *In Search of Adam*, which traces many ideas that, from a modern perspective, appear quite bizarre. How could anyone seriously think that the bones of a mammoth were those of a unicorn? Excursions into the thoughts of previous generations frequently leave us wondering, "Why were they so stupid in those days?" "How could they believe such things?" This is particularly true of those who today are committed to a strict empiricist's position. The strict empiricist believes that *to be a good scientist one must clear one's mind of bias and observe nature objectively;* if this is done properly and the observer is astute and honest, then the truths of natural history will be clearly apprehended. In the strict empiricist's view of the world, those who do not see nature in the same way must be suffering from a lack of objectivity; all unbiased, objective observers should see the same things, since "nature does not lie." Disagreements among observers are generally considered to derive from flaws in the character of at least some of the disputants.

It appears to me that Freeman (1983) is attempting to demonstrate flaws in my character as a basis for dismissing the research I reported in my book *Bones*. One can hardly miss his message that he does not trust my work. He suggests that it aims to deceive readers with "the prospect of good fight." He expresses his belief that "scientific inquiry requires a calm and impartial evaluation [presumably as exemplified by his own discussion] . . . and is inconsistent with ridicule and unsubstantiated bluster" [presumably characteristic of mine]. He characterizes my work as "disguised by complex logical gymnastics and impressive-seeming mathematical manipulations" which incorporate "much sleight-of-hand." He concludes that the errors he finds in it "betray a cavalier treatment of data that undermines one's confidence in Binford's conclusions." If I do not see the world the way he does, then, it is because he is objective and impartial, while I am devious and an untrustworthy observer.

Looking backward nudges us into the realization that the strict empiricist's view is shortsighted and largely inaccurate as to how science proceeds. Those predecessors who appear so "stupid" when they parade across the pages of our histories were not really unobjective, illogical, biased, overgeneralizing sophists. They were, for the most

Originally published in *Current Anthropology* 24:372–377, © 1983 part, honest, dedicated researchers fettered by their ignorance and their conceptual paradigms. They sought, as many of us do, to use the knowledge available to them to warrant their views of the world. From our contemporary perspective we can see that that "knowledge" was generally inadequate, inaccurate, or conceptually distorted. We all work with the knowledge and understanding available to us. As our ignorance is reduced, we necessarily realize that the knowledge we had at an earlier point was inadequate. This viewpoint directly challenges the strict empiricist's view of our search for understanding. Success flows not from righteousness, but from the quality of the intellectual tools with which one approaches experience. Disagreements among scientists generally derive from differing judgments as to the utility of the conceptual and intellectual tools available and the appropriate procedures or tactics to use in attempting to reduce our ignorance, not from character flaws that prevent the unworthy from seeing nature clearly.

Freeman suggests that I advocate the "method of multiple working hypotheses" in my book but fail to use it. I must point out that I argued *against* that method as it is generally practiced by most archaeologists (see Binford 1981a:247). The method of multiple working hypotheses *as commonly used* by archaeologists is a warranting argument rather than a research tactic. This approach recognizes that there may be ambiguity in the facts of the archaeological record to which we attempt to give meanings and recommends that the archaeologist confronted by this ambiguity *prudently weigh* the possible alternatives and then reach a judgment as to which is most likely. This is an epistemology which accepts *plausibility* as the criterion for judging the truth of a statement. (A good example is seen in Isaac and Crader 1981.) This method has been described as one of assessing the "prior probabilities" of a proposition (Salmon 1982b:42). We must realize that plausibility is a judgment concerning the degree to which one has prudently used the information available to him for deciding which alternative is most likely. What is advanced as true remains dependent on this judgment, and, of course, the information available for making it *may be false.* The pursuit of plausibility in the face of acknowledged ambiguity assumes that we have the knowledge necessary to reach a correct interpretation. This means that most arguments are, in the long run, *ad hominem* in form, since disputants must basically question an adversary's prudence or scholarship (see Bunn's 1982 review of my *Bones* book). Any person making an interpretation is essentially forced to defend his judgment tenaciously, since yielding to an alternative could be seen as prima facie evidence that he was either a lesser scholar or imprudent in his original reasoning. Disputants working within the framework of the "multiple working hypotheses" warranting argument generally adopt an *advocacy position,* conducting research with the aim of strengthening their original interpretations. If successful, this allows them to avoid having to acknowledge any implied imprudence or lack of scholarship.

The advocacy character of argument and research carried out under the rubric of a "multiple working hypotheses" approach is well illustrated by recent argument with regard to the early hominid sites of Africa. One of the key arguments advanced to explain the extensive carnivore damage on bone from Olduvai sites has been that animals scavenged the food remains left behind by the hominids on their abandoned "home bases" (see Leakey 1971:43; Bunn 1982a:495; Isaac 1971:288, 1982:7–8). This is indeed a plausible suggestion. It could as reasonably have been argued, however, that hominids scavenged bone already ravaged by other carnivores or that both non-hominid carnivores and hominids contributed to the faunal accumulations at the site. With the information available, the animal gnawing had no unambiguous meaning. Isaac's response to this ambiguity was to dump bones from his camp debris at a peg and then record the frequency of parts remaining after scavengers (jackals and hyaenas) had consumed and transported parts. From this he concluded that scavengers do indeed ravage garbage at human camps and went on to cite the experiment as justification for believing that the animal tooth marks on bones from the Olduvai sites were made after the hominids had abandoned their sites—in other words, that this explanation was a plausible one. I don't believe anyone judged it implausible, but I certainly questioned whether it was true. Isaac's "experiment" was not designed to reduce interpretive ambiguity.

An approach that accepts plausibility as the criterion for truth is a gross distortion of the method of multiple working hypotheses as it was originally conceived. That method was advanced as a research program aimed at reducing ambiguity by seeking new knowledge. My book is concerned with this program. Basic to its argument is the observation that a configurational type of inference has characterized archaeological interpretation in the past; the researcher has identified the "whole" and then cited it to lend plausibility to the interpretations offered for its parts. I criticize this approach, suggesting that instead of employing tactics which border on the fallacy of affirmation of the consequent we need to conduct the research that will permit independent interpretations of the parts prior to presenting a view of the whole. We need independent diagnostic procedures for giving meaning to the independent types of material remains the archaeologist may observe (see Binford 1982a for a discussion of this view of "objectivity"). My focus is on bones and the properties of faunal assemblages which may be understood independently of any association with stone tools or assessments of "prior probabilities" based on holistic inferences about the deposits in which the bones are found.

Freeman ignores these points and comments: "I . . . wish that Binford had taken more time to inform himself about the Morín site and its Mousterian levels, their contents and their contexts, before deciding so definitely on their interpretation" (1983:366). I am fairly familiar with the Morín materials and did study Freeman's work, but I considered a discussion of the site irrelevant. My basic point was that we should seek to develop methods that permit us to assign meanings to the parts or elements of a deposit independently of the configurational argument of plausibility a gestalt "identification" of the deposit may make possible. If I accept the premise that man was the agent responsible for a deposit, I can certainly invent a post hoc argument that renders the things in the site consistent with that premise. Animal-gnawed bone can be seen as pressure-flaked tools made by man, broken human bone can be seen as evidence for cannibalism, and generalized animal gnawing can be seen as evidence that scavengers visited sites after man had departed. In the case of Cueva Morín, I have no doubt that man was a major contributor to the character of the deposits there. This does not, in my opinion, render secure the interpretation that the flaked bones illustrated by Freeman are tools produced by man.

What I said originally (1981a:55) about Freeman's materials was this:

> The most enthusiastic recent advocate of "retouched" bone flake tools in the Paleolithic is Leslie Freeman, who comments on his analysis of such "tools" from Level 17 at the cave of Morin: "If the bone pieces were omitted from the study of recovered artifacts, an impressive richness of detail concerning the technology of the Mousterian cave occupants would obviously be lost" (Freeman 1978a:49).
>
> Without taking them up piece by piece, I will assert that the chipped pieces illustrated by Freeman (1971, 1978a) are classic examples of chipped-back flakes produced by gnawing animals, probably canids.

In my comment on White's article I stated (1982c:177; emphasis added): "The specimens illustrated by Freeman (1971, 1978a) are without exception *indistinguishable from canid-gnawed bone fragments.*" In this latter opinion Freeman appears now to agree with me. He states:

> I am convinced that there is no certain way to distinguish consistently between bone flaking produced by carnivores and flaking done by man by simple visual inspection of scar morphology. . . . Binford has conclusively shown that carnivore gnawing may produce forms that look astonishingly like deliberate flaking of bone by humans. . . . The fact that it may never be possible to differentiate perfectly between gnawing and human trimming on some bones is a bit of new information we owe to Binford. (1983:371–372)

He is not content, however, to accept my arguments as they were made. Instead, he proceeds to set up a straw man with his claim that I have argued about more than the illustrated bone: "admitting that carnivores could have been occasional agents of the flaking of some bones in the Upper Level 17 assemblage is a far cry from proving that they were the only agents, or the major agents, of the transport and flaking of the Morín bone, as Binford implicitly claims." I never even mentioned transport and offered no judgments at all about the conditions under which the bone assemblage was accumulated. In the context of this distortion of my ideas Freeman then proceeds to present an almost textbook example of the "method of multiple working hypotheses" as a warranting argument.

The first hypothesis considered is that Morín was a carnivore predator kill site. This alternative is rejected as implausible. A second hypothesis is that Upper Level 17 was a carnivore den or lair, and this alternative is also rejected as implausible. Finally, the hypothesis is offered that it is an archaeological site produced by hominid actions, and this is judged plausible. I never questioned this interpretation; all I suggested was that the alleged bone tools illustrated by Freeman are indistinguishable from canid-gnawed bone.

In the course of this argument, observations by Klein regarding contrasts between hyaena accumulations and archaeological sites in the frequencies of cranial and postcranial remains are cited (Klein 1980:252). I have searched in vain, however, for any suggestion by Klein that these contrasts are generically diagnostic "for differentiating the hyena bone accumulations from those made by man." If seriously proposed, such a criterion would force me to conclude that a very large number of the Nunamiut Eskimo sites reported by me (Binford 1978a) were accumulated by hyaenas.

Addressing the interesting problem of identifying the agents responsible for the flaked bones he alleges are tools, Freeman states: "We still cannot rule out carnivores as major (or minor) agents of bone alteration, even though it is not clear what attraction cultural accumulations of clean, broken bone would have had for them" (1983:368–369). Here we see Freeman engaged in a little bit of "logical gymnastics" or perhaps even "sleight-of-hand." Isaac's work has shown that scavenging of hominid sites by carnivores is not "implausible." To me it would only seem unlikely if (a) evidence of gnawing were extensive, as is reported at Olduvai sites (Potts and Shipman 1981), and (b) such sites were considered to have been permanently occupied or residentially "permanent." Under the latter conditions one could reasonably question how scavengers could have had uninterrupted access to the bones, since, as Isaac's experiences verify, nervous scavengers tend to carry bones away rather than chew them in place. This little contribution to the "weight of evidence" implies a number of hidden assumptions. It is obviously assumed that any bone alteration by carnivores had to be made on the site. It must further be assumed that the bones were clean and broken before the carnivores arrived. I suspect that these assumptions follow from a belief that the site was a permanently occupied residential location with a house or structure (see Freeman 1978a). I wonder how Freeman calculates the contribution of this query to the "weight of evidence" when it must rest on so many tenuous, and unexamined, premises.

Continuing, Freeman mentions two types of marks on bones that he considers to have been produced by hominids. At least one of these seems to correspond to marks previously described as tooth-inflicted (see Binford 1981a; Potts and Shipman 1981, Bunn 1981), yet Freeman does not identify any tooth scoring within his assemblage. If his assessment is correct, then our dispute is over. If there are no tooth-scored bones at Morín, then the pieces I suggested are chipped-back pieces produced by gnawing canids cannot be such. Strangely, Freeman does not argue this point or defend his novel identification of two types of hominid-inflicted marks. He simply *asserts* that both are hominid-generated. My experience leads me to doubt this argument from authority. First, I have given a great deal of research time to trying to develop an unambiguous way of recognizing tooth scoring as opposed to tool-inflicted marks. Secondly, while there are certainly statistical differences between the populations of marks produced by animal teeth and those produced by tools, there remain ambiguous cases that could be attributed to either. Freeman, with no claimed experience in observing animal tooth marks and certainly no history of research on tool-inflicted marks, seems totally comfortable in diagnosing the latter. No tooth marks are reported, and no ambiguity is acknowledged.

Next it is noted that there seems to be a bias against flaking on the bones from cervids. I have checked this claim and confirm Freeman's observation. In discussing this bias, he asks, "Why wouldn't the more easily manageable remains of deer or juvenile animals be more extensively altered, if carnivores were involved?" I can only respond, Why would a carnivore gnaw and worry an "easily manageable" bone to the extent of producing chipped-back edges? Most of the chipped-back types of canid gnawing I have observed occur on bones *not* easily managed by the gnawing animal. Freeman's (1983:367) Table 1 shows that only for the large bovids are the upper limb bones well represented. These would of course be the ones most "challenging" to a gnawing canid and the ones therefore most likely to remain at least partially identifiable if gnawed. Plausibility is a function of the knowledge and assumed context in terms of which one's guesses are made and one's "expectations" are phrased.

In his discussions of the placement of flaking, the patterned occurrence of gnawing related to other morphological traits, and the occurrence of "chips," Freeman speaks of "extensive" flaking, yet very few pieces of extensively flaked bone have been illustrated; on the other hand, he notes my description of extensively chipped-back bone and comments that such marks are "not abundantly represented." He goes on to suggest that animal-gnawed assemblages should have high frequencies of extensively gnawed bones; this is simply not the case. The use of nonfacts as the basis for a judgment of plausibility is further illustrated in his discussion of "chips," where he suggests that there were probably quite a few of them but then goes on to note that no fragments "such as one would expect in scat" were observed. I must point out that the reason chips are not generally present in gnawing areas is that the animals swallow them, and they are therefore the very items most common in scat.

The assertion of nonfacts is most evident in Freeman's discussion of the size of the bones showing alteration: "the size of some retouched pieces and the size of flake removals can be an argument that the retouch is not gnawing. Even hyenas don't habitually break and gnaw ungulate long bones 13–15 cm (or larger) in diameter with walls 1.5–2 cm (or more) thick, but a great many of the flaked bones at Cueva Morín are fragments of such large pieces" (1983:370). The following is taken from my field notes regarding the remains of an adult moose (clearly approaching the size classes Freeman discusses) killed by bear and fed upon by wolves (see Binford 1981a for a description of this episode):

> The carcass is scattered around with the head and neck lying close to the axial skeleton. The ribs and processes of most vertebrae are heavily gnawed and broken off. The pelvis is extensively gnawed and part of the ischia has been removed. The gnawing areas (three of them) where the wolves dragged off anatomical segments are located in a rough semicircle back from the death site about 25 meters (the head and axial skeleton). In one is the left rear leg of the moose. The femur has been broken through at the femoral neck and the greater trochanter has been chewed off. *The shaft below the hole where the greater trochanter had been is channeled with typical chipping back along the margin of the channel.* The meat and skin have been stripped from the leg down to a point about four inches above the distal articulation of the tibia. The distal femur remained partially articulated with the proximal tibia but the femoral trochlea has been punctured and furrowed as has the tibial crest.

Again, Haynes (1982), who has been conducting a long-term study of wolf predation on American bison (an animal within the size range of the Morín bovids), reports (pp. 273–74):

> Long bones from fully utilized carcasses of adult bison or moose are rarely fractured, although the entire articulating ends of many are chewed or broken off. Wolves and bears frequently remove the proximal end of the humerus . . . the

greater trochanter, and much of the distal end of the femur . . . and the proximal
end of the tibia. . . . It is characteristic of fully utilized kills that one or both humeri
are modified by removal of the proximal end into partly or fully open-ended
tubes. . . .

Haynes illustrates (fig. 5) a flake scar produced by gnawing wolves on a bison long-
bone splinter 7 cm wide (considerably bigger than the 4-cm-wide flake which Freeman considers beyond the capacity of wolves to produce).

The pattern of long-bone destruction indicated in these examples has been repeatedly noted by field observers. Mech (1966:81), perhaps our most experienced observer of wolf behavior, reports of adult moose carcasses fed upon by wolves that "the
skull and anterior half of the backbone [are] in one piece, and the pelvis and posterior
part of the backbone in another. The legs are detached from the skeleton, but most of
the bones of each remain together. The ends of the ribs and long bones and the edges
of the scapula and mandibles are ragged from being chewed." Figure 8.1 shows a
white-tailed deer carcass fed upon by canids. The head and neck are largely unravaged, and, although pulled around and disarticulated, the legs largely remain as
articulated anatomical segments, with the proximal ends of the upper limb parts
stripped of meat and gnawed as described in the above accounts. This means that
bones showing marks of gnawing will be generally restricted to proximal shaft sections of upper limb bones, the lower limb bones remaining untouched unless they are
gnawed in den or rendezvous site contexts.

Freeman is simply wrong in believing that wolves, much less hyaenas, are unable to
gnaw bones in the size range he is discussing. In fact, the patterns of bone modification by animals may explain the bias toward large bovid bones in flaking that Freeman
notes. His Table 1 (Freeman 1983:367) shows that it is only for the large bovids that
there are many fragments of upper limbs—particularly the humerus and the femur-
tibia, the very bones cited by all observers of carcasses fed upon by nonhuman
predator–scavengers as the ones most likely to be modified by gnawing animals.
Freeman's earlier-cited query as to why carnivores would not gnaw the bones of the
red deer as commonly as the larger bones of the bovids may well be illuminated here;
the parts of red deer and horse most likely to have been gnawed at kill locations are
reported to be generally absent from the Morín deposits.

A "working hypothesis" Freeman has not considered is that at least some of the
bones of Morín Upper Level 17 were transported to the site by hominids from carcasses already ravaged by other predator/scavengers. It is possible that much of the
bone in Cueva Morín comes not from hominid-hunted animals, but from the kills of
other predators or the death sites of large animals already ravaged by other scav-
enger/predators. This is not the place to follow up this interesting possibility. Instead,
I want to summarize the arguments Freeman has employed here. First, he has suggested that I have "character flaws." Then he has set up a straw man and proceeded to
guess at both the context of site formation and the facts relevant to the interpretation
of the site's properties. These imagined "facts" would, if true, lend plausibility to his
interpretation; however, the formation contexts are unknown, and the alleged facts
regarding animal-gnawing behavior and cut marks are generally nonfacts. Freeman,
surveying this house of cards, concludes from his assessment of the weight of evi-

Figure 8.1 A white-tailed deer carcass fed upon by canids.

dence that there is "the strongest circumstantial case that humans also flaked bone." If we have no sound middle-range research to aid us in giving meaning to what we see in the archaeological record, we can always generate a post hoc argument rooted in our beliefs, partial knowledge, ignorance, and bias which will tend to reinforce our original ideas. The strict empiricist is always committed to a defense of the "knowledge" and conceptual framework of the moment, since it is that on which he draws to render his position plausible.

Freeman seemingly accepts my argument that there is evidence of carnivore activity in Cueva Morín Upper Level 17 ("Like many other Pleistocene sites, Morín Upper Level 17 is a tapestry of interwoven strands of hominid and carnivore activity"). It should be pointed out that the only evidence cited thus far for the role of carnivores in the formation of Cueva Morín Upper Level 17 is the alleged worked bones illustrated by Freeman. How is then, that he can go on to conclude that "the case for a major carnivore role in accumulating and flaking the Upper Level 17 bones is weak"? This claim only makes sense if he is assuming that because man is represented at the site, he is also the major agent responsible for all the properties of its contents. I disagree with the knowledge base from which Freeman works and the intellectual and philosophical tactics he is prone to use. I wonder what the "prior probabilities" might be for a situation in which flaked bones produced by gnawing animals are mixed into a site with flaked bone tools that have never before been recognized in the Mousterian and are indistinguishable from the animal-gnawed pieces. Standing behind this extraordinary situation is the additional fact that there are quantities of independent evidence showing that animals produce such flaked bones but only a poor analogy to stone tool making and a replicative experiment performed on a cow bone by Freeman to lend credence to the opinion that ancient hominids produced these "mimic" bone tools.

Archaeologists (more accurately, prehistorians) have for years operated with no well-researched foundation to which to appeal in justifying their interpretations of the past. There has been no science of the archaeological record, only a vague belief that prehistorians could somehow directly understand archaeological facts. I tried to point out in my book that studying the past is a matter of creating a past through inference. In order to create an accurate past we must be able to justify our inferences in the strongest possible terms. Such strong justification can only come from the scientific investigation of the archaeological record. We must understand how the static characteristics we observe came into being. We can never advance as long as we are content to accept our current state of understanding, ignorance, and/or myth as adequate to the task. If we pursue the past with a standard set of interpretive conventions, then we simply reach conclusions consistent with what we already "knew" over and over again. *Science seeks ways of using experience to illuminate the adequacy of our ideas about the world.* If one seeks to break into the intellectual stagnation of conventional thought in the hope of stimulating the scientific pursuit of knowledge, then one must show how the interpretive conventions in common use can lead to false or at least ambiguous interpretations. This was the basic thrust of my 1981 book, and it has upset the empiricists and conventional thinkers.

As we gradually grow in understanding through middle-range research, appeals to plausibility made from a poor conceptual and factual understanding of the archaeological record by honest, smart, and dedicated prehistorians will begin to take their places on the pages of our history. Future generations may well wonder "how they could have believed such things."

"Brand X" versus the Recommended Product

THE ANALOGY PROBLEM

In a recent series of publications Richard Gould (1971, 1974, 1977, 1978a, 1978b, 1980a) has presented his views on what he considers the major problems of contemporary archaeology. He has offered suggestions as to how these might be solved. His efforts have received mixed responses within the field.

> Gould crafts a persuasive alternative to explanation by direct analogy. In so doing, *he renounces several propositions fundamental to modern archaeology. . . . Serious doubt is cast upon the pervasive assumption that archaeological sites represent fossilized human behavior. . . .* He cautions against uncritical applications of the principle of *uniformitarianism, which is more appropriate to the physical sciences than to archaeology* but which is a central assumption in the use of argument by direct analogy. . . . *Living archaeology is among the more profound statements on archaeological theory and practice to appear in recent years.* (McIntosh 1980:117–118; emphasis added)

Quite clearly the reviewer considers Gould's work to be a major, even classic, contribution to our field. On the other hand, the same book was reviewed by Patty Jo Watson (1982), who obviously found it difficult and somewhat obscure.

> The book is entertaining, but it is not easy to extract from it precisely what Gould believes ethnoarchaeology is and should be, and thus to compare his position with previous views. (Watson 1982:455)

After discussing Gould's positions, Watson seems to come to the conclusion that far from being one of the more profound statements on archaeological theory and practice to date, nothing very new or profound was to be found. Watson's position has been summarized by Wylie (1982b:385) as follows:

> . . . Watson draws the critical conclusion . . . arguing that Gould is only able to differentiate his position from its forebears as sharply as he does by rhetorical sleight of hand and that, in doing this, a considerable amount of confusion has been introduced into the ethnoarchaeological literature. . . . This is a serious charge when directed, as it is, against a position intended to clear away confusion

Originally published in *American Antiquity* 50(3):580–590, © 1985.

and provide ethnoarchaeology with a comprehensive and unifying conceptual framework.

I reviewed Gould's book (Binford 1980b) and reached negative conclusions as regards his contribution. On my recent rereading of Gould I found, as Watson did, that his writing is opaque and hard to follow. More serious, however, was my impression that his presentations was frequently illogical and philosophically "innocent."

Paradoxically, however, I found myself in general agreement with Gould's (1980b) comments and criticism of Carol Kramer's (1979) book and particularly Watson's contribution:

> The theoretical basis for ethnoarchaeology is the use of analogies derived from present observation to aid interpretation of past events and processes. (Watson 1979:277)

If Watson is correct, then I would have to side with Gould in pointing out that analogies are reasoned inferences from observed similarities. The simple faith that similar forms had similar causes seems to be a very naive position, particularly when it is realized that the judgment of similarity is at least partially dependent upon how we choose to conceptualize our observations. Viewed in this context, Gould's objections seemed to be germane and to echo objections that I raised long ago (Binford 1967). Watson would reply with the claim that analogies are only trial "interpretative hypotheses" floated by the investigator as ideas to be tested (Gould and Watson 1982:359). We are also instructed that the major way to increase the "plausibility" of our arguments from analogy is to increase the scope of the similarities between the cases being compared (see Gould and Watson 1982:362–363). I need not point out that this is not a test of an inductive argument, it is simply an extension of it. Watson does not offer any suggestion as to how such arguments are to be "tested" regardless of how limited or extensive the positive analogies among compared cases might be. Her suggestion is what I consider to be a simple expansion of an operational definition for the properties to be inferred (see Binford 1977a:3–7, 1983a:7–13). I consider the term *definition* appropriate here since most inferential arguments that appeal to analogies use the analogy as a justification for adopting a definition for the properties to be inferred. Under normal conditions the argument from analogy serves as a warrant for adopting a definitional equation between dynamic conditions and some static properties of the archaeological record. This situation exists because the archaeological record is static and hypotheses regarding the relationships between statics and dynamics *cannot* be tested by an exclusive appeal to the static properties of the archaeological record (see Binford 1983a:14–17). Watson does not recognize this problem and in fact suggests that testing is possible using the archaeological record.

> Gould stresses alertness to anomalies in the process of checking the fit of interpretive models to archaeological data. . . . I stress use of a procedure that centers on testing to confirm or disconfirm the fit between hypothesized relationships (based ultimately on analogy with living systems) and the empirical reality of the archaeological record. (Watson in Gould and Watson 1982:363)

On the issue of analogies Gould seems to have put his finger on a major problem for archaeologists and Watson seems oblivious to the problem, as I see it. At least on the issue of problem recognition Gould has taken up an important issue. In fact, on this issue I am more comfortable with Gould's position than with that of Watson. Why then have I been critical of Gould? Why do I find it difficult to understand his arguments and views? Why have I largely been negative toward his works? These were questions that I asked myself as I read the Gould-Watson (1982) dialogue and the additional comments by Alison Wylie (1982b).

GOULD, NEW ARCHAEOLOGY, AND PARADIGM CONFLICT

I suppose my reactions to much of Gould's work were conditioned by a hostile and misleading review by Gould (1979) of my (1978a) Nunamiut book. A negative approach was common to most of Gould's statements about the "new archaeology." For instance, speaking of what he is clearly setting up as the popular position represented by the "new archaeology," Gould likens the situation to a commercial on television in which the popular "Brand X" is compared to the "real thing" sponsored in the commercial. As everyone knows, "Brand X" is *always set up as the inferior product relative to the one named in the commercial.* Gould's choice of metaphor is perhaps more appropriate than he realized, since he has either misunderstood the major thrusts of Americanist archaeology over the past 20 years or has, as in many of the commercials to which he alludes, quite literally "set up" the new archaeology as a straw man for showing off his own commercial product.

One could analyze Gould's works using traditional tactics, as he has done to others, so that *ad hominem* questioning of his professional competence (see Binford 1981a:239–240; Thompson 1956) would be considered the appropriate procedure for evaluating his arguments. Following this approach we might ask, is he well educated, is he a nice guy, is he honest, is he fair, etc., with the quality of the answers serving as the basis for accepting or rejecting his arguments and ideas. Rejection of this approach was, however, at the very root of what I hoped would develop into a truly "new" archaeology (Binford 1983a:8). I suppose it was the widespread character of this type of personal attack and evaluative innuendo that originally prompted me to advocate a more "scientific" approach to archaeology in which we sought to use our experiences in the external world analytically as arbiters of our ideas instead of the traditional procedure of evaluating the worth of a person as the basis for accepting or rejecting his or her ideas about the external world.

Basic to my position was recognition of the need for exploring our own ideas as conditioners for how we approach experience. It seemed clear to me that the archaic idea that objectivity was a state of mind that "honest" people could achieve was most certainly incorrect (see Binford 1983b). Our ideas and assumptions condition quite fundamentally what we see and what we accept as fact. We need to explore new ways of achieving objectivity. We need to gain new perspectives on the arguments we mount (see Binford 1982a) and we desperately need to "lose our innocence" (see Clarke 1973) regarding the role of our paradigm—the culture that we bring to experience, as a conditioner of what we see, how we judge significance, and how we use our observations.

Much of the argument in contemporary archaeology stems from paradigmatic incompatibility among the disputants. Unfortunately, most of the time the paradigmatic issues are not discussed and the argument proceeds as if it were the "objective" empirical world or the personal characteristics of the disputants that were at issue. We need to become much more skilled at paradigmatic criticism because paradigmatic self-awareness is basic to the growth of knowledge and understanding. I have insisted on this point numerous times but most commonly it is not understood, or it is ignored (see Binford 1978b:357—358, 1983b, 1983c, 1984; Binford and Sabloff 1982). Becoming self-aware regarding the intellectual role of our paradigms and increasing our ability to specify their contents so that they can be subjected to evaluation should be major goals of practitioners within a maturing field.

Gould advocates a particular world view regarding the nature of humankind and the world of archaeology. As part of this paradigm he adopts a particular philosophical position as regards the way we should proceed in our search for knowledge and understanding. I suggest that it is Gould's uncritical adoption of both a paradigm and a particular epistemological theory that guides his behavior and his thought as an archaeologist. These "ethnocentric" views lead him to criticize the works of others who do not subscribe to his views as if their work were misguided, poorly conceived, or motivated out of "churlishness" (Gould 1979:738). *I will try to demonstrate that Gould's behavior does not necessarily derive from character flaws or "bad" motives on his part,* instead it is considered here to be a consequence of his paradigm. I hope to show in this critique that, given his viewpoint, his arguments and his treatment of others' ideas possess a legitimate internal logic. I hope further to illustrate that the inadequacies in his argument and views reflect negatively on his paradigm and therefore that one should not "innocently" adopt it, as some of the positive reviewers cited earlier seem to have done.

GOULD'S GOALS

> As anthropologists we are interested in questions of symbolism and meaning, but as archaeologists we are inclined to examine such questions from a materialist point of view. (Gould 1980a:160).

> Only in living human species . . . could one expect to understand the operation of the *really important and interesting aspects of human behavior, namely those having to do with the human use of symbols.* Since these are mainly non-material in nature, it seemed reasonable to conclude that archaeologists with their reliance on material remains . . . could never hope to do more than deal *with a limited and rather unimportant part of the story of the human species.* (Gould 1980a:3; emphasis added)

I think it should be clear that Gould's position assumes that we should be studying symbolism and ideology, yet acknowledges that unfortunately all we have are material things. His assumption seems clear; it is ideas that guide human history. This position is not up for evaluation by Gould, it is simply assumed to be self-evident and, of course, "true." For him the paradox is clear: archaeology provides the only direct source for potential information about the non-literate history of the human species. This must be understood in terms of the symbols and ideology used by ancient people, yet the *archaeological record is a material record.* The challenge for the archaeologist is to find ways of studying the material record as a means to illuminate the symbolic and ideological domain considered basic or "causal" in human history.

Gould as a Strict Empiricist

It is in dealing with the apparent paradox—idealist's goals and material remains—that Gould, to my mind, makes his first big mistake: he accepts as accurate the traditional arguments regarding the limitations of the archaeological record. Gould notes, ". . . the problem is basically the same as it has always been since the beginning of archaeology . . . finding and improving ways to overcome the limitations posed by the nature of archaeological evidence" (Gould 1980a:2). The limitation to which Gould alludes is, of course, the material character of the archaeological record. The magnitude of this perceived limitation is made clear when it is realized that Gould operates as a *strict empiricist.* That is, he views the scientific approach as one that considers the source of knowledge to be derived directly from one's sense perceptions. Reason, in turn, supplies only analytical tools—that is, conventions and statements true by definition. Furthermore, all important synthetic knowledge is observational in character. For the strict empiricist, theory is conceived of as being synthesized from observational or empirical "laws," and these are simply confirmed empirical generalizations. We offer hypotheses from our experience, and if these trial laws tend to be confirmed by future observations then the hypotheses may be raised to the status of laws. Theory is knowledge synthesized or built up step by step. For the strict empiricist, laws are things we *discover* about the world.

> Patterned regularities in our evidence would . . . lead us to discover laws of human behavior [Gould 1980a:40]. . . . On the basis of this single case we can posit a general principle . . . assuming, for the sake of argument, that cross cultural testing proves that such a principle exists, we can then apply this principle as an explanatory prediction . . . in the archaeological record. (Gould 1981:280)

More surprising than Gould's adherence to the traditional archaeologist's view of science is his belief that I and other "new archaeologists" also adhered to such a position! When Gould comments on the new archaeology's criticism of particularism he states:

> Underlying the overall attack on archaeological particularism was the notion that *it is the regularities in the archaeological data that will provide the basis for laws or lawlike propositions about human behavior.* (Gould 1981:40; emphasis added)

Gould's belief that everyone subscribes to the strict empiricist view of science leads to his distortion of my work and that of others. I do not think Gould consciously assumes this posture from sophistic motives—I believe that Gould really thinks all persons are empiricists like himself.

The position I adopted regarding the traditional archaeologists' views on the limitations of the archaeological record was stated in 1968:

The practical limitations on our knowledge of the past are not inherent in the nature of the archaeological record: the limitations lie in our methodological naivete, in our lack of development for principles determining the relevance of archaeological remains to propositions regarding processes and events of the past. (Binford 1968:23)

Standing behind this statement was the philosophy that theory represents *inventions* of the human mind, that we cannot observe cause, that we mold "thought experiments" as to the dynamics of causation. In short, we invent, rather than discover, theories or parts of theories. Theories are arguments as to how the world works, not what it is like.

The transition from data to theory requires creative imagination. Scientific hypotheses and theories are not derived from . . . facts but invented . . . to account for them. (Hempel 1966:15)

I have said many times that empirical generalizations, the building blocks of theory for the strict empiricist, are only statements about how the world appears to be (see Binford 1978b:358). Theories are arguments or causal models regarding dynamics that seek to deal with the question of why the world appears as it does (see Binford 1981a:25). In short, empirical generalizations are the things we seek to explain, they do not themselves explain. "At each juncture of explaining observations from the archaeological record, we must question anew to what variables operative in the past our observations refer" (Binford 1968:25).

His misunderstanding of this issue plus his commitment to empiricism serves to rationalize Gould's recent interest in defining a domain to which we should limit our generalizations. He has called archaeology the "anthropology of human residue formation" (Gould 1978c:815). That is, we cannot properly study or discuss most or even many of the aspects of human behavior that social and cultural anthropologists discuss because we do not have direct access to the relevant empirical domains. We cannot generalize about phenomena to which we do not have access. We do have access to the archaeological record, and following Schiffer, Gould (1978a:2) sees the archaeological record as essentially "rubbish."

Thus the empirical attitude of the ethnoarchaeologist in studying anthropological processes leading to human residues enables him to move from his discovery of "rules" of behavior as they occur in particular human societies to the possibility of discovering in residue formation "laws" of behavior that are universal to mankind. (Gould 1978a:8)

This statement makes explicit Gould's belief that we generate empirical generalizations. For him, it is perfectly clear that we cannot generate generalizations about domains of phenomena that we do not have *empirically* available. Gould's failure to understand that the issues and arguments of the 1960s were aimed at *rejecting* the principles of strict empiricism leads him to assume that I and others must also operate from the same perspective that he adopts—the traditional perspective. Given his viewpoint, my attempts, as well as those of others, to talk about features of the past not "recoverable" archaeologically, such as social organization, were viewed by Gould as misguided attempts to "enliven" our discipline.

> The more archaeologists tried to enliven their interpretations of the past by apply-
> ing ideas about the past derived from social and cultural anthropology, the more
> they exposed themselves to the criticism of social and cultural anthropologists
> whose studies encompassed a wider and presumably more satisfying range of
> human behavior. (Gould 1980a:3)

This statement illustrates Gould's empiricism. Properties of social organization,
ideas of how cultural systems work, etc., could be studied only by social and cultural
anthropologists. Only they observed the appropriate empirical domain about which
only they could offer generalizations. Archaeologists did not study a domain of social
phenomena, they studied material things. Gould seems to see the discussions of social
organization during the early 1960s as misguided attempts to "make a silk purse out of
a sow's ear."

> Not all anthropology is appropriate to the aims of archaeology, and what is perhaps
> even more important we cannot allow archaeology to be presented as a kind of
> imperfect anthropology of the past. Archaeology sailed perilously close to this
> particular intellectual iceberg during the 1960s when it set out to discover ma-
> trilineal pottery and other "signatures" of prehistoric social organization. I concur
> with Roland Fletcher's recent arguments (personal communication) that such
> efforts created false expectations for archaeologists while at the same time de-
> meaned the discipline of archaeology. (Gould 1980a:250)

Gould's beliefs have not only led him to advocate very outdated positions, but he
has also assumed that everyone else is or should be a strict empiricist. Given such an
assumption he has great difficulty with the writings of those of us who had rejected
such positions. He sees our actions as illegitimate, stemming from questionable
motives, or perhaps chauvinistic. For him, any thinking person can see that many
interpretations offered by some of us have not been based on empirical generalizations from the data!

GOULD'S DESCRIPTIONS OF MY WORK

> In seeking uniformitarian linkages between past and present day human behavior,
> Binford has invoked the biological concept of adaptation as a potential source of
> uniformities, and he goes on to construct a detailed model of human behavioral
> adaptations in relation to immediate circumstantial facts (seasonality, terrain and
> distances, modes of transport, movement of game species, and so on). Whatever
> variability in Nunamiut meat use and faunal residues occurs is seen by Binford as
> arising from human adaptive behavior in relation to differences in situational and
> circumstantial factors under which animal products were procured, transported,
> stored, consumed and ultimately discarded, rather than being due to mental tem-
> plates or any other kind of normative cultural category shared by these Eskimos.
> For Binford, it is circumstance rather than culture that determines human behavior
> in relation to meat procurement and faunal remains. (Gould and Watson 1982:366)

This is a distortion of both my work as well as the implications of the Nunamiut
studies for anthropology. I will begin my critique of Gould's distortions with a comment I made many years ago, which Edmond Leach seems to have enjoyed greatly,

namely: "Behavior is the by-product of the interaction of a cultural repertoire with the environment" (Leach 1973:762). Given this viewpoint, I designed my Nunamiut studies to demonstrate that when we hold *culture* constant, that is, the repertoire of convention and knowledge, we nevertheless see variable behavior. This variability must be seen as responsive, flexible behavior that the repertoire facilitates in the face of variable environmental conditions. The sites and contexts that I studied among the Nunamiut were largely occupied at different times *by the same individuals.* One could hardly argue that there was a cultural change or ethnic difference between a fall site occupied by Frank Rulland in 1948 and a winter site occupied by Frank Rulland in the same year! Nevertheless, significant differences were demonstrated between the faunal assemblages at two such sites. These differences were referable to differential transport, dependence upon storage, phase of consumption from stores, etc., characteristic of each occupation. The purpose of my studies was to demonstrate that sites generated by the same men, carrying the same culture, were nevertheless formally different in archaeological content. The point of contention between myself and F. Bordes had been over the degree that cultures were internally homogeneous, that is, recognizable by their consistent similarities as noted among assemblages, or whether assemblages could be formally different and still referable to a single sociocultural system. In no place was the argument made that some behavior was ecologically determined and other behavior culturally determined. My research was about how culture works and the character of the behavior that culture facilitates and organizes. The statement by Gould (Gould and Watson 1982:366) that "for Binford, it is circumstance rather than culture that determines human behavior" is a misrepresentation of just about everything I have ever done.

This pattern of misrepresentation is continued when Gould suggests that my ecological arguments were warrants for making uniformitarian assumptions. Gould clearly suggests that my uniformitarian assumptions were about the way humans would respond to such environmental conditions as seasonality, terrain, and distance. This is simply not correct. I made uniformitarian assumptions about the economic anatomy of caribou and sheep. I used these assumptions to evaluate the character of behavioral biases manifest in the differential distribution of anatomical parts on sites.

> To use the principle of uniformitarianism effectively in ethnoarchaeology we must not only ask the right questions but also ask them in the right order. What about hunter-gatherer societies which procure, transport, consume, and discard meat products in a manner patterned altogether differently from the Nunamiut? (Gould and Watson 1982:366)

My uniformitarian assumptions made possible an evaluation of the degree that past peoples responded differently to constant conditions, not, as Gould suggests, an assumption that all people must behave like the Nunamiut. After his telling criticism of my work, Gould goes on to note that he has observed episodes of kangaroo butchering and that, regardless of circumstantial variability, the Australians always butchered the animals into the same nine anatomical units. He notes that he looked for variability in "eco-utilitarian" terms, but found none, at least with respect to butchering.

> The strict adherence to a fixed pattern of initial divisions of meat was explained more parsimoniously with reference to social relations based upon kin-based

sharing of food and access to resources . . . than to direct influence of the immediate circumstances under which hunting occurs. While the "extra step" involved in this initial butchering and sharing of meat is ultimately adaptive, it would be hard to explain if one adhered to a simple deterministic notion of how human behavior relates to circumstances. In other words, one must look first at the eco-utilitarian relationships that occur in the situation one observes and see to what extent variation in the observed behavior can be accounted for by these immediate circumstances. If one has exhausted this level of explanation without totally satisfactory results, then one is entitled to go on to the next higher level of explanation, namely the ideational realm of shared traditions. (Gould and Watson 1982:367)

We see in these statements the confusion wrought by Gould when he translates the works of those who are not his kind of empiricists into his paradigm. Gould saw my discussions of Nunamiut behavior not as directed toward the understanding of the archaeological record and its variability but instead as a search for empirical patterns that through ethnographic analogy could be projected as universally relevant to all people. His experiences in Australia seemed a "spoiler" (Yellen 1977a:133) for what he thought I was projecting as potential laws of human behavior. As I have pointed out, I was not making the argument that Gould attributes to me, hence his counterpoint is misdirected.

GOULD'S POSITION: A PHILOSOPHICAL PARADOX

When I discussed Gould's goals I cited him to the effect that symbolism and ideology were the "aspects" of the human experience that we needed to study if we were to understand human history in human terms. This is a common component of most idealist philosophical positions, of which historicism is one expression.

Historicism in extreme form is the view that human behavior has a special character which precludes explanation by scientific methods because it is not governed by scientific laws; understanding is attained not through scientific explanation but rather through our peculiarly human ability to empathize, to enter into passions, fears, calculations, and aspirations of past humans. (Bamforth and Spaulding 1982:179)

True to the above characterization of historicism, Gould argues for the "special character" of human behavior and against the position that scientific explanations could be developed for human phenomena. Gould acknowledges that for "natural phenomena" other than human behavior the methods of science are perhaps sometimes applicable. He also acknowledges that human beings live in a naturalistic matrix, hence the findings of the natural sciences are relevant as a framework in terms of which to view human behavior, but not to explain it (see Gould 1980a:112, where nature is viewed as a limiting factor). This is just another way of stating the ancient folk wisdom expressed in the Mother Goose rhyme "Wear you a hat or wear you a crown, all that goes up must surely come down."

Gould sees human behavior as a strictly human product variable from place to place and time to time. This human "expression" could not be understood in terms of the naturalistic matrix, but instead must be understood in terms of the local characteristics of ideology, philosophy, and symbolism, which presumably vary among societies "historically." Culture conceived in these terms becomes the explanation for variable human behavior and it is considered to be particularistically distributed and variable, both temporally and spatially, in form and content.

It is from this perspective that Gould argues against the search for "laws" of human behavior (see Gould 1980a:36–39). If one believes that laws are discovered and that they are "successful" empirical generalizations, then empirical material—which for Gould appears to be unique, idiosyncratic, or not subject to generalization—would of "necessity" be inappropriate. It appears self-evident that cultural "data" could not serve the goals of generalization as viewed from his perspective. Gould's idealistic philosophy leads him to believe that the results of important human behavior, conditioned by symbolism, philosophy, ideas, values, etc., are not subject to understanding by scientific methods. As an empiricist he expects science to proceed by generating empirical generalizations, then raising such generalizations to law-like status through arguments from enumeration. He suggests that the use of such procedures would overlook the unique and particular, for him the human characteristics, and hence the important aspects of the archaeological record. Gould abhors this "waste" of the particular and unique. It is in this context of reasoning that Gould suggests that the search for "laws" is a shortsighted and wasteful use of archaeological data.

> To this might be added the further recognition that it may be precisely those aspects of human behavior that prove least susceptible to measurement and scientific analysis that could prove, in the end, to be the most decisive. Could it be that the more restrictively quantitative archaeology tries to become, the more trivial it becomes, too? (Gould 1980a:38)

Here we see Gould's dilemma. On the one hand, he is an idealist committed to the study of uniquely human characteristics that are thought to require a special kind of explanation. In the latter we use our own human capacities to empathize with those of the past by virtue of our ability to recognize our own humanity in others. At the same time, he is committed to an outdated idea of science, which proposed that knowledge was obtained not as a result of intellectual activity but directly through sense perceptions. In this view, scientists clear their minds of bias and observe the world in good faith. They seek to generalize their observations, and over time these generalizations may be raised to the status of laws by the accumulation of an increasing number of confirmed cases.

> All statements of regularity are provisional to a degree, since they are always being tested. . . . (Gould 1980a:161)

> . . . like anomalies, laws and lawlike statements are relative and must be understood in relation to the process of testing in which they are constantly subjected in science. (Gould 1980a:161)

Given this view, Gould sees science as inappropriate to his humanistic, particularizing goals for understanding human behavior. The logic is clear; culture is a human expression otherwise called ideology, philosophy, symbolism, or tradition, which does not vary with respect to "natural laws" and, therefore, represents a domain not amenable to study by the basic procedures of science. Since archaeological remains are presented to us in confused units, we can recognize the role of past culture as a conditioner of pattern in archaeological remains by the very fact that "natural laws" appear to be broken—an anomaly appears.

Gould's objections to ethnographic analogy as cited in the beginning of this paper derive neither from an understanding of its logic nor from philosophical insights into inferential argument. They derive from his strict empiricist views coupled with his belief that human behavior is guided by an "inner" logic derived from local philosophy, ideology, and symbolism. The latter relativistic position leads Gould to view arguments from ethnographic analogy as misguided attempts to offer one's ethnographic experiences as if they were governed by uniform tendencies of human nature. This viewpoint makes it appear to him that we assume "the very things we should be trying to find out" (Gould 1980a:29).

If we view Gould's reading of my (1978a) Nunamiut report as an attempt by me to describe "human behavior" and then project this experience, suggesting that all humans would in turn behave in analogous ways, then his distortion of my work makes some sense as does his insistence that other peoples do not behave like the Nunamiut. Given such a view of analogy, the argument that Gould offers regarding anomaly also makes some sense. That is, an anomaly is an ethnographic or archaeological experience that differs empirically from the "standard" that had been presented from some prior ethnographic experiences and by analogy projected as if it applied to all peoples. In short, an anomaly is an example of Yellen's "spoiler" tactics relative to analogical arguments.

Gould views archaeologists, misguided by scientific models, as seeking out experiences and then attempting to generalize these experiences as trial "laws" of human nature. In turn, when we meet an empirical case to the contrary, relative to such generalizations, we then know we are not dealing with universalistic phenomena and must, in his view, shift perspectives from the universalistic to the particular—the particular ideological and symbolic context of the peoples involved.

> Anomalies discovered by means of ethnographic studies *compel* archaeologists to expand their explanations in many cases to aspects of the socio-ideational realm of human residue behavior. (Gould 1980a:229; emphasis added)

"Spoiling" arguments from ethnographic analogy, as he sought to do with my Nunamiut writings (see Gould and Watson 1982:365–368), is one route to discovering "anomalies"; however, the recommended way is to use the findings of natural science to enlighten the historicist's domain.

> Instead of trying to discover laws of human behavior, the living archaeologist is concerned with using relationships that have already achieved the status of law in other fields as frameworks for making discoveries about human behavior. (Gould 1980a:140)

> . . . one must look first at the eco-utilitarian relationships that occur in the situation one observes and see to what extent variation in the observed behavior can be accounted for by these immediate circumstances. If one has exhausted this level of explanation without satisfactory results, then one is entitled to go on to the next

higher level of explanation, namely the ideational realm of shared tradition. (Gould and Watson 1982:367)

Patterns, characteristics, and properties of the archaeological record that do not "fit" the natural science laws as conceived by Gould are anomalies and as such betray the role of unique, idiosyncratic, and idealistically based human behavior. This paradigmatic belief renders it possible for Gould to pursue his goal:

> If we can put aside analogies and laws, with their uniformitarianist assumptions about how humans *ought to behave,* and instead explore methods that will help us find out how they really do behave, perhaps we will develop wider and more satisfying explanations. (Gould 1980a:39)

Statements such as this are perhaps the most ironic of Gould's writings because they suggest that his procedures will lead us to "objective" truths and "accurate" insights into human behavior!

Gould's writings are not unique in strangely combining philosophies. What renders Gould's writings most interesting and unique is his naivete regarding the role played by his own beliefs and philosophy in conditioning how he sees the world and particularly how he sees the works of others. As an empiricist, he believes he sees nature clearly, not distorted or filtered by his own thoughts—his paradigm (see Binford and Sabloff 1982). As an empiricist, he believes that his philosophy is given by nature and therefore must be shared by any other honest observer. His empiricism blinds him to the reality that there are others who do not share his empiricist views. Consequently, when he reads my writings he re-creates me in his image. He imparts to me his own strong convictions. As pointed out, he discusses the Nunamiut study as if I were seeking to project the particular behaviors observed among the Nunamiut as universalistic expressions of human nature and hence expectable in the behavior of others. He criticizes the search for laws as if the only meaning of the word was empirical generalization. In his view, the single-minded search for such general phenomena would overlook the unique and, for him, the interesting. He is unaware that laws need not be conceived as successful empirical generalizations (see Binford 1978b). He must be puzzled by such statements as "The relevance of theory is . . . this, a statement of universal form, whether empirically confirmed or as yet untested, will qualify as a law if it is implied by an accepted theory" (Hempel 1966:58).

Gould's work is perhaps the best demonstration I know of the bankruptcy of the traditionalist's position. His view of "reality" is not given by nature, but through its interaction with the assumptions and intellectual biases he holds. Ironically, his own insistence on the general utility of the empiricist view of science contradicts his alleged commitment to the cultural relativist's position, where the symbols, ideas, and values of different cultures dictate that their practitioners see the world differently, evaluate rationality differently, and behave differently in similar environments or "limiting situations." Why shouldn't this also be true among archaeologists coming from different "traditions"?

I do not adhere to either of the positions advocated by Gould. I am fully convinced that our paradigms condition in awesome ways how we conceive of experience. On the other hand, I am not committed to the sterile skepticism of cultural relativism. I think we can learn how paradigms constrain our thought and conceptualizations of experience. I think we can learn how to use different conceptual approaches to nature. "Science is a method or procedure that directly addresses itself to the evaluation of cultural forms. That is, if we view culture as at least referring to the particularly human ability to give meaning expediently to experience, to symbol, and, in turn, view experience through this conceptual idiom, science is then concerned with evaluating the utility of the cultural tools produced" (Binford 1977a:3).

I consider the "new archaeology" as a move toward achieving a more sophisticated self-consciousness regarding the problems inherent in trying to infer a past from contemporary observations. Phrasing the problem this way emphasizes the creative role that the archaeologist plays in constructing a past. This creative role is always in terms of ideas concerning the meanings that contemporary artifacts and other archaeological traces hold for the events and dynamics of the past. The new archaeology advocated a move toward the difficult task of evaluating the cultural tools that we use to aid in our task of constructing a past.

The paradigmatic dependence illustrated in the writings of Gould should emphasize the utility of this position. The critique presented here should also illustrate some of the concerns that were recognized years ago and that prompted many of my suggestions favoring a "new archaeology."

Traditional archaeology was largely an approach that assumed a strict empiricist view of science. Traditional archaeology in its "theoretical" posture assumed an idealistic historicist's perspective for viewing humankind and its works. I have tried to show that these postures are also representative of Gould's views. Gould is trying very hard to reject "Brand X"—the new archaeology—as a laxative for purging intellectual particularism from archaeology. He suggests that he has developed a "recommended brand." As I have studied the recommended product, I have come to realize that, strangely enough, it has all the properties of the disease!

Chapter 10

"Righteous Rocks" and Richard Gould:
Some Observations on Misguided "Debate"

by Lewis R. Binford and Nancy M. Stone

In 1912, W. H. R. Rivers published what, we, as students, regarded as a "classic" in anthropology. We have reference to an essay called "The Disappearance of Useful Arts." Rivers's point is framed in his introduction:

> The civilized person, imbued with utilitarian ideas, finds it difficult to understand the disappearance of useful arts. To him it seems almost incredible that arts which not merely add to the comfort and happiness of a people but such as seem almost essential to his very existence should be lost. (Rivers 1912:109)

After reviewing the evidence regarding the loss of the canoe, pottery, and the bow and arrow by various groups in Oceania, Rivers comes to the conclusion that utilitarian considerations are apt to be inappropriate for anticipating the character of cultural growth. In addition, he points out that the persistence of "useless" cultural elements presents us with a paradox analogous to the demonstration of the loss of useful arts. "This persistence of the useless combines with the disappearance of the useful to make us beware of judging human culture by purely utilitarian standards" (Rivers 1912:130). What Rivers concludes is simply that religious or magical factors may motivate people to behave in ways that seem anomalous if only utilitarian considerations are taken into account.

More than 50 years later Richard Gould (1978c) offers to the field of anthropology a surprisingly similar insight. In fact, he went a step further and proposed that the recognition of an anomaly relative to utilitarian considerations could even be taken as evidence indicative of the operation of "ideational or nonmaterial factors" (Gould 1978c:833). In later commentary on his earlier studies Gould says that

> symbolic systems can play an essential role in human adaptation . . . as the case of "righteous rocks" among Western Desert Aborigines and at Puntutjarpa shows. . . . (Gould 1980a:160)

> . . . if . . . silicrete is less than ideal in relation to the local materials, then we once again have an anomaly that is more economically explained by a social-ideational than a utilitarian argument. (Gould 1980a:228)

The above comment has reference to the observation that the local materials around Puntutjarpa shelter were more appropriate as raw material for adzes than

Originally published in *American Antiquity* 50:151–153, © 1985.

were the exotic cherts also found there. Gould had noted that 26.7% of the adzes from the site of Puntutjarpa were manufactured from the inferior exotic chert, which in his judgment was more costly to procure. This "surprising" situation was then judged to be a "significant anomaly" (Gould 1980a:149). Gould had previously commented:

> Was the efficiency of exotic cherts great enough to lead the Aborigines to make the extraordinary efforts needed to obtain them for adze making? I very much doubt that it was. . . . We can reasonably infer that some other consideration led the ancient Aborigines to make the extra efforts needed to obtain them. (Gould 1978c:288)

In comments on Gould's arguments Binford (1979:260–261) simply pointed out that Gould's assumptions regarding lithic procurement were not necessarily warranted. Binford noted that no extraordinary procurement efforts, as postulated by Gould, were necessarily required and hence no anomaly, relative to utilitarian considerations, need be assumed to explain the data reported, if one adopted a more realistic view of raw material procurement. In short, Binford pointed out that most raw material is obtained incidentally during the course of the normal subsistence-related mobility in the habitat and one should not estimate procurement cost as if it were a direct cost incurred by an exclusive trip made to obtain materials. Binford's comment was directed toward what he considered to be unrealistic a priori assumptions made by Gould in recognizing his anomaly, which in turn permitted him (given his beliefs) to point to ideological reasons for such "anomalous" behavior.

One might well imagine our surprise on reading in the article by Gould and Saggers (1985:117–118) that Binford (1) "discount(s) the importance of technological criteria in explaining the occurrence of lithic materials among mobile hunter-gatherers"; (2) "doubt[s] the usefulness of relating such variables as distance from source, difficulties of terrain, transport capabilities, or artifact utility"; and (3) dismisses as unimportant "lithic procurement and technical factors of tool use."

This peculiar distortion of Binford's views is further emphasized by such statements as "unlike Binford, however, Goodyear is not content to assume that the functional prerequisites of tools are insignificant factors in procurement" (Gould and Saggers 1985:124).

We do not mind criticism; in fact, we think criticism is one of the major means we have to clarify thought, expand our ideas, and thereby grow intellectually. What is not productive, however, is self-serving criticism that misrepresents the positions of others. That misrepresentation of Binford's work occurs in this article is undeniable and baffling; however, in the interest of clarification we have chosen to elaborate on these points rather than focus on their distortions.

We think a naive reader of the paper by Gould and Saggers would draw the conclusion that Binford had written a position paper on the meaningful analysis of stone tool assemblages with particular emphasis on the interpretation of lithic source variability. No such paper has been written. The paper to which Gould refers (Binford 1979) is a summary of some observations made on the organization of Nunamiut Eskimo technology. The purpose of that paper was to emphasize that (a) technologies are organized, (b) organizations may vary from one society to another, and (c) there are indicators, or "signatures" as Gould might say, for at least some of these organizational differences. During the course of these discussions Binford sought to warrant the claim that the procurement of resources, replacement of materials, recycling of items, and the mobility of items in the technology varied with whether the items were organized as components of site furniture, personal gear, or situational gear. Binford further noted that at any given time the system state conditions with regard to gear (that is, whether items are in storage or actively organized for use) would condition assemblage variability. It was hoped that the reader would be impressed with the need to seek an understanding of the organization of past technologies from the static patterns of variability that we as archaeologists might note. It was thought that this was particularly important at the level of intersite lithic assemblage variability. As regards Binford's alleged discounting of "the importance of technological criteria in explaining the occurrence of lithic materials among mobile hunter-gatherers" we can only reply with what Binford in fact had to say on these issues, remembering, however, that his paper did not deal with explaining lithic source variability per se.

> Gear produced for inclusion as "personal gear" or even "household gear" is much more likely to be manufactured according to quality considerations unaffected by constraints on time or immediate availability of appropriate material, since this activity is intended to meet anticipated future needs. (Binford 1979:267)

Here we see Binford's discussion of the quality of lithic raw material as it varies relative to the production of tools designed to perform different roles in the technology. In fact, this statement anticipates rather nicely the facts reported by Gould from both Puntutjarpa and James Range East, namely that a hafted tool, such as the adze, is likely to have been personal gear and hence a curated tool. This means that adze producers would be biased toward good raw material regardless of where such material was found within their normal range. This, in fact, seems to be the pattern described by Gould and Saggers. At Puntutjarpa the best material was local, and that was the dominant material used for adzes. At James Range East the best material was exotic to the area, and much more exotic material, relative to Puntutjarpa, was in fact used for adzes. It would be interesting to know if at James Range East there was also a more exhaustive use of the adzes of exotic material than was observed at Puntutjarpa; we would expect such a pattern.

As regards the charge that Binford doubts the usefulness of such variables as "distance from source, difficulties of terrain, transport capabilities . . ." it can only be viewed as absurd in light of the fact that Gould himself has only recently negatively criticized Binford's work for emphasizing these very variables! "For Binford, it is circumstance rather than culture that determines human behavior in relation to meat procurement and faunal remains" (Gould and Watson 1982:366). Explaining to the reader what Binford means by circumstance, Gould is rather specific:

> Whatever variability in meat use and faunal residues occurs is seen by Binford as arising from human adaptive behavior in relation to differences in situational and circumstantial factors under which animal products were procured, transported, stored, consumed and ultimately discarded, rather than being due to mental templates or any other kind of normative cultural category shared by these Eskimos. (Gould and Watson 1982:366)

Gould may try to salvage the logic of his position by pointing out that his criticism was directed at Binford's arguments about meat and animal products and here we should be talking about stone tools. This would be a weak and poorly taken point since it would miss the significance of the literature. Binford's original comment about Gould's work was not that seeking to estimate costs relative to transport costs, distance to sources, etc., was wrong or inappropriate, it was only that Gould was doing it poorly. It is clear that he still does not understand the problem, much less visualize appropriate approaches to its solution.

It is perhaps doubly ironic that Gould's early criticism of Binford's work asserted that he ignored ideological and cultural variables in favor of utilitarian concerns. In fact, as noted previously, Gould's point was reminiscent of the quaint speculations of W. H. R. Rivers cited in the beginning of this essay. Surprisingly, however, the Gould and Saggers paper concludes that Binford's shortcomings rest with his dismissal of utilitarian variables! It would certainly be helpful to our field if in his future writings Gould would decide what he thinks is important and link this with an accurate understanding of the literature.

Chapter 11

Richard Gould Revisited, or Bringing Back the "Bacon"

INTRODUCTION: SEQUENCE OF PREVIOUS EXCHANGES AND ISSUES RAISED

In recent years Richard Gould has regularly been addressing the field of archaeology with a number of programmatic suggestions. I consider these ideas to be poorly thought out yet seemingly seductive to those who wish to avoid the basic intellectual issues facing archaeology as a science. I began to criticize Gould (Binford 1979) when I realized that his easy, stylistically soft form of rhetoric was being taken seriously by students and some teachers. In a recent analysis of Gould's positions I advanced the view (Binford 1985a) that the basic assumptions from which Gould operated were strict empiricists' ideas of science (a point that Gould 1985 has now conceded), but that at the same time he paradoxically adopted an idealist approach when seeking explanations for culture and therefore history. Gould states,

> It may be precisely those aspects of human behavior that prove *least susceptible to measurement and scientific analysis that could prove, in the end, to be the most decisive.* Could it be that the more restrictively quantitative archaeology tries to become, the more trivial it becomes, too? (Gould 1980a:38; emphasis added)

It was my contention that the simultaneous adoption of these positions leads Gould to (a) complex problems of epistemology and (b) frequent illogical postures in his arguments. Gould himself recognizes some of these problems, and he tries to solve the paradox of adopting a scientific (although outdated) approach while at the same time maintaining that the interesting aspects of human history may be those that are the "least susceptible to measurement and scientific analysis [but] could prove, in the end, to be the most decisive." Gould, of course, has in mind what he calls "the really important and interesting aspects of human behavior, namely those having to do with the human use of symbols" (Gould 1980a:3). It is quite clear that Gould adopts an idealist posture when considering explanations for human behavior and human history. He seeks to solve this seeming paradox (the adoption of science while at the same time denying its relevance to the investigation of human history and behavior) by advocating his method of argument from anomaly:

> By applying uniformitarian assumptions we can use empirical science to infer accurately when nonmaterial, cognitive, or ideational factors are affecting out-

comes (the argument by anomaly) that differ from our predictions. (Gould 1985:642)

As I have pointed out (Binford 1984b), this attempted solution fails on epistemological grounds. I commented on Gould's method of argument from anomaly as follows:

> What Gould does not consider is that our ignorance of the material conditions and organizational properties of past systems represented archaeologically may be the cause of anomalies and irrationalities in our terms. Something may appear anomalous simply because of our ignorance of factors considered by the ancients in their reasoning processes. Because we are unable to reconcile the behavior of a group of people in the past with what little we know about their environment, social setting, and situational state is no justification for seeing a "social-ideational" explanation, nor for moving to a new level of explanation as has recently been advocated by Gould.

Gould's argument from anomaly is a form of argument from lack of evident alternatives. The argument takes the following form: if we see something we do not understand, it must therefore derive from symbolic or ideational causes. As I have pointed out, "Gould's argument from anomaly is a fancy phrase for the old practice of calling something a ceremonial object when you do not know what it is" (Binford 1984b:180). It should be mentioned that this is the same form of argument used for years to "prove" the existence of God. An observer would look out at the natural world, express wonder and admiration for its regularity, beauty, and organizational properties, and then conclude that, since there was no explanation for such phenomena, the world must have been created by God.

Equally interesting is the failure of Gould's advocated approach at the practical or applied level. In 1980 Gould introduced his argument regarding the "anomalous" use of lithic raw materials at Puntutjarpa rockshelter (Gould 1980a). This is generally referred to as the "righteous rocks" argument. In fact, this argument was introduced as the initial demonstration of the utility of his argument by anomaly (Gould 1980a: 138–160), although it had been made earlier (Gould 1978c:288). Gould's research team had measured the "utility" of different raw materials for use as adzes. They had found that the exotic raw materials have fewer edge-holding properties than the local material. Gould stated the anomaly this way:

> There is an anomalous relationship in this case, which is: if white chert was obviously the most efficient lithic raw material for adzemaking, both in terms of efficiency of procurement and use, why was exotic stone used at all for this purpose? (1980a:153)

Gould has made much of his demand that we work from empirical foundations, yet he uses an imagined set of "laws"—all men behave in terms of efficiency considerations, and all men conceive of the manufacture and use of tools relative to their eventual discard location. I know of no body of empirical data that supports either of these assumptions. *If either of these assumptions is not granted, there is no anomaly.* Even if we ignore this point for the moment, there are other internal problems with Gould's practical demonstrations of his advocated procedures.

Gould offers argument by anomaly as a replacement for argument by analogy. He titles his chapter "Beyond Analogy" and tries to argue that analogy is no longer a reasonable base from which archaeologists should work. Ironically, however, it is ethnographic analogy to which he appeals in order to justify his conclusions that his alleged anomaly can be understood in ideational and symbolic terms; he simply cites the use of exotic artifacts and raw materials as "ritual items" (e.g., Kimberley points), *yiraputja* (items of "special substance"), and additional examples that have been documented by explorers, field anthropologists, and other researchers in Australia. He then uses these ethnographically documented phenomena to justify both his belief that the use of exotic stones at Puntutjarpa are referable to the same behavioral phenomena and his search for an ideological basis for explaining his "righteous rock" patterning at a site said to span 10,000 years. Since this is the type of logic Gould uses, there is little doubt as to why he finds little difference between the present and the past in the Warburton area of Australia. Gould's bluster regarding analogy's "last hurrah," and his simultaneous use of analogy as the very basis for his arguments, has been criticized previously (Wylie 1982b).

Such basic problems were obvious to most readers of Gould's work, and I have addressed this issue in a direct fashion. As noted, Gould cites the use of exotic raw materials for adze manufacture at Puntutjarpa as the basis for declaring an anomaly and therefore the justification for seeking ideological motivators standing behind the selection of exotic raw materials (Gould 1978c:288) by the occupants of Puntutjarpa rockshelter. I countered his suggestion (Binford 1979:260–261) by noting that variability in the quality of utilized raw materials might be understandable in terms of (a) the embedded nature of raw-material-procurement strategies known to characterize some societies and (b) biases in the use of materials of different quality for tools with different anticipated roles in the organization of the technology (Binford 1979:267). Gould has apparently abandoned his original argument in the face of criticism— "Saggers and I had already backed away from the 'righteous rocks' explanation (Binford and Stone are beating a dead horse here)" (Gould 1985:641). Nevertheless, he apparently sees no relationship between this change of heart and the implications for his proposed strategy of argument by anomaly. As was previously pointed out, these "anomalies" may frequently be apparent to an investigator only in the context of the investigator's ignorance of what the world is like.

In 1982 the dialogue between Gould and Watson regarding analogy in archaeological reasoning was published, and Gould sought to defend his positions on the importance of idealism to the understanding of human history, his solution to the paradox of his own metaphysics, the argument from anomaly, and the arguments presented in his earlier book, *Living Archaeology* (Gould 1980a). In the Gould and Watson (1982) article Gould made reference to my research and misused and misrepresented my work. This prompted several articles in which I sought to clarify both Gould's misrepresentation of my work and the failure of Gould's approaches to deal realistically with archaeologists' problems.

After the Gould–Watson dialogue I began a detailed reading of Gould, and the result of this research was published in 1985 (Binford 1985a). Before its appearance, however, Gould and Saggers (1985) sought to counter my suggestions (Binford 1979) regarding alternative ways of thinking about Gould's lithic raw material data from Puntutjarpa. Gould and Saggers's article is strange in more ways than one. First, they completely missed the point to which my initial criticism was addressed—namely, that the *assumptions* used by Gould as if they were demonstrated laws for the purpose of recognizing an anomaly were not laws; therefore, there was no anomaly. Binford and Stone (1985:152) note this in their reply. The second strange aspect to Gould and Saggers's (1985) paper was a series of fallacious arguments classifiable as *ignoratio elenchi*. Such arguments are characterized by missing the point or attempting to discredit one's opponents by disproving assertions that they have not actually made. We (Binford and Stone 1985) answered these arguments. Another strange charac-teristic of the paper (relative to Gould's earlier emphasis on ideology and symbolism) was the attempt by Gould and Saggers to emphasize such utilitarian concerns and situational variables as transport costs and artifact utility as conditioners of patterning in the archaeological record, facts that Gould was earlier willing to characterize as "simple" (Gould and Watson 1982:367) when discussed relative to Nunamiut use of animal resources. We heard nothing about arguments from anomaly or ideological determinants of lithic raw material utilization. One might suspect that Gould's ide-alism was fading. Shortly thereafter, however, my analysis of Gould's assumptive position in argument was published (Binford 1985a), accompanied by a reply from Gould (1985). In the latter rejoinder he reiterates his earlier position on anomaly (Gould 1985:642); however, he now states that the study of cognition requires a different kind of ethnoarchaeology than the one he previously advocated (Gould 1985:643). He also states that there is another kind of ethnoarchaeology—"dirt ethno-archaeology"—concerned with culture-historical interpretation. What is interesting is that Gould has answered none of the criticism and has consistently replied to critics with *ignoratio elenchi* arguments.

THE LATEST ROUND—SOME THINGS DON'T CHANGE

Gould (1985) has "answered" my analysis of his position by openly declaring himself an empiricist, and he seeks once again to impress the field with the value of his personal approach to doing archaeology. I find this reply an excellent example of the weaknesses of the metaphysical postures that he adopts; in the interests of clarifica-tion, I point out those weaknesses.

1. The paradox rendered by his choice of philosophical positions ensures that his arguments are internally inconsistent.

> [a] Perhaps now is a good time to consider the alternative to Binford's views; namely that there is a real world out there, and ask to what extent it is knowable to us through our observations. To accept such a view would mean, of course, that the evidence does speak for itself if we will allow ourselves to be guided by it. (Gould 1985:638)

[b] Binford is not wrong when he stresses the importance of ideas with respect to their role in organizing the observations one makes of the world or the universe, as such "paradigm shifts" as the Copernican Revolution demonstrate. Yet these same shifts can also be interpreted as the result of a willingness by the observers to be *guided by the evidence* of their observations. (Gould 1985:638)

In these paired quotes we can see very clearly the incompatible ideas with which Gould works. If one acknowledges, as he does, that our ideas may condition the way we organize our observations on the external world, how then can we ignore this recognition and demand that we be "guided by the evidence of . . . observations" in the sense that "evidence speaks for itself" as an accurate reflection of the "external world"? What about the role of those ideas as organizers of our observations? Gould's suggestions for how archaeology should be done internally conflict, yet he nevertheless advocates the position of strict empiricism in spite of its long-recognized inadequacy. This is simply another example of the kind of paradox that Gould sets up for himself, such as his advocacy of "empirical science" while adopting an idealistic approach to explanation. Science seeks measurement and the use of analysis as a means to knowledge, but the idealistic philosophy denies that this approach helps us to learn and maintains that when dealing with human actions we must seek empathy with the workings of the minds of the human actors if we hope to gain understanding. It is this type of situation that has led me to describe many of Gould's arguments as "self-serving" and "misleading." These are assessments of Gould's *arguments* and not *ad hominem* "attacks," as Gould has characterized them.

> *Argumentum ad hominem*: An irrelevant or malicious appeal to personal circumstances; it consists in diverting an argument from sound facts and reasons to the personality of one's opponent, competitor or critic. (Runes 1979:19)

2. *Gould's form of argument obscures the issues.*

I seek here to respond to Gould's claim that I engage in *ad hominem* attacks while pointing out the character of Gould's arguments. As is clear from the quote (a) given above, Gould implies that I do not believe that there is a real world "out there" since he offers the existence of a real world as an alternative to my views. This implication is self-serving, misleading, and simply wrong. I strongly subscribe to the view that there is a real world out there, but I also recognize that what is the real world for a grasshopper is very different from the real world for a color-blind dog or for persons bringing their own cultural conventions to the mediation of their experiences with that real world. A basic assumption of science is that the external world is knowable in terms of itself. The challenge for the scientist is to face the fact that we seek to know the real world on our terms, using cognitive devices, descriptive conventions of our invention, and so forth, for learning about the real world.

One of the basic, naive assumptions of strict empiricism was the failure to acknowledge the role of our own culture as a filter conditioning how we observe the "real world." Gould cites my earlier statements of this position as indicative of an "extreme mentalist position" (Gould 1985:638). I believe that his remarks are based on a self-serving and misleading form of argument that results in misguided debates and distortions. My response is not *ad hominem ad nauseum,* as Gould (1985:643) suggests. It is a judgment regarding the character and quality of Gould's arguments and written statements, not regarding his character or personality traits.

Gould's claim that I advocate an extreme mentalist position is an example of *argumentum ad ignorantiam.*

> *Argumentum ad ignorantiam*: An argument purporting to demonstrate a point or to persuade people, which avails itself of facts and reasons the falsity or inadequacy of which is not readily discerned; a misleading argument used in reliance on people's ignorance. (Runes 1979:19)

The generally accepted definitions of mentalism and idealism are given below. I attempt to demonstrate that Gould has used such terms in a form of argument consistent with the definition of *argumentum ad ignorantiam.* As such, the judgment that his rhetoric and arguments are misleading, self-serving, and leading to misguided debates and distortions is a logically justified conclusion and, as such, is in no way a personal attack.

> *Mentalism*: Metaphysical theory of the exclusive reality of individual minds and their subjective states. (Runes 1979:195)

> *Idealism*: Any system or doctrine whose fundamental interpretative principle is ideal. . . . Metaphysics . . . identifies ontological reality . . . exclusively with the ideal, i.e., . . . Mind, Spirit, Soul, Person, Archetypal Ideas, Thought. (Runes 1979:136–137)

I am neither an idealist, pure or otherwise (Gould 1985:640), nor a mentalist (Gould 1985:638). I fully accept the view that there is ontological reality outside individual minds and their subjective states; in fact, my philosophical bias is materialistic in that I consider culture conceived idealistically to be explicable in materialists' terms. In addition, the adoption of a scientific posture assumes that we all are capable of modifying our idealistic, culture-bound views through disciplined interaction with the external world, an ontological reality independent of our ideas about it (see Binford 1986d). This is not, however, a denial of the existence of ideal phenomena. I believe that their explanation is one of the goals of science and, even more important, that a clear and hardheaded understanding of their role in our lives as scientists is in fact crucial to the advancement of science. This well-documented posture can in no legitimate manner be described as an extreme mentalist position, nor can it be said to represent an idealist posture derived from Hempelian doctrine (Gould 1985:640). I conclude that Gould is engaged in *argumentum ad ignorantiam.* The other possible conclusion would be that the ignorance rests with Gould himself as to my position concerning the arguments of Hempel and to the nature of the arguments that are well documented in the literature. I prefer the kinder interpretation, but of course readers must make up their own minds.

3. Gould's simultaneous commitment to an "empirical science" and to idealism conditions his view of priorities in a way that ensures his inability to participate in archaeological science.

It is because of Gould's belief that the external world is directly accessible through observations that he mounts his appeal for the "oath of measurement" as well as his criticism of my search for more useful ideas as guides to examining the world of experience. Gould's confusion is nowhere better demonstrated than in his opening statements in his "Oath of Measurement" section. After tipping his hat to the fact that we can learn and can expand our abilities to understand the archaeological record through methodological research, he reveals his thoughts in a most provocative manner.

> Yet if we look again we can see important domains of human behavior that are not likely to yield themselves to archaeological explanations, no matter how theoretically sophisticated we become. This was the point of the first chapter in *Living Archaeology*. Is Binford seriously implying, for example, that we will ever be sure of the specific phonological or grammatical characteristics of prehistoric languages through archaeological research? . . . I would ask the same about the details of prehistoric social organization that several of the "new archaeologists" of the late 1960's were then claiming to have . . . inferred from archaeological evidence. . . .
>
> In fact I would go further and argue that application of inappropriate theories . . . can be counterproductive. (Gould 1985:639–640)

Here we see the bias of a strict empiricist. What we see is what we have. What we have are the only legitimate phenomena to discuss since they provide the only data available for generalization. Generalization is the only legitimate road to the recognition of regularities. Regularities are what empiricists seek; in the old days of strict empiricism, these regularities were "trial laws" to be confirmed by expanding our arguments from enumeration. Strict empiricism grew up during the sixteenth and seventeenth centuries, when the goal of researchers was to know more about the world of "nature." At the same time, most people accepted the theory of creation as the "explanation" for the properties of nature that were uncovered. Strict empiricists did not seek explanation for their observations; they had an explanatory theory —God made it that way. Beginning in the mid-nineteenth century, roughly coincident with the "birth" of modern anthropology, the theory of creation was challenged. An era of theory building began—we wanted to know why the world was the way it appeared to be. Once theory was recognized as the basis for explanation, the entire question of evaluating the accuracy and utility of theories became important, and the old naive view that we could see nature accurately and understand it directly disappeared in the active sciences. In America the founding anthropologists reacted adversely to most of the early, postempiricist theories in anthropology (racism, vital progressive determinancy, etc.) and advocated theories more in line with the social values of the founding fathers. In this context, empiricism was revived for anthropology.

The work of the new archaeologists recognized that empiricist anthropology was out of line with the rest of modern science; these persons, to whom Gould refers, were working with an understanding of science that acknowledged the role of theory and the importance of evaluating these inventions of ours. We were convinced that sound explanation for the phenomena of the archaeological record was the only productive approach to describing the past accurately. This meant that we sought understanding for properties of the archaeological record, not that we were trying to milk from the archaeological record unjustified inferences to the past for which there was no phenomenological basis, as Gould implies. The works dealing with social organization were exploring the archaeological record and the possible effects of social forms that might differentially condition the spatial and temporal structure of components of the archaeological record. Traditionally, these differences were thought to be related to stylistic variability and to be simply reflective of normative shifts in the "popularity" of different "mental templates" standing behind pottery types (Rouse 1939; Krieger 1944; and see Dunnell 1971 for a discussion of this point). In short, we were examining the feasibility and adequacy of a traditional "theory" or, more realistically, a set of sterile conventions for assigning meaning to variability in "style." Clearly, Gould was upset because as an empiricist he could not directly "see" any preserved social organization in the archaeological record. (I might point out that he could not "see" any mental templates, stylistic norms, etc., in the archaeological record, either, but because of the conventions traditionally used by archaeologists, most traditionalists believed that they could; see Dunnell 1971 for a good discussion of these conventions, as well as Binford 1986d). For him, therefore, discussing social organization was counterproductive.

This outdated empiricist's bias is clear in other critical postures assumed by Gould. For instance, he disapproves of my attempts (in Binford and Binford 1966, reprinted in 1969) to view lithic assemblages as constituted by organizationally based components that mix in varying patterns of association to yield assemblages of differing aggregate forms. His criticism is "the failure by Binford and Binford (1969) to demonstrate the relationship between different tasks and the factors produced in their factor analysis" (Gould 1985:640). One can only wonder what Gould expects of science. We had demonstrated provocative patterning of a type anticipated by our reasoned guesses as to the ontological "real world" that could stand behind assemblages. We had done a pattern-recognition analysis. To demand that we have a proven "theory" at the instant of recognizing that the problem was reasonable to consider, and by implication that the previous theory used for giving meaning to patterning was likely to be inadequate, is ludicrous. We learn by (a) recognizing problems, (b) seeking explanations, and (c) testing the utility of such explanations. Theory building is just that—not some immediately perceived "truth" that is slapped onto our data as a convention for interpretation. If Gould does not like our suggestions, as a productive scientist he should seek to demonstrate something of their inadequacy, not simply reject them as inadequate because they do not meet his outdated demands for empirical expression.

This same empiricists' dogma is revealed in Gould's criticism of my Nunamiut work. He states that he has

> lingering doubts about the utility indices developed by Binford (1978a) in his caribou butchering and meat-use study. . . . The utility indices used rigorously throughout this analysis were based on the anatomical study of a single animal . . . [but] there is a real caribou population out there. (Gould 1985:640)

Here we see Gould's strict empiricist bias raised to truly amazing heights. In the Nunamiut study I wanted to develop a frame of reference considered to be possibly relevant in the decision making of the Nunamiut people. I would have liked to have had more experimentally butchered animals, but even if I could have butchered as many animals as I wished, probably no more than five or six would have been killed. The reasoning was simple: why invest many man hours, much money, and large numbers of animals in a project aimed at accurately estimating values for the "real caribou population out there" when it was not known (a) if this approach was useful, (b) what level of accuracy was needed for estimates of utility in order to monitor Nunamiut decision making, and (c) whether we were dealing with a species-specific or a generalized knowledge of ungulate anatomy on the part of the Nunamiut. One can only imagine the looks on the faces of the National Science Foundation grant reviewers if I had sought to kill and butcher a random sample of all living caribou so that the utility indices would refer to a "a real population of caribou" before it was realistically known whether that was a relevant and productive "fact" to establish! The robust patterning demonstrated in the Nunamiut report (Binford 1978a) and the subsequent successes of other workers (e.g., Blumenschine and Caro 1986; Legge and Rowley-Conwy 1985; Speth 1983; Will 1984) using my "poor" indices recognized interesting and consistent patterning. Now that we know something of the utility of the approach and something of the level of accuracy needed, it is time to design research to improve the indices (Kevin Jones, Galen Burgett, and Luis Borrero are all working on this research).

I agree with Gould that we need to "assign priorities" but not that we need to prioritize our "choices of theories and the levels to which we apply them." Productive research results from assigning priorities to the facts we need to establish and the methods we need to develop for evaluating theories. Gould seems to view archaeological science as being advanced by adopting well-established theories and then uncritically applying them to our data (see Gould 1980a:140). Archaeology must be actively engaged in theory building and evaluation, not in accepting or rejecting theories in terms of some false, absolutist criteria rooted in outdated empiricism. Such a strategy defeats the process of learning in which we are supposed to be engaged.

A good example of Gould's arguments of misplaced concreteness resulting in his nonparticipation in science is provided by his discussion of our comments on his own work.

> The Binford–Stone critique presents a good example of how inappropriate theory can be when it does not adhere to the empirical facts it purports to explain. Binford and Stone have what sounds like a good idea when they propose that the relative frequencies of local versus exotic lithic material from stone adzes . . . are best explained as being due to curation from use as personal gear. Perhaps these adzes qualify as . . . "personal gear," in Binfordian terms, but that whole idea remains a mentalist construct until some measurements that are external to the cultural system of either the producers (in this case the Nunamiut) or the observer are available to connect this argument to the material world. (Gould 1985:640)

Here we see very clearly Gould's demand that theory be presented in operational terms—namely, that somehow theory comes *de nova,* presumably from nature. Theory comes from us, and it is incumbent upon us to evaluate its utility. Such evaluation is not provided by discussion of the origin of the idea. I developed the idea of personal gear and other organizational properties that stood behind the differential distribution and patterns of association for artifacts during my Nunamiut experience, unlike what Schiffer (1985) suggests—that my presentation of such ideas as personal gear and site furniture are "emic categor(ies) of the Nunamiut Eskimo" (Schiffer 1985:192). This is simply untrue. I was developing these ideas in the context of analyzing mortuary practices in the early 1960s (Binford 1962, 1963b:138). More to the point, suppose it were true? Is the utility of an idea for uncovering the dynamic factors conditioning the content of the archaeological record to be evaluated by reference to the character of its source? The answer must be a resounding no. The utility of an idea for advancing the sophistication of a science can only be evaluated in the context of the scientific activities of the scientists.

Schiffer and Gould miss the importance of the Mask site study (originally discussed in Binford 1978b). Let us put the situation as follows: if no ethnographic observation had been made on the Nunamiut and an archaeologist had approached the study of their archaeological materials, would his conceptual tools and analytical devices be adequate to recognize the organizational basis standing behind the statics remaining for the archaeologist to see at the Mask site? Schiffer suggests that his concepts of use rate, use life, duration of use period, and reuse rates are the important variables that condition "cultural deposition . . . regardless of technology or organization" (Schiffer 1985:192). This appears to me to be an honest acknowledgment by Schiffer that his conceptual tools would be inadequate for isolating organizational properties of the Nunamiut system, and I have demonstrated with the Nunamiut case that these properties are basic to understanding "cultural deposition." It is my posture that we must seek to infer organizational properties, and that building such a methodology is dependent upon the recognition of phenomena of relevance. That was the point of the Mask site example. Schiffer seems unhappy with that demonstration, presumably because, as he admits, his concepts would be of little utility for recognizing organizational properties.

Gould's approach is similar, rejecting an idea that even he admits has potential because he cannot think of a way to operationalize methods for monitoring implicated properties in the archaeological record. I can only suggest to Gould that there was and is a real world of dynamics out there, and if we cannot dedicate ourselves to developing methods for monitoring real-world dynamic conditions of relevance to the archaeological record, then we end up with a fantasy past arising from our own lack of imagination and dedication to learning.

> The practical limitations on our knowledge of the past are not inherent in the nature of the archaeological record; the limitations lie in our methodological naivete, in our lack of development of principles determining the relevance of archaeological remains to propositions regarding processes and events of the past. (Binford 1968:23)

The veracity of the above quote is demonstrated by Gould's own tactics. I have previously suggested that "it would be interesting to know if at James Range East there was a more exhaustive use of the adzes of exotic material than was observed at Puntutjarpa; we would expect such a pattern" (Binford and Stone 1985:153). Gould acknowledges that he too would like to know these things, but since he could not think of any way of learning, he abandoned the issue. He states,

> It was quickly put aside because an empirical consideration of desert Aborigine adze-making, use, and discard showed that this test is unworkable. In order to apply it, one would have to know the size of the original stone-adze flake before it was progressively worn down by use and resharpening. The worn out remnants of these adze flakes . . . provide no reliable clues as to the original size of the flake from which each one was derived. (Gould 1985:641)

This conclusion will certainly come as a surprise to lithic analysts, who have faced this same problem for many years. There *is* a relationship between the size of the original lithic piece and the size range of the flakes removed. Are the sizes of the resharpening flakes from the two classes of tools (exotic vs. local material) different relative to the sizes of the exhausted items? Gould may not have saved small chips, so he might not be able to take advantage of these strategies; nevertheless, is such a situation a limitation of the archaeological record?

Let us try another workable test. The thickness of an exhausted (non-bifacially worked) piece is related to the size of the original flake because there is a direct relationship between the size of the bulb of percussion and the size of the flake. In most cases the thickest part of an exhausted adze is the thickest part of the original flake, since retouch proceeds from the edges toward the point of greatest thickness, particularly on adzes. This understanding and the empirical work already accumulated on this point (see Dibble 1984, 1987), taken in conjunction with the numbers of retouching scars relative to the thickness and size of the flakes, could be used to compare the two classes of tools with an expectation of quite reliable results. Gould did not think of such relationships.

There are still other approaches that have been worked out by many different lithic analysts. Gould simply does not try. Instead, using an analogy (which, as we have seen, he says we should not do)—an analogy to modern Aborigines that was probably not germane to his problem—he simply gives up and concludes that because of the "limitations of the archaeological record" we cannot learn. Hence, the production of ideas regarding the *real-world* conditions known to affect the archaeological record should not be thought of, introduced for discussion, or taken seriously. He concludes, from his outdated empiricist's position, that "another stimulating Binfordian idea bites the proverbial dust for want of a reliable empirical basis" (Gould 1985:641). Following this example, Gould could be led to the conclusion that we cannot make any statements about the past at all since there is no empirical past remaining for us to see. The past is gone, Richard. There are only contemporary static data. Our job is to understand those contemporary facts in such a way as to reliably construct (infer, if you wish) a "real-world" past. Insisting that the "real-world" past was the same as the "real-world" present of the archaeological record is sheer nonsense. Insisting on discussing the past only in terms of the "real-world" present (the archaeological record), when it is conceived of only in unimaginative and uninvestigated ways, fails to understand the very nature of archaeological research.

As I have said before, Gould's argument and his view of archaeology are strongly influenced by his ideological framework. If one is an idealist, believing that the only important and interesting aspects of the past are ideological and symbolic phenomena and that science is an inappropriate approach to learning about such phenomena, then one does not participate in science. In fact, Gould has said as much: he wishes to use the products of science as the basis for recognizing anomalies so that he can then talk about an idealist past in nonempirical terms. It is this desire to use science rather than participate in it that leads Gould to his lack of appreciation for the process of science, a learning process. If something advanced by a scientist appears to be incomplete or not directly usable, he rejects it. At the same time, he cites examples of lack of completeness as examples of failure. Both of these postures exhibit a near total lack of understanding for the scientific process.

4. Gould's paradoxical view of archaeology also accounts for his argumentative tactics.

I have pointed out many examples of Gould's use of false and misleading forms of argument. I have also repeatedly commented that these are self-serving, misleading, confusing, and generally invalid. He constantly uses such invalid forms of argument as *ignoratio elenchi* and *argumentum ad ignorantiam,* and he has certainly not been above *ad hominem* argument and innuendo (see Gould 1979 for numerous examples). What is the point of all this avoidance of the issues and misrepresentation of critics? I believe that the answer rests in the empiricist assumptions adopted by Gould. For one who believes that the properties of the real world are accessible directly through observation and measurement, unincumbered by theories and prior ideas, such objectivity is achieved by clearing one's mind of prior ideas and potentially distorting theories. If one does this "properly," then all such "objective" observers should see the same "independent reality." What happens when one observer discovers one thing and another sees something different? The answer is clear: one or the other did not achieve the righteous state of objectivity! There must be something wrong with at least one of the observers. Disagreements among observers therefore naturally take the form of probing exploration of each other's character, reliability, and so on in search of character flaws. If the latter are recognized, then the "truth" rests with the righteous.

It is no accident that the only explicit discussion of epistemology by a traditional archaeologist came to the following conclusion:

> The final judgment of any archaeologist's cultural reconstructions *must therefore be based on an appraisal of his professional competence,* and particularly the quality of the subjective contribution to that competence. (Thompson 1956:331)

In short, the focus of debate regarding conflicts in interpretations is necessarily the *subjective* contributions to competence or simply the personal characteristics of the persons involved. *Ad hominem* argument is all that really matters in debate!

The righteousness of those empiricists who believe in their ability to see nature truly is well illustrated by Gould's comment:

> Perhaps the Nunamiut really are as "simple" as he [Binford] suggests, in the sense that one can account simply for their behavior in relation to meat products on a

circumstantial basis without recourse to more complex explanations involving ideas and symbols. (Gould and Watson 1982:368)

Here we see the righteousness of the empiricist. If someone else sees the world differently, then according to the empiricist there must be something wrong with the other person. To protect the field from such questionable characters, one continually structures arguments against them and their competence, not against the issues. The only issue acknowledged is the issue of who sees reality truly.

GOULD'S VIEWS ON CURRENT ISSUES

Gould's writings are strong verification for the proposition that the power of one's paradigm is truly awesome. He nevertheless adopts the position that the problem really rests with

> Binford's failure to distinguish between the role of mental constructs in the history of ideas . . . and the empirical realities of the world of behavioral phenomena that exists independently of those theories and that can be discovered through controlled observation and measurement. (Gould 1985:639)

This is the same person who comments,

> Stanislawski (1975) and I (1968) have even suggested that one can explore the possibility of "deep structures" in human residue formation that approximate the search by linguists and linguistically oriented anthropologists for universal patterns in human cognition. (Gould 1980a:117)

Speculation on how Gould would discover "deep structures" without the aid of conceptual tools and approaches that could be wrong or inappropriate fairly boggles the mind. I can only comment by repeating a statement I once made to the University of Chicago faculty during a particularly boring discussion of incompatible points of view: "Only two things can happen to a man who insists on standing in the middle of the road: he is either run over or passed by."

Returning again to Gould's recent arguments, there are some new twists. Most of these arise in the context of his discussion of ethnoarchaeology. It is no surprise that he again advocates his method of argument from anomaly, using "empirical science" in its "uniformitarian" posture to spot anomalies that then permit him to turn off science and shift to an idealistic approach in which the "emic" ideas and values of the participants are thought to dictate the character of "anomalies" as well as provide the "really important" phenomena for understanding both the past and cultural phenomena in general. Originally, Gould (1980a:25) defined "living archaeology" as follows:

> The operations needed to carry out the data collecting and reasoning for discovering and explaining anomalies in human material and residue behavior.

Judging from Gould's discussion, "living archaeology" was conceived of as the centerpiece of a unified theory of ethnoarchaeology (Gould 1980a:250), since in his view, "as long as living archaeology addresses problems related to general principles in human residue behavior, it will serve as the baseline for archaeology as a social science" (Gould 1980a:242).

Because he proposes "living archaeology" as the centerpiece for a unified theory of ethnoarchaeology, it came as something of a shock to read Gould's recent comments on ethnoarchaeology. In his latest statements he recognizes three approaches: (1) the "etic" approach, which he says "focuses on observation and inference to discover uniformitarian relationships between human behavior and material remains" (Gould 1985:643); (2) the "emic" approach, which "concentrates on cognitive realities within the context of particular cultural systems" (Gould 1985:643); and (3) the "dirt" approach, which "attempts to account for the specific features of particular culture-historical sequences by appeal to ethnographic analogies" (Gould 1985:643). While I generally disagree that these are equally useful or even feasible approaches, what is interesting is the near-complete turnaround in Gould since the publication of *Living Archaeology*. There Gould claimed that his approaches were the centerpieces for modern archaeology. Where is this approach in the above triad? It is not there. Instead we are told that it is not to be considered "an empirically satisfying way of moving from one kind of archaeological reality to another" (Gould 1985:643). What are these kinds of reality among which Gould wants to move? They are the material properties of the archaeological record among which Gould hopes to "recognize" anomalies as a justification for abandoning science and moving into the ideational domain of the past, the "particularistic and more cognitive or more historical" (Gould 1985:643) aspects of the past. How do we evaluate arguments about what was in the heads of the ancients? How do we evaluate the claim for unique "causation"? We cannot. We can only accept such arguments if we *believe* such phenomena or conditions are causal in the first place. Arguments about the ideas of the ancients only make sense if we believe a priori in these phenomena as causal agents. Similarly, arguments about unique, "particularistic" events only make sense if we *believe* in them as causal phenomena. Given such a belief, it is only "reasonable" to invent them for the past so as to render the remnants of the past understandable in the terms we will accept.

There are neither linkages argued nor standards for evidence provided between the empirical material remains of the archaeological record and the historical, cognitive, and particularistic speculations that one might imagine as being relevant to one's alleged anomalies. Where is Gould's oath of measurement here? Where is his righteous demand for empirical grounding? Gould's approach is paradoxical. He seeks to use science as a means of escaping the empirical bonds of the present archaeological reality in order to be free of empirical concerns when constructing a past that is consistent with his prior beliefs as to what must have been important and meaningful in that past.

I have said that Gould is a traditional archaeologist. Strictly speaking, I was wrong. Traditional archaeologists, as idealists, sought to reach the minds of the ancients by stipulating the relationships between the material properties of the archaeological record and the ideas in the minds of the long-dead (see Dunnell 1971 for a fine discussion of these stipulative procedures). Such arguments can be evaluated, as many have been in the last 25 years. On the other hand, Gould's approach works with material remains as a way of justifying the leap away from data, testable argument, and questions of evaluation. An anomaly serves to justify the move away from science into the world where "essentially qualitative or even non-scientific approaches . . . address the cultural and historical particularities" (Gould 1985:642). At best this is traditional archaeology with an unrealistic and "romantic" twist that is mystical to the scientist and certainly an anachronism to the traditional archaeologist. Even for modern idealists, Gould's "middle of the road" position makes him inconsistent and subject to telling criticism (Patrik 1985:48–50).

Gould's posture is eclectic (see Harris 1979:287–314 for a telling criticism of this posture) in that he literally attempts to "have his cake and eat it too." Such approaches never really deal with problems in the field; they are simply attempts to argue around the issues. We need hardheaded research designed to cope with problems, not confusing discussion that avoids the issue.

Chapter 12

An Alyawara Day: The Stone Quarry

by Lewis R. Binford and James F. O'Connell

Ethnoarchaeological fieldwork involves many dull and uninteresting days. Now and then, however, one is included in events one thought one would never witness. We are about to describe one of those days.[1]

Several characteristics of the day made it special. First, we witnessed events that to our knowledge had never previously been observed by anthropological or even casual Western observers. Second, this opportunity was made possible by a rather uncommon commitment on the part of our Alyawara informants to do things in the "old way." Binford (1984b) has recently used another set of experiences among the Alyawara to illustrate the point that as an ethnographer it is frequently difficult to know what one is observing. It is especially difficult to know the conditions being considered by the informants when they decide to organize a demonstration in a given manner.

Our experiences provide clues to the past organization of Alyawara stone tool technology. No claim is made that we saw Alyawara stone tool technology "in action"; their traditional technology has been obsolete for many years. However, knowledge, training, and skill in lithic work were still part of the cultural repertoire of the old men we accompanied on a trip to a traditionally exploited quartzite quarry.

We must emphasize the point that the traditional technological system was gone. By this we mean that all the organized use of information regarding the need for tools, the degree to which those demands could be met in the context of other planned activities, etc., had ceased; the conditioning factors no longer operated. Similarly, there was no longer any organized use of information regarding the provisioning of the group with tools and the use of tools that had given an organized and understandable character to the execution of roles by the participants in the past system. The request for stone to make "men's knives" had come from us; the number of tools to be made was what our informants judged necessary to satisfy our request.

Nevertheless, the men processed much more material than would have been needed simply to satisfy our curiosity. It is our opinion that the men were acting out past situations, in a nostalgic mood triggered by the events of the day and their interest in the place we visited. This is, of course, our own judgment. Because we felt that we were seeing much more than just a straightforward demonstration of antique skills in

Originally published in *Journal of Anthropological Research* 40:406–432, © 1984.

response to our requests for a look at behaviors of the past, we have tried to report as accurately as possible the events and the ambience of that day at the quarry.

A DAY AT THE QUARRY: JUNE 15, 1974

We had been uncomfortable in our small tent at Bendaijerum, a camp of Australian Aborigines near the cattle station at MacDonald Downs, Central Australia.[2] It was morning and there was a touch of frost in the air as we milled around camp, trying to get warm in the Australian winter. In spite of the cold, we were excited, for we were going on a trip with three Alyawara men to a quartzite exposure, where their people had quarried stone to make tools before the Europeans came. The Aborigines had first gathered around our tent, talking on the sunny side of the canvas wall, then had moved up to the men's camp. The adult men sat around small fires, with blankets draped over their heads and shoulders like so many old Pueblo Indians. They sat silently, as if getting up courage to move in the chilly air. Then suddenly they got to their feet, a small group of old friends and close relatives, talking in the rhythmic, rumbling tones of their language. From the start the Aborigines seemed more interested in our project for that day than they had been in most others. And yet we could not seem to get away; there was always someone who needed to be consulted, something had to be found, something forgotten.

By ten o'clock the sun was high and the chill of the winter morning had receded. In the growing warmth, we left the brush windbreaks of the Aboriginal camp, driving out across the Bundey River and onto a short-grass plain sprinkled with mulga trees. As we crossed the plain, the unbroken character of the flats gave way to Australian sand savannah—red-rock boulder hills, sand dunes, spinifex grass, acacia, and red-bud mallee trees.

The savannah sand (Figure 12.1) was pitted with many small tracks, most made by lizards; during the day, this is a world of lizards and birds. We think of hawks and eagles as rare, but in the Australian savannah, they are the dominant predators. From the sky they search the land continuously. Flocks of small green parrots bring the eye back down to earth, where fifty or more may streak across the tops of the grass.

Our reflective observation of the landscape was interrupted by the excited Aborigines, who were pointing to some bustards feeding in the grass. The Australian bustard is a long-legged bird that primarily eats grasshoppers; it is about the same size as an American great blue heron (Figure 12.2) and looks surprisingly like the African bustard. Shots rang out and the Aborigines ran off to retrieve three dying birds. After they were tossed in a pile against the back wall of the truck, we resumed our drive across the dunes. About an hour from the forest of Bendaijerum, we sighted a group of three kangaroos in the shade of an acacia tree. Again shots rang out, and a large female fell. The Aborigines rushed up just as she was raising her bewildered head and used a stick to strike down this attempted revival; the animal died under a flurry of blows. In her pouch was a small joey. It was pulled out by its long legs and its head was struck against its mother's thigh. The two were loaded in the truck and again we drove into more dunes that seemed indistinguishable from those we had already marked with tire tracks.

Figure 12.1. Australian sand savannah (photograph by L.R.B.).

Figure 12.2. Sandy and Jacob after having killed three bustards (photograph by L.R.B.).

We drove for another hour. As the sun approached its highest point in the sky, we noticed more large animal tracks. We slowed as we passed sandy bald spots where the green vines of *anatia*—bush potato, or wild yam—were observed by the interested Aborigines.[3] Normally the men would have stopped to dig up the good-tasting tubers, but today they waved us on with the backs of their hands. The farther we went, the fewer the signs of cattle, their grazing, or other tire tracks. Nature seemed to be reasserting its dominion with more tracks of emu (a large, ostrich-like bird) and other wildlife. Even the rare rabbit-like hare wallaby had left its tracks. We had clearly entered a place not much visited by Europeans.

The three natives, Sandy, Manny, and Jacob, talked less among themselves and interrupted the silence of travel only to point out interesting animals, plants, and situations.[4] Riding with the same men around their present camp was strictly an economic experience. There they talked about or pointed out game (tucker, as they called it), firewood, and edible plants. In contrast, today they talked of the landscape and of earlier times, before large-scale European intrusions.

We had been driving for hours across country that to our untutored eyes seemed undifferentiated, yet to the eyes of the Aborigines the environment was filled with information. Around two o'clock, Jacob, who was the navigator, pushed his hand out and indicated a little turn to the right. Within about fifteen minutes, we pulled up at the end of a small rise. The men got out, almost before the truck had stopped, and spread out, looking for assurances that their recollections were correct. This initial reconnaissance seemed tense; the Aborigines paid scant attention to us or to each other. Gradually their heads began to raise up, they walked about with less concentration, and they smiled, satisfied.[5] It seemed they were saying that things were as they remembered, no European had disturbed their character, everything was as it should be.

As the Alyawara were assuring themselves of their world, we were examining the small rise of sand-covered boulders, peppered with small trees. Between each rock exposure and clump of trees was a dense scatter of flaked and modified stone, a fine-grained quartzite. To one accustomed to seeing stone tools on archaeological sites, all the flakes and worked stones appeared large, oversized.[6] We archaeologists are accustomed to using complicated techniques to permit the observation of patterning; here the patterning was clear and obvious. Undulating depressions encircled by high densities of flake debris alternated with clusters of large blocks from which only a few flakes had been struck.[7] Away from these clusters of "big stuff," scattered on the sandier slopes or tucked under the edges of vegetation, were small half-moon scatters of large flakes and a few chunks and blocks (Figure 12.3).

As we took all this in, Sandy and Manny moved away from us across the stone quarry, talking as they pointed to stones lying on the surface; some of them they picked up. It was clear they were not doing this for us; in fact, they no longer noticed us. They were doing what they had been taught to do by their elders, what was at one time expected of all men.

We were disappointed. What we had seen thus far had already been described for Australian quarry work. Aborigines were said to have few if any specialized lithic-working techniques. In fact, one of the authorities on Australian peoples had described their behavior at quarries as follows (Tindale 1965:140):

Figure 12.3. Surface of the quarry as first seen by us. The tufts of grass in the foreground mark the spot where the knapper sat when this debris was generated. Note the arc-like distribution of the debris. The very small debris scatter in center right was identified as the remains of an episode of retouching, probably unrelated to the large flake distribution in the center of the photograph (photograph by L.R.B.).

> On arrival at Pulanj-pulanj two of the younger men pried out slabs and fractured boulders of the siliceous rock up to two feet in diameter from the red earth covered walls of the dry creek. Boulders lying in the open were considered to be not suitable for attention. The largest boulders they could lift they raised high above their heads and hurled down onto the rocky pavement, attempting to shatter them into smaller pieces. They endeavored to stand on more elevated places, seemingly both to increase the effect of their throws and to escape flying splinters of silica.
>
> Smaller pieces were then struck, virtually at random, either with the above mentioned hammer stone, which was passed from hand to hand as required, or with a piece of the mother rock. When a suitable-sized flake was detached by the hit-and-miss process, it was set to one side. When a boulder of particularly good stone was discovered it was alternatively hurled down and struck at with the hammer until no further flakes could be obtained from the core which remained.

Other workers have given similar reports. Brian Hayden, who was recently engaged in trying to recover some Aborigines' last memories of earlier days as stone-tool makers and users, comments (1979:122):

He mentioned that the old men used to dig deep into the ground to get large pieces of opal. . . . It is hard to know how to interpret this since we saw no pits of any antiquity at any of the quarry sites . . . and no other Western Desert ethnographers have noted such practices.

Manny and Sandy were walking about the rock-strewn surface talking about the quality of the quartzite. They would reach down and pick up chunks, examine them, then toss them back. Given the descriptions by Tindale and others, one might imagine that they were simply looking for flakes appropriate to their needs. But Sandy and Manny were not interested in flakes; they were picking up big chunks and using them like hammers to remove flakes from other large chunks (Figure 12.4). They then examined the freshly exposed surfaces of the stones, talked briefly, then tossed everything down. It seemed clear that they were not looking for flakes; they were testing the quality and character of the materials.

In answer to our questions, Sandy explained to us that they were looking for the place where the really good material could be found. We asked what the good stuff would look like. Sandy's answers were not very satisfactory. There was an allusion to purity of color and smooth texture, but we certainly did not glean enough information to permit us to join in the search. We asked if they had, thus far, seen any of the good stuff. They had, but they really did not know where it was coming from. We then asked

Figure 12.4. Manny Lewis testing cores. The hammer being used is a large quartzite chunk picked up at the quarry (photograph by L.R.B.).

them why, if they had found some of the good stuff, they had not kept it. Sandy smiled and looked around for a chunk of stone. He picked up a large flake and struck it. It split into several pieces, the fractured surfaces stained with iron oxide. Clearly the chunk had previously been cracked so that water had percolated into it. When Sandy struck the chunk it fell apart, breaking along the old fracture planes. He pointed to the weathering cracks and noted that the stone was "rotten," so that it broke with a "mind of its own." The cores that littered the surface of the quarry had all been weathered; they were thus considered unsuitable for making tools.

Meanwhile Manny had wandered off; when we caught sight of him, he was down on the side of the boulder outcrop, poking in the sand with his feet. Sandy walked briskly over to him. They became absorbed in conversation while Sandy pulled at a partially exposed boulder. He first struck it "in place" with the butt of his steel ax. Both men agreed that the material was good. Nevertheless, they moved farther downslope and focused their attention on an area of boulders just barely visible under the reddish sand. Sandy dug around one with his ax handle and Manny scooped sand away with his hands. A smaller boulder, weighing perhaps forty-five pounds, was uncovered (see Figure 12.5, area 1, for the location of these actions). Sandy pushed and shoved it free. He then carried it down to the flat area (Figure 12.5, area 1) at the foot of the slope and began to remove flakes by striking the boulder with his ax. Meanwhile, Manny went up into a grove of trees, where he cut a large branch, about four inches in diameter, from a mulga tree. This he trimmed into a stout pole about six feet long. Manny returned with this pole and began using it to pry up the edge of a large boulder. It did not move. He then made a narrow trench around a corner of the boulder. Once the corner was exposed, he took up a rock weighing about twenty pounds and threw it down on the edge of the exposed boulder. A large flake was removed, which he scooped up and quickly carried down to Sandy. Both men agreed that the buried boulder was the good stuff, that is, the material they wanted to make tools from. Sandy and Manny resumed their digging around the boulder, but after a short time, Sandy returned downslope to his core (Figure 12.5, area 2).

Squatting behind the core, Sandy directed heavy blows with the butt of his ax, so that large flakes were removed. As each flake was detached, it was picked up, examined, and then placed at arm's length in front of him. He turned the core frequently and examined the scar where the previous flake had been removed. Sometimes he struck off another flake adjacent to the earlier scar, and sometimes he used the flake scar itself as the striking platform.

Throughout all this, Sandy worked kneeling or squatting behind the core, which was positioned on the ground in front of him (Figure 12.6).[8] A flake struck off the core could be driven downward into the sand. We later learned that the flakes were picked up "so you know what you were making," and then placed out of the way so that the next flake would also fall into the sand, preventing its edges from being dulled by hitting previously struck flakes. It was clear from watching Sandy that he knew the type of flake he wanted to produce. It was also clear that he knew that he had to alter the core's shape and then strike its edge relative to the shape of the face in order to produce a flake of desired form. In short, Sandy was using a direct percussion technique to preform a core. It was only after he succeeded in producing a core of desired

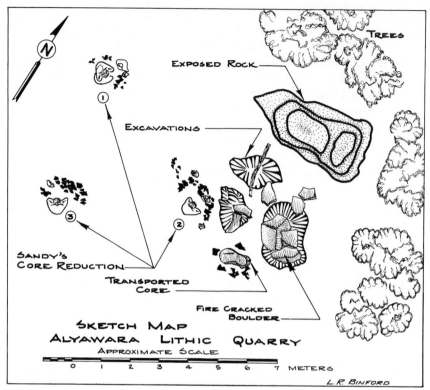

Figure 12.5. Sketch map of quarry area. Several characteristics are of interest. First, Sandy's orientation while reducing the cores was always into the light, so the placement of his arcs of debitage were also oriented relative to the source of light. Their orientation shifted with the progress of the sun across the sky. Reduction area no. 1 shows Sandy's initial position and orientation directed toward us as observers, but as soon as he started to reduce the core, he moved around, facing into the light. Second, the clear independence between the areas where the boulders were excavated and roughed out versus the areas of core reduction illustrates nicely the principle that men working simultaneously on different tasks do them in different places. This is particularly true of special-use sites, where there are no major constraints on space use (see Binford 1983c:144–194).

shape that we understood that he was trying to produce a core with a transverse cross-section shaped like a high-angled triangle (Figure 12.7). Once he was successful, he could then strike off blades or flakes along the flat face of the triangle.[9]

Once the core had been roughly preformed, a number of blades or flakes were then struck alternately from either side of the nose of the core (Figure 12.8). After this more detailed preforming of the core face, a blow was struck farther back from the core rim, just above one of the ridges running down the face of the core. This procedure yielded blades of the desired shape: long triangular pieces with sharp edges on the converging sides. These blades had either one or two medial ridges on the dorsal surface (Figure 12.9).

Figure 12.6. Sandy White reducing a core to produce blanks for men's knives. Sandy is squatting at point no. 3 on Figure 12.5. Note the arc of flakes (photograph by L.R.B.).

Figure 12.7. Sandy White about to strike a core prepared for the removal of blanks for men's knives. Sandy is working in reduction area no. 3, Figure 12.5 (photograph by J.F.O.).

Figure 12.8. "Nose" of core prepared for the removal of initial guide flakes (photograph by J.F.O.).

Figure 12.9. Blades removed by Sandy White from prepared core shown in Figures 12.7 and 12.8 (photograph by L.R.B.).

Once we understood what we had seen, Binford jotted down some questions that we later put to Jacob, who spoke better English than Sandy. Jacob explained that although today had been "special" in that the stoneworking was being done for our benefit, things were not too different from what they might have done before the appearance of Europeans. He related that a particular type of blade was needed to make a good men's knife, the tool we had asked the Alyawara men to manufacture for us. Sandy had worked his core to produce the particular flakes needed as blanks for the men's knives.[10] Jacob continued that there were other tools requiring the same kind of blank, e.g., "ordinary men's knives," "fighting axes," and "spears."[11] He had only heard of the latter two tools being used by the "old ones" in the north. In any event, flakes of the form produced by Sandy were not needed frequently, since the tools he mentioned were not manufactured "too often." It was explained that shaping the core was the "big job" and was always done in the quarry, where all the big chunks and "mistakes" could be thrown away before one had to carry anything. Jacob noted that once one got a "good one," that is, a well-prepared core, "everybody hit 'em off as many as you can get before you make mistakes." Binford asked what would be done if one made more flakes than one needed; Jacob commented that they could leave them "somewhere" until they were needed. The comments by the informants made it clear that the manufacture of blades as demonstrated by Sandy was normally done in the quarry. The resulting blanks would then be introduced to the residential site as manufactured items.

O'Connell suggested to Sandy, who was working on another core, that he demonstrate the kind of flake suitable for retouching into a "women's knife" or a "spoon" (see O'Connell 1974 for a description of these tools). Sandy removed a flake from the core in much the same way as he had for the "men's knives." The only difference was that the flake was slightly less symmetrical. He then took up a linear chunk of raw material lying nearby and used it as a percussor, retouching the flake so as to round the distal end. He also retouched the flake along one lateral edge (Figure 12.10). Later, Jacob commented that if flakes for men's knives were not carried properly, the edges would sometimes get dull. These dulled pieces might be made into women's knives, back at camp. Jacob also noted, however, that women's knives were most commonly made from flakes struck from cores at the camp, rather than from the special blades produced in quarries and used for men's knives.

This point—that many tools were produced from flakes struck from cores back at the camp—can serve to refocus attention on what Manny was doing while Sandy finished reducing his core. Manny had been digging out the largest boulder in the excavated area. After the "women's knives" demonstration, Sandy got up and joined Manny. Sandy piled up sizable chunks and slabs just back from the edges of Manny's trench. These slabs were to be used as surfaces on which fulcrum blocks were placed. The latter were used to pry up the large buried boulder with the mulga tree limb previously mentioned. As Sandy adjusted the lever, Manny motioned for Binford to come and lend a hand. Binford took over the end of the lever, thinking that his greater weight would be of some help. Gradually the boulder was inched out of its bed. As the boulder was raised by the lever, Manny slipped a pyramid-shaped stone under it. All this time Binford could only guess what the men intended. He thought they were

Figure 12.10.   Sandy White behind an exhausted core in reduction area no. 2 (Figure 12.5) secondarily flaking a blank for a women's knife. Note the typical arc of flakes (photograph by L.R.B.).

trying to raise the boulder so they could knock off a large chunk as they had done earlier when testing the stone.

After the boulder was raised into a tilted position, resting its weight on the apex of the pyramid-shaped stone, the two men left us and spread out into the nearby trees. They returned with armloads of sticks, dry branches, and small twigs. They arranged the fuel under the boulder and kindled a fire (Figure 12.11). As the flames grew, the men added more fuel and sat back, speculating on how the boulder would break.

We had seen suggestions in the North American literature and elsewhere that fire was sometimes used in the quarries (see Elkin 1948:100 for an Australian reference). Boulders were said to have been heated and then cooled by throwing water on them, "causing flakes to come off." Such references are fairly common in the early American literature, but many recent investigators have been skeptical of them (Crabtree and Butler 1964; Ellis 1940:45; Purdy 1981a, 1981b). By contrast, Akerman (1979) reports experiences similar to our own.

Before us was a large block resting on a pointed fulcrum, with a fire burning underneath (Figure 12.12). The two Aborigines drew imaginary lines across the top of the boulder, speculating as to how the block would break. Before long there was a musical "ping," as a crack developed completely across its width, above the point where it rested on the fulcrum. The fire continued to burn for about half an hour. We

Figure 12.11. Close-up of fire being kindled under the large boulder. The flake scar on the edge of the boulder was produced when Manny threw down a sizable rock on the exposed corner to test the quality of the material before excavating the boulder (photograph by L.R.B.).

Figure 12.12. Sandy White sitting on rock outcrop watching fire burning under boulder. The large slabs in the foreground were moved to the edge of the excavation to help lever the boulder up onto the fulcrum (photograph by L.R.B.).

did not hear a second "ping," but the block was broken into three large pieces when the men stepped forward to begin the task of levering out the broken sections.

Manny took the lever and hoisted one section out of the hole (Figure 12.13). A few spalls had popped off the surface on the underside where the fire had been most intense, and the surface was somewhat smudged. Otherwise, however, there were no obvious effects of the burning beyond the dramatic breaking up of the large boulder. The first major section to be removed was rolled over the edge of the hole onto a level area, where Sandy began chipping large flakes off the original surface, using the heat crack as a striking platform. He was reducing this piece much as he had the previous one, removing large, thick flakes from the cortical surface. The chunk was gradually reduced in size and modified into the "nosed" form of the earlier core, with the parallel flake scars around the end, from which the long blades could be struck. Sandy struck off two good blades, then left this core lying on the surface and returned to the excavation, where Manny had inched the largest of the firecracked boulder sections onto the nearby surface (Figure 12.14).

Using the newly cracked surface as a striking platform, Sandy again removed flakes from the cortical surface (Figure 12.15), gradually reducing its size and modifying its form. It was dressed into a core weighing about fifty pounds. Later, Jacob explained that in old days the men would have done essentially the same things we had seen: namely, made cores from which the blanks for men's knives were struck, as well as other cores to be transported back to the base camp.

Figure 12.13. Removal of the first section split from the parent boulder by differential heating (photograph by J.F.O.).

Figure 12.14. Manny Lewis levering up a second section of fire-split boulder. Sandy White is already beginning to dress the first section of the split boulder—the section shown in Figure 12.13—into a core. Sandy is working in area no. 3, Figure 12.5. The scattered flakes and exhausted core are visible in reduction area no. 2, Figure 12.5, along the far side of the excavation (photograph by L.R.B.).

Jacob elaborated that one would never leave a quarry "empty-headed"; the men would all carry back roughed-out cores on their heads, using a cushion of grass wrapped with fur string to make a "nest" for the cores. Jacob noted that the transported cores would have been prepared as Sandy had done, except that they would have been smaller.

Binford asked Jacob why they did not make all the tools in the quarry, rather than carrying cores back to camp. Jacob explained that the tools most commonly employed at the camp were small flakes used for "cutting up things." He noted that these need not be any particular shape, only fresh and sharp. With a core in camp, the flakes could be struck off as necessary. One could even use the mistakes, since tools such as adzes and women's spoons were made by secondary retouch, not by preshaping on the core.

The men stressed the fact that they should be very careful in preparing flakes for transport and in transporting blanks from the quarry. Lack of care would result in dull edges on the blanks when one wanted to use them. We did not have to ask the men how they "took care" of the blanks produced in the quarry, since they went quietly about doing things in the "old way."

Figure 12.15.   Sandy White trimming the sides of a large section from fire-split boulder. This large section, after having the cortical surface removed, was carried back to the men's camp at Bendaijerum (photograph by L.R.B.).

Manny went to a grove of trees and returned shortly with four rectangles of fresh bark from a paper-bark tree (*Malaleuca lasiandra*). The pieces were about thirteen inches long and six inches wide. The bark is soft and composed of compacted, thin sheets, much like the birch bark of North America. Manny and Sandy wrapped in paper-bark pouches the few flakes they had judged adequate. Manny wrapped one women's knife blank and two blanks for men's knives in his pouch. He placed the flakes on one section of bark, then shredded off a wad of thick bark layers and rolled them in his hands, placing the fibrous, tinder-like padding over and around each flake. He then placed the other half of the paper bark over the arrangement and carefully lifted up the pouch. A ball of "hair string" was then brought out. Holding the ball and pouch in one hand, Manny unwound the free end of the string and punched holes through the pouch between the flakes. The free end of the string was then laced through the holes. Finally, the ball of string was tucked into the pouch. It was noted that one "never cuts string if one can help it." Sandy did the same thing with his flakes, except that he used grass padding in the pouch and packed five flakes for transport.

We were told that in the old days these paper-bark pouches would have been carried under the arms in the string belts of the men returning to camp. Today, however, we loaded them, along with the oversized core, into our truck, where they lay beside the dead kangaroo and three birds.

During our experiences at the quarry, we had not noticed the time; everything had been done in an unhurried manner. As soon as we had loaded the core onto the truck, however, we realized that we would have to hurry to get back to camp before dark. It was clear that the important landmarks known to the old men would begin to fade with the diminishing light, so that nightfall would force us to make an "overnight." We had food, but little except the clothes on our backs of the day to counter the icy chill that would return at sunset.

We pulled into camp after dark. The men were intent on distributing the meat from the kangaroo and the three birds. We went to our tent. Later, Jacob came by with some meat from the kangaroo, but he did not stay long. We were already working on our notes. It got colder and finally we built a fire in the floor of our tent and hovered around it with blankets over our heads. We wrote until later and then went off to sleep, knowing that we had seen some special things.

ANTHROPOLOGICAL REFLECTIONS

The impact of what we had seen gradually struck us. We had seen Australian Aborigines quarry stones by digging up large buried boulders. We had seen them split a boulder by building a fire under it. We had seen two men prepare a special core from which convergent-sided blades were struck. These blades—the blanks for men's knives—were carefully packed in small pouches for transport back to camp. At the same time, the men roughed out another core to be transported back to camp. In the past, similar though somewhat smaller cores would have been transported to camp for use in replacing a variety of general-purpose tools. These things seem self-evident, but what else can we make of the experience?

The Working Postures of the Men

In all the core-preparation and core-reduction events we observed, the basic working posture was squatting or kneeling behind a core that was resting on the ground.[12] This is not a unique observation. For instance, we are fortunate to have a comparable description from another area of the Central Desert (Spencer and Gillen 1912:374):

> He chose a small lump of quartzite which measured about eight inches in length and roughly six in diameter, the surface at one end being approximately flat, whilst toward the other it is slightly tapered away. The latter was placed on the ground and then, holding the block upright in his left hand, he gave a series of sharp blows with a little quartzite stone held in his right hand.

Binford has searched the ethnographic and ethnohistoric literature for descriptions of stoneworking; while there are regrettably few, every one that describes the working or preparation of a core suggests or explicitly describes the core as *resting on the ground in front of the worker,* except one very influential example. This is, of course, the description of the Brandon gunflint knappers.

For more than a century, the Brandon knappers have provided a major ethnographic analogue for the interpretation of stone tools and a model for lithic experimentation. In his seminal discussion of lithic work, John Evans (1872) described the Brandon knappers and provided early illustrations of their products. In the classic work by E. B. Tylor (1881:184–186), illustrations taken from Evans are reproduced and a discussion of lithic working technique is provided, based on Evans's observations at Brandon. On the continent, there was experimentation with stone tool production by the end of the nineteenth century (Johnson 1978). Most attempts at learning something about tool-production sequences seem to have taken as a model the techniques used by the Brandon workers or (less often) French gunflint manufactures (Schleicher 1927). Both of these reflect the common European pattern of working while seated on a stool or chair.[13]

Denise de Sonneville-Bordes (1967:57) credits only Coutier (1929) as an inspirational predecessor to François Bordes's accomplishments as a master flint knapper (see also Bordes 1978). Bordes has commented to Binford on a number of occasions that the descriptions by Evans and the published work of Rainbird Clarke (1935), both of which were inspired by the Brandon knappers, provided a model for his own perfection of stoneworking techniques.[14] Given that sitting in a chair or on a raised surface is a habitual working posture in Europe and America, and that this same posture was characteristic of the Brandon knappers (Figure 12.16), it is not surprising that almost all the contemporary lithic experimentors adopt a seated posture, in which the core rests on the thigh. The thigh is normally protected by a special covering or by thick clothing (as seen in Figure 12.16). Bordes almost always worked cores and manufactured core tools in this way (see photographs in Howell 1965:118–119, where Bordes is shown roughing out a core, making a hand ax, and using an antler hammer to flake a biface).

Many of the recent lithic experimentors learned from either F. Bordes or Don Crabtree. It is well documented that at the time of the Les Eyzies conference on lithic technology (Jelinek 1965), Crabtree had primarily perfected the skills of pressure flaking and blade production, whereas Bordes was the acknowledged master of percussion techniques. Not long after their meeting, Bordes also became very skilled in pressure-flaking techniques, which he learned primarily from Crabtree, while Crabtree similarly mastered Bordes's techniques of percussion work.

Since most of the current group of lithic experimentors are also Western "chair sitters," and many have learned knapping techniques from either Bordes or Crabtree, it is not surprising that most habitually adopt the on-the-thigh working posture when using percussion for both working cores and shaping tools. Errett Callahan (1979:25) has recognized this potential bias and has commented on it in the context of describing his preferred "holding position":

> The ideal seat—bear in mind that this is personal opinion now and may/may not exactly fit other knappers, past or present—was a rather low stool, block, log, or rock which elevated the knees slightly above horizontal. At the time most of these experiments were performed, I did not favor resting the biface atop the padded left thigh except for the removal of particularly stubborn flakes on rather large bifaces.
>
> Rather unfortunately, I think, this leg position is used to the exclusion of almost all other positions by many Western knappers. [See Bordes and Crabtree 1969:16

Figure 12.16. Working posture of the Brandon knappers (photograph reproduced from Pond 1930).

for illustration.] A personal study of the techniques of numerous "self-evolved" knappers, professional, commercial, and amateur, revealed to me that the leg-pad holding position is only one of many techniques suitable for generalized biface percussion work.

The Western European bias in holding position may misdirect many phases of archaeological interpretation. For instance, in recent experiments treating the patterns of debris accumulation during lithic reduction, three postures are almost always employed by the experimentors: on-the-thigh while seated, hand-held while seated, or hand-held while standing (see Fischer et al. 1979; Newcomer and Sieveking 1980). These postures and the distributions of debris they produce may have little to do with the common non-Western work posture of squatting and using the ground as a work surface. The latter is more likely to be relevant to the interpretation of those archaeological remains, particularly Paleolithic, with which we are most often concerned.

It has occurred to Binford that much of the Paleolithic material currently interpreted as resulting from a "block-on-block" reduction strategy is most likely the result of cores resting on the ground being worked from a squatting position, as described here. This would certainly make much more sense to anyone who has tried to dodge the flying shatter produced when using a block-on-block technique. Similarly, most geometrical evidence cited to justify the inference of a block-on-block technique could just as well have arisen from a holding posture similar to that of the Alyawara. Recall the classic arguments over the significance of the "Clactonian" (Ohel 1979) and the differences between assemblages called Clactonian and those called Acheulean.[15] Many of the technical differences, astutely noted by Newcomer (1970, 1971, 1979), could well reflect differences between cores reduced from a squatting position and materials detached when using a different holding posture, one that is more appropriate to working bifaces.

Binford has always been interested in the fact that many early reports from North America on stone knapping report a padded "anvil" used as a rest while working bifacial tools. This was reported by Cushing (1895; see also Fowke 1891, 1892). In addition, experimental workers have used wooden anvils during their work (see Pond 1930). For a worker who habitually uses a squatting posture, the use of a slightly raised work surface when shaping a biface would seem to be almost a necessity.[16] In most hunter-gatherer camps we have seen, firewood is commonly pulled in front of a worker to serve as a raised work surface. We would not be surprised if early observers' reports of American Indians using wooden anvils as rests are indeed accurate. Such anvils could be an accommodation to habitual squatting or cross-legged work postures. Under such conditions, a wooden "anvil" would be a resting surface equivalent to the thigh of a habitual chair sitter.

Levallois Techniques in Australia

The prototypes of the prepared cores with which archaeologists have been concerned for so long are the Levallois core and the pyramidal blade core. The classic description of the Levallois core is as follows (Burkett 1933:43):

A suitable nodule of flint was chosen and a selected upper surface worked over by flaking until a flattish face resulted. The sides of the nodule were now boldly trimmed away so that the future tool was, as it were, blocked out, though still attached to the core. A striking platform was next prepared and a single blow then detached the required tool which would consist of an object whose upper surface was flat as a result of the primary flaking while still on the nodule and whose under surface was a flake surface resulting from the blow of detachment.

Cores of this type have been widely illustrated and are well-known to most prehistorians. There are several alternative techniques of preparing the Levallois core (see Bordes 1980, as well as Tixier et al. 1980:44–45).

What we saw the Alyawara men doing fits none of the above descriptions. They were preparing a pyramidal core from which blades were regularly struck. This core had the form of a large keel or a "nosed" block of material (Figure 12.17, 1). The striking platform was a large flake scar on a split surface of the original nodule (Figure 12.17, 2). The keel-shaped block with a "nose" was then struck in regular successive ways, as indicated in Figure 12.17, yielding preshaped blades with sharp, convergent sides and parallel ridges on the dorsal surfaces (Figure 12.18, 1, 2, and 3). The butt of the blade was regularly unfacetted. The exhausted cores are referred to by Australian pre-

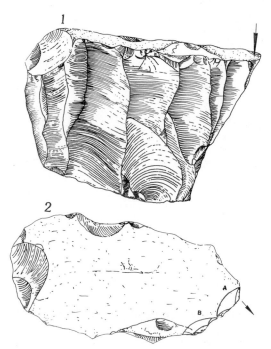

Figure 12.17. Side and top view of core prepared for removal of blanks for men's knives (Leilira blades).

historians as "horse hoof cores" (Mulvaney 1969:140). The exhausted form is achieved by working back the nose of the core until the face from which the flakes and blades were struck approaches roughly a ninety-degree angle relative to the striking platform. At this point, further attempts to remove additional flakes or blades produce very short, often hinged-fractured pieces. The core itself displays a "stepped," or "chattered," platform edge, correlated with a series of stacked hinge fractures, each terminating closer to the platform edge (Figure 12.18, 4).

Having seen these procedures in the Alyawara quarry, it is clear to us that Sir Baldwin Spencer saw the same thing among the Central Desert Warramunga, around the turn of the century (Spencer and Gillen 1912:374):

> We came across a quarry which had been worked for many years past. The ground was strewn with numerous discarded flakes, because, for every one that is considered good enough to use, there are at least a score thrown aside as useless.
>
> At this quarry we watched with much interest the process of manufacture as

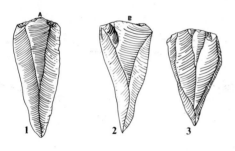

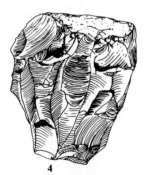

Figure 12.18.   Blades removed from core illustrated in Figure 12.17. The exhausted core shown as item no. 4 illustrates several common features: the nose, or keel, has been worked back; the platform-core face angle approaches 90°; and abortive removals leave hinge fractures near the platform. Exhausted cores of this form are commonly called "horse hoof" cores in Australia.

carried out by a Warramunga man. First of all he chose a small lump of quartzite which measured about eight inches in length and roughly six in diameter, the surface at one end being approximately flat, whilst towards the other it is slightly tapered away. The latter was placed on the ground and then holding the block upright in his left hand, he gave a series of sharp blows with a little quartzite stone held in his right hand. The first two blows were in spots close together, just within the margin, each resulting in the detachment of a flake, in such a way as to form two surfaces that ran down the face of the block and met toward the lower part. As a general rule these two surfaces are not in contact with their whole length. How far this is or is not the case depends simply upon whether the first two flakes lie closely side by side or are separated from one another at their upper ends by a longer or shorter face, with the result that where this is present the blade is tetragonal in section.

Two field observations from Central Australia, ours and Spencer and Gillen's, made more than sixty years apart, clearly show that the Central Desert Aborigines worked cores for the production of blades in nearly identical ways. What is more interesting is that in both of these documented cases, the Aborigines were working cores for the production of blanks for use in the manufacture of men's knives. These blanks are widely known in the literature of Australia as *Leilira blades* (Spencer and Gillen 1899:592–593, 1912:374–376). In this light, it is interesting that François Bordes (1967a) identified the Leilira blades as illustrated by Spencer and Gillen as "Levallois points." This identification carries the clear implication that they were produced from Levallois cores.

In 1974, C. Dortch delivered a major paper in Canberra in which he discussed the history of suggestions regarding the presence of prepared-core techniques in Australia (1977:117). In the same paper, Dortch describes a series of core and flake forms that do appear to be Levallois in both form and technique. These were recovered in late-phase assemblages of the Ord Valley, in the Kimberley district of Western Australia. These materials, described in detail by Bordes and Dortch (1977) and further commented on by Bordes (1980), were taken as support for Bordes's earlier recognition of the Levallois technique in Australia. It will be recalled that this identification was based on his suggestion that the Leilira blades were products of the Levallois technique. We think it is clear, however, that the cores from which the Leilira blades were struck were not Levallois in form. Bordes (1967a, 1980) had not based his identification of Levallois technique on formal properties of cores. Instead, arguing from analogy, he identified the Leilira blades as Levallois points and then inferred a type of Levallois preparation used in their production. Examples of "equifinality" are certainly not new to lithic studies, but it is interesting to see what some of the different paths to the final form might be.[17]

The Organization of Technical Options

The men had produced blades in the quarry. These blanks were transported back to the residential camp, protected in small paper-bark pouches. Nevertheless, while in the quarry they had also processed a core for transport back to the residential camp, where it was anticipated that the core would yield materials to be used as everyday cutting tools (utilized flakes when seen archaeologically) as well as blanks for the manufacture of a number of woodworking tools. We later had the opportunity to observe the reduction of cores in the men's camp at Bendaijerum.[18] These observations clearly suggest that the Aborigines had different procurement and reduction strategies for different types of tools. Similarly, different staging decisions characterized the production of different tools, all manufactured from the same raw material.

Archaeologists have noted for years that different techniques might be represented in the archaeological remains from a single occupation. It has been frequently suggested that techniques varied with the kinds of raw material used; sometimes that does appear to be the case. In the Alyawara situation, the kind of raw material is not the factor conditioning their decisions to use different techniques and different logistical strategies for provisioning the group with different tools. In this case, we see rather that different techniques were used because different perceived costs were associated with different demands for different tools within the system. The decision to transport manufactured blanks versus cores was, in the Aborigines' view, related to differential tool demand and the potential use life of the special blades versus the "everyday" flakes or blanks for woodworking tools.

In the technology, as in almost all other aspects of a cultural system, we are dealing with an internally differentiated subsystem. Tools are not just tools, procurement strategies are not just procurement strategies. Each is differentiated and organizationally adjusted to the other, so that there may be one kind of procurement strategy appropriate to the supply of one class of tools and another considered appropriate to replacing other kinds of tools. In the case of the Alyawara, as observed by us and as they described their tactics to us, the stone tools that appear to have been curated (see Binford 1977b and 1979) were more commonly produced in ways similar to that used for the blanks for the men's knives; that is, the blanks were produced in the quarries. On the other hand, tools that dulled quickly or were otherwise used rather expediently were produced as needed, from cores that were transported to living sites from the quarries.

We can expect many other technologies to be internally differentiated and to exhibit different procurement, production, and staging strategies (Bradley 1975; Muto 1971), organized with respect to differences in use life, demand periodicities, and assemblage specializations (personal gear versus site furniture, etc.; see Binford 1979). For instance, if the tools being produced are to become curated components of personal tool kits, then one set of strategies might be appropriate.[19] On the other hand, if everyday, expedient tools were being produced, very different replacement strategies could be expected. Since most of these decisions are conditioned economically, they might also be expected to vary within a system depending upon its spatial positioning within a region (see Binford 1982b for a discussion of changes in the placement of a system in geographical space as a conditioner of changing provisioning tactics at a single site).

Certainly the traditional Alyawara technological system was extinct at the time of our observations. Nevertheless, the internal differentiation in lithic procurement strategies and particularly in the staging of manufacturing sequences among different sites provides the archaeologist with food for thought regarding organizational factors as major contributors to interassemblage variability among sites generated by a single cultural system. If Binford is even close in his suggestion that the common hand axes of the Acheulean were portable tools (see Binford 1983c:74–75), then it is not unlikely that such tools were manufactured differently and the use of raw material was staged differently than were the common, expediently produced tools found on regularly used locations.[20] There may well be important reasons for restudying the many early assemblages that have generally been sidelined because they were thought to be mixed Clactonian and Acheulean.

CONCLUSIONS

We have had the opportunity to observe events that have not generally been described before. These events obviously prompted us to think anew about some of the practices and interpretive conclusions of contemporary archaeologists. This is basic and a necessary component of intellectual growth. It is hoped that the events we have taken pains to describe will prompt others to reflect on archaeological methods and interpretations. The growth of theory is dependent upon the use of our informed imaginations. Sharing our experiences here will hopefully inform readers' imaginations in new ways and so prompt the growth of productive ideas about both the past and our attempts to learn about the past.

NOTES

1. We wish to thank Prof. Jack Golson and Dr. Peter Ucko, who arranged our collaboration. The Australian Institute for Aboriginal Studies and the Department of Prehistory, Australian National University, provided much-appreciated financial support.
2. For additional information on the Alyawara, see Denham (1975); Hawkes and O'Connell (1981); O'Connell (1974, 1977, 1980); O'Connell and Hawkes (1981); O'Connell et al. (1983); and Yallop (1969).
3. The scientific name is *Ipomoea costata*.
4. At this time Sandy was about seventy-four years old, Manny was about sixty-four, and Jacob was in his seventies.
5. Although the men did not discuss the folklore of this place with us, it was our impression that this was an important place in their cultural landscape.
6. Few flakes appeared to be smaller than five to nine inches long, and most of the worked chunks weighed four to twelve pounds. The scene was much like those in photographs published in Holmes (1919:204, 212).
7. See Holmes (1919:202–203) for a description of very similar features.
8. The squatting posture was the form most commonly adopted by Aborigines while working cores. This is a very common work posture among many different peoples; judging from

anatomical data, it was a habitual posture among ancient populations as well (Trinkaus 1975).

9. By convention, blades are defined as flakes that are at least twice as long as they are wide.

10. The term *blank* is used here consistent with its definition and use in Binford and Papworth (1963:84), but obviously is also referrable to the work of W. H. Holmes (1894:122, 128).

11. There are several good descriptions of ordinary men's knives in the literature; see Spender and Gillen (1899:Figure 117 and pp. 591–594) and Allchin (1957: Figure 1 and pp. 125–126).

12. This day we observed four episodes of core preforming. On an earlier trip we had observed two episodes of core reduction, and on still another day, we observed three men working on a single core.

13. Note the description of the most comfortable posture given by Knowles (1944:12–13) as well as by Barbieri (1937:100).

14. Other descriptions of the Brandon industry have appeared from time to time; see Lovett (1877) and Knowles and Barnes (1937).

15. Most modern workers believe that Clactonian flakes were not generally produced by a block-on-block technique. Nevertheless, such a technique is commonly identified in many early lithic industries.

16. See Binford (1983c:151, Figure 86) for an example of a modified squatting posture.

17. D. Crabtree (1972) and others are certainly aware of the fact that very similar-looking end products may be achieved using different production techniques.

18. Observations made on that day provide the material for a future article.

19. Brian Hayden (1976) has argued that Binford's discussion of curation was misguided because the Nunamiut Eskimo used metal tools. He simply missed the point.

20. On this point we seem to be in agreement with Brian Hayden (1979:15).

Chapter 13

An Alyawara Day: Flour, Spinifex Gum, and Shifting Perspectives

We had made a deal with the locals, the men of the Alyawara camp at Bendaijerum, near the cattle station at MacDonald Downs, Central Australia (Figure 13.1).[1]

When I was introduced to the older, initiated males at their men's camp, they asked why I was there. I had replied that I was there to learn as much as possible about how they used the land, how they got enough to eat, and how they lived in general. This precipitated a kind of joke. One of the old men stood up and spoke at length, to the obvious amusement of the others. The gist of his speech was the following: What you want to know is what every Alyawara boy wants to know and begins learning from the responsible men when he is very young. You will have to get up very early each morning and work hard, since there is so much to learn and your beard is already gray!

It seemed clear that the old men had agreed that I should be permitted to seek this knowledge, but the problem was to decide which men were responsible, that is, which men would teach me. The issue was settled by a series of adoption agreements, whereby I was assigned to a moiety and to a dreaming tract, etc.[2] These assignments determined my relationship to the other men and, in turn, settled the question of which men would be my teachers. The particular characteristics of the kinship conventions are the cultural mechanisms that integrate biological reproduction with the reproduction of social roles, thereby insuring that the culturally organized system also reproduces itself. Minimally, kinship conventions assign social roles to individuals and simultaneously specify the role responsibilities of others toward the individual. This placement of a person within the social matrix specifies the cultural content that must be learned (men's roles, women's roles, etc.) and the persons who are responsible for preparing the young person for gradually stepping into the anticipated roles. In short, kinship conventions are the mechanisms that organize cultural reproduction, articulated to the flow of biologically generated persons through the system. In a very real sense, kinship conventions may be the basis of an educational system: the system that organizes the reproduction of the cultural system itself.

At least part of our deal consisted of the Alyawara men giving us a social status through their kinship conventions.[3] In turn we then were expected to behave appropriately, to cooperate, to learn, and to become enculturated, at least in certain ways. To make this possible, a set of men were responsible to us, as teachers. We were quite

Originally published in *Journal of Anthropological Research* 40:157–182, © 1984.

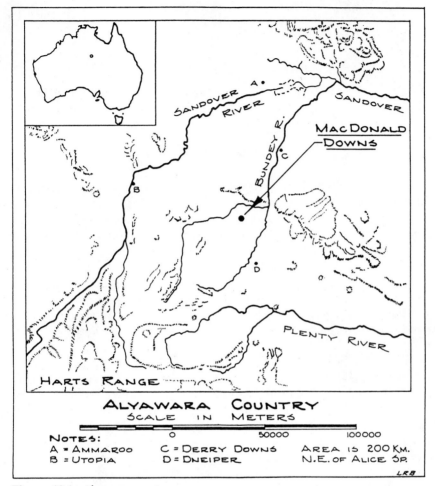

Figure 13.1 Alyawara country.

literally enrolled in Alyawara school, with the goal of learning how to perform as an Alyawara, appropriate to the kinship-defined statuses given us. It is certainly true that after this agreement we were frequently awakened very early, to start a day of learning. Why would they do this for some stranger who happened to show up?

ONE DAY IN JUNE

The day I am about to describe did not start as a schoolday for us. The events of the morning of 16 June 1974 were dictated by the laws of modern Australia and the conventions of paternalism, exploitation, and abuse that often characterize the interaction between Aborigines and white Australians.[4] The other half of our deal was well exemplified by the events on this Sunday morning.

There was to be a handout of food, mostly bags of flour, to the Aborigines living on the cattle station at MacDonald Downs. We were sleeping near the men's camp and were aroused by groups of talking men walking past our tent. It should be explained that the Aboriginal camp at Bendaijerum was composed of four kinds of habitation units: a men's camp, several women's camps, conjugal camps, and a boys' camp (see O'Connell 1977 for a good description).

A men's camp consists of a shelter, cooking hearths, and work areas used by the adult males. Most tools and craft items are manufactured there, and most cooperative social and economic planning goes on in the men's camp. Visiting males, widowers, and unmarried but initiated males sleep in the men's camp.

A women's camp is similar, in that most of the daytime activities of women—child care, grinding seeds, roasting grubs and small animals, etc.— are both planned and executed from it. Cowives not currently sleeping with their husbands, widows, and unmarried but eligible girls all sleep in the women's camp.[5]

Conjugal camps are generally distributed as satellites of women's camps. A wife and her husband sleep in a conjugal camp and take evening and morning meals there. Such camps are generally abandoned during the day, when the husband's activities center in the men's camp and the wife's in a women's camp.

The boys' camp is commonly a poorly constructed shelter where the teenage males sleep and center their activities. At Bendaijerum there was still another kind of camp—the ethnographers' camp— occupied by uninitiated, postpubescent males, so that it was a kind of boys' camp, but sometimes the older men congregated there, as though it were a funny kind of men's camp. This ambiguity became clear on the Sunday morning I am about to describe.

As the sun began to warm our tent, the women could be seen moving off toward the cattle station in small groups, with children running ahead or lagging behind (Figure 13.2). As the women moved toward the station, the men gathered in the men's camp. We observed both from our camp. The men walked toward the station in several larger groups. We got the truck running and went down to the station, arriving before some of the men. I had decided to stay out of things and take photographs of the events; the gathering would be a fine time to get pictures of most of the people.

On the other hand, O'Connell became very active, helping the cattlemen distribute flour, asking questions for some Alyawara, and generally smoothing out the event. This was a manifestation of the other side of our deal. We had skills—knowledge of Euro-Australian culture, good use of English, and a truck and other gear useful in the Aborgines' situation. We were *expected* to act in the "whitefellow" world on behalf of our Aboriginal relatives. We clearly had roles in the Alyawaras' eyes that were non-traditional but important in their contemporary situation.

That day Jim O'Connell performed very well in this role. He helped two Aboriginal men get some gasoline, which otherwise might not have been possible that day. He acted on behalf of a woman who wanted to purchase some clothes, and he arranged for a young man to ride on a cattle truck to Alice Springs to visit relatives. All these things were observed by O'Connell's Aboriginal "relatives."

The consequences were dramatic. On their return to Bendaijerum, the men did not go to the men's camp. Instead, they collected in our camp, just as if they were visitors

Figure 13.2 Alyawara women and children walking to the cattle station, 16 June 1974.

in another group's men's camp. They talked and sat around precisely as they do in the men's camp. At least that afternoon, our boys' camp was behaviorally transformed into a funny kind of whitefellows' men's camp.

I recall being very flattered and did not really know how to act. Nevertheless, I relaxed into asking questions. We talked a great deal that day about kinship. We also talked of periodic aggregations and how local group composition varied before and after corroborees. Their answers always seemed to come around to "territories." My notes record the following:

> When I took up their mention of "territories" there was an explosion, "Alyawara not like whitefellow with fences between countries—say you can't go here and there. We go everywhere, back and forth, all good friends. Whitefellow fences bad—people fight—we different."
>
> All the men were excited pointing out that "countries" were not owned.
>
> "Today people live in camps—(mobs)—countries made up by dreamtime things—people belong to countries because people come from dreamtime business. Camps come from how today people get along, how they like or not like each other, camps don't come from dreamtime business. How can camps have "countries"? Whitefellow has "countries" which belong to mobs, this is bad. Our countries make people, people make mobs (camps) live well because people carry on dreamtime business in their countries. Mobs go wherever they want."[6]

Clearly we were being taught more than technology and something of the traditional settlement pattern; we were being taught their views on the intrusive, whitefellow ideas of ownership and property. This was proper men's talk in a men's camp.

I wonder if we could ever have obtained such clear statements regarding property, territory, and the differences between "estate" and "range" (see Stanner 1965) if these Aborigines had been unacculturated, or at least unfamiliar with whitefellow ideas of property.

The men had earlier agreed to take us step by step through the process of manufacturing men's knives. We had already been to the stone quarry and had observed the production of cores and blanks, particularly the blanks for men's knives (see Binford and O'Connell 1984). After our talk about territories, one man had said that we would be taught some more about men's knives that afternoon. The older men left, and after about an hour we went up to their men's camp. There were six men present, sitting at a white ash hearth. The men said that Jacob was at the young men's camp looking for resin, but shortly he appeared, commenting that the women had not gathered the material for the gum, so we would have to do that today.

Jacob and Sandy White left with us for our tent and the truck, parked nearby. We piled in and left camp, crossing over the Bundey River and into a flat area of short grass fringed with mulga trees. As we went north, the plain appeared to be bounded by red-rock boulder hills, arranged against the northern horizon. We were directed through a draw in the loaf-shaped hills and then into a narrower area between a wash and a rocky hill. The particular grass they needed evidently tended to grow on rocky areas. As far as I could understand, the blowing winds insured that the grass stalks would be abraded against the stones. This continual abrasion resulted in the bleeding out of resin, which then formed "scabs" over the abraded areas of the stems. These scabs of resin could be collected and transformed into a mastic, or gum.

We parked the truck at the base of the red-rock ridge. One of the men went over to a "ghost bark" tree and began chopping an oval-shaped section of bark from the trunk (Figure 13.3). A healed scar attested to the fact that this had been done before. Two oval-shaped pieces of bark were removed from the tree, from opposite sides of the tree. The removals were made at different heights, so that the tree would not die. A third piece was cut from another tree nearby. Three winnowing trays had just been manufactured on the spot.

It was explained that in the past an ax would not have been available, and "somefellow" would have used a "big chunk" of rock to cut the winnowing trays. Not far away a fair accumulation of stones was pointed out as probably being where a "big tree used to be." The stones were large, from four to eight pounds in weight, with at least one fairly sharp cutting edge. It was the opinion of Jacob that there were "lots" around there, since people came here for making resin ever since "dreaming time." He also noted that he liked cutting the trays from the bark of a previously scarred tree; it shows that he is doing things like men should. At about this time, Sandy came down from the hill and talked excitedly with Jacob—he seemed to have sighted some kangaroos across the flats, along a line of trees bordering the wash to the north. They both climbed the rocks to look, but they evidently couldn't be sure. We had all now moved up the hill.

Figure 13.3   Removing a bark tray from a ghost bark tree. Note scar from a previous removal.

While Jacob was cutting the winnowing trays, Sandy White had been moving across the upper slopes of the rock ridge, examining clumps of grass; whatever he was searching out was not visible from my vantage point beside the trees where Jacob was working.

When we moved up the hill, I had carried one tray and Jacob had carried two. We now saw what Sandy had been doing. He had searched out a large, flat rock that was to serve as a threshing floor. When we arrived it was already partially covered with clumps of uprooted spinifex grass. He demonstrated that he had previously swept the rock floor. After giving up on the kangaroos, both men turned to pulling up grass and adding it to what soon became a very large, haystack-like pile about three feet high (Figure 13.4). While Sandy continued collecting grass, Jacob went up the hill to a clump of small trees and cut one about 1½ inches in diameter and trimmed it to a straight pole about 3½ feet long (Figure 13.5). Then he came back down to the growing pile of grass.

There he took his newly manufactured flail and began beating the pile of grass with a rhythmic movement, interrupting the flailing to turn the pile, which was becoming somewhat more compact as a result of the pounding (Figure 13.6). The flailing continued for about seven minutes, and then the pile of grass was pulled back off the large rock. Covering the threshing floor was a thin coating of what appeared to be gray dust and many small, dry sections of grass stem and other chaff. Sandy made a small broom from grass stems and then swept the gray dust into a pile in the center of the floor. At the same time, Jacob scooped up some of it into one of the ghost-bark winnowing trays.

Figure 13.4   Collecting grass to be piled on the threshing floor.

Figure 13.5   Cutting a flail.

Figure 13.6 Threshing the pile of grass.

Jacob started a rocking motion with the tray, one end slightly higher than the other, and one could see the lighter grass stems migrating to the high end of the tray. As the stems accumulated, Jacob would blow on the high end and the chaff would fly away, leaving an increasingly clean accumulation of gray dust at the low end of the tray. He would sometimes reach in and pick up larger sections of grass stem and leaf. As the rocking, picking, and blowing process continued, Jacob would occasionally stop and pour off the clean gray dust into one of the other winnowing trays, then add more dust from the pile on the floor. This process continued in silence until all the dust from the central pile on the threshing floor had been processed into roughly equal piles, resting in the two other trays.

During most of this operation, Sandy sat quietly watching Jacob work (Figure 13.7). Near the end he got up and began searching the horizon; after Jacob had finished his cleaning of the dust and stood up to stretch, Sandy engaged Jacob in conversation, pointing in an animated fashion to the draw where the kangaroos might have been. Finally Jacob began running down the hill in a low crouch, toward the truck. There he got the .22 rifle, owned by O'Connell, and began running in a continued low crouch from one clump of vegetation to another, across the relatively flat area in front of the draw or wash, about half a mile away. As this was going on, O'Connell, Sandy, and I moved away from the threshing floor and up the hill, so that he could get a better view of the hunting. We began questioning Sandy as to what he had seen; this time there was no mention of kangaroo. All Sandy would say was that maybe there was "something" out there!

Figure 13.7 Gray resin dust on the threshing floor.

We all stood high on the hill watching, but we were looking northwest into the early afternoon sun, and we soon lost sight of Jacob. It seemed a long time, about forty minutes, before Sandy finally pointed out Jacob walking steadily across the flats toward the truck. He stopped there, left the rifle, got a drink of water, and began climbing the hill toward us. When he arrived there were only a few unintelligible words exchanged between Jacob and Sandy, and both then moved off briskly toward the threshing floor. O'Connell followed closely and asked if he had seen any kangaroo; Jacob simply said he had not seen anything, and the episode was closed.

Later I questioned Jacob about this episode. He commented that men are always watching for game. Everywhere men stop to do something, such as making spinifex gum, they always watch for game. If he had killed a kangaroo that day, he would have brought it back and made a roasting pit at the bottom of the hill near the trees, where there was wood, and "cooked 'em up." We had seen this very procedure near the lithic quarry we had previously visited (see Binford 1983c:165–169).

Jacob and Sandy resumed their work at the threshing floor as if nothing had ever interrupted them. When Sandy returned, he carried two elliptical stones about seven inches long and four inches thick. These he placed in the center of the floor, and both men then moved around, picking up small sticks and dried bark. They both returned with several handfuls of firewood. The two stones were placed in the center, aligned parallel to one another, about ten inches apart. The kindling and firewood were placed between the two stones (Figure 13.8). One of the winnowing trays full of cleaned resin dust was then set across the firewood pile, with its ends on the two rocks

Figure 13.8 Laying the fire.

(Figure 13.9). The fire was kindled and the flames grew up around the green bark trays. The men stirred the resin dust with small sticks; as the heat increased the dust began to be transformed into little lumpy balls. As this happened the men would pick the lumps out, molding them into a growing round ball. In the meantime, Sandy placed another tray on the fire, so that both men were doing the same things (Figure 13.10).

As Jacob finished his ball, which was by this time about two inches in diameter, he got up and began looking over the surface of the ground. He shortly returned with a large, flat stone, about twelve inches across and three inches thick. He set this down in front of where he had been sitting, and at the same time seated himself. He took from his pockets three smaller stones, all about the same size, four inches across and three quarters of an inch thick; all were very flat. Jacob adjusted the large stone in front of him as one might adjust a work surface, and he added some more kindling to the fire (Figure 13.11). He then placed the three smaller stones on the new fuel in the center of the fire. He sat back as the fire flared up, then broke four sticks to a length of from ten to twelve inches (these were about half an inch in diameter; two of them had been used earlier to stir the resin dust).

The fire was fanned with Sandy's hat, so that the three small stones got quite hot. Jacob then took two of the previously prepared sticks and removed one of the flat stones, now hot, from the fire and placed it on top of the resin ball that was sitting on the flat table rock in front of Jacob (Figure 13.12). Jacob placed his stick across the flat

Figure 13.9 Initial cooking of the dust.

Figure 13.10 Hand-molding a resin ball.

Figure 13.11 "Ironing rocks" being heated.

Figure 13.12 "Ironing rocks" being removed from the fire.

Figure 13.13 "Ironing" the gray resin balls.

Figure 13.14 Shaping the gum tablet.

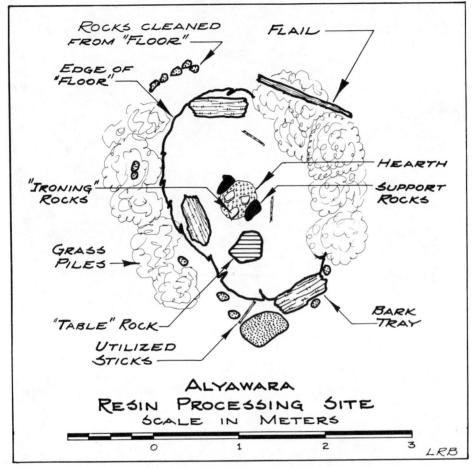

ROCKS CLEANED FROM "FLOOR"

FLAIL

EDGE OF "FLOOR"

HEARTH

SUPPORT ROCKS

"IRONING" ROCKS

GRASS PILES

BARK TRAY

"TABLE" ROCK

UTILIZED STICKS

ALYAWARA
RESIN PROCESSING SITE
SCALE IN METERS

0   1   2   3

LRB

Figure 13.15   Alyawara resin-processing site.

rock and began "ironing" the ball with the hot rock (Figure 13.13). As the hot rock was moved across the ball, rocking back and forth, the gray resin ball was transformed into a black, tar-like substance that shone and glistened around the edges of the hot rock. Jacob would put the rock back on the fire and then fold the black, glistening gum into the center of the ball, exposing more gray resin on the surface. This ironing, folding, and ironing again continued until the round, gray ball was transformed into a black, tar-like gum tablet, 6½ inches long and 2 inches wide at the widest point, with rounded edges and rather flat top and bottom surfaces (Figure 13.14). While Jacob had been working so had Sandy, and both men finished their tablets about the same time. Jacob got up and brought the two tablets over to show to us. At the same time, Sandy took one of the winnowing trays, scooped up sand, and smothered the fire with several trayfulls. While the others returned to the truck, I took a photo and made a quick map of the processing site (Figure 13.15). The following items remained at the site:

1. Three bark trays, two badly burned.
2. One small hearth with two large tray support stones on either side and three flat, burned stones used for the ironing tossed back into the fire. These were covered with three scoopfuls of sand.
3. A flat, table rock used by Jacob to iron his resin ball on. Left in place where it was used.
4. The flail used to beat the resin dust from the grass.
5. Piles of grass tossed back from the flat rock threshing floor.
6. Four charred sticks used in stirring and ironing.

When we piled into the truck, the men immediately began to talk of hunting. It was decided that we would hunt until dark. O'Connell drove the truck according to Jacob's directions. We sighted eight bush turkeys and fourteen kangaroos. Several shots were made from the truck and only two stalks were attempted. We bagged no game. As the sun began to set, Jacob directed us into a low area with many dead trees. We all got out and began breaking off dead branches and piling the top and back of the truck full of firewood. After this we drove steadily back to the camp at Bendaijerum and unloaded the firewood behind Jacob's conjugal camp, where he proceeded to make a distribution to relatives and to Sandy. We left as soon as possible, since we had to wash. We were invited to the cattle station owner's house for dinner that evening. Dinner conversation was largely dominated by the woman, who told us story after story of how the Aborigines could not "take care of themselves" and how time and time again she and her husband had stepped in to save or otherwise protect the Alyawara from harm.

ANTHROPOLOGICAL REFLECTIONS

Obviously I chose to describe this day because I thought there was some significance to the events, with implications beyond the events themselves.

Internal Analysis

We, as investigators, were obviously not participants in the traditional system of the Alyawara; we were important participants with unusual roles in the intercultural situation of the Alyawara during 1974.[7] By including us to some extent in their traditional system, the Alyawara themselves could at least sometimes be seen as having legitimate calls on us and our outside role skills. Similarly, we were expected by the Alyawara to perform roles that extended, *in their interest,* into the broader, intrusive whitefellow system. Finally, we had certain claims on the Alyawara for knowledge and information, insofar as we were included in their world through kinship ties. Since our roles were new, and the status of ephemeral participants in the Alyawara system was new, there were uncertainties as to how important it was to behave toward us, even when in a seemingly traditional context, in traditional ways. Let me take an example from the day just described. I should caution that I do not *know* the possibilities I suggest were in fact realities. Nevertheless, even my suspicions should be sufficient to point out some of the problems inherent in making observations on a living system.

It will be recalled that after it was decided that we should be exposed to more traditional knowledge regarding the manufacture of men's knives, there was an episode where Jacob was said to have been in the boys' camp and then later commented that "the women had not gathered the material for the mastic." On questioning, Jacob had indicated that gathering the resin was normally a woman's task. Clearly, preparing the spinifex gum is basic to the making of men's knives, yet it would appear that they had not intended to demonstrate its manufacture. My first guess was that this was a case of "abbreviation," in that the men, while having agreed to show us "everything" about making men's knives, had judged that we were not really interested in everything. On the other hand, if in the course of things the women or boys normally brought in the resin, then the men were simply behaving normally and modeling the normal adult male way of dealing with the situation. In their eyes this may not have been an abbreviation, since the collection of spinifex resin was normally done by women or boys.

Nevertheless, as the events of the day demonstrated, the men were both skilled and knowledgeable about collecting and processing the resin. Several facts obtained later led me to believe that boys normally learn how to do this not from their male teachers but from their mothers, while they still live in the women's camp and accompany women on their daily foraging trips. The manufacture of resin is not learned from his male sponsor after a boy leaves the women's camp and moves into the novice camp, where the men take over most of the cultural instruction. I would guess that what we saw in the resin processing demonstration was most likely abnormal from the Aborigines' perspective.

Almost certainly on initially reading this description, the reader would have considered my descriptions of the resin collecting and processing to be a "traditional" episode, likely to be an abbreviation by the men. Instead it might well be an *abnormal condition,* arising from our lack of enculturation over the course of our normal growth and maturation. We were culturally young male novices who did not even know how to make spinifex gum, something we should have learned as small boys! Whether this interpretation is accurate or not, it illustrates a very real point: an outside observer coming into a system cannot participate in a normal manner, no matter how dedicated both he and his teachers may be. In addition, the teachers frequently do not realize the problems inherent in such a situation themselves, since they take for granted the normal maturation and scheduling of role growth in their culture.

When I worked with the Eskimo, I found that commonly the men would be surprised to realize that I did not know something that every child should know. They would then be embarrassed at talking to me as a child in a situation structured for peer-peer interaction. Rather than stop and teach me, they would often change the situation so that the knowledge was not needed or so that they no longer dealt with me as a peer—in short, my learning was stopped. This happened because I was not a "traditional" person. I was in need for a kind of ethnographic head start program that they did not have. As a result, I received baffling signals and my learning situation was frequently aborted, but certainly not through malice or lack of concern. They were simply not prepared to deal with a baby with a gray beard.[8]

In the case of the spinifex resin episode, the Alyawara men had no resin, so they had to make some if they were to complete the tasks they had set for themselves. They probably decided to teach us along the way. In short, it was not a traditional episode at all!

Shifting Perspective

When we place this event in the larger context of comparative ethnology, we face another scale of information; we gain another perspective (see Binford and Sabloff 1982) on our experiences. As we will see, their significance may change dramatically.

In shifting to a comparative frame of reference, the first thing to note is that published descriptions of resin processing are rare. My reading has turned up only two accounts. John Greenway (1972:201–204) had resin processing demonstrated to him, in the course of making an ethnographic film, by Pitjantjatjara who had been living at Musgrave Park station but who had gone out on a walkabout (in Greenway's truck) to the vicinity of Piltardi Gorge, some fifty-five miles west of Musgrave Park. The second account also describes Pitjantjatjara speakers, observed by Brokensha (1975) either at Amata Settlement or in the new, decentralized settlement at Pipalyatjara, in the Tomkinson Ranges.

In the latter case the spinifex gum was evidently being produced in the context of a home crafts industry, where the Aborigines were making "traditional" items for sale as a means of gaining cash. Brokensha (1975:64) observed that

> the process . . . commences with thrashing the . . . spinifex needles with a stick into a piece of canvas or cloth to dislodge the gum. . . . The [next step] is concerned with separating the gum from pieces of vegetable matter and it will be noted that a modern adaptation in the form of a flywire sieve is used. Traditionally this separation would have been performed by winnowing. . . . Great skill is required in the heating process, by movement of the mulga bark torch across the gum to ensure it is softened sufficiently to be pliable but not over heated which would cause the gum to melt and become brittle and useless on cooling.

An interesting set of documentary photographs accompanies this description; in all the photos the people processing the resin are men.

The former description of resin processing comes from a group of Pitjantjatjara-speaking Aborigines who lived in the vicinity of Musgrave Park station in 1967. Greenway (1972) reports that the spinifex resin is extruded along the stems of the plant by virtue of their infestation by an organism that presumably eats holes in the grass stems. He comments that he could not figure out how the Aborigines knew which strands of grass were infested and which ones were not (Greenway 1972:202).[9] The early steps in the description provided by Greenway are very similar to those observed among the Alyawara. The men search out a flat rock threshing floor, pile the appropriate grass on it, and beat it with a flail. The grass is then pulled back, and the resin is brushed up into piles of gray dust with an expediently manufactured broom. But here we meet a major contrast. Greenway reports that the dust gathered by the men is then turned over to the women for cleaning by essentially the same methods used by the Alyawara men: rocking, blowing, and picking over the dust in a shallow container. However, in this case the container was a manufactured wooden bowl, and *the cleaning was done by women*. Once cleaned, the dust was returned to the men, who processed it with burning brands as in Brokensha's descriptions; however, the resin is said to be folded onto a stick, on which it is then transported.

Table 13.1 summarizes the points of comparative interest noted among the cases available. I have already suggested that the pattern of action observed among the Alyawara was responsive in its details to their immediate situation, including our ignorance. In the face of the comparative data, however, it can be argued that the situation is not this simple. For instance, I do not know for sure what we saw. *Did the men demonstrate the manufacture of spinifex gum the way the women would have done it, or did the men demonstrate a men's mode of production, used when the women would or could not do it?* From the Alyawara data alone this could not be determined. When I was in the field it never occurred to me to wonder whether the action of the men was really a normative demonstration of the way the Alyawara, considered in an ethnic sense, characteristically manufacture spinifex gum. I did not know enough about Alyawara life to appreciate the situational factors considered by the men when deciding on their course of action. It is only on reflection, and by comparing my experiences with the two cases summarized in Table 13.1, that I have been able to come to some tentative assessment as to the organizational significance of what O'Connell and I witnessed that Sunday in 1974.[10]

Several facts made explicit by the comparisons are very important. First, curated (see Binford 1979) wooden bowls were used in both the Pitjantjatjara cases for cleaning the resin dust. In my experience, such bowls are "women's gear." In *none* of my interview data from the Alyawara men were wooden bowls mentioned as part of their portable gear, carried normally into the field. The Alyawara reported that men commonly carry spears, a spear thrower, throwing sticks, a hair string belt, string to tie up their hair bun, an extra hook for the spear thrower in the pierced septum of their nose, and stone tools tied up in their hair bun. On some occasions they may also carry shields, men's knives, and other weapons used primarily in fighting (see Edwards 1973:p. 29, plates 3 and 4, and p. 35, plate 1; Tindale 1974:black-and-white plates 25, 57, 58, 61 and 66). In marked contrast are the tools that were described as habitually carried into the field by women: wooden bowls, digging sticks, head pads that also served as sources of string, and flake knives (and/or "women's knives") tied up in their hair. As in the case of men's portable gear, many documentary photographs show women in the field with most of the above-mentioned items (Binford 1983c:205; Edwards 1973:p. 7, plate 7, p. 31, plate 1; Tindale 1974:black-and-white plates 19 and 23; Tonkinson 1978:4, 5, 23, 34).

What this rather strict differentiation of portable gear implies is that when winnowing or processing in a wooden bowl was considered necessary, it was generally left to the women, who used their curated wooden bowls. This also means that if resin dust

Table 13.1

Three Records of Spinifex Gum Preparation

	1967 Pitjantjatjara (Greenway 1972)	1972–1975 Pitjantjatjara (Brokensha 1975)	1974 Alyawara (Binford)
Cause of resin deposits			
Grass infested by parasites	No data	Grass abraded on rocks	
Initial Procedures			
(1) Threshing grass on natural rock floor	Threshing grass over cloth	Threshing grass on natural rock floor	
(2) Sweeping up dust with expedient grass broom	Dust collected in cloth	Sweeping up dust with expedient grass broom	
(3) Transfer of dust to manufactured and curated wooden bowls	No transfer to other container noted	Transfer of dust to expediently produced bark winnowing trays	
Cleaning of resin dust			
(1) Winnowing and cleaning *by women*, using curated wooden bowls	Passing dust through a fly screen *by men*, to remove large grass stems	Winnowing and cleaning *by men*, using expediently produced bark trays	
(2) Cleaned dust heated, placed on/in unknown surface	Cleaned dust transferred to table rock for further processing	Cleaned dust collected in bark containers	
Methods of heating resin			
(1) Heating of surface using fire brands	Passing fire brands over dust exposed on table rock	Placing bark trays directly on fire and stirring	
(2) Resin molded into a ball, mounted on a stick[a]	Resin compacted into a hand-compressed ball	Resin compacted into a hand-compressed ball	
(3) ?	?	Gray ball ironed with heated flat rocks	
(4) ?	?	Melted resin dust, transformed into black gum, folded so that gray ball is transformed and shaped into a tablet	

[a] It is not clear whether the ball was a dark gum ball or a gray ball like the hand-compressed balls reported by Brokensha.

was gathered by the men, it would most often be carried back to the residential camp and turned over to the women for processing. In actual practice, I suspect that most commonly the resin is collected and processed by the women, who then turn over the cleaned product to the men for use in tool manufacture.

Use of the curated wooden bowls for cleaning precludes the heating of the resin in such containers, since these curated tools would be damaged. Instead, in all cases where wooden bowls are used, some method of heating is employed in which fire brands are passed over the resin dust, making it slightly sticky and therefore capable of being molded into a ball. Another method, indicated in a photograph in Edwards (1973:33, plate 1), involves a man moving a hot stone around in the dust contained in a wooden bowl. It seems clear that there were at least three methods of initial heating: direct heating in a container placed on the fire, passing burning brands over the dust, and moving hot stones around in the dust.

Second, it is equally clear that direct heating is not something that would be done using the women's curated wooden bowls.[11] This means that the techniques demonstrated by the Alyawara men were most likely expedient techniques, used when spinifex gum was needed; when manufacture could not be delayed until after return to the residential camp, where the women would normally process the resin; and when women were not with the men who needed the gum. My conclusion is that the process observed among the Alyawara was a truly male process, employed by men when the field manufacture of resin was required. Under those conditions they manufactured expedient processing bowls from bark, which could be used to heat the resin dust directly because they were expendable. The more common procedure was for the women to gather and process the resin using their wooden bowls. When curated bowls were used, the initial heating had to be done so as not to damage them. The differences between the Alyawara and the 1967 Pitjantjatjara cases are most likely situationally conditioned, *functional* differences between processing by a mixed sex group and processing by an all-male group.

A final comment must be made regarding the contrasts between Brokensha's observations and those by Greenway and myself. Clearly different and foreign tools were being used in Brokensha's experiences, such as the fly screen. In addition, the men processed the resin dust using women's bowls. That there had been a new role created for the men, that of commercial craftsman, may well have contributed to the breakdown of the accommodative division of labor that seems to have characterized the Aborgines' mobile, traditional life style. It would be interesting to see what different functions and contextual associations tools such as wooden bowls take on as the role structure of the society changes, in line with Brokensha's experiences. The important conclusion, however, is that aside from "acculturative" variability, differences between the Pitjantjatjara and the Alyawara descriptions should be understood as *situationally* different. The degree to which there may also be *ethnically* related differences in resin processing between the two groups cannot be evaluated given the available evidence.

Looking out toward Colleagues

This paper has several purposes. First, it is valuable simply to document the experiences I had among the Aborigines. It is also valuable to analyze in some detail the complicated patterns of interaction and accommodation that characterize the relationships between ethnographers and the people they study. Unfortunately, most ethnographers portray themselves as moving into a group of people, seemingly free to move about within the system and to see things objectively. They are frequently depicted as participating naturally within the system.

This is a myth. All ethnographers are outsiders, and the locals accommodate to their presence in various ways. It is rarely clear how these accommodations condition what ethnographers will in fact see, how it will be explicated by the locals, and how it will be modified by them to deal with the fact that ethnographers are naive outsiders. Ethnographies are inferential interpretations made from the ethnographers' experiences, but most ethnographers present their interpretations as objective facts. The myth is thus perpetuated that ethnographers do not need to be skilled and self-conscious about their inferential methods. This has not been generally appreciated, as the following statement indicates: "the ethnographer-social anthropologist has no black box problem, he can observe the workings of the system at first hand" (Leach 1973:767). Archaeologists who seek to use ethnographers' data in their arguments must be even more cautious.

Second, I have sought to discuss the variability noted among several descriptions of resin processing, as still another probable example of situationally variable behavior characteristic of people who share a common body of culture. While in this case the sharing of a common body of culture is not as easy to demonstrate as was the case in my studies of Nunamiut behavior (Binford 1978a), the issue in contention is the same. If people share a common body of culture but behave differently under different conditions, then the behavior must be referred to situational factors considered by actors when choosing a course of action.

In humans, as culturally conditioned animals, the very rationality of behavior relative to measured environmental features is also relative to culturally abstracted experience, transmitted both intergenerationally and among peers. Culture is our extra-somatic means of adaptation. To illustrate that it works well relative to what we know about environments is not to deny culture, nor is it to observe a simple system, as Richard Gould has recently suggested (Gould and Watson 1982:367). Gould believes that somehow there is an opposition between circumstantial, or functional, arguments and cultural arguments: "For Binford, it is circumstance rather than culture that determines human behavior in relation to meat procurement and faunal remains" (Gould and Watson 1982:366).

In the study to which Gould refers, I observed the behavior of a small group of Nunamiut men in a variety of situations. They were all Nunamiut, and from the same small group. I conducted my study so that culture could be held constant. There was no question that all the sites I described and all the events I observed pertained to the same ethnic group and were performed by a limited number of known men who did not change their culture from one episode to the next. My Nunamiut study was not an "anticultural" study. It was a demonstration that there was substantial variability in the behavior of the same individuals, resulting in very different archaeological remains from site to site. Such differences obviously could not be due to cultural differences. This is not to deny that there are cultural differences that might also be demonstrated among different groups of people. In no way have I ever opposed a functional point of view to a cultural point of view. However, I have frequently asked how, in the face of demonstrated situationally responsive behavior when culture is held constant, can archaeologists assume that all archaeological variability is isomorphic with cultural variability? My studies have been generally middle range in character, intended to evaluate the accuracy and utility of the conventions that archaeologists have used to interpret variability among archaeologically observed units.

In the past, it was generally assumed that all archaeological variability was a direct measure of cultural variability. Unfortunately, this point of view remains with us. Sackett (1982:72), for instance, has suggested that style concerns a "highly characteristic manner of doing something which by its very nature is peculiar to a specific time and place." I can only point out that characteristics of the environment are also referable to specific times and places. Why then, when we observe distinctive products of human behavior, must they be referable to postulated, ethnically distinct human groups, said to be differentially distributed temporally and geographically?

All culturally aided behavior is not necessarily ethnically organized, nor is the most productive explanatory framework for temporal and spatial variability in the archaeological record to be sought in the historical dynamics of ethnic group interaction. Sackett's statement of faith that archaeologically observed geographical and temporal variability refers to ethnic histories makes no sense to me. The little case of resin processing presented here documents behaviors that are certainly peculiar to a given time and place. I have argued, nevertheless, that the differences involved are primarily functional, or referable to differing situations that are not necessarily ethnically significant.[12]

The same acceptance of unfounded existential assumptions about the nature of the archaeological record dominates the works of Ian Hodder. For instance, *"excavated artefacts are immediately cultural, not social,* and they can inform on society only through an adequate understanding of cultural context" (Hodder 1982c:10, emphasis added). If excavated artifacts are immediately cultural, then differences in either forms or frequencies of artifacts must document cultural differences. This is the position refuted over and over again in my Nunamiut study (Binford 1978a). Sweeping existential assumptions are simply not necessary, because the nature of the archaeological record can be studied in its formation context.

If I am correct in interpreting the differences between my description of the Alyawara and Greenway's description of the Pitjantjatjara, then a spinifex resin processing site produced by a male hunting party and a site generated by the same men of either group in a residential setting would be seen as culturally different, given Hodder's view. This is not to say that material symbols do not exist, nor that symbolic codes do not exist in the archaeological record; they most certainly do. The problem, however, rests with our abilities to recognize the kinds of phenomena we are observing. Put another way, we must identify the formation contexts that structured the archaeological remains with which we work. Hodder advocates a limited view, in which all archaeological remains derive primarily from only one context—the cultural context, the context of symbol and belief. Like all other single-dimension conventions, this is distorting and misleading when used as the basis for interpreting multivariate phenomena, that is, phenomena that arise from the interactive conditioning of many different causal and conditioning factors. To force all this multidimensional variability into a single interpretive convention is to misrepresent the past and to abuse the archaeological record.

Even as the crippling repetition of traditional conventions continues to retard archaeological growth, still other workers offer suggestions that miss the point of what I seek to accomplish. Richard Gould is fond of pointing to actions that from our

Western perspective are counterintuitive, but which simply derive from a non-Western rationality: "Anomalies discovered by means of ethnographic studies compel archaeologists to expand their explanations in many cases to aspects of the social-ideational realm" (Gould 1980a:229). Ethnographic demonstrations such as those alluded to by Gould take the form of citing anomalous behaviors that become rational given a different belief system. The inferential leap is then made that when one encounters counterintuitive conditions in the archaeological record, one must therefore postulate a different basis for rationality operative in the past. The reader will no doubt recognize this as a classic example of argument from ethnographic analogy. Oddly enough, however, Gould disapproves of the use of such inferential strategies and in fact maintains that argument from anomaly should replace argument from analogy!

Leaving this logical problem aside, what Gould does not consider is that our *ignorance* of the material conditions and organizational properties of past systems represented archaeologically may be the cause of anomalies and irrationalities in our terms (see, for instance, my discussion of one of Gould's anomalies; Binford 1979:260–261). Something may appear anomalous simply because of our ignorance of factors considered by the ancients in their reasoning processes. Because we are unable to reconcile the behavior of a group of people in the past with what little we know about their environment, social setting, and situational state is no justification for seeing a "social-ideational" explanation, nor for moving to a new level of explanation, as has recently been advocated by Gould (1980a:228; Gould and Watson 1982:367). Once again this is not to say that ideological, or culture context, differences may not in fact separate past actors from contemporary archaeologists, but the simple argument from analogy that such differences exist ethnographically is not sufficient to justify the leap to post hoc accommodative arguments. The complexity of the contingencies considered by actors in other systems is illustrated here in the resin processing comparisons. This complexity should serve as a warning against the all too ready judgment that something is "anomalous."

CONCLUSIONS

This description of an ethnographer's day should be relevant to the ethnography of the Alyawara and of the anthropologists. I hope these joint perspectives can aid in the better practice and use of ethnoarchaeological research. I hope in addition that my discussion of the situational factors that are apt to have conditioned variability among the documented cases of Aboriginal resin processing will serve as an object lesson to those who regard documented variability as an unambiguous measure of cultural differences, and to those who might accept reported experiences and implicated materials as normative or characteristic of ethnic units, while they remain uninformed about the situational conditioners that molded what they observed. I also hope to expose the argument from anomaly, as illustrated by Gould (1980a), as a kind of arrogance of ignorance, where appeals to socioideological causes are made whenever one faces a reality that is not understood. Gould's argument from anomaly is a fancy phrase for the old practice of calling something a ceremonial object when you do not know what it is.

NOTES

1. The research reported here was financed by a grant from the Australian Institute for Aboriginal Studies. It was extended to me through the kindness of Peter Ucko. James O'Connell was already in the field, working with the Alyawara, when I joined him for a short but most instructive bit of research. An earlier piece describing another Alyawara day was coauthored by O'Connell (Binford and O'Connell 1984). I have not added his name to this essay, since he is in the field (in Australia again) and is unable to approve or disapprove of this product. He shared every event described herein, but I wrote the essay and have chosen the context for discussing the events presented. It would be interesting to have him comment on my treatment of these events.

2. My adoption was made easy in this case, since O'Connell had been there some time and had already been adopted. When I appeared the Alyawara decided that we were "brothers," and I was given essentially the same kinsmen as O'Connell had.

3. There has been a long and confusing literature treating Australian social organization. One of the first great synthesizers was A.R. Radcliffe-Brown (1930, 1956), who insisted that the social organization was based on the family and the horde, which he identified as a group organized in terms of patriaffiliation and associated together by virtue of virilocal post-marital residence. The horde was said to be a land-holding group. These ideas appear to me to be simply the projection of Western ideas of territoriality (see Binford 1983d) onto the world of Australian hunter-gatherers. Radcliffe-Brown's position was advanced by Elman Service, who, while acknowledging that on-the-ground groups may not strictly speaking be "patrilocal bands," concluded that social organization of the "patrilocal band" type (Service 1962:75–76) was exemplified by the Central Australians (Service 1962:61–62), elaborated by what he called sodalities. Perhaps the most bizarre example of ascribing to the Australians one's own ideas of human nature is James Woodburn's recent suggestion that elaboration of ritual, etc., characteristic of Central Desert Australian life is an "enterprise whereby men, in their political maneuvering, seek to gain control over a woman's potential labour" (cited in Morris 1982:175). I have commented previously that it has always seemed strange to me that anthropologists have not given any attention to the possibility that culture itself is organized; that is, the transmission of culture—particularly as manifest in culturally defined roles—is organized so as to insure descent "without modification" (Binford 1983a:222). Much of what has been discussed as social organization in Australia is almost certainly cultural organization, in my opinion.

4. For some of the recent discussions and controversy concerning Aborigines and archaeologists, see the June 1983 issue of *Australian Archaeology* (no. 16), which contains a fascinating series of articles presenting differing points of view on this very emotional issue.

5. Many of the Alyawara are polygynous, with some men having as many as three wives.

6. The allusions here are to the *fact* that on-the-ground groups are not structured in their composition in terms of jural rules of either postmarital residence or any single kin- or sodality-based mode of affiliation. The Alyawara men are here confirming the position

described by Stanner (1965) regarding local-group organization among the Central Desert Australians.

7. I doubt that any anthropologists are truly participants in the traditional systems they frequently see themselves as studying. The very presence of the anthropologist implies an interactive situation such as we experienced among the Alyawara, a small-scale system interacting with the larger systems out of which the anthropologist comes.

8. It is important to point out that the very collection of ethnographic data is not a simple, straightforward "objective" procedure. What we observe is conditioned by the interpretation of the situation *by the informants*. The question then becomes one of how situations, structured by our characteristics and roles in the social events of our study experience, can ever be viewed as traditional.

9. It will be noted that this conflicts with the interpretation I made from what the Alyawara said. My guess is that Greenway did not get his views from his informants, but from Tindale (1974:caption to color photo 37), who reports that the resin is obtained from "scale infested Triodia grass." The Alyawara may indeed have told me this, but what I understood from their description, given the language problem, was that the grass stems were damaged by abrasion.

10. There have been critics of cross-cultural comparisons who claim that they are only feasible if "the particular historical and cultural dimensions of activity were denied" (Hodder 1982c:5). By making these cross-cultural comparisons I deny no historical or cultural dimensions; I simply seek useful clues to explanation.

11. Long ago I suggested that Australian technology was highly curated. Brian Hayden (1978) attempted to illustrate that this was not true, since most lithics he observed in use were expedient tools used for manufacturing wooden tools, the basic technology used in coping with the environment. One thing he did not consider was the impact on stone tool distributions if they were used to make primary tools (largely of wood) that were curated; most of the lithics end up in residential sites where the curated wooden tools are apt to be made. In turn, the archaeological record of special-activity sites would be improvised, because the *curated* wooden tools were used there. This was the point of my comments on curation and assemblage variability, which Hayden obviously missed.

12. As in all my earlier arguments regarding functional variability, I am denying neither the existence of ethnicity nor its potential importance as a conditioner of variability in the archaeological record. My only concern is for the unambiguous identification of archaeological properties with a clear ethnic, symbolic, or ideological referent.

Chapter 14

An Alyawara Day: Making Men's Knives and Beyond

THE SITE AND THE SETTING OF TOOL MANUFACTURE

On Monday, June 17, 1974, our day started with a visit from two Alyawara men, Dave and Jacob.[1] I asked them about the use of heated stones while O'Connell and I were trying to have breakfast and get some of our notes together in preparation for the upcoming day's work. When the subject of heated stones was actually talked about, given all the other conversations that seemed to be going on, the two men suggested that the roasting of grubs was frequently accomplished by heating stones in a fire and then pulling them back from the coals where it was easier to work. With the stones in an easy access position, the grubs would then be placed on them for cooking. It was also mentioned that in winter sand was frequently heated and spread on one's bed at night.

Our "at home" ethnography was not too successful that morning, so we left our camp and walked to the men's camp where the manufacture of men's knives was beginning.

The men's camp is the place where visiting males sleep, where old men and men having trouble with their wives might also stay, and, most importantly, where the men of the local group spend most of their daylight hours when they are not in the field. Men's camps are constructed only in those Aboriginal settlements at which several families reside and the projected duration of occupation is at least several weeks. In such settlements the men's camp is the spatial focus of "male culture." Essentially all the tools manufactured by men while living in a fairly large residential camp are made in the men's camp. Importantly, craft activities and other kinds of activities requiring considerable space or continuity of placement (see Binford 1983c:165–172, 185–192 for a discussion of space) from one day to the next are carried out in the men's camp. There the daily schedule of family meal preparation and the care of children does not intrude on male activities.

Figure 14.1 shows the internal arrangement of features on the men's camp at Bendaijerum. The main activity areas are the structure with internal bedding areas and hearths (F-H); the windbreak area, with a brush screen and hearths (B-E) positioned in front of the windscreen; a shaded conversation area, with a single white ash hearth (L); and a roasting pit area (A) behind the brush windscreen. In front of the wind-

Originally published in *American Antiquity,* 51:547–562, © 1986.

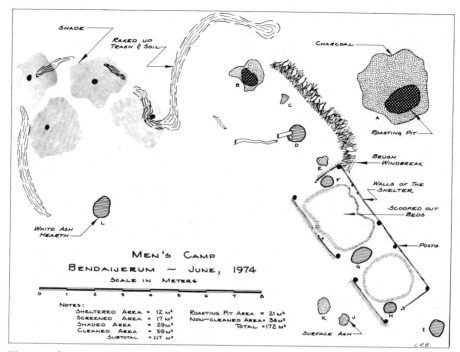

Figure 14.1 Map of the men's camp where the knives were made.

screen and the shelter is an area that was kept clean and used for a variety of activities (the practice of dances, reduction of stone cores, stacking of firewood, etc.). This portion of the site is best described as a maintained, generalized use area.

The overall site area, as recognizable by pulled or trampled vegetation, comprises approximately 272 m². The entire site area can be broken down into several subareas: a shelter (12 m²), the windscreen area (17 m²), the shaded conversation area (29 m²), the generalized use area (59 m²), the roasting pit area (29 m²), and approximately 34 m² of rough work area behind the windscreen where automobiles were repaired. These specific areas, conservatively defined, account for 172 m². This means that there is an additional 100 m² taken up by paths and "dead spaces," such as areas with trash and areas expediently used but not maintained.

On the day of the manufacture of men's knives all of the men were outside. Their activities were centered in the area protected by the windscreen. When we arrived there were eight adult men and two children in the camp. One man was at hearth B preparing *damper*, a large, unleavened bread cake, which is buried into a white ash hearth for cooking. Three men were engaged in tasks directly related to the manufacture of men's knives, and the other four adults were sitting or lying on bedding placed between the brush screen and the hearths (particularly Hearth D in Figure 14.1). The two children were moving around and periodically ran off to other camps in the settlement.

THE MANUFACTURE OF MEN'S KNIVES

On previous days we had worked with the three principal toolmakers while they gathered the raw materials necessary for the manufacture of the knives. These materials were displayed in the men's camp (Figure 14.2). The blanks of fine-grained quartzite had been carried to the camp at Bendaijerum in a paper bark pouch from a lithic quarry (Binford and O'Connell 1984), and the two tablets of spinifex resin (Binford 1984b) were set out on a large firewood "anvil" in front of Hearth D (Figure 14.1).

One of the components needed for the manufacture of men's knives, which we had not previously observed the workmen obtain, was the wood for the handles. Upon our arrival in the camp, Sandy White was working on a section of a tree branch about two and one half inches in diameter and seven inches long that had already been stripped of bark and roughly shaped. Using an ax, he trimmed this piece of wood while it rested on the firewood "anvil" in front of Hearth B (Figure 14.1). Figure 14.3 shows this activity and the simultaneous preparation of damper at Hearth B. The wood was worked into a roughly shaped oval tabloid and passed to another man, Jacob, who began the final shaping of the handle with a metal knife. Meanwhile, Sandy and another man, Johnny Hunter, each selected one of the blanks from the paper bark pouch and began to assess their suitability as blades for men's knives. They also placed the two tablets of spinifex resin close to the smoldering log burning in Hearth D

Figure 14.2 Displaying the raw materials used in assembling the knives.

Figure 14.3 Making the wooden handles.

(Figure 14.4). The heat rendered the resin soft and plastic. While the resin was heating the flakes were fitted to the handles that Jacob had made. For instance, if the blank was wider than the handle, the width of the flake was reduced by lateral retouch (Figure 14.5). At least in this case, retouch is unrelated to the production of the working edge; in fact, in the Aborigines' view retouching renders the lateral edge dull and unsuitable as a cutting edge.[2]

While the resin was warming and the blanks were being prepared for hafting, Jacob had put the finishing touches on the handles. After having been roughed out, the wooden tablet was smoothed and shaped. The 18 cm (7 in.) long tablet was cut into two handles, each about 8 cm (3.25 in.) long. Jacob placed a metal butcher knife across the wooden tablet and pounded it with a hammer. The resulting deep cuts were dug out with the knife tip until the wooden tablet was cut in half. Then the end was trimmed and the two handles were considered ready for use. It was explained that "in the old days" a stone flake would have been used like a saw, working around the wooden piece until a controlled break was possible, and then the break would have been smoothed by rubbing it on a rough stone.

Once the resin was soft the warmest surfaces were pushed onto the butt end of the flake as well as onto the end of the handle that had been selected to fit with the flake. After an appropriate amount had been applied to each of the parts (Figure 14.6) the flake and the handle were separately placed next to the smoldering log so the resin on each would be rendered plastic again. When the resin was pliable the parts were

Figure 14.4 Warming the resin. Note the piece of firewood, which is also used as a work surface.

Figure 14.5 Retouching a flake blank to make it fit the handle.

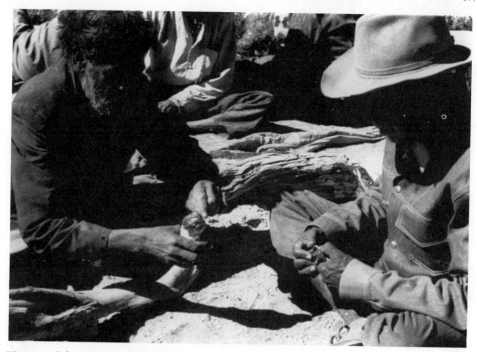

Figure 14.6 Applying mastic to the handles and knife blades.

joined and the resin welded together to form a strong bond between the two elements. After cooling, the fit between handle and flake and the balance of the knife were examined. After the "feel" of the knife was judged correct more resin was applied to the haft, building up the surface into a thicker area at the joint. As new material was added it formed irregular blobs on the tool. These were allowed to cool and then small sticks that had been put in the fire were picked up while still flaming and were rubbed along the resin surface. The men then used their fingers to smooth the surface (Figure 14.7). The result was an even, almost burnished appearance to the resin-covered area of the hafted knife.

During the time that these actions were being carried out by the craftsmen a variety of other activities were occurring in the men's camp. The larger damper or unleavened bread loaf was removed from the ashes (Figure 14.8) and some men began eating chunks of the bread. There had been much conversation in the camp, and some uninitiated young men had joined the group to watch the craftsmen work. Children had spread the news of what was going on, and several additional adults arrived with broken tools to be repaired while there was resin available in the camp. It was explained that when materials were introduced to a men's camp word spread quickly and others would be attracted to the camp to see what was happening and to repair specific tools. For example, Figure 14.9 shows a man binding an adze with kangaroo sinew. This binding was later secured with melted resin.

This focus of attention on tool manufacture and repair prompted the people in the

Figure 14.7 "Ironing" the mastic with a burning stick.

Figure 14.8 Removing the damper from a white ash hearth.

Figure 14.9 Repairing an adze using stone tools and available mastic.

camp to take stock of their tool needs. As a result, the men knew what additional raw materials were needed in the camp as a whole. When any one of them had the opportunity to obtain the needed things, commonly in the context of normal hunting and reconnaissance, they would bring the desired material to the men's camp. In turn, this would frequently precipitate another technological "stock taking," tool-manufacturing, and tool-repairing event. In this manner the group maintained a high level of technological provisioning.

The reality of this situation was played out for us that day in the men's camp. The tool-oriented discussion and the arrival of other men with differing tool needs prompted still further craft activity. The large core that had been returned from the lithic quarry (Binford and O'Connell 1984) was brought out from the brush beside the shelter where it had been cached. Several men worked at reducing this core and produced numbers of flakes, which, in very short order, were distributed throughout the residential encampment for use as utilized flakes, women's knives, and other incidental tools.[3]

The distinctive half-moon flake distribution, previously described from experiences in the lithic quarry (Binford and O'Connell 1984), was repeated in the debris produced by the men reducing the core in the men's camp (Figure 14.10). The blanks that the men wanted to save for particular manufacturing needs were generally placed near the right knee of the worker and picked up when the worker abandoned the core. We repeatedly observed the situation in which another worker would take up

Figure 14.10   Reducing a core in the men's camp. Note the distribution of flakes, with the "keepers" to the right of the worker.

the core reduction, remove his blanks, etc., while his debris accumulated over that of the previous workers. During the lulls between different episodes of workers reducing the core, other men and boys would recover from the arc of debris flakes that were then taken to other family camps at Bendaijerum. After the craft-activity session little remained in the place where the core was reduced except the tiny impact splinters and pieces of small chunky shatter. Later in the day, even this small remnant deposit was obliterated when the men raked and swept the area with branches.

After the men had made the knives—that is, achieved the hafting of the quartzite blanks to the wooden handles—they started to manufacture the sheaths for the knives. Using modern metal knives the men cut up paper bark pouches into shaped pieces designed to fit the stone knife blades. After adjusting the paper bark sheaths to fit individual knives, a large ball of "fur string" was obtained from inside the shelter. This string is best described as a kind of felt. A long human hair used as a "starter" is rolled with a greased hand, which has been lightly rubbed in ocher, over the fur of a very young kangaroo (joey). The short, soft fur is wound around human hair, producing a red felt string. The length is increased by overlapping additional hairs on one end of the string and continuing the winding process. The string is then rolled up into large balls. The large ball of fur string that was brought from the shelter for use in making the sheaths for the knives had been made in this manner. The string was simply wrapped around the paper bark, which in turn was placed around the stone knife blade (Figure 14.11). A great deal of string was wound around the paper bark, enough to cover the sheath.

Once all the men had completed their knives, each was placed on a small leaf of paper bark and all the products of the day were displayed in the men's camp (Figure 14.12). This act marked the end of the men's knife-making activity as they conceived of it. At that point the conversation shifted to the question of who was to receive the various products of the day.

Later we questioned the men and talked a bit about the men's knives. Everyone agreed that these were "fighting knives," used generally after combatants had already fought at close hand with throwing sticks. When the men got in close they would draw their knives and try to cut each other across the abdomen or the back. The knives were tucked under the hair-string belts that the men wore around their waists.

In spite of the rather specific function assigned to these knives everyone mentioned the fact that they could be dismantled and the parts used for a variety of expedient functions. The large amounts of string could be unwound and used for many things "in the field." Similarly, the paper bark sheath could be pulled apart and used for tinder, something particularly useful during the rainy season. The wooden handle could also be used for kindling fires. A throwing stick could be drawn back and forth across the handle to produce a fire plow for making fires in the field. The resin could be reheated and removed for use in tool repair, as medicine for cuts, and for repairing containers. Finally, the stone tool blank could be reworked into other forms and

Figure 14.11 Wrapping the fitted sheath with string.

Figure 14.12 Displaying the finished items.

reduced into multiple flakes if major cutting tasks presented themselves. All in all, the men's knife is perhaps best thought of as a portable repair kit that may only rarely be used as a fighting knife. Men regularly carry them when they travel.

REFLECTIONS ON WHAT WE SAW

Archaeologists have frequently questioned the utility of ethnographic observations to archaeological research. It is common to hear the claim that "this is just another cautionary tale" or "I cannot see how this helps the archaeologist." I have chosen to report the events of a single day in some detail. Many may have similar queries regarding this report. I will attempt to treat such questions in the following discussion.

I consider ethnographic reports of activities and events germane to products archaeologists recover to be important in their own right. I have frequently had the experience when reading ethnographic descriptions of seeing important implications for us in observations made by others in completely different contexts of description. Surely there is value in an archaeologically trained observer's descriptions of events in which items germane to archaeologists were being processed in a living system. What are some of the implications that come to mind as a result of both having observed and written about these experiences?

There is a generic relation between archaeologists' observations on living systems and the interpretative tools they use for inferring the character of past dynamics. If we bring these interpretative tools to bear in a test case, a situation in which both the patterning archaeologists might see and the causes of patterning we would infer are known, then we clearly have the opportunity to test the validity of the principles standing behind our inferential arguments. This is very different from a cautionary tale, which frequently takes the form of an object lesson to archaeologists suggesting that the archaeological record is limited and not capable of yielding information about one or another form of "ethnographic reality." I have suggested many times (e.g., Binford 1987a) that the testing of the validity of our interpretive principles must be made in actual situations in which the dynamic (causal) and the static (derivative) effects are both observable. Clearly, if our inferential techniques and conventions lead to false interpretations when applied to a test case, then we learn something of the limitations of those techniques, conventions, and concepts.

In reflecting on the events of the day described, what about archaeological "culture"? What concepts, conventions, and techniques of inference seem to be implicated? Perhaps the first point to come to mind is that we rarely saw a single craftsman start the manufacture of an item and carry the procedure through to the completion of the tool. Much more commonly, one man might begin making an item, and then it would be passed to another worker who would carry the manufacturing process several steps further and in turn pass the item on to still another man. The one-producer–one-tool equation, assumed in so many stylistic studies, does not seem to characterize Alyawara tool production. I do not mean to imply that such an assumption is always wrong, only that the relation between worker and product seems to be culturally variable. This *fact* is strikingly illustrated by the contrast between my Alyawara experiences and those I had among the Nunamiut Eskimo. In the Eskimo context a craftsman starts a task and almost invariably the same man takes the item to completion. In addition the manufacturer has a strong personal identification with the products of his handiwork. Another worker would not pick up a partially finished item and add his bit, as would occur commonly in an Alyawara men's camp, for such an act would be interpreted as an invasion of the personal space of the artifact's owner.

This simple observation clearly has implications for at least some of the assumptions made about the past by archaeologists who utilize the concept of style. Rather than exploring other implications, I will expand from this particular day to consider other ethnographic experiences as they may affect the concept of style as advocated by some archaeologists.

> Whenever we employ the term "style" we are invariably referring to a highly specific and characteristic *manner of doing something which by its very nature is peculiar to a specific time and place*. . . . What is stylistic is by definition diagnostic, and concerns the manner in which morphological, or formal, variation among artifacts reflects culture-historically significant units of ethnic tradition. (Sackett 1982:63; emphasis added)

> Style . . . is formal variation in material culture that transmits information about personal and social identity. (Wiessner 1983:256)

In both of the above definitions there is an agreement that style is formal variation that conveys information about social-cultural identities. In the case of Sackett, however, we are given a convention for recognizing variability that has stylistic significance. Given such a conception, the question is not, "What does the word style indicate?" Instead, it is "What in the concrete world of archaeological materials is unambiguously stylistic?" This is a middle-range research problem in spite of Sackett's definition (see Binford 1981a:21–30): How do we justify the assignment of stylistic significance to specific formal properties of the archaeological record? Most people have approached this problem with what I (1978a:2–3) have called the *fabrication model* of determinacy.

> Few would disagree that planning is characteristic of acts of fabrication and that fabrication plans are guided by some ideas regarding the desired outcomes. This "fabrication model" comes into question when we ask whether it is relevant to all facts and patterns observable in the archaeological record. Is it an adequate and accurate dynamic model that accounts for the frequency variability in an archaeological assemblage? (Binford 1978a:3)

As suggested above in the ethnographic example, the relation between maker and product is something that is itself culturally variable; hence, the patterning that could result from differing organizations of producer-product relationships is also likely to vary. This relationship is not something that we can expect to be similar from one case to the next, as has been assumed by archaeologists who think that they have a general interpretative procedure for use in stylistic analysis. I must agree with the following:

> The choice of attributes in which to invest style appeared to be the result of historical events, rather than following coherent principles (Wiessner 1983:273)

Wiessner's observation that the infusion of stylistic information is itself culturally variable renders a pan-cultural convention (as proposed recently by Sackett 1982) for measuring ethnic identity an unlikely procedure to discover or invent. My experiences documenting variable relations between manufacturers and their products justify a skeptical view of pan-cultural conventions for the assignment of stylistic significance.

Perhaps even more important to the development of productive skepticism regarding the general utility of defined concepts, such as *style*, is the degree to which we can expect variable assemblages to be produced by participants in a single sociocultural system. If members of a single sociocultural system produce formally variable assemblages of archaeological remains deposited at different locations, then how can we use described differences among assemblages as unambiguous measures of differences in ethnic identity, as Sackett's concept of style would lead us to do? The answer is quite simple. We cannot.

The events described in this article might be developed as a concrete example or demonstration of this position. The men were making men's knives in a men's camp. The organizational basis of the settlement system—a cultural phenomenon—clearly conditions the patterns of debris distribution among localizations of archaeological materials. Organization of the same tools into tool kits useful in carrying out different activities certainly results in formal differences in archaeological by-products of both production and use. If we understand the relation among such properties as lithic debris, food remains, and personal items, particularly as they might vary among different occupied locations, we might begin to diagnose the organizational properties of the settlement system when we see it only as archaeological phenomena. Clearly such concerns are *functional* in that they seek to understand the relations among classes of material remains as differentially structured by the internal organization of a sociocultural system. This view of function is not, however, the view most commonly assumed when the word *function* is used among archaeologists.

Generally, archaeologists assume that function refers to the intended or actual use made of an item in a sociocultural system. Function in this latter sense is more akin to the idea of tool roles (see Camilli 1983) in a pan-system or normative sense of the word. Function, in the sense that I have tried to develop over the years, has reference to the interactive conditions within a system that ensure that the role performance for similar tool forms will regularly differ from one situation to the next (see Binford and Binford 1966). I have also suggested that situational conditions are important in conditioning the use of different tool forms for accomplishing analogous tasks in different situations (Sackett's 1982 isochrestic variation; see Binford 1979, 1984b) and have shown how members of the same ethnic group produce highly variable archaeological remains on the different sites they occupied (Binford 1978a). These are facts of ethnographic experience. They are facts that demonstrate that the concept of style as used by Sackett and many other archaeologists will lead to erroneous conclusions about the past.

What is commonly missed in much discussion of my work is that the term *function* has reference to variability arising as a result of the internal operation—the functioning—of the sociocultural system of interest. More importantly, the functional argument has reference to variability in the composition of the archaeological record. The question of interest is how to distinguish compositional variability arising from the normal internal dynamics of a living system—a condition that regularly exists and that has been repeatedly demonstrated—from variability referable to differences between different systems. The answer to this problem must rest in the development of an adequate and discriminating inferential methodology. This is a middle-range archaeological problem that cannot be solved by polemical or sophistical argument, nor by operational definitions such as Sackett's. If we are to make progress in the accurate construction of the past, we must solve these basic problems accurately and unambiguously. It is the evaluation of the adequacy of our paradigm, the concept of style itself, in dynamic contexts that permits us to recognize the limitations of our conceptual tools. *Style,* as commonly used by archaeologists, is a misleading concept.

The style/function problem is illustrated in additional ways by the events that took place in the Alyawara men's camp. During the description it was emphasized that a variety of different raw materials were required to produce the men's knives. These raw materials had to be obtained at very different places (Binford 1984b; Binford and O'Connell 1984). The processing and transportation problems associated with aggregating a variety of materials are considerable and take a long time. These factors ensure that men's knives will not be manufactured just anywhere, nor immediately as the need arises. Rather, they will usually be manufactured in a men's camp or in male-activity areas associated with conjugal camps that serve for extended periods as the logistical focus of the subsistence-settlement system. Other tool types, such as expediently produced flake knives, may well be produced in almost any site or social context, however, and therefore any debris that is distinctive to each context may be distributed differently among different types of sites.

This argument may be too intuitive for many. Perhaps a better example is provided by the comparison of the formal characteristics shown in the Bendaijerum site plan (Figure 14.1) with those in Figure 14.13. Figure 14.13 is a map of a men's camp we visited on June 6, 1974. It was located in the dry steam bed of the Sandover River and was used by a group of males different from those at the camp shown in Figure 14.1. Nevertheless, they are all Alyawara and had all camped together in the past in various combinations at various times; in short, they are ethnically the same people. Nevertheless, the internal arrangement of the camp, its surroundings as regards the placement of the conjugal camps, and the presence or absence of permanent structures and types of contents (automobiles were present at Bendaijerum and not at Sandover River) all make these two camps formally different from one another in a variety of ways. Similarly, these distinctive properties are characteristic of particular times and places, meeting, for instance, Sackett's (1982) criteria for style. This is functional variability.

Such variability, while it may characterize certain places and time periods (Sackett 1982:63) is, nevertheless, not stylistically diagnostic of ethnic identities, nor it is a by-product of stylistically conditioned isochrestic options and choices. In such cases, style

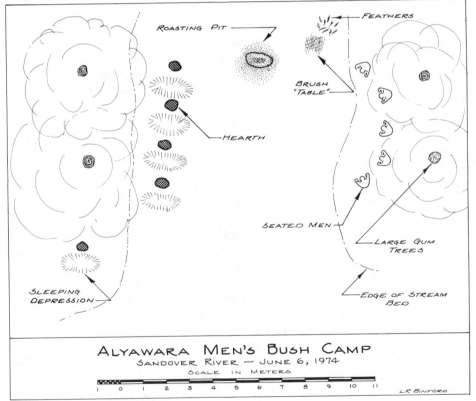

Figure 14.13 Organization of a men's camp on the Sandover River.

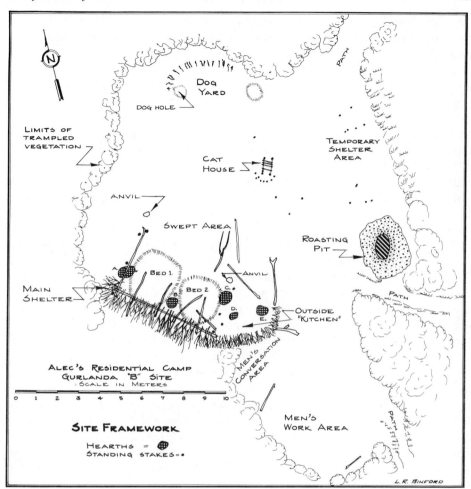

Figure 14.14 Conjugal camp, Gurlanda "B" site.

is certainly not "function writ small" (Sackett 1982:75). Functional variability is never stylistic in the sense discussed by Sackett because it has reference to formal variability within a unit that is ethnically homogeneous in the culture-historical sense or to variability that has independent culture-historical origins unrelated to the conditions of ethnicity.

Perhaps this point may be made again by comparing the men's camp at Bendai-jerum (Figure 14.1) with a conjugal camp (Figure 14.14). The site structure of a conjugal camp—the camp in which a family unit lives within the larger residential encampment—is somewhat different from the men's camps (for a detailed description, see Binford 1987a). In such a camp one or more wives may sleep, children and dogs are commonly present, and all the activities associated with female roles are represented, whereas these are absent in the men's camp (see O'Connell 1977, 1979 for a description of Alyawara settlement types). Viewed archaeologically, these camp types are formally very different. The activities of tool manufacture described in this essay would not be carried out in a conjugal camp that was part of a large encampment. The men's camp and the conjugal camp are not spatially contiguous, so the archaeologist would see them as separate sites. They are formally different in spite of simply being different components of a single residential encampment. Once again they are each distinctive of place. Given the resolution of current dating techniques, an archaeologist could well infer them to be temporally distinct as well, and the differences could be interpreted as measures of ethnic distinctiveness.

The challenge is to develop methods for distinguishing in the archaeological record formal properties that are informative about the organizational properties of a given system from those properties that are stylistic in their meanings or have determinants independent of those conditioning ethnic variability. Style is a concept of the paradigm that considered culture as an explanation. Now we need to explain culture itself.

An anonymous reviewer of this article wrote that Sackett is primarily concerned with how we can use isochrestic style to say something about ethnic groups, even if they are not congruent with those that may have exited prehistorically. I strongly disagree with this statement, which I am afraid describes a common attitude. Most of the justifications for the operational definition of our concepts are made on the basis of common-sense experience in the contemporary world. We look around us and see formal properties of things and behaviors that are "characteristic of time and place" and can in fact be used to make ethnic identity inferences. I can tell the difference between Chinese ceramics and Navajo ceramics, so these experiences seem to justify the use of the style concept as advocated by Sackett and many others. When it is pointed out that the real world is more complex than our naive experiences may have led us to believe, are we really to ignore the complex realities and just go on regardless of the likely lack of congruence between our constructions of the past, as guided by such inadequate concepts as style, and the reality that was the past? Those who answer yes to this question are reactionaries who do not seek to improve the intellectual tools with which we seek to know the past.

This situation was brought home forcefully to me in a session for which I was a discussant at the 1985 SAA meeting in Denver. Research was reported where a chronological sequence was observed in the "styles" of projectile points. Because style was the central concept in terms of which these stratigraphic observations were assimilated by the archaeologists, it was assumed that each distinctive form of projectile point in the stratigraphic sequence was "unique to time and place"; thus, undated sites could be arranged chronologically using the identified "styles" of points. Later research yielded "bad" radiocarbon dates from other sites and also indicated that some of the "styles" might not be temporally unique. What was the response of the investigators? They questioned the radiocarbon dates and the "new" data, because they believed that the original stratigraphy was correct, and more importantly, they thought that they understood the dynamics of stylistic phenomena—it should be unique to time and place.

In such a situation, excavation and the making of new observations cannot increase our knowledge. Because we think our present knowledge and understanding is adequate, we question the empirical world but we never question our knowledge and alleged understanding. The concept of style is a bad concept, as it is commonly used by archaeologists. We need much more work like Wiessner's (1983). We need to address seriously the problem of identifying formal variability that has reference to independent determinant processes, and we need to stop kidding ourselves that all variability is stylistic, as discussed by Sackett (1982). His soul searching regarding the concept of style has failed to address the basic issues. He is still seeking a convention to save the procedure of our traditional approaches to time-space systematics. In my opinion these approaches are obsolete and indefensible. Sackett is engaged in mounting a "re-endorsement" argument.

> Re-endorsement theories are those which, after profound reflection, reach the conclusion that all is well with the existing bank of beliefs, or at least with a substantial part of it, simply in virtue of it being the existing bank of beliefs. (Gellner 1974:46)

The field is not advanced by backward orientations. We must move on to new concerns as we recognize the limitations of old ideas and approaches. Denying limitations ensures stagnation.

NOTES

1. This research was financed by a grant from the Australian Institute for Aboriginal Studies. It was made possible through the kindness of Peter Ucko. James O'Connell and I were working together when the events described here were observed.
2. The retouch is very similar to "backing" but it was produced by hand holding the piece not by retouching on an anvil, as is normally associated with backing tactics.
3. See O'Connell (1974) for a discussion of Alyawara tools.

Chapter 15

Butchering, Sharing, and the Archaeological Record

INTRODUCTION

Richard Gould (1978c, 1980a; Gould and Watson 1982) has made positive claims for his inferential approach, at the same time implying that approaches used by others are limited in various ways. His arguments touch upon important issues currently under debate. For instance, Gould addresses patterns of butchery and the sharing of meat in his discussions of method and procedure. These are issues currently discussed among archaeologists trying to elucidate the behavioral significance of very early archaeological sites. Glynn Isaac (1978a, 1978b, 1980) has been a strong advocate of the view that early man lived in base camps and was organized into social groups within which the sharing of the meaty parts from animals was basic to their way of life. I have challenged this view (Binford 1981a, 1985a) and have been concerned to learn how we might render from the archaeological record an unambiguous interpretation as to whether or not early man was sharing meat (see Binford 1978a:272–273).

A totally different context of arguments stands behind Gould's interest in sharing and in its potential influence on behavior, and, by implication, on patterning in the archaeological record. Gould has stated his case as follows:

> Philosophically, I can regard Binford's analysis of his Nunamiut data as similar to the approach I am advocating here except for the fact that he has not made any explicit effort to incorporate possible ideational factors into his overall argument. Perhaps the Nunamiut really are as "simple" as he suggests, in the sense that he can account simply for their behavior in relation to meat products on a circumstantial basis without recourse to more complex explanations involving ideas and symbols. But the Western Desert Aborigine case contains anomalies that cannot be fully accounted for at this level of reasoning and must be referred to the ideational domain to achieve a satisfactory explanation of all the behavior that was observed. . . . (Gould and Watson 1982:367–368)

> *The strict adherence to a fixed pattern of initial division of meat was explained more parsimoniously with reference to social relations based upon kin-based sharing of food and access to resources . . . than to the direct influence of the immediate circumstances under which hunting occurs.* (Gould and Watson 1982:367; emphasis added)

Originally published in *Journal of Anthropological Archaeology* 3:235–257, © 1984.

In summary, Gould suggests that among the Ngatatjara a rigid and unvarying pattern of butchery is practiced. This rigidity is cited as *anomalous,* presumably in comparison to the great variety of butchering tactics which I (1978a:47–62) reported from the Nunamiut Eskimo. Given Gould's (Gould and Watson 1982:368) belief that when one recognizes an "anomaly" it signals the ideational domain as a conditioner or determinant, he naturally seeks such an explanation in the face of this alleged anomaly. Gould focuses on the ideology of sharing and the ethics of kin-based altruism as the most parsimonious "explanation" for the Australians' rigid butchery pattern. Given Gould's "archaic empiricist" (see Binford 1985a) views, he considers my behavioral descriptions of the Nunamiut as misguided arguments from ethnographic analogy aimed at establishing empirical laws of human behavior. Gould states:

> For Binford, it is circumstance rather than culture that determines human behavior in relation to meat procurement and faunal remains. (Gould and Watson 1982:366)

In fact, in my Nunamiut study, I was examining the archaeological record as manifest in faunal remains. I sought to understand patterning and interlocational variability in terms of the behaviors executed by the Nunamiut actors at places studied archaeologically. My concern was *how the same actors, bearers of a constant "culture" or ideational domain, generated variable patterns of association and covariation among faunal assemblages.* Gould appears to misunderstand this research if he sees it as an attempt to establish that the patterned behavior observed among the Nunamiut was generalizable directly to all hunter-gatherers. Given such a view, Gould cites that different formal behavior of the Ngatatjara Australians as anomalous relative to my Nunamiut descriptions. This difference is then considered a justification for his seeking explanations in the "ideational domain" (Gould and Watson 1982:368).[1]

In the following sections I will consider Gould's use of ethnographic experiences and his advocacy of "living archaeology" as a way of addressing the important issue of assigning meaning to the archaeological record. *I will consider Gould's suggestions in the context of seeking to understand how sharing might be manifest archaeologically.*

My work with the Nunamiut was conducted with the archaeological record as the subject of research. Gould's actualistic studies among the Aborigines do not seem to have been conducted with a similar focus. Instead, he studied the behavior of the aboriginal peoples in the same way an ethnographer might conduct research (see Binford 1983a:391). Having observed the ongoing dynamics of a living system, *Gould then seeks to infer the character of the archaeological record.* This is an argument from ethnographic inference, and it is this very tenuous practice that Gould advocates to all archaeologists under the label of "living archaeology":

> By observing the adaptive behavior of any living human society, we can *derive predictions* about the society's discards, *we are doing living archaeology.* (Gould 1980a:113; emphasis added)

It is these derived "predictions" which should constitute "archaeological signatures"[2] for the "adaptive behaviors" observed.

In the case of Gould's work we are left in the dark regarding the properties which would constitute an "archaeological signature" for the rigid butchering procedure he discusses. Whatever this "signature" might be, Gould would explain it most "parsimoniously" by reference to a strong sharing ethic. It would appear that the "derived prediction" is that the archaeological "signature" would also be rigid and a direct reflection of the butchering pattern, but on these issues Gould is silent. I find this surprising. Why is Gould not addressing the problem of the material correlates for the behavior and mental phenomena which he considers important? I think that the answer hinges on the realization that Gould is not arguing about the archaeological record. A different issue is at stake!

EVALUATING GOULD'S POSITION

In beginning an evaluation, one of the first thoughts to come to my mind is that essentially the same butchering procedure observed by Gould (1967) among the Australians was used by the Nunamiut Eskimo when butchering large to moderate-size birds such as Canada geese, whistling swans, etc. The only difference was (a) the wings were generally removed discretely and did not remain attached to the breast, (b) the breast was not cut into halves at the time of initial butchering, and (c) there was no tail. Otherwise, the butchering procedure was the same as described by Gould for the kangaroo. The butchering pattern which fascinated Gould, when seen in the Nunamiut context, can be understood as another practical behavior pattern accommodated nicely to such situational variables as body size and the proportions of the animals being butchered.[3]

In all fairness, however, Gould has not stressed the formal properties of the butchering sequence as requiring a "cultural" explanation. Instead, he has pointed to the rigidity with which the Australians butcher animals in a "standard" manner as requiring explanation in the ideological domain.

Do the Nunamiut Lack a Strong Sharing Ethic?

Approaching Gould's argument as a scientist, it would seem rational to ask, in the face of a proposed explanation for a given phenomenon, whether the explanation holds up in contexts different from the one which it was invented to accommodate? The strength of a scientific explanation is at least partially measured by the degree to which it facilitates understanding of experiences more comprehensive than those which seemingly rendered the argument rational in the first place. Gould's argument, translated into a scientific frame of reference, would appear as a proposition which suggests that *the greater the adherence to a sharing ethic with regard to meat products, the more rigid will be the butchering procedures employed by the people in question.* Given this general proposition, linked to the observation that the Nunamiut practice extremely variable butchering procedures, we would expect, if the proposition was generally true, that the Nunamiut lacked or had only a very limited commitment to a sharing ethic. Is this true?

One of the inevitable sources of gossip among the Eskimo is a situation, in a context considered appropriate for sharing, where a hunter either failed to share or failed to do it in terms of the kin-based conventions for sharing. Whether men immediately share meat on their return to a residential camp or whether they place their game in the stores of the households they represent is primarily a function of a set of distinctions made by the Nunamiut between hunting for stores versus hunting for immediate consumption. This distinction is commonly associated with hunting for caribou versus local game. Most of the time, local game is considered a target in backup hunting strategies and hence such animals are commonly introduced when the group is poorly provisioned. The animals which fall into this category are mountain sheep, moose, and grizzly bear. These are also the animals most likely to be sought in the mountains during summer when hunting for fat to supplement dried meat stores (see Binford and Chasko 1976:101–111; Speth 1983:143–159).

The factor which primarily conditions whether a hunter shares or places meat in storage in his judgment as to whether or not everybody already has meat. If the verdict is yes, then the hunter turns over his kills to his wife (places them in storage). On the other hand, if kinsmen are judged to have little food and to be in a needy state the hunter shares out anatomical segments much in the same way the Australians share out meat. If the hunter's judgment is incorrect and there are poorly provisioned families in the camp, yet he did not distribute meat, then the gossip circuit is sure to start, aimed at the "insensitive" hunter. Sharing among the Nunamiut is always a combination of kin-based obligations and sensitivity to need. The importance of the latter factor is illustrated by the fact that in actual sharing situations the quantity distributed is at least partially adjusted to the size of the family receiving the food. If the hunter renders the judgment that there are kinsman in need, he then distributes butchered anatomical segments to others in terms of ego-centered (male) kin relationships. Each person who receives a share then generally gives at least part to his wife, and if she prepares it for a meal she may then share out again in terms of her kindred.

> Once meat is brought to the household, the woman takes charge of the cooking. It is also her function to present gifts of meat and fat to other persons. During times of stress her first responsibility beyond the members of her household, is to her parents and other lineal relatives. The second is to her siblings, especially if they reside close by or in the same village, the third is to her husband's parents. Beyond these persons the woman may distribute meat to such close relatives as cousins, aunts, uncles, nieces and nephews of any member of the family, and to friends. No particular cut of meat or part of an animal is associated with or customarily reserved for any particular relative. A gift should be a good piece of meat with fat on it if possible. (Gubser 1965:81–82)

This important distinction between the sex-based responsibilities for sharing is linked among the Nunamiut with the nearly continuous fact of delayed consumption. That is, most of the time consumption is out of stores;[4] hence, sharing is commonly a woman's responsibility carried out at the time of meal preparation and/or serving. If males are hunting for food to go into stores, there is no sharing by the men beyond the division of game among the participants in the hunting party. Only in situations of direct consumption, judged appropriate in terms of general need, does a hunter conduct a meat distribution using the male-centered kinship conventions on his return to camp.

I must conclude that among the Nunamiut there is a strong sharing ethic. Given Gould's "law" we should, therefore, expect them to have a rigid butchering pattern. Alas, this expectation is not met. Long before I studied the Nunamiut, Gubser (1965:81) noted:

> There are many variations in butchering caribou; the determining factors are how the meat is to be transported and how long it is to be stored. If it is to be stored for a long time, the caribou is not skinned but only quartered, beheaded, and eviscerated; then it is stacked up on a hillside. If, say, a woman is planning to carry the meat home by dog pack, she may even sever the meat from the legs and separate the leg bones from each other with her ulu.

My research confirmed and elaborated the earlier observations of Gubser:

> What has been described is probably viewed as a great deal of variability and certainly a consideration of many different factors—means of transport, amount of meat available, outside temperature, and so on. I find it difficult to provide an "idealized" description of what may be called the "Nunamiut method of butchering" (Binford 1978a:87).

These observations support the view that *there is no necessary relationship between the strength of the sharing ethic and the lack of variability in butchering pattern.* In all fairness to Gould he might argue that he never expected there to be a "necessary relationship" between the strength of the sharing ethic and the rigidity of the butchering pattern. He could point out that such a claim would have to be based on an argument from "ethnographic analogy." Such an argument would, in this case, be justified by his experience with the Ngatatjara, from which he has told us there was a strong sharing ethic that explained the rigid butchering pattern. Gould has come out strongly against projecting ethnographic descriptions from one group of people as expectations to be realized among another group. *Why then, does the Nunamiut material bother Gould?* If each society can be expected to culturally unique, exhibiting differing ideological justifications for manifest behavior, why is Gould not content to accept my descriptions of Nunamiut culture? Unfortunately, Gould does not tell us. As in previous discussions, we find that Gould is silent on an issue one might anticipate him to speak out about. As we have queried before, why?

THE NUNAMIUT DATA AS A PARADIGMATIC CHALLENGE

The Nunamiut study presented data which would have been distorted and misrepresented if the traditional interpretative conventions used by archaeologists had been applied to Nunamiut sites. In short, *the variability manifest within the Nunamiut system challenged the normative expectation of internal homogeneity for behavior executed within a given culture.* Gould's reaction to this challenge is sketched out in the following:

> Perhaps the Nunamiut really are as "simple" as he suggests, in the sense that one can account simply for their behavior in relation to meat products on a circumstan-

tial basis without recourse to more complex explanations involving ideas and symbols. (Gould and Watson 1982:367–368).

> On over 70 observed occasions in 1966–1970, the Western Desert Aborigines of Australia, . . . invariably divided macropods (mainly red kangaroo, *Magalaeia rufa*) into the same initial nine pieces, . . . *Clearly some kind of normative principle was at work in the Aborigine case.* (Gould and Watson 1982:366; emphasis added)

In the above quotations we see the issue isolated; Gould expects there to be normative ideological guides to behavior. He expects there to be "mental templates" standing behind manifest behavior and he further expects "cultures" to be internally homogeneous in their repertoire of such templates. Gould observed a pattern, a very repetitive pattern, and assumes along with many others that

> culture is patterned . . . (therefore) the patterning which the archaeologist perceives in his material is a reflection of the patterning of the culture which produced it. (Deetz 1967:6, 7)

Gould is a traditional archaeologist. He assumes certain properties of culture—it is patterned—this patterning is then thought to be manifest in the regular behavior characteristic of the participants in a culturally organized unit. If we do not see regular, internally homogeneous behavior, something is clearly wrong. Gould sees regular behavior in the butchering behaviors of the Ngatatjara. Everything is as it should be. On the other hand, I reported extremely variable behavior as characteristic of participants in a single ethnic group. This is contrary to his paradigmatic expectations. Does he use such seeming contradictions as an opportunity to evaluate the degree to which his preconceived assumptions are productive and appropriate? No. What Gould does is try to cast doubt on the accuracy of my reporting:

> As in much of Binford's earlier work, there is a persistent and high level of ego-involvement that affects the presentation of his findings. In a case like this, where we have a book that will be referred to often by archaeologists in their efforts to explain their own faunal evidence and by ethnoarchaeologists for comparison with findings for other contemporary human societies, this becomes a matter of some concern. (Gould 1979:739)

I have commented previously on the tactics of strict empiricists:

> In the strict empiricists's view of the world, those who do not see nature in the same way as he does must be suffering from a lack of objectivity; all unbiased, objective observers should see the same things, since "nature does not lie." Disagreements among observers are generally considered to derive from flaws in the character of at least some of the disputants. (Binford 1983b:372)

In this vein, Gould chooses to question my "objectivity" rather than his assumptions or his paradigmatic views as to what the world of culture should be like.

Gould's bias is further illustrated by the fact that he ignores my discussions of the variability at issue. I had long ago recognized that the behaviors I witnessed among the Nunamiut were different from others that I had experienced and differed from descriptive accounts of butchering in the literature. My response had been to accept the challenge, to try and explain the differences and similarities noted. For a traditional archaeologist, differences and similarities are not in need of explanation, they are simply accepted as measures of cultural differences and similarities. The latter, in turn, are to be understood in terms of differential histories. Not being a traditional archaeologist, I had offered suggestions as to how we might understand cultural variability itself:

> When inputs to the system are few but large as in the case of the Nunamiut, each consumer unit is participating in homologous logistical, storage, and consumption sequences. Evaluations as to the utility of parts are made along these sequences. On the other hand, when inputs are small few decisions are made along an extended sequence related either to logistics, preservation potential, or consumption priorities. Instead, anatomical parts are differentially distributed among consumer units. In short, differential distributions occur at the locations of processing and differential consumption in the Nunamiut case, whereas among a group like the !Kung differentiation of parts among consumption units occurs by virtue of a distribution of parts to persons, differentially evaluated in terms of kinship, status, or other social idioms. (Binford 1978a:132)

It should be clear that I was well aware of the differences between the Nunamiut, who are logistically organized (see Binford 1980a) and heavily dependent upon storage, and societies where inputs are small but fairly continuous, as in the cases of the !Kung and Gould's Australians. I noted in my Nunamiut studies the following contrasts:

> In the Nunamiut case anatomical parts are differentially evaluated and this scale of evaluation is mapped onto different places and times evaluated in terms of transport consideration, anticipated differentials in storability, and so on. On the other hand, the !Kung most certainly have some similar understanding of the differential utility of anatomical parts but this is mapped onto persons differentially evaluated in such terms as kinship associations. (Binford 1978a:133)

Instead of seeking an explanation for the differences, Gould would have us believe that either (a) the Nunamiut were misrepresented by me, or (b) they were "simple," or (c) I failed to investigate the important symbolic determinants standing behind their use of meat. In other words, Gould is attempting to counter a warranting argument. My descriptions, which rendered it rational to expect cultural systems to be internally differentiated, is simply doubted. My argument that the archaeological record is not simply a material manifestation of mental templates, but instead the actual consequences of concrete behavior, is rejected.

I have argued that many may attempt to execute wonderfully integrated plans but the contingencies of the natural world in which he lives frequently force modifications of these plans. The real-world contingencies, in terms of which men rationally modify their plans, ensure that the archaeological record will vary with these contingencies and not be a simple material projection of the plans and mental images held in the minds of cultured men. It is as a counterclaim regarding the nature of the cultural world that Gould's descriptions of Aborigine behavior take on significance. He claims that in Australia the Aborigines are not "simple" and, to understand their behavior, we must refer to the beliefs which guide and stand behind it. In turn, their behavior is thought to be "properly" normative and internally homogeneous. In short, the

Nunamiut challenge to the traditional paradigm may be dismissed as somehow biased and poorly reported. The world which Gould wishes to see, the world of his paradigm, is restored. The Ngatatjara's repetitive and redundant butchering pattern is to be taken as confirming the old view of culture. Gould's "objective and unbiased" work should therefore save archaeology from demeaning (Gould 1980a:250) itself as it sailed "perilously close to this particular intellectual iceberg" (Gould 1980a:250)—the "new archaeology."

HOW IS THE ARCHAEOLOGICAL RECORD IMPLICATED?

One would expect that since all this argument is taking place among archaeologists there would be some discussion of the properties of the archaeological record. *Gould is totally silent on this issue.* This is not surprising since for traditional archaeologists the meaning of archaeological remains was never considered an issue, they are simply material manifestations of "culture." The problem of what "culture" means is not something that can be solved through the study of material products, since it is a mental phenomenon. As Gould (1978c:833) is fond of telling us, "just because the Western Desert aborigines do it this way today does not mean they did it that way in the past." This is just another way of asserting that there appear to be no necessary linkages between material things and the meanings assigned to them by different peoples. This has always been a troublesome paradox arising from the traditionalists point of view. If one accepts the argument that patterning in material things derives from the ideas and beliefs which guided the observed order being discussed, e.g., the ideological patterns standing behind the material remains, then all one can do is systematize the materially manifest patterns. Then, by an appeal to one's belief as to the nature of culture, the archaeologist may interpret his systematics in terms of the historical dynamics that are believed to condition the differential distribution of "culture" among different populations. This has always been the posture of traditional archaeology.

Today there is an attempt to argue that one can, even must, understand the nature of the ancient ideas and beliefs assumed to guide the observable patterning in material things. This is the posture of Ian Hodder (1982a, 1982b) and many of his colleagues. Hodder's approach is rationalized by his belief that there are certain characteristics of the human mind which condition ideologies in general. With a knowledge of these principles, used artfully in interpretation, one can reconstruct the "cultural context," the actual world of symbols, which is said to have determined the reorganization of matter characterizing the different systems of ideas and values—cultures—of the past. This posture differs from the mainstream of traditional archaeology. It is true that traditional archaeology shared with Hodder and other "contextualists" and "structuralists" the belief that it was ideas and values which guided the actors' behavior and hence "stood behind" observed artifact patterning. Hodder's position, nevertheless, differs in that he denies that similar forms may refer to similar ideas. It was, of course, the latter proposition that made possible historical interpretations from patterned similarities. Hodder argues that any form or artifactual pattern can only be understood in terms of the ideological framework which integrated cognitively the actions and lives of the ancient peoples responsible for it.

For classic traditionalists, ethnoarchaeology can play only a very limited role. If one can justify the argument that there had been no relevant culture change between the archaeological past and the social present, then one can study a modern society for purposes of "fleshing out" a picture of the past. This is the strategy advocated by Oswalt (1974) and described by Gould as a "continuous model" (Gould 1974:39) of ethnoarchaeological analogy. The reason for studying a living group is then to find out about the "culture" which served to motivate and condition the way the "makers" of the artifacts designed their products, restructured their environments, and conceptually integrated action with philosophy. *Under this approach one never really studies the formation processes of the archaeological record, only the rationalizations of the actors for their participation in the processes which might condition an archaeological record.* As I suggested earlier, Gould does not report on the archaeological record as such. He only reports on the dynamics as played out by a series of actors, in the same way an ethnographer might report on experiences (see particularly Gould 1980a:6–28). It would appear that, for Gould, documenting the relationships between actions and ideology proves the reality of his paradigm. The paradigmatic assumptions are therefore vindicated and may be used again as conventions for assigning meaning to the archaeological record. In his terms, we may "derive predictions about the society's discards" (Gould 1980a:113). If his view of culture is correct, and the archaeological record is simply a material manifestation of the ideas and values of ancient men, then, given an understanding of "culture," Gould can "derive predictions" about the properties of the archaeological record. Given this perspective, *ethnographic experience would be cited in justifying assumptions about culture, while archaeological remains would be considered simple patterned reflections of culture.*

Ethnoarchaeological approaches in the hands of Hodder and some of his colleagues are more directed toward the archaeological record, but only from an advocacy perspective. That is, Hodder's recent works (1982a, 1982b) are both organized to illustrate, using ethnographic examples, how patterning in material remains is unintelligible in the absence of a knowledge of the cognitive ideology of the actors that produced it. Once again, the research is not directed toward understanding how patterning in archaeological materials comes into being. It is designed to demonstrate that patterning is dependent upon ideological or cognitive schema. Like Gould, we are generally left to infer the archaeological patterns which are thought to flow from the cognitive schemes "ethnographically" presented. Rarely is any attempt made to document the patterns actually generated. We are expected to "derive predictions" about the archaeological record from verbal descriptions of ideological "guides" to behavior thought to actually control action. Once again, what passes for ethnoarchaeology is not an attempt to explain an archaeological record or develop reliable methods for understanding its formation. Ethnoarchaeology, as practiced in this context, simply becomes studies conducted among living peoples for use as warranting arguments for believing certain things about culture. If one accepts this perspective, or paradigm, interpretive conventions to be used in assigning meaning to the archaeological record simply flow from the internal logic of the paradigm adopted. Under these approaches, the archaeological record is not investigated, and its properties are not explained. Instead, abstracted properties of the record are simply interpreted according to the beliefs of the investigator. Such accommodative arguments serve as middle-range theories for traditional archaeologists. Given the cultural paradigm of your choice, the archaeological record is traditionally linked to this paradigm by the assumption that the patterning in the record is a material manifestation of culture. Dunnell (1971:122) pointed out some years ago that for traditional archaeologists culture "is a means of explanation."

My approach has been different. I have argued that the challenge to scientific archaeology is to investigate the archaeological record. It is only with an understanding of how this record is formed that we will be able to infer accurately properties of interest about the past, including properties of past cultural systems.

Given this perspective, I am interested in how sharing is manifested in the archaeological record. In addition, given the claims by Gould about rigidity in butchering procedures, I am interested in how such procedures might affect patterning in the archaeological record.

EVALUATING GOULD'S ARGUMENT: CONTROL DATA ON SHARING

The Nunamiut Data

While I worked among the Nunamiut Eskimo I had the opportunity to observe many acts of sharing (see Binford 1978a:132–133, 142, 456–457, 471–472, 478). However, the archaeological "signatures" derived from these acts were more difficult to document. Unambiguous data referable to sharing were obtained from only two sites, Ingstad (Binford 1978a:323) and Palangana (Binford 1978a:437). Table 15.1 summarizes the anatomical part frequencies for Dall sheep recovered from different consumer units within each site. On the Ingstad site there were known to have been four sheep killed during the course of the occupation. Two were introduced by unidentified hunters believed to have been of the Tulugak Lake band while the other two sheep were killed by known individuals. The bones from the houses of the two known hunters are summarized in columns 1 and 2 while the faunal remains from the other Tulugak band families are tabulated in columns 3 and 4. Sheep remains from all the residential sites of the Killik River band's families (a visiting band at this site) is summarized in columns 5 and 6. Inspection of the table illustrates the first important point, namely, that *the anatomical parts common at the residence of one family are generally low or absent on the locations of other consumer units within the same site*. This condition derives from the fact that different anatomical segments are the units shared out by hunters. This means that the anatomical units which are represented by only one element from a single individual, such as the skull or the neck, if present within one site will only be present at the residence of one of the consumer units within the site. On the other hand, parts which may be broken down into multiple segments, such as ribs, may tend to exhibit overlapping distributions among a set of consumer locations within a single community.

In these examples, data were selected because they represented rarely killed animals which are almost always shared among the Nunamiut. Since only a few such animals are represented, the mutually exclusive form of anatomical-part patterning expected among separate consumer units within a single community is clearly visible. We may reason that this pattern may tend to break down if *the duration of the*

Table 15.1

Frequencies of Anatomical Parts among Different Residence Groups Derived from "Shared" Dall Sheep

Ingstad site[a]												Palangana site[b]					
Sheep bones at tents of two Tulgakmiut hunters		Sheep bones at tents of other Tulugakmiut families		Sheep bones at tents of Killikmiut families				Sheep remains, House 1		Sheep remains, House 2		Sheep remains, total	
MAU	%	MAU	%	MAU	%	MAU	%	MAU	%	MAU	%	MAU	%
1.0	50.0	0	0	0	0	1.0	29.0	0.5	33.0	0.5	50.0	1.0	67.0
1.0	50.0	0	0	0	0	1.0	29.0	0	0	1.0	100.0	1.0	67.0
2.0	100.0	0	0	0	0	2.0	57.0	0	0	0.5	50.0	0.5	33.0
1.0	50.0	0	0	0	0	1.0	29.0	1.0	66.0	0	0	1.0	67.0
1.0	50.0	0	0	0	0	1.0	29.0	1.0	66.0	0	0	1.0	67.0
1.0	50.0	0	0	0.5	100.0	1.5	43.0	1.5	100.0	0	0	1.5	100.0
0	0	1.5	50.0	0.5	100.0	2.0	57.0	0.5	33.0	0	0	0.5	33.0
0	0.	1.5	50.0	0.5	100.0	2.0	57.0	0.5	33.0	0	0	0.5	33.0
0	0	2.5	83.3	0.5	100.0	2.5	71.0	1.0	66.0	0	0	1.0	67.0
1.0	50.0	2.7	90.0	0	0	2.7	77.0	0.23	15.3	0	0	0.2	13.0
1.0	50.0	0.9	30.0	0	0	1.9	54.0	0	0	0	0	0	0.0
0	0	3.0	100.0	0	0	3.0	86.0	0	0	0.5	50.0	0.5	33.0
1.0	50.0	1.5	50.0	0	0	2.5	71.0	0	0	0.5	50.0	0.5	33.0
2.0	100.0	2.0	66.6	0	0	2.0	57.0	0	0	0	0	0	0.0
1.0	50.0	1.0	33.3	0	0	2.0	57.0	0	0	0	0	0	0.0
1.0	50.0	0	0	0	0	1.0	29.0	0	0	0	0	0	0.0
0.5	25.0	0	0	0	0	0.5	14.0	0	0	0	0	0	0.0
0.5	25.0	0	0	0	0	0.5	14.0	0	0	0	0	0	0.0
0.5	25.0	0	0	0	0	0.5	14.0	0	0	0	0	0	0.0
0	0	2.5	83.3	0	0	2.5	71.0	0.5	33.0	0	0	0.5	33.0
0	0	2.0	66.6	0	0	2.0	57.0	0.5	33.0	0	0	0.5	33.0
1.5	75.0	1.0	33.3	0	0	2.5	71.0	0	0	0	0	0	0.0
1.5	75.0	2.0	66.6	0	0	3.5	100.0	0	0	0.5	50.0	0.5	33.0
0.5	25.0	1.0	33.3	0	0	1.5	43.0	0	0	1.0	100.0	1.0	67.0
0.5	25.0	0.5	16.6	0	0	1.0	29.0	0	0	1.0	100.0	1.0	67.0
0.5	25.0	1.0	33.3	0	0	1.5	43.0	0	0	1.0	100.0	1.0	67.0
0.5	25.0	0.5	16.6	0	0	1.0	29.0	0	0	1.0	100.0	1.0	67.0
0.5	25.0	1.0	33.3	0	0	1.5	43.0	0	0	1.0	100.0	1.0	67.0
0.5	25.0	0	0	0.5	100.0	1.0	29.0	0	0	0	0	0	0.0
0.5	25.0	0	0	0.5	100.0	1.0	29.0	0	0	0	0	0	0.0
0.5	25.0	0	0	0.5	100.0	1.0	29.0	0	0	0	0	0	0.0

[a] Information taken from Binford (1978a: Table 6.21, p. 323, columns 20–25).

[b] Information taken from Binford (1978a: Table 8.4, p. 437, columns 17–20).

occupation is increased and/or there are different hunters representing most of the consumer units present within the community who regularly distribute meat during the course of the occupation. How the pattern diverges from the one illustrated in Table 15.1 will depend upon variability in the hunting success of hunters occupying different nodes within the kinship matrix relative to those receiving shares. I stated the situation with regard to sharing and patterning in the archaeological record some years ago:

> Food distributions are activities conducted in terms of a set of cultural conventions, a mental template if you will, of the proper pattern of distribution in relation to a set of cultural conventions that evaluate people. Since the activities in which such conventions are employed are egocentric, and despite the fact that all members of a group may share common cultural conventions, we can expect two things. The first of these is that the patterning manifested in the faunal remains will vary with the number of persons making distributions. In addition, patterns may change even if only one person is making distributions relative to any changes that may occur in the composition of the group receiving food. The structure of this situation is such that redundancy in patterning, or a lack thereof among segments of a community, would bear *no* relationship to the degree that they shared a common convention for conducting meat distribution! This example illustrates the differences between patterning that results from the execution of a strategy and the conventions used in [guiding] its execution. The archaeological remains derive from the conditions of execution. (Binford 1978a:471–472)

The San Data

Gould might object to my use of Nunamiut observations, given his claims for my overly involved state of mind, so it is important to establish the fact of the signature patterning associated with sharing with observations made by others.

Yellen collected an important and provocative body of data from San camps during his fieldwork in the Kalahari. I have summarized from his maps, descriptions (Yellen 1977b), and inventories (Yellen 1977a) data referring to Camp 10 (//Gakwe/Dwa). This site (Figure 15.1) was occupied for 12 days by 13 adults and 11 children. During that time two gemsbok were killed and parts introduced to the site for distribution by sharing:

> All men go out after the gemsbok that =toma had wounded the day before. They find it dead and butcher it, eating all the marrow from the cannon bones, some ribs, the liver and the head. The rest of the animal is carried back to camp and consumed there. Later during their stay, =toma wounds another young male gemsbok at !kau !kasi. The men go after it the next day and find it alive but unable to run, and they kill it with a spear. At the kill site, the men eat the marrow from the cannon bones, some ribs and part of the liver. The skin and horns are left at the kill, and the remainder of the animal is carried back to camp. (Yellen 1977a:207)

Of course, the above description has only reference to the behavior of the hunters and the particular events taking place before the parts of the introduced animals were actually shared. In another article Yellen (1977b) has an excellent description of the

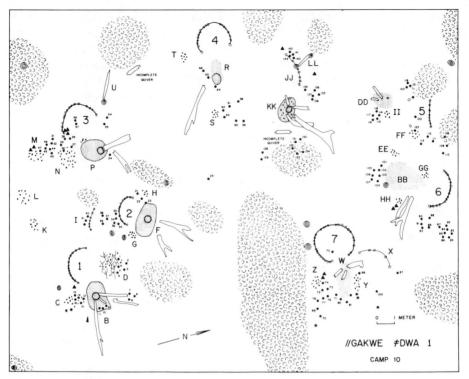

Figure 15.1   Site plan, !Kung Camp 10 (from Yellen 1977b).

meat sharing within a residential camp. This takes place after animals are introduced to the site. Yellen generalizes that there is commonly a three-stage pattern of sharing associated with meat distributions:

> Meat moves from the hunters and carriers upward through the kinship network to parents and in-laws, and then outward and downward again. When sharing is viewed in a specific instance, such as this one, it can be clearly seen why hard and fast distribution rules cannot apply; each kill must be considered as a specific case; the relationships between families who happen to compose a group at that moment and family size must both be taken into account. (Yellen 1977a:289)

It is clear that Yellen is warning the student that the archaeological record reflects the actual behavior as executed, not the normative "culture" which might be thought of as "counciling" such behavior. Ironically Gould, himself, has supplied descriptive material with similar implications. He notes that with smaller kangaroo and euros there is a two-stage pattern of sharing among Ngatatjara hunters (see Gould 1967:58). During his fieldwork Gould was able to trace the acts of sharing in six observed episodes and found that the final size of portions consumed after the two stages of dismemberment and sharing was remarkably the same, averaging 1.23 pounds per share (Gould 1967:59). What this means is that *the faunal remains, as finally introduced into the archaeological record at a residential camp, will most likely be deposited (a) in units of consumption, not units of initial butchering and sharing, (b) in forms resulting from the modifications made during preparation of parts for consumption (cooking, drying, pounding, etc.), and (c) distributed and associated spatially in terms of disposal modes relative to the locations of consumption.* This last point has been astutely made by Yellen as follows:

> Thus in [many] . . . studies . . . patterning is related to a single variable based usually on either primary butchering or tool use. It is instructive that, in the !Kung case, these factors have . . . little effect on the final form of the faunal remains, and that far more important are the last stages of butchering for cooking and direct consumption and selective destruction by natural processes after the bone and bone fragments have been discarded. (Yellen 1977a:327)

Yellen's experiences are in essential agreement with my own when investigating formation processes in ethnographically controlled situations. Keeping this in mind, it is important to return to a consideration of the control data collected by Yellen in the context of known sharing behavior. Table 15.2 summarizes the frequencies of anatomically identified bone fragments listed by Yellen (1977b:207–210) from each of the seven residential locations used by the occupants of Camp 10. Figure 15.2 summarizes the data graphically. What is strikingly illustrated is the same structure of variability as was documented among the Nunamiut. The anatomical parts from the two gemsbok are *differentially* distributed among the separate residential units within the community. The next characteristic to notice is that parts which are capable of easy segmentation are those which are most ubiquitously distributed. Vertebrae appear in six of the seven house sites, ribs occur in all, and pelvic parts were recovered from five of the

Table 15.2

Frequencies of Identified Gemsbok Bone Fragments Associated with Each of the Residential Locations Used by the Occupants of Camp 10

| | Hut area | | | | | | | | | | | | | |
| | 1 | | 2 | | 3 | | 4 | | 5 | | 6 | | 7 | | |
Fragment	No.	%	No.	%	No.	%	No.	%	No.	%	No.	%	No.	%	Total
Cranium	1	.06					1	.04							2
Vertebrae	4	.25	3	.25	0	.00	5	.20	7	.47	12	.63	6	.38	37
Sternum	1	.06													1
Ribs	1	.06	2	.17	6	.40	10	.40	3	.20	5	.26	1	.06	28
Pelvis	7	.44	3	.25	2	.13	1	.04	0	.00	1	.05	0	.00	14
Femur	0	.00	0	.00	2	.13	1	.04	0	.00	0	.00	3	.19	6
Scapula	0	.00	0	.00	4	.27	4	.16	5	.38	0	.00	3	.19	16
Humerus	2	.13	0	.00	0	.00	1	.04	0	.00	1	.05	2	.13	6
Radius-ulna	0	.00	4	.34	0	.00	0	.00	0	.00	0	.00	0	.00	4
Extremity	0	.00	0	.00	1	.07	2	.08	0	.00	0	.00	0	.00	3
Unidentified fragment	0	.00	0	.00	0	.00	0	.00	0	.00	0	.00	1	.06	1
Total	16		12		15		25		15		19		16		118

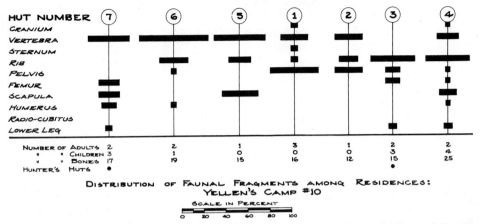

Figure 15.2   Distribution of faunal fragments among !Kung residences in !Kung Camp 10 (data from Yellen 1977b:206–211).

seven residences. In marked contrast, the bones of the upper legs—femur, humerus, scapula—appear in three residences only for each bone.

In the case of Yellen's data, the head and lower legs were not reported to have been returned to the site; nevertheless, traces of these parts are present. It is not clear from the ethnography how they were introduced. I think it is germane, however, that the lower leg parts occur at the residences of the men who killed the animals or at the location of the storage rack. In my experience with the Nunamiut, parts which are "consumed" by the hunting party, i.e., distributed for consumption among the field party in hunting camps or at kill sites, etc., may occasionally be introduced to the residential site by hunters who did not consume all their shares while in the field. These parts are considered as already allocated to the hunter even though the bulk of the meat he transported to the camp may be distributed to kinsmen. Put another way, parts which are considered "field food" and already allocated by whatever convention to the members of the field party may be returned as part of the hunter's share not subject to further distribution within the camp. Such parts are most commonly lower legs as well as head and neck elements, with the occasional addition of some ribs and organ meats. Among the Australians, the parts of the kangaroo that are sometimes consumed in the field are the lower rear legs and the tail. In spite of Gould's skepticism, the pattern of consumption or disposal of marginal parts in the field is a general characteristic among modern hunters, commonly varying with the size of the prey relative to the transport potential of the field party.

I mentioned earlier that meat distributions among the Nunamiut were conducted in terms of kinship conventions but at the same time involved considerations of need. For instance, families positioned at roughly similar kinship distances from the person making the distribution would receive different amounts of meat depending upon the size of the families represented. Figure 15.3 illustrates the relationship between the number of bones and the number of consumers on each residental location. It is clear that there is a generally strong positive linear relationship between the size of the

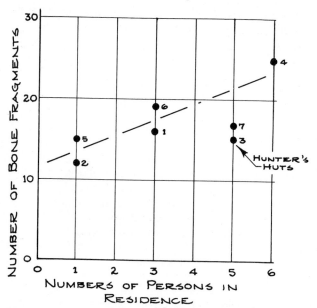

Figure 15.3 Number of bone fragments per hut for hunter and nonhunter residences in !Kung Camp 10 (data from Yellen 1977b:206–211).

shares as measured by numbers of bone and the size of the consumer unit. The two exceptions are the families of the hunters, both of which exhibit anomalously how values for numbers of bones. There is in the literature a kind of "myth" that the sharing ethic is so strong that successful hunters give away all their meat and, hence, tend to eat less well than the dependents of the less skillful hunters. I can understand how some ethnographers might be deceived into thinking this but my experience leads to opposite conclusions. *Successful hunters' families eat better, not only in times of food scarcity, but all the time.* The presence of high frequencies of ribs, pelvic parts, and femurs at hut 3 (Figure 15.2)—the hunter's residence—shows that high-quality food was common at the hunters' hearths. If you add to this the common occurrence of the hunter getting organ meats (no included bones), the lower frequency of bones per number of consumers can be taken to indicate a dominance of higher-quality meat parts introduced to the hunter's camp.

Comparing the San data with that for the Nunamiut, we note the dominance of anatomical parts with a high utility value (see Binford 1978a:15) on residential sites in both cases. The abandonment or consumption of parts of marginal utility by members of the hunting parties at kill or field butchering locations was also noted among the Nunamiut. Finally, there is an extreme assemblage variability among the residential units as also noted among the Nunamiut. This variability does not arise from the fact that each family in the community has a different culture, or practices a different primary butchering strategy, or differentially adheres to a sharing ethic. It arises from the fact that sharing may be guided by a strong ethic and even by normative rules as to how one should share meat parts; but, nevertheless, *the archaeological record is not isomorphic with regard to either the rigidity or the form of the guiding ethics or to the form and sequence of initial butchering activities.* The situation is perhaps best explicated by reference to my thoughts after considering this problem as experienced among the Nunamiut Eskimo:

> This is an interesting situation in terms of the archaeologist's notions of linkage between culture and the structure of archaeological remains. Food distributions are activities conducted in terms of a set of cultural conventions, a mental template if you will, of the proper pattern of distribution in relation to a set of . . . conventions that evaluate people. Since the activities in which such conventions are employed are egocentric, and despite the fact that all members of a group may share common cultural conventions, we can expect two things. The first of these is that the patterning manifested in the faunal remains will vary with the number of persons making distributions. In addition, patterns may change even if only one person is making distributions relative to changes that may occur in the composition of the group receiving food. The structure of this situation is such that redundancy in patterning, or a lack thereof among segments of a community, would bear no relationship to the degree that they shared a common convention for conducting meat distribution! This example illustrates the differences between . . . patterning that results from the execution of a strategy . . . [versus] the conventions [guiding] its execution. The archaeological remains derive from the conditions of execution . . . These . . . are . . . situational conditions. (Binford 1978a:471–472)

Put another way, there is clear interlocational variability in faunal assemblages generated by the San. As in the Nunamiut case the people producing this within-system variability share a common culture. In addition, the San appear to practice a "rigid" primary butchering procedure, yet marked internal or "functional" variability is produced among their sites.

I must conclude that at least two of Gould's criteria for dismissing my Nunamiut-based arguments are rendered suspect by the San data. (1) I did not collect the San data; hence, my alleged biases cannot be said to explain the facts. Yellen can hardly be accused of trying to prove my point of view while he was in the field. If anything, his bias was in the reverse direction. (2) The San can hardly be described as either lacking a sharing ethic, being "simple," or having been poorly investigated in terms of their ideological and belief systems. Gould's objections to my Nunamiut-based arguments are countered by the San data.

There is, however, an additional posture which Gould might assume. He could insist that the Australian materials be considered in terms of themselves. His experiences among the Australians could be cited as providing an empirical case to the contrary and therefore a "spoiler" for generalizations projected from other cases. As I have suggested in this paper, Gould has not thus far made such an argument since he has not demonstrated any archaeological patterning said to be a result of the alleged rigidity or strong commitment to a sharing ethic, which he ascribes to the Australians. I am quite confident that such an attempt would fail, since the patterning among faunal remains within archaeological sites is much more likely to be referable to units of consumption, not units of initial butchering and sharing. This situation is further complicated by patterns of breakage and dispersion arising from cooking, drying, pounding, etc., during processing and consumption, as well as by the disposal modes common at the site. These factors all ensure that explanations other than references to idealized "rules" for sharing would be required for understanding the archaeological record at any given site. At the level of between-site comparisons, the level which Gould criticizes in my Nunamiut analysis, a regular adherence to sharing ethics results in considerable intersite faunal variability and *not site-to-site similarities or cultural homogeneity* imagined by Gould and other traditionalists. Guessing the nature of the archaeological record from abstracted ethnographic observations is at least as dangerous as guessing the ethnographic past from abstracted archaeological observations.

Ironically, it is the intersite variability, the lack of homogeneity, and the lack of formal similarities among a set of culturally identical units that provides the information which makes possible the recognition of patterning indicative of the butchering pattern and perhaps also of sharing. This fact is well illustrated by the multivariate analysis of the Nunamiut faunas from a number of functionally different sites (Binford 1981a:93). The analysis isolated the basic primary butchering units which were the units generally introduced to, or abandoned on, sites. A similar analysis of numerous residential sites where the major source of intersite variability was the differential distribution of anatomical parts among sharing consumer units, as is documented here for both the Nunamiut and the San, should yield the patterned manner of dismemberment and provide some clues as to how rigidly butchering procedures had been adhered to by the ancients. What would not be clear, however, would be whether interassemblage variability was a consequence of functional differences among sites, or if it arose, as has been illustrated in this paper, from sharing anatomical parts of differing size and abundance among independent consumer units. The challenge to the archaeologist is to develop ways of reducing ambiguity and increasing the accuracy with which we may analytically identify past causes of variability in the archaeological record. Gould's strategy of doubting my descriptions of variability and suggesting that the Australians were not as "simple" or perhaps were more "cultured" than the Nunamiut since they appeared to have a more ideologically regulated butchering pattern simply misses the point of archaeological investigations and misleads the unsuspecting as to the nature of archaeological research, particularly the role of ethnographic information in such research.

NOTES

1. This approach is logical only if Gould accepts the Nunamiut descriptions as lawlike propositions. They were never presented as such.

2. Gould claims that he first heard this phrase from James O'Connell in Canberra (Gould 1980a:253). However, his first use of the phrase is in a review of Binford's (1978a:131) book, in which it is used repeatedly.

3. Many writers, such as Hodder (1982a, 1982b), condemn cross-cultural comparisons. They claim that the meanings of similar things must be different in different cultural contexts. Gould probably agrees on this point.

4. There has been considerable confusion in the recent literature regarding factors conditioning storage and its role as a conditioner of complex social roles (see Meillassoux 1973; Testart 1982; Woodburn 1982; Wiessner 1982; cf. Binford 1980a; Ingold 1983).

Chapter 16

Styles of Style

It is very clear from Sackett's recent reply to my comments on his arguments regarding style that he is upset (Sackett 1986a). I am really sorry about this, but nevertheless I consider his earlier writings and his reply to my article both to have missed the issues involved and to have misrepresented them. Perhaps the following comments will bring the literature back to a discussion of issues.

I do not think there is an archaeologist alive who has not sorted his artifacts into gross "functional categories," such as projectile points, and then proceeded through various operations to recognize "styles" of projectile points thought to have socioethnic referents in the past. This basic procedure has characterized archaeological approaches to formal variability since essentially the beginning of the discipline. Archaeologists have always either implicitly or explicitly recognized that both style and function may be manifest in the same artifacts. There has been much discussion about how to cope analytically with the distinct possibility that style may have "causes" of variation that are different and operate independently of properties that have more direct "functional causes" or conditioners. Contrary to what Sackett suggests, early in my career, while I was almost exclusively engaged in a detailed and long-term study of lithics, it seemed to me that there were no unambiguous ways of recognizing these different potential contributors to overall formal variability. My studies of lithic reduction were quite extensive (for the time) and included details of formal variability that might be referable to traditionally learned motor habits as well as seemingly "artisan-specific" details of lithic modification (Binford 1963a, 1963b, 1963c, 1963d; Binford and Papworth 1963; Binford and Quimby 1963). Much later, while reading Sackett's extended discussions of style, I discovered that like most archaeologists I had been studying "isochrestic style" without the benefit of Sackett's discussion! The principle seemed simple: You do not compare apples and oranges. Given that there may be several sources of variation observable in the entities we recover, analysts must seek to hold one potential source of variability constant in order to see another unambiguously (see Binford 1965). This old principle seemed to me to be the importance of Sackett's discussion of isochrestic style; however, he elaborates:

> I argue that the specific forms assumed by objects of material culture represent what amounts to series of specific choices made by artisans, whether consciously or not, from a broad spectrum of equally viable alternative ways of achieving the

Originally published in *Journal of Anthropological Archaeology* 8, © 1989.

same end. I refer to such choices as constituting *isochrestic* (literally, "equivalent in use") variation. (Sackett 1986a:630)

One can hardly ignore the similarity between this statement and Ruth Benedict's famous idealistic statement regarding the "great arc of culture" (see Benedict 1934). When I read such statements, I see an introduction of idealism and the traditional ideas of where culture comes from—i.e., human choices. I will return to this point later. My first reaction as a methodologist was to ask how in fact we can establish "functional equivalents" and how we know the range of "equally viable alternatives" available to an artisan. Back in the early 1960s I was already having great difficulty with this problem when I was "unknowingly" using an isochrestic approach to the study of style. What is a functional equivalent? For instance, in 1963 I discussed the problem this way:

> In any system there are elements which, for certain tasks, can be considered functionally equivalent but not functionally isomorphic. For instance, horseback riding and bicycle riding in certain situations may be functionally equivalent modes of transportation, both serving to transport a single individual at rates exceeding that of foot travel. On the other hand, they are not functionally isomorphic in that a bicycle cannot be efficiently used to traverse a stream or rugged terrain, whereas a horse may be efficient in such a context. (Binford 1963a, 1972a:298–299)

The requirement that functional equivalents also be functionally isomorphic if "choices" of one alternative versus the other were to be exclusively referable to tradition or ethnic distinctiveness seemed clear to me. If what we considered to be functional equivalents (a judgment made by us about the organization of reality in the past) were not functionally isomorphic, then choices of alternatives by past artisans and persons could well be rational and practical selections of differing alternatives made with respect to the organizational context in which they found themselves. These types of choices could vary independently of simple notions of ethnicity, and of the guiding hand of isochrestic tradition as conceived by Sackett. In short, for Sackett's isochrestic approach to work, it is my understanding that (a) the traits or characteristics of interest have to be selectively neutral, and (b) we have to be able to distinguish selectively neutral traits from those that were conditioned in their distribution and spatial patterning by selective factors operating on the choices of actors independently of their notions of self-identity and their commitment to traditionally learned ways of doing things. Only when these conditions were met could we claim that differences between "time and place" and unambiguously referable to "who the actors were" versus "what they did and why."

A second argument may be mounted in favor of "isochrestic" or other forms of stylistic variability—that is, the difference between unconscious and conscious "choice." Certainly, many formal properties of artifacts may be the result of unconscious, traditionally guided behavior. When this is the case, rational or conditioned choice of alternatives would be irrelevant and the problem of functional isomorphism and selectively neutral phenomena would not be troubling, at least for some places and times. (This view, however, recognizes that things unconsciously conditioned at one time could be raised to the level of consciousness at others.)

Long ago I explored the possibility of recognizing functional equivalents, and I basically gave up. First, I learned that from my modern perspective what might be considered functional equivalents, arrowheads were arrowheads, hearths were hearths, pots were pots, etc., frequently turned out on increased knowledge not to be bounded classes of artifacts that were in any way functional equivalents. The variability meant something. Hence, there seemed little chance of meeting the procedural requirements of the "isochrestic" approach that Sackett has recently resurrected. Each time I subdivided the class of things I initially thought represented "functional equivalents," I learned that given a greater knowledge of technology and techniques of production even my subdivisions did not turn out to be functional equivalents. Instead, they indicated good, rational, well-informed responsive action on the part of the artisans who were operating in practical contexts that I initially did not appreciate. As we worked at increasingly fine grained levels of pattern recognition in the archaeological record linked to increased study of technology, I came to the conclusion that the major determinant of my judgment as to what was a functional equivalent turned out to be my own ignorance or blind commitment to a belief about culture itself.

For instance, the classic model of stylistic variability presented years ago by Jim Ford (1954, 1962) seems to me to fail completely because of his argument that candles and electric lights are "functional equivalents" and, in another of his examples, that house forms or architectural designs are "functional equivalents." Surely the forces leading to the development and adoption of electricity are far more complicated than a selectively neutral choice to replace candles with their "functional equivalent"— electric lights. An additional problem arises as a "rider" to the isochrestic approach. That is, how do we deal with changes in tradition as they are operationally recognized using stylistic concepts such as the one Sackett proposes? If isochrestic variability is referable to tradition, and to all that the term *tradition* conventionally implies regarding the question "who the people are," we may reasonably ask, to what does a change in tradition refer? It seems to me that Sackett's suggestions lead us back again into the dilemma of traditional archaeology.

Sackett's arguments make assumptions about several important points. First, the appearance of an isochrestic form of "style" has no explanation; it represents a choice on the part of "culture participants" for which no explanation can be given from the perspective of the archaeological investigators. It simply marks the act of choice on the part of ancient persons. Similarly, the disappearance of a stylistic form equally has no explanation; it again represents the acts of choice on the part of ancient participants. Finally, our ability to "see" patterning is simply a function of the scale at which choices were shared among ancient populations. It is this last assumption that makes possible the equation of "styles" with ancient ethnic units, since such units are conceived as segments of the population who share a common "culture."

With this approach there can be no explanation of culture itself, nor can there be any explanation of culture history. By assumptive definition, our ability to see "culture history" directly informs us about continuities or the lack thereof in the temporal and spatial distributions of populations who shared more cultural elements—assembled by choice-making participants—in the past. This posture requires us to infer that a change in social identity (regardless of how this change was conceived by the ancients) is indicated when we are faced with patterns of punctuated change in those properties chosen by us to be indicators of shared "culture-style" seen in the archaeological record.

If one assumes, as Sackett does, that the unit of socioethnic identity is recognizable by its traditional stability in isochrestic choices, what do we infer when we encounter a punctuated instability in archaeological sequences? Sackett's arguments follow the same logic as that which forced the common interpretation by traditional archaeologists of many migrations in the past. All such argument is dependent upon the assumption that what is traditional is selectively neutral and not subject to perturbation except by reshuffling the bearers of tradition. One can also argue that *the fact that characteristics may be stable does not ensure that they are selectively neutral.* All that may be indicated is that, given relative stability in the selective regime, some reliable responses have been worked out. If there is change in the selective regime, then new or different "choices" may be more appropriate and, importantly, differentially appropriate to segments of the populations previously seen as sharing a high order of common practices.

What I am suggesting is that "choice" may well be conditioned and even determined in an evolutionary sense. Sackett's definitional approach—which amounts to a series of stipulative arguments about the meaning of variability in the archaeological record—ensures conventional interpretation but does not allow a search for explanations of the properties being interpreted. Under the logic of "isochresticism," as presented by Sackett, we have essentially three interpretative choices (as did traditional archaeologists): new isochrestic alternatives were introduced from elsewhere (diffusion), new isochrestic alternatives were introduced within the local population (independent invention), or the continuity of tradition was interrupted by a change in the identity of the actors (migration). I think we should seek a level of understanding far beyond these simple interpretive conventions.

If we adopt a processual approach we can certainly imagine interruptions in the continuity of a tradition without any change in the actual identity of the breeding populations or socially organized segments participating in the changes, and we can expect that explanation does not simply rest with "accidental" infusions of new or greater ranges of "isochrestic choices." There may in fact be an explanation for the changes: the alleged isochrestic choices may not be selectively neutral! A regular and understandable process may be at work that may be understood in terms other than post hoc inventions of events.

This is not to say that events conceived as traditional archaeologists imagined did not take place, only that the methodology of traditional archaeology and "isochrestism" as presented by Sackett ensures that all change and variability will be assimilated into an ethnic-history model of the past. We must have approaches that will permit us to differentiate events of history (what we seek to explain) from the explanations of those events. This means we must not only see the archaeological record as reflecting ethnic histories but that independent of our ability to "see" such phenomena we must also be able to monitor the organizational properties of past interactive dynamics that may well have conditioned those events and "choices" that signal for us the ancient operation of interesting dynamic phenomena. Simply reducing the interesting patterns of variability to "choices" only demands that we understand what conditioned those "choices."

I have seen nothing in Sackett's discussion that admits the possibility of explaining culture change and variability other than an implicit assumption of "free will" in choice-making by ancient individuals. If such an assumption is denied by Sackett, then the alternative seems to be simply that culture causes culture, in that choice may be conditioned by "compatibilities" with earlier cultural choices. I find these ideas stifling to science, and to the search for explanations of culture process. Evolutionary processes could well bring about change in the range of "isochrestic alternatives," in the relevance of "isochrestic alternatives" already known or present, as well as a restructuring of identity groups themselves. I have thought that the search for such understanding is worth investigating. As I read Sackett, his discussions and definitions tell us what meanings to attach to variability, how such patterning comes into being, and where the locus of causation rests—in the minds of choice-making individuals. With such a posture, research designed to explore the causes of culture change and variability is truncated, and we are urged to return to the easy task of making up culture history using Sackett's conventions.

I do not consider it silly to entertain the possibility that sometimes traits may be selectively neutral while under differing selective contexts the same traits could be selectively conditioned in enlightening ways. If this is a reasonable set of possibilities to investigate, then how do we recognize unambiguously the processual roles of traits in order to be able to assert that their patterning in time and space is an unambiguous measure of tradition or clue to the simple intergenerational or regional disposition of ethnic units? Selective forces can also be expected to have characteristic placements in "time and space." The only answer I have heard is offered by traditional archaeologists who, recognizing the problem, acknowledge that the only way was by studying the spatial and temporal continuity in the patterning among selected traits. Those traits that meet our a priori expectations as to how culture "behaves" would then be chosen by the archaeologist as stylistically significant (see Binford and Sabloff 1982). This is conventionalism of the worst kind.

Returning to a more practical consideration, I thought that the problems discussed above were built into the traditional approach, although at the time we did not call such problems *isochrestism*. I long ago considered the problem of selective "neutrality" and concluded that its solution was beyond my abilities during the era when I was working on the problem of style. Because of this I suggested that we explore an approach that was not dependent on our a priori and, certainly, limited ability to isolate "neutral" or functionally equivalent classes of artifacts. If style can result from unconscious phenomena, then rational choices would not condition stability in the results of such unconsciously learned or habitually acquired characteristics, and we might be able to develop a means of identifying actors independently of what might be conditioning what they did when consciously coping with a dynamic world. It was this shift in approach that prompted my suggestions that we seek traits reflecting motor habits and other learned, habitual actions that could be expected to *cross-cut or to appear on functionally different classes of phenomena*. This was a suggestion regarding a potentially useful approach not, as we will see, a claim about the ontological nature of style. It certainly was not a move toward the conception of style in exclusively iconological terms, as Sackett (1985:154) has claimed. In short, I reasoned that we might profitably seek style where functional variability appears irrelevant to its expression, rather than trying to control or hold function constant. Sackett seizes upon this suggestion (made originally in the context of lithic studies; see Binford 1963a, 1972a:299; Binford and Papworth 1963:78; Binford and Quimby 1963, where it was emphasized that lithic reduction strategies may "crosscut" or stand behind formal tool design) for his own purposes—that is, to argue that I have proposed a rival ontological argument regarding the locus of style, which he identifies as iconological and rooted in "ceramic sociology" (Sackett 1977:376).

Let us see what I have said on this issue. After discussing what Rouse (1960:314) had termed procedural and conceptual modes (Binford 1965, 1972:200), which clearly recognized the differences between "symbols" and unconscious traditions dictating habitual variability, I proceeded to discuss potential sources of variation conditioned by the sociocultural context or, as Sackett would say, "who the actors were."

> With regard to the sociocultural context of formal variability, two broad classes of variation can be recognized which crosscut the categories mentioned above. *Primary functional variation* is that which is directly related to the specific use made of the vessel in question; for example, the differences between a plate and a storage jar. *Secondary functional variation* is a by-product of the social context of the manufacturers of the vessel or of the social context of the intended use of the item, or both.

> This variation may arise from a traditional way of doing things within a family or a larger social unit, or it may serve as a conscious expression of between-group solidarity. Certain design characteristics may become standardized as symbols appropriate to vessels used in specific social contexts. At this level of analysis we may recall Linton's (1936:403–421) statement that any given cultural item may vary with regard to form, meaning, use, and function in variable cultural contexts. (Binford 1965, 1972a:200)

> What is idiosyncratic secondary functional variation in one group may symbolize political ties in another. Primary functional variation in one social system may be partially incorporated as secondary functional variation in another. (Binford 1965, 1972a:202)

Despite these statements, which sought to guide us to the isolation of different sources of variability in the archaeological record, Sackett reduces my position to that of advocating only the "iconological approach." Such misunderstanding of my writing is apparent in many of Sackett's articles. One example is Sackett's (1982:82–94) discussion of the well-documented interassemblage variability problem regarding the interpretive challenge offered by the Mousterian. For instance, in the 1965 paper cited above I clearly identify secondary functional variability as having reference both to unconscious formal properties arising from traditional or habitually learned ways of craft execution and to consciously acknowledged, socially conditioned symbols. I then proceed to suggest that when temporal patterning is being considered the term *tradition* should apply to

> continuity in those formal attributes which vary with the social context of manufacture exclusive of the variability related to the use of the item. This is termed *stylistic variability* (Binford 1971, 1972a:220), and on a single time horizon such a tradition would be spatially defined as a *style zone.* (Binford 1965, 1972a:203)

Clearly these distinctions presuppose an analytical ability to recognize function, in my sense of the word. Since, in my experience, this turns out to be very difficult when only morphological criteria are used, I therefore chose to focus on those properties that seemed to have a chance of unambiguously telling us "who the actors were." I was not offering an ontological argument about the "locus" of style.

It should be pointed out that on this issue Sackett begins to reveal his own goals in discussion. For instance, he notes that Upper Paleolithic assemblages tend to be distributed in a spatial mosaic, where spatial comparison results in what I referred to above as *style zones,* a term he erroneously attributes to Sally Binford (Sackett 1982:86). He then proceeds to assert that the use of this term implies a commitment to his straw man position, that of the ceramic sociologist! Clearly my use of the term *style zone* had reference to both habitually executed patterns and symbolically conscious organization of formal variability, not only to the latter, as Sackett suggests. (Today, in the face of strong empirical evidence that they may vary independently, I would not lump these two sources of variability together; see Wiessner 1983 and, particularly, 1985). Sackett (1982:86) nevertheless asserts that "iconology plays a highly visible role in Binford's interpretation. It equally pervades his chain of argument." To paraphrase Sackett's own words in reply to this situation: "We are not simply dealing here with a difference of informed opinions. The gulf between what my article[s] actually say[s] and [Sackett's] characterization of it is so great as to cast doubt upon the veracity of his reporting and to raise the question of whether he himself believes I hold the position he attributes to me" (Sackett 1986a:631; I have substituted Sackett's name for mine). In developing his representation of my arguments, Sackett then goes on to suggest the following: "For example, at one point we find him [Binford] maintaining that Mousterian variation has to be functional because a scraper index (one of the key criteria for drawing divisions among Middle Paleolithic industries) could not possibly have ethnic significance (Sackett 1982:86)."

It is true I offered such an argument, but not in the context in which Sackett presents it—that is, because of my commitment to an iconological argument as to the nature of style. The fact is, I was arguing against an undifferentiated idea of style, one in which Sackett's isochrestic variation was lumped with iconological ideas, as presented by Bordes. Bordes's arguments regarding the interpretation of Mousterian variability were rooted in his belief in the self-conscious maintenance of ethnic distinctiveness by members of Mousterian "tribes." Bordes himself gave just an example regarding Quina scrapers in his arguments with me (see Bordes 1968:144–145;

Bordes and Bordes 1970 for a very explicit statement of his position on style as conscious group pride). I was attacking the very idea Sackett claims I was committed to! I was also attacking the position Sackett advocates.

Sackett then goes on to make further erroneous conclusions regarding my alleged commitment to iconological notions of style, which

> allows [Binford] to dismiss out of hand certain kinds of evidence his opponents could consider to be highly relevant. It might be admitted, for example, that a scraper has no direct symbolic value in the iconological sense. But if one were to define ethnicity in terms broader than iconology alone and to note that different sets of tools may be used by different groups of people in alternative isochrestic "styles" of activities such as butchering and carpentry, a scraper index might not be dismissed so easily as a potential means for drawing ethnic distinctions in the archaeological record. (Sackett 1982:86)

This statement seems to me to have all properties of taking Alice by the hand and walking right through the looking glass. It presupposes the existence of selectively neutral "alternative tool designs" for use in such activities as butchering and carpentry, but it fails to acknowledge that the scraper index being discussed is an index that describes the relative frequency of a single form of scraper retouch in contexts of other scraper forms and combinations present in the *same* assemblage. It seems clear to me that if one accepts the scraper index as an ethnic marker, then all the other scraper traits that do not covary or that sort independently in associational contexts, for instance simple convex scrapers, but nevertheless consistently co-occur with the indexed scrapers (Quina, in this case), must not be ethnic markers! In short, isochrestism as presented by Sackett assumes variety but at the same time presupposes that archaeologists can magically identify the variants that have ethnic significance. This seems to be a heavy methodological burden to bear.

The Quina index covaries positively with young animals of all species, clearly suggesting spring and summer animal exploitation, while it varies inversely with the amount of introduced lithic material not rendered into formal tools as well as with flake size and, when environment is controlled for, with frequencies of burned pieces of lithic material. It also varies positively with exotic raw materials. I could go on and on describing other patterned relationships exhibited by Quina scraper index (for example, I find it fascinating that the index covaries positively with the occurrence of mineral crayons). The clear indication seems to be that the index has a high value in cold environments, it is high when there are good seasonal indicators of summer, and it is also high when relatively few Levallois materials are found in the same level and when most flakes produced at the site are small. I find it difficult to imagine an ethnic group that only exists in summer and has an isochrestic bias in favor of young animals coupled with what appears to be a cultural bias for high mobility and longer maintenance of tools introduced from elsewhere. Yet such isochrestic ethnic indicators disappear in other seasons! Clearly we have to imagine an extreme form of ethnic seasonal migration while acknowledging that local people were using the same region in fall and winter but conveniently disappearing in summer. *It appears much more likely that the "isochrestic" variability in scraper design is varying with changing organizational contexts of persons responding differentially to the dynamics of their environment.* In this instance I think a very strong case can be made for isochrestic variability in Sackett's sense being not the result of ethnic choices but representing functional variability in the organizational dynamics of a single cultural system. This position was not drawn because of an irrational choice made by me as to the nature of style.

Sackett assumes that he can recognize functional equivalents a priori; I do not; He also assumes that isochrestic variability arises from choices made in the context of a shared culture, where there is a normative, static commitment to the production of traditional forms handed down from original choice-makers. In my experience, isochrestic variability (in Sackett's sense of the term) is the very essence of organizational variability within ethnic groups, providing them with the adaptive flexibility to deal with the dynamics of the environment (both natural and social) in which they live. What may appear to be "functional equivalents" to us may not have been conceived as such by the ancients. Sackett does not address this real world ambiguity confronting our analytical methods. His lack of commitment to analytical resolution of perceived ambiguities (which, in my opinion, his approach ensures we will not see) means that he will do exactly what he suggests that I do—namely, dismiss the scraper index as a clue to organizational phenomena and interpret it "conventionally" as an ethnic indicator.

I generally do not agree with a priori assumptions asserting that we know how culture works and how it is manifest in the archaeological record. I think that that is the prime subject of our investigations. I am against the simple definitional approaches as expounded by Sackett. I am against his suggestions that by virtue of immersion in a data base we will miraculously be guided to accurate interpretations of the ethnically structured past. I am against arguments that begin with ontological assumptions and proceed to the stipulation of interpretative principles as Sackett is doing. All of these approaches put the cart before the horse in scientific approaches to learning. We want to seek a knowledge of "ontological" conditions, not assume we know beforehand based on analogical arguments with sales catalogues of tools or simple arguments about World War II weapons.

That Sackett has not understood this is indicated by his suggestion (quoted above) that I dogmatically dismiss the scraper index as used by Bordes as a major ethnic identifier. None of my discussions with Bordes concerned this issue. I did not suggest that Bordes's interpretations were incorrect, only that I could see no sound methodology ensuring that they were. I was presenting arguments to the effect that the same observations could reasonably have different referents in the past. If such a reasonable possibility exists, then clearly the challenge is to conduct the needed research to permit us to resolve interpretative ambiguities. I was advocating research, not a simple judgment based on someone's belief as to what was true of the past. Sackett's suggestion that my arguments imply a simple dismissal of the scraper index as a potential ethnic marker reveals his failure to understand the issues.

Sackett's stipulative argument basically ensures that we do not need to do methodological research; instead he asserts there is an adequacy in his reasoned speculations about processes operative in the past. From this august position Sackett sees no value in my globe-trotting efforts to conduct methodological research. I should be a "real" archaeologist and dedicate myself to a lifetime study of a provincial segment of the archaeological record. How this can lead to a better understanding of the past is suggested to rest solely with the empirical insights that would naturally flow from such an intimate knowledge of a data base. Sackett's position "dismisses" functional, ecological, or evolutionary explanations—only accidents of culture history, which mediate traditionally conditioned choices. This a priori "insight" should guide our interpretations. This is equivalent to Bordes's suggestion that the correlation between denticulate tools and horses at Combe Grenal is to be understood not in functional terms but as evidence of cultural distinctiveness, where the Denticulate Mousterian ibe had a "tradition" of horse hunting (Bordes and Bordes 1970:71). This position is xactly what Sackett has in mind:

> That artisans strongly tend to conform to and perpetuate the isochrestic options dictated by their craft traditions is presumably no different from their conforming to and perpetuating the specific motor habits, cuisines, hunting practices, attitudes and supernatural beliefs appropriate to and characteristic of the social grouping in which such traditions are fostered. Isochrestic choice permeates all aspects of social and cultural life. While its root causes may be obscure, its need is obvious. . . . Life would simply be chaotic or altogether impossible without it. Order, skill, facility in human relations and technology require the definitiveness and effectiveness that come from choosing specific lines of procedure from the nearly infinite arc of possibility and then sticking to them. (Sackett 1985:158)

Here we have one of the clearest statements of traditional archaeology I have seen. Isochrestic choice is in fact what stands behind cultural variability. Cultural variability results from having made choices from that great Benedictine "arc" of variability. Making such choices is to be understood in classic "functional" terms (as argued by Radcliffe-Brown [1965]), where social solidarity is the currency with which we can understand variability among cultures, and cohesive social life is made possible by conservative commitment to order, made possible by making a set of choices and then "sticking to them." This is an essentialist argument in which conservatism in all aspects of human life is essential to the continuation of human life divorced from the interactive world of coping with reality. Variability among cultural systems simply has reference to this essential principle of human action; no explanation in evolutionary, ecological, or organizational terms can be offered.

Given such a view, it is no accident that Sackett's "clarification" of the issue of functional variability as argued in the Bordes-Binford debate takes a predictable form. He denies the dynamic of tactically flexible behavior that varies with goals and situations as recognized by people and is in turn subject to selection as to whether or not varying goals can be achieved through similar means in different environmental or situational settings. He offers instead his belief that man behaves in a nonresponsive, conservative fashion, perhaps eating horses because of who they are ethnically.

Culture is mankind's extrasomatic means of adaptation, and seeing it only as a conservative, stability-fostering phenomenon does not help us to understand its variability or its changes. Functional variability for me always has selective implications, and the contexts of selection can be expected to crosscut and frequently to vary independently of the "social identities" of the actors and, more importantly, may actually be a causal agent in ethnogenesis. For all his discussion of functional variability, Sackett denies such variability and the explanatory challenge it presents. This was the problem with normative, sharing approaches to archaeological variability in the traditional paradigm. It was in fact what justified commitments to simple measures of similarity and difference as adequate measures of "cultural" distinctiveness. Sackett appears to be a man caught in the middle. On the one hand he discusses functional variability (Sackett 1982:76–77, 1986a:628–629) and seems to acknowledge variability that is independent of "who the actors were" (see his 1985 reply to Wiessner, who is pointing to just these kinds of dynamics), while at the same time he suggests that we should ignore these documented processes and "go further" by seeing them as variant properties in macro–style zones, which he sees as resulting from choices from his great arc of selectively neutral variability. For Sackett, functional variability appears irrelevant to understanding cultural variability and, more importantly, variability as presented to us in the archaeological record. Sackett views the challenge to the archaeologist as simply to somehow see the boundaries between choice suites and then we would be accurately isolating the boundaries of choice-making populations who were corporately committed to maintaining "law and order" in their social lives. I said I thought that Sackett was offering a reendorsement argument, and I can find no reason to change this appraisal.

Further, I have begun to note a characteristic in some of Sackett's recent work, which I term here the "Sackett switch" in argument. A good example of this may be found in his discussion of the curation argument. He distorts what I have to say in many ways while seeking to recast my suggestions into a *reductio ad absurdum* form of critique. Perhaps the best example is to refer to my criticism of the traditional approaches to time-space systematics regardless of where and when they are practiced (see Binford 1982b) and then to cite the results of those classificatory exercises that I specifically criticized (e.g., those conducted on European Upper Paleolithic remains) as arguments against my criticisms (see Sackett 1982:91–92). This is simply not an answer to my criticism. In fact, Sackett's entire discussion of curation is based on a distortion of my arguments; he has apparently made no attempt to understand the issues involved. For instance, "to date Binford has provided no specific evidence of what he has in mind by curated tools in the Paleolithic save for two vague clues: that their manufacture should entail considerable investment on the artisan's part and that they may not appear until the 'later phases' of Upper Paleolithic times" (Sackett 1982:93–94).

This is a good example of the "Sackett switch." I have not attempted to analyze the Upper Paleolithic. I have not addressed my attentions to explaining Upper Paleolithic variability. I originally introduced the curation argument into the literature on interassemblage variability as an example of Bordes's violation of his own principles of argument when he introduced the results of White and Peterson's Australian research into his argument (see Binford 1973). I suggested that some of the differences between Mousterian and Australian assemblages might be a consequence of organizational differences, giving curation as an example of one such possible contrast. I attempted no analysis of the situation—I only suggested that it could be important, noting that contrasts between Upper Paleolithic and Mousterian assemblages could have reference to similar organizational contrasts, especially since Bordes believed that the Mousterian was an example of expediently produced and used lithics. Sackett makes it sound as if I am misleading Upper Paleolithic researchers by not doing analysis and thereby demonstrating the utility of my ideas. I am not an Upper Paleolithic researcher.

Is this "failure" on my part the reason Sackett fails to read accurately what has been said? I think not. Instead, as I see it, his treatment of the literature stems from his commitment to traditional ideas of cultural variability (read ethnic variability, which nevertheless may not correspond to how ethnic groups are actually partitioned). Given Sackett's commitment to "choices" seemingly made solely to reduce chaotic living, anything can happen. There can be no analytical methods for exploring why culture or "ethnicity" is variable, since any combination of behaviors, beliefs, actions, etc., can be chosen by the ancients. Our only recourse is to recognize cohesive suites of end products exhibiting some redundant patterning spatially and temporally and then display this recognized pattern in terms of our time-space systematics. Not surprisingly, this same belief in choice permeates his procedural suggestions to other archaeologists:

> Given the potentially enormous range of alternative ways style may be expected to express itself, readers who might wish to apply the isochrestic approach can safely assume that *their own insight into a data base they know at first hand will likely prove of greater value in designing an appropriate strategy for attacking its stylistic component than any methodological suggestions of a general nature that I might propose.* In fact, the most useful comments I can offer may have greater relevance to the state of mind of the researchers than to their methodology. . . . [S]tyle soon comes to be regarded as a pattern to be pursued rather than a problem to be resolved. . . . Its pursuit will not in fact be ended until the potential of the archaeological record itself is exhausted. (Sackett 1982:108–109; emphasis added)

Herein lies Sackett's message. All his discussion seems to be directed toward an ontological claim as to the nature of style, and his position is simply that all patterned cultural variability is stylistic. It arises from choices made by actors. There are no explanations to be sought. If we were to realize this, then all this silly discussion of methods for isolating variables, seeking to understand variability, etc., would be recognized as useless. We should proceed by "getting to know" our data and by developing our artistic skills for recognizing patterns. Patterning referable to time and place is, after all, style, and as Sackett suggests, its systematics is the desired goal of our research.

This is an approach that is rooted in an essentialist explanation for phenomena, and in turn it makes the empiricist's assumption that, given the "essential" nature of style, any good observer should be able to recognize its essential characteristics. Those who do not see the same things as Sackett are either limited or consciously obstructionist. In his most recent essay Sackett follows just such an argumentative procedure, suggesting that my failure to answer his earlier articles arises from my hope that others would not read them (Sackett 1986a:632).

While I have covered the issues as I see them, Sackett has introduced another dimension into the literature that must receive comment. This dimension borders on the level of *ad hominem* argument although it is clothed in other forms. For example, he states (1986a:632) that I do not understand his arguments, presumably because of my limitations, or because I have a chauvinistic commitment to my own personal "style" as unfolded in the literature. He reiterates his belief that there is only one way to understand the archaeological record: "wrestling simultaneously with style and function in a body of relevant data that one controls at a high level of detail. It calls in short for a specialist's intimate working knowledge of a given block of the ethnographic or archaeological records" (Sackett 1986a:632). He then goes on to state that [Binford] is not a "journeyman scientist in the usual sense of the word and [Binford] commands no such body of data. Nor is he likely to so long as his research is restricted to the lines of his 'short but instructive' stay among the Alyawara" (Sackett 1986a:632). This statement clearly questions my qualifications to comment on the problem of style, and at the same time asserts that his pronouncements are well founded because of his long-term initial commitment to stylistic recognition. In the Alyawara instance cited by Sackett, I was forced to change my research plans in Australia for personal reasons (the death of my son). Nevertheless, Sackett is willing to accept the Australian research episode as indicative of a normative personal style "chosen" by me. So much for Sackett's ability to intuitively recognize style!

Sackett's final argument of dismissal is that my motives in archaeological research are questionable, stemming not from a commitment to learning but from my attempts to write a revisionist's history of archaeology in which I place myself in a central position by presumably falsely opposing what I am trying to do with what was traditionally done in archaeology. Sackett is astonished by my suggestion that the concept of style is so intimately tied to the traditional position that we might better discuss the problem of reliably recognizing archaeological properties that have reference to "who the actors were" from properties that have reference to "what they did" in terms other than style. As I have tried to illustrate, Sackett argues that these are not different problems or properties with perhaps independent distributions and differing explanations but instead a dual manifestation of a single phenomenon—ethnicity.

I simply think that Sackett is wrong, that his suggestions regarding the "ontological" character of style are misleading and unproductive, and that given his approach one could not recognize the difference between assemblages produced by members of the same ethnic group and formally analogous assemblages produced by members of different ethnic groups. All he has done is to deny that his approach holds to the view that gross assemblage similarities are a direct measure of ethnic distance. What then does Sackett propose? How do we recognize ontologically "true" style? All I have heard is that we should "wrestle" with our data, make a long and journeymanlike commitment to a single data base, and then pursue "patterns" (which, as Sackett cautions, can be anything). If we use this methodology, somehow the truth of the past will be forthcoming. This is to be done in the intellectual context of belief that equates what people do with who they are. In short, the problems I have raised and addressed do not exist, yet it is implied that Sackett could solve them if they did!

Finally, Sackett suggests that his isochrestic approach represents an exposure of the false nature of previously discussed problems and points the way to a new "synthesis free of the doctrinaire baggage that now encumbers them" (Sackett 1986a:633). This is not the result of research to which Sackett claims to be committed. It is word magic, which exempts him from facing some of the interesting issues in contemporary archaeology, thereby permitting him to practice his *art* in a field substantially committed to scientific procedures.

Chapter 17

Researching Ambiguity: Frames of Reference and Site Structure

I have made the point several times that one of the goals of ethnoarchaeological research should be to aid in the development of methods for inference justification. Research aimed at the justification of inferences has been called middle-range research. There is, however, a great deal of confusion over what is meant by this phrase, and there are dissatisfactions with the point of view (Raab and Goodyear 1984) as well as alternative approaches for which claims of superiority have been made (Gould 1980a; Schiffer 1985). This paper represents a further attempt at clarification.

It has been claimed, for instance, that middle-range research is just another name for "formation processes" (sensu Schiffer 1976 [Raab and Goodyear 1984]). This is misleading. I have consistently suggested that middle-range research should be aimed at the isolation of organizational variables characteristic of past systems. On the other hand, most ethnographers and many archaeologists view the past in episodic terms, with the expectation that understanding of the archaeological record will somehow emerge from the exposition of the cumulative consequences of past events and episodes seen in their particularistic characteristics. It is fully acknowledged that we should research such details and develop our analytical and recognitory skills in this direction. Nevertheless, the latter approach, while generally accepting the view that the archaeological record may be a compound or at least an aggregate of remnants from past events, draws the archaeologist's attention to increasingly particular conditions and events, with the expectation that after each particular is "understood" somehow a picture of a greater "whole" will emerge. This is a classic inductivist approach and, in my opinion, will never lead to an understanding of organizational facts. An important job of the archaeologist is to focus on organizational facts and not on the particular behaviors executed in the constraining contexts of organizations.

If we consider organization to be the determinant and the conditioning factor structuring behavioral process, and we recognize that the archaeological record is a result of different episodic or incidental punctuations of a process, then clearly the knowledge needed to understand variable events is the organized conditioners for those events. A cultural system is simply another way of labeling the organizational components that condition the processes in which human actors participate.[1] If we hope to understand event sequences or patterned indicators of process, we must seek

Originally appeared in *Method and Theory for Activity Area Research*, edited by Susan Kent, published by Columbia University Press, New York, pp. 449–512, © 1987.

to understand the organizational frameworks within which such events and processes proceeded. In addition, we must realize that organizations may be considered to exist at differing structural levels. For the archaeologist, it is sometimes very important to recognize the past relevance of certain organizational conditioners of behavior. I have suggested, for instance, that cultural forms of adaptation may be relatively recent (Binford 1982c). If such a suggestion is even minimally warranted, it is of interest for the archaeologist to develop reliable ways of recognizing culturally (as opposed to nonculturally) organized hominid systems. Obviously, behavior would be conditioned differently in such differing organizational contexts.

One very heated current debate in paleoanthropology revolves around the question of whether the early hominids lived like culturally organized human foragers, characterized by sexual division of labor, food sharing, and perhaps speaking a primitive language (Isaac 1978a, 1978b). Or were these hominids nonculturally organized and different from modern foraging peoples in their subsistence strategies (Binford 1981a, 1982c, 1984c)? Clearly we would like to know these things as well as being able to recognize other clues to perhaps distinctive organizational properties of the ancient past. Given the way current arguments are framed, the challenge to the archaeologist is to develop, through middle-range research, unambiguous archaeological diagnostics for the strategies we thus far have conceptualized. If the archaeological record presents us with patterned facts that are ambiguous with regard to the strategies we have conceptualized, then new middle-range research is clearly demanded. Such research could lead to the recognition of other, previously unrecognized strategies or of inadequacies in our knowledge of the relationship between the strategies as dynamically conceptualized and the statics as manifested archaeologically. One important strategy is to reduce ambiguities in the recognition techniques used to identify organizational phenomena archaeologically.

As an example more germane to the material to be developed later, it should be pointed out that I have proposed two contrastive forms of organization characteristic of hunter-gatherer subsistence-labor organization, collector and forager strategies (Binford 1980a). In very general terms, collector strategies operate to move resources to consumers while forager strategies operate to move consumers to the resources. It is recognized that both strategies may appear in the organization of a single society, perhaps differentiated seasonally or with respect to other contingencies. It is also recognized that both strategies may appear to be operating simultaneously at different levels of organized behavior within the organization of a single society. In other words, while individuals are hunting they may act as collectors, although the pattern of residential movement throughout the year may exhibit characteristics of the forager strategy in that consumers are being repositioned relative to resources in the habitat.

The land use and "site types" generated in the context of an almost pure collector strategy have been studied (Binford 1978a). At the time of the Nunamiut study the Eskimo were essentially sedentary, hence there were few "forager" characteristics to the residential pattern. It is true that they had been mobile in the recent past and that the archaeological patterning characteristic of their residential sites reflected some "positioning" with respect to resource distributions. Nevertheless, at the level of labor organization they were collector strategists.

Faced with the problem of identifying types of sites, many archaeologists might uncritically adopt, through an argument from ethnographic analogy, the distinctive patterns that I was able to demonstrate among the Nunamiut (Binford 1978a) between functionally different types of sites and the contents of faunal remains found therein as a form of operational definition of a "hunting camp" or a "processing location," etc. This approach represents the classic abuse of ethnographic analogy (see Binford 1977a:3–51 for a criticism of such an approach). It fails to take into account the archaeological consequences of similar behaviors that may be organized differently (see Binford 1983a:392 for a discussion of the phenomenon). Behavior is not the only phenomenon documented in the archaeological record. The organizational framework within which behavior is executed is also documented. Without an understanding of the framework, the behavior may appear to be erratic or particularistic, and the remains from that behavior may be ambiguous. It is the view advocated here that research designed to resolve this apparent ambiguity is one of the major avenues to organizational understanding.

The research discussed below is designed to provide case material on a system that is traditionally organized in the forager mode. It is hoped that this analysis of behaviors, which are similar to those of the previously described Nunamiut Eskimo but are executed in the context of a very different subsistence/settlement system, is informative regarding middle-range research and illustrates the limitations of a strictly behavioral approach.

FAUNA: APPROACH TO RESEARCH

In earlier work I developed an approach to faunal study that examined the economic anatomy of animals actualistically (Binford 1978a), and this knowledge was used to evaluate the behaviors of past peoples in their use of animal products. Economic anatomy can be considered quite literally as a *frame of reference,* functioning much like a screen upon which slides are projected. Different consequences of past decisions or behavioral strategies are reflected in anatomical-part frequencies when they are projected against a knowledge of economic anatomy. The varying patterns of bias in the frequencies of anatomical parts provide some clue to the organization of past behavior when referred to the frame of reference—the differential distribution of usable materials on the skeleton of an animal. By using this approach, I will of necessity be describing the ethnographically observed behavior relative to known skeletal morphology. Later I will be studying the biased occurrences of bone frequencies as recovered from Aboriginal sites, viewed with the same frame of reference. This approach renders unnecessary such arguments from ethnographic analogy as, for example, the argument that high frequencies of phalanges and metapodials indicate a kill site or a hunting camp when judged from the Nunamiut experience. As pointed out, however, we want to learn about the differing ways that similar or analogous behaviors may be differently organized cross-culturally. The use of ethnographic analogy in the above manner prevents such understanding. The important question is how, under different systems of organized behavior, similar behaviors (for example, the discard of anatomical parts of marginal utility) are differentially integrated systemically with other behaviors. Surely, most archaeologists must realize that this is an essential feature of cultural variability!

The important statement in the above general discussion is *how, under different systems of organized behavior, similar behaviors are differentially integrated with other behaviors.* What this means for the archaeologist is that analysis must be aimed at the elucidation of differing forms of interaction among otherwise similar things. Many archaeologists consider the search for categorical or signature "correlates" for discrete aspects of past systems to be our goal. Ambiguity for such persons signals failure and a reason for turning away from the discussion. *"I am convinced that using Binford's procedures one ought to be able to 'prove' that any assemblage is a carnivore accumulation"* (Freeman 1983:366, emphasis added). This statement represents a classic case of failure to understand the important role of recognizing ambiguity when interpreting archaeological observations.

Failure to appreciate the important research opportunity provided by the recognition of ambiguity is well illustrated in the current debates surrounding the interpretation of early hominid sites. I have emphasized that the original excavators of the Olduvai sites noted numerous clues indicating that the integrity of those sites was low or at least suspect (Binford 1981a). Multiple agents, notably hominids, hyenas, and lions, had been identified as potential contributors to the composition of the faunal assemblage. Nevertheless, the response of most investigators has been to dismiss the implications of the data. Animal coprolites, extensive animal tooth marks on bones, and anatomical-part frequency patterning indistinguishable from that known to be produced by animals quite independent of any human involvement are all explained with post hoc arguments that save the investigator's view of the past, in spite of the facts. For instance, the coprolites and gnawing marks have been dismissed as a consequence of animals being attracted to meat and garbage accumulations generated by the hominids (Bunn 1983:28; Isaac 1983a:11; Potts 1983:51). Given this interpretation, the assemblage can be attributed to hominid behavior and the evidence of non-hominid agents dismissed as epiphenomenal. In short, the site contents are treated as unambiguous relative to hominid behavior. What is even more surprising is that some investigators acknowledge the lack of exclusive integrity for the deposits and yet blissfully interpret the content and characteristics of the deposits as if the hominids were the exclusive agents responsible for their character (see Potts 1983; Shipman 1983; and, more recently, Jones 1984). The failure to acknowledge the importance of demonstrated ambiguity is irresponsible at best. The failure to recognize the important research opportunity that the recognition of ambiguity presents is simply shortsighted.

The substantive debates cited above are not the only examples of failures to acknowledge key issues in archaeological research. For instance, the use of ethnographic analogy to warrant the interpretation of a "head and lower leg" anatomical-part frequency graph as indicative of a kill site never addresses the issue of how the simple behavior of disposing of marginal anatomical parts differs in the context of differentially organized subsistence-settlement systems. On the other hand, merely citing a noted difference as "cultural" begs the question of understanding cultural differences (e.g., Hodder 1982a:159–161). I am convinced that selection operates on cultural systems at the organizational level, resulting in analogous behaviors being differentially integrated with other behaviors, each of which might well have cross-systems analogues.

The use of a frame of reference conceived in the sense of the economic anatomy of an animal permits us to recognize analogous behaviors relative to that framework, and then we can turn our attention to the structural context of these behaviors as archaeologically documented for differing systems. This means that research is not oriented strictly to behavioral "correlates" (Schiffer 1976:13) but to the differential manner in which recognizable behaviors are integrated relative to other archaeological indicators of past behavior as a clue to recognizing different forms of culturally organized systems. In this paper I will be focusing on how faunal remains studied from the perspective of their economic anatomy are related to facts of site structure, and how this relationship can be used as a clue to recognizing differently organized subsistence-settlement systems.

ETHNOGRAPHIC OBSERVATIONS: THE ALYAWARA CASE

In 1974 I had the opportunity to work with James O'Connell while studying the Alyawara, an Arendic-speaking group of Central Desert Australian Aborigines.[2] While working among the Alyawara we mapped and collected the fauna from a residential site on the Gurlanda "B" site, which had been occupied by an Alyawara family for approximately six months. The observations made relative to the composition of the faunal assemblage collected from this site are integrated below with site-structural facts.

General Characteristics of the Faunal Assemblage

There were 816 bone fragments in the site assemblage. Of these, kangaroo bones represent 92.4 percent (752 bones). There were 38 bones from domestic cattle, representing 4.8 percent of the assemblage, and an additional 20 bones from domestic sheep, representing 2.5 percent. Reptile, rabbit, and two unidentified innominates were the other 6 bones recovered from the site. Table 17.1 summarizes the bone frequencies for red kangaroo, cattle, and sheep by minimal animal unit (MAU; Binford 1984c).

Several points are of interest here. First, the kangaroo body-part frequencies are dominated by heads and lower rear legs. This is a frequency pattern that has been commonly seen in parts abandoned on kill-butchery sites and hunting camps by people who are logistically organized (Binford 1980a). This pattern is also seen in faunal remains transported from kill sites by nonhuman predator scavengers (Binford 1981a:229). In both cases the common feature is that the head and lower legs are marginal parts. They are parts with high bone-to-meat ratios and they are the parts that are consumed last, if at all, by primary carnivores. In addition, they are the parts least likely to be transported by humans when hard decisions must be made as to which

Table 17.1

Gurlanda "B" Site Faunal Assemblage

	Kangaroo			Cow and domestic sheep		
Element name	No. elements in whole animal	Site MAU	Indexed MAU[a]	No. elements in whole animal	Site MAU	Indexed MAU[a]
Skull[b]	2	15	60.0	2	5	100.0
Mandible	2	17	68.0	2	3	60.0
Incisor	—	—	—	—	—	0
Atlas vertebra	1	0	0	1	1	40.0
Axis vertebra	1	0	0	1	1	40.0
Cervical vertebrae	5	2	3.2	5	0	0
Thoracic vertebrae	13	8	5.4	13	1	3.2
Lumbar vertebrae	6	2	2.6	6	6	40.0
Caudal vertebrae	24	12	4.0	24	0	0
Ribs	26	36	9.6	26	0	0
Scapulae	2	4	16.0	2	1	20.0
Humeri	2	3	12.5	2	0	0
Radii	2	2	8.0	2	1	20.0
Innominates	2	9	36.0	2	5	100.0
Femurs	2	2	8.0	2	1	20.0
Tibiae	2	4	16.0	2	3	60.0
Fibulae	2	13	52.0	—	—	—
Calcanei	2	14	56.0	2	0	0
Tarsals	10	4	3.2	10	3	1
Metatarsals	2 (4th)	25 (4th)	100.0	2	0	0

[a] Indexed MAU values are derived from the MAU values. The MAU values are calculated by taking the observed frequency of the bone and dividing it by the anatomical frequency of the bone. The indexed MAU values are derived by taking the highest value of MAU and dividing all other values by it, then multiplying the quotient by 100.
[b] Skulls are given an anatomical frequency of two in this study, although this would appear contrary to common sense. Because the skulls of kangaroos are relatively fragile, the Aborigines frequently split them sagitally while consuming them. The easiest way to monitor this consumption pattern is to give skulls (i.e., crania) an anatomical frequency of two. This figure is also used for cow and sheep crania to maintain a consistent and comparable figure.

parts should be carried to the residential location. These are typically the parts that logistically organized hunters consume in the field so as not to reduce the quantity of high-quality meat that they would be able to return to the residential unit. This same pattern has been observed among such nonlogistically organized hunters as the San (Yellen 1977a:207), who regularly share all meat for immediate consumption. While kangaroos are anatomically different from the animals thus far studied in the context of recent taphonomic research, it would appear (Tribe and Peel 1963) that the lower rear legs and the heads of kangaroos are as marginal a food source as those parts are on mammals that have been studied with respect to economic anatomy.

The pattern of kangaroo-part frequencies documented here is consistent with patterns known from other residential sites where contemporary hunters were living (see Binford 1978a:323, columns 20–25) or where whole animals were being processed. That is, hunters returning whole animals to camps, where meat distributions are made, commonly keep the marginal parts for themselves or simply dispose of them at the butchering site. This is not to say that they keep only the marginal parts, rather that low-quality parts are rarely distributed as "gifts" during sharing episodes. This pattern also has been recently observed among the !Kung, where meat distributions similar to those conducted by the Alyawara are carried out (Binford 1984d).

In the Alyawara case, we have ethnographic knowledge that we are dealing with a system organized differently from that of the Nunamiut. Among the Eskimo there are extended logistical aspects to the settlement system, and many logistically related sites are produced. Disposal of marginal parts occurs in the initial stages of processing carcasses and, hence, occurs at kill-butchering sites, hunting camps, and some processing locations. Among the Alyawara, where storage is not practiced, hunting is conducted for direct consumption and the prey are small- to medium-sized animals. Whole animals are commonly introduced into the residential sites, and hence disposal of marginal parts occurs there.[3]

The ability to see the organizational context of behavior is made possible by the use of a knowledge-based frame of reference. It is the facts within this frame of reference about which uniformitarian assumptions are made, not the behavior of humans or "symbolic principles" as advocated by idealists and "contextual" archaeologists (Hodder 1982a:215) or as criticized by traditionalists like Gould (see Binford 1985a for a discussion of this issue). The frame of reference permits us to see similar behaviors arising from different past organizations of behavior when archaeological facts are arrayed against this framework and then studied from the perspective of the structural context provided by the archaeological record. This point is further illustrated with the remains of animals other than kangaroo.

Shifting to the anatomical parts from cattle and sheep we see a totally different pattern. Pelvic parts and lumbar vertebrae are common from both domestic species, suggesting that Alec (the occupant of the site) was a common recipient of these high-quality food parts when other band members were distributing the meat. Heads were also represented, as were some marrow bones from the lower rear legs of both sheep and cattle. It should be pointed out that kangaroos are extremely deficient in fat relative to animals domesticated or hunted in other parts of the world (Tribe and Peel 1963:284). For this reason it is suggested that minor concentrations of fat may be "overexploited" by aboriginal Australians relative to users of other types of animals elsewhere (see Speth 1983 and Speth and Spielmann 1983 for discussions of the importance of fat). It is well known that the Aborigines regularly pound up bones, particularly vertebrae, and consume them in this pulverized fashion. This is equivalent, from a consumption standpoint, to processing bones for bone juice or rendering bone grease, as practiced by other peoples for maximizing the consumable fat from the animals taken.[4] I think that some of the low body-part frequencies at our site arose from differential amounts of destruction during processing and are therefore not directly reflective of sharing or of the patterns of butchery, which are behaviors upon which many archaeologists focus when discussing body-part frequencies. Of course this hunch can only be evaluated by reference to additional facts that can be warranted as measures of processing and other destructive behaviors.

The anatomical-part frequencies represented in the faunal assemblage for the domestic species are very different from the frequencies of kangaroo parts. The kangaroos were all hunted, and certainly many of those represented were killed by the male occupant of the site. The hunter shared these animals with other families in the camp. On the other hand, the domestic animals were killed by a band representative and Alec was the recipient of meat shares from another man. *It should be clear that even if both men had an identical "mental template" regarding the proper way to butcher and distribute an animal, the faunal assemblages at several residences within the camp would be different.* This effect has been discussed elsewhere (Binford 1984d) and should lay to rest any arguments about direct ideological imprinting on the archaeological record (see Gould and Watson 1982:367–368).

The important point of this discussion thus far is simply that an Alyawara residential site exhibits an anatomical-part frequency graph with strong analogies to those commonly recovered from Nunamiut kill and hunting-camp locations. If one had argued from ethnographic analogy using the Nunamiut as a model, the Alyawara case, with the presence of marginal skeletal elements, would signal clear ambiguity in our ability to assign meaning accurately to archaeological facts based solely on ethnographic analogies.

Dealing with Ambiguity

For those who want an unambiguous signature for behavior, we are probably close to having one when we use the patterns created by the unprocessed disposal of lower leg parts and heads (depending upon the body size of animals) as an indicator of the initial steps in the human use of animal products. On the other hand, it should also be clear that this behavior is not a "signature" for types of sites, except when one is working with variability within a stable system. Put another way, an anatomical-part frequency graph dominated by heads and lower legs may be indicative of a kill-butchering site only within a logistically organized subsistence-settlement system. When viewed cross-culturally, the pattern of lower-leg dominance is ambiguous. Are we then to despair and dismiss anatomical frequency data as "misleading" and useless? That would defeat the purpose of science. Assuming that science represents a procedure for learning, we must pursue ambiguity and attempt to understand the relationships between this pattern and other facts indicative of organizational conditions. On elucidation, such relationships would permit us to see the linkages between this behavior and other clues to organizational differences. The development of middle-range understanding must proceed hierarchically in that we successively use knowledge considered secure to expose ambiguity in another domain of our knowledge. This is what is meant by "relative objectivity" (Binford 1982a)—using alleged knowledge warranted with one set of theory-based arguments as the basis for assessing knowledge that has been warranted or justified in terms of an intellectually independent argument. In short, we seek to set up an interactive usage of our knowledge, or of what we think we understand, in order to gain a different perspective on both sets of knowledge. This procedure maximizes the opportunity for recognizing ambiguity. In turn, we then conduct research to reduce or eliminate such ambiguity and, if successful, learn of new and organizationally indicative relational facts. In attempting to illustrate this procedure I will turn my attention to the facts of site structure.

Approaches to Site-Structural Analysis

The study of site structure is an area of research that has grown up in the context of relatively modern approaches to archaeological investigation. In this endeavor, it is recognized that archaeological sites may be internally differentiated, structured arrangements among artifacts, ecofacts, and features. Addressing the archaeological record in this manner forces the archaeologist to be concerned with two types of problems: (a) the analytical techniques most appropriate to the task of pattern recognition, and (b) the relationships between various forms of recognized patterning and the organization of life and work among the humans responsible for the production of the archaeological remains.

Since these ideas have been regularly emphasized in the archaeological literature there have been a number of distracting discussions and incorrect characterizations of the approach. Perhaps the most remarkable distortion of the writings and thoughts of those of us who have worked on the problem of site structure has been the idea that I and my colleagues believed that human activities were cross-culturally organized so that each activity would be uniquely placed in space, with the result that each activity would be characterized by a unique tool kit.[5] The most explicit statement of this confusion was made by Yellen:

> It is unfounded to assume that activities are spatially segregated or arranged by type within a single camp. Most tasks may be carried out in more than one place and in more than one social context; and conversely, in any single area, one can find the remains of many activities all jumbled together. Unfortunately, many archaeological analyses are based on just such an erroneous assumption, and their resulting conclusions must be called into question. A corollary of this simple area activity assumption is that associated remains are functionally related, and Whallon (1973) indicates that this single idea underlies all present-day spatial analyses. !Kung data make this a priori model untenable. (Yellen 1977a:134)

Another misrepresentative claim was made by Schiffer (1975), who was trying to convince an audience that "the new archaeologists" advocated a "direct" interpretive posture in which artifacts were taken at "face value" as directly reflecting behaviors and activities that are commonly described ethnographically (Schiffer 1976:11–12). Schiffer (1985) continues to make such claims in spite of evidence and argument to the contrary (see Binford 1981b and, particularly, 1983a:161–167).

Schiffer was not the only person to misrepresent the thrust of site-structural studies. Many other workers translated the site-structural approach into the more traditional paradigm and proceeded to interpret spatial patterning in terms of conventions uninvestigated at the middle-range level of research. The transfer of this traditional approach onto site-structural studies has led some researchers to summarize the assumptions of uninvestigated and rarely justified interpretive conventions as if they were basic to site-structural investigation. For instance, in a recent study Kent organized her research to test such ad hoc propositions as (a) "that most activity areas are sex specific" and (b) "that most activity areas are monofunctional" (Kent 1984:8–9). Not surprisingly, she reports that "most subsistence-oriented artifacts were found as isolated occurrences, and the second largest concentration was found in ash areas" (Kent 1984:170). That is, the artifacts were not distributed unambiguously relative to the context of use about which the investigator sought reconstructionist knowledge. This kind of reasoning derives from the false idea that we are looking for "lawlike generalizations" about on-site behavior per se. Given such a view Kent's findings, like Schiffer's, appear to many as "cautionary tales" warning against generalizations. In turn such findings are then commonly cited as evidence that general statements such as the following have been proven invalid: "the form and composition of assemblages recovered from geologically undisturbed context are directly related to the form and composition of human activities at a given location" (Binford 1983a:122).

The question is not about the validity of this proposition, which has been sustained by all ethnographic research thus far conducted to investigate the link between static patterning in the archaeological record and the causal and conditioning factors operative in the dynamic "formation" situation for the record. The point of controversy is not the principle stated above but the relationships between particular types of patterning and the particular behaviors reconstructivists want to "see." If one seeks to identify where ancient peoples ate their meals, and all the remains of consumption have been removed to a dump, then the discard behavior is seen by Schiffer (1976:12) as "distorting" the archaeological record. This view is then said to demand a "transformational" approach where the distorted data can be "transformed" into statements or control conditions for making the desired inferences. This is nonsense. In the above example the archaeological record remains an accurate reflection of the cleaning and maintenance activities of the ancient peoples involved. This behavior is no less referable to the "systemic" context than is eating. The challenge to archaeologists is the investigation of the archaeological record itself and the development of recognition criteria for accurately referring observed patterning to past activities and organizational characteristics of behavioral systems. This was the message of the "new archaeology" as I envisioned it, and it remains, in my opinion, the most productive approach for guiding present and future research.

In addition to the above distractions, some confusion has appeared in the more technically oriented literature concerned with the tactics of pattern recognition. One of the first such discussions was by Speth and Johnson (1976), who provided a useful summary of the assumptions and limitations of the use of correlational approaches to pattern recognition. Nevertheless, they seem to assume that there is an optimal technique to be found or developed and that archaeologists should use this technique in the analysis of spatial data for the purpose of recognizing patterning. Their research, however, is offered as a cautionary tale. They argue that recognized patterns may be ambiguous in that they could be spurious or refer to differing conditions (equifinality) in the past. In spite of this caution they appear to assume that the results of pattern-recognition studies can be directly interpreted by convention into meaningful statements about the past if we can isolate and identify all the "distorting" conditions that may stand between the contemporary patterning and the past dynamic reality. This position is reminiscent of the Schiffer approach to "formation processes." This type of approach can also be identified in the recent works of Carr (1984). Carr has, however, added a hypothesis-testing component to what I consider to be essentially a pattern-recognition program:

> The techniques one chooses for analysis should make only those assumptions that are congruent with the expectable and empirical structure of one's data. . . . For intersite spatial analysis, these requirements translate as follows. (1) Given any hypothesis of the kinds of activities that occurred at a site, test implications stating the expectable spatial patterning of artifacts and derived with the aid of principles of formation of the archaeological record should be expressed in mathematical terms reflecting the analytical method to be used; also, (2) the mathematical techniques one chooses . . . should make only those assumptions that are logically concordant with the activities and the formation that mapped them into spatial configurations of artifacts. (Carr 1984:104–105)

This is truly remarkable set of statements. It quite literally says that it is inappropriate to analyze data except in terms of one's preconceived ideas. Even more strange is the implication that we must know the past before we can analyze the archaeological record. I have always thought that we analyzed the archaeological record in order to learn something about the past! In all fairness it must be pointed out that Carr acknowledges that perhaps it is not always possible to know the past first, so in situations of uncertainty he suggests that one should use very general techniques (Carr 1984:105). As the reader will see, this is the strategy I follow later in this paper. I do not seek to pick on Carr but I wish to point to a major problem in analysis that has been well described by Christenson and Read (1977) as the "methodological double bind." Archaeologists must become aware of this problem and seek solutions rather than taking a formalist's approach and simply using conventions.

I should not imply that Carr's critiques of techniques and methods are not valuable, because they most certainly are. I feel that it is equally true that he is well aware of the analytical problems facing archaeologists, judging from a number of unpublished papers in my possession. Nevertheless, what is disturbing about Carr's (1984) recent statement is the reader's impression of his view of search techniques and the role of such techniques in archaeological procedure. There is little question that Carr sees the assumptions of the techniques as "problems." If one cannot know the past sufficiently to determine if the assumptions are justified with regard to the particular data set in question (i.e., mount a robust argument of relevance; Binford 1983a:157–167), then one should not use the technique. Carr seems to be saying that our inability to justify making certain assumptions renders ambiguity in the results obtained and a potential basis for spurious results. This posture is reasonable from a mathematical perspective but totally impractical for an archaeologist. Our task is to use a variety of techniques in such a way as to permit the diagnosis of ambiguity. It is in the recognition of ambiguity that we learn of the inadequacy of our identification criteria and our prior knowledge. It is largely through the recognition of ambiguity that we identify problem areas in our alleged knowledge and, hence, areas in need of investigation. We must consciously use assumptions in the analysis of archaeological data. One productive way is to study identical data using observations structured by differing assumptions as a basis for the inductive recognition of ambiguity and/or the identification of inappropriate assumptions rather than to demand that we know which assumptions are applicable before proceeding with analysis.

One cannot approach the pattern recognition problem from the perspective of identification when the problem for the archaeologist,[6] at least in our current state of knowledge, is one of inductive inference. Just as the paleontological approach was generally of little utility to the archaeologist, and we consequently had to develop our own taphonomic and archaeozoological approaches (although this accomplishment is not seen in Grayson's [1984] book), so can we look forward to the replacement of the mathematical perspective by an "in-house" development of analytical methods or tactics designed to serve our needs. One such set of tactics will be demonstrated later in this paper.

As has been suggested, much of the discussion of site structure has thus far operated with false assumptions as to what is being discussed; has suffered from a failure to appreciate the nature of the problem in the first place; or, as in the case of Schiffer, has confused a general set of approaches for a relative set of particular arguments. This has generated an even more confusing situation for students. Acceptance of their teachers' synthesis of this mess has led some to suggest that activity areas and tool kits are not useful concepts for archaeologists (Simek 1984)!

Through the years (Binford 1972b, 1973, 1977a, 1978a, 1978b, 1979, 1980a, 1982c, 1983a, 1983b, 1983c, 1984c; Binford and Binford 1966; Binford et al. 1966) I have been concerned with interassemblage variability, its relationship to intrasite structure, and the more general problem of diagnosing the nature of past activities from archaeological remains. This paper is a continuation of my research, making use of actualistic controls (Binford 1981a:21–30); a site-framework approach (Binford 1983c:144–192); and what I will call here experimental approaches in analysis, rather than the unrealistic identification approaches commonly advocated by the "hypothesis testers."

Internal Site Structure: An Alyawara Site

While O'Connell and I were working together, we mapped a number of Alyawara sites. One residential site was mapped and then the faunal remains were collected to permit the evaluation of how Aboriginal sites differed archaeologically from Nunamiut Eskimo sites, with which I was very familiar. O'Connell advised the documentation of a site that had been in use during the tenure of Denham's (1975) fieldwork among the Alyawara. The particular residential unit chosen for study was headed by a man named "Alec," who had lived on this site with his two wives for approximately six months.[7]

The data to be presented in this chapter were collected in the context of a plane-table survey of the site. A detailed map was made of the recognizable features, modified vegetation, and major surface materials that were judged to have been part of the site structure during use. Much of the scattered building material clearly visible on the site referred to the period when the site had been at least partially "pulled down" to recycle building materials and to obtain firewood during postabandonment camping in the adjacent area.[8] Figure 17.1 presents the site framework (see Binford 1983c:144–

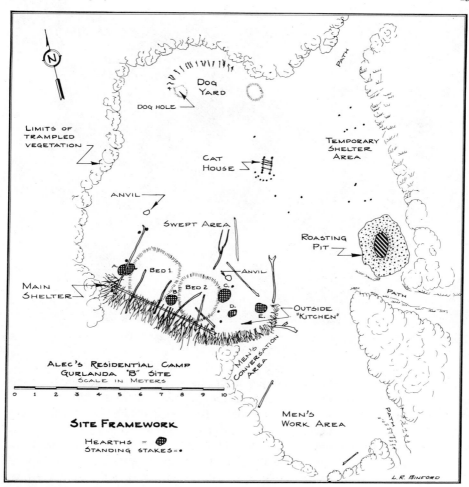

Figure 17.1 Map of site framework at an Alyawara residential site.

149). The major features on the site were a shelter, swept area, inner marginal-use area, dog yard, temporary shelter, roasting pit, butchering and distribution area, and a men's activity area. These are discussed separately below.

Shelter. This structure resembled a combination of a windbreak and what would be called a ramada in the American Southwest. That is, it was a roofed sunshade, although the roof was certainly not waterproof. The structure was oriented in a rough east-southeast to west-northwest fashion with the open side facing the sun on the north and east.[9] Figure 17.2 shows this structure as it appeared when we began mapping. The view is looking slightly south-southeast across the collapsed structure. The structure was approximately 4.8 m long and 2.6 m wide, representing 12.46 sq m of sheltered space. The interior can be thought of as a central bedding area, with other usage zones encircling this space. The bedding areas were two shallow, scooped-out zones (Figure 17.1). The eastern bed was approximately 2 by 2.10 m, while the western bed was larger,

Figure 17.2   Photograph of shelter at time of mapping—Alyawara Residence.

2.3 by 2.5 m. This "bed" was less well defined and may have primarily served other functions. Most of the personal gear of the occupants was stored between the beds and the back wall of the structure. This included clothing, bedding, household containers, and personal gear of both the males and females. To the rear and between the beds was a small "white ash" hearth (Figure 17.1, hearth B). This is a "bedside hearth," as has been described for many hunter-gatherers (Binford 1983c:163–164). Closer to the front of the structure and along the outside of each bed were two additional hearths.[10] These hearths were described as being cooking hearths, where most of the food was prepared. (They are shown as hearths A and C on Figure 17.1.)

On the eastern end of the structure was an attached shelter, a windbreak that was not covered. Two hearths still visible in this area (Figure 17.1, hearths D and E) were used on days when outside cooking and eating were more "comfortable" than such activities would have been indoors. The orientation of this "outside kitchen" was slightly different from that of the main structure, almost certainly reflecting the differences in the position of the sun between winter and summer, when the main structure was most likely constructed. Most family daytime activities during the cooler months would have taken place in this open windbreak.

Swept area. Directly in front of the structure was an area described as the "clean" or swept area (Figure 17.1). This area was maintained by the women; trash was tossed to the edges and the area was actually raked periodically to remove rubbish from in front of the structure.

Inner marginal-use area. Just beyond the swept area was a crescent-shaped area where various occasional activities of the women might be localized. For instance, this was the area in which debris from the swept area tended to end up. It was also a "toss zone" for larger items removed from the maintained area of the shelter. Posts and vertical sticks betrayed other usage of this area, but unfortunately the details are unknown. This area could be thought of as the place between the paths and the regular activity areas. This was where debris and some unusual activities were "tucked away." On this particular site there was a rather unusual feature, a cat house. This feature is shown in Figure 17.3, to the right of center. It was reported to us that a feral cat had been captured and a cage had been made for the cat in an attempt to tame it. Although the effort to tame the cat was unsuccessful, it had nevertheless been kept in its cage and cared for as a curiosity. The cat cage was considered something of a focal point for children's play and hence this zone had been the location of an extra amount of children's activity.

Dog yard. The dogs were tethered along the back side of the crescentic "dump" or trash area. There was one very distinct dog yard on the outer side of the main arc of trash near the northwest edge of the site. The dog shelter was clearly marked by a very dense concentration of bone and by a line of small brush placed like a miniature windbreak. This feature is shown in Figure 17.4 at the upper left. Holes typically dug by dogs are seen at both ends of the windbreak. Dense scatters of cans continue the definition of the trash arc, which defines the marginal use area on the site.

"Temporary shelter". On the northeast edge of the site a few vertical sticks were still in place; they were of the type that commonly forms the supports for a brush windbreak (Figure 17.3, upper left). At the time of mapping, the area's appearance prompted me to suspect that the shelter had been "pirated" or had been partly torn down,

Figure 17.3 Photograph of "cat house" and temporary shelter—Alyawara residence.

Figure 17.4 Photograph of dog yard (upper left)—Alyawara residence.

presumably for purposes of "recycling" the construction materials. The amount of debris immediately adjacent to this area suggested that it represented a temporary shelter in which the occupants had not engaged in the kind of regular clean-up that is obvious in front of the main shelter. The identity of the occupants of this shelter was unknown at the time of mapping. Nevertheless, the distribution of materials was such that this structure appeared to be a component of the occupation being described.

Roasting pit area. On the east side of the site, forming the south and east margin of the trash arc (Figure 17.1), was the roasting pit used in cooking kangaroo and other "large" animals, such as emu. The partially collapsed pit was still visible, as was the highly diagnostic, dense concentration of large charcoal chunks. There were very few bones in this area, and it was explained by informants that bones removed during the roasting process, such as lower rear limbs, were generally tossed directly to the dogs in the nearby dog yards.

Butchering and distribution area. Directly south and west of the roasting pit area and just to the south of a path leading into the site from the east was an area where butchering, after cooking, was said to have taken place. Men who would visit the site to receive shares of meat distributed by Alec would normally stand around during the butchering, receive their shares, sometimes eat a portion of the meat on the spot, and then leave for their own residences with what remained of their share (see Binford 1983c:171 for a photograph of this situation). This is a male-centered activity and is generally performed near the male activity area and outside the residential space maintained by the women.

Men's activity area. East-southeast of the structure was a well-defined cleared area that was identified as the men's work area. This is clearly seen in the upper center portion of Figure 17.2. During the time this site was occupied the Alyawara men were hunting from old automobiles. They would obtain these cars from junk areas around cattle stations, get them running (for short times), and use them for hunting kangaroo. This "extensive activity area" was where Alec kept his car and probably repaired it every time he wanted to use it (Binford 1983c:165–172). In this case the car would be pulled into the center of the area and the workers would move around it, performing different tasks. In structure the locus was much like a butchering area in that there was a focal item, work was done around it, and discarded materials were thrown back along the periphery of the walk zone. The marginal distribution of the oil cans, old car parts, and other items is visible in Figure 17.2. Once the car was removed the pattern remaining was a circular scatter of debris around the "empty" center.

Summary. In a very real sense the site may be thought of as essentially reducible to a male region and a female region. The male region consisted of the male work area, the butchering and distribution area, and the roasting pit area. In addition there was a kind of men's sitting area or zone where visiting males might sit and chat with the resident male and not intrude into the women's household activities. This area may be thought of as a specialized segment of the male activity area and was located just south of the windbreak at the east end of the main shelter. The most distinctive characteristic of these areas was the presence of automobile parts, oil cans and, in terms of more traditional artifacts, numerous grinding stones used in making pigment. Pigments were used heavily in male ritual, and manufacture was quite obvious at this site judging from the pigment-stained grinding stones.

Areas considered "female" were the shelter, the outside extension, the swept area, the trash arc, the dog yards, and the other marginal use areas along the trash arc.

Only the temporary shelter was ambiguous as to the gender of the occupants. There are several possibilities in this case. My initial judgment was that it represented the sleeping area of visiting young men who may commonly attach themselves to a family camp, particularly if the male family head has kin-based educational responsibilities to the "boys." There was food debris associated with this structure, suggesting that meals were prepared there. This is consistent with the known pattern of camp visitors. Nevertheless, subsequent research by O'Connell has identified this shelter as having been occupied by a single male just prior to the establishment of Alec's camp. Thus, its origin was prior to the building of this residential site but it obviously was used by the occupants for unknown purposes while the residential site was in use.

Distribution of the Faunal Assemblage

In order to view the relationship between the site framework, as defined by the features, and the assemblage of faunal items, the density of bones is expressed in "contour" lines imposed on the map of the site (Figure 17.5). Several properties of this map are informative. Perhaps the most impressive fact is that within the domestic areas, the main shelter, the swept area, and all the male activity areas, there are very low bone densities. Years ago I identified a similar distribution on a Late Woodland site in southern Illinois. In both examples, the houses and other features that served as

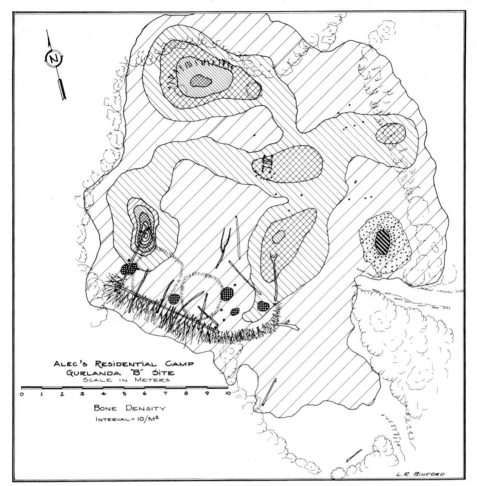

Figure 17.5   Map of bone density relative to site framework.

the focus of common activities were located in areas "marginal" to the major concentrations of "cultural items," the discrete entities making up debris concentrations
(Binford et al. 1970:70–71, 88). There is a moderate concentration of bone in the area
of the temporary shelter, which is consistent with the interpretation of this feature as
"temporary" since maintenance of sites is generally a partial function of occupational
duration.

An interesting characteristic of some small localizations of bones (Figure 17.5, B and
C) is that they are associated with structures and positioned as "door dumps," which
have previously been described (Binford 1983c:165). These are small "accumulation
points" for debris originally deposited around the bedding areas, most commonly
from morning snacks and meals taken in the bedding area during inclement weather.
Such materials may be "temporarily" dumped to one side of the doorway on an
almost daily basis, although in many cases of long occupancy these dumps may be

cleaned up periodically. Nevertheless, there will commonly be a residue of small materials remaining where the door dumps were habitually located.

Another concentration appears to be an in situ accumulation just beyond a processing facility. (Compare the localization in Figure 17.5 just north of the end of the windbreak with the position of an anvil shown on Figure 17.1 at the northeast end of the house "wall.")

In the center of the site is a distinct accumulation of faunal remains concentrated around the "cat house." This zone was not maintained, either by picking up or by sweeping. It represents what might be described as a "dead space" trap for artifacts and debris. This "catch-all" character is nicely illustrated in Figure 17.3, where cans, drums, and a highly visible cluster of clutter are concentrated around the feature. Additional debris had accumulated from the feeding of the cat, which according to informants was fed nothing but meaty foods. This feature was placed on the outer edge of the domestic space presumably because it was a focus of interest and curiosity.

The localizations noted above were all associated with the domestic space. This is well defined as a U-shaped distribution around the swept area in front of the main shelter plus a minor localization to the east of the temporary shelter. Beyond this "domestic" boundary is the most dense concentration of bone at the site, found directly in association with the dog yard. This fact reflects several conditions; perhaps the most important for understanding the faunal assemblage is that the dogs were fed the "leavings" from human meals as well as marginal parts disposed of at the time of butchering.

We should now have a firm grasp of the site framework, the skeleton of structures and features around, among, and within which activities were conducted. The density plots of bones betray locations of activity as well as something of the character of refuse disposal. Quite clearly, the domestic area was maintained; the inside of the shelter and the "swept area" were regularly cleaned, resulting in a peripheral ring of debris accumulated through sweeping and tossing. We can also see that the dog yard was the final depository for most of the faunal remains. Except for this area, the activity zones beyond the domestic area yield little faunal material. These include the roasting pit area, the men's work and conversation areas, as well as the zone identified by informants as a meat-distribution area. In terms of what we know, the site can be considered to have a "core" domestic area that was regularly maintained, as defined by the main structure, the swept area, and its encircling ring of debris. Beyond this domestic zone there is a peripheral zone where largely male specialized activities were carried out, in addition to the housing of dogs. This model corresponds nicely to the generalizations of Yellen (1977a:99) regarding "nuclear areas" versus peripheral "special activity areas," as he observed them behaviorally among the !Kung. On the other hand, the archaeological manifestations of such an organization are quite different. In the !Kung case the nuclear areas are indicated by high densities of debris (see Yellen's 1977a:103–108 definition of nuclear areas) while in the Alyawara case, "nuclear" areas are indicated by low densities and are bounded by high densities of debris. Finally, the special activity zones in Yellen's experience are characterized by low densities, and on the Alyawara site the dog yard exhibits the highest densities. Such differences may betray interesting organizational contrasts between the two systems, or they may simply reflect situational differences between the cases being compared, a point to which I will return.

The next question we seek to resolve is to what degree are the areas of dense debris (clear localizations of activity) also areas where anatomically different body parts were disposed of differentially. We also want to know whether there are clues to the nature of the use areas reflected by the manner in which anatomical parts may be spatially segregated among the faunal localizations and features of the site framework.

Factor Analysis of the Faunal Remains

Unlike so-called deductive approaches, in which techniques are to be matched to expectations, I have chosen to use a single technique, factor analysis,[11] and to apply it to data conceptualized in a variety of fashions as a way of gaining some relative perspective on the criteria used in setting up "typologies." It is almost trivial to comment that any item or entity can be considered to have a potential infinity of attributes in terms of which it might be classified. Basic to archaeology is the stage of research when we *decide* which attributes to use and how they are to be arranged for use in classificatory schemes. Ideally we are seeking to generate instruments for measurement. The question when we do such things is always what we are in fact measuring. This is the perpetual problem for the archaeologist who uses a stipulative "first step" procedure in organizing his/her observations. In this situation, the archaeologist uses judgment, based on his/her current knowledge of how the world works, as a guide for selecting the properties of "things" to be used in generating classifications. Always we must face uncertainty, is our knowledge adequate and relevant to the actual processes of the concrete world that we seek to know and measure? Most strictly mathematically reasoned strategies never permit the data to "talk back" and implicate the properties selected for manipulation analytically. Holding techniques constant and varying the schemes of data description permit such evaluation, as I will seek to demonstrate.

In performing a factor analysis, we are searching for patterning in an array of data organized by provenience unit. We are hoping to isolate units definable as patterns of covariation exhibited among the entities classified independently by the observer. The demonstration of patterns of dimensional covariation is then taken as a strong indication that the items exhibiting a grouped pattern were treated in similar ways in the past. The factor analysis does not, however, tell us in what ways the recognizable pattern of covariation actually came into being or, therefore, what the demonstrable patterning means. Archaeologists must accept the challenge of explaining patterning that we might be so fortunate to recognize within the archaeological record.

We thus face an enormous problem. First, how may we recognize patterning with different kinds of organizational referents in the past? Second, how do we reliably assign meaning to the recognized patterns? The specific analytical challenge considered for the materials reported here is to seek answers to the following questions: (1) What patterns exist? (2) Are there any clues as to the meanings of the isolated patterns? (3) How is the past implicated? (4) How are our procedures implicated?

Setting up the analysis. Each listing in the original fieldnotes was coded onto a separate line (so that each element or fragment was one observation unit). The coding techniques were modified from those developed by Todd (1983) for use with artiodactyls. Obviously they had to be modified by the addition of extra codes to take into account the fact that kangaroos have a more differentiated anatomy than artiodactyls (Table 17.1, above). The tabulated attributes of each observation unit are provenience, species, anatomical element, and anatomical portion of the fragmented identified segment. Finally, evidence of gnawing or other modifications was noted, as were evidences of butchering, such as cut marks and breakage characteristics.

Factor analysis design. The observations were organized in three different ways for analysis by factor analytic techniques. The first approach was to treat each item listed in the original fieldnotes as a unit for analysis. For instance, equal weight was given to a single long-bone splinter and to a complete innominate. Each provenience was summarized in terms of the complete inventory of fragments recovered. These inventories by provenience unit constituted the "cases," while the fragment descriptions defined the variables used in the analysis. This organization of data will be referred to as the matrix of fragments. It is justified by taking the archaeological record at "face value" and designing ways of describing the items recovered in terms of their recovered form without attempting to treat them as indicators of parent or original forms. If the archaeological record is structured by relatively "immediate" conditioning factors, it was thought that these "final form" characteristics should exhibit the greatest or most robust patterning.

The second way of organizing the observations was to sum the fragments as quantitative indicators of anatomical categories; that is, fragment counts were used as some measure of the frequency of the anatomically defined segment present. In this procedure the anatomical segments judged relevant were known from ethnographic observation to be those into which the Alyawara most commonly segmented the carcass of a kangaroo. In addition, two categories of processing by-products were also included as clues to whether processing or dispersal of butchering segments was the framework primarily conditioning the final disposition of parts on the site. The following anatomical segments were used as the variables in this analysis.

Skull—all fragments of the head, including mandible, cranial fragments, sections of orbit and occiput, etc.

Upper vertebrae—all vertebrae above the pelvis: axis, atlas, cervical, thoracic, and lumbar.

Forelimb—scapula, humerus, radius, ulna, carpals, metacarpals, and phalanges.

Pelvis—pelvis proper, sacrum, caudal vertebrae.

Upper hind limb—femur, tibia, fibula.

Lower hind limb—tarsals, metatarsals, phalanges.

Ribs—all fragments.

Long-bone splinters—both large splinters and small chips (visually discriminated)

Cancellous bone fragments—small, unidentifiable fragments of cancellous tissue.

The third way of defining the variables was in terms of minimal number of elements, which I have commonly used in other studies (Binford 1984c:50–53). In this procedure the actual anatomy of the animal is treated in terms of articular ends for single bones and for certain grouped categories, such as thoracic vertebrae. Using this procedure I have been very successful in analytically monitoring the actual behavior of Nunamiut Eskimo as they differentially use the anatomy of caribou for different purposes along a logistical and spatially variable organization of activities.

Once the variables were defined for each provenience unit, the values for each variable were indexed by taking the highest frequency value within the given provenience unit,[12] assigning it a value of 100, and then expressing all other frequencies as a proportion of this highest value. After calculating the index values for all the real numbers in the array, all zero entries were assigned a value of one (1) in anticipation of the next step in preparing the data for factor analysis (log transformation). The indexing was done so as to eliminate the variance in the matrix that is referable to sample size differences among the cases. We are interested in structural relationships among the variables themselves and not in patterns that may be referable to an underlying variable—size differences among the cases.

After all the variables in all three different matrices were transformed in the above ways, the values were converted to natural log values. This conversion was made because factor analysis is conducted with measures of *linear* correlation. Previous experience with faunal assemblages has shown that correlations among faunal variables may commonly be curvilinear. The log transformation renders such data into a form that meets the assumptions of the analysis.

Each matrix was then factor analyzed using the Statistical Analysis System package and the PROC FACTOR procedure with a minimum eigenvalue retention criterion of 0 or 1. An initial unrotated factor analysis was followed by a varimax rotation.

Factor analytic results. The original intent of this analysis was to seek a recognition of patterning that might have arisen in the context of the preparation of food for consumption as well as during consumption, since it is generally agreed that (except for such postdepositional conditioners as trampling, etc.) breakage most commonly occurs in the context of food preparation and consumption. After a trial run it was realized that the manner of setting up the matrix was inappropriate because there were so many cells with zeros. We therefore edited the matrix, eliminating all variables that had two or less occurrences among the proveniences, and a rerun analysis was performed. Table 17.2 summarizes the results obtained in the rerun.

Several kinds of information are supplied by the factor solution. First, except for long-bone splinters and chips, none of the most common items on the site appear as diagnostics of the factors generated. In fact, most diagnostics are relatively low frequency items. This strongly suggests that, while some weak structure is indicated, the faunal assemblage is relatively undifferentiated across the site except with respect to breakage diagnostics.

Although it must be acknowledged that the structure is weak, it is interesting to examine its form. Perhaps most striking is the fact that groupings of variables indicated by the factor loading do appear to reflect secondary and tertiary processing of parts and not earlier stages of the treatment of animals. This is clearly suggested by the fact

Table 17.2
Factor Analysis of Gurlanda "B" Faunal Assemblage

Elements	Factor 1	Factor 2	Factor 3	Factor 4	Factor 5
Mandible	0.098	0.410	−0.089	−0.005	0.059
Maxilla	−0.117	0.635	−0.090	0.074	−0.046
Cranial fragment	0.055	0.700	−0.091	0.137	−0.093
Incisor	0.127	−0.039	−0.007	0.108	0.766
Unidentified molar	0.854	0.128	0.054	0.085	−0.070
Thoracic vertebra	0.163	−0.055	0.746	0.119	−0.121
Caudal vertebra	0.074	−0.102	−0.087	0.046	−0.041
Rib	0.234	0.598	0.139	−0.009	0.060
Unidentified vertebra fragment	0.016	−0.015	0.019	0.067	−0.047
Scapula	−0.115	−0.055	−0.056	0.060	−0.043
Pelvis (complete)	0.018	0.025	−0.022	0.117	−0.079
Tibia	0.031	0.004	−0.078	−0.600	−0.048
Calcaneus	−0.076	0.022	0.026	0.136	−0.035
Tarsal	−0.069	−0.030	0.767	0.048	0.122
1st metatarsal	0.014	0.229	−0.100	0.021	−0.163
2d metatarsal	−0.040	−0.061	−0.104	−0.145	−0.065
Metacarpal	−0.084	−0.058	−0.077	−0.041	−0.059
Unidentified bone fragment	0.582	−0.024	0.087	−0.104	0.382
Fibula	−0.101	−0.049	−0.033	−0.264	−0.074
Fibula shaft	−0.061	0.158	0.107	0.756	0.055
Long bone splinter	0.676	−0.114	−0.021	−0.238	0.386

that bone size and fragmentation patterning seem to be the dimensions in terms of which the variables group, and not anatomical parts per se. For instance, a very common anatomical part on the site is the metatarsal, yet it does not appear grouped to other elements in the first five factors to be extracted.

By referring back to Table 17.1, the reader will see that factor 1 is defined by isolated molars, unidentifiable cancellous fragments, and small bone chips. These are all small, and they are all items that can be expected to be associated and to occur in areas that are used for consumption. These are the items that may quite literally "fall out" during processing and consumption and, being small, may be missed during clean-up. Factor 2 is defined by cranial fragments, maxilla fragments, and rib fragments. These items have in common the fact that they tend to be flat and also tend to be items that are not pounded up during consumption. They are gnawed, sucked, or "picked," in that small nuggets of edibles are extracted from the crevices. These are all items that are judged to be the most likely to be raked aside or tossed away from consumption areas (Binford 1978b). Factor 3 is primarily defined by thoracic vertebrae and tarsals. These are both anatomical units that were commonly observed as complete and were not pounded or broken during food processing. At this point the "meaning" of this grouping is unclear. Factor 4 is a very satisfying grouping since it makes so much sense in terms of what is known of Alyawara behavior. It is defined by long-bone shaft splinters and is negative relative to tibiae. In the kangaroo, the only bone that yields substantial amounts of bone marrow is the tibia; thus, breaking up tibiae reduces the number of tibiae. The factor results reflect this fact. Factor 5 is diagnostically recognizable by incisors, while factor 6 is largely defined by mandibles and scapula, both large and relatively flat bones. It seems quite clear that the groupings revealed by the factor analysis are referable to associations derived during the processing and disposal of food, and not during butchering and/or sharing of food.

The other two factor studies conducted, one on grouped body parts and the other on minimal number of elements (MNEs), both yielded results that were less robust than the first procedure. Parts appearing as diagnostic almost always are the variables that appear infrequently; factors tend to be defined by single variables; and the groupings, although weak, make no anatomical sense with regard to the assumptions of variable definition. Nevertheless, if we take the indicated structure seriously, it appears to be some "translation" into anatomical units of the findings reported from the first procedure, where size and condition of bone, not anatomical origin, are more important. This supports the earlier suggestion that the meaningful associational patterning on the site derives from processing and disposal acts, in which an entire animal is the target of treatment, and not from decisions made with respect to anatomical segments of an animal judged appropriate to different use contexts, as is common on Nunamiut sites.

These findings have two important implications for faunal analysis: on sites of logistically organized hunter-gatherers the differential segmentation of anatomical parts for different purposes dominates the final pattern; on the Alyawara site, faunal descriptions phrased in anatomical terms are largely irrelevant. The final form of the assemblage at a forager residential site derives from the uniform processing of whole animal carcasses at a single place; hence, attributes of bone size and breakage are the properties that exhibit intrasite patterning. What is demonstrated is that comparison among assemblages from systems organized differently may be most indicative of organizational differences when a common technique is used. These differences only become apparent, however, when the attribute sets in terms of which the data are described for analysis are varied analytically. In this example the use of a frame of reference for classificatory purposes is illustrated. The anatomy of the animals is a given, and uniformitarian assumptions can be made. The interesting question is how past peoples differentially behaved with respect to this known condition. By holding analytical technique constant and varying the attribute systems, some perspective on this question can be gained.

The Distribution of Covariant Patterning Relative to Site Structure

I now turn to the interesting question of the fit, spatially speaking, between the patterns isolated by the first factor analytic procedure and the framework of the site as it is known. Table 17.3 summarizes the factor loading for an inverted matrix, in which the provenience units are grouped according to the character of the information that serves to define the factors, as summarized earlier in Table 17.2.

Figure 17.6 illustrates the distribution of information definitive of factor 1. The proveniences exhibiting a factor loading greater than .50 are shown as shaded isopleths. The defining proveniences for factor 1 are on either side of Bed 2 (Figure 17.1) and in front of the bed across the swept area. This U-shaped distribution covers the

Table 17.3

R-Mode Factor Analysis of Gurlanda "B" Faunal Assemblage

Provenience Unit	Factor 1	Factor 2	Factor 3	Factor 4
B01	0.822	0.174	0.135	0.215
B02	0.609	0.059	0.047	−0.096
B03	−0.233	−0.025	0.337	0.829
B04	0.802	0.117	0.105	0.129
B05	0.339	0.233	0.366	−0.156
B06	0.386	0.839	0.095	0.032
B07	0.412	0.072	0.461	0.453
B08	0.177	0.887	−0.020	0.019
B09	0.674	0.333	0.039	0.189
B10	0.713	0.147	0.137	0.080
B11	−0.190	0.649	0.112	−0.138
B12	0.609	0.133	0.542	0.183
B13	0.342	0.790	0.299	−0.115
B14	0.866	0.220	0.248	0.139
B15	0.631	0.209	0.608	−0.061
B16	0.057	0.120	0.746	0.174
B17	0.686	0.172	0.540	0.236
B18	0.541	0.286	0.411	0.462
B19	0.546	0.106	0.192	0.013
B20	0.375	0.095	0.478	0.574
B21	0.789	0.095	0.282	0.088
B22	0.152	0.840	0.341	0.204
B23	0.373	0.129	−0.001	0.631
B24	−0.107	0.234	0.104	−0.032
B25	0.510	0.004	0.210	0.525
B26	0.004	0.911	−0.098	0.094
B27	0.390	0.069	0.046	0.119
B28	0.248	0.001	0.758	0.312
B29	0.624	0.054	0.181	0.440
B30	0.388	0.369	0.434	0.173
B31	0.274	0.072	0.826	0.217
B32	−0.028	0.189	−0.106	−0.008
B33	0.463	0.493	0.175	0.416
B34	0.718	0.193	0.597	−0.011
B35	0.708	0.183	0.549	−0.041

"outside kitchen" area as well as what was called "Bed 1." There is an additional localization in the middle of the area occupied by the temporary shelter. It will be recalled that factor 1 is defined by bone chips, unidentified fragments of cancellous tissue, and isolated molars. As previously pointed out, these are small items that were probably dropped in situ where bone was processed for marrow or simply crushed for consumption along with meat and fat. The small chips have been noted elsewhere as very good diagnostics of in situ marrow-bone breakage (Binford 1978a:153–157). Because this material is small, some would certainly have been left after "cleaning

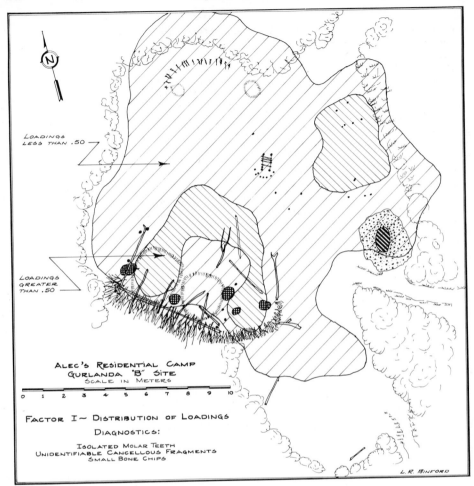

Figure 17.6 Map of distribution of factor 1 diagnostic provenience units.

up"; thus, I think it is clear that this factor is indicative of in situ meat and bone consumption. It is only distributed in known domestic areas and in some of the least-dense areas of bone accumulation. The interpretive coherence seen here throws some light on the "function" of Bed 1 within the main shelter. It will be recalled that there were only three adults and no children living on this site. The bed space (Binford 1983c:97) is about three times that needed to sleep three people. The distribution of factor 1 diagnostics strongly suggests that we misinterpreted the internal arrangement of the main shelter at the time of recording. "Bed 1" is likely to have been primarily an internal kitchen/eating area, not a sleeping place. This insight renders the spatial organization much more realistic. There were optional "kitchen" areas, an outside one (which is very common among hunter-gatherers, see Binford 1983c:172–176) and an inside kitchen used during inclement weather.

The provenience units serving to define factor 2 exhibit a distribution peripheral to the dog yard and the area along the west side of the house as well as the swept zone of the domestic area (Figure 17.7). An independent localization occurs on the east side of the domestic unit, forming a distinct arc relative to the roasting pit. This arc overlaps and is interrupted by a small cluster in the domestic area, which encircles the "outside kitchen." A very minor concentration is seen due east of the temporary structure. As with the previous factor distribution, the dispersion is largely in low-density areas or peripheral to high-density areas. This can be taken to mean that the context of deposition was somewhat independent of the actions that concentrated bone in high-density areas. It is also interesting that this is the only diagnostic set that has a substantial localization within one of the men's areas.

The diagnostics of factor 2 are cranial fragments, maxillary fragments, and ribs. These are all parts that are picked, sucked, and "gnawed." These are hand-held parts that are commonly tossed aside during consumption. Tossing is a mode of disposal that can be done either in a standing or a seated position, whereas the small by-products definitive of factor 1 are almost exclusively the consequence of seated work postures. The differences in the distributions (Figure 17.6 versus Figure 17.7) almost certainly reflect this condition, plus the additional fact that eating in a standing position is common at the time of meat distributions conducted with the roasting pit as a focal feature. The distinctive arc oriented to this feature (Figure 17.7) portrays this situation. On the other hand, individuals seated in the domestic arc described by the factor 1 diagnostics most likely tossed the diagnostics of factor 2 back into the "rim" of debris around the domestic area as well as in the direction of the dog yard. Persons seated in the outside kitchen tossed their discards toward the "door dump." This model accounts for the distributions and the properties of the factor diagnostics. One could argue against this interpretation, but the indications that the covariant patterning derives from a different "eating" and disposal mode than was indicated by factor 1 seem very secure. There is nothing to suggest that the differences relate to planned or sequential consumption and/or processing of anatomical parts for storage or differential use along a logistical sequence. Everything points to the differences as being incidental consequences of differential contexts of consumption and food preparation and associated disposal modes.

Finally, factor 3 appears as a peripheral distribution around the dog yard and cat house, with minor localizations along the right and left sides of the northern edges of the domestic area (Figure 17.8). The area with the highest factor loading is the arc around the eastern edge of the dog yard, which was noted as having the highest density of dog feces at the time of mapping. It is not clear what is causing the diagnostics to covary, but it seems likely that it has reference to some peculiarity of dogs' eating habits. For instance, I have noted many times that both dogs and wolves eat the skin off lower limbs. They do this by scoring the bone around a round section of the bone and then stripping the skin away. This commonly leaves tarsals and carpals isolated and articulated in tight skin sheaths. I do not know how such behavior would affect kangaroo anatomy, but I strongly suspect that something of this nature stands behind factor 3. This certainly appears to be a pattern reflective of animals' eating habits and not arising from feeding special anatomical parts to the animals, as occurs among the Nunamiut.

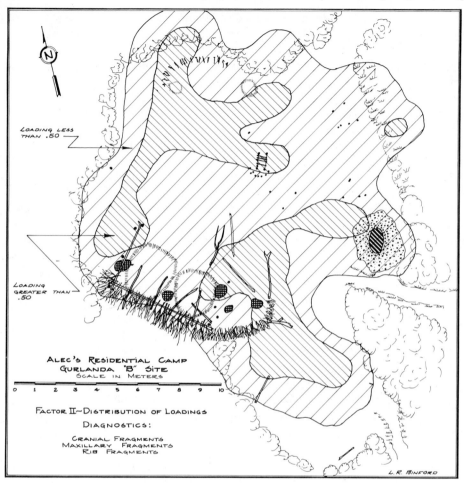

Figure 17.7 Map of distribution of factor 2 diagnostic provenience units.

What is striking about the distributions is that they grade into one another, varying from areas with in situ by-products of processing and consumption to peripheral areas with raked, tossed, or deposited accumulations marginal either to high-density areas or to low-density areas known to have been cleaned up. The single dimension characteristic of this variability appears to be fragment size, which results from consumption and processing and is further restructured by clean-up and dog feeding. The variability seems to be conditioned by disposal mode and by the entropy from cleaning operations. The distribution does not betray any specialized or planned differential use of anatomical parts, nor does it reveal any differential spatial disposition of anatomical segments, such as butchering units (which might occur on sites of logistically organized hunter-gatherers, e.g., Binford 1978a). In the case of butchering units, parts are differentially placed and used depending upon whether they are selected for storage (as dried or frozen meat) or cached for future processing. The fact that the

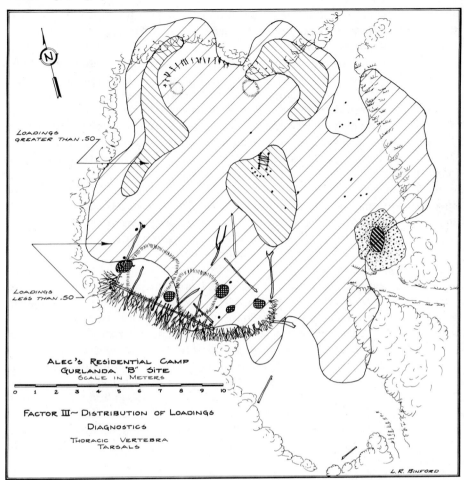

Figure 17.8 Map of distribution of factor 3 diagnostic provenience units.

choices regarding parts to be consumed are conditioned by such prior decisions ensures that, even in debris from consumption, anatomical part differentiation will occur as a function of consumer sequencing of food options and will be manifested in terms of anatomical segments. Such variability underlies or is integrated with patterned variability from human consumption and independent selection of parts for dog feeding. No such complex structure is evident on the Alyawara site.

Two important sets of conclusions derive from this study: (1) the faunal distribution on the Alyawara site is undifferentiated except in terms of the degradation and disposal sequences associated with animal-product consumption; and (2) the observational units appropriate to the study of Alyawara residential fauna are different from those that were found to be appropriate to the study of Nunamiut residential sites. It is known that the Nunamiut were logistically organized collectors who practiced a variety of storage strategies. Methodologically speaking, I found the most interesting conclusion to be that the structure of faunal remains reflects the organizational character of the Alyawara situation—the introduction of complete animals and the undifferentiated treatment of the anatomical parts. Only in very minor, consumption-related ways is there differential treatment of parts—namely, tibiae are processed for marrow, vertebrae are commonly pounded up and eaten, and a biased consumption of heads and ribs occurs at the time of meat distributions. The overall pattern of part disposal is undifferentiated by area except as reflected in fragmentation and part association arising incidentally from processing, consumption, and disposal differences. Such variability contrasts dramatically with the situation in which parts are distributed in different places as components of different activities conducted in the context of an organized system of delayed consumption. Additionally, on Nunamiut sites there is an "overlay" differentiation of anatomical parts in dumps arising over the course of a consumption sequence. This effect derives from the biased consumption from stores as well as from selections made among alternative methods of storing food (e.g., drying vs. freezing). The undifferentiated pattern that is seen on the Alyawara site could not occur on a Nunamiut residential site.

We can almost certainly use the contrasts in results obtained when classifications based on breakage and "final form" are used in faunal analysis as opposed to the use of anatomical segment indicators, such as MNE or MAU, as signatures for distinguishing between hunting situations organized for immediate or for delayed consumption. The weak factor resolution, indicative of density-dependent associations, may well turn out to be a good clue to lack of structure and hence to immediate consumption situations rather than the more "statistical" interpretations commonly given to such results. Techniques of using multiple classifications, with analytical techniques held constant, can generally be expected to yield clues to diagnostic indicators of organizational significance. This can be accomplished because we gain some perspective on the stipulated properties we originally employed when setting up the classificatory conventions later analyzed by mathematical or statistical means. With this strategy the archaeological record gets to talk back!

I think it has been demonstrated that we can distinguish between direct and delayed consumption situations through the analysis of faunal remains in terms of different attribute systems. Taking a systems approach, we may anticipate that when we shift to another domain of facts (for instance, site structure) we can expect there to be additional properties that may derive from organizational differences among systems. I will compare the Alyawara residential site with a Nunamiut site to highlight additional clues to organizational differences and then return to the problem with which this discussion began—how to tell a residential site from some other type of site with a method that is independent of their faunal content.

SITE STRUCTURAL COMPARISON: FORAGER AND COLLECTOR SYSTEMS

As we have seen, the Alyawara roasting feature was repeatedly used to process the continuous flow of hunted food into the site. On the other hand, the Nunamiut segment differentially use anatomical parts of caribou for different purposes, and on their residential sites one finds hearth-centered processing areas used for short periods but dense with artifacts (Figure 17.9C, grease-processing hearths). Processing is commonly a timed series of activities comprising several processing steps (Binford 1978a:299). This results in functionally differentiated processing areas and, importantly, in highly specialized dumps—specialized both with respect to the breakage and processing consequences as well as to the types of anatomical parts deposited. The presence of specialized dumps is consistent with the general contrast between patterns of disposal at Nunamiut and Alyawara residential sites. For example, on the Eskimo site (Figure 17.9C, "bone dump") there is a dense pile of marrow-cracked long-bone fragments that were probably deposited after relatively rare long-bone-processing episodes. Such processing episodes were periodic responses to the bulk of accumulated long bones piling up during the course of the occupation. Other examples of such features have been illustrated previously (Binford 1981a:129, 1983c:136–137).

In marked contrast, there were no specialized dumps on the Alyawara site. Instead, a diffuse scatter of refuse was concentrated in the dog yard and around the periphery of the "swept area." The anatomical-part contents of one area of this diffuse scatter were typical of the composition of the entire zone of refuse accumulation. While Nunamiut sites may also have diffuse refuse scatters accretionally built from discrete acts of discard that result from the regular maintenance of the residential space, there will in addition be highly specific bulk-processing features and locations sometimes accompanied by specialized dumps, such as is seen in Figure 17.9C. Specialized processing and disposal areas for different kinds of food products are likely to be major site-structural clues to the differences between forager and collector systems.

All differences between the two residential sites shown in Figure 17.9 are not simply indications of the differences between forager and collector organizations. For example, the Eskimo house has a major concentration of artifacts inside, while the Alyawara residence had very few visible at the time of our work. These differences are probably more a reflection of the climate than of any major "cultural" difference (see Binford 1983c:176–187 for a discussion of constrained work space at Palangana). In addition, the situational contrast between the Eskimo, who use a willow floor, and the Alyawara, who kept a "swept" soil floor, further conditions the amount of artifacts and debris in the two houses. The Eskimo house floor acts as an artifact trap as well as a structural inhibitor to the act of sweeping inside the house. The result is that everything but very large items tend to remain where they were dropped in the Nunamiut house, while in the Alyawara house such items are swept away.

The major structural difference between the Alyawara site and the Eskimo site that is not referable directly to climatic conditioners and/or organizational differences between collectors and foragers is the expansive nature of the men's work area at the Alyawara site. This area is divisible into two components, the conversation area and the extensive activity area where automobiles were maintained and repaired by the male household head and his friends.

In the case of the male conversation area there is an analogous locale on the Nunamiut site (Figure 17.9C, "men's outside area") directly outside the house, facing the source of winter light. This area is recognizable by a small scatter of tools outside the house walls, a distribution that covers an area of 4.7 sq m. On other Eskimo sites,

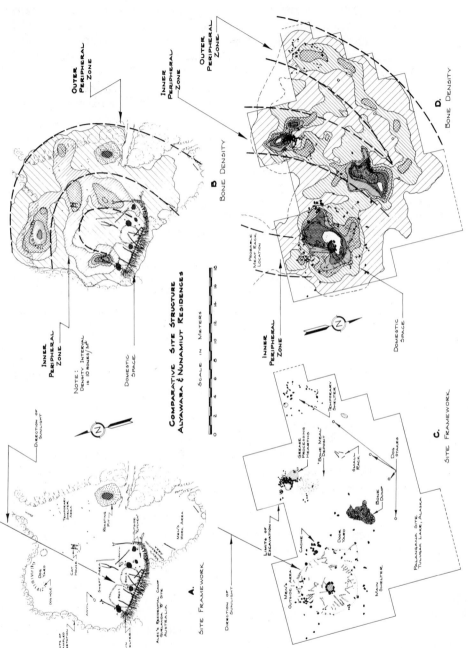

Figure 17.9 Site structural comparison—Nunamiut and Alyawara residences.

where the occupations were in fall or spring, such areas are similarly placed but may extend over an area of 6.8 sq m. (This situation is modeled in Binford 1983c:175 and labeled "Nunamiut residential model.")

The male Alyawara conversation area is marked by several grinding stones covered with ocher and other pigments as well as by at least two gun parts and a wooden spear head. The extensive work area where cars were repaired has no direct analogue on the Palangana site but is analogous to other extensive work areas observed among the Nunamiut. In fact, the circular distribution of car parts, oil cans, and parts of wooden crates and long pole levers (the latter two items being used to jack up automobiles) exhibits a spatial pattern directly analogous to butchering areas (Binford 1983c:122–123, 165–172), where the central area is occupied by the focus of work and the circular periphery consists of by-products of the work that were dropped or tossed aside. The extent of the Alyawara work area is analogous to the Nunamiut counterpart. There are 23.7 sq m within the roughly circular distribution of items, while most Nunamiut butchering areas require between 17 and 24 sq m for "stand up" activities.

As suggested here, there appear to be major differences between the disposal modes and associated attributes of refuse patterning that are distinctive to forager and collector systems. These differences, when seen in a modular fashion, aid further in recognizing organizational differences among systems. When we can recognize modules, as in the case of the extensive work area, we can begin the interesting task of discovering how such work areas are related to other recognizable activity modules in the structured composition of sites. In turn, across such recognizable modules we can study the patterns of refuse association and degrees of formal content segregation as a means of understanding organizational differences among sites.

IDENTIFYING RESIDENTIAL SITES GENERICALLY

In identifying generic residential sites from special activity loci, we need to know (a) if there are general residential site characteristics that might be recognizable, and (b) how residential sites, as a generic class, are different from other types of sites. The following comparison is not intended as a demonstration of secure knowledge of residential site structure. Instead, it is offered as an example of how we might proceed with the learning process. At present there are so few well-documented sites that attempts to do pattern-recognition work are premature. Nevertheless, Figure 17.9 compares, at the same scale, the internal site framework of an Eskimo winter residential site with the Alyawara residential site described above.

There were dog yards at both sites, one in the Alyawara site and four in the Eskimo site. On both sites there were temporary shelters. The Eskimo example had been occupied first by the males while they were building the substantial house later lived in by the family unit. In the case of the Alyawara site the first occupant was an unmarried man, and his structure was obviously later used by the main occupants. On the Eskimo site a near-complete skeleton of a wolf was recovered adjacent to a small rack, where there was also a concentration of fishing gear. On the Alyawara site a rack had served as the support for a cage for a "pet" cat. On both sites a substantial "hearth" was located away from the house. On the Alyawara site, men cooked whole, unskinned kangaroos in a roasting pit prior to distributing meat to sharing recipients (see Binford 1983c:165–172 for a discussion of this activity). On the Eskimo site the outside hearth was a surface feature where women had processed the accumulated articular ends of long bones for bone grease, largely in one operation. *The most important characteristic is not the similarity between the features listed above but the fact that they were all placed peripherally with respect to the central focus of the site plan, the domestic area* (compare Figures 17.9B and 17.9D).

The site structure of a residential site might be summarized as dominated by domestic space/sheltered sleeping and "kitchen" areas as well as alternative, inclement weather work space within the shelter. Quite literally the site serves to maintain the domestic social unit. It is the base of operations for the domestic unit. As such, the domestic facilities are almost always maintained. For instance, outside the sheltered area there are frequently door dumps, which betray the cleaning-up of the sheltered life space. There may also be alternative activity areas against the shelter, such as men's conversation and work space, along a sunny wall in cool settings and in the shade of the structure in warm places. The domestic space is *focal* relative to the rest of the site framework and debris distribution. Commonly, around or beside the domestic space is a wide band of activity areas and debris accumulations that forms a pattern peripheral to the domestic space. On both the Eskimo and Australian sites "inner" and "outer" bands of refuse and activity localizations parallel one another. These inner and outer lines of features make up the wide peripheral zone (Figure 17.9).

I am suggesting that there is a generic pattern distinctive to residential sites.[13] Basic to this configuration is the fact that domestic space is focal to all other activities. This is not to say that all residential sites are alike in their details, only that the maintenance of the domestic unit is the primary function of the facilities at such sites. The way utilized space is developed during an occupation is a manifestation of planning depth. If one plans to occupy the site for some time and does not care to have the debris from one activity inhibit the performance of another, one develops special use areas peripheral to the domestic area. During the course of residential site occupation many different role-specific tasks may be performed at the site. Such special "use areas" are generally peripheral to the domestic space, resulting in a kind of generic site "plan" as shown in Figures 17.9B and 17.9D.

Over this generic structure debris is laid down in patterned response to the site maintenance tactics employed by the occupants. One could think of site maintenance (cleaning up) as some measure of planning depth or of the degree to which activities are performed in anticipation of future actions. Considered in this manner, the quantity of secondary refuse might be generally correlated with duration of occupation since the amount of planning is likely to be correlated to the scale of anticipated use at a given place. It must be realized, however, that one cannot expect a perfect correlation, since situational factors or unanticipated conditions can always upset the "best laid plans of mice and men." Similarly, we can expect that environmental factors will condition the degree to which clean up is necessary for sustained use of organized space.

My experience in Eskimo winter houses is a case in point. In that situation, outside use areas are gradually covered by both falling and blowing snow, resulting in uncluttered space on the surface in spite of the build-up of clutter under the snow. The archaeologist sees the accumulation as it has dropped after the snow melts, which certainly gives the appearance of unmaintained space in spite of the fact that during use the debris did not cause cluttered space. It should also be mentioned that maintenance activities appear to be related primarily to planning depth and not to pan-systemic "values" or attitudes toward "dirt" (cf. Hodder 1982a:192–193). This point is illustrated by the variability seen on the Alyawara site itself. For instance, the extensive men's work area was not cleaned up. Similarly, the area around the temporary shelter was not cleaned in the same manner, nor at the same scale, as the domestic area around the main shelter. In fact, the temporary shelter exhibited a pattern of door dumps and proximate debris accumulation similar to that noted on very short-term occupations, as documented by Yellen (1977a).

Moving from the problem of diagnostics used to identify residential sites to the problem of recognizing sites of different function, we find that we must again focus on patterned characteristics of secondary refuse. If the general relationship to planning depth suggested above can be sustained, we would have an important characteristic to aid in the recognition of residential sites versus hunting camps. In general, the anticipated duration of use of hunting camps is short, hence they are rarely cleaned up and primary refuse from immediate processing and consumption tasks tends to be common. Consistent with this manifestation of lack of planning depth is the fact that different types of activities yielding sometimes large quantities of debris may all be performed in generalized work space, commonly around an outside hearth.[14] This fact contributes further to the appearance of "primary" refuse from a variety of activities occurring side by side or in overlapping distributions in a generalized work area. In spite of this unspecialized organization of space the faunal remains should exhibit some patterned differentiation by anatomical part since, on most hunting camps, animals are processed for storage and/or transport to consumers in other places. This results in the biased consumption of anatomical parts of marginal utility, or the processing of parts that were removed in order to reduce the bulk to be transported. One might obtain evidence of anatomically biased consumption, but this would commonly be contrasted with butchering areas, processing areas, etc., unlike the undifferentiated pattern seen on the Alyawara site.

This comparison hopefully makes certain points explicit: (a) the size of generalized work areas versus specialized activity areas in these data is basically conditioned by the habitual posture of the workers (e.g., sitting versus standing) taken in conjunction with the sizes of the targets or focus of work and of the work force; (b) sites with some planning depth are made up of regular work areas and special activity spatial modules arranged so that relatively uncommon activities do not "intrude" on normal repetitive work schedules. The latter fact conditions the distribution of extensive work areas, such as the men's work area, dog yards, and hide-scraping activity areas, and of the loci of activities that yield large quantities of debris, such as primary flint working. All of these loci would normally be peripheral to domestic use areas (Yellen 1977a:92). The basic physiological requirements of living, eating, sleeping, child care, etc., condition the internal spatial accommodations found in domestic life space. Of course, the way these activities are organized will be responsive to the climate and how it impacts the ability of humans to work in unsheltered or unlighted places (see Binford 1983c for a discussion of these effects). In addition we can expect there to be more secondary refuse on residential sites as a function of the longer occupational durations commonly associated with these sites, although it is fully realized that mobility is itself variable among systems.

Pan-human characteristics may condition very general spatial patterns characteristic and diagnostic of certain types of hunter-gatherer settlement (see Binford 1983c for a discussion of this modular approach). For example, if butchering is the primary function of a location, butchering areas will be the primary focus and subsidiary activities, such as snacking, napping, and localized processing of butchered parts for transport, will be peripherally located (Binford 1983c:122–123). It is certainly possible, and quite likely, that some butchering sites of logistically organized groups may have residential components as well as special processing areas, but these will be peripheral to the focus of the occupation. On the other hand, hunting camps and stands may be characterized by very short-term "maintenance" with regard to human needs, such as warming up, snacking, conversation, and embedded craft activities during dull times. The site structure of the Mask site (Binford 1978b) illustrates just such a focus of use, where regular sleeping, child care, daily meal preparation, and a division of labor with regard to meal preparation and consumption were activities for which no accommodation was provided in the organization of utilized space. In short, the focal area of the site was around hearths. All activities were centered around these features, and the space was neither maintained nor organized to accommodate independent activity and work schedules characteristic of a residential camp. By working between faunal domains and site structural domains we should be able to recognize hunting camps from residential camps.

IMPLICATIONS FOR LEARNING

The basic message of this discussion is that we are developing ways for giving meaning to certain broad characteristics of site-structural patterning, which should make it possible to distinguish between, for example, a hunting camp and a residential site. Given these capabilities, if we observed an anatomical-part frequency graph from an Australian site dominated by heads and lower legs, and based on the Nunamiut analogy it was thought that such a graph was indicative of a hunting camp, we should recognize the ambiguity from site-structural facts and be in the position to conduct research to broaden our understanding of organizational facts. By investigating apparent ambiguity, and by bouncing our knowledge back and forth between contexts and frames of reference, we could recognize organizational differences between the Alyawara and Nunamiut systems. We might be able to grasp the difference between forager and collector systems, even in the absence of direct ethnographic knowledge of such differences. This type of knowledge growth should be a major aim of our comparative research.

The approach being advocated here is one in which we seek to analyze our data and partition our knowledge into general, uniformitarianistic knowledge that can serve as a frame of reference (as did the economic anatomy of animals). Against this frame of reference we can project or compare other properties of the archaeological record that are also understood in generalizable but independent terms (e.g., site structure) in order to isolate the organizational characteristics of past systems. In both cases, we would initially be seeking to recognize and understand properties that have general relevance to human actions, as in the case of extensive activity areas versus domestic activity areas. These broad generalizable properties would then serve as an analytical frame of reference against which we could discern extensive behavioral variability. In the context of such similar organizations, very different "behaviors" (in Schiffer's sense of the word) might be carried out. One example of different behaviors that occur at work spaces with similar organizations is illustrated by the Alyawara men's activity area, where automobiles were repaired, versus the Nunamiut butchering areas.

Past organization has reference to the different ways in which similar behaviors are put together and juxtaposited spatially at both the intrasite and intersite levels of archaeological pattern formation. In like fashion, similar behaviors may be differentially organized or put together so as to yield very different formal "assemblages" or spatially patterned archaeological arrangements of items and features. Alternatively, there may be very similar organizational arrangements for differing behaviors. We must understand the interrelationships between behaviors, and their integration with other behaviors, in order to understand the patterning manifested in the archaeological record.

Organization is not just behavior. It is the manner in which behaviors are juxtaposi-tioned and integrated with one another, and these generalizations cannot be seen simply by the identification of discrete behaviors themselves, nor by inventorying the different ones present at different sites. It must be realized that social units that perform very different behaviors may exhibit similar organizations and, in turn, that similar behaviors may be organized in differing ways. It is by working back and forth between independently reasoned frames of reference for behaviorally relevant archaeological materials that we obtain clues to the nature of past organization.

I would argue that the development of frames of reference phrased in terms of cross-culturally valid determinant conditioners of behavior are necessary before the differing organizations of behavior, characteristic of differing cultural systems, can be seen by archaeologists. It is the description of organizational variability that we seek to achieve in our study of past systems. It is such variability that helps us understand behavioral facts, and in turn it is organizational variability that we seek to explain as cultural scientists, not just behavior per se.

This approach implies that, for archaeologists, developing relevant laws of human behavior per se primarily serves middle-range research goals, while understanding the factors that condition the differing organizations in terms of which humans behave represents the goals of general theoretical development. One cannot be "built-up" from the other. They refer to differing orders of phenomena. The advocates of a "behavioral archaeology" have failed to appreciate this point, as have those (e.g., Raab and Goodyear 1984) who advocate strictly inductive theory-building procedures.

IMPLICATIONS FOR ARCHAEOLOGICAL RESEARCH TACTICS

Clearing up misrepresentations of the relationships between dynamics and statics identifies my study as middle-range research. As stated earlier, middle-range research is aimed at explicating the dynamic/static linkage that must be understood before inferences from the statics to the dynamics can be justified.

We must accept the fact that testing or evaluating the causal character of such linkages cannot be studied through the investigation of statics alone (Binford 1983a:12–17, 157–167). It is equally true that evaluation of proposed linkages cannot be accomplished through the study of dynamics or through ethnographic research alone. Gould's failure in this regard is a good illustration of this point. He studied the Ngatatjara Aborigines ethnographically and tried to infer the nature of the linkages between his experiences in the dynamic domain and patterning in the archaeological record (Gould 1980a). He was wrong (see Binford 1984d, 1985a; Binford and Stone 1985). Gould noted that I had observed a great range of variability in the butchering tactics of the Nunamiut Eskimo. Because he observed a "rigid" butchering procedure among the Ngatatjara, he concluded that the rigidity was referable to a strong "sharing ethic" among "his people." By implication, no such strong sharing ethic should have been present among the Nunamiut! This is simply not true. The main contrast between the Nunamiut and the Ngatatjara is a vast organizational difference: the Nunamiut participate in a logistically organized system, where butchering occurs in many different contexts and for different purposes, whereas the Ngatatjara system is representative of a foraging strategy. This difference is exacerbated by enormous environmental contrasts, where freezing conditions a different set of butchering strategies than those that occur in fly-infested, warm settings. Linked to these differences are differences in how the sharing behavior is organized in a Australian (forager) system and a Nunamiut (collector) system (Binford 1984d). Attempting to refer the variation to a quantitative difference in the degree to which the two ethnic units are dedicated to a sharing ethic misses the major point of cultural anthropology—namely, that it is not the biological character of the people nor other "essential" attitudinal contrasts that account for differences, it is primarily how similar things and behavioral tendencies are differentially organized and hence emphasized. In turn, the challenge is to explain how such organizational diversity arises and is perpetuated.

Failure to play off general behavioral characteristics against clues to organizational differentiation is a major failure of those who pursue reconstructionist goals. The examples of the important and indicative properties of "secondary refuse" for understanding organizational differences suggested in this paper demonstrate that secondary refuse is not a "distortion" of the systemic properties of past systems. I have previously treated this point (Binford 1983a:157–167, 213–227), but many still insist that the archaeological record is limited and distorted in its ability to yield information about past systems. At the practical level what is commonly distorted are our views about how to research the archaeological record and how to learn about its implications for the past. Learning how to learn is the challenge of science.

Returning to the archaeological perspective, I must emphasize that middle-range research is the only way to evaluate propositions that seek to link dynamics and statics in a controlled fashion. The example illustrated here shows how ethnoarchaeology can play an important role in providing the controlled information necessary to productive middle-range research.

The role of analogical reasoning is central to any discussion of middle-range research. In my opinion, analogy is a basic and fundamental tool of middle-range research and a necessary part of the "tool kit" of intellectual tools to be used by middle-range researchers. This is not to say that it cannot be abused. Nevertheless, I have suggested here that the active investigation of ambiguity can be a useful research tactic. Commonly, arguments from ethnographic analogy serve as the starting point for our alleged understanding of the archaeological record. It is against such an understanding that tactics for recognizing ambiguity are played out. The recognition of ambiguity should be viewed as a caution or as an alert flag signaling some limitations in our knowledge. Even more importantly, the recognition of ambiguity frequently isolates for the researcher a domain of information needed or an area of intellectual inadequacy that, if addressed, may help clear up the apparent ambiguity. If the astute researcher heeds this flag and pursues the growth of knowledge in the implicated area, the resulting understanding will contribute to the growth of our field.

I have tried to illustrate this point with the classic form of argument from ethnographic analogy. Among the Nunamiut a distinctive graph of anatomical-part frequencies dominated by heads and lower legs occurs on kill sites and hunting stands. One could then reason from analogy that, if such a pattern were observed elsewhere, the site yielding the distinctive faunal pattern was a hunting stand or kill site. In the case discussed here it was a residential site that yielded a similar anatomical-part frequency graph, demonstrating ambiguity in the meaning of such a phenomenon. For some, this would be taken as a justification for rejecting the use of ethnographic analogy (Gould 1980a:29–42) or perhaps as just another "cautionary tale" showing how archaeologists should beware of generalizations. Other archaeologists might even see this as a lesson in how they should respect the uniqueness of each culture. I would agree that the use of unevaluated propositions for interpreting the archaeological record is a mistake (Binford 1981a), but the use of ethnographic analogies in the context of middle-range research procedures is perhaps crucial. When linked to an active search for an investigation of ambiguity, it stands as a basic element in the learning process (Wylie 1985).

I have tried to illustrate another important component of the learning strategies that archaeologists must perfect. This is the development of cross-cultural comparative studies aimed at the recognition of general behavioral "regularities," which in turn serves as frames of reference useful for recognizing variability in the way different cultural systems are organized. In the case discussed here, I already had a clue to some fundamental organizational differences between the hunter-gatherer systems being compared (Binford 1979). By pursing middle-range research in an ethnoarchaeological context I sought to understand how differently organized systems might be manifest archaeologically with respect to behavioral patterns whose recognition criteria I had already investigated (Binford 1978a).

It is perhaps important to stress that this paper has been about how we learn. Much of the emphasis in relatively recent literature has been on how we evaluate alleged knowledge. This is of course important, but the most important aspects of science have to do with the tactics we employ in using the knowledge available to us at any one point in time as a springboard for exploring our ignorance, or the limitations of our ideas of the moment. This paper has addressed the latter issue. Seen in this manner, many of the arguments recently generated in the archaeological literature appear to be misguided and out of place. For instance, the citation of facts about the Bushmen (as described by Yellen 1977a:132–136) as "empirical cases to the contrary" relative to my experiences with the Nunamiut, or Gould's (1980a) similar arguments, only make sense if it is believed that the only goal of science is to isolate general "laws" of human behavior. This point of view fails to understand that theories are not a recitation of "laws."

I hope I have illustrated that generalizations function as backdrops useful for recognizing organizational differences among systems. It is the specification of such differences that provides the basis for the science of culture, the investigation and explanation of cultural differences themselves. It is these differences and similarities and their distribution that must be explained. Explanatory theories will never consist of lawlike generalizations; rather, they will be integrated arguments as to what conditions both the similarities and the differences. When variability is cited solely as the basis for denying generalizations, the entire productive process of learning about fundamental cultural differences is aborted. The recognition of variability and difference is not a justification for the argument of uniqueness and particularism. If we take as our task the explanation of cultural differences, then their fundamental character must be elucidated before we know what it is that is in need of explanation. There has been much spinning of wheels and misguided argument on this point in the recent literature. It is time to stop nonproductive argument and get on with the business of science.

ACKNOWLEDGMENTS

I am most fortunate to have had able assistance during the research, analysis, and manuscript phases of the development of this paper. James O'Connell worked with me while mapping and researching the Alyawara site reported here. Eric Ingbar did much of the work in preparing and executing the factor analysis of the Alyawara site data. Nancy Stone lived through the writing of this manuscript and contributed greatly to the final form it has taken. To these people I am most grateful.

NOTES

1. Culture is assumed to be extrasomatic in that it is not dependent upon genetic mechanisms as the determinants of its form (White 1949:23–39).
2. This work was financed by a grant from the Australian Institute of Aboriginal Studies.
3. Ironically the argument for hunting and the "Schlepp effect" was based on a failure to understand this point (see Perkins and Daly 1968).

4. Gould (1980a:193–195) considers this behavior "extreme" and to be understood as an adaptation to game scarcity in the Western Desert of Australia. My guess is that the behavior is more general and reflective of the low fat yields from kangaroo.

5. Binford (1983c:238, note 10) answers such claims.

6. See Binford (1977a) for a discussion of this distinction.

7. For additional information on Alyawara settlement see Binford (1986a) and O'Connell (1977).

8. I do not mean that the postabandonment patterning was to be ignored, only that we sought to describe the site framework relative to which the occupational debris accumulated.

9. This orientation is analogous to the common southeast orientation found in the northern hemisphere.

10. The wind had blown the ash away so that these hearths were documented by a scatter of very fine charcoal and some minor soil oxidation.

11. The choice of a "global" technique is justified by the fact that it has been demonstrated as an appropriate technique for the Nunamiut data. Here I am seeking some comparative perspective relative to those data.

12. It is acknowledged that this procedure can obscure lower-scale manifestations of patterning; however, my target in this analysis was the total site level of structure.

13. In his ring model, Yellen (1977a) recognized many of the same conditions that I am stressing here. The difference is that he was looking at a band camp, which is of course the modular result of combining many of the patterns characteristic of residential units themselves. I will address the topic of multiresidential camp planning in a forthcoming article.

14. Perhaps the best archaeological demonstrations of what I am discussing are the debris concentrations around the "outside" hearths on Pincevent 36 (Leroi-Gourhan and Brézillon 1972). I am convinced that these features represent a series of hunting camps, not residential sites.

Part IV

Models and Accommodating Arguments versus Pattern Recognition: What Drives Research Best?

Chapter 18

Multidimensional Analysis of Sheep and Goats: Baa-ck and Forth

The organization of this book is focused on debate. When seriously conducted by professionals, debate is one avenue that can be used to sharpen our abilities for recognizing germane targets for receiving our research attentions. I wish at this point, however, to shift the focus to another avenue that I think needs serious consideration. Simply stated, it is doing archaeology. In the introduction I cited the definition of our field I have basically accepted throughout my career. I am suggesting that most archaeologists do not act in ways consistent with Spaulding's astute description. Basic to Spaulding's discussion is an emphasis on the study of relationships among observations made on formal properties of artifacts—read "archaeological record"—and in turn the relationships among these formal properties and the spatial and temporal dimensions. The focus here is on relationships. I introduced this point in Chapter 1 and I wish to continue exploring this concept here.

Before powerful microcomputers became readily available, intensive study of relationships was almost impossible. Faced with huge mounds of artifacts, archaeologists described various formal properties (made first-order observations) and sought to generalize or systematize these observations into taxonomies. These taxonomic syntheses could then be reviewed relative to time scales, the familiar chronological charts of archaeological monographs and textbooks, or against a backdrop of geography, the familiar map with dots, circles, and arrows. There was little else archaeologists could do given the literally overwhelming task standing behind the call for the study of relationships. Facing the quantity of observations archaeologists routinely made on artifacts and the archaeological record and attempting to investigate the relationships among these observations was practically impossible using a slide rule, a hand-crank calculator, or even mainframe computers that were largely noninteractive. Most archaeologists did not appear to be frustrated by this limitation, since they had a paradigmatic insulator against even thinking of trying to explore relationships. These were the normative assumptions about the meaning of artifacts that I have criticized so often.

As pointed out in Chapter 2, archaeologists believed that the observations they chose to make on artifacts implicated static "mental templates" for the proper way to make artifacts. These templates were conceived as discrete and differentiated, and the goal was to inventory them as the basis for tabulating the intellectual content of a "culture." No study of relationships as we might think of them in a modern sense was considered necessary; only a summary of associations among these synthesized taxonomic aggregates in time and space was thought appropriate for discussion. These summaries were followed in turn by various convention-driven "interpretations" of culture history.

Such common conceptual distinctions as "industries versus assemblages" betray something of the lack of concern for the study of relationships. An industry is a subset of the general class "artifacts" that has reference to all those artifacts made of the same raw material. We could then speak of a ceramic industry, a lithic industry, a bone industry. The thought standing behind such a primary distinction is in simple deference to such guiding principles as "don't compare sheep and goats" or "don't mix apples and oranges." There was a practical consideration as well: the formal characteristics considered germane for describing ceramic properties were judged to be different from those seen as appropriate to describing lithics, faunal remains, or the others.

In traditional archaeology, where the goal was the recognition of mental templates or design models, the generalizing tool was suites of formal categories. We were seeking to isolate "natural units" thought to have been given "by nature" in the form of the designs for manufacture held in the minds of the ancients (see Chang 1967b:78). This minimally veiled essentialist position only makes sense to those who believe that there are natural units out there which it is our task to discover. Given that archaeological types or classes of artifacts were viewed in such ways, the "don't mix apples and oranges" admonition makes some sense. As is not surprising, our monographs and archaeological reports are a wonderful testament to the lack of interest in studying relationships among classes in any systemic sense of the word. "Good" monographs are a series of chapters (e.g., lithics, ceramics, ground stone) with essentialist subheadings (e.g., projectile points, hand axes, knives; for a modern example see Thomas 1983). Generally speaking, an archaeologist might make summarizing generalizations about properties or attributes for the entities assigned to classes or even make comparative statements regarding subsets within classes, but one can search long and hard for any analytical comparisons made by archaeologists among classes or industries of artifacts. For the traditionalists, such activities would make little sense. Why should one think of studying the character of relationships among separate classes of artifacts or other properties of the archaeological record when our task was to isolate "natural units"? That would be viewed as violating the empiricist's wisdom that one should not compare sheep and goats or mix apples and oranges.

My early arguments with F. Bordes focused on this point. If our taxonomies of artifacts are considered to reflect natural units, and success as a typologist is success as an empiricist (the ability to see nature clearly), then taxonomic units are thought to have direct reference to the nature said to be under investigation—the design templates standing behind the formal variability we observe. Given such a view, it is inconceivable to ask what our taxonomies are measuring, as I did with regard to the Bordes taxonomy. Similarly, it is inconceivable to question the character of the organized interaction among properties discussed with reference to one artifact class and (different or analogous) properties used to describe another artifact class. While known to be possible, such isolation of properties was considered a violation of the way nature was organized and hence a commission of the error of mixing apples and oranges. No good archaeologist wanted to be cited as having committed such an error.

Archaeological reports diligently seek to keep their "natural units" all neatly separated. This is nowhere better illustrated than in the treatment by archaeologists of the descriptive products of "specialists." Our reports are padded by independent chapters on fauna, basketry, pollen, sediments, phytoliths, coprolites, and wooden objects, and there is no integration, no study of the relationships among observations made by the "specialists" and the archaeologist or among the various specialists. Each specialist describes a different unit of segmented "nature," and all of them have different ideas as to the characteristics of nature standing behind their observations. After all, artifacts are products of fabrication designs by humans, whereas pollen has reference to the reproductive properties of plants; you cannot mix apples and oranges. This essentialist view of nature, linked with empiricist guidelines for studying this assumed nature, still dominates much of archaeology.

When I worked with Bordes during 1968, he was clearly a bit annoyed with my interest in bones. The study of bones is the proper domain of the specialist, the zoologist who understands the criteria for species identification and in turn what the presence or absence of those species implies about nature, the character of the environmental setting in which the ancients lived. One afternoon Bordes was particularly annoyed with me because I was lamenting to him that many of the bones had not been piece plotted during the excavations at Combe Grenal (in fact none of them were supposed to be piece plotted, but many diggers did so anyway). Nothing like the care given to the stone tools was evident. Bordes walked up and down along the drip line at Combe Grenal, expounding at great length: the bones were a product of the animal world, the world of zoology; differences in the "typology" of the bones only told us who the animals were; we wanted to know who the people were; only the typology developed by a "good" artifact observer could tell us that. I tried to suggest that knowing how the animals were used by people could tell us many things about seasonality, the degree to which persons practiced storage, whether provisioning of central places was going on, even the spatial organization of labor or activities within the environment. Bordes's response was better than most. First he noted that, if the ancients responded to their environments in rational ways using different products at different seasons, processing animal products differently for storage, and so forth, then the only way I could give meaning to patterning observed for the bones was dependent upon my ability to understand what was rational. Such rationality should be general to man and in no way informative about who they were—and would therefore be useless. Unlike him, I would not be engaged in any quest of discovery; I would be a little boring person simply describing over and over again what we already knew—that man was rational. I then countered with the age-old observation that what is rational to one person is not necessarily rational to another. Rationality is something that we cannot claim to appreciate directly, something we cannot intuitively see as the empiricist might imagine. Bordes did not like this argument. He strode back and forth, puffing on his pipe and telling me that although I was an American I argued like a "G— D— Anglo-Saxon." I just wanted to confuse the issues with meaningless words, whereas any "rational Frenchman" would never do such a thing. He would never waste his time with such meaningless conversation.

Bordes was great fun, and one always knew when his irritation overpowered his involvement in argument. I pushed him still further that day at Combe Grenal, talking about what we could learn from bones. Finally, he was "fed up," as he was apt to say, and said, "Binford you are wasting your time. All this stuff about bones, you can learn nothing except who the animals were. I can see the situation here in this cave clearly. The big chief walks into the camp, looks down, and sees this old bone lying in his path. He reaches down, picks it up, and throws it outside the cave, saying 'who put this G— D— bone in my way?' What does that do to all your statistics on bones?"[1]

That afternoon Bordes and I talked back and forth about this issue and about the degree to which cleaning up was something that varied in organizational terms and was itself an interesting property of past behavior to investigate. Although Bordes was never convinced by my arguments, he did acknowledge that perhaps there was something to be learned since the differences between peoples might be reflected in their choices as to which animals to eat. Bordes, however, never thought that this was something requiring the attention of the archaeologist. "I can tell this from the specialist's report," he would say, "and during the time I am digging. There are clearly more horses from level 14 at Combe Grenal than from any other level; anybody can see that. Those denticulate people chose to eat horses."[2]

The point of all this has been to illustrate that, given traditionalist assumptions about archaeology linked to empiricist assumptions about how to learn, there is really no reason to study relationships among "fundamentally" different things. It was this view that I challenged long ago by trying to suggest that culture was not a catalog of beliefs or mental templates; instead it was a system and was characterized by all that the term "system" implied organizationally. One could document the use of stone pebbles to smooth pottery, shells to scrape it, wood to support a vessel being built, even stone tools or antler tools used in procuring clay and decorating pots. The archaeological record was produced in the context of many variable ways of organizing natural materials, including the organization of human labor itself. It could therefore be profitably explored for patterning in terms of relationships among different things for the purpose of understanding how the past was organized. Archaeologists had to begin the difficult job of pattern recognition; as Spaulding pointed out, they had to behave as archaeologists and study the relationships among formal, temporal, and spatial properties of the archaeological record. At the methodological level they also had to study the relationships between organized behavior and the material consequences of that behavior. They had to engage in middle-range research if they ever hoped to understand the relationships they might discover. They had to begin the difficult task of seeking knowledge about what these relationships, once recognized, might have reference to in the organization of past systems. In addition, they had to know whether patterning simply had reference to the way archaeologists chose to look at the archaeological record (thus the emphasis on sampling; Binford 1964) or to other conditions that might produce patterns that had no reference to past human systems at all.(See the literature of the 1920s regarding what was or was not to be included in the category "artifact," and my excursion into this problem in *Bones:* Binford 1981a.)

All of us realized that, if we were to expand archaeological endeavor from the examination of entities to the examination of relationships among entities and classes of entities, we too would have to face the situation of any researcher seeing something unfamiliar. In turn we would have to seek knowledge beyond the archaeological record itself to have a good idea as to the character of the dynamics to which the patterning might have reference (see my discussion of this frustration in Binford 1983c:98–100.) The issue of what our taxonomies measured, as argued in the "Mousterian debate," would have to be expanded in more complicated ways to deal with patterning in relational terms that we might be able to demonstrate and therefore "see." Traditional archaeology only addressed this issue through stipulation and normative arguments from casual observations on dynamics linked to assumptions about human nature. Since the question had not been previously faced, there was precious little accumulated knowledge to draw upon; hence my push for ethnoarchaeological, experimental, and other forms of controlled observation. If we accepted the challenge to conduct pattern-recognition studies at a sophisticated level, we also had to face the problem of "seeing" many new things for which our received knowledge was inadequate to guide accurate interpretation.

Many of the articles reprinted in the following section are probes in the direction of expanding our pattern-recognition endeavors. Clearly my work with bones and the directions I have pursued with faunal study as well as the beginnings of integration of faunal facts with stone tool facts represent moves to expand our pattern-recognition exploration. Most of my arguments with Africanists arose from my attempts to expand our pattern-recognition frontiers while at the same time criticizing the conventionalism that has stood behind much interpretation of early hominid materials (see Chapters 19, 20, 22, 23, and 26).

As I viewed the literature of most Lower Paleolithic research, stipulation played a clear central role in the same fashion as the stipulations dear to the hearts of traditional archaeologists (see, e.g., Isaac's 1971 operational definitions for recognizing a "base camp" and the stipulations guiding the recognition of "living floors" discussed in Chapter 26, which clearly but tautologically make possible discussions of base camps and "central-place foraging" behavior on the part of ancient hominids). The use of the idea of "industries" by many archaeologists was consistent with the essentialist idea that there were natural units out there to be discovered by astute empiricist observers.

The "assemblage" was another "natural unit" used by archaeologists to make possible synthetic statements linking observations on industries and other "natural units" such as faunal remains or pollen. The assemblage is the spatially associated aggregate of industries, fauna, pollen, and so on. This spatial aggregation was assumed (as we see in Isaac 1971) to be the consequence of human/hominid actions. Thus the association was seen as the justification for any statements made about the past in any synthetic sense. For example, the popular literature on Torralba is only justifiable if one assumes that all things found together go together and have unambiguous reference exclusively to past hominid behavior (but see Chapter 25). It was this assumption that I questioned in my review of Glynn Isaac's book on Olorgesailie (Binford 1977c) and that was the point of departure for my arguments over the Olduvai fauna in *Bones* (Binford 1981a). Clearly Isaac got the message on this point; hence his happiness with the "smoking gun" argument about cutmarks (see Bunn 1983a). He missed the more general argument, however, that relationships once seen may have no self-evident reference to the past.[3] Relationships between tools and fauna, for instance, may potentially have reference to hominids (use of the word "potentially" here simply acknowledges the possibility that multiple agents could be involved; see, for example, the problems encountered in interpretation of the Abri Vaufrey materials; Binford 1987c); it in no way justifies what may be said about relationships that one may recognize (see Chapter 24).

Most of the articles reprinted here are about early man studies and represent my debates on Lower Paleolithic issues. I began participation in this literature for a number of reasons, but I fear that understanding the literature is as much a function of knowing something about the "faunal" composition of the field of archaeology as it is a function of comprehending the issues.

Argument with Yippies, Yuppies, Puppies, Puppies with Guppie retouch, Lollies, and self-proclaimed Guppies is very different from argument with Guppies. Guppies do not argue, they pronounce and pass judgments. True Guppies are above all the argument, secure in their knowledge and with their monopoly on truth. Guppies find debates vaguely disgusting in that they are seen as public admissions of non-Guppiehood. Debates are for Puppies and the insecure youth trying to get ahead. It should be pointed out that the only place Puppies, Yuppies, Yippies, self-proclaimed Guppies, and Lollies get to behave like Guppies is during the research grant review process, where they can hide behind their anonymity; there they can pronounce and pass judgments in the Guppie Way: it is wonderful for them and, I might point out, quite vicious.

Much of the "heat" of the early years of the new archaeology came from Guppies who saw such dissatisfaction as an insult to their Guppiehood. Being Guppies they did not confront my articles or argue with me, they simply tried to use their Guppie status to eliminate me. Guppies are sometimes quite dangerous beasts. Puppies, seeing the examples of their Guppie guides to success, frequently adopt Guppie tactics and at every juncture contribute to the character assignation as modeled by Guppies. It is interesting that a number of conditions not controlled by Guppies in the United States contributed to their loss of some power here. Perhaps the single most important factor was the growth of the field, both in terms of personnel and, more important, jobs during the 1960s. During the growth period, as far as American archaeology was concerned there was a place for everyone—even those heaped with Guppie disapproval. Many foreign centers of Guppie power (see Wright 1977) saw the discussions going on in the United States accurately as a threat to Guppiehood as it had traditionally operated in archaeology. In addition to there being a nationalistic character to Guppie protection, there was perceived to be safety in research subject areas outside the United States, since what has been called the excesses of the new archaeology or the demeaning of the discipline of archaeology (Gould 1980a:250) was thought to be contained within that country. Workers in foreign areas or time periods totally unrelated to the American Southwest or eastern North America had been spared. They were thought to be above all the hoopla. I was aware of such attitudes but did not pay much attention until my visit to Australia in 1974, where Isaac (1977b) delivered a paper entitled "Squeezing Blood from Stones." There it was made quite clear in a very tactful manner that all the interesting discussion and honest investment in learning more about the archaeological record that I and my colleagues had been attempting was irrelevant to the Guppie-controlled domain of the Lower Paleolithic. (This point was made even more explicit in conversation.) This was not a new experience, but it was one that particularly bothered me since every student of archaeology was required to study at least something about the Lower Paleolithic. In short, very traditional ideas were ubiquitously taught to all archaeologists by virtue of a Guppie monopoly.

I did not act immediately, since I was hard at work trying to write up the Nunamiut material and many other pieces representing a research backlog that at the time appeared to me to be mountainous. As I cleared this backlog I realized that I was finishing off one phase of my research investment and began to think about what I would do next. I obviously had the Combe Grenal data and the Mousterian problem to address. In Australia, however, I had spent much time with Bordes, and he was clearly fed up with the Mousterian and was seriously flirting with the idea of working in Australia, which he later did. Bordes's original plans for the Combe Grenal data were to publish it in two volumes, one written by Bordes and another by me, with a clear and cooperative discussion of the Mousterian problem. Bordes did not want to do it then, so I too left the Combe Grenal data for a time when we both felt like getting it out. How could anyone have imagined that Bordes would die before we even got started? His death was certainly one of the saddest events in my life.

In any event, I began reading the literature of the Lower Paleolithic with an eye to opening up a debate. The opportunity came when I was asked to review Isaac's (1977a) publication on Olorgesailie (Binford 1977). I was very restrained, very polite, and quite Guppie-like in this review since I was well aware that Guppies do not debate. Slightly later Isaac was invited to Albuquerque to deliver one of our Harvey lectures (clearly a "Guppie accident of history"). Glynn was very keen on his "sharing" argument, and one of his major papers on the subject was that Harvey lecture (Isaac 1978b). Unfortunately, I was very ill with the flu when Glynn arrived in Albuquerque. He graciously consented to brave the flu bug and came out to see me for an afternoon and evening. In spite of my runny nose and reddened eyes, we had what he described as a great "down-to-earth discussion of our differences," which were all about his sharing argument being based on the assumption of hunting by the early Pleistocene hominids. What was clear to me, however, was that I was acting like a Guppie in our conversation since I kept introducing to him my knowledge and experiences with animals in the Arctic, which was not publicly available. Of course neither he nor anyone else knew anything about those things, since the germane material had not been covered in the Nunamiut book (1978a).

After the brave Glynn Isaac left my house that afternoon, waving back at my flu-droopy eyes, I decided that I had to write an article on taphonomy as the basis for beginning a debate with Isaac. He seemed willing, even though he was certainly a Guppie by then, and to get one into debate is not easy. What started out as an article quickly turned into *Bones* (Binford 1981a). But I wanted a debate only if it could be clearly focused on issues, not clouded by personal and nonpublic knowledge. It was just another accident of history that I chose to use the published faunal data from Olduvai Gorge as an analytical exercise in *Bones*. Clearly in all this I was behaving like a Guppie, setting a trap to get a debate partner. On the other hand, Isaac was a Guppie and I knew Guppie ways. He later admitted to me that many of his "suggestions" to his students and associates as to what might be good research projects between the years 1977 and 1981 were also Guppie accidents of history, since he knew in a general way what my arguments were likely to be.

Much to my surprise Isaac did not review *Bones* for *Science*. Instead, another Guppie accident of history occurred when Isaac's student Henry Bunn (1982a) reviewed the book. This is heavy Guppie tactics. Nevertheless, I still thought that productive debate might be possible, so I did not answer the review in public; I wrote a letter to Bunn outlining my objections before the publication date, thinking a serious consideration might result in some modifications and hence an indication that serious debate was possible. I have included in the following section (Chapter 20) a copy of my letter to Henry Bunn dated February 15, 1982. It should be clear from this letter that my concerns were how knowledge claims are made about the past. Equally important to me was the need to address the issues and not develop a debate based on every fallacious argument known to logic. The best of all motives is rarely enough in dealing with Guppies. Puppies are ambitious and are not interested in debate, only in being right; their confidence comes from their favored Puppie status, not from any properties of substance. After the exchanges reprinted in the following section (Chapters 20 and 21), Isaac invited me to Berkeley for a debate and I was encouraged by our conversations. Later he invited me to Harvard, where we had productive conversations, so in spite of the nonsense of the response to *Bones* I was encouraged as to the possibilities that a substantive debate might still be possible. In the midst of the "sniffing and circling" between Isaac and myself, however, complicating events, including press conferences and the publication of an article (Shipman et al. 1981) defending the traditional interpretation of Olorgesailie location DE/89B criticized in my review of Isaac's book, burst onto the scene.[4] I considered then and still consider Shipman's arguments to be some of the best examples in the literature of how *not* to deal with a problem of archaeological interpretation.

If two professionals are to participate in productive and honest debate, they must trust one another. I enjoyed that kind of relationship with François Bordes and knew well the value of such a relationship and its importance if each participant, as well as the field, were to profit by any debate. The Shipman affair made me very suspicious, since her choice of research topic and her stand on the issue looked to me to be a clear Guppie accident of history and a repeat of the book-review situation, where the Guppie's Puppie is sent out to engage critics and thereby protect the Guppie in his self-assured position of nonparticipation. If I was to continue pursuing my goal of productive debate, I had to be able to trust the potential debate partner and be assured that he or she considered the issues worth debating. Information made available to me suggested that, while the choice of research topic by Shipman was probably a Guppie accident of history, her approach and style of treatment was not authorized Puppie behavior; instead it was judged ambitious Yuppie behavior.

In order to clear the air I wrote the article reprinted here (Chapter 22). I had several goals in this article. First, I wanted to point out that the scavenging interpretation of "data" was introduced into the recent literature by Isaac. He and I had discussed this issue and the application of the criteria he actually employed while sitting in my flu-infested living room in 1977. I wanted to pat Isaac on the back for having taken our genial discussions seriously. Second, for readers and interested persons I wanted to treat the recent literature as an aggregate composed of independent participants and not simply a Guppie-directed corporate action. Most important of all, I wanted to identify what I considered to be the most profitable issue to discuss if productive debate was to be forthcoming, namely, the assumption by Isaac and his team that the reported animal gnawing on the bones from the Zinjanthropus floor was to be dis-missed as having been inflicted after the hominids had abandoned the site. This unjustified assumption cleared the way for the repeated interpretation that the homi-nids who used the Zinjanthropus floor had a meat-rich diet and were likely to have been hunters. All the cutmark arguments seemed to me to be essentially irrelevant since, unlike what has been claimed, neither I nor anyone else seriously doubted the hominid involvement in the accumulation of the bones on the Zinjanthropus floor. The "smoking gun" arguments from cutmarks were directed to a nonexistent issue.[5]

At the Zinjanthropus site the issues were first the nature of the hominid involvement and second whether all the materials on the floor were categorically assignable to hominid behavior. In addition, I knew of no reliable procedures for unambiguously assigning meaning to cutmark patterning. This concern is difficult for empiricists to understand, since they believe and behave as if the links between observations and the use of those observations as evidence in argument are self-evident. This incorrect assumption is the central issue standing behind my dissatisfaction with the literature on the early time periods in general. Returning to the "Changing Views" article (Chapter 22), I also made clear my attitudes toward the Yuppieism that had been introduced into the literature on the Lower Paleolithic.

I had just returned from China when I heard of Isaac's tragic death. At that point all my hopes for productive discussion of the Lower Paleolithic issues were completely wiped out. This judgment has certainly been validated by the subsequent develop-ments in the literature. As I have suggested, productive debate is totally dependent upon the participants knowing what the issues are. Productive debate does not devel-op from committing all the basic fallacies of logical discussion. Productive debate is not a war. It is not a series of public insults and little ploys of one-upmanship. It is a logical focus on issues. The issue is not who is right but instead how we should proceed in order to gain a basis for judging which arguments may be justified regard-ing the nature of the past. Blind empiricists have difficulty with this posture. As I pointed out in my reply to Freeman (Chapter 8), the logic of empiricism and the Guppie ethic in general ensures that the only method of disagreement about the world of experience is to discuss the credentials (*ad hominem* argument) and the qualifications of another to make observations on nature and to have the gall (in the view of empiricists) to offer interpretations from that experience. As I have tried to point out, the only logical tactic available to empiricists is to demean the qualifications (personal and professional) of persons engaged in that privileged (and impossible) activity of seeing nature truly.[6]

The article republished in the following section (Chapter 23) was a serious attempt to cope with much misrepresentation about the Zinjanthropus floor introduced into the literature, but more importantly to introduce some knowledge and observations about cutmarks, since Bunn and Kroll (1986a, 1986b) seemed upset that I had not addressed what they clearly thought was the centerpiece of their position. As noted earlier, I considered this view a non sequitur because there was no tested or even minimally justified basis for interpreting cutmarks in terms of what they might mean behaviorally—for example, the state of the bones at the time the cutmarks were inflicted, the goals of tool-using hominids, and the signatures for inferring early access to carcasses. Observations cannot be transformed into evidence for or against an interpretation when Lollie strategies are used. Of course, I do not think that Bunn and Kroll were conscious of their tactics. As empiricists, they behaved (at least they acted) as if the transformation of observations into evidence were not a necessary step in reasoning but could be accomplished by simply "seeing" nature truly. I have no doubt that they really believed that their observations, the "data," directly imply meat eating, and my objections were simply seen as annoying attempts to break into the Guppieland of Lower Paleolithic studies. What presumption on my part! After all, they have "seen" the bones and in other ways communed with the "facts."

My approach was to introduce what I had observed about cutmarks and to cite serious descriptive summaries of cutmark patterning produced by other researchers as the only knowledge available, at least to me, that might reasonably be used to evaluate their unjustified interpretations. In no way do I consider this knowledge adequate to justify accurate interpretation, as I point out in the article. Much pattern-recognition work is required to establish the nature of the interpretative problem. How many different patterns are there in cutmark form, abundance, and placement? With what does such formal variability covary: body size, species, ethnicity, geography, system state? In short, no archaeological investigations of cutmarks have been performed in the sense that I outlined in the introduction as at the heart of archaeological science—the study of relationships among formal, spatial, and temporal dimensions. In the absence of this type of investigation, we have no clues as to the character of the problems we might face in seeking to give meaning to patterning, particularly since no useful patterns have thus far been described by those who seek to interpret their observations on Lower Paleolithic materials. One cannot draw justified positive conclusions from ignorance, no matter how badly one would like to do so.

Another issue has been introduced into the debate regarding my earlier pattern-recognition work. The claim has been endlessly repeated that because I used Mary Leakey's data my conclusions are suspect since "better" data were allegedly available. To some readers, particularly empiricists, this criticism seems to make sense. It makes no sense to me. There is no such thing as "good" data in any absolute sense. The only way such a claim could be made is if it were assumed that observations have direct and magical implications to knowledge and understanding. Observations are neutral until they are infused with meaning by us through our arguments as to their significance: thus my emphasis on how we justify our inferences from observations. There *are* germane data, observations made in such a way as to eliminate known and identified sources of bias. There are more or less complete sets of observations, as judged by the knowledge standards of the time. But in the absence of a methodology there are no "good" or "bad" observational sets, only observational sets whose value lies in the potential they hold out to the astute investigator of relationships.

For instance, many persons have voiced the opinion that I should have sought to produce a better typology of Mousterian tools before moving to pattern-recognition studies in the early 1960s. I could see no reason to do this. This position is lost on empiricists, who somehow know what is good data. Such postures are astonishing to me. Because we do not know what is implicated by such observations, and we have few reliable methods for using them, we therefore have no meaningful frame of reference for judging their quality. There is simply no way of knowing such things when phenomena not previously investigated by hard-headed, middle-range research are being addressed. There is simply no way to judge what are good or bad data except by some vacant stylistic criteria of the era (measurements should be made in the metric system; all bone splinters should be recorded; data should or should not be expressed as tabulations of the forms as they present themselves to us, such as broken fragment description vs. MNI estimations, etc.). In the absence of a methodology for the use of observations in investigated and understood forms, there is no guide for the production of good data beyond the vague goal of seeing as much as one can in the hope that future investigators will figure out some way of using these observations. Empiricists do not think this way. They believe that they can see meaning in nature directly; they believe that this ability is dependent on having a good observer, that good data are observations made by good observers, or that good data meet the stylistic criteria of the time for recognizing the good observer. If the reader detects some circularity here, then the reader can see through empiricism.

It is quite true that archaeologists can expand our potential for learning about the past by identifying properties and characteristics of the archaeological record not previously given systematic descriptive attention by previous workers. This is akin to expanding our exploration of relationships only at the primary observational level. Just as in the case of discovering new and previously unseen relationships, the new properties observed do not carry self-evident meaning. We must conduct hardheaded middle-range research in order to understand any generalizations made from these "new" observations or from any patterns recognized through second- and third-derivative pattern-recognition studies. In the absence of methodological research, the "new" observations stand only as potential sources of knowledge going beyond our current level of either ignorance or knowledge, depending upon one's evaluations of the state of our art.

As pointed out in some of the essays in Part I of this book, we cannot think with ideas we do not have and, I might add, cannot argue about the relevance of observations in the absence of a methodological framework for evaluating relevance. Most of our research strategies, as with our concerns in debate, should be directed toward motivating research into zones of ignorance that can be identified as potentially productive. Empiricists never consider such things. If a good observer simply looks, he will see truth, and nothing further is needed. Research is thought to progress as a simple function of ensuring that only "good" observers using "good" data are taken seriously. All this guarantees is that our textbooks will be filled with arguments from authority and that no productive research will be forthcoming except as a result of sheer accident since no priorities can be assigned to our search for knowledge beyond the recitation of where "good" observers have previously "looked" and where they have not.

In spite of all the problems with the debate as it has developed, I have not given up on the Lower Paleolithic. In Chapter 24 I present some observations that are argued to be germane to the assumption that has been basic to the position of the East African group as to the proper interpretation of the Zinjanthropus floor. I think one can anticipate that their response will consist of attempts to dismiss these observations as not good and the observers as not good rather than taking up the challenge to learn more in hopes of gaining some knowledge that might move our interpretations closer to our learning goals, to have at least some glimmer of insight as to what the ancient past was like.

With regard to this last point, the final chapter in the following section (Chapter 28) represents what I consider to be another way to stir productive debate. I have employed still another approach to the use of observations on our contemporary world. I have tried to generalize some characteristics of cultural variability resulting from my long-term interests in hunter-gatherers. Unlike others who employ the common technique of using such knowledge as the basis for making arguments from analogy, and hence accommodating the past to our knowledge of the present, I seek to use generalizations (hopefully defensible ones) about modern hunter-gatherers as a frame of reference in much the same way as when I sought to develop the "economic anatomy of animals" as a frame of reference. One can think of a frame of reference as something like a screen for projecting slides. It is a "knowledge screen" against which cases, when projected, can be evaluated as to their fit with what we think we know. This procedure minimally permits us to see differences and become aware of clues to perhaps more fundamental differences, since the cases here are very ancient ones indeed. A lack of fit in this situation may well clue us to the possibility that there were fundamental differences in the organization of life at these early times. This strategy is an expansion of the challenge to study relationships to a very large scale indeed.

In Chapter 28 I am not engaged in developing specific methods; to the contrary, very general procedures are employed. The aim is not to engage in debate over specific methodological points but instead to explore large-scale patterning almost at the intuitive level for the purposes of recognizing characteristics that might well be most productive to pursue at the methodological level. I have tried to make a case to the effect that planning depth is a variable for which we might reasonably seek justified methods of measuring. I am reversing the situation of the Mousterian debate, where a typology had already been developed and the real question was what that typology is measuring. In this chapter I am suggesting that we might do well to seek ways of measuring the important variable of planning depth. It is a call for middle-range research developed to deal with issues presented to us by the archaeological record and its patterning.

If it is to be successful, the growth of science must be slow, deliberate, and painstaking. This growth must be guided by serious discussion regarding what we need to know and where our ignorance gaps rest. Such discussion is not developed by sticking safely with the alleged knowledge we have; we must be willing to probe the "great unknown" for guides as to where we might profitably invest research efforts. If we stick closely to the data, as empiricists advise, we stay where we are, frequently stagnating in "puzzle solving" rather than advancing the frontiers of our field. I am making no claims that the "Transition" article will turn out to serve to advance the field, only that trying one's wings is a necessary activity of the archaeologist dedicated to learning. One can be sure that debate will follow, and we will almost certainly learn from investing in such debate.

As noted previously, following debate in the ongoing literature is difficult because it is laced with fallacious forms of argument, misreading of authors' positions, and, also important, "games people play." I have switched back and forth between the issues and the games—but not because of some newly realized disenchantment with the reality of life in the field of archaeology. I have talked about things normally not discussed because my experience with teaching students has shown over and over again that they are idealistic and do not expect to see in our literature the low quality exhibited by debates, and they do not expect to need an understanding of the nature of the fauna inhabiting our world. The result is that our literature is very confusing to honest readers. My contention is that there is "much less there than meets the eye" because there is "much more there than meets the eye." The young archaeologist must be educated as to properties on both sides of our professional coin, particularly when reading debates. Skill in the recognition of the power of paradigms, individual "negotiations" within a competitive field, and finally substantive issues are all woven together in our literature. The student must develop skills in pulling these things apart; it can be an education in itself.

NOTES

1. Who would have guessed that shortly after my return home from France I would have to contend with many less-colorful renditions of this same argument extending over many years.

2. Bordes did not know it, but in the sense of the debates illustrated in the last section he was taking an "isochrestic" position on style. Different animals represent functional equivalents with regard to food; the culturally aware ancients made choices among these functional equivalents, thereby expressing themselves isochrestically. Food is obviously functional; since their choice of alternative was stylistic, relative frequencies of species is seen as a marker of isochrestic style! Bordes and I were naive in those days. We did not know we were arguing over such important issues as "cultural formation processes" and "isochrestic style." We thought we were exploring in terms of common sense as seen from different perspectives. I did not even realize that Bordes's argument about the "big chief" struck down fundamental principles of the new archaeology, as Schiffer was to discover. Oh well, we live and learn.

3. Isaac was fond of advocating a method of "multiple working hypotheses." This tactic is well illustrated in his article "Bones in Contention," where he notes that "considerable numbers of the bones bear numerous carnivore tooth marks. This is consistent *either* with their being the primary residue of carnivore feeding—or with the carnivores taking advantage of fresh

bone which had been abandoned by some other exploiting agency—meat eating hominids for instance" (Isaac 1983a:11). Here we see Isaac imagining only two possible "hypotheses." If one is capable of sitting in the armchair and imagining all the possible causes for observed phenomena, one's prior knowledge must be truly staggering. This is a "looking back" strategy in which one feels secure in one's prior knowledge and ignorance is not acknowledged. This problem is the same as that with Gould's method of anomaly (see Chapters 9–12). One is not seriously considering the possibility that there might be something left to learn. In short, one big alternative "hypothesis" could be simply that we do not know what causes the phenomena we see. My introduction of the argument that the carnivore gnawing could have been inflicted prior to the transport of bones to the location by hominids was not considered by Isaac (see comments to this effect in many of the following articles). This type of approach is regrettably common in archaeological interpretation. When regularly practiced in situations in which archaeologists are seeing new things, it is sure to be a disaster.

4. The growth of knowledge in archaeology is a slow process and requires disciplined attention to our ignorance. This view is at odds with the Guppie Way. I suppose one of the practices that betrays Guppieism more than any other is the press conference. Holding press conferences to announce "important" discoveries has a long tradition in Paleolithic studies. Typically, an archaeologist "finds" a new site and not infrequently even "finds" something in it. After the first season of excavation or surficial examination, a press conference is held to announce to the world the important findings. These press conferences may allude to what was found, but what they most commonly announce is something "new" about "our" ideas of the past. Without exception the press conference conveys the idea to the public that the meaning or "idea of the past" being presented flows self-evidently from the data—what was found or cited in the press conference.

I have been a teacher for many years, and the empiricist's fallacy is the most common layman's view of science. It is the idea most difficult to combat in young students arriving from our public school systems and "other" universities. The behavior of professionals, as presented through press conferences and news releases, is the model to the layman as to how science works. Almost without exception this presentation is false.

Guppies commonly have differential access to the media, and as a result the public is bombarded with very misleading ideas as to how science works. Time-Life books, Nova programs, and *National Geographic* "living color" presentations all perpetuate misleading ideas as to how archaeologists learn. This false presentation is not the fault of the media editors and publishers, as is frequently claimed by those who call the press conferences, but is to be laid directly at the feet of those who use the media for their own purposes.

The Torralba situation is an example. Before excavations were even well along and certainly before any analysis had been done (analysis has still not been done at the relational level), far-reaching interpretations of the past were presented to the media and popular press. The same is true for many other sites. The press-conference reconstructions of life in the past become our "knowledge" of the past. These popular stories about the past are immediately written into our textbooks, and our own students are presented with views of the past that are unjustified in any scientific sense simply because the textbook author is judged as not being current if they are not presented (see, e.g., John Gowlett's (1984) *Ascent to Civilization*). Thus our culture marches on, but learning stops.

Once such interpretations are part of our "culture," a ripple effect of Guppie protectionism sets in. For instance, I presented a short summary of my Torralba paper (Chapter 25) at the Field Museum of Natural History symposium on the evolution of human hunting. The full text of the paper as reprinted here was to be published in a book edited by M. Nitecki, the symposium organizer. The original plan of the editor was to publish the volume in the University of Chicago Press's Prehistoric Archaeology and Ecology series. I have been told that the volume was rejected by the series editors because of the inclusion of my paper. Whatever the case, Plenum Press is now doing the job. Guppies do not debate; they manipulate, and at the same time they see truth clearly (see Chapter 8). Certainly such a miraculous skill needs to be protected. If the paper was so awful, one would expect a convincing criticism of issues raised in the paper to have been easily handled by a Guppie or even a self-proclaimed Guppie with access to self-evident truth and possessed of superhuman insight. There is more to archaeology than an honest search for understanding and a reliable knowledge of the past.

5. This was not, however, the case at many other sites.

6. Some recent literature on Lower Paleolithic issues are textbook examples of this nonproductive legacy from the philosophical past. The "I'm right and you are dump" strategy has been unrelentingly pursued by Henry Bunn in writing and in public presentations. Bunn's paper at the Field Museum symposium on the evolution of hunting was the single most outrageous distortion of issues and the views of others I have ever witnessed in my professional life, and believe me I have seen some lulus. My initial attitude toward Bunn's self-appointed defense of Isaac was simply to ignore his Puppieism. (Bunn had put on a performance similar to that of the Chicago presentation at the earlier symposium held in Berkeley to honor Desmond Clark. I had heard about it in some detail—including a tape-recorded excerpt.) I could not imagine Glynn Isaac approving of such nonprofessional street fighting. I changed my mind about responding, thinking that if Bunn was affecting the profession he had to be answered regardless of how nonproductive such engagement might be. As Bunn shifted from public performances to published pursuit of his goals, I was astonished again at the response of readers. It was clear from reader response and conversations that real professionals were taking seriously all this bluster. What a field we participate in.

Chapter 19

The Hunting Hypothesis, Archaeological Methods, and the Past

Paleolithic archaeology is the offspring of two intellectual parents: the progressive evolutionary arguments, which sought to document the "emergence" of man out of the bestial "ooze"; and the culture history arguments, which sought to trace the several "cultures" or "races" of man back to their primordial beginnings. More recently, Paleolithic archaeology has developed into an independent science of the archaeological record, dedicated to understanding the past and its dynamics through fine-grained study of the processes that brought that record into being. To the extent that such an investigation is successful, archaeologists may direct their study of the past toward an evaluation of the theories previously advanced to explain human evolution, in addition to providing their own constructions of the past, which then demand explanation and hence theory building.

In the past, the Paleolithic archaeologist was essentially dependent upon the particular "culture" within which he or she was educated. Methods for archaeological inference appear, on reflection, to have been largely a series of conventions for assigning meaning to archaeologically observed phenomena. The justifications for such conventions were normally derived from whatever "theory" the worker accepted as an explanation of the conditions in the past that brought into being the properties to which meanings were assigned. This situation ensured that our views of the past, seemingly warranted by the citation of archaeological evidence, were most often consistent with our views of the past prior to doing archaeological work! The conventions used by archaeologists to assign meaning to the archaeological record were conventions that accommodated the properties of the archaeological record to the a priori views of the archaeologists and their colleagues as to what the past had been like.

It is remarkable how "adaptable" to a priori intellectual postures the archaeological record has been in the past: that is, how "clearly" the archaeologist could organize the facts of the archaeological record to support the currently preferred rendering of the past. The "facts" of the archaeological record were cited with conviction to prove the existence of various nomadic Neanderthal "tribes" of south-central France whose distinctly different material cultures remained essentially unchanged for thousands of years. The "facts" of the archaeological record were cited with conviction to prove that the australopithecines were "blood-thirsty killer-apes" living in caves and behaving as

Originally published in *Yearbook of Physical Anthropology* 30:1–9, © 1988.

skilled predators. The "facts" of the archaeological record were cited with conviction to prove that at least some hominids at the Plio-Pleistocene boundary were organized into "bands" of approximately 25 individuals, in which males of the group did the hunting and females gathered plant foods and made heavy investments in parenting. Similarly, males made significant parental investments by provisioning both females and offspring. The "facts" of the archaeological record miraculously revealed to us a hominid past that was much like the human present—a hominid past in which the major behavioral features of modern man that distinguish us from other primates were also present.

These characteristics—heavy dependence upon meat, by primate standards; a tendency toward lasting associations between males and females; and significant investment by both male and female parents in the support of offspring—were judged to have been already present at the time of the initial appearance of tools. This meant that all of the arguments from evolutionary biology that sought to explain the origins of human biosocial characteristics had to be mounted with respect to the time period prior to the eras of relevance for archaeological research, prior to the appearance of tools. This was wonderful! You could hear the sighs of relief coming from Paleolithic archaeologists around the world. Observations of properties related to bone morphology, biochemistry, and geo-environmental context became the basis for inferences about evolutionary process, because once stone tools appeared, our ancestors were thought to be living in fully "human," culturally deprived, Bushmanlike bands.

This interpretation of the past was not only comforting to unimaginative archaeologists, it was also reassuring to those "theorists" whose behavioral arguments depended upon there being no way of falsifying them. If one's arguments are behavioral and one has little behaviorally relevant "data," then "acceptance" inevitably becomes an argument from authority. Of course, most so-called authorities like that situation.

Given this paradigm, all the archaeologist had to do was to interpret the archaeological record from the past in terms of an "understanding" of contemporary hunter-gatherers. The unsettling arguments as to what the evolutionary past had been like must be faced by others. The archaeologist enjoyed a stable, known past; the past was like the present, although human ancestors definitely were in need of a kind of cultural "Headstart" program. The archaeologist had only to imagine an impoverished past. All the tricky problems of imagining a past inhabited by creatures unlike ourselves could mercifully be left to physical anthropologists and human paleontologists. Archaeologists had nothing to say on these issues.

Beginning in the 1960s some researchers (e.g., S. Binford 1968a:274; Freeman 1968; Howell 1968) suggested that perhaps the hominid past was *not* like the human present. This point was increasingly emphasized in the 70s and 80s (Binford 1972b, 1973, 1981a, 1982c, 1985b). If this was not an unreasonable proposition to entertain, then the challenge to archaeology was direct, devastating relative to traditional interpretive practice, and extremely exciting all at once. The admission that we did not know what variability in the archaeological record meant, and did not understand the conditions under which patterning in the archaeological record was generated, was accompanied by the optimism and excitement of any real science. The recognition of one's ignorance is the very basis for the commitment to learning and the belief that we can learn by virtue of our own efforts. For those of us who accepted this challenge, archaeology became a fascinating field, one bursting with challenge and potential for new and different kinds of understanding. For those committed to the old, safe, and paradigm-dependent use of conventions for interpreting the archaeological record our actions and arguments appeared to be totally bizarre, irrational clashes with the self-evident; misguided skepticism, perhaps arising out of hidden motives; and most of all, a lack of commitment to "the facts."

Modern archaeology has repeatedly dealt with this kind of charge and countercharge, and it continues to plague the field (see Courbin 1981). Most serious archaeologists realize that we create the past through inference, and that the methods of inference justification are therefore the pivotal factors conditioning the quality and accuracy of our product. This is equally true whether we are "inferring" a past for general descriptive purposes or inferring conditions in the past that are of direct relevance for evaluating theories of past dynamics. The central problem for the archaeologist is simply how to create evidence from observations. Archaeology has been successful in its move to address such problems, although much remains to be learned. The excitement of the early years of post-traditional archaeology has continued despite attempts to discredit the development of a methodology for inference (see Hodder 1984b; Moore and Keene 1983) that will enable us to learn about the past.

In the late 1970s the growing understanding of properties of the archaeological record and their potential meaning was turned to the very interesting issue of what life had been like for our early hominid ancestors who lived during the era when tools were first used (Binford 1977c, 1981a, 1985b, 1986b,d; Binford and Stone 1986). When this problem was addressed from the perspective of archaeological science, a new tension was established between archaeology and its sister disciplines, and this is increasingly true for the relationship between archaeology and human paleontology. It is interesting to note that this tension regarding the nature of the hominid past appears today among paleoanthropologists with widely divergent views, some of which it is worthwhile to examine.

In 1966 a milestone paper entitled "The Evolution of Hunting" (Washburn and Lancaster 1968) was presented at the "Man the Hunter" conference in Chicago. Although many earlier writers had suggested that hunting was a key element in human evolution, it was the Washburn and Lancaster paper that, to my knowledge, first outlined an argument as to the nature of its importance and "how things had worked," in an evolutionary sense. As in all theories, an argument was presented that tells us why the world is the way it appears to be. Washburn and Lancaster first sketched out what hominid history was thought to have been like. It stated as a given what the researchers sought to explain, and at that time, no one, including myself, would have argued with Washburn and Lancaster's characterization of the Paleolithic: "Probably all experts would agree that hunting was a part of the social adaptation of all populations of the genus *Homo,* and many would regard *Australopithecus* as a still earlier hominid who was already a hunter, although possibly much less efficient than the later forms" (Washburn and Lancaster 1968:293).

Since early man was assumed to have been a hunter, the challenge at the theoretical level was to explain how this important feature distinguishing "us" from the other great apes came about. More important to their argument was the challenge to explain how hunting behavior was essential to the development of our distinctively human way of life.

The archaeological data base then available consisted of information from many early sites that appeared to exhibit a bias in favor of very large animals (see Sampson 1974:128). Archaeologists had interpreted these faunal assemblages as the product of systematic and extensive big-game hunting, best exemplified at the site of Torralba, where it appeared "self-evident" that early man had been a truly spectacular hunter of the biggest game of all—elephants (see Howell 1965). The apparent success of early hominids as hunters led to the suggestion that perhaps the early hominids replaced the saber-toothed tiger as the major predator on big game and may even have contributed to their extinction (Washburn and Lancaster 1968:295). For nearly everyone in the 1960s the world of early man was a hunting world; thus, hunting was judged to be the only appropriate phenomenon for which theories should be built.

Washburn and Lancaster pointed out that big-game hunting would foster male-male cooperation and that this in turn would intensify tendencies toward a male-female division of labor, with males hunting and females gathering small animals and plant foods. Such a division of labor would be a prerequisite to food sharing between males and females and provisioning of the young by males. The independent exploitation of the environment by males and females and the subsequent sharing of their differing products presupposes a common place where sharing must occur. It also presupposes the transport of products obtained to such jointly occupied places. Hence, "home bases" could be expected. Further, a shift to big-game hunting would also mark an increase in range size and a greater mobility among the hominids than is commonly seen among other primates. This increase in range size would make increases in intelligence "pay off," and the ability to plan for the future in terms of seasonal variation in resource availability would be favored. In short, an argument was made for a set of functionally linked characteristics within the human pattern from which a very recognizable contemporary social unit was said to emerge: "When males hunt and females gather, the results are shared and given to the young, and the habitual sharing between a male, a female, and their offspring becomes the basis for the human family" (Washburn and Lancaster 1968:301). In the hunting hypothesis, these phenomena appeared to flow naturally from the shift to big-game hunting.

For archaeologists, who operate with few independently justified methods for inference, a wealth of interpretive potential seemed to be embedded in these insightful arguments. First, if all of these human traits were tightly linked, then the identification of one of them should imply the presence of the others (archaeologists were comfortable with arguments from analogy). Second, if identification criteria for more than one of these traits could be generated, then we could "flesh out the bare bones of archaeological remains" by analogical argument to the model and thereby provide a picture of socioeconomic life in the Paleolithic. In short, archaeologists operated as intellectual dependents, seeking to find ways to justify the existence in the past of what others had reasoned must have occurred. Among archaeologists addressing the remains of events from the Plio-Pleistocene boundary, the physical juxtaposition of animal bones and stone tools was viewed as self-evident support for an inference of hunting (Isaac 1971; Isaac and Crader 1981). The dense aggregation of bones and tools on ancient surfaces was taken as self-evident evidence of "home bases." The inference of a sexual division of labor, sharing between adult males and females, and male provisioning of the young therefore seemed justified (Isaac 1976, 1978a,b); why else would there be a "home base" (see Leakey 1981; Leakey and Lewin 1977, 1978)? The impressiveness of the hunting hypothesis as presented by Washburn and Lancaster served as the justification for inferences to the past by the archaeologists.

I need not point out that there is no logical independence here. The theory is being "tested" by stipulated (unjustified) identificational criteria—in short, definitional conventions—and inferences reasoned analogically from the theory itself. The simple association between bones and tools is stipulated to mean hunting and home bases, and then an elaborate interpretation is made possible by extending through analogy the impressive functional linkages specified in the hunting hypothesis. The picture that this type of reasoning facilitated for our early hominid ancestors has been graphically presented to the world in full color in *National Geographic* (Leakey and Walker 1985; Weaver 1985), Time-Life books (White and Brown 1973), and numerous publications by Richard Leakey (Leakey 1981; Leakey and Lewin 1977, 1978) and others. Our textbooks abound in this view of early man. They were like us, perhaps only needing a little cultural enrichment to render them into a contemporary San hunting and gathering band.

During the time of this interpretive posturing, made possible by the hunting hypothesis, advances were being made in the field of evolutionary biology. At roughly the same time, alternate views of early man were being pushed from a feminist's perspective, which sought to render the life of early man into a model of "woman the gatherer" (Zihlman 1981) or to see early men as having been like other great apes, chimps being a common model (Tanner 1981; Tanner and Zihlman 1976). The latter attempts have recently been criticized, I think correctly, as "referential models" (Tooby and DeVore 1985)—that is, simply taking a known or summarized condition and seeking to argue that the past was like the conditions in the chosen model.

An alternative strategy has been suggested—the building of "conceptual models" (Tooby and DeVore 1985), or what the advocates take to be "true" theories. The theory discussed is neo-Darwinian, which few would dispute in its biological essentials. But how does this theory make possible an understanding of the evolutionary processes that actually led to our humanity? It is a theory of mechanism, not of process. As presented by Tooby and DeVore, the "conceptual model" being advocated is the updated hunting hypothesis and only requires that whatever historical scenario one builds for the past, it must not violate the principles of neo-Darwinian theory. What is missed here is that the validity of neo-Darwinian theory does not ensure that the processual scenario is accurate.

It is true that the authors are able to convincingly criticize the "woman the gatherer" model, and the positions advocated by Owen Lovejoy (1981) and Johanson and Edey (1981), and to defend the functional linkages made in the original hunting hypothesis. The latter ability is not surprising, however. First, many believe that the emergence of our humanity came about as a result of neo-Darwinian principles at work. Second, most would agree that the modern human condition, as characterized by male-male cooperation; sexual division of labor between males and females; and variable but consistent parental investment in offspring by both males and females, involving reciprocity, sharing, and social exchange—in short, a distinctive organization to the human family—is in fact linked to hunting in the modern world in many cases. In addition, we know there was a reduction of sexual dimorphism through time as well as increases in brain size, and an increase in the habitats in which hominids were successful. Given what we know of the results of evolution, it is not surprising that we can build a scenario that accounts for this known condition and does not violate principles of neo-Darwinian theory. This ability does not, however, ensure that the results of evolution are also its causes. The restated hunting hypothesis assumes just this. On reflection, the proposed "conceptual model" is in fact a "referential model" (simply, the known human condition), and it then builds a series of functional linkages among the properties in the known condition that are consistent with neo-Darwinian principles. This is certainly an advance over the "anything can happen in evolution" view, or referential models that violate neo-Darwinian principles. The scenario nevertheless remains a logical exercise that seems to be evolutionary in character but lacks any secure knowledge of the behavioral contexts of selection that actually operated to bring into being the traits of the modern human condition it seeks to explain. For evolution to work, in neo-Darwinian terms, there must be an interaction between fitness and life context; or, in a "cultural" context, perhaps currencies other than "fitness" are at work. Our knowledge of the contexts and currencies are assumed in the hunting hypothesis as it is currently being used: early hominids were hunters and hunting made us biologically human.

The tension that I mentioned earlier between human paleontologists and archaeologists and among archaeologists has largely arisen since the early 1980s. It seems clear that we had a self-reinforcing system in operation between the Paleolithic archaeologists and the human paleontologists. Archaeologists were scratching the backs of the biological colleagues by interpreting their "data" with reference to the evolutionary biologists' models. The archaeologists were building wonderful pictures of the past reasoned from the hunting hypothesis, and in turn, the archaeologists' arguments regarding big-game hunting by early man were taken by the evolutionary biologists as validating the basic assumption of their evolutionary models. This seems to me to be a situation that violates all the assumptions of the scientific method. Tension broke out when archaeologists, realizing the conventionalist and tautological character of our interpretive justifications for creating a past, began to demand justifications for inferences that were intellectually independent of the theories and models being "tested." How can we recognize hunting on the part of ancient hominids in reliable ways and, importantly, by virtue of warranting arguments that were not embedded within the theories we sought to evaluate? Since the late 1970s, some archaeologists have been trying to accomplish just this shift in archaeological interpretive methodology.

Using the knowledge we had of how hunting by modern humans is manifest archaeologically (Binford 1978a, 1983b,c, 1984c, 1987d) linked to a fast-growing knowledge of the actions of other agents (particularly nonhominid predators and scavengers, as well as geological processes; Brain 1981), we begin to examine the archaeological record of the hominid past in new ways (Binford 1981a, 1985b, 1986b; Binford and Ho 1985; Binford and Stone 1986; Bunn et al. 1980; Potts and Shipman 1981; Shipman 1984b). The results have been surprising and certainly controversial, and will likely remain so for some time. There are good reasons to suspect that much, if not most, of the bone behaviorally related to stone tools from the early Pleistocene is the result of scavenging, not hunting (Binford 1981a, 1985b; Binford and Stone 1986; Blumenschine 1986). During the middle Pleistocene the pattern seemingly continues, with an increased attention to the exploitation of carcasses for meat, which frequently may have been consumed on the spot (Binford 1985b). Restudy of the published data from Torralba yields no support for the earlier arguments that big game was being hunted there; instead, the pattern of scavenged lower limbs and heads of mainly horses, bovids, and cervids is indicated, with the occasional exploitation of naturally occurring carcasses of elephant, horses, and cervids for what must have been small amounts of meat (Binford 1987d), judging from the low frequencies of associated tools.

I might also point out that hunting per se is not the only problem. Long ago prehistorians recognized what were once summarized as "parallel phyla" under the assumptions of the culture-historical school. Persons of my age all learned that there was a cultural tradition of great antiquity where tools, such as hand axes, were made from cores and other tools were made on flakes. While today we approach the interpretation of variability in the archaeological record much differently, the observations our predecessors made about variability have not been contradicted; instead, modern research continues to document a major dichotomy in the archaeological record of the early time ranges in expanded detail.

For instance, I have recently completed a reanalysis of the published data from Olduvai Gorge beds I and II (Binford 1986c). It is demonstrable that near the very dawn of tool use there is a major dichotomy in the depositional context of tools. In one context there are a number of different "core" forms of choppers, discs, and polyhedrons associated (rarely) with whole flakes and resharpening flakes as well as utilized nodules. Rarely does this suite of tools covary with lithic manufacturing debris or such small flake tools as scrapers and utilized flakes. This suite of tools is commonly made of raw materials not available (and therefore not reduced) where the tools were found—in short, it appears to represent tools that were transported from other places and abandoned largely as discrete items. In contrast is a suite of artifacts that includes manuports, lithic debris, a few core tools, and flake tools such as scrapers and utilized flakes. These tools are generally manufactured of locally available (within 6 km) stone and discarded where they were manufactured. Disposal appears as a linked suite of forms representing nearby procurement, processing, use, and discard of tools. We can think of this as an expediently produced and used aspect of the technology, as opposed to the transported aspect of the technology.

Even more provocative is the statistical association of different patterns of faunal remains with the two kinds of tool assemblage. The small tools and lithic debris suite (expedient aspect) associate with an anatomically biased faunal assemblage of largely leg and skull parts. These frequently show clear evidence of having been processed for "marrow" and other fatty filling of bone cavities. On the other hand, the transported aspect associates with carcass remnants, where minimal exploitation of more meat-yielding parts is indicated. These remains do not appear to have been moved far from the locations where they were found, however. Two types of feeding strategy seem to be associated with two different aspects of the technology.

This organizational pattern continues with some modifications through the Acheulean and into the Middle Paleolithic. There are formal changes, but the basic behavioral regime appears largely unchanged over this enormous period of time. With some exceptions (e.g., Torralba) in the Acheulean the hand axes and cleavers appear as the transported component, while many of the small tools continue to be made and used on the same spot. The pattern as thus far explicated does not fit well with a sharing, division-of-labor model of subsistence. The transported component appears at the "end" of the system, in which meat appears to be consumed at the spot or very near where it was encountered. The expedient component is associated with transported animal parts, but they are parts that yield very little food indeed. It seems likely that the latter sites represent processing locations rather than base camps, and the transport of potential foods is more related to processing for gaining access to the food rather than provisioning of a group of consumers. Otherwise, foods encountered in the environment that can be consumed without processing are eaten on the spot and not returned to a base camp for sharing. Either the entire group (males, females, and children) eat together at the points where food was encountered, or very few foods were transported to locations where they could be processed for consumption.

In light of this suggestion I must mention a very provocative set of observations made recently with regard to the important archaeological remains from Zhoukoudian. I have just completed (but have not yet written up) an analysis of the stone tools recovered from this site and found the by-now-familiar dichotomy in the technology. One aspect is composed of choppers, cores, and large flakes manufactured of nonlocal materials and the other consists of debris from the bipolar reduction of locally available raw materials associated with the modified flake tools. The number of hominid remains recovered from the Zhoukoudian site is sufficient to enable investigation of the possibility that there is a different age association with the two technical aspects of the technology. The statistical analysis showed that while adult *Homo erectus* are found with both transported and expedient tool suites *the children associate only with the expedient component!* This is thus far the first concrete clue to relationships between technology and social organization. It is far too early, however, to speculate on the nature of early hominid social organization. Nevertheless, it is clear that the dichotomous technological pattern, the suggestions of scavenging, and the hint that both may be linked to different feeding strategies (with the expedient aspect more regularly involving children) have no analogies to anything known among modern human hunting and gathering peoples. It is tempting to speculate that the processing of bones with high fat content but limited quantities of meat might simply represent the activities of women supplementing the diet of children with high-quality foods at the time of weaning. If so, there is little evidence of other introduced foods, as would be expected in a food-sharing context. We are really just beginning to put in place the techniques for gaining a realistic picture of early hominid behavior.

At present, convincing evidence for hunting of moderate- to large-body-sized game seems delayed until around 70,000–90,000 years ago in Europe, and maybe equally late in southern Africa (see Binford 1984c). Elements of the hunting hypothesis may be correct, but current work suggests that if so, it is relevant to the time period of the emergence of fully modern man, not the ancient hominid past. This of course leaves unexplained the increase in brain size, the successful radiation into temperate settings during the mid-Pleistocene, and quite likely the loss of estrus and many other properties that had previously been treated as a linked, atemporal, neo-Darwinian package by the hunting hypothesis.

Of course, the archaeological methods for inference justification currently being developed could be wrong. It is, however, in the context of archaeological middle-range research that this condition would be exposed, not by upset evolutionary biologists who feel secure with intellectually dependent archaeologists confirming their views through tautological interpretive argument. Even if our currently used inferential strategies turn out to be faulty, I strongly doubt that methodological advances will ever return us to the view that hominid life at the Plio-Pleistocene boundary was a watered-down version of modern man. One conclusion arising from the current research is that early hominids were very different from us. It will be nice when archaeological methodology has advanced sufficiently to say with some assurance of accuracy just what their life was like. Once we can do this, we can all engage in productive theory building that seeks to explain a past reality, rather than being in the posture of explaining the existence of a flat earth, blind to the fact that the earth is round.

Chapter 20

Letter to H. T. Bunn

Dear Mr. Bunn:

I was disappointed by your review (Bunn 1982a) in that you misrepresented my material and continuously entered into "arguments against the man" rather than treating my arguments in a serious research-oriented manner.

As I tried to outline in *Bones,* the philosophy of traditional archaeology was one in which the "truth" of a proposition was judged by the reputation of the individual making the statement. From the beginning of your review you attempt to discredit my scholarship, my knowledge, as well as my "fairness." This is *ad hominem* argument and the tactics of traditional archaeology.

You say my history is rather "selective." I know of no history that is not selective since it normally involves a classic form of argument from example. I chose my examples to illustrate the point that the problem of *inference* was pervasive and widespread. My purpose was not to cite everything that had ever been written about bones or to provide an annotated bibliography or even to document that someone in 1865 did not have the problem. My purpose was to demonstrate the general pervasiveness of a problem in need of solution. You ignore my treatment of the subject by suggesting that I have been unfairly selective, with the clear implication that I am misleading someone. Yet you never let us in on how I have been misleading. *This is the worst kind of innuendo.*

You cite my failure to mention "cut marks on bones from Old Crow Flats," presumably as evidence of my lack of "fairness." This is again a "cheap shot," since Morlan mounted his arguments in terms of bone breakage. My interest was in Morlan's arguments and how they were made. I was criticizing his inferential procedures. I have no position on the age of man's entry into the New World. If we were to find a skeleton buried complete with birth certificate and dead in the arms of a sabertooth cat, that would not render Morlan's inferential argument from fractured bones a sound argument in my opinion. My book is not about various scholars' "visions" of the past but how we may go about using evidence to evaluate the accuracy of inferences to the past. Cutmarks may strengthen Morlan's "vision," but they do not render his inferential argument from bone breakage robust. Your mentioning this kind of point, irrelevant to my book and my arguments, *can only be seen as another argument against the author through innuendo.*

Your impatience with my treatment of Dart is similar. Brain's work did not permit some *persons* to dismiss Dart's arguments over a decade ago; in fact most did so without any evidence whatsoever. In my opinion the Hottentot goat work and the leopard work was misused by East Africanists, particularly since the implications of Brain's work for their data was never followed up in detail (see my discussions of this in *Bones,* 1981a:191–192). Dart's work is central to the development of middle-range research in Africa. You may disagree with me, but I see his questioning the nature of early man's behavior as basic to the development of productive middle-range research. Why do you want me to "dismiss" Dart?

You suggest that I am "unfair" to Isaac. You suggest that I cite Isaac's "most informal popularized writings and do not acknowledge Isaac's advocacy of taphonomic research on both human and nonhuman processes affecting bone and artifact accumulations." You may not like my opinions of Isaac's work, but to suggest that I have been unfair is sophistry. I basically disagree with him; is that *unfair?* I do not think Isaac's dependence upon arguments of "plausibility" and commitment to truth through prudent "judgment" will advance the field. I do not think Isaac understands the nature of inference. Isaac's considered judgments in a "fair" and "prudent" context of "multiple working hypotheses" lead him to accept the most plausible "working hypothesis," which then becomes *the popular view* of the past at the time. This is just another way of presenting the old traditional criteria in which our views of the past were a function of the *judgment* of scholars such as Isaac. Most of Isaac's advocacy of "taphonomic research" has been in the character of replicative experiments and post hoc modeling from analogy. One can look, for example, at the way Isaac treats the problem of faunal backgrounds based on mean density figures from Behrensmeyer. Using a mean value from transects across space, Isaac then identified some of the "living floors" as containing anomalously high densities. This is silly since we do not know anything about the variance around the mean. I would be very surprised if all the bones in Behrensmeyer's survey were evenly distributed over the landscape. She says, "Occasionally the remains of several individuals were found together. Also it seems that scavengers may carry single bones of one carcass to the vicinity of another" (Behrensmeyer and Boaz 1980:75). Isaac acts as if patches of bone are unnatural; this is just not true. Knowing the factors that condition density of bones quite independent of hominid intervention will never be even addressed following the logic of Isaac's procedure— that is, comparing patches to mean values for major transects described without some measure of clustering (in fact where variance is ignored). We don't know what is anomalous with respect to a mean until someone measures variance around a mean. I am quite sure that Isaac's idea of anomalously high densities as the basis for recognizing hominid sites will amuse most paleontologists.

I thought I was being very fair to Isaac by not using his work as an example of faulty approaches to inference. Being a nice guy (which Glynn is), being dedicated (which he also is), and conducting germane research (which Glynn also does) does not solve the problem of inference (which I don't think Glynn even recognizes as a problem). My book was about inferential problems; in this light I think I bent over backwards to be "fair" to Glynn.

Your failure to grasp the message of my book is nowhere better illustrated than in your discussions of the Olduvai chapter. You suggest that I conducted a "factor analysis . . . in an attempt to demonstrate that most of the assemblages result from nonhominid predator scavenger behavior." This is simply not true. I was not attempting to demonstrate anything. I had no axe to grind. I was simply using a powerful and controlled search technique to isolate patterning in the data as reported. If there is no difference between the fauna generated by hominids and that deposited by any other predator-scavenger, then how can we recognize either one? I was seeking to recognize patterns that were outside the range of documented patterns for predator-scavengers. This is hardly trying to "demonstrate that most of the assemblages result from nonhominid behavior."

You then go on to suggest—pass the judgment—that "because of a variety of weaknesses in Binford's analysis it is doubtful that his results on Olduvai are useful contributions to scientific archaeology." This is some pronouncement! *It would be fine if you could defend your position.* What are these weaknesses according to your review?

1. *I used Mary Leakey's data on Olduvai Gorge* in spite of her clear statement that they were preliminary. I am fully aware that one can make an infinite number of observations on a body of materials. The generation of subsequent facts does not render previous observations faulty or misleading as long as one is faithful to their internal logic. In one sense all observations are preliminary relative to observations that might be made in the future. We must work with what we have.

2. You suggest that the weakness of using her preliminary facts rests with my analytical dependence upon MNI estimates. You point out that I do not cite Gentry and Gentry (1978) for their MNI estimates. The latter point is true but it is also totally irrelevant since my method of calculating MNI is a truly minimal method based on the original suggestions of the person who introduced the technique in the U.S. (T. White) and not the estimate best described as *Maximal Number of Individuals* conducted by Gentry and Gentry. I explained in some detail my methods of and reasons for calculating MNI values as being the most sound and rational approach given the aims of my analysis. I don't give a damn how many dead animals are represented. I have pointed out that neither man nor beast eats in units of whole animals. I am interested in the numbers of anatomical parts expressed in animal units that are represented by different bones. Expressing frequencies in terms of animal units renders the use of a ratio scale possible (which is the most powerful scale available for comparing quantitative information such as bone counts; I have explained all this in my Nunamiut book [Binford 1978a], as I note on page 263 of *Bones*). You obviously did not read the Nunamiut book, nor do you understand my use of MNI values since maximum estimates such as those given by Gentry and Gentry and apparently also made by you are totally inappropriate to my work. *The MNI problem is yours, not a weakness of my analysis.*

In the middle of the MNI misrepresentation you mention my failure to cite an unpublished article by Isaac and Crader (unpublished at the time the *Bones* book came out). It is true that I had seen a copy of this "widely circulated" paper, but I judged it not to be in the public domain and therefore not yet usable. You suggest that Isaac and Crader come to many of the same conclusions I do with regard to vertically diffuse deposits. This is a truly off-the-wall statement since it was Mary Leakey's conclusion (1971) that these deposits were not "living floors." I simply accepted her judgments on that point. You suggest that I arrived at such a conclusion after "numerical acrobatics." This is gross misrepresentation.

You then resume the demonstration of your ignorance about the MNI problem by suggesting that errors of great magnitude are inherent in my results because your MNI estimates do not agree with mine. Several points can be made here. I am quite sure your estimates have nothing to do with the way I calculate MNI values, as I have suggested. Nevertheless, you obviously don't understand a ratio scale. It would not matter if I chose a constant value at random to be used in calculating a ratio. *The structure of the array is not modified when all values are divided by a constant.* I was analyzing the arrays for structural properties that would be unaffected by changes in the values of the constants used. *The weaknesses here are in your understanding of what was being done and in your logic, not in my methods.*

3. After your irrelevant discussion of MNI values you move to the meat of your perspective—namely, your belief that hominids generated the sites and carnivore scavenging occurred after the hominids had left. Isaac made this point in 1971 ("The Diet of Early Man," p. 288):

> In contrast to Makapan, the problem at Olduvai camp sites is not to determine how many of the bones were introduced by non-hominid agencies, but how many may have been removed by scavengers.

This position amounts to simply "explaining away" the facts which do not fit your a priori view that the Olduvai sites were living sites generated by hominids. As I pointed out in my book, we are all inventive enough to imagine a set of conditions that, if true, would accommodate our observations and preserve the view of the past we prefer. This is what K. Popper (1972:39) has called "immunization."

> Whenever the "classical" system of the day is threatened by the results of new experiments which might be interpreted as falsifications . . . the system will appear unshaken to the conventionalist. He will explain away the inconsistencies which may have arisen; *perhaps by blaming our inadequate mastery of the system.* Or he will eliminate them by *suggesting ad hoc the adoption of certain auxilliary hypotheses,* or perhaps of *certain corrections to our measuring instruments.* (Popper 1959:80; emphasis added)

4. Moving on to still further alleged weaknesses, you bring up the question of "natural background bone density." I have already noted that the standard being used by Bunn and Isaac is a mean value derived from modern field experiences. No measure of variance is presented. With this idea of "background" any aggregation is an "anomaly." With this wonderful reasoning established you go on:

> Recognizing that the sites are high-density anomalies does permit a fairer understanding of Mary Leakey's reasons for viewing the bones as hominid food debris.

This is an astonishing statement. I think most of us have understood for a long time the reasoning that led to the interpretation of the Olduvai "sites" as living floors. The question has been, Are there necessary links between the cited facts and the inferred conditions that render such inferences secure? I think most must realize that a high-density association between bones/artifacts and other items is insufficient to render secure the inference that hominids "acting alone and first in a sequence" produced the aggregation.

At this point you launch into another attempt to discredit my analysis by pointing out that hyenas are not wolves and that other actions, such as trampling, may produce attritional results analogous to animal gnawing on bone assemblages. The motives for this discussion are not quite clear (are you setting up a "hidden" data source, such as a thesis submitted to the Faculty of Science, University of Pretoria, in 1980?), and I see no relevance for these paragraphs. My analysis sought to remove from consideration the patterning referable to identified agents so we might see if there were residual patterns that might refer unambiguously to hominids. Pointing out that the ambiguous materials may be even more ambiguous does not seem to impact my analytical strategies in any way.

5. Continuing with the alleged weaknesses, you give us one of the most revealing paragraphs in your review. You state (p. 495):

> Still another weakness . . . is . . . viewing sequentially modified assemblages first in terms of canid predator-scavenger data and attributing only residual variations to other factors. . . . Why should the opposite sequence—hominids as principal agents of bone transport and modification followed by attrition due to scavenging carnivores—escape Binford's serious consideration?

Clearly you missed the point of the book. We must start from what we know and work toward the unknown. If I had any reliable idea of what a "hominid" assemblage might look like, then yes, I could reverse the analytical procedure and extract the diagnostically unique hominid material. *But that is of course what we want to learn, e.g., what hominid-generated materials look like!* I have been kind here. You totally confuse an analytical procedure with a set of historical conditions in the past. Presumably you are suggesting that my procedure precludes the interpretation of the Olduvai material as hominid-generated sites—this is sheer nonsense and is simply sophistry. In fact my analysis permitted the recognition of faunal patterning that relates to transported materials and is likely referable to the hominids. The analysis does not permit me to assess an absolute sequence, but the patterning, if referable to hominids, points to the second-order assemblage (that is, parts selected from an already scavenged carcass). This interpretation is not dictated by my analytical procedure; it is a post hoc interpretation offered by me based on my experience with faunal assemblages. You seem very confused by the difference between a controlled pattern-recognition strategy and the justification for the inferential interpretation of patterns once they are recognized. My interpretations are not dictated by my pattern-recognition strategies (see Binford 1981a:282).

These sites could well be places where scavenged materials were aggregated—near water—for processing and consumption. The proposal that hunting was practiced to a significant degree does not appear to be a robust possibility based on the patterning isolated. Similarly, the possibility that sleeping or food sharing took place at such locations is not at all evidenced by the data available. In fact the recognized patterning renders such an interpretation difficult (to my way of thinking). Such suggestions only make sense in the context of treating the Olduvai materials in terms of conventional concepts, such as "base camps." I see no justification to postulate such phenomena.

Research is the development of methods for using what we know to probe what we do not know. I think it is reasonable to recognize that the character of life among the hominids at the Plio-Pleistocene boundary is something we don't know. Imposing on this ignorance characteristics of the behavior of modern man does not reduce our ignorance, it only covers it up. You seem content to accept the presence of cutmarks on bones as sufficient justification for assuming all kinds of conditions in the past. I am not content with that type of flimsy warrant for conventional interpretations. I would get to work with the difficult task of carrying out research.

One final set of comments. You allude to "unnecessary errors" in my book but never cite specific errors, which would have certainly have aided the readers and rendered your comment helpful rather than just another cheap shot. This is like the comments you started with—simple innuendo. Are these errors on every page? Do these errors impact the arguments? You further suggest that there is "misquotation of other researchers' published and even unpublished writings." My God, am I trying to misrepresent the world? Where are these misquotations? What about the misquotations of others' unpublished writings? (The only unpublished [at the time] works cited by me were one of yours and the companion article written by Potts and Shipman; see Binford 1981a:286–288.) It should be noted that elsewhere you criticize me for not citing an unpublished paper! This whole book review is an *ad hominem* argument effected through innuendo and self-serving misrepresentation.

Sincerely,

Lewis R. Binford

Chapter 21

Bones of Contention: A Reply to Glynn Isaac

Glynn Isaac's review (Isaac 1983b) of *Bones: Ancient Men and Modern Myths* (Binford 1981a) is in many ways a fair descriptive presentation of the contents of the book. However, he has brought to his reading certain expectations, and it was in terms of these expectations that he critically evaluated some sections of my work. I believe that his expectations were mistaken, that they have misguided his criticism, and that his review distorted the intent of my work in important ways.

An example of his attempt to make my work fit his expectations occurs early in the review. Isaac states,

> His treatment goes back and forth between the observations and the explanatory factors, and it is not entirely clear to me the extent to which his final conclusions are predictions being tested for fit, or the development of explanations that fit the data. (1983b:417)

Clearly, Isaac is demanding something which I did not intend and which I don't consider necessary or appropriate. I was simply trying to share with the reader the experiences with predator-produced faunal assemblages which led me to recognize certain factors as potential contributors to variability and to demonstrate that variability does in fact exist. Technically these were warranting arguments, that is, arguments advanced to illustrate that it is reasonable to think certain thoughts about assemblages. I was engaged in an exercise of inductive reasoning, yet Isaac seems to be expecting all discussion to be some type of hypothesis testing or explanation for patterning.

That Isaac brings to *Bones* expectations which I consider inappropriate, and then demands that my tactics of presentation and organization meet his standards, is obvious in other comments in the review. For instance, Isaac states,

> Binford introduces some data on bone assemblages where humans are the dominant processing agency. He uses only his own Nunamiut data, and although he comes up with interesting points of contrast, I was disappointed. What would the values of other assemblages that are undoubtedly human home-base refuse look like if they were put through the same chain of ratio calculations and correction computation? This is something that still needs to be done. (1983b:417)

Isaac clearly fails to understand the major thrust of my arguments regarding middle-range theory as presented in *Bones*. As repeatedly emphasized, "control" case com-

Originally published in *American Antiquity* 49:164–167, © 1984.

parisons were used specifically as controls in the scientific experimental sense of that word. Controls must be just those situations in which the properties being compared are understood in terms of causal conditioners. We must understand that the factors which contribute to observed similarities and differences in the archaeological record are what we seek to understand. We must realize that comparisons and assessments of gross similarity or difference among archaeologically observed cases are the very phenomena which we seek to explain and understand. Isaac is suggesting that he can use some archaeological cases as "controls." I frankly do not know what those cases might be, particularly if we chose sites earlier than 35,000 years ago. The use of one case whose meaning is understood through inference as the justification for making the same inference for another site in no way addresses the validity of the inference justification in the first place. It was of course the latter problem which I addressed in the *Bones* book. Would Isaac accept the very set of conditions which I criticized in the *Bones* book, namely the coincidence of shelter, fire and/or food remains, the old conventions for recognizing the "homes" of early man?

In other comments, Isaac is equally concerned with my procedures for calculating ratios from counts, and with my using survival percentages as a "correction computation" for assemblages which have suffered attrition. These kinds of "suspicions" are difficult to treat without extensive discussion. First, conversions of raw counts to ratio values eliminates the problem of autocorrelation among cases which may derive from size differences among the cases. Since we are interested in similarities which do not simply reflect allometric patterns of similarity, and since dividing an array of numbers through by a constant does not change the relationships among the numbers, the disputed procedure eliminates the potential autocorrelation which can be expected from size differences among the cases, while preserving the structural similarities and differences of interest among the cases. Second, the "correction computation" to which Isaac refers is the use of a set of survival percentages which were experimentally developed through the study of the relative durability of different bones in the anatomy. I used these to overcome the ambiguity characteristic of an assemblage which had suffered heavy attrition. As illustrated in *Bones,* an unravaged assemblage of one form and a ravaged assemblage of another form could appear similar even though their "pre-ravaged form" was very different. My entire discussion of ravaged assemblages was designed to illustrate that the resulting formal properties generally masked many of the formal properties that characterized the population prior to its having suffered attrition. In fact, it seemed that the assemblages with completely opposing forms approached a more similar form after they had been ravaged. I do not consider these demonstrations to be equivocal, and with them in view it is hard to understand Isaac's profound "skepticism."

In another place, Isaac misrepresents the book as essentially a substantive set of arguments about Olduvai Gorge and criticizes me in terms of this interpretation. However, my book was clearly about methodology, and the Olduvai exercise was presented as one example to demonstrate my approach. Isaac acts as though I am advancing a new theory of early man, when, in fact, I am only trying to illustrate that the limitations of our current inferential strategies reveal a past which is a far cry from the "technicolor" reconstructions common in our textbooks. In particular, I was not primarily interested in using the Olduvai material for reconstruction; rather, I was interested in illustrating the important "distorting" role of differential survivorship in respect to faunal assemblages. As I noted, assemblages which started out with very different forms, when subjected to attritional agents, begin to look alike if the scale of attrition is substantial. This expectation is realized in the factor analysis and permits us to recognize the other Olduvai assemblages which had been ravaged in ways similar to the control cases. The implication is simply that ten of the cases are palimpsests in the causal sense and hence ambiguous with respect to diagnosing the agents originally responsible for their forms, since survivorship properties dominate the statistical remnants of the original faunal assemblages. Given analytical techniques then current, we could not diagnose these assemblages beyond reference to their ravaged conditions.

In another instance, Isaac accuses me of not using the best evidence, since I used Mary Leakey's published data on fauna from Olduvai Gorge. While it is true that her tables did not present the faunal attributes in exactly the form required by my analytical procedures, Isaac's suggestions that I should have gone to Africa and studied the Olduvai fauna myself, or failing that, obtained other data, are silly. I had no interest in studying the Olduvai data myself, but had I generated my "own" facts through direct observation, Isaac would certainly have been quick to point out the discrepancies with Mary Leakey's data, or with those of Gentry and Gentry (1978), or with anyone else's. Had I used the "facts" of Gentry and Gentry, Bunn et al. (1980), or Potts (1982), they too would not have been in the form required by my analytical procedures, and I would have had to "extrapolate and adjust" as much or more. I believe Isaac's comment points up his naive empiricist belief in one and only one set of "true" facts. Recent philosophy of science has undermined this view and we now almost universally accept the premise that facts are a function of the conventions used in their production. My book accepts the basic premise that there is not some *absolute truth lying out there* waiting to be described by superior observers. Hence, I made the necessary adjustments to suit the purposes of my procedures.

After the above criticism Isaac asserts that the comparative data I incorporated in the matrices are not empirically observed bone-part frequencies but are values generated by correcting for percent survivorship. *This is simply not true.* No survivorship corrections were made on the African data sets used in the factor analysis.

In still a further example of misrepresentation Isaac suggests that my comment to the effect that the factor analysis was a robust solution was inaccurate (1983b:417–418). He interprets values presented in my table 6.07 under a heading "VP" as percentage figures. Isaac then goes on to suggest that the first factor only accounts for 10.5 percent of the variance; therefore, my assessment of the quality of the solution was wrong. What is wrong is Isaac's understanding of a factor analysis. The value of 10.5 is the proportion of the sum of the diagonal values assimilated by factor #1, which in this case would be slightly over 50% of the total. How this information is considered by Isaac as reflecting on how robust the solution might have been is not at all clear. What is clear is that Isaac was very willing to use "facts," even those he did not understand, to belittle my work.

Another example of Isaac's failure to discern my intent appears in his summary of my conclusions. He states, "Binford suggests that a crucial adaptive innovation by the early hominids was breaking *bare* bones which had been abandoned by primary predators and by dominant scavengers" (1983b:418). In fact, I don't think I used the phrase "bare bones" anywhere in the book, and this distortion, when used in the context of arguments about cut-marks, makes my observations appear silly. Ancient hominids did not cut and dismember already bare bones and I never suggested that they did.

Proceeding with his criticism, Isaac states, "it is not clear to me why some of the numerous data sets from undoubted late Quaternary human middens were not included" (1983b:418). I can only answer that I see no reason to include uncontrolled data. All archaeological data sets must be inferentially interpreted, and when we are seeking to evaluate our inferential methods we must use controls which are not based on the very inferential techniques we seek to evaluate. Here again Isaac reveals his failure to understand the differences between models of the past and models of the relationship between dynamics and statics, whose understanding we must have in order to construct an accurate past.

Finally, Isaac notes that he is unclear why, among the various multivariate techniques available, "factor analysis alone was used. This would seem to me a prime instance where *discriminate function analysis* would be better" (1983b:418). Again, Isaac has misunderstood my point. I was seeking to evaluate the degree to which multiple sources of variability contributed to the form of cases. Discriminate function analysis assigns cases to categories, and I was seeking to dimensionally partition cases for the possible contribution to their aggregate form by multiple independent agents.

Understanding achieved from reading, as with observing the world, is at least a partial function of what the reader brings to the experience. In this case, I am confident that Isaac has brought to the *Bones* book a frame of reference which is generally inappropriate to it. I believe the message of the book has merit, that Isaac has misread the message, and that by implication the frame of reference with which Isaac operates is of limited utility. I suggest that this is the critical message in my book, which Isaac acknowledges has raised his blood pressure.

Chapter 22

Human Ancestors: Changing Views of Their Behavior

INTRODUCTION

I think it is safe to say that during the latter years of the 1970s there developed in paleoanthropology a kind of "consensus" view of our hominid ancestors. This view was largely developed by Glynn Isaac (1971, 1978a, 1978b, 1983c), then of the University of California at Berkeley, and popularized in many articles and in several books aimed at lay audiences authored or coauthored by Richard Leakey (Leakey and Lewin 1977, 1978; Leakey 1981). Fundamental to this construction of our ancient past was the view that early man was a hunter. It was admitted that the early beginnings of mankind were impoverished relative to the achievements of later men; nevertheless, the history of the emergence of our modern condition was thought to be a story of progress. It was a history of gradual and accretional accomplishment, given the original presence of certain fundamental "human" characteristics. Isaac argued in a seemingly convincing manner that, at the very dawn of our appearance as tool-using hominids, "men" were hunters living in social groups characterized by a male–female division of labor. The products of the hunt were returned to sleeping places (home bases) in which altruistic sharing took place among adults as well as provisioning of children. Crucial to this construction of early man's lifeway was Isaac's belief that food sharing was a major conditioner for many of the "essentially" human characteristics that he believed to have been already present at roughly the Plio-Pleistocene boundary (Isaac 1971, 1976, 1978a, 1978b; Isaac and Crader 1981). Food sharing thus was believed to have set the stage for much of the progressive emergence that seemed to characterize the later evolution of mankind.

FORESHADOWING OF CHALLENGE—SOME SKEPTICISM

During the time that this "consensus" view of early man was being formed I had been conducting research for purposes of developing a methodology for making behavioral inferences from animal bones believed to represent archaeological traces of ancient human–hominid behaviors (Binford and Bertram 1977; Binford 1978a). During the course of this research the potential of the application of my nascent methods

Originally published in *Journal of Anthropological Archaeology* 4:292–327, © 1985.

to the questions of the nature of ancient man's behavior appeared obvious. As a result of this interest I began to read more critically the literature dealing with the factual basis for the consensus view and to examine the rational basis for the inferences then being made, particularly by Africanists. My first excursion into this field of argument came in my review (Binford 1977c) of Glynn Isaac's (1977a) monograph on the important early site of Olorgesailie. I noted that, while Isaac was an innovator in considering the integrity of deposits yielding traces of early man, he never questioned that the *associations* among the items found in such modified deposits were all indicative of hominid behavior. He simply accepted the conventional "wisdom" that they were present because hominids had caused the association. This reinforced Isaac's beliefs that stone tools associated with animal bones were evidence of hunting. This permitted, even required, that he speculate on the hunting techniques used by ancient hominids to account for the extraordinary association between stone tools and the remains of a large number of now-extinct baboons found at the Olorgesailie site of DE/89B.

> A killing pattern such as is observed . . . might have been achieved if the baboons had been driven against a hazard or if their waterhole had been poisoned. But driving baboons or geladas against a hazard is almost inconceivable, since the species shows such guile and agility. Poisoning of waterholes, while a possible explanation for the killing pattern, would have resulted in a much broader spectrum of species in the refuse.
>
> An ethnographic analogy provides for a plausible . . . reconstruction. . . . [During] a communal baboon hunt . . . [the hunters] encircle the roosting place of a baboon troop in a grove of trees or on a small rock outcrop . . . [and] dislodge the baboons by . . . making a great noise. As the baboons try to break out of the circle they are clubbed to death. (Isaac 1977a:91)

I questioned that Isaac's acceptance of the facts of assemblage composition and faunal association were directly referable to past hominid behavior.

> I have said many times that one cannot reconstruct the past in ignorance of the processes which operated to bring the archaeological facts into being. . . . *A frontal attack is now needed on assemblage composition and tool–faunal associations for the earlier ranges of time. We need to know more of the formation processes for the archaeological record.* (Binford 1977c:203)

This statement, simply put, means that I did not think that archaeologists knew how to diagnose the different processes that could stand behind the early deposits that also yield evidence of hominids. What is most interesting is that during the next several years many different researchers were engaged in activities largely designed to address these very issues.

THE ACCOMMODATION OF NEW EVIDENCE

1980 and 1981 were big years in the literature of paleoanthropology. The results of the previous several years of focused research from Isaac's team were reported in *World*

Archaeology (Bunn et al. 1980). In that report discussion was focused on the important site of Koobi Fora, FxJj50. This article reported pioneering work on faunal analysis, particularly concerning inspection for cut marks and breakage patterns that might be cited to link the fauna behaviorally to acts of hominid tool use. Site structural studies, designed to illustrate the spatial patterning in tool and faunal remains, were also reported. While clearly showing concern for inference justification, Isaac's team nevertheless drew the following conclusions:

> Many of our observations will have relevance for testing hypotheses about the nature of early hominid behavior. . . . Suffice it to say that the concentrations of artifacts and bones, the cut marks and the conjoining sets are all consistent with (but not final proof of) interpretations that attribute meat-eating and food transporting activities to the early tool makers. . . . Further, the characteristics of the bone assemblage invite serious consideration of scavenging rather than active hunting as a prominent mode of meat acquisition. (Bunn et al. 1980:133)

In other words, the facts from Koobi Fora were cited to justify the continued defense of the consensus view of early man—with the caution, however, that scavenging might have been a mode of meat procurement. In spite of this insight, the site was seen as a "base camp" where the behaviors thought to be critical to the emergence of many of our basic human traits, such as sharing, regular meat eating, and perhaps early "language," were considered to have been present.

Taking up my challenge to the hunting interpretations rendered by Isaac for the Olorgesailie site of DE/89B, Pat Shipman reported her conclusions gleaned from a restudy of the DE/89B fauna (Shipman et al. 1981). In this publication the identification of a "distinctive breakage pattern" was used to justify the conclusion that butchering and probably hunting had occurred.

The Olorgesailie materials were not the only target of Shipman's investigations. Roger Lewin (1981a:211) reports on the events at the annual meeting of the American Association for the Advancement of Science (January 3–8, 1981). Lewin cites reports by Alan Walker on observations made in independent studies by Shipman and Richard Potts regarding

> "cut marks superimposed on marks made by carnivore teeth." This is the kind of incontrovertible evidence for prehuman scavenging that paleoanthropologists will welcome enthusiastically. "They've also found extensive cut marks on fossil horse limbs from Olduvai at a point where virtually no meat would be present, only tendons and skin," he added. "Either these creatures weren't smart enough to know where the meat was, which is unlikely, or they were interested in something other than meat. One can only speculate what they were after." (Lewin 1981a:372–373).[1]

In another review article in *Science,* Roger Lewin (1981b) summarizes conclusions from the previously published articles by Potts and Shipman (1981:577) and Bunn (1981:574) in *Nature.* Lewin comments,

> Two intriguing aspects of interpretation emerge from Potts and Shipman's work. The first concerns possible competition between early hominids and carnivores. The second relates to the uses to which protohumans put animal products.

Then Lewin summarizes accurately the thinking of the researchers on these subject as follows:

> Clearly, the hominids sometimes had first access to a carcass, and sometimes they followed carnivores. This is good evidence that at least some of the hominids' meat-eating was the result of scavenging in competition with carnivores rather than direct hunting. . . .
> There is apparently some indication that skin and ligaments from animals were important products for our ancestors. . . .
> It has frequently been stated that one of the earliest technological inventions made by our ancestors must have been some form of carrier bag in which to transport collected plant foods, though evidence for such receptacles is virtually nonexistent. It is intriguing to speculate that some of these cutmarks do in fact constitute such evidence, indirect though it is. (Lewin 1981b:124)

My review of the major points made in literature through the summer of 1981 points out several things.

1. Isaac is the first (in the sequence of current arguments) to suggest that there is evidence from early time periods perhaps indicative of scavenging.

2. Later, the observation of tool marks overprinted on carnivore tooth marks is cited by Potts and Shipman (1981) and emphasized by Lewin (1981b) as being further evidence for scavenging. In addition, however, it is noted that tool-marked bones are commonly those from the lower legs of ungulates. This bias is interpreted as arising from the processing of tendons for the manufacture of carrying bags (Lewin 1981b).

3. Finally, an additional idea appears in the literature, namely "that the hominids and carnivores were competing for carcasses or bones, perhaps to obtain different substances" (Potts and Shipman 1981).

While these arguments were developing regarding the Lower Paleolithic materials, Shipman was staunchly defending hominid hunting of fierce animals, perhaps in a ritual context, as an explanation for the data from Olorgesailie (see Shipman et al. 1981, 1982; Shipman 1983).[2]

Thus, by the summer of 1981 scavenging had been suggested by Isaac and inferentially supported by the observations of Potts and Shipman (1981) of cut marks overprinted on carnivore gnawing. At no point, however, had the "consensus" view been basically challenged. It was still maintained that "meat eating" was important, thereby defending the argument emphasizing the importance of such behavior for a division of labor and the "sharing" hypothesis (Bunn 1981). Shipman appears also to support the consensus view with her claims for the hunting of giant geladas at Olorgesailie. She stresses the "human" appearance of mid-Pleistocene hominid behavior, adding that the biased presence of cut marks on ungulate lower limbs from Olduvai perhaps arose in the context of tendon removal for use in the production of carrying bags; this suggestion had previously been made by Richard Leakey regarding what was considered to be the most fundamental tool of home-base-living early hominids (Leakey and Lewin 1977:174). In addition, Shipman et al. (1981:260) examined cercopithecid remains from Olduvai "camps and living floors" as a clue to how hominids might have treated such species. The authors concluded that the remains were not hominid altered since the Olduvai data were similar to "nonhominid" data from Lake Turkana. The original research design indicates to me that Shipman believed that the Olduvai sites were high-integrity living or base-camp locations. In short, all the new data and observations were being accommodated to the then prevailing view of early man.

THE CONSENSUS VIEW IS CHALLENGED

In April of 1981, between the burst of publications cited above, another book appeared: *Bones, Ancient Men and Modern Myths* (Binford 1981a). This book represented the state of my knowledge regarding factors conditioning the character and composition of faunal assemblages and the methods then available for unambiguously recognizing the agents responsible for, or the determinant conditions influencing, site formation. I discussed, among other things, patterns of bone modification (breakage and inflicted marks) as they may indicate the identity of agents contributing to deposits remaining from the past.

Archaeologists beginning the task of investigating the limitations of the knowledge of their time change their views of the past and the meanings that they give to their experiences as new knowledge is generated. This is done as they gain new perspective through their investigations on the limitations of the knowledge with which they work. In my book I summarized what was then known about the composition of ungulate bone populations remaining on animal kill sites and bones accumulated in animal dens. The reasoning was simple: if we cannot tell the difference between the faunal assemblages associated with stone tools and forms of assemblage known to occur independent of human agency, then what, if anything, is implied by such ambiguous faunal remains as regards the behavior of the early hominids? Ambiguity must be resolved before defensible interpretation can be put forth. If it cannot be resolved, it must be eliminated from consideration—not because the ambiguous facts are not interesting, but because of the limitations of our present knowledge to resolve the ambiguity.

I chose a procedure that would permit the elimination from consideration of the faunal facts, as recorded, that were ambiguous in terms of our current knowledge. The results of the analysis were informative, since the faunal composition at the Olduvai sites (tool associated) was more complex than simple compounds of "kill" versus "den" assemblages common in nature. A "residual" pattern was isolated that, it was thought, could be informative about hominid behavior.[3] This pattern was characterized by parts of animals biased in favor of those yielding the least meat (Binford 1981a:281). The most common bones in these assemblages were identified as those yielding only bone marrow as a potential food. It was pointed out that these are also the bones commonly surviving at kill–death sites after exploitation by nonhominid predator–scavengers. Inferences from this pattern were summarized as follows:

> 1. They (the hominids) were scavenging the consumed kills and scavenging death sites of animals after most of the other predator–scavengers had abandoned the carcass and scattered some of its parts.
> 2. The parts scavenged were primarily leg bones that appear to have already had the meat removed, or they were lower leg bones that had little meat present. . . .

3. The major, or in many cases the only, usable or edible parts consisted of bone marrow.

4. Hominids were using hammer tools to break open the leg bones and thereby expose the usable marrow. . . . There is no evidence supporting the idea that the hominids were removing food from the locations of procurement to a base camp for consumption. In fact, the covariant patterning among anatomical parts shows that the parts selected by hominids for use were taken from already consumed and abandoned carcasses: the coincidence of both the residual components of such an animal kill and the modified elements used by the hominids at the same site demonstrates nicely that the consumption was at the place of procurement. No evidence for base camps exists. Similarly, the argument that food was shared is totally unsupported. (Binford 1981a:294)

These conclusions were warranted by citing the information then available on the nature of large mammal faunal assemblages at "natural" kill–death sites where humans were known not to have been involved in modifying the materials. In addition, previous studies of the economic anatomy of ungulates (Binford 1978a:15–46) were cited to warrant the conclusions regarding the economic or food potential of different bones. The conclusions regarding base camps were justified by the argument that the only usable material indicated by bone frequencies—bone marrow—occurred in far too small a "package" for it to have been shared.[4] It will be recalled that the importance of the hunting hypothesis depended upon hunters killing animals of moderate to large size, therefore obtaining much more food than a single hominid could consume. It was thought that the only "motive" for killing such animals would have been if they were being returned to a base camp and shared among a large group of consumers. The conclusions were further justified by the fact that the frequencies of lower legs occurring on the Olduvai sites matched frequencies occurring on natural death sites. This strongly suggested that the hominids were not initially dismembering carcasses but that most commonly they were picking up already dismembered anatomical segments for consumption of the remnant food morsels.

It was pointed out that scavenging tactics would favor the biased exploitation of carcasses from animals of moderate to large body size, since these would be more likely to yield usable parts after other scavengers had finished feeding (Binford 1981a:296). This suggestion was, of course, consistent with the already known pattern that many early sites consistently yielded bones from large animal species (see Sampson 1974:128, 215–216).

Very importantly, my analysis supported the observations of the excavators that other animals, particularly carnivores, had played a major role in conditioning the content of the faunal assemblages found in the same places as the stone tools. This meant that the total faunal assemblage could not simply be interpreted as resulting from hominid behavior. In addition, the analysis demonstrated that the archaeologically remaining faunal assemblages had been modified by destructive agents, in that a "signature" pattern of biased bone destruction was demonstrable. These facts condition the degree that interpretations about hominids can be made directly from the faunal frequencies as they were recorded by archaeologists. If sustained by further evidence, it means that interpretations of hominid behavior cannot be made directly from the raw data recovered from the Olduvai sites. In short, most of the Olduvai sites appear to be palimpsests, further modified by attritional agents.

The arguments in *Bones* challenged the models of the past then commonly accepted regarding the organization and behavior of early hominid life. I also challenged Shipman's interpretations of the data from Olorgesailie (Binford and Todd 1982) by pointing out that she lacked any clear form of inference justification and that the pattern that she claimed to be a distinctive indication of hominid butchering was the normal survival pattern expected in nature for bones of differing density.[5]

While of importance, these challenges to the prevailing views of the past were not as important as were the methodological challenges, which went directly to the root of interpretation. How does one use the knowledge of the time to justify or warrant interpretative conclusions offered regarding observations on the archaeological record? My major point had been that there was sufficient evidence available to clearly suggest that the Olduvai sites were palimpsests resulting from the perhaps semi-independent actions of a number of formation agents. Thus, one could not accept the raw data from these sites as directly referable to hominid behavior without first measuring or controlling for the effects of other agents on the form of the assemblage. The second major point had been to show that, when we did control for ambiguity, the composition of the faunal assemblage, which may well refer unambiguously to the hominids, did not appear to represent carcasses transported or processed for meat; instead, the tiny morsels of bone marrow from the lower limbs seemed to have been the food targets of the early hominids. The challenge went to the heart of both the then-current view of the past and the methods of inference justification then commonly being employed by the Africanists.

COPING WITH THE CHALLENGE

Just about a year after the publication of *Bones,* Shipman delivered a paper at the 4th International Council for Archaeozoology in London.

> Potts, Bunn, and I (Potts and Shipman 1981; Shipman 1981a, 1981b; Bunn 1981) have shown that the stone tools and bones at some early sites (FxJj50, Koobi Fora; various Bed I and II sites, Olduvai Gorge) are causally, not casually, associated. The main thrust of these papers had been to demonstrate the existence of cutmarks on various bones. Such evidence in part refutes Binford's claim that the sites were formed by carnivore or hydraulic activities, in that we know that at least some of the bones were acted upon by early hominids wielding stone tools. (Shipman 1983:35–36)

It should be clear that Shipman had not read the *Bones* book very carefully, since nowhere did I question the relationship of stone tools to the processing of animal remains. I had even offered suggestions as to how it was done! Nevertheless, in her paper she proposed to "test" the arguments of Lovejoy (1981) and Isaac (1978a) regarding provisioning, sharing, and living in base camps. This was to be accomplished by using a set of stipulated conventions for inferring or denying meat eating, food sharing, food carrying, base-camp living, and division of labor among ancient hominids. These stipulated indicators are asserted to be what recent hunter–gatherers "do," and a knowledge of these activities would therefore provide a "signature" for the behaviors she sought to recognize archaeologically.[6] Her criteria are as follows (from Shipman 1983:36):

Behavior	Correlate
Meat-eating	Cutmarks on bones
Food-sharing	Disarticulation of carcasses
Food-carrying	Differential carcass utilization
Base-camp-living	Disarticulation of medium to large carcasses, defleshing of very large carcasses
Division of labor	Combination of bony and plant remains at the base camp

I think it should be clear that almost anyone familiar with hunters and butchery could point to situations in which any one of Shipman's correlates could occur and not indicate what she claims. In fact, even she discounts the correlate of cut marks on bones as indicative of meat eating by recounting her belief that the biased marking of lower leg bones was because of tendon removal! After a short discussion of her criteria she proceeds to demonstrate that the frequencies of cut marks and tooth marks are essentially the same on shafts as they are on articular ends of the Olduvai bones, with a minor cut mark bias in favor of shafts. In turn, the frequency patterning of cut marks at Olduvai was shown to be different from that observed by Gifford et al. (1981) on archaeological bones recovered from a Neolithic site, where a much higher proportional frequency of marks on articular ends was observed. This was taken as evidence that the Olduvai hominids rarely disarticulated carcasses! Such a conclusion is not warranted even given the data she presents. First, there are cut marks on the articular surfaces of bones reported by Potts and Shipman (1981) as well as by Shipman (1983). Second, a proportional difference as noted by Shipman could be understood to represent a different processing strategy with respect to bone shafts at Olduvai while a similar disarticulation strategy could be common to Olduvai and the Neolithic site. In short, arguments from proportions or ratios are always ambiguous with regard to the sources of observed differences. Nevertheless, Shipman gave the following meanings to her observations.

> The *conclusions must be* that the Olduvai hominids are rarely if ever disarticulating carcasses. Thus both Isaac's and Lovejoy's hypothesis are refuted by these data: food-carrying and food-sharing (and by implication, base-camp-living) did not occur at these sites. (Shipman 1983:40; emphasis added)

Here we see that her entire position on the significance of the early sites is based on her rejection of the proposition that the hominids were disarticulating carcasses. This is a point that, as I have suggested earlier, cannot be defended even with the data as she has presented them. Nevertheless, after linking the above suggestion with those previously advanced by Vrba regarding how one might identify scavenging, Shipman claims that she has formulated her own criteria for recognizing hunting versus scavenging: (1) "early hunters were more likely to have hit upon a strategy suitable for hunting a single type of animal rather than a more broadly applicable strategy" (Shipman 1983:45). [Author's comment: they would be specialists.] (2) ". . . smaller carcasses, whether juvenile or adult, are less likely to be available for scavenging than larger ones" (Shipman 1983:45).[7]

There appears to be no justification at all for the argument that early hunters would be species-specific specialists except perhaps her knowledge that the early sites contained many different species and hence she could strengthen her "position" by such an assertion. It is unclear why the second claim is made, since there is a relatively large small-mammal and rodent fauna from the Olduvai sites, which has regrettably remained largely unanalyzed.

Undaunted, however, Shipman seeks to warrant the following conclusion. "I propose as an alternative to the human-type hunter–gatherer models that early hominids were predominantly scavenging for meat and foraging for plant foods" (Shipman 1983:45). Shipman again reports her observations on cut marks but this time long after the appearance of the *Bones* book. In this setting she presents "her" insight that early hominids were scavengers! Citing as evidence a biased tool-using attention to shafts rather than articular ends, she then unjustifiably asserts that this pattern means a lack of dismemberment activity! Ironically, by failing to demonstrate that meat-yielding bones were relatively rare at Olduvai she defeats her own argument, since one can imagine the scavenging of already dismembered relatively large meat-yielding parts linked with the transport of such parts to a base camp where sharing could be as reasonable as it is in the hunting hypothesis!

This irony is further extended since she adds the previously stated idea that, for her, scavenging places hominids in direct confrontational competition with other predator–scavengers. Such a situation is only realistic if the early hominids were going primarily after meat, the target of many other predator–scavenger feeders.

> Perhaps the unusual distribution of cutmarks at Olduvai relative to the Neolithic site . . . is a direct consequence of the opportunistic foraging–scavenging mode of life. Removing meat and other useful materials from a carcass as rapidly and efficiently as possible makes sense if the hominids were likely to be displaced or attacked by carnivores. (Shipman 1983:45)

It should be clear that Shipman has in mind a meaty carcass being stripped without disarticulation by tool-using hominids. In such a case, it would seem that the tool-marked bone (from filleting) would remain at the carcass or kill site. Is she saying the Olduvai sites are natural death locations where hominids sneak in and cut off food morsels? On the other hand, if she has in mind confrontational competition, why would the hominid not disarticulate parts (a more rapid strategy) and carry them to safe locations? Alas, we are not enlightened; we are only told that hominids were in direct competition at carcasses, yet they were not dismembering them—instead, they were essentially filleting or removing tendons for carrying bags!

There is perhaps another issue that is even more important than the organization of Shipman's arguments. This has to do with her attempt to model a "way of life" from patterning manifest in essentially medium to large mammal bone. It should be recalled that the participants in the arguments being summarized are talking about some of the "first" archaeological manifestations of hominid behavior. We are discussing the very dawn of tool use and its "early years." From what we know of technological change in general, how likely is it that the earliest experimentation with tool use would constitute the "core" of the tactical array used by a creature in the adaptive exploitation of its environment? The hominids performed archaeologically invisible activities previously; how wonderful it would be if their early use of tools would in fact inform us about their total adaptation! I think this is the most unlikely state of affairs one could imagine. The challenge in this situation is to understand the context of initial tool use and then to see how this context changes through time. We know that, much later, man and late hominids used tools in many facets of their adaptation; was that true in the early years? Based on the facts that only the medium- to large-sized mammals have been studied taphonomically and that the only unambiguous pattern in these remains seems clearly to point to scavenging for bone marrow and perhaps to the incidental eating of tiny morsels of dried or desiccated meat, it is hard to see this behavior as the normative core of their adaptation.

During the spring of 1984 several articles by Shipman regarding the "scavenging hypothesis" appeared. Perhaps the most important of these "new" arguments relates to bias in the anatomical parts exhibiting cut marks.

> Meat-eating would be indicated by the presence of cutmarks on the meat-bearing bones (upper forelimb and hindlimb bones) of prey animals; very few cutmarks would be present on non-meat-bearing bones, like those of the feet. (Shipman 1984a:9)

Now we are told that Shipman actually carried out her work on the Olduvai materials with this argument in mind and that, much to her surprise, more than half of the cut marks occurred on non-meat-bearing bones. She then returns to her earlier idea that perhaps the cutmarks were produced while the hominids were removing tendons: "Many of these marks were on non-meat-bearing-bones. Many of these marks must have resulted from skinning and tendon removal as well as butchery."

The next article to appear was in the popular magazine *Natural History* under the title "Scavenger Hunt," and here a more sophisticated discussion of disarticulation versus filleting of meat from bones was introduced into the discussion (Shipman 1984b:22). It was suggested that the bias in favor of "meat removal" (from bones that do not have meat) was evidence that the hominids did not carry "their kills back to camp to share with others, since both transport and sharing are difficult unless carcasses are cut up" (Shipman 1984b:22). (This again implies that we are looking at kill sites?)

> When I looked for cut marks attributable to skinning or tendon removal, a more modern pattern emerged. On both the Neolithic and Olduvai bones, nearly 75 percent of all cut marks occurred on bones that bore little meat, these cut marks probably came from skinning. Carnivore tooth marks were much less common on such bones. Hominids were using carcasses as a source of skin and tendon. This made it seem more surprising that they disarticulated carcasses so rarely. (Shipman 1984b:22)

If the early hominids were scavengers, what did they scavenge? The answer that Shipman gives us is "tendons." How can she postulate an overall way of life based on tendon extraction? Given the original context of this suggestion (tendons used for making carrying bags) it would seem that her arguments would lead her to propose that the hominids were more likely foragers of vegetal food! Nevertheless, in an article by Roger Lewin (1984) entitled "Man the Scavenger" the essential features of Shipman's arguments as seen in the *Natural History* article were recapitulated. The contents of the article are not new but the tone is surprising. For instance, "the idea that scavenging might have represented a complete ecological adaptation is only now being articulated" (Lewin 1984:861). Later in the article we are told, "In developing the scavenging hypothesis, Shipman has documented the various physical and behavioral characteristics among carnivores and compared them to hominids of 2 million years ago" (Lewin 1984:862).

We have gone from a biased distribution of cut marks on the shafts of lower limb bones at the Olduvai sites to a discussion of the overall niche occupied by early hominids in an African setting. The whole time, Shipman bases her reconstruction on the unjustified interpretation of (a) proportional differences in cut marks between Olduvai and Neolithic sites, and (b) the assumed significance of carnivore evidence at the site—direct competition between hominids and carnivores.

At the 4th International Council for Archaeozoology in London (April 1982), Richard Potts presented a paper designed to clarify the problem of early hominid subsistence. Potts launches into a series of arguments warranting his analytical strategy, which begins with the following assumptions:

> representation of different skeletal remains on sites in part relates to the timing of hominid access to carcasses. Hunting implies that the complete carcass is acquired by the predator. In contrast, scavenging produces wider variation in the availability of skeletal parts. Processing of an animal recently dead (early scavenging) may permit access to the entire skeleton and its resources. On the other hand, late scavenging—after other animals and agents have acted on the carcass—allows access only to skeletons which have undergone disarticulation and bone dispersal. (Potts 1983:52)

The careful reader will recognize this as the same principle that I used earlier to argue that the residual pattern noted on the Olduvai sites was most likely the result of scavenging (Binford 1981a:253). This is the principle upon which I based my earlier studies of human hunting and faunal assemblage diversity. A biased deletion of parts was made from an original population, resulting in a derivative population found elsewhere (see Binford 1978a:81, 242–245). There is, however, a major difference, which Potts has overlooked, between the forms of the original population and the derivative population. It was shown empirically time after time that the first derivative population, the one removed from a parent population, was in fact different from the parent population. This difference derives from the fact that modern humans exploit a carcass in a biased manner. They do not just pick what is most common or accessible but what is most useful to them in the context of availability. It is the pattern inherent in the first derivative population that is a clue to the exploitive bias standing behind the selection of parts from a parent population. Potts simply assumed that early hominids were not interested in usable material, that they picked up bones in direct proportion to what was available to them as already disarticulated parts. I think such an assumption is very hard to justify. The hominids must have been interested in some usable materials on a carcass and not just in the bones themselves considered in anatomical terms. One could easily argue that the most usable material would remain on those parts that were least likely to have been exploited earlier by other kill-scavengers! Of equal importance must be the recognition that the hominids *had tools* and could and apparently did *disarticulate* animal parts, presumably with reference to judgments as to their utility. Such behavior would ensure that the removed or transported assemblage of parts would be different from the parent population of parts from which selections were made.

Ignoring such problems, Potts proceeds to justify the argument that there was a signature pattern to anatomical parts remaining on nonhominid kill–death sites. Potts focuses on an observation by A. Hill (1975, 1979) that forelimbs tend to be disarticulated early in the normal sequence of anatomical disorganization expected among carcasses. It should be noted that research conducted on decaying bovid carcasses in the New World, where it is known that no active scavengers were present, does not yield such a pattern (Todd 1983). On such sites both front and rear legs do not "fall off" in the sequence noted by Hill. Presumably the pattern Hill observed is related to predator dismemberment rather than a regular pattern of anatomical disorganization independent of mammal agents. Nevertheless, Potts proposes an analytical strategy to determine whether hominids consistently had access to carcasses early or late in the alleged normal sequence of anatomical disorganization. His proposal is a simple one: calculate two ratios from the actual counts of bones on the Olduvai sites, the ratio of front to rear leg elements and the ratio of axial skeleton parts to all limb parts. He calculates his ratios for a number of key Olduvai sites and finds that there is little patterning recognizable, an exception being noted for bovids of medium size.

At this point we are forced to ask why Potts insists on treating the remains on the Olduvai sites as if hominids were responsible for all the bones present. There is clear evidence in the form of extensive animal gnawing (Potts and Shipman 1981; Shipman 1983), coprolites believed to be from lions and hyenas (M. Leakey 1971:43, 50), as well as breakage and part-survival patterning (Binford 1981a:256–262) that is nearly identical to control cases where gnawing animals broke and consumed a faunal assemblage. In addition, water sorting can be expected to condition at least three of the assemblages he studied.[8] Finally, there is an anatomical part association pattern that is partially indistinguishable from that known to result from ravaged carcasses where man played no role in their modification (Binford 1981a:262–288). In spite of the evidence to the contrary, Potts proceeds as if all the bones on the studied Olduvai sites were directly referable to hominid actions. This procedure is simply not defensible. The problems of potential transport of parts by animals and by water, and the differential and biased destruction of anatomical parts by gnawing animals, are simply ignored. We see here a failure to deal realistically with the archaeological record.

With this unrealistic approach Potts moves directly to inferences about hominid behavior and concludes that they were nonspecialized omnivores using a "broad base of faunal exploitation and a varied mode of foraging . . . that at least occasionally utilized animal resources" (Potts 1983:61). Such conclusions are simply not warranted. First, the model used for monitoring hominid strategy was not a realistic one, in that it assumed that the hominids did not exploit carcasses in terms of the subsistence potential of parts, only the simple availability of bones anatomically considered. Second, the analysis assumed that all the bones on the Olduvai sites were accumulated by hominids and that the anatomical frequencies present were directly reflective of hominid behavior, unmodified by scavenging animals. These assumptions are demonstrably inappropriate. Finally, his conclusions tell us that we can expect great flexibility and variability in the subsistence behavior of the early hominids. Such conclusions simply do not add to our knowledge since they derive from the vague lack of patterning that always results from treating a complex, multidimensional phenomenon unidimensionally.

In the beginning of his paper, Potts (1983:51) asserted that he considered the Olduvai sites to have been "stone caches which were used repeatedly for carcass processing." The "stone cache" argument to which Potts alludes was developed in his dissertation (Potts 1982) and has recently been expounded in a more complete fashion (Potts 1984a). This argument starts with the observation that most of the stone found in the Olduvai sites had been transported from "several kilometers away." From this observation the suggestion is made that the hominids transported the stone to appropriate places in their environment in anticipation of subsequent use. Later, when hominids secured a carcass or parts thereof, they would transport the animal parts and perhaps other foods to these caches for processing. This strategy is evaluated as being more efficient than having a single home base and also tending to reduce competition at carcasses.

> Because many animals were attracted to carcasses, it was necessary for hominids to transport portions of them away from the death sites at which they had been obtained. . . . Time and energy spent in handling and transporting portions of meat could be minimized by taking the bones to the nearest cache, where there remained stone tools. . . . Time spent at the cache was then minimized by processing the new material quickly to obtain whatever . . . were needed. By abandoning the site immediately, hominids could probably often avoid direct confrontation with carnivores attracted to the remains. (Potts 1984a:345)

These arguments are interesting in that they attempt to model a non-home-base formation context for the Olduvai sites. They are seemingly plausible, in that currently popular appeals to efficiency and risk reduction are built into the arguments. They further imply a very different subsistence–settlement pattern than is common with modern man. Thinking of this sort is needed when treating the early materials. However, the model fails in several ways. Perhaps the greatest difficulty lies with the fact that it cannot be tested as presented, beyond its plausible accommodation of the facts as known or admitted at present. As such, it is a classic post hoc accommodative argument. Secondly, it fails to acknowledge the data relative to nonhominid roles in site formation since it accommodates ambiguous data. It makes the convenient assumption that the evidence for nonhominid presence at the site was added after the hominids had abandoned the site. Finally, it assumes a set of planning strategies on the part of the hominids that is only known among the most complex modern hunter–gatherers, namely a caching strategy for materials and the outfitting of places. This strategy is presently documented only for complex, logistically organized, modern hunter–gatherers (Binford 1980a).

In a more recent paper, Potts (1984b) acknowledges some of these problems but adopts what is best described as an "uncertainty averaging" strategy rather than treating the analytical problem presented by the Olduvai sites realistically. Not surprisingly, he concludes that things are uncertain and resorts to opinions warranted by appeal to general ecology and the plausible suggestion that life was different in the Lower Paleolithic (Potts 1984b:159–161).

I applaud Potts for his attempt to introduce new ideas into the field of early man studies. I agree that the Olduvai sites are not home bases, and I agree that they are more likely multiple occupational, "functionally specific" locations. I doubt strongly that they are tactically planned locations of the type he suggests. I will have more to say on this point in the summary.

The third paper of interest delivered at the London conference was by Glynn Isaac (1983a). This paper summarized the knowledge that he considered to be secure about the behavior of the early hominids. It essentially acknowledged the skeptical excitement of the preceding years and then emphasized the evidence for the transport of anatomical parts by hominids. In addition, it emphasized that the evidence indicated "meat eating" on a significant scale (Isaac 1983a:13). (This is a misleading statement since we actually have no evidence bearing on the relative contributions of different food sources to the overall diet of the early hominids.) Isaac then goes on to suggest that, while his earlier position on "home bases" was probably premature (he made early man appear "too human"), nevertheless the "significant" role of meat eating and the evidence for transport of animal-derived "foods" justifies what he calls, the "central-place foraging" view of early man. He then cites his earlier papers (Isaac 1978a, 1981a, 1981b; Isaac and Crader 1981) as well as one by Jane Lancaster (1978) as germane to this view. These are all statements of the old "home base" consensus view. This position was well summarized in Isaac and Crader (1981:93) as follows:

> In devising models of early stages in the evolution of a system in which food-sharing became a pivotal ingredient, meat does have critical importance: it is a highly concentrated, highly portable form of nourishment. Portions of a carcass are readily carried and are an important food prize when consumed at the destination. We thus favor a model in which the active delivery of some meat to fellow members of a social group developed in a reciprocal relationship with the practice of transporting and sharing some surplus plant foods. We see the model as representing a functionally integrated behavioral complex, in which any attempt to isolate one or another component as an initial or prime mover is probably misleading.

Since 1983 Isaac has presented his views many times and currently concedes that the hominids were probably not sleeping at "central places," but he continues to insist that the transport of animal products (and "significant" meat eating) are sufficient empirical indicators of the accuracy of his "model" of early hominid behavior and in turn of the conditioning role that such behavior played in bringing forth our human characteristics.

The point made by Isaac about "significant" meat eating seemingly stems from work done by one of his former students, Henry Bunn, who also delivered a paper at the London conference. Bunn's paper was short and to the point. He analyzed the form and distribution of what he judges to be tool-inflicted marks on the bones from Isaac's site (Fxjj50) at Koobi Fora and from the important floor at Olduvai Gorge (FLK-22) that yielded the "Zinjanthropus" hominid remains. He reports the *proportion* of different anatomical parts that, in his judgment, yield tool-inflicted marks. He stresses the fact that cut marks consistently occur in high proportions on the articular ends of long bones. This clearly conflicts with the claims by Shipman, discussed earlier, that "hominids are rarely if ever disarticulating carcasses" (Shipman 1983:40). Like Shipman, however, Bunn (1983a:27) does report high frequencies of cut marks on the shafts of long bones, seemingly indicative of different behavior than is commonly reported from relatively modern assemblages.

Like earlier apologists for the tooth marks from Olduvai, Bunn notes the high frequency of carnivore marks on the bones and offers what can be considered the "standard" argument for their dismissal (see previous statements of this position: M. Leakey 1971:43; Isaac 1971:288; Bunn 1982a:495, as well as my comments on it: Binford 1983b:373).

> The simplest explanation for the presence of several hundred bones with carnivore gnaw marks, some of which occur on bones that also retain cut marks, is that scavenging carnivores, possibly hyenas, were attracted to the FLK Zinjanthropus bone and artifact concentration after hominids created it. (Bunn 1983a:28)

This may be the "simplest" assumption, but it is also the assumption that saves the "consensus" view of the past. If animals were admitted to have played a role in the accumulation of the deposits, the case for bone transport by hominids would be rendered at best ambiguous. Secondly, if animals were to be admitted as potential bone transporters, then the case for "significant meat eating" would be less secure. Seeing scavengers coming on the site after the hominids had produced it makes it possible to salvage the consensus view. It also makes it possible to offer alternatives to the consensus view and still not face the issue of the methodological sophistication needed to analyze data when multiple agents are suspected as having been operative in site formation, as was done in Potts's (1983) arguments.

SUMMARY OF CRITICISM

What seems clear is that essentially all the major authors treating the early eras of tool use agree that much of the fauna on the sites was accumulated by virtue of hominid scavenging activities. It appears that all currently also agree that these lake- and waterside locations were not places where the hominids slept. All authors (except perhaps Shipman, who is unclear on this issue) seem to agree that the hominids transported parts of animals to the places we see today as sites. All also recognize a major role of nonhominid predator–scavengers in the formational history of the sites. These views represent major and deeply provocative changes in our ideas about early man, which have largely come about since 1980. Major disagreements remain regarding (a) the presence and, if so, the quantity and character of hunting carried out by the early hominids, (b) the motives for transporting animal parts, (c) the functional character of the sites with respect to the broader subsistence–settlement pattern of the hominids, and (d) the role of the nonhominid predator–scavengers both in site formation and in the ecology of the early hominids. It seems appropriate to summarize the arguments regarding these points of controversy.

I think it should be clear that the role of carnivores as contributors to the site formation processes is the central and currently unresolved issue complicating much of the interpretation of the data from the early hominid sites. I argued that nonhominid predator–scavengers were important agents responsible for some of the characteristics of the Olduvai faunal assemblages (Binford 1981a). I also suggested that what appeared unambiguous at these sites was an assemblage of bones biased in favor of ungulate lower-limb bones, which were probably selected and transported for purposes of processing for bone marrow. I used my analysis to challenge the view that hunting and transport of meat-yielding parts to base camps for sharing were justifiable interpretations of the Olduvai data. It should be emphasized that the challenge was offered by reasoned argument from the facts of faunal assemblage composition, both in terms of anatomical part frequencies and in terms of breakage categories justified by the independent study of the economic anatomy of ungulates.

The response was interesting. Shipman did a complete about-face. She had quite obviously been defending the consensus view with her "very human" interpretation of middle Pleistocene hominids. This clearly implies humanlike characteristics for the earlier hominids. All at once, using two data sets (the proportions of animal-tooth to tool-inflicted marks on bones and the proportions of tool-inflicted marks on bone shafts versus articular ends), she argues that early hominids were not hunters, they were scavengers. The alleged lack of evidence for disarticulation in the Lower Paleolithic is said to show that hominids were not transporting meat-yielding parts to "home bases." Finally, the evidence of carnivore tooth marks is suggested as indicative of direct competition between hominids and other scavenger–predators for animal products. As previously pointed out, there is no lack of evidence for disarticulation by the hominids, and the proportional data cited by Shipman is inappropriate to her argument. The important facts of faunal assemblage composition are not mentioned, nor are the problems of multiple agents as contributors to the Olduvai assemblages dealt with except by avoidance. The argument for competition with carnivores is hard to accept in the absence of any clear suggestion as to how the tool- and tooth-marked pieces came to be associated at sites. Consideration of this problem should lead directly to an evaluation of the kinds of sites represented by the Olduvai material, and we see that this issue is generally ignored except to say that they are not base camps (although implications seemingly unappreciated by Shipman haunt her arguments). Of all the contributors to debate, Shipman seems to be the only writer who suffers from problems with both the appropriateness of the analytical procedures chosen and the internal logic of her argument, even if one grants her the assumptions made.

This is not to say that someone skilled in analysis could not use Shipman's observations, but she would have to present her data on gnawing and cut marks broken down by anatomical part since *the only frame of reference we currently have for evaluating biased behavior* is relative to the use of anatomical parts of known utility. If she were to present her material in this fashion she might be able to demonstrate a biased use of animal products in favor of non-meat-yielding parts. She could not, however, demonstrate the absence of disarticulatory behavior or the absence of transport. The second major problem with Shipman's conclusions rests with her argument for direct competition among hominids and other predator–scavengers. Instead of a hard-headed attempt to understand the common occurrence of tooth-inflicted marks on bones associated with hominid remains she moves directly to arguments of "evolutionary functionalism," which appear to be implausible and poorly grounded.

The work of Richard Potts appears somewhat more sophisticated. Rather than denying transport, he clearly goes with the data that seem to indicate the transport of animal parts by hominids. Potts's work suffers from two major weaknesses: (a) the failure to treat the problem of the integrity of the deposits, adopting the explanation for animal-tooth-inflicted marks as inflicted *after* the hominids had accumulated meat at "stone caches;" and (b) the assumption of the very behavioral characteristics for the hominids that we would like to monitor—that is, planning depth in their subsistence strategies. Potts points out that the stone was transported to the "sites" in both tool and manuport form. He assumes that this was done in *anticipation* of the use of such locations for processing animals and perhaps other food products. Such behavior requires considerable abilities in *planning ahead.* I have stressed elsewhere (Binford 1982c:178; 1984c:97, 98, 195, 224) that planning depth with regard to technology is not something in which the early hominids appear to have been very skilled.

Potts's model assumes motivation and, in so doing, suffers from the same tautological properties that I will show characterize Glynn Isaac's arguments—namely, the facts of the case are argued in a post hoc manner to result from an assumed motivation. The evidence for the motivational component of the argument consists of the very facts that it is supposed to explain (see Potts 1984a:345)! In fact, the only data currently available for which there is some independent basis for inferring motivation would permit recognition of a bias in the use of animal body parts (see Binford 1978a), yet these investigators strangely avoid these data. We need much more work at the middle-range level to provide independent frames of reference against which to evaluate motivational arguments. At present the only basis for believing Potts's accommodative argument is that it fits the data. Of course, it was developed to accomplish just that and hence remains a tactical tautology.

The arguments of Glynn Isaac and his student, Henry Bunn, both fail to treat the problem of the integrity of the Olduvai sites by assuming the "standard" explanation for the evidence of nonhominid predator–scavenger presence—these animals gnawed the bones after the hominids had left the sites. Isaac's current defense of his slightly modified "home base" argument, central-place foraging, assumes that the motive for transporting animal parts is for sharing; hence, the evidence he is willing to accept for sharing is the demonstration of transport, another tactical tautology. Finally, both Isaac and Bunn appear willing to accept the bones as evidence for meat eating by arguing for disarticulation of anatomical segments by the hominids, and by citing the quantity of bones. Once again, the only evidence currently independently justifiable for demonstrating a bias toward the use of meat is from anatomical part frequencies, a data domain they both seem to judiciously avoid!

In general the responsive arguments have been encouraging in that the challenge to the consensus view is taken seriously and even supported by some, while all are struggling to view the data from the early hominids in new ways. What is perhaps regrettable is that the types of work necessary to forging a more realistic view of the past are not thus far forthcoming. We need solid descriptive studies of the important Olduvai sites in terms consistent with current methods of analysis. The faunas need to be described in detail: the frequencies of cut marks, animal gnawing, and breakage patterns must be reported in such a way that the patterning regarding the interaction among agents, which most certainly stands behind the archaeological record, can be recognized. Short articles that merely summarize "new facts" in ways that are not amenable to alternative analyses do not help. I look forward to a period of more substantive research and more meaningful argument than has thus far materialized.

BEYOND THE REACTIVE ARGUMENTS

It is perhaps appropriate to point out that I became involved in arguing about the lifeways of the early hominids from the perspective of working with archaeological materials from a later time period, the Mousterian of Europe (see Binford and Binford 1966; Binford 1972b, 1973, 1982b, 1982c, 1983b, 1983c). During the course of work on the "Mousterian problem" I became convinced that the organization of the hunting and gathering way of life, among these relatively recent ancestors, was quite different than that among fully modern *Homo sapiens sapiens.* If this was true then the almost "human" lifeways depicted in the "consensus" view of the very early hominids stood out as an extremely unlikely condition. It was for this reason that I began to "worry" about the early Pleistocene materials. I think that I have been successful in casting strong doubt on the characterizations of hominid life that were so current in the 1970s. As suggested in the summary, many of the points of the challenge are currently conceded by many Africanists.

It might be reasonably asked, where does this leave our understanding of the processes leading to our own characteristic humanity? It should be clear that large-game hunting has been considered by many as a formative step in our evolutionary background. As suggested here, the practice of such predation during the early phases of hominid experience has been strongly challenged, and there is a growing suspicion that active large-game hunting may not have been a part of the early hominid lifeway. In view of this uncertainty some have simply shifted the hunting argument to later time periods, suggesting that hunting was a behavior characteristic of *Homo erectus.*

> There are after all some persuasive records of systematic hunting later in human
> history. One of the oldest of these is at Olorgesailie in Kenya, where hominids

repeatedly killed and butchered giant baboons. . . . The hominids of the time were *Homo erectus,* which had appeared in Africa some million years earlier than the Olorgesailie site.

As there are no equivalent records of systematic hunting between 1.5 million and 0.5 million years ago, the question of when the practice began and when the scavenging mode ended remains a matter of speculation. (Lewin 1984:862)

As has been pointed out, the evidence presented by Shipman et al. (1981) for systematic hunting at Olorgesailie is far from convincing;[9] nevertheless, it is appealing to some to hold to the old view that it was hunting that "made us human" and hence translate the argument to a more recent era.

At the same time that the history of early hominid large-game hunting was being reevaluated, there were intellectual challenges to the idea that hunting was a crucial behavioral context for understanding the emergence of our "humanness." I have already discussed the consensus view of early man, but Glynn Isaac's argument is not totally dependent upon hunting although a sexual division of labor seems crucial to his arguments.

> Once food transport was initiated, novel selection pressures would come to bear on (1) ability to communicate about the past, future, and the spatially remote, and (2) enhanced abilities to plan complex chains of eventualities and to play what one might call "social chess" in one's mind. That is, the adoption of food-sharing would have favored the development of language, social reciprocity, and the intellect. (Isaac 1983c:535)

Another view has been articulated by Owen Lovejoy (1981), writing from a more biological perspective, in which he suggests that reproductive advantages and disadvantages accrue to differing kinds of social arrangements and, by implication, subsistence behavior. His arguments have the advantage of suggesting mechanisms for the appearance of food transport and "provisioning," while Isaac's take a more historical approach and postulate such conditions as necessary prerequisites to the human characteristics we know must have appeared more recently. Given the implied importance of a male–female division of labor in Isaac's argument, Lovejoy makes a most provocative point regarding male–female subsistence activities.

> Greater seasonality and the need to increase both birthrate and survivorship would also favor at least partial separation of male and female day ranges since this strategy would increase carrying capacity and improve the protein and calorie supply of females and their offspring. . . . Lowered mobility of females would reduce accident rate during travel, maximize familiarity with the core area, reduce exposure to predators, and allow intensification of parenting behavior. . . . Monogamous pair bonding would favor feeding divergence by "assuring" males of biological paternity and by reducing feeding competition with their own offspring and mates. (Lovejoy 1981:344–345)

Although Lovejoy is making the above argument with respect to changes he believes occurred during the Miocene, the argument is perhaps more germane to the conditions facing a radiating hominid population penetrating the temperate zone during the mid-Pleistocene. It is interesting that when Lovejoy's argument is considered in a Miocene context the focus would be exclusively on equatorial and subequatorial environments, where temperature-related seasonality is not a major factor exacerbating patchy food distributions.[10] If, as many have thought, hunting is strongly tied to a male–female division of labor, a separation in feeding ranges would provide a natural basis on which a division of labor and sharing could later be developed between the sexes. The latter characteristic, sharing, could be related to the beginning steps toward a more hunting-dependent subsistence strategy.

As we have seen, recent research strongly supports the view that the early hominids living in essentially equatorial and subequatorial environments were not large-mammal hunters in any systemic way. On the other hand, a separation in feeding ranges could well be exacerbated by the lowered food abundance in temperate settings and in turn could provide the selective context upon which hunting and a more systematic division of labor could be biologically favored. I have long thought that hunting was a strategy that would increasingly serve an omnivorous primate in environments with shorter and shorter growing seasons (Binford 1981a:296). A temperate-zone context of selection could be summarized as the need to cope with the overwintering problem. One solution to this problem is to eat animals who have already solved this problem in their region. Viewed against a suspected pressure to separate the feeding ranges of males and females, plus the advantage of predation as a means of solving the overwintering problem in temperate settings, we can envision a more realistic framework to investigate the important changes in adaptation that must have occurred in our remote past. In support of the temperate-zone focus there is evidence from modern hunter–gatherers that clearly indicates the advantage of hunting in environments with short growing seasons. Richard Lee (1968) has demonstrated that dependence upon nonplant foods increases as one moves away from the equator. I have shown (Binford 1980a) that, in addition, modern hunter–gatherers deal with the overwintering problem by increased dependence upon storage as one moves farther from the equator. Surely, early man had to cope with these same problems!

I cannot imagine that the earliest hominids to radiate into temperate settings practiced storage strategies, but one can imagine them being under pressure to become at least seasonal predators. Harking back to Lovejoy's arguments, we could also expect that one of the first moves in this direction might well have been an increased separation in the feeding ranges of males and females. In addition, the increased shelter requirements in the temperate zone would render it even more reproductively advantageous to reduce the mobility of females and their offspring, providing still further advantage to increases in provisioning behavior on the part of males.

Arguments such as these may turn out to be wrong, but at present they can provide provocative guides for the development of research programs aimed at furthering our understanding of hominid evolution. It was in the context of such speculations that I turned my attention to the study of temperate-zone sites with an eye to isolating both when and where unambiguous evidence of hunting appears and, further, how we might use archaeological traces to enlighten us concerning the interesting possibility of semi-independent feeding ranges among hominids as well as the interesting question of recognizing the presence of a division of labor.

WHEN AND WHERE DID HUNTING BECOME A MAJOR HOMINID STRATEGY?

At the southern tip of Africa is a geographically small temperate environment. In 1981 I had the opportunity to study the fauna from the South African site of Klasies River Mouth, which spans the period from around 125,000 until about 35,000 years ago and documents the shift to the presence of fully modern forms of man. Based on my European experience I had fully expected the occupants of this site to have been regular hunters. Much to my surprise, however, my interpretation of the data indicated that scavenging of medium- to large-body-sized animals was still a regular and significant subsistence strategy. Also, while hunting of small mammals was practiced, there was a trend toward increases in hunting through the sequence at Klasies that was roughly coincident with the anatomical shift to more modern types of humans. It is true that the scavenging appears more regular than thus far indicated for the early hominids at Olduvai Gorge, and that fire and other technical aids to processing food and almost certainly protecting sleeping areas are indicated; nevertheless, the overall pattern of life appeared remarkably similar to the strategies of the hominids of the Plio-Pleistocene boundary, particularly for the earlier phases of the sequence. While there were other provocative results of this study, certainly the most surprising was the conclusion that not only was early man not a "mighty hunter" but very late hominids on the very threshold of the appearance of our own species were also *not technically aided hunters and gatherers* in the sense that archaeologists have generally assumed for the earliest hominids or have considered likely for mid-Pleistocene *Homo erectus.*

A LOOK AT THE NORTHERN TEMPERATE ZONE

Since the small and relatively recently settled temperate zone on the southern tip of Africa may have a very different history than the large and anciently colonized temperate areas of Europe and Asia, it was clear that the next research step was to investigate the early evidence for hominid radiation into Europe and Asia. During the spring and summer of 1984 I had the opportunity to conduct such investigations. These studies are as yet incomplete in that all the planned analysis has not yet been performed. Nevertheless, I have gained some interesting impressions of the data at this stage of their preparation for publication.

I have studied the fauna from the lower gravels and the lower loam, as excavated by John Waechter, from the famous site of Swanscombe–Barnfield pit (see Wymer 1968:322–361; Roe 1981:67–72). These materials are associated with a Clactonian tool industry and are generally assigned to the Hoxnian interglacial (Mindel–Riss in the old Alpine sequence), which is estimated to have occurred between 350,000 and 400,000 years ago. I have also studied the fauna, excavated by John Wymer, that was found in association with a hand axe industry (Lower Industry) from the famous site of Hoxne. This is thought to be more recent than the Swanscombe material and could be as recent as 200,000–240,000 years old (see Wymer 1983:187).

Several preliminary observations are of interest with regard to these faunas. At Swanscombe only six bones exhibited tool-inflicted marks.[11] Three of these were related to disarticulation: a mandible, an atlas vertebra, and a distal tibia. The other three marked pieces bore clear evidence of meat removal. These were on a proximal tibia, the shaft of a distal tibia, and the shaft of a distal humerus. Importantly, no metapodial bones bore tool-inflicted marks and there were no scraping or chop marks on any of the bones from Swanscombe. This suggests that the hominids were interested in meat and that their involvement as agents responsible for the accumulation of much of the fauna at Swanscombe was minimal. The latter inference is born out by high frequencies of shed antler and a pattern of anatomical part frequencies strongly suggestive of a normal "background" fauna, which might be expected to have accumulated naturally on an exposed waterside location where some hydrological sorting had also occurred. There was very little evidence of marrow bone breakage and there was also minimal evidence pointing to the action of other carnivore–predators. Very few animal-gnawed bones were present.

At Hoxne, as at Swanscombe, there were only a few bones with tool-inflicted marks. One astragalus of fallow deer had been cut by stone tools during disarticulation, and all other cut marks were on horse bones. Nine horse bones bore tool-inflicted marks, of which three are believed to be related to disarticulation while six are thought to have been inflicted during meat removal. Two of the latter were ribs, one was a metacarpal, and the remainder were on long-bone splinters. In marked contrast to the fauna at Swanscombe there was considerable evidence of systematic marrow-bone breakage, particularly of horse bones. In terms of anatomical part frequencies the horses were represented by a head- and lower-limb-dominated frequency graph, as were the clearly scavenged large-mammal remains from Klasies River Mouth. On the other hand, the fallow deer were represented by primarily meat-yielding bones while red deer exhibited a graph with properties of both horses and fallow deer. As was true at Swanscombe, animal gnawing, while present, was relatively uncommon. For all intents and purposes the Hoxne fauna has the characteristics of a transported and accumulated assemblage scavenged from medium to large mammals, in which heads and marrow-yielding bone were the parts most commonly transported for processing. In addition there is a meat-biased assemblage evidenced by the remains of fallow deer, but these creatures are infrequent at the site. The latter pattern is very similar to that noted at Klasies River Mouth for the time period around 125,000 years ago; however, the degree that these smaller animals were hunted cannot be established from these data.

While preliminary, it is my impression that the Swanscombe fauna represents hominid scavenging at the source of carcasses. There appears to be a meat bias in the treatment of bones and there is no evidence for systematic marrow-bone processing. The assemblage does not appear to be transported or aggregated. In marked contrast is the fauna from Hoxne, where transport and aggregation of heads and marrow-yielding bones of both horse and red deer is indicated. Systematic marrow-bone processing is the most robust evidence for hominid modification of the bones. There is a provocative suggestion that the small fallow deer may have been rarely killed for meat. This site has much in common with the much earlier Olduvai sites; however, the situation is clarified by the general absence of evidence indicative of carnivore involvement in the accumulation of the deposits. Thus, by the much later era, when hominids made their first appearance in the British Isles, the way of life indicated by the medium to large mammal remains does not appear to be greatly different from that of their much earlier ancestors at Olduvai Gorge!

In further search of evidence for changes in subsistence practices I studied the deep, stratified sequence of deposits from the French site of Abri Vaufrey (Rigaud 1982). This site is particularly interesting in that it is a cave, and its deposits span the period from the Mindel/Riss interglacial (Hoxne) through the first interstadial of the Würm (300,000 to about 60,000 years ago). Thus far I have analyzed the remains from layer VIII (235,000 years ago, perhaps roughly contemporary with Hoxne) and am familiar with the tabulation and recording of the more recent layers. Layer VIII yielded a "flake" industry that is "typical Mousterian" in the Bordean sense of later Würm Mousterian assemblages. The fauna that is referable to hominid transport to the cave was primarily red deer, horse, and rare occurrences of aurochs. Surprisingly, *there were no tool-inflicted marks on these bones resulting either from dismemberment or removal of meat.* Equally surprising was the fact that the anatomical parts commonly represented were upper-limb bones or the meat-yielding bones from these animals. These bones had been gnawed by nonhominid predator–scavengers in exactly the same pattern as is shown by controlled data from predator-exploited kill and death sites, indicating that the hominids had transported meat-yielding bones from previously ravaged carcasses, not from hunted animals. In the Vaufrey level VIII assemblage there were few lower-limb bones, and *even these were rarely exploited for bone marrow.* There was little evidence for the regular use of fire in this level and no evidence for cooking.

In marked contrast was the fauna of level VII, believed to date around 200,000 years ago. In this assemblage tool-inflicted marks from both dismemberment and filleting meat were relatively common, as were numerous long-bone splinters exhibiting longitudinal scrape marks. Long-bone splinters with numerous pitted scars, known in the European literature as "compressors," were also present. There was clear evidence for regular processing of long bones for marrow. The regular use of fire was clearly indicated, and there was a biased pattern of burning on bones. In terms of anatomical part frequencies, preliminary tabulations suggest a head- and lower-leg-dominated assemblage. Except for the greater frequency of tool-inflicted marks and the evidence for the regular use of fire, this assemblage resembles that from Hoxne. On the other hand, the associated tool assemblage, like level VIII, is classifiable as typical Mousterian! As in the case of level VIII there is a regular pattern of animal-tooth markings that is indistinguishable from the known pattern remaining on ravaged carcasses after nonhominid predator–scavengers have finished feeding. This is taken as evidence that, as in the case of level VIII, the majority of the transported fauna was scavenged from previously ravaged carcasses. This view is further supported, in the case of level VII, by tool-inflicted marks that overprint animal-tooth marks.

Very little analysis has been thus far conducted on materials from the upper levels of Abri Vaufrey; nevertheless, it can be reported that the levels deposited during the Würm I phase of the French sequence exhibit a very different treatment of fauna. The pattern is very similar to that with which I have become familiar from having studied the remains excavated by F. Bordes from the important site of Combe Grenal. Combe Grenal spans the first two phases of the Würm, dating between 85,000 and 45,000 years ago; like the previously discussed Klasies River Mouth site in South Africa, it documents the period just prior to the appearance of our species. At Combe Grenal the large animals, such as aurochs and horses, tend to be represented by essentially meat-yielding upper-limb bones (see Binford 1981a:99) but unlike at Vaufrey level VIII some of the marrow-yielding bones occur in reduced numbers, suggestive of "riding" or transport of more complete limbs back to the site. Additionally, marrow-bone cracking was seemingly done as "matter of course" at Combe Grenal. That is, most marrow-yielding bones that were introduced showed evidence of cracking. What is most variable at Combe Grenal is the incidence of their introduction. For moderate-sized animals, particularly red deer and reindeer, there is good evidence that a much more representative anatomical inventory was introduced into the site. Meat-yielding bones are common, and there is considerable variability among the levels in the degree to which lower limbs were introduced. The lower-limb bones that were introduced were regularly exploited for marrow; sometimes even the phalanges of reindeer were broken. Particularly striking is the general absence of nonhominid gnawing of the bones from moderate-sized animals. This contrasts markedly with Klasies River Mouth and all the earlier sites discussed here. This is taken as good evidence that the majority of the moderate-body-sized animals at Combe Grenal *were hunted for meat.* This pattern is particularly striking for the faunas of Würm II levels at the site.

Particularly interesting is the distribution of tool-inflicted marks on the Combe Grenal bones. First, the number of such marks is relatively rare compared to the frequencies reported at Olduvai Gorge (see Binford 1981a:99; cf. Bunn 1983a:27). In addition, most of the marks are clearly related to dismemberment of carcasses and removal of muscle tissue. As has been pointed out before, many of the tool-inflicted marks on the much earlier faunas are biased in favor of lower-limb bones and along the shafts of nonmeaty bones. This was also true of many of the marks from the Vaufrey level VII bones. These summary statements should not be read to imply that there is little variability at Combe Grenal; there most certainly is. Nevertheless, the overall picture contrasts markedly with the earlier European sites thus far known.

The European sites from the Rissian age (100,000–300,000 years ago) exhibit a very different pattern than that noted above. It is my impression that hunting seems most likely indicated for only small animals and rodents—particularly rabbits, which are common in such early European cave sites as Lazaret (Jullien and Pillard 1969) and the earlier Rissian levels of Combe Grenal (personal observation). Scavenging appears to have been the major method of meat procurement, and it should be emphasized that there is a bias in favor of scavenging meat as opposed to marginal, marrow-yielding parts, which dominate the exploitation pattern for moderate to large animals at Klasies River Mouth. On the other hand, the exploitation of marginal parts is certainly carried out in Europe, as is evidenced at Vaufrey level VII and Hoxne. Particularly interesting are the observations at Swanscombe (Mindel/Riss interglacial) and Vaufrey level VIII (early Riss). As noted, there are very few tool-inflicted marks at Swanscombe, which is believed to be a "field" location roughly at the source of scavenged carcasses. At Vaufrey, where there is definitely a bias in favor of meat-yielding parts transported to the location, there were *no tool-inflicted marks* on the bones. It is my guess that this situation reflects the fact that meat was frequently eaten directly from the carcass and rarely transported. This view is consistent with the situation at Swanscombe.

Tool use appears to be primarily related to processing of parts for rendering foods accessible. This suggestion is consistent with the pattern noted at Klasies River Mouth, where many of the lower limbs appear to have been at least partially desiccated before they were processed for marrow removal. When this was the case there appears to be much more tool-assisted processing related to the removal of dried skin and tendon prior to marrow removal than there is tool-assisted processing of fresh meat. If this suggestion is sustained by future research, then the high incidence of tool-inflicted marks reported from the Olduvai sites (Bunn 1983a) may well be telling us that scavenging there was primarily of at least partially desiccated carcasses and consequently that meat would not have been a significant component of the scavenged diet.

I think it can be safely inferred that by Würm II times in south-central France hominids were regularly hunting moderate-body-sized animals. In addition, they were scavenging large-sized animals, such as aurochs and horses. Unlike the situation in southern Africa at roughly the same time, however, *scavenging was systematically for meat, not for marginal parts (such as marrow bones), although head parts appear to continue to be a major target of scavengers*. It is also my impression that, as hunting of moderate-body-sized animals increased in the Würm, less use was made of such small animals as rabbits, which are common in some earlier European cave sites.

During the Riss glacial episode and earlier the picture is quite different. There is no convincing evidence in the studied cases for regular hunting of anything except perhaps very small mammals and rodents. Scavenging appears to have been the primary method of obtaining meat from moderate- to large-body-sized animals. There appears to be a clear contrastive pattern between locations where essentially non-meat-yielding marrow bones were processed and sites to which meat-yielding bones were transported. There is also the hint that when meat was available, either at carcasses or as transported body parts, consumption was direct and largely not tool-assisted except perhaps in disarticulation tasks.

CONCLUSIONS

The picture that emerges from these studies is very different from what is generally considered to be the history of hominid subsistence evolution. At the dawn of tool use the early hominids appear to have been scavenging carcasses largely for marginal foods and using tools to gain access to these tiny morsels, mainly bone marrow. That this can be taken as evidence for a "scavenging" mode of adaptation is highly unlikely, since the tactics indicated must have contributed only slightly to the modal subsistence security of these creatures.

Jumping far ahead in time to the period of the first appearance of hominids in the British Isles we see a very similar pattern but with perhaps a slightly different focus—

scavenging appears to be much more meat oriented. This is also in a context that demonstrates much less nonhominid predator–scavenger involvement in the formation history of the sites and may point to regular consumption of meat largely unassisted by tools. At this time there is little that can be reliably inferred regarding "home bases" or sharing of food.

By the early phases of the Riss glacial sequence we note some interesting variety in the faunal assemblages associated with tools. There appears to be at least a dichotomous pattern of sites where marginal parts were transported for marrow-bone processing versus sites where meat-yielding bones were transported for meat consumption; however, there is little evidence that in the latter situation consumption was strongly tool assisted. Surprisingly, the tool assemblages associated with these two types of faunal assemblages are "typologically" the same, differing only in the amounts of exotic raw materials used in tool manufacture. Exotic raw materials were more frequent in the assemblage from the "meat"-dominated site than in the assemblage from the marrow-bone-processing site.

During the Würm some major changes occur. Hunting for medium-sized animals seems to be indicated. A more integrated exploitation of animal products seems to have been practiced, and the transport of parts regularly yielding more food than a single person might reasonably consume is present. In the geographically distant southern tip of Africa an analogous trend seems to be indicated in which hunting of small animals increases throughout the sequence and scavenging of marginal anatomical parts begins to fall off as a regular strategy.

Given differences in geography and environment the patterns from the northern temperate zone appear remarkably similar to the pattern seen in South Africa. *At present the inevitable conclusion seems to be that regular, moderate- to large-mammal hunting appears simultaneously with the foreshadowing changes occurring just prior to the appearance of fully modern man.* According to the principle laid down by Gilbert and Sullivan, "You can't be your own grandpa." *Systematic hunting of moderate to large animals appears to be a part of our modern condition, not its cause.*

IMPLICATIONS

It is perhaps even presumptuous to open up this topic since these are revolutionary and even "shocking" conclusions. I am convinced that the taphonomic study of faunal remains must be integrated with our more traditional studies of tool assemblages and site locational data. We have long recognized problems of tool assemblage variability, such as the alternation of developed Oldowan with Acheulean tools at Gadeb (Williams et al. 1979) or the alternation of flake- versus biface-dominated industries at Olorgesailie (Isaac 1977a) and the arguments over the Acheulean and Clactonian of Europe (Collins 1969; Ohel 1979). We still do not know what these fascinating patterns indicate in terms of past behavior. It is true that the old idea that they represent "cultural traditions" is still common in the literature and most current textbooks present the known patterns of variability in this paradigm. Regardless of the conservative adherence to the "cultural tradition" point of view, the fact remains that we do not know what such variability indicates in terms of hominid life ways. The arguments being currently set forth regarding the early hominids and the conclusions presented here about later hominid history clearly point to the fact that we are dealing with creatures very different from ourselves. The imposition of the assumption of culture on the pre-modern ancestors of man is no more justified than the imposition of a Bushman-like way of life on the early hominids.

The first important step in research growth is the recognition of ignorance, the acknowledgment that we do not know something. It is time to abandon our assumptive "knowledge" regarding hominid behavior and begin the hard-headed task of reducing our ignorance and hence contributing to our greater understanding of man's ancestors. This will not come about by fanciful "reconstructions" of the past or arguments about the plausibility of a "scavenging" adaptation. It will come about by the development of sound methods for reliable inference regarding the characteristics of the past implicated in such speculations. It may not be a bad place to start by considering the possibility that much of the interassemblage tool variability could have arisen in the context of independent feeding strategies between males and females in particular ecological settings during the Pleistocene. We may be seeing more female versus male "culture" tempered by situational conditions rather than ethnic "culture," as has been commonly assumed by archaeologists.

ACKNOWLEDGMENTS

I thank Glynn Isaac and two unidentified readers for their helpful criticism of the original draft of this paper.

NOTES

1. Shipman has consistently speculated that they were after skin and tendons (see Shipman 1984b:22).
2. One could argue that in fact the materials referrable to *Homo erectus* do not bear on the arguments regarding the behavior of early hominids. This is not likely given the materials I will discuss later, which represent hominids even more recent than *Homo erectus*.
3. My strategy was one in which recognized ambiguity was eliminated from the assemblages being considered. Shipman (et al. 1981) followed no such strategy.
4. This same argument would apply to small rodents and other animals that might have also been part of the early hominids' diet.
5. Shipman et al. (1982) answered these criticisms by referring to her results of a chi-square test. Such a technique is inappropriate when a curvilinear relationship is known to exist, as it does between her data on known baboon carcasses unmodified by humans. Nevertheless, Shipman continues to maintain her interpretations (see Shipman 1983:43).
6. Shipman (1983:37) is vague on the utility of these "signatures." She nevertheless uses them as if no ambiguity exists (see Shipman 1983:40).
7. This is one of the points I made in the *Bones* book.

8. Potts (1982) considered the evidence for water sorting in his dissertation, and after demonstrating much ambiguity on this issue he nevertheless concludes that water sorting played no significant role in conditioning the composition of the Olduvai fauna. Based on the data that he presents, this judgment is unjustified.

9. This argument is presented as fact in recent textbooks; see Gowlett 1984.

10. I do not imply seasonal "stability" in equatorial settings, only that temperature-related seasonality increases temporal and spatial variability in food availability by a large measure.

11. I am well aware of the controversy (Shipman 1983 vs Bunn 1983a) regarding the recognition criteria for cut marks. I am very skeptical of Shipman's claims for lack of ambiguity in identifications when her methods are used. I have seen many bones from geologic contexts in North America where human presence is unequivocally *absent* yet marks having all the characteristics she describes are nonetheless present! Similarly, many marks reported by Bunn as cut marks are in my opinion matched in control collections where young carnivores gnawed bones. At present I trust my experience in cut-mark recognition, which is based on a great deal of experience and employs a configurational approach (see Binford 1984a) and recognized ambiguous cases.

Chapter 23

Fact and Fiction about the Zinjanthropus Floor: Data, Arguments, and Interpretations

Bunn and Kroll's (1986a:431–452) analysis of the fauna from the Zinjanthropus floor in Olduvai Gorge makes three major points. The first of these is that because Bunn's (1982b) bone counts do not correspond to the values I used in my analysis of the Oldowan faunas (Binford 1981a) my arguments should be dismissed. In their Table 2, they compare my values with the MNE and MAU values based on their observations. Because Leakey (1971:276) did not distinguish between mandibular and maxillary teeth, I calculated MNE values for the total suite of teeth present in an animal's head and used the result as an indicator of variation among sites in the frequency of heads. They report the frequencies of mandibular versus maxillary teeth and conclude that many mandibles and few maxilla are represented. Using MNE values for mandibular teeth, they produce an MAU value of 38.0, while I reported one of 13.07 using total teeth as an indicator of number of heads present. There is no implication of error in this demonstration; Bunn and I counted different things and, not surprisingly, got different results.

Bunn and Kroll go on, however, to a critical discussion of differences between our analyses in *percentage MAU values*. For example, "metacarpals and metatarsals . . . are overrepresented . . . , and his [Binford's] high rib and vertebrae patterns are strikingly reversed by the facts" (1986a:435). Both analyses use the number of teeth to determine the maximum MAU; that the value I used (13.07) is lower than that used by Bunn and Kroll (38.0) ensures that all other skeletal parts will have higher relative values in my list than in theirs. Put another way, the values in the two lists may be identical (e.g., 13 proximal metatarsals in each), but if they are standardized using different figures (in this case, 13.07 for heads versus 38.0 for mandibles), the percentage values for proximal metatarsals will be 69% in my list and 23% in theirs. Bunn and Kroll's comparisons of percentage MAU values have to do not with the facts of the Zinjanthropus bone assemblage but with the basis for displaying them. The only meaningful comparison that can be made with the figures presented in their Table 2 concerns the MAU values, the values that refer to what was counted.

An inspection of those values indicates that my estimates (based on Mary Leakey's data) are in general slightly higher than theirs. This is hard to understand, since Leakey was reporting on 1,023 bones and Bunn and Kroll presumably on 3,500 (p. 433). The

Originally published in *Current Anthropology* 29:123–135, © 1988.

most obvious difference between my figures and theirs occurs in the estimates for ribs, between my 8.97 and their 1.19. What is the source of this discrepancy?

Investigating the derivation of Bunn and Kroll's values. I first turned to their Table 4. The values listed under "total number of pieces" here could refer to MAU values, but this seems unlikely, since percentages of cut marks are only reasonably expressed relative to MNE (Binford 1984c) or NISP (Grayson 1984) values. The values for head parts (e.g., mandible = 180) seem to indicate that these are NISP values, since there is no way of using them to obtain an MAU value of 38.0. In addition, from the values for their category "rib proximal end plus shaft" we obtain a count of 76, which when divided by 26 (the number of proximal ribs in an animal) produces an MAU estimate of 2.92. Because their Table 2 gives an MAU value of 1.19 for ribs, we must conclude that they did not use the data summarized in Table 4 as the basis for Table 2.

Seeking further enlightenment, I consulted Bunn's (1982b) dissertation and found that the only way of obtaining the count of 31 (26 × 1.19) proximal ribs implied by Table 2 is to include only those from animals in the discrete Size-Groups 1–3, excluding those from animals in the combined Size-Groups 3 and 4. Thus the figures for ribs are derived from a selected group of animals; Bunn (1982b:285) lists 89 proximal ribs for the total fauna exclusive of carnivores, while Bunn and Kroll report only 31. Again, for vertebrae, Bunn and Kroll list an MNE of 35 in Table 2, and the bones from animals of Size-Groups 1–3 as listed in Bunn's dissertation yield a value of 36, in striking contrast to the 238 vertebrae listed for the total fauna (1982b:285). We must conclude that Table 2 is constructed not from counts of the fauna from the Zinjanthropus floor but from a selected segment of that fauna, consisting only of bovid Size-Groups 1–3.[1]

Bunn and Kroll's data are primarily biased in the same way that the treatment of faunas from old excavations used to be biased—against skeletal parts that cannot be assigned to species, which tend to be vertebrae, ribs, cranial fragments, and long-bone splinters. At the same time, they argue that ribs and vertebrae are "overrepresented" in tabulations not biased in this fashion. The value of Leakey's listing of skeletal parts rests precisely in her reporting of data on parts that are difficult to identify but clearly present on the Olduvai sites and certainly meaningful. Bunn and Kroll's editorial decision is consistent with their position on the meaning of the Zinjanthropus fauna, but it inaccurately describes that fauna.

Their second major point is that MAU estimates should be based not on articular ends but on long-bone shaft splinters. This suggestion seems to be prompted by the observation that "metapodial . . . epiphyses are relatively more abundant than Binford's numbers indicate. Metapodials are the pivotal skeletal element in Binford's arguments that hominids had access mainly to nonmeaty, low-utility bones, and the seemingly high overall representation of metapodial epiphyses could be taken as corroboration of his original interpretations." Bunn has produced MNE values for complete long bones by "detailed specimen-by-specimen comparisons among all specimens in each limb and animal size category" with attention to "overlap of homologous parts, to conjoining, to differences in size and morphology, and to other attributes that could . . . rule out the possibility that two specimens originally formed parts of the same complete bone" (1986a:435). Articular ends were the original focus of MAU estimation because MNI values calculated from partial or fragmented faunal remains may be distorted. For example, the presence of a distal tibia does not necessarily indicate the former presence of a proximal tibia, since butchering may cause the latter to be separated from the distal end and transported with parts of the femur. Units that can be expected to have had independent histories must be described independently, especially when carnivore agents are suspected. If Bunn and Kroll had wished to invest in identifying long-bone shaft units, they should have done so in terms of proximal and distal segments (central segments could have been joined to either end and therefore cannot be used for postulating the existence of an additional complete bone in the absence of conjoining elements, except under rare conditions, e.g., age differences), which would then have had to be compared with the articular ends to determine whether the reconstructed shaft segments could have come from the same bones. It is not clear whether they did this, although comparison with articular ends was evidently made.

Table 23.1 compares Bunn and Kroll's MNE estimates using long-bone shaft fragments with my MNE values. There is a dramatic difference between our estimates for femur and tibia and a somewhat smaller one between our estimates for radius-ulna. We may ask whether these differences are simply a function of variables not considered by Bunn and Kroll when deciding which combination of features on diaphysis fragments constituted unambiguous evidence for the presence of a complete bone. Given the variation in length, smoothness, and other morphological traits exhibited by the types of bones listed in Table 23.1, one could reasonably expect the number of shaft splinters generated when a given bone is broken and the number of bones present as estimated from articular elements to differ for each type of bone. These values could be estimated quite accurately for each type of bone if the number of articular elements present had not been differentially reduced by scavenging animals after humans had broken the bones, as Bunn and Kroll (1986a:435) suggest. Put another way, if Bunn and Kroll's values for tibia and femur were correct, we would expect these types of bone to relate very differently to the total number of shaft splinters than do the other bones in the list.

Table 23.1
Relationships between Various Expressions of Zinjanthropus Floor Data and Control Data on Bone Breakage

Skeletal part	No. of articular ends[a]	No. of shaft fragments[b]	MNE (Binford)	MNE (Binford's MNI method)	MNE (Bunn and Kroll)	Expected no. of shaft fragments[c]
Humerus	24	58	12.0	19	20	420
Radius-ulna	19	57	9.5	14	22	228
Metacarpal	23	32	11.5	15	16	184
Femur	12	58	6.0	6	22	198
Tibia	21	128	10.5	11	31	420
Metatarsal	25	28	12.5	15	16	162

[a] Bunn and Kroll 1986a: Table 2.
[b] Bunn and Kroll 1986a: Table 4.
[c] Based on Binford's (1978a:155) table of breakage for MNE values in column 3.

Table 23.1 also presents expected values for shaft fragments calculated from the data obtained during experimental breakage of limb bones. The number of splinters was originally summarized (Binford 1978a:155) in terms of counts per articular end. Since Bunn and Kroll report whole-bone MNE values, the expected values were calculated by doubling the summary counts listed in my original table and then multiplying these figures by my MNE values. While splinters longer than 1.5 cm are few for the bones listed in Table 23.1 (Binford 1978a:155), subsequent experiments have shown that when bones are broken to yield more large splinters [which is normally accomplished by breaking the bones before the periosteum has been removed), there is a corresponding reduction in the number of small chips and impact chunks produced. Thus, the total number of fragments reported by Binford (1978a:Table 4.6) for each type of bone is a good predictor for the total number of large splinters produced regardless of the method used to crack the bones and hence of the size of the splinters characteristically produced.

Figure 23.1 displays the relationship between the numbers of articular ends reported (column 1) and the numbers of splinters expected on the basis of my marrow-cracking experiments on the homologous caribou bones (column 6). One distribution links the metapodials with the radius-ulna and the femur and is slightly negative because the longer the bone the more splinters per articular end are apt to be produced. The other is defined by the humerus and tibia, which occur in the expected inverse relationship to one another but yield more splinters per articular end than do the bones of the other suite, presumably because of differences in their gross morphology. Figure 23.2 displays the relationship between the numbers of articular ends and the numbers of shaft splinters observed in the same segment of the Zinjanthropus-floor fauna (columns 1 and 2). The only difference from figure 1 is the slopes of the lines; the negative relationship for the metapodials, radius-ulna, and femur is more linear, and the line for the humerus and tibia is strongly contrastive. To evaluate the possibility that the humerus is somewhat underrepresented by shaft splinters in the Zinjanthropus data, the relationship between observed and expected numbers of bone splinters was plotted (Figure 23.3) using only the observed articular ends reported by Bunn and Kroll to calculate the expected numbers. The humerus proved to be the only exception to a near-perfect linear relationship between the observed and expected numbers. When a straight line is fitted to all the values except the humerus, the relationship is described by the formula $y = -29.406 + 0.37743x$, where y is the count of bone splinters observed and x is the count of bone splinters expected on the basis of my previous experiments. The correlation coefficient is a remarkable 0.98. When the above equation is used to estimate the number of humeral splinters that should have been observed, we find that instead of 58 there should have been 129. This means that 54% of the articular ends present are not represented by shaft splinters on the Zinjanthropus floor. Since the proximal humerus is easily destroyed by taphonomic agents (particularly by carnivores), it is not uncommon for substantial portions of the humeral shaft to remain attached to the distal end on carnivore-gnawed bones (see, for example, the upper two bones in Binford 1981a: 172, Fig. 4.56). Remarkably, 58% of all distal humeri observed at wolf kills (Binford

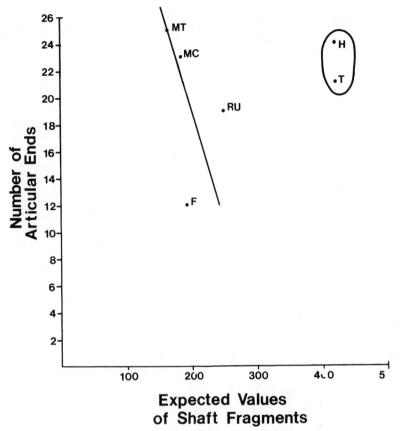

Figure 23.1. Relationship between number of articular ends observed and number of shaft splinters expected on the basis of experimental evidence. MC, metacarpal; MT, metatarsal; RU, radius-ulna; F, femur; H, humerus; T, tibia.

1981a:194) were essentially composed of the complete shaft minus the proximal articular end, and 54% of the articular ends on the Zinjanthropus floor appear to be unrepresented by shaft splinters. This similarity in the data suggests that the reported distal humeri from the Zinjanthropus floor were essentially distal ends with considerable amounts of attached shaft that had not been reduced to splinters after they were introduced to the site.

We must therefore conclude that the numbers of shaft splinters recorded by Bunn and Kroll are an accurate reflection of the numbers of articular ends recorded at the site with the exception of the humerus, which is 54% underrepresented. There is no support whatsoever for their position that originally many more tibias and femurs were present than is indicated by articular ends. The objection might be raised that the experimental data on bone breakage were derived from the study of caribou, which is certainly not represented on the Zinjanthropus floor. The similarity between the two

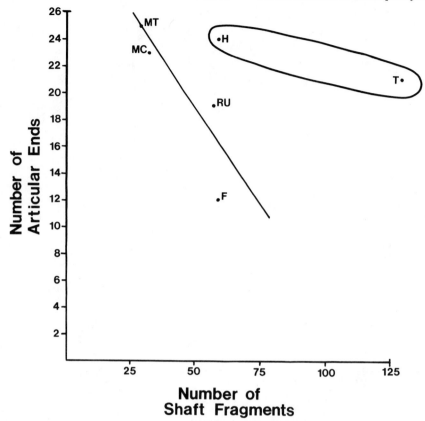

Figure 23.2.   Relationship between number of articular ends observed and number of shaft splinters recorded on the Zinjanthropus floor, MC, metacarpal; MT, metatarsal; RU, radius-ulna; H, humerus; F, femur; T, tibia.

graphs (Figures 23.1 and 23.2) would be hard to explain, however, if the data on caribou were not relevant, and these data are a good predictor of the breakage data from other species in this case.

How are we to understand Bunn and Kroll's large estimates for the inferred number of tibias, femurs, and radio-cubiti originally present? The relationships between articular ends and shaft splinters observed on the Zinjanthropus floor may in fact accurately reflect the general relationship between broken bones and splinters derived from those bones for the skeletal parts whose numbers remained relatively unchanged. Bunn and Kroll argue for this point as follows: "the total MNE values for the humerus, metacarpal, and metatarsal are almost identical . . . , because those values are based on epiphyses of relatively low nutritional value that would not have been particularly susceptible to selective removal by scavenging carnivores" (1986a:436). Using these skeletal parts, we can calculate the expected numbers of original bones from the numbers of bone splinters observed on the Zinjanthropus floor for the other skeletal parts whose numbers were drastically changed by Bunn and Kroll. (There

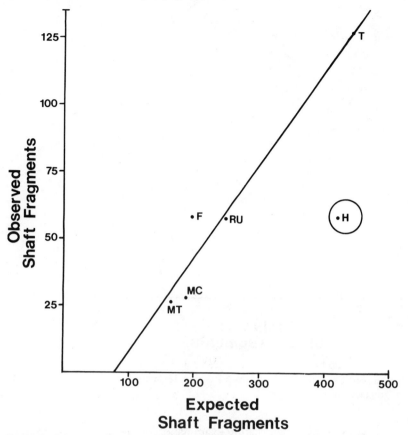

Figure 23.3. Relationship between number of shaft splinters observed and number of shaft splinters expected on the basis of experimental evidence. MC, metacarpal; MT, metatarsal; RU, radius-ulna; F, femur; H, humerus; T, tibia.

would be no advantage in increasing the numbers of these bones on the site, since Bunn and Kroll's belief in meat eating would not be served by such an increase.) Taking the metacarpal, metatarsal, and humerus MNE values from Table 23.1, column 4, we can investigate the relationship between the numbers of inferred bones (using MNI techniques to obtain MNE values) and the numbers of shaft splinters observed (Figure 23.4). If one calculates a regression line for this relationship, the following equation is obtained: $y = 10.799 + 0.140704x$, where y is the MNE for whole bones and x is the number of shaft splinters reported. We may now solve this equation using the observed numbers of bone splinters for each bone (Table 23.1, column 2) and obtain the expected number of complete bones under the assumption that MNI-based calculations for the metatarsal, metacarpal, and humerus define the "real" relationship between articular ends and bone splinters for all leg bones. The results are given in Table 23.2.

The similarity between the two lists is striking. We are told by Bunn and Kroll that

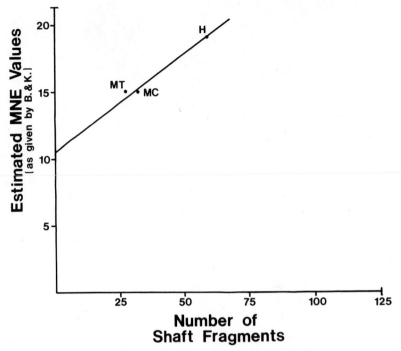

Figure 23.4. Relationship between MNE values estimated by Bunn and Kroll and number of shaft splinters observed for skeletal parts whose frequencies were not changed by them. MC, metacarpal; MT, metatarsal; H, humerus.

their estimates are the result of painstaking examination of the actual bone splinters, taking great care to conjoin pieces and to evaluate whether splinters could have come from the same bone using such criteria as diaphysis wall thickness. Yet these estimates are nearly identical to mine, which are based on false assumptions about the relationships between numbers of bones and the numbers of bone splinters produced

Table 23.2
MNE Values Obtained by Two Methods of Estimation

Skeletal part	By regression equation ($r = 0.99$)	By Bunn and Kroll's method
Humerus	18.9 = 19	20
Radio-cubitus	18.8 = 19	22
Metacarpal	15.3 = 15	16
Femur	18.9 = 19	22
Tibia	28.8 = 29	31
Metatarsal	14.7 = 15	16

when those bones were broken. Ironically, the only skeletal part that seems to vary independently of the numbers of bone splinters present—the humerus—is a major control element. I must conclude that Bunn and Kroll's estimates are conditioned by the same variable that guided my model—the number of bone splinters. One could speculate that the numbers of judgments of independence made by Bunn was a simple linear function of the number of bone splinters with which he worked. Referring to my earlier work (Binford 1978a:155), we note that for every large bone splinter produced during marrow cracking many small chips and very small splinters are also produced. If one is working only with rather large splinters, the probability of being able to refit them is quite low, since the intervening small chips and splinters are missing. Since the numbers of large splinters and small chips vary in a regular way with the different limb bones, one's inability to match pieces (hence one's judgment that the pieces had independent origins) would be expected to increase as a simple function of the number of pieces one had available for comparative study from each skeletal part.

Whatever the explanation for the astonishing near-identity between the results of my methods of estimation and Bunn and Kroll's procedure, I am forced to conclude that the estimates for limb bone MNEs given by them are incorrect and misleading. I have already shown that all bone splinters can be accounted for by the bones that according to Bunn and Kroll were originally broken on the Zinjanthropus site. They postulate that the "inferred" bones are missing because they were removed by hyenas. If that had been the case, there should have been a striking overabundance of shaft splinters from the tibia, femur, and radio-cubitus relative to the numbers of articular ends remaining. Bunn and Kroll's methods for estimating the numbers of bones originally present are not more accurate than mine, and their inflated values for tibias and femurs appear to be a function of their perceptions and/or assumptions about the relationships between bones and splinters rather than of the number of bones originally present. On the basis of what can be demonstrated with the numbers before us, the only thing that can be said is that the humerus is underrepresented by shaft splinters on the Zinjanthropus floor.

Bunn and Kroll's third major point concerns the significance of cut marks—whether their placement and frequency are clues to the original state of the skeletal parts that were impacted by tool-using hominids. They state that the cut marks were inflicted during dismemberment and filleting of meaty animal limbs. The principle that underlies this interpretation (1986a:449–450) seems to be that

> inflicting deep slicing cuts into the surfaces of limb shafts does not further the efficient removal of meat from the bones, and it dulls the cutting edge of the knife. The slight miscalculations regarding the relative positions of meat and bone that produce such cuts are most likely to occur when it is difficult or impossible to see where the bone is, as when complete, meaty limb bones are being defleshed.

There is more concealing tissue on the upper rear limbs than on the upper front limbs of most animals, and there is a clear contrast between the upper and lower limbs of any animal in this regard. I do not know how Bunn and Kroll distinguish meaty upper limbs from nonmeaty lower limbs, but I consider the lower rear limb to begin at the neck of the distal tibia and the lower front limb at the neck of the distal radio-cubitus. These criteria are used in the summary of Bunn and Kroll's Table 4 cut-mark frequencies presented in my Table 23.3. According to Bunn and Kroll's principle, we would expect higher frequencies of tool-inflicted marks on large-animal parts than on small-animal parts and on upper rear limb parts than on upper front limb parts and a lower frequency of marks on lower limb parts than on upper limb parts regardless of body size. Only in the relationship between upper and lower limbs for small animals are the expectations met. In the light of their reasoning regarding cut marks ("the partial defleshing of meaty limbs prior to hominid access to carcasses would have rendered the surface of the limb bones more readily visible and thus reduced the number of cut marks"; 1986a:450), their data strongly support the view that the so-called meatiest bones were scavenged.

One might argue that Bunn and Kroll may still be right about the significance of cut marks because their interpretive principle is wrong. In fact, I do consider it wrong; my experience suggests that the number of cut marks, exclusive of dismemberment marks, is a function of differential investment in meat or tissue removal. When a butcher who is filleting meat seeks to get all the adhering tissue off the bones, there will be many cut marks; if little effort is made to clean the bones, relatively few cut marks result. In addition, the numbers of cut marks and their frequencies on different bones may reflect very different processing operations. Skinning, for instance, will result in unambiguous cut-marked limb bones only in the area of the phalanges and the necks of metapodials, regardless of how much care is invested in the processing. Rational discussion of cut marks requires that we be able to recognize marks inflicted during different operations. For this reason I will summarize my observations on the cut marks inflicted during filleting operations and then discuss the effect on bones of subsequent marrow removal and of dismemberment prior to (one pattern) versus

Table 23.3
Frequency of Cut-marked Bones
on the Zinjanthropus Floor

Skeletal part	Percentage of elements bearing cut-marks[a]	
	Small animals	Large animals
Upper limb[b]		
Front	29.5	24.0
Rear	24.0	10.0
Lower limb		
Front	17.0	8.0
Rear	12.0	22.0

[a] Data from Bunn and Kroll (1986a: Table 4)
[b] Values for the shafts of both the tibia and the radius-ulna are included in the values for upper limb bones, although this most certainly biases values in favor of upper limb elements.

after (another pattern) filleting. These generalizations are based on personal experience and the analysis of bones resulting from filleting operations performed by the Nunamiut. They have particular reference to observations of cut marks on bones abandoned after meat had been removed from complete, largely articulated limbs (Billy Morry's drying camp; Binford 1978a:223–235) and bones "gang-processed" for both meat and marrow.

As a result of the removal of meat from the femur we can expect to see many longitudinal marks on the posterior surface along and parallel to the linea aspera and at the base of the greater trochanter. Fewer marks should occur on the anterior surface, with longitudinal cuts visible primarily on the proximal quarter of the shaft. A few transverse or slightly oblique "short chevrons" (Binford 1981a:131) may appear on the distal quarter of the anterior shaft. Typical patterns of marks are illustrated in the composite drawing of cut marks on mountain sheep femurs from the Bugas-Holding site (Figure 23.5). The tibia (Figure 23.6) has much less meat than the femur, but successful filleting requires attention to the attachments of the sartorius muscle in both medial and lateral areas of the tibial tuberosity. In essentially the same place are the insertions for the patellar ligament; hence, cut marks can certainly be expected in this area. In addition, removal of the gastrocnemius muscle requires that attention be focused on the proximal posterior surface of the tibia. One can expect long (fre-

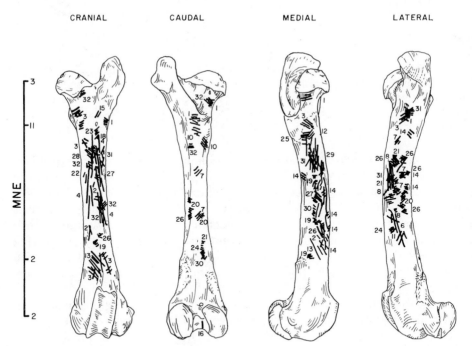

Figure 23.5. Composite of cut marks observed on mountain sheep femurs from the Bugas-Holding site (Todd and Rapson 1987; illustration by L. Todd). Numbers are specimen numbers of bone fragments bearing the cut marks indicated; scale at left shows distribution across the bone of specimens with cut marks.

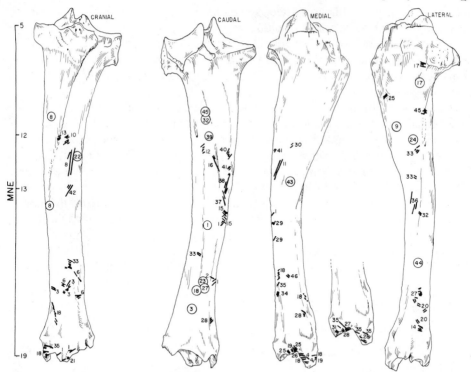

Figure 23.6. Composite of cut marks observed on bison tibias from the Bugas-Holding site (Todd and Rapson 1987; illustration by L. Todd). Numbers are specimen numbers either of bone fragments bearing the cut marks indicated or (where circled) of bone fragments showing impact points at the locations shown; scale at left shows distribution across the bone of specimens with cut marks.

quently single) longitudinal or only minimally oblique marks here, concentrated on the upper half of the shaft. Marks on the distal end of the tibial shaft are more apt to be groups of transverse or short chevron marks inflicted when tendon bundles (flexor digitorum and flexor hallucis) on the posterior surfaces are cut, while the tibialis anterior and peroneus longus would attract attention on the anterior surface. If much of the meat has been removed prior to the use of tools for recovery of adhering pieces, there will be many more short chevrons and transverse cuts on the proximal half of the tibia, a much higher frequency of such marks on the femur, and relatively long scrape marks on both bones.

The scapula (Figure 23.7), which yields considerable meat, presents an interesting situation. Its irregular shape renders it somewhat difficult to fillet, and its flatness ensures that a large number of cut marks will result from filleting. The number of cut marks on the scapula is generally inflated relative to the amount of meat that is procured. Because this bone contains virtually no marrow, all cut marks are referable to filleting and/or dismemberment.

On the humerus we expect a filleting pattern analogous to that for the femur, although the longitudinal marks will tend to be somewhat shorter. On the proximal

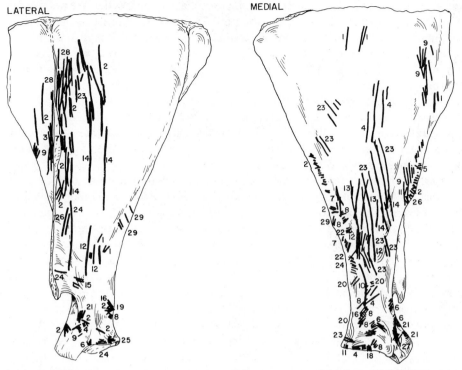

Figure 23.7. Composite of cut marks observed on mountain sheep scapulas from the Bugas-Holding site (Todd and Rapson 1987; illustration by L. Todd). Numbers are specimen numbers of bone fragments bearing the cut marks indicated.

half of the shaft they will be concentrated on the anterior surface, along the pectoral ridge. On the distal half they may occur at the convergence of the supercondyloid ridges. Some short chevrons may occur at the base of the pectoral ridge, but the vast majority will lie across the supercondyloid ridge.

The radio-cubitus or fused (adult) radius and ulna of most ungulates can be expected to exhibit few truly long longitudinal cut marks, although when they do occur it will be from the anterior surface of the radius along the lateral and medial edges (most often they are slightly oblique). Similar marks will sometimes occur along the posterior crest of the "ulna," opposite but just below the level of the coronoid process. More common will be transverse cuts (inflicted during dismemberment) along the anterior face of the articular circumference of the radius, with numerous short chevrons almost exclusively characterizing the marks on the distal half of the shaft and much more common on its anterior surface (Binford 1981a:133).

When meat has been filleted from complete limbs, one can expect more longitudinal marks on the proximal half of the radio-cubitus and tibia, and the marks will be almost exclusively longitudinal on the humerus and femur. The relatively few short chevrons will be largely restricted to the distal half of the radio-cubitus and tibia, and few if any marks (except those inflicted during the original dismemberment) will appear on the tarsals, carpals, or metapodials. If the removal of meat has been the

primary concern, the metapodials will exhibit essentially no marks that are not referable to skinning (few result from skinning per se) and/or to alternative methods of
dismemberment such as the removal of the metapodials prior to filleting. If the bones
have been processed for marrow after the meat has been removed, we can expect
many marks on the metapodials and a minor increase in dismemberment marks
covarying with marks inflicted during marrow extraction. These expectations are
again well illustrated by the bones from the Bugas-Holding site; most cut marks occur
on shafts and result from filleting and marrow cracking, while very few dismemberment marks occur on articular ends of limb bones. Other data from the site support
the view that the bones were filleted before dismemberment, and therefore this latter
task was relatively easy and resulted in very few marks.

   In 1981, at the same time that the cut marks from Olduvai were first reported, I
noted that the Nunamiut not only cleaned metapodials of tendon and other tissue but
sometimes scraped bones to remove the periosteum prior to marrow cracking (Binford 1981a:134). I pointed out that the many transverse marks or short chevrons
reported in the first discussion of the East African cut-mark data were what one would
expect when "lower limb bones or bones remaining from meat consumption by
carnivores are exploited" (Binford 1981a:287). I went on to say that longitudinal
marks on metapodials can be expected to result from removal of the periosteum and
to suggest that the many marks on lower limb bones, at that time considered puzzling,
could result from extensive investment in marrow extraction. Bunn and Kroll (1986a:
437) now inform us that Bunn has shown that cleaning is not "a necessary step in the
efficient fracturing of limb bones for marrow." Examination of his dissertation reveals
that he butchered some goats and cattle using stone tools and "broke the limb bones
and mandibles for marrow" (Bunn 1982b:43). One wonders whether he went on to
use the marrow and to consider the differences in the remains resulting from the
aggregate processing of bone for marrow, high-investment processing for limited
individual returns, and casual processing of bones for individual consumption. No
one has ever suggested that bones cannot be broken without removing the periosteum, but ethnographic observations attest to the fact that regular users of marrow
do frequently clean the bones prior to breaking them.

   In addition to the cleaning of bones prior to cracking, I have reported a method of
processing that among the Eskimo is largely restricted to situations in which individuals consume marrow on the spot; I have published photographs of marrow-
cracked bones processed essentially unskinned (Binford 1984c:157–158). This low-
investment strategy results in larger bone splinters and cut marks, if any, that are
generally restricted to the anterior surface midshaft. This example illustrates my
suggestion that cut-mark frequencies tend to reflect the amount of labor invested in
the recovery of usable material.

   The expected pattern of cut marks on metapodials if they are processed with
investment for the removal of marrow is much more analogous to that which will
occur on the distal radio-cubitus and the distal end of the tibial shaft than it is to that
on any other limb bone. Short chevrons will dominate the marks on the distal ends,
and on the metacarpals there will be about equal numbers on the anterior and
posterior surfaces. On the metatarsals there will be more short chevrons on the

posterior surface because the tendon bundle is frequently embedded in the deep channel on this surface. If longitudinal marks occur on the metacarpal, they are apt to be either on the crest of the posterior medial edge or on the anterior lateral surface just below the proximal articular circumference. On the metatarsal longitudinal marks (rare on fresh bones) will be generally on the proximal half of the shaft, concentrated on the medial ridge of the anterior surface or inside the tendon channel on the posterior surface midshaft. Transverse cuts (inflicted during dismemberment) are rare but may occur just below the articular circumference and extend as far as 4–6 cm below it. Short chevrons occur on proximal as well as central portions of the shaft and are more common on the anterior than on the posterior surface. Short chevrons are more common when tissue is thin and tightly connected to the bone, while long longitudinal marks are more common where substantial meaty units of muscle occur. The proportion of cut marks (particularly short chevrons) reflects not the accidental impacting suggested by Bunn and Kroll but investment by the butcher in the removal of difficult, tightly adhering particles.

When butchers have access to complete or near-complete limbs and meat is the desired product, there is little advantage in dismembering the bony segments of the limb before filleting. The meat may be filleted quite easily from the articulated limb bones. This activity results predominantly in longitudinal cut marks on the scapula, the proximal halves of the humerus, femur, and tibia, and, minimally, the radio-cubitus and short chevrons on the distal half of the shaft of the tibia and radio-cubitus and, less frequently, on the distal half of the femur and humerus. No dismemberment marks need accompany these marks, and there will be few if any marks on the metapodials.

Marrow cracking, in contrast, is most easily done with single bone units; thus in this case we can expect the filleted limbs to be disarticulated. The bones will have been cleaned of both skin and meat; in this situation leverage is much more useful, and disarticulation can be accomplished with very few cuts indeed. Thus, if we observe a pattern in which marks inflicted during filleting are common but dismemberment marks, particularly on the upper limb bones, are rare and unrelated to the normal flexing pattern of the limb when muscles are attached, we may suspect that meat removal was the first processing operation to occur. Fewer marks will be noted on the articular ends of the lower limbs, since the joints are easily spread by leverage.

The above generalizations assume that at the beginning of marrow extraction the metapodials have not been skinned; skinning of complete limbs frequently begins with the carpals and tarsals. This often means that the skin on the metapodials at the time of marrow processing has already begun to dry out. Thus the pattern of expected cut marks for metapodials presupposes at least some drying and stiffness of the lower limb bones at the time of processing for marrow. On the upper limb bones we expect an overlay of short chevrons inflicted during cleaning, primarily on the shaft near the ends and in the areas where the longitudinal marks also occur. In the final stage the bones will be broken, resulting in patterned frequencies of impact locations on each bone.

When bones are scavenged from ravaged carcasses, in contrast, first, given what is known of carnivore feeding behavior (Binford 1981a; Blumenschine 1986; Richardson 1980a), much of the meat from the upper limb bones, particularly from the upper rear limb, can be expected to be missing. Second, usable parts remaining after animal feeding are apt to be unskinned except in areas where heavy feeding occurred. The lower limbs are likely to be intact and encased in skin, and even if they have been gnawed the skin is still likely to remain around the articular junctures of the meta-podials and the distal tibia and distal radio-cubitus and the articulation of the proximal radio-cubitus and the distal humerus. Third, even though usable meat may remain and usable marrow may be present, the skin and the exposed tissue will have begun to dry, making removal and disarticulation more difficult. Under these conditions we can expect few longitudinal filleting marks on the upper limb bones; instead, short chevrons and short transverse marks will be more likely to occur as a result of the removal of meat remnants. There will be few dismemberment marks on the proximal or distal femur, the proximal tibia, the proximal humerus, and the scapula. Such marks will be more frequent on the distal humerus and the proximal radio-cubitus, around the metacarpal-carpal articulations, and at the distal tibia–tarsal–metatarsal joint, the result of disarticulation of bones for marrow cracking. Finally, short chevrons from the cleaning of bones for marrow cracking should be common on the metapodials, distal radio-cubitus, and distal tibia. If longitudinal marks occur, they should be most often seen on the metapodials, since these are apt to be the most difficult to skin in a scavenging context.

Since modern hunters dismember limb bones at a carcass primarily to transport large quantities of meat, we can expect that in a scavenging context dismemberment is less likely to occur at the carcass than at a processing site. If dismemberment does occur at the carcass, it will be related to the procurement of a usable limb section: the choice of this section will be a function of the pattern of consumption characteristic of the carnivore that had previously fed on the carcass. Any dismemberment will most likely be related to marrow extraction and not to meat recovery, which can be done most effectively before the fresh limb bones are disjointed.

Against this background we may examine the cut-mark frequencies reported from the Zinjanthropus floor in comparison with data from the Bugas-Holding site and from the important Magdalenian site of Petersfel (Albrecht et al. 1983), both representing faunas extensively processed for meat and subsequently processed for marrow. On the basis of my knowledge and the opinions of the excavators it seems quite clear that essentially complete limbs were filleted and then bones were disarticulated for mar-row cracking and that all of this took place after initial skinning of the animals. Thus investment was made in the removal of the skin in usable form, a task that leaves few cut marks on limb bones (even on bones with little meat, like metapodials), and finally additional investment was made in the preparation of bones for marrow cracking. Table 23.4 compares the Petersfel and Bugas-Holding data on percentages of bone fragments assignable to given bones exhibiting stone-tool-inflicted cut marks with Bunn and Kroll's data. The varying frequencies of cut marks on the Petersfel and Bugas-Holding bone imply that extensive labor was invested in the limbs of the animals in an attempt to recover all edible material, with some bias in favor of the rear limb, where in sheep and reindeer there is a greater amount of edible material. Bison has different body proportions, and this is reflected in the cut marks. Such differential investment of labor is visible with regard to the meat-yielding upper limb bones, not

Table 23.4

Cut-mark Frequencies in Zinjanthropus Floor, Petersfel, and Bugas-Holding Assemblages

| Skeletal part | Zinjanthropus floor[a] | | Petersfel[b] | Bugas-Holding[c] | |
	Large animals	Small animals	Reindeer	Bison	Sheep
Front limb					
Scapula	9	0	?	62.5	89.2
Humerus	21	36	28	46.7	50.7
Radio-cubitus	18	17	29	37.7	46.9
Metacarpal	9	14	24	26.1	32.4
Rear limb					
Femur	15	15	35	42.9	59.3
Tibia	9	31	30	34.2	44.7
Metatarsal	13	10	22	29.2	27.6

[a] Data from Bunn and Kroll (1986a: Table 4).

[b] Data from Albrecht et al. (1983: 112–116), where shaft fragments are identified in the same manner as by Bunn and Kroll.

[c] Data from Todd and Rapson (1987).

the marrow-yielding lower limbs. In the bones from the Zinjanthropus floor we see no such pattern. For both large and small animals, the greatest attention is given to the upper front limbs and less to the femur than to the radio-cubitus. I would conclude that the femurs had very little usable meat at the time of processing. If the marks on the humerus were indicative of filleting (Bunn and Kroll do not supply descriptions), then we would have to infer that meat-oriented processing, if any, was aimed at the humerus.

No scapulas were found at Petersfel (for reasons related to the drying of meat; see Binford 1978a:115–123), but they are well represented at Bugas-Holding. Tool-inflicted cut marks were found on 62.5% of the bison scapulas and 89.2% of the smaller mountain sheep scapulas. None of the scapulas from small animals and only 9% of those from larger animals in the Zinjanthropus floor assemblage had tool-inflicted marks. The lack of investment in this meat-yielding bone suggests that there was little meat on it at the time of acquisition.

Remains from the Zinjanthropus floor represent comparable but low amounts of investment in the radio-cubitus and an even lower investment in the metacarpal relative to the Petersfel and Bugas-Holding remains. This low investment seems to me to reflect not a lack of interest in marrow but a different context of marrow extraction. Most ethnographic examples of heavy investment in marrow extraction refer to the processing of many bones at once not for immediate consumption but for eventual sharing. This was demonstrably the case at Bugas-Holding and is inferred for Petersfel. The relatively low frequencies of cut marks on the Zinjanthropus metapodials suggest that these bones were discretely processed for individual consumption and/or were difficult to process. (Bunn and Kroll's suggestion that the metapodials were marked as a result of skinning is unrealistic given the levels of marking recorded; 1986a:438). My guess is that the Zinjanthropus floor occupants invested in the recovery of marrow for individual consumption but that the task was made difficult for them by the state of the bones at the time of processing. This interpretation is supported by the contrasts in the cut-mark data between tibias and metatarsals. Given what we understand about the results of processing fresh bones for both meat and marrow, there is no way to accommodate the fact that for small animals from the Zinjanthropus floor only 15% of the femoral fragments but 31% of the tibial fragments have tool-inflicted marks. This contrast is even more striking when it is noted that 28.6% of the distal tibia fragments but only 7.6% of the shaft fragments are cut-marked. Again, little meat removal seems indicated.

Against this background the data from the large animals become even more interesting, since we see very low values for cut marks on the tibia, and these correspond to the low values for the femur. The Zinjanthropus floor occupants appear to have been less interested in the tibia (compared with the femur) than they were in the radio-cubitus (compared with the humerus). This makes no sense in light of what we know about meat distributions on a living animal or, I might add, about marrow-cavity volumes (there is more marrow in the tibia than there is in the radio-cubitus). These observations can be clarified by examination of Table 23.5, in which percentage values for fragments exhibiting cut marks are taken as a measure of the relative tool-assisted investment in processing (maximum processing investment being indicated by 100%). Especially for the scapula (essentially absent in the Petersfel assemblage), we see a striking contrast between the Bugas-Holding data and those from the Zinjanthropus floor that once again leads us to suspect that the Zinjanthropus floor hominids did not have access to meat-laden bones. If we continue the comparison overlooking the scapula, we find that the Bugas-Holding bison humerus, the sheep femur, and the Petersfel reindeer femur received the greatest numbers of tool-inflicted marks. The slight bias in favor of the humerus over the femur for the bison may reflect its particular body proportions. Bunn and Kroll report that the most common

Table 23.5
Percentage Investment in Various Skeletal Parts as Indicated by Cut Marks[a]

| | Zinjanthropus floor[a] | | Petersfel[b] | Bugas-Holding[c] | |
	Large animals	Small animals	Reindeer	Bison	Sheep
Front limb					
Scapula	42	0	?	100	100
Humerus	100	100	80	75	57
Radio-cubitus	85	47	71	60	53
Metacarpal	42	38	68	42	36
Rear limb					
Femur	71	41	100	69	67
Tibia	42	86	85	55	50
Metatarsal	61	27	62	43	31

[a] Percentages transformed from Table 23.4.

Figure 23.8.   Male waterbuck (photograph by L. R. Binford).

animal in their assemblage is a Pleistocene relative of the modern waterbuck (*Kobus*). The waterbuck (Figure 23.8) does not exhibit the extremes in amount of meat yielded front and rear that are seen in American bison (Figure 23.9), with its huge shoulder hump and massive concentration of meat and tissue in the front limbs. Thus, the bison data are no exception to the rule of maximum investment in the most meat-yielding parts. The anomalous investment of the Zinjanthropus floor hominids in the humerus relative to both the scapula and the femur strongly suggests that removal of meat from meat-laden bones was not the context in which the biased infliction of marks on the humerus occurred. Consistent with this strange "over-marking" of the humerus is a simple pattern on the radio-cubitus, which received more attention in the Zinjanthropus floor data than the femur, scapula, and tibia. I conclude that there was little meat present on the scapula, femur, and tibia, particularly of large animals, to which attention could be directed.

At Petersfel maximum investment was in the femur and the tibia, clearly parts related to meat removal, while for the Zinjanthropus floor the maximum investment for large-animal parts was in the humerus and radio-cubitus. I conclude that there was little meat on the femur and tibia at the time of processing by the Zinjanthropus floor hominids. In addition, more attention was given to the metatarsal than to either the femur or the tibia, and from this I conclude that marrow extraction exceeded meat removal from the "meaty" rear limbs of large animals. On the front limbs, even though the scapula data strongly suggest that only a small amount of meat was present, the bias may have been in favor of meat remnants rather than marrow. This seeming shift of emphasis from meat to marrow in the possible context of differences in meat

Figure 23.9.   American bison (photograph by A. Osborn).

availability (high mark frequency on the humerus) suggests that (in contrast to the situation at Petersfel and Bugas-Holding) little effort was being made to extract all the usable products available. Instead, only enough for a meal was taken. There is no support for Bunn and Kroll's assertion that large animals were hunted or scavenged in "aggressive ways," resulting in early access to prime, meaty parts and in a build-up of large quantities of meat and marrow that would implicate food sharing.

When the Petersfel and Bugas-Holding data are compared with the Zinjanthropus floor data for small animals (which Bunn and Kroll claim were probably hunted; 1986a:442) we see essentially the same pattern. Biased attention to front limbs is evident in the Zinjanthropus data, and little support is apparent for the inference of intact muscle masses on those limbs if one considers the data for the scapula. Nevertheless, when marginal meat packages were available there again appears to have been an underexploitation of marrow, as indicated by the presence of complete metacarpals and by the pattern of cut marks on those bones. This again suggests immediate consumption—investment conditioned by individuals' appetites rather than by concerns for maximum exploitation of available products for purposes of sharing. Similarly, examination of the data from the rear limbs shows an investment in marrow (cut marks were frequent on metatarsals) almost equal to that for the femur. Since metatarsals are six times as common as femurs, we must conclude that, as in the case of large animals, there was little meat on the femur. In addition, cut marks on the small-animal tibias are most likely related to marrow removal. Again we are forced to conclude that (a) little meat was available to the hominids, (b) the meat available was primarily on the humerus, and (c) marrow was the primary animal product exploited with regularity at the Zinjanthropus site. Finally, the lack of correspondence between suggested indicators of marrow exploitation is consistent with the view that processing was not maximized; instead, individual feeding behavior is most consistent with the facts. When meat was available marrow was less regularly processed, but when meat was unavailable marrow was extensively exploited. It is hard to imagine the occurrence of sharing with this pattern of processing investment.

Finally, Bunn and Kroll note that "the cut marks are predominantly oriented obliquely relative to the long axis of the limb bone" (1986a:437) and that there are "numerous, oblique slicing marks on muscle attachment areas of the meaty limb bones" (1986a:439). Although the long longitudinal marks described here as resulting from meat removal can exhibit this orientation (in a very low relative frequency, however), the most common obliquely oriented cut mark results from the cutting of tightly attached small tissue elements along the major muscle attachments on the bone. If we can trust Bunn and Kroll's generalization, it would appear that the form of the cut marks recorded by Bunn primarily supports the view that few bones processed at the Zinjanthropus site had substantial quantities of meat on them.

Bunn and Kroll point out (1986a:450) that I have largely ignored the published cut-mark data. I have done so for two reasons. First, I judged Bunn's (1982b, 1983a) early descriptions of cut marks difficult to accept, and I agreed with Shipman (1986) that when better techniques of identification were used these data could be expected to be modified. In this regard it is interesting that Bunn and Kroll now base their arguments on their "micro-sample" (Table 4), which reduces the claims for the frequency of cut marks in the Zinjanthropus assemblage. In spite of the fact that the micro-sample lowers the estimated number of cut-marked bones by only 10%, while Shipman (1986) suggests that a 40% reduction is perhaps more realistic, I have chosen to take these questionable data seriously. Secondly, I avoided discussing the cut-mark data because I did not know of any reliable control data that could be used to guide their interpretation. Cut marks occur on bones as a result of sequential and independent acts of processing. When we summarize archaeological cut marks we are producing a composite description of the results of potentially different and independently varying steps in the processing of animal products. I still know of only one control case (Binford 1984c:73); therefore, comparative diagnosis of the results of processing steps that appear to us as a flat composite statistical summary is impossible. At a minimum, I have tried to provide a description based on my ethnographic experiences that is germane to the study of the processing of bones for meat.

Unfortunately, I did not know while I was working with the Nunamiut what we would need to know in order to evaluate cut-mark frequency data. I should have obtained control data on marks produced (a) exclusively during carcass butchery as opposed to secondary butchering associated with sharing, storage, and preparation for cooking and (b) during marrow extraction in different contexts of intended use, such as meals (when upper limb bones are commonly processed) and "gang-processing" episodes (when lower limb bones are more commonly processed). How does a composite pattern of sequential dismemberment compare with a composite pattern produced by filleting and subsequent dismemberment of bones for marrow extraction? In the absence of good control cases I have used in this discussion two

extremely well-documented cases in which the researchers used the most sophisticated methods possible to describe and interpret their results. The conclusions fit very
closely with those based upon actual Nunamiut butchering of animals and with the
observations I have made on the resulting cut marks. In my judgment, these archaeological cases are likely to be good examples of animal processing as I have described
it from experience, but because they are archaeological cases the meaning of the
patterning is inferred; they are not control cases. To my knowledge, we have not a
single body of cut-mark data on modern bones for which the causal behavioral
conditions are known. In my ethnographic data the cut marks are still a consequence
of several processing steps, and distinguishing one from another is still a matter of
inference. Bunn and Kroll discuss cut marks as if they were self-evidently meaningful
in terms of what they want to believe about the past.

    I do not care to spend much time on their response to my comments on their
paper, but I do want to correct certain errors in it. Seeking to diminish the significance
of gnaw marks on the bones from the Zinjanthropus floor, they note that the proportion of gnawed bones is lower than that in spotted hyena dens. I know of no one who
has suggested that the Zinjanthropus floor was a hyena den, and the fact that the
frequency of gnawing on the bones there is less than on bones in a den says nothing
about its importance. My point was that the gnaw marks could have been present on
the bones at the time of their introduction to the site. Animal gnawing would be expected at a site to which bones scavenged by hominids from already ravaged carcasses
were transported. In response to this suggestion, Bunn and Kroll state that "Binford
reverses the sequence of site-forming events as reported by Kroll and Isaac (1984)
in their discussion of spatial patterns at the FLK Zinjanthropus site" (1986a:450). But
Kroll and Isaac never established a sequence of site-forming events; they simply
offered an opinion on them. What I did was to suggest that the sequence they adopted
is unsubstantiated and another sequence at least equally plausible. Perhaps their most
astonishing statement is "Abandoning his earlier argument that the FLK Zinjanthropus
site is a location where carnivores repeatedly killed animals, Binford now alleges that
hominids transported bones to the site" (1986a:45). I quote from the only work in
which I seriously considered the site's character (Binford 1981a:276, 282):

> That numbers of different situational contexts are represented on the Zinjanthro-
> pus floor is supported by the analysis. . . . This is the most heterogeneous or
> situationally mixed site, as judged from the factor analysis, within the studied set
> from Olduvai Gorge. A scavenged natural death of animals appears represented, as
> do some transported items, scavenged, perhaps by hominids, from animal kills
> somewhere else. . . . It might be possible, using detailed studies of breakage mor-
> phology and association, to isolate . . . clusters of material referable to hominid
> behavior on a floor such as Zinjanthropus; however, given its demonstrably low
> integrity and resolution, arguments about base camps, hominid hunting, sharing of
> food, and so forth are certainly premature and most likely wildly inaccurate. The
> only clear picture obtained is that of a hominid scavenging the kills and death sites
> of other predator-scavengers for abandoned anatomical parts of low food utility,
> primarily for purposes of extracting bone marrow.

I concluded that a mixture of agents and conditions contributed to the assemblage. At
no time did I suggest that the Zinjanthropus floor was "a location where carnivores

repeatedly killed animals," nor is it new for me to suggest that hominids transported bones to the site.

Bunn and Kroll turn next to the value of their "new" data on skeletal-part frequencies and my alleged reluctance to deal with it (1986a:450–451). The idea that their Table 2 is incomplete has been examined and found indefensible. That I performed a multivariate analysis on their "bad" data is incorrect—a simple cluster analysis was the method used. There was no "uncertainty" about the placement of the assemblage, which was unambiguously grouped with the kill-site assemblages used in the comparisons (1986a:445). My suggestion that the Zinjanthropus assemblage would be likely to distribute "between the Combe Grenal bovids and the ravaged-kill data" is quoted out of context as a summary of my findings and then found hard to reconcile with my previous conclusion (Binford 1985b) that the moderate-body-sized animals at Combe Grenal were hunted. But I clearly identified the moderate-body-sized animals as red deer and reindeer (Binford 1985b:319) and stated, "In addition, they [the occupants of Combe Grenal] were scavenging large-sized animals, such as aurochs and horses" (1985:320); it was the aurochs that was compared to the species on the Zinjanthropus floor.

Bunn and Kroll assert that their Tables 2 and 3 "expose Binford's conversion of the FLK *Zinjanthropus* bone data and his resulting patterns and interpretations as seriously in error." I think that this discussion is sufficient to demonstrate that no such exposure has occurred and no such conclusions regarding my interpretations are warranted. I must conclude that both the skeletal-part frequency data and the cut-mark data are most consistent with and indicative of the scavenging of marginal foods from previously ravaged carcasses. Bunn and Kroll's attempt to defend the traditional home-base hunting hypothesis fails on every point.

NOTE

1. These revelations redirect attention to the controversial mandibles. Can we assume that the MAU value for "CRA/TTH" in Table 2 was calculated in a manner similar to that used for ribs and vertebrae? Bunn (1982b) lists 36 mandibles plus teeth (MANT)—since lefts and rights are indicated, we can assume this actually means mandible halves—for animals of Size-Groups 1–3. A generous interpretation of this figure would indicate an MAU value of 18 for mandibles. A total of 116 isolated teeth from animals of this size is listed. If all of these teeth were in fact mandibular, an additional 10 individuals would be indicated, giving us a total of 28. Bunn and Kroll list an MAU value of 38, leaving us with a difference of 10. Perhaps since Bunn wrote his dissertation the additional 196 isolated teeth listed under the combined Size-Groups 3 and 4 have been identified more accurately and the additional 10 MAUs come from this unreported work. If this is the case, however, it is apparent that similar attention has not been given to the ribs or vertebrae.

Chapter 24

Hyena Scavenging Behavior and Its Implications for the Interpretation of Faunal Assemblages from FLK 22 (the Zinj Floor) at Olduvai Gorge

by Lewis R. Binford, M. G. L. Mills, and Nancy M. Stone

During the 1970s, archaeological remains from the period of the earliest appearance of stone tools were frequently interpreted as evidence for a complex set of functionally linked hominid behaviors (Isaac 1978a, 1978b). These included a sexual division of labor, significant investment by adult males and females in the care of offspring, the development of language, and a family-based form of social organization. All of these behaviors were viewed as the evolutionary consequence of a shift to hunting on the part of our ancient hominid ancestors.

This model of causation, which was originally proposed by Washburn and Lancaster (1968) and termed "the hunting hypothesis," was not adopted by archaeologists as a theory to be tested; it functioned instead as the intellectual justification for stipulative arguments linking archaeological remains to inferred behavioral dynamics. As an essential preliminary step in the interpretation of the archaeological record in terms of the hunting hypothesis, archaeologists had to develop criteria for identifying components stipulated by the model. The identification of hominid hunting, and the behaviors it was believed to have stimulated, was derived from the clustered association of stone tools with animal bones at "home bases" (Isaac 1971). In response to a methodological imperative of "seek and ye shall find," archaeologists opened a door to the past through which the view of hominid behavior appeared surprisingly like that of modern hunter-gatherers.

In 1977, Binford began to question the inferential procedures of proponents of the hunting hypothesis (Binford 1977c, 1981a, 1984c, 1985b, 1986b, 1986c; Binford and Ho 1985; Binford and Stone 1986). The present research is a continuation of this program of investigation. Because the relevance of this study may not be apparent to those who are not specialists in early man studies, we will outline briefly the major points of controversy leading to the present discussions of the nature of early hominid food procurement strategies.

In *Bones: Ancient Men and Modern Myths,* Binford (1981a) presented the argument, based on knowledge of the behavior of modern hunters (Binford 1978a), that the anatomical part frequencies reported by Mary Leakey (1971) from important sites in Olduvai Gorge did not appear similar to those produced by the various strategies that modern hunters follow when they are exploiting carcasses. In addition, it was observed that if hominids *had* accumulated at least some of the bones found in

Originally published in *Journal of Anthropological Archaeology* 7:99–135, © 1988.

association with stone tools, they were differentially transporting bones that would yield little, if any meat! The Olduvai assemblages were commonly dominated by anatomical segments from the heads and lower limbs of animals; other bones were present but in lower frequencies. It was reasoned that if hominids had had initial access to carcasses by virtue of having killed them, the parts introduced into sites identified as home bases would not be parts of marginal utility but instead would be anatomical parts yielding far greater amounts of edible tissue. Binford argued that the most plausible implication of the anatomical part data was that the hominids were not exploiting carcasses as the feeders but instead were scavenging still useful parts that had been abandoned at kill sites by the initial feeders, most probably nonhominid carnivores. It was recognized that other, more meaty parts might sometimes have remained for the hominid scavengers, but for the most part the amount of available edible tissue could not be directly inferred by the archaeologist exclusively on the basis of anatomical part representation.

Although this argument continues to be dismissed by other researchers on a number of grounds (Behrensmeyer 1986; Bunn 1982a; Bunn and Kroll 1986a, 1986b; Freeman 1983; Isaac 1983b), it did precipitate a shift in the vocabulary used to describe postulated hominid behavior. "Hunting" and living in "home bases" were replaced by "central place foraging," a term whose apparent neutrality allows advocates of the hunting hypothesis to retain all of the behavioral components of their argument except actual hominid provisioning tactics.[1] As Glynn Isaac observed, "Meat eating on a significant scale is indicated, but the existing data do not yet allow one to distinguish acquisition by hunting from acquisition by scavenging, though the assemblages from several sites are fully consistent with scavenging modes" (1983a:13). Hominid transport and consumption of meat may have replaced hunting as the pivotal behavioral mechanism in this argument, but the evolutionary consequences remain unchanged:

> it could well be that whether or not sharing was "intended," the recurrent transport of prime food to predictable, favorite places led to *de facto* dissemination of nourishment. This would constitute incipient central place foraging regardless of motivation. (Isaac 1983a:15)

Critical to this interpretation was the clarification of certain other data regarding the properties of the early sites that had emerged from the work of Bunn (1981) and Potts and Shipman (1981). These workers had presented evidence of relatively high frequencies of bones from the Zinj floor at Olduvai Gorge with tool-inflicted cut marks and carnivore-inflicted tooth marks. The cut mark data had become the centerpiece of Bunn's arguments that hominids were consuming considerable quantities of meat (Bunn 1982b; Bunn and Kroll 1986a). The carnivore tooth mark data were problematical, however, since Binford (1981a) had observed that such patterns would be expected if hominids had been scavenging bones from carcasses previously ravaged by nonhominid carnivores.

An accommodative argument originally presented by Mary Leakey (1971) was revised to account for modifications produced by carnivore gnawing.

The simplest explanation for the presence of several hundred bones with carnivore gnaw marks, some of which occur on bones that also retain cut marks, is that scavenging carnivores, probably hyaenas, were attracted to the FLK *Zinjanthropus* bone and artifact concentration after hominids created it. (Bunn 1983a:28)

Glynn Isaac even presented the results of an experimental exercise conducted earlier to demonstrate the plausibility of such an argument.

In 1964, as part of our Olorgesailie work, we dumped our domestic bone refuse for several months at a peg out in the wilderness. At the end of the experiment the scavengers proved to have won game, set and match—only a few measly splinters remained. . . . Similarly at Koobi Fora, Bunn tried to make a collection of experimentally fractured fresh bone. With the slightest relaxation of precautions, the local hyaenas and jackals would slip into camp and remove the specimens! There is nothing hypothetical about carnivore reworking of hominid bone discards! (Isaac 1983a:11)

An undetected paradox was therefore built into the arguments presented by the Isaac team. Carnivore gnaw marks on the bones from the Zinj floor were attributed to scavenging animals who visited the site after hominids had abandoned the remains of their meaty meals. Yet Isaac's own experiments had documented that scavenging hyenas regularly *removed* bones from the location where they were discarded and left only "a few measly splinters." These observations of hyena scavenging behavior had major implications for the interpretive arguments adopted by Isaac and his associates. If scavenging hyenas behaved in the past as they had in Isaac's experiment, then one could expect certain consequences for the faunal remains on the Zinj floor. First, in its anatomical part frequencies the faunal assemblage would be heavily biased away from the form originally abandoned by the hominids. This bias would be against large bone pieces and in favor of "measly splinters." Any argument that accepted the anatomical part frequencies as directly indicative of hominid behavior (Bunn 1983a; Bunn and Kroll 1986a) would therefore be unjustified.[2] Second, Isaac's experiment clearly illustrated that hyena behavior would considerably alter the spatial patterning of the bones relative to their original placement as debris from hominid feeding. Applying Isaac's observations to a feeding sequence in which hominids preceded carnivores as modifying agents of the bones, one would expect the spatial patterning of carnivore-gnawed bones to be peripheral to and largely independent of the distribution of stone tools, *except* for small bone splinters. Was this true?

In 1984 Kroll and Isaac reported on Kroll's study of the spatial patterning of artifacts and faunal remains from the Zinj floor. This important study graphically demonstrated that the spatial distribution of animal-gnawed bones was isomorphic with the stone tool and cut-marked bone distributions. Figure 24.1 is reproduced from Kroll and Isaac: in Figure 24.1A the total distribution of stone tools on the Zinj floor is presented; Figure 24.1B presents the total bone distribution on the Zinj floor; Figure 24.1C shows all of the carnivore-gnawed bones; and Figure 24.1D presents all of the cut-marked bones relative to the unmodified bones. The researchers summarized their observations as follows:

The overall distribution pattern [here Figure 24.1B] consisting of the dense circular concentration, the elongate concentration, and the lower density scatter of other

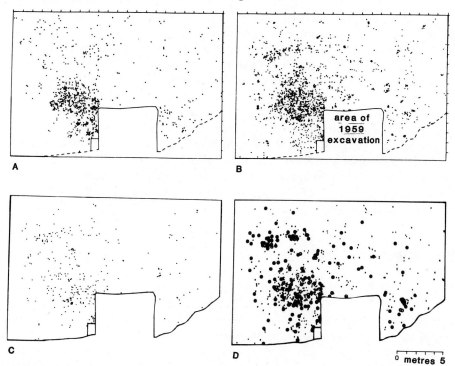

Figure 24.1. Plans of the excavations of Olduvai Gorge (FLK Zinj) showing the positions of (A) plotted stones, (B) bones, (C) carnivore-gnawed bones, and (D) cut-marked and unmodified (neither gnawed nor cut) bones (1 scale mark = 1 m). Some of the smaller pieces were not individually plotted. The dashed lines mark the edges of the erosion slope (from Kroll and Isaac 1984: Figs. 2 and 14).

> bones, persists through the apparent carnivore filter (here Figure 24.1C) and seems to have been the pattern left from hominid involvement with the bones (here Figure 24.1D). . . . The working hypothesis that hominids formed the spatial pattern of bones is consistent with the fact that the spatial pattern of stone artifacts (here Figure 24.1A), which would not have been a major attraction for carnivores, largely coincides with the bone pattern. (Kroll and Isaac 1984:25)

We agree with this conclusion. However, if the distributions of animal-gnawed bone directly overlap the distribution of stone tools—and no independence between these distributions can be supported by the facts as reported—then these findings are incompatible with the distributions that one would expect as a result of Isaac's observations of scavenging hyenas. Bones modified by hyenas would be expected to have been moved to a location peripheral to or beyond the boundaries of the hominid site, and only small bone fragments would remain associated with stone tools. The actual distribution of animal-gnawed bones from the Zinj floor reported by Kroll and Isaac was difficult to reconcile with the argument that carnivore tooth marks were imposed on the bones after their discard by hominids.

While these distributions appeared to implicate directly Binford's argument (based on anatomical part frequencies) that carnivore gnawing preceded hominid scavenging of carcasses, some important observations were missing from Isaac's report of his experiments. The condition and distribution of whatever bones remained after hyena scavenging are types of information that would be crucial to the interpretation of the materials from the Zinj floor. In addition, since this was the only experiment known to be relevant to the issues under debate, some might claim that other circumstances could have rendered Isaac's results atypical of hyena behavior. For these reasons, we undertook to make a further study of hyena scavenging behavior during the summer of 1986. In collaboration with M. G. L. Mills, the Senior Research Officer at the Kruger National Park game reserve in South Africa, Binford and Stone carried out four experiments with bones in different states of processing in order to evaluate claims that scavenging carnivores had gnawed bones previously processed and discarded by hominids on the Zinj floor.

EXPERIMENTS 1A AND 1B

Limb bones of African buffalo (*Syncerus caffer*) were obtained from the herd culling operations of the Nature Conservancy staff of the game reserve. These bones had already been butchered, but all connective tissue between adjacent bones was still intact and some meat still adhered to the bones.

Experiment 1A

Experiment 1A was set up at the Skukuza camp dump, where hyenas were known to scavenge regularly. Two metal stakes were placed 2.5 m apart in a north–south orientation so that the location of the bones could be established relative to fixed reference points. The site of this experiment was a cleared area of the dump with no trees or debris that could obscure the distribution patterns.

The following butchered African buffalo bones were brought to the site: seven complete femora with attached patellae and proximal tibiae, and five complete humeri with attached fused radio-cubiti. Some of these bones were then processed by Binford to simulate modified bones remaining on the Zinj floor. All humeri were cracked open. In a procedure designed to evaluate any preference that hyenas might exhibit in selecting bones for transport, three humeri were simply cracked transversely in mid-shaft and the marrow was left in the shafts. Two others were broken with long spiral fractures that exposed the medullary cavity longitudinally. Marrow was removed from these bones. In the case of distal ends, the joint attachments were left intact and the proximal radio-cubiti remained articulated. Four femora were left as unmodified complete bones with attached proximal tibiae; one femur was broken transversely in mid-shaft but the marrow was not removed. The two remaining femora were cracked with long spiral fractures and the marrow was removed. In addition to the bones listed above, four large bone splinters were detached during marrow cracking; other splinters remained attached to the parent bones by periosteum and tissue. In all, 24 bone units were then placed in an arrangement between the two stakes as shown in Figure 24.2. This arrangement was left in place at 4:15 P.M. on August 19, 1986.

Bone displacement. The first agents observed at the dump site were scavenging birds (Figure 24.3). By 5:30 P.M. many Marabou storks (*Leptoptilos crumeniferus*) and two ground hornbills (*Bucorvus leadbeateri*) surrounded the experiment. The storks were more interested in the small pile of marrow that had been removed from some of the bones and placed near the north stake than they were in the bones themselves. The ground hornbills were tugging at some of the tissue on the bones, displacing one distal humerus with attached meat a distance of 2.8 m to the west of its original position. The storks later pulled two of the bone splinters 1.8 and 2.2 m to the east of their original positions. By 6:16 P.M. the storks were roosting in nearby trees, the hornbills had left the site, and impala (*Aepyceros melampus*) were now walking over the experimental area, although they appeared to ignore its contents. The experiment remained untouched by carnivores through 9:30 P.M.

We were unable to observe the experiment during the night, but on our return at 9:00 A.M. the following day (Figure 24.4) hyena spoor surrounded the experiment area. Jackal spoor was concentrated near the south stake. *No bones remained in the area of their original placement.* Only 10 bone elements could be found, and of these 10 only 8 belonged to the original group of 20 bones and 4 bone splinters. A new bone splinter had been produced by gnawing hyenas, and a proximal tibia had been disarticulated from its original element. The mean distance of all 10 bones from their

Figure 24.2. Arrangement of meaty bones at the dump site (Experiment 1A).

Figure 24.3.   Birds that consumed marrow and moved bones at the dump site (Experiment 1A).

original placements was 17.1 m; the closest bone had been moved 6 m, while the most distant was 25.1 m from the position illustrated in Figure 24.2. *There is little ambiguity in these results.* Hyenas had removed the bones from their original location, and none of the bones gnawed by hyenas remained where we had placed them. In addition, the four original large bone splinters were recovered, two in situ and two in the location where they were abandoned by storks. None of these large bone splinters had animal tooth marks on them. Table 24.1 summarizes the numbers and condition of recovered bone elements and compares them to the number of bones originally present.

Of the 12 original bones with marrow present, only 2 (17%) were recovered; of the 8 original bones with marrow removed, 6 (75%) were recovered. This suggests a bias toward removal of bones containing marrow. With regard to bone size and amount of edible material, the distal ends had more adhering tissue than did proximal ends. This was also true of complete bones. There appears to be a bias favoring the complete removal from the location of larger bone elements with more edible tissue. The details of this bias are presented in Table 24.2. Table 24.3 lists the number of remaining modified bones attributable to different scavengers.

Gnawing patterns. No complete bones were recovered, so gnawing patterns will be described in terms of portions of bones.

Proximal humerus. Two proximal humeri were recovered. Both were heavily

Figure 24.4. Mills and Binford recovering transported bones (Experiment 1A).

tooth-scored, with tooth pitting on the upper articular surfaces and scooping out of the lower edges of the humeral head. No radial tooth marks were present on the shafts, and no tooth punctures occurred on adhering shaft elements.

Proximal femur. Three proximal femora were recovered. One was gnawed by hyena, with heavy tooth pitting and scoring on the dorsal surface of the femoral head. Transverse tooth scoring occurred just below the greater trochanter, which was partially eaten away. Two femora were gnawed by jackal and all adhering meat was removed. The dorsal surfaces of both femoral heads had minor tooth scoring. There was tooth pitting and some longitudinal tooth scoring on both greater trochanters.

Table 24.1
Experiment 1A (Dump site)

	Articular end[a]		Complete bones with marrow
	Marrow present	Marrow removed	
Number of bones in original distribution	12	8	4
Number of bones re-covered	2 (17%)	6 (75%)	0

[a] Includes whole bones with marrow, tabulated as one unit each.

Table 24.2
Experiment 1A (Dump site)

	Proximal ends (small)	Distal and complete bones (large)
Number of bones originally present	8	12
Number of bones remaining	5 (62.5%)	3 (25%)

Distal humerus. Two distal humeri were recovered, both gnawed by hyenas to the extent that almost all adhering tissue had been removed. Both radio-cubiti were still attached, although both projecting proximal cubiti were gnawed away. The only visible marks on the radii were two longitudinal tooth scores on the anterior face of one proximal radius and a deep tooth pit on the sawed-through surface of the other radial section. Tooth pitting occurred on the medial condyles of both distal humeri, with tooth scoring on the exposed surface of one condyle.

Distal femur. One distal femur with attached proximal tibia was recovered. Heavy hyena tooth pitting was noted on the sawed surface of the tibial shaft. Tooth pitting and minor scooping out occurred on the medial and lateral edges of the tibial condyle. Corresponding tooth scores occurred on both the lateral and the medial surfaces of the femoral condyle. The greatest destruction was along the proximal edge of the femoral channel, at the point where it merges with the femoral shaft. Scooping out and deep pitting were visible on both femur and proximal tibia.

Experiment 1B

Because the habitual scavenging of hyenas at the dump site could conceivably bias their behavior at this location, a second experiment was placed in a more remote area of the game reserve. Bones prepared by the cull butchers as in Experiment 1A were placed on a prominent bedrock exposure adjacent to a tree. Downslope was a large grass-covered area of bushveld. Since the bedrock prevented the use of stakes as locational markers, a brick that had been used as an anvil for cracking the bones was used as a marker (Figure 24.5).

The following elements obtained from the cull butchers were brought to the site:

Table 24.3
Experiment 1A (Dump site)

	Agent of modification	
Recovered bones	Jackal	Hyena
Large with marrow present	0	1
Small with marrow present	3	2
Large with marrow absent	0	2
Small with marrow absent	0	0
Total	3	5

Figure 24.5. Overall view of bushveld location; bones in Experiment 1B in center.

six buffalo femora (three complete with attached patellae and proximal tibiae, one complete with no attached parts, and two proximal femora and complete shafts with butchering saw marks through the distal articular ends); one complete humerus with attached proximal radius and fused radio-cubitus (ulna); and five meaty units, each consisting of a proximal tibia and attached patella, which had been butchered during the preparation of bones for Experiment 2 (described below).

At the bushveld site, all three femora and attached proximal tibiae were split with long spiral fractures and the marrow was removed. The complete humerus with attachments was processed in the same way. The one complete femur without attachments was split transversely and the marrow was left in the bone. The two femora with sawed distal ends and the five meaty units of proximal tibia and patella were not modified further. This processing produced four additional large, long, detached bone splinters and 19 small impact splinters.

Bone displacement. These units were arranged as shown in Figure 24.6 and were left in place at 5:00 P.M. on August 20, 1986. At 10:20 P.M. it began to rain, and it continued to rain until approximately 12:30 A.M. When we returned to the experiment area the next morning we discovered hyena spoor that had been overprinted by raindrops, which suggested that hyenas had visited the experiment prior to or during the rain. Three long bone splinters remained at the site along with the 19 small splinters produced when the bones were cracked the previous day (Figure 24.7). All of these appeared to be in their original positions. None of the bone splinters exhib-

Figure 24.6. Arrangement of meaty bones in Experiment 1B; note brick anvil in center.

ited any tooth-inflicted modifications. As in Experiment 1A, *all bone units other than splinters and chips had been removed from the experiment location.*

The following bones were recovered during a thorough search of the bushveld surrounding the bedrock outcrop: one proximal femur and shaft (unbroken), saw-cut through the distal end; one proximal tibia, disarticulated and cleaned of meat by the hyenas; one distal humerus with attached proximal radius and fused cubitus from which we had removed the marrow. Of the original 21 units (exclusive of impact chips), only 6 could be found: one-half of these were long-bone splinters. Only 17.6% of the 17 original major bone elements were recovered, and none of these were found where they had originally been placed. The three recovered elements were clustered in thickly matted grass, a mean distance of 34.9 m from the experiment location (actual distances were 35.4, 35.9, and 33.2 m). Comparisons between the number of recovered bones and the original inventory appear in Tables 24.4 and 24.5. Unlike the bias indicated by Experiment 1A, no preferential removal by hyenas of bones containing marrow or of meatier pieces is evident. All indications from spoor suggest that hyenas were the only scavengers present and that birds played no role in modifying the distribution of bones.

Gnawing patterns. Only one of the two complete bones was recovered. This was a femur with the greater trochanter gnawed away and deep tooth scoring on the dorsal surface of the femoral head. Scooping out characterized the ventral surface of the femoral head and neck. No radial scoring was indicated. Tooth pitting was present on

Figure 24.7. Experiment 1B location after removal of bones by hyenas; only bone splinters remain (compare with Figure 24.6).

the cut surface of the distal femur, and deep pitting was apparent along the medial aspect of this surface.

The recovered distal humerus (with attached proximal radio-cubitus) had been stripped of meat and most tissue. Deep tooth scoring occurred on the dorsal or upper surface of the humeral head. Pitting was visible along the ventral margin of the humeral head.

The proximal tibia was tooth-pitted in the cancellous tissue of the saw cut and along the anterior margin of the articular surface.

Comparison of experiments 1A and 1B. The experiments differed both in their

Table 24.4
Experiment 1B (Bushveld site)

	Articular ends[a]		
	Marrow present	Marrow removed	Complete bones with marrow
Number of bones in original distribution	8	4	2
Number of bones recovered	2 (25%)	1 (25%)	1 (50%)

[a] Includes whole bones with marrow, tabulated as one unit each.

Table 24.5
Experiment 1B (Bushveld site)

	Proximal ends (small)	Distal ends and meaty elements
Number of bones in original distribution	5	12
Number recovered	0	3

setting and in the types of scavengers attracted to the bones. At the dump site (Experiment 1A) birds and jackals in addition to hyenas modified the bones and their distribution. The experiments also differed in the scale of movement. At the dump site, 40% of the original bone elements were recovered, while at the bushveld location only 17% of the original elements were recovered. Some of this difference may be referable to the differences in vegetation at the two locations. Dense grass may well have affected our ability to locate bones carried off from the bedrock but not completely removed from the area. On the other hand, the dump location was essentially devoid of surface vegetation in the area around the experiment, and recovery of bones was relatively easy. Another point of contrast was the indication at the dump location of a transport bias favoring meaty bones or bones with marrow. No such bias is indicated by the few remaining bones at the bushveld location.

These differences notwithstanding, no ambiguity exists with respect to the primary conclusion from both experiments: all major bone elements involved in the two experiments were either removed completely from the location (70%) or were moved considerable distances from their original placement (30%). Only long-bone splinters and impact chips remained at their original location. In addition, none of these in situ items were gnawed or in any way modified by scavenging animals. It is apparent that these observations provide no support for the proposition that scavenging animals, particularly hyenas, will gnaw bones in the locations where they are encountered.

Follow-up observations. In the case of both experiments, follow-up observation revealed that the location of recovered bone did not change significantly after the first night of exposure. Because we wanted to use the same locations for subsequent experiments, we removed the bones used in Experiments 1A and 1B after 2 days, prior to placing new experiments in the same locations.

EXPERIMENTS 2A AND 2B

Experiments 1A and 1B involved bones with some attached meat and tissue, which would clearly have been of interest to scavenging animals. If hominids had processed animal parts for food, however, it is likely that very little meat would remain on the subsequently abandoned bones. In order to evaluate whether the presence or absence of tissue would result in different treatment of bones by scavenging hyenas, two additional experiments were carried out. For both of these experiments bones were cleaned of all adhering meat and tissue. After cleaning, the bones were allowed to dry for 1 (Experiment 2A) or 2 (Experiment 2B) days. In this time even the smallest remnants of tissues had hardened and were reduced in size.

Experiment 2A

The location at the dump site used for Experiment 1A was also used for Experiment 2A. Seven completely defleshed buffalo femora were carried to the site, along with three complete humeri. None of these bones had any attached elements. The following bone units were placed between the two stakes in the pattern shown in Figure 24.8: two complete, unbroken femora; five proximal femora, three of which were broken with long spiral fractures and had the marrow removed; five distal femora, three of which no longer had marrow; two proximal and two distal humeri in which the marrow remained; and one proximal and one distal humerus with the marrow removed. In the process of breaking the bones, 19 large, unattached bone splinters and 13 impact chips were produced.

Bone Displacement. The arrangement of bones was completed by 4:35 P.M. on August 20, 1986. Shortly afterwards, Marabou storks appeared and quickly consumed the pile of bone marrow left between the two stakes. By 5:15 P.M. the storks had abandoned the location, and two bones had been moved: a proximal humerus with

Figure 24.8. Arrangement of defleshed bones at the dump site (Experiment 2A); note bone splinters in center.

marrow had been dragged 1.2 m south of its original location, and two long-bone splinters were moved 1 m east of their original position.

The next morning the following modifications had occurred in our original experimental arrangement. First, all of the articular ends or basic bone units had been removed from the experiment area. Second, remaining on the site in essentially the same position were 12 of the original 19 long-bone splinters and the 13 impact chips. *As in the previous experiments, none of the bones remaining at the site showed any tooth-inflicted modifications.*

Of the 18 major bone elements exclusive of long-bone splinters and chips, only 6 could be found nearby. Their distribution was similar to those from Experiment 1A; they were an average of 17.7 m west of their original positions, the closest distance being 10 m and the farthest being 30.9 m.

A comparison between Experiments 1A and 2A in terms of the numbers of recovered bones and their condition is presented in Table 24.6. The results of the two experiments are similar, particularly the percentages of recovered bones with marrow present versus marrow removed. There seems to be a consistent bias in both experiments in the removal of bones with remaining edible marrow. An unexpected result was the recovery of more original bone elements from Experiment 1A (40%) than from Experiment 2A (33%) despite the presence of adhering meat and tissue on the bones from the first experiment.

Gnawing patterns. Six bone elements were recovered with the following visible modifications.

Proximal femora. One proximal femur (marrow originally removed) exhibited tooth pitting and scoring of the greater trochanter. Tooth scoring was present on the dorsal surface of the femoral head, and a large tooth puncture was apparent on the ventral margin. Two radial tooth scores occurred on the shaft just below the articular end.

Another proximal femur (marrow originally removed) exhibited extensive scooping out of the greater trochanter and considerable tooth scoring on the dorsal surface of the femoral head. Three deep tooth punctures were present along the ventral margin of the femoral head.

The third proximal femur (marrow originally present) was extensively damaged.

Table 24.6

Relationship of Recovered Bones to Method of Experimental Preparation (Experiments 1A and 2A)

	Articular ends[a]		Complete bones with marrow	% Original elements recovered
	Marrow present	Marrow removed		
2A: number in original distribution	10	8	2	
2A: number recovered	1 (10%)	5 (63%)	0	33
Comparison with 1A	2 (17%)	6 (75%)	0	40

[a] Includes whole bones with marrow, tabulated as one unit each.

The greater trochanter was completely absent. The dorsal surface of the femoral head had multiple, deep tooth scores. The ventral margin of the femoral neck was extensively tooth-pitted and partially eaten away. Minor radial tooth scoring was present at the base of the articular end, and the marrow cavity had been split open by two tooth punctures.

Proximal humerus. One proximal humerus (marrow originally removed) was missing one-half of the articular head. There was extensive tooth scoring on the remaining one-half, with tooth scoring, punctures, and scooping out of the ventral margin. The trochanter was scooped out, and three transverse tooth scores were visible on the shaft.

Distal femur. One distal femur (marrow originally removed) had scooping out along the anterior surface of the articular channel at the juncture with the shaft. Several transverse tooth scores occurred on the shaft just proximal to the scooped out area.

Distal humerus. One distal humerus (marrow originally removed) appeared to be unmodified.

Experiment 2B

On August 21, 1986, the bushveld location described for Experiment 1B was again used as the site of Experiment 2B. Two complete humeri and four complete femora of African buffalo, all defleshed and dried for 2 days, were transported to the site. The two humeri were unmodified complete bones, but all four femora were broken at the site. The marrow was removed from the medullary cavities of three proximal and three distal ends and was placed near the anvil. The three bone splinters and 19 impact chips produced in Experiment 1B were left in place, and the additional 15 long-bone splinters and 49 impact chips produced by fracturing the femora were left where they fell around the anvil. Figure 24.9 illustrates the distribution of bone elements involved in Experiment 2B.

Bone displacement. The experimental arrangement was completed by 5:15 P.M., and there was no further monitoring until the following morning at 8:30 A.M. At that time fresh hyena spoor was visible around the periphery of the outcrop, and no major bone elements remained on the experimental site (Figure 24.10). A search of the area resulted in the recovery of three bone elements in the same general area as the bones from Experiment 1B. The two proximal femora and one distal femur (all with marrow originally removed) represent 30% of the bone elements originally introduced to the experiment location. The most distant bone was 37.0 m from its original position and the nearest was 18.2 m, yielding a mean transport distance of 30.7 m.

The results of Experiment 2B, summarized in Table 24.7, are consistent with the observations recorded for Experiments 1A and 2A at the dump site location; there is a clear bias in the complete removal from the location of bones that contained marrow. In contrast, in Experiment 1B the bias was in favor of removal of bones without marrow. We conclude that although there is some variation there does appear to be a bias favoring the complete removal of bones with edible tissue.

Gnawing pattern. One distal femur was recovered with several tooth pits on the

Figure 24.9. Original distribution of bones in Experiment 2B.

Figure 24.10. Resulting distribution of bones in Experiment 2B after hyena gnawing.

Table 24.7

Relationship of Experimental Preparation to Number of Bones Recovered

	Articular ends[a]		
	Marrow present	Marrow removed	Complete bones with marrow
Experiment 2B: Bones originally present	4	6	2
Number/percentage recovered	0	3 (50%)	0
Experiment 2A: Number/percentage recovered	1 (13%)	5 (63%)	0
Experiment 1B: Number/percentage recovered	1 (13%)	1 (25%)	1 (50%)

[a] Includes whole bones with marrow, tabulated as one unit each.

articular surfaces of both condyles. Two proximal femora were heavily tooth-scored on the dorsal surfaces of the femoral head. One was so heavily scooped out in the area of the femoral neck that the articular end was split into two parts, a portion of shaft adhering to both parts. The greater trochanter of this femur was tooth-pitted and partially gnawed away. The second proximal femur was missing a portion of the greater trochanter, and transverse tooth scoring was visible just below the distal end of the greater trochanter.

Follow-Up observations. The bones remaining from Experiments 2A and 2B were left where they were found and were monitored for one week. In both cases there was essentially no change in their inventory or distribution after the first night of exposure. At the dump site the distribution was modified slightly by the repositioning (possibly by birds) of some bones an average of 90 cm from the locations noted after the first night of exposure. There appeared to be no pattern to this subsequent movement. Similarly, there were no additional modifications to the bones.

SUMMARY OF EXPERIMENTAL FINDINGS

Bone Displacement

Two general observations are apparent regarding the removal of bones from their original locations. First, all bones gnawed by hyenas were moved from their original locations. Second, the bone elements remaining in their original positions were either long-bone splinters or impact chips, and none of them had been gnawed by hyenas.

Spatial patterning. Table 24.8 summarizes the spatial data derived from the four experiments. Since a general correspondence is clear between the locations where experiments were conducted and the mean distances and ranges of transported bones, we suspect that the locations to which hyenas move for gnawing scavenged bones vary considerably with local topography or types of vegetation. For this reason the specific hyena transport distances in these experiments cannot be considered typical of all hyenas; rather, we can expect hyenas to respond to local conditions from one encounter situation to another. If we use the data from these experiments as a

Table 24.8
Summary of Findings

	Mean transport distance (m)	Range of distances (m)
Dump site	17.1	6.0–25.1
Experiment 1A	17.7	10.0–30.9
Experiment 2A		
Bushveld site		
Experiment 1B	34.9	33.4–35.9
Experiment 2B	30.7	18.2–37.0
Summary	21.4	6.0–37.0

guide to the spatial patterning of faunal assemblages expected to remain at archaeological sites after hyena scavenging, however, we would expect to recover only impact chips, long-bone splinters, and perhaps nonmeaty, fragmentary by-products of hominid food processing. None of these items would exhibit tooth-inflicted marks. Bones with evidence of animal gnawing would be expected to occur as a peripheral distribution varying in concentration as a result of topographic and vegetational conditions between 6 and 38 m from the original localization of bones abandoned by hominids. Using the mean distance of 21.4 m for the bones we recovered following hyena transport, we might expect a peripheral distribution of larger, originally more meaty bone elements arranged peripherally to the center of the original distribution at a mean distance of 21 m.

Bias in the bone distribution. In our study we have reported that hyenas often completely remove bones with some adhering meat or containing marrow. This means that there is a bias in the recovered bones that favors those without adhering meat and marrow. What does this bias mean strictly in terms of anatomical parts? Table 24.9 summarizes the anatomical part frequencies involved in all four experiments and compares these frequencies to the number of parts that were subsequently recovered. It is clear from this tabulation that fewer distal segments of femora were recovered than proximal segments. In two of the four experiments, the distal segments were attached to other bones by connective tissue; they represented more food potential and therefore were more often totally removed from the site. Binford maintains that two factors—the degree of bone breakage and the presence or absence of adhering

Table 24.9
Comparison of Anatomical Part Totals Originally Present in Experiments versus Those Recovered[a]

	PH	DH	PR	PC	PF	DF	PT	PAT
Originally present	11	11	6	6	24	22	15	15
Number recovered	3/27%	4/36%	3/50%	3/50%	9/38%	3/14%	2/13%	0/0%

[a] PH, proximal humerus; DH, distal humerus; PR, proximal radius; PC, proximal cubitus; PF, proximal femur; DF, distal femur; PT, proximal tibia; PAT, patella.

meat—condition carnivore bone selection and the subsequent pattern of tooth marks inflicted by gnawing. At an archaeological site, the selection by scavenging carnivores of bones for gnawing should be a reflection of the degree of hominid exploitation of the same bones, prior to abandonment of the site. If bones with meat or marrow are discarded, then we could expect considerable carnivore transport and gnawing, with only bone fragments and splinters remaining in their original position. Our experience would lead us to expect the removal of complete bones and articular end segments from any site in which hominids were only marginally exploiting such segments.

Gnawing Pattern

Mills has studied hyena behavior extensively (Mills 1978, 1984a, 1984b, 1985; Mills and Mills 1977, 1978) and notes that this carnivore species regularly exploits the marrow contained in long bones devoid of meat, although they also consistently gnaw on and digest bones without either adhering meat or marrow. Hyenas get access to the marrow of large, disarticulated bones by holding the bone upright with their forefeet (Figure 24.11) and licking and biting at an articular end until it is destroyed. Sometimes this process is interrupted and a partially consumed articular end is abandoned. In either case, bone splinters are produced and may be eaten in the process of bone destruction and marrow consumption or they may be ignored. It is unlikely that unconsumed bone splinters would show tooth-inflicted modifications from gnawing, since hyenas either consume a splinter completely or leave it unmodified except for any marks that occurred on that portion of the bone before it became detached. In any event, scavenging hyenas do not gnaw bone splinters—they eat them or ignore them.

The following gnawing patterns were observed on the bones used in our experiments and are consistent with observed scavenging hyena behavior.

Proximal femora. In our experiments, nine of the proximal femora were gnawed and abandoned by hyenas and then recovered by us. The dorsal surface of the femoral heads were heavily tooth-pitted and -scored in all nine cases. Because of butchering disarticulation, this surface was accessible for gnawing. The pattern of tooth scoring indicates that hyenas used the upper surface of the femoral heads for seating their maxillary or mandibular teeth while using their opposing teeth to puncture and scoop out the ventral edge of the femoral head and adjacent femoral neck. Eight of the nine recovered bones had modifications in this area, and two had sufficient bone tissue removed to justify a description of being partially gnawed away. In addition, the necks of two femora were scooped out, while four others had only tooth punctures along the ventral margin of the femoral head and neck.

This pattern is very different from that which is commonly observed at a kill-site carcass (see Binford 1981a:75, Figures 3.48 and 3.49). In such a situation, the greater trochanter is most often tooth-pitted and partially destroyed, while the femoral head and neck normally remain unscarred. In our experiments the modifications to the greater trochanter ranged from almost total destruction to very minor tooth scoring, but the heaviest carnivore modification was focused on the femoral head and neck, which are unavailable for gnawing at a fully articulated kill-site carcass. Another

Figure 24.11. Spotted hyena gnawing bone (photograph by Mills).

divergence from the kill-site gnawing pattern is the relatively rare occurrence in our specimens of heavy transverse tooth scoring just below the greater trochanter. This pattern is common when animals gnaw the femur while it is articulated, but it was not a common observation in our experiments.

Distal femora. Three distal femora were recovered: one from Experiment 1A, involving a bone with attached meat, and one each from Experiments 2A and 2B, in which cleaned bones were used. These bones displayed patterns of destruction most common in situations in which the patella is attached to the joint, implying articulation with the proximal tibia. This is characterized by scooping out and tooth puncturing of the trochlea at its juncture with the anterior surface of the femoral shaft (see Binford 1981a:74–75, Figs. 3.46 and 3.47). This pattern is a common by-product of the removal of the patella by gnawing animals, although occasionally it is observed on disarticulated femora. Tooth scoring on the ventral face of the articular condyles is common on disarticulated distal femora, and the specimens in our experiments were modified in this way. Tooth pitting along the outer edges of both the lateral and medial condyles was also apparent on these three bones, which is also a feature of the gnawing of disarticulated segments. Transverse tooth scoring was noted only on one specimen, which also exhibited heavy scooping out of the proximal trochlea.

Proximal humeri. Three proximal humeri were recovered, and all were gnawed in similar ways. As on the proximal femora, the dorsal surfaces of the large articular balls were heavily tooth-scored and -pitted, as were the corresponding ventral surfaces where gnawing animals seat their teeth. In all cases tooth pitting was adjacent to the scooped out margins and on both the lateral and medial tuberosities. The destruction was much less extensive than that produced when an animal gnaws a humerus still articulated with a scapula. In that case, the tuberosities will be heavily damaged and the surface of the articular head will be essentially free of tooth pitting and scoring. In gnawing of articulated humeri, transverse tooth scoring is frequently a feature below the humeral head and around the neck of the shaft. Tooth scoring of this type, observed on only one specimen, consisted of two short tooth marks.

Distal humeri. Four distal humeri were recovered, three with attached proximal radio-cubiti. One was unmodified except for some tissue removal; no tooth scoring was noted. Two specimens had been stripped of all meat and exhibited minor tooth scoring and pitting on the medial margins of the condyles. The remaining element had no attached radio-cubitus and displayed moderate tooth scoring on the head of the condyle. The modifications made to the proximal cubitus, however, were typical of articulated bones in which the proximal ends are simply gnawed away (Binford 1981a:73). In Binford's experience this is relatively rare at carcasses and occurs more often in dens or situations in which the joint is being gnawed for bone marrow rather than for meat.

Proximal Tibiae. Two proximal tibiae were recovered. Both bones had been disarticulated by the cull butchers, who sawed either through or just below the articular ends. The placement of the saw cuts appears to have affected the ways in which animals gnawed these bones since both had heavy tooth punctures inside the saw cut. This type of damage is not associated with carnivore processing of either articulated limb bones or disarticulated whole or broken bones.

COMPARISON WITH ISAAC'S EXPERIMENTS

In his seminal experiment directed toward understanding the consequences of hyena scavenging of faunal remains generated by humans, Glynn Isaac (1983a) found that 82 (71%) of the original population of 115 bones "placed at a peg" had been completely removed from the location by scavenging animals. In our experiments the results were somewhat different, in that fracturing the bones produced a high frequency of very tiny impact chips, which may have been much smaller than the bones discussed by Isaac. If we ignore these impact chips, our experiments included a total of 65 large bone units and 42 long-bone splinters. We recovered 20 large bone units (69% removed) and 34 long-bone splinters (19% removed), resulting in an average of only

44% of the total assemblage being removed. In short, more small bones remained in their original positions in our experiments than in Isaac's. The percentage of large bones relative to small bones removed from the location is similar to Isaac's results, however: 69% of ours were totally removed compared to 71% in Isaac's experiments. We may then generalize that more of our small bones remained in their original positions and more of our large bones were recovered than in Isaac's experiment. Large bones were more often removed completely or were moved greater distances than small bones.

When we consider the spatial patterning produced by the "carnivore filter" that repositions faunal remains modified by humans, our data are somewhat more "radical" than Isaac's. For instance, 80% of the total number of recovered large bones in Isaac's experiment remained within roughly 9 m of their original locations, while only 4.5% of our large bones were recovered within that distance of their original locations. The mean distance from the original location of Isaac's recovered large bones was approximately 4.2 m, while in our experiments the mean distance of recovered large bones from their original locations was 17.1 m. An opposite pattern is observed for recovered small bones; 66% of the small bones that Isaac recovered remained within 3 m of their original locations, whereas all of our recovered small bones remained in their original locations.

For both large and small bones, Isaac's remnant pattern is more diffuse or carries a suggestion of smearing outward from the original distribution. In contrast, in all four of our experiments the result is a discrete placement in which 81% of the small bones remained exactly where we left them and larger bones were moved a minimum of 6 m, with the majority having been moved an average 21.4 m and all but one of the transported bones located between 10 and 37 m from their original positions. Perhaps some of this difference is referable to the fact that Isaac presented a summary of distributional data reflecting cumulative forces acting on an assemblage deposited accretionally over a 2-month period. Our data reflect primarily hyena behavior, and each experiment involved the restructuring actions of hyenas on discrete deposits in only a single night. Even when samples remained exposed for longer periods of time, no subsequent activity by hyenas was noted. In contrast, Isaac's experiment may reflect some simply mechanical displacement of bone occurring as a by-product of animal movement or dragging of bones.

Another possible cause of the diffuseness noted in Isaac's experiment may be the behavior of birds, which can relocate bones but which do not leave gnaw marks. In our discussion of Experiment 1A we reported that birds had actually moved one large bone 2.8 m from its original location, and two bone splinters had been moved 1.8 and 2.2 m, respectively, prior to the arrival of hyenas at the site. In a supplementary experiment described only briefly here, six large bones that had previously been gnawed by hyenas were placed in a discrete localization along with 10 long-bone splinters not previously used in the experiments; these bones were later studied for indications of modifications in their distribution produced by birds. Two large bones had been moved 2.1 and 1.9 m, while five bone splinters were moved 2.4, 1.8, 2.2, 0.8, and 0.9 m, respectively. Five bone splinters and four large bones remained undisturbed.

A summary of our observations at Experiments 1A and 2A, where scavenging birds had access to a total of 38 large bones, showed that 3 (8%) were moved a mean distance of 2.4 m from their original locations. Similarly, when birds had access to 23 long-bone splinters, 7 (30%) were moved a mean distance of 1.62 m. Although we do not know whether scavenging birds were additional agents of bone movement in Isaac's experiment, the scale of movement documented here for birds could well account for much of the smearing characteristic of Isaac's spatial distribution.

With regard to the important issue of the distribution of gnawed bones, Isaac unfortunately did not describe the bones remaining in his experiments in terms of gnawing patterns. We think it is likely that most of the small bones were not gnawed, but it is regrettable that we do not have detailed information about the large bones. In our experiments, however, the pattern is clear: no bones remaining in their original positions were gnawed, whereas all but one of the larger bones transported a mean distance of 21.4 m from their original positions were distinctively and identifiably gnawed by hyenas.

CONCLUSIONS

Four experiments were conducted to investigate the impact of hyena scavenging on faunal assemblages created by humans. The results of all four experiments are clear and unequivocal and can be summarized by two general observations. First, *all bones gnawed by hyenas were moved from their original locations.* Second, *the bone elements remaining in their original positions were either long-bone splinters or impact chips, and none of them had been gnawed by hyenas.* These findings are incompatible with the argument that hyenas gnawed in place the bones recovered from the Zinj floor (FLK 22) at Olduvai Gorge after hominids had abandoned them. If we position our experimental results over the actual Zinj floor artifact distributions, we find that most of the gnawed bones would be expected to occur outside the excavated area (except perhaps for a concentration in the southwest corner). Similarly, all bones remaining in the centers of dense stone tool concentrations should be small, un-gnawed bone splinters.

Two interesting features are evident from an examination of the distribution of gnawed (Figure 24.1C) and cut-marked (Figure 24.1D) bone at the Zinj site relative to the artifact distribution shown in Figure 24.1A. First, gnawed bone occurs within the zone of dense artifact concentration, but it appears to be less dense and distributed over a slightly larger area than are the artifacts. Second, the distribution of cut-marked bone is similar to the gnawed bone; also centered in the areas of high artifact density, it similarly expands beyond the borders of dense artifact localization. We may generalize that both the gnawed bone and the tool-inflicted cut-marked bone, although centered isomorphically with the artifact distributions, are distributed over a slightly larger area. In addition, there is slightly better definition in the bone distributions of the elongate concentration (Kroll and Isaac 1984:23). These recognized areas are shown schematically in Figure 24.12).

What is clear about the distributions is that while the elongate concentration is

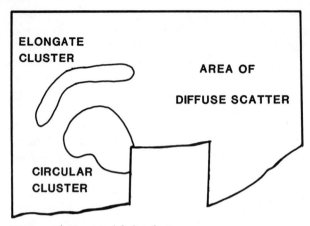

Figure 24.12. Model distribution.

peripheral to the circular distribution, there is no peripheral concentration of gnawed bone relative to either. Second, the bone distribution as a whole is slightly more extensive than the artifact distribution, and if one acknowledges that the elongate distribution is a spatial component of the hominid-generated site structure, then there is no independent distribution of either gnawed bone or cut-marked bone peripheral to this compound structure. The distribution of conjoining pieces reported by Kroll and Isaac (1984:26) demonstrates nicely that for carnivore-gnawed and cut-marked bone specimens the refits regularly link the elongate distribution and the circular distribution, strongly supporting the view that both localizations are the result of a single set of formation conditions arising in the context of hominid activities. We therefore conclude that there is no independent distribution of gnawed bones arranged peripherally to the original hominid-generated placement of bones. Such a pattern would of course be expected if scavenging hyena had gnawed the bones after hominid processing, and in addition we would expect the bone remaining within the processing area not to be gnawed.

In this regard, Mills has noted that the behavior of hyenas in any bone-chewing situation will vary in response to several factors. The numbers of hyenas involved, as well as their species, may determine how far and in which directions the bones will be carried. A solitary spotted hyena is less likely to transport bones from a central site than is a group of hyenas; however, any accumulation of bones is likely to attract several spotted hyenas, in which case the bones would be carried off for consumption away from possible competitors, as was seen in our experiments. The greater the number of hyenas involved, the further the bones might be dispersed from the original site. On the other hand, a single brown or striped hyena would be likely to transport bones from an accumulation and store them nearby. Even with these species, however, it is likely that an accumulation of bones would attract more than one individual.

It is extremely unlikely that carnivores, particularly hyenas, would not severely disrupt the arrangement of bones at a hominid "home base"; therefore, the bones that show evidence of hyena gnawing at a site such as FLK 22 (the Zinj floor) were probably chewed on prior to hominid acquisition and disposal. The most plausible implication of the anatomical part distribution data at the Zinj site is that the hominids were scavenging still-useful parts from carcasses abandoned by other, nonhominid carnivores.

This observation brings us to the second point in our discussion of site structure. Kroll and Isaac's (1984) distribution study does not distinguish among bones in terms of size. Nevertheless, the very first discussion of the Zinj floor included the observation that the bone occurring at least in the circular concentration was highly fragmented and generally small. Subsequent pattern recognition studies by Ohel (1977) using Leakey's (1971:Fig. 24) map of the floor showed that the clustered circular distribution defined by the stone tools (Figure 24.1A) yielded some 700 (97%) small bone fragments and only 12 (3%) large bone units. If this bias in size is sustained by the more complete data presumably available to some researchers, then our experimental results would lead us to expect few if any gnawed bones in the circular concentration, and gnawed larger bones should be distributed peripherally. As Figure 24.1C indicates, however, there is a significant amount of gnawed bone in the circular concentration on the Zinj floor.

Even if the elongate area were to be considered a peripheral distribution, this area would only be 2–3 m from the edges of the circular distribution or 5–6 m from its center. As we have pointed out, Isaac's experiment showed a smeared distribution of larger bone at roughly this scale, but we do not know if any of his bones were gnawed. Based on our experience, we would not expect such bones to be gnawed. Smearing of a localization at this small scale is much more likely to result from physical activity on the location and/or from the action of birds, neither of which would produce hyena-gnawed bone.

All of the currently published data on the site structure of the Zinj floor strongly support the conclusions advanced by Kroll and Isaac (1984:25) "that hominids formed the spatial pattern of bones" in the circular and elongated clusters. The high frequency of gnawed bones within these clusters is contrary to all experimental data on hyena gnawing behavior thus far known. We suggest that a hominid-produced spatial pattern that incorporates animal-gnawed bone as an essential component of that pattern could only occur if the gnawing had been present on the bones prior to the hominid production of the "site."

We began our discussion of the Zinj floor by pointing to a paradox inherent in the interpretative arguments as they have appeared in the literature. We noted that while it was argued that the animal gnawing on the bones from the Zinj floor was inflicted by hyenas who scavenged the site after hominid abandonment, at the same time it was simply assumed that the summary properties of the faunal assemblage from the total excavation could be used as the basis for the reconstruction of hominid diet (see Bunn 1982b, 1983a). In the most recent restatement of the hunting hypothesis, Bunn and Kroll (1986a) attempt to neutralize the paradoxical aspects of earlier arguments by maintaining that post-hominid scavenging hyena behavior accounts for the fact that the anatomical part frequencies reported from the Zinj floor do not indicate a bias in favor of meat-yielding parts. By postulating the original presence on the site of meaty limbs not present at the time of excavation because of removal by scavenging hyena, they bolster their view that the occupants of the Zinjanthropus floor were consumers of large quantities of meaty animal parts. As a result of this new argument, the reality of the postulated scavenging hyena at FLK-22 becomes a crucial piece of knowledge needed for the meaningful interpretation of the Zinj floor.

The meat-yielding bones that Bunn and Kroll claim were removed by scavenging hyenas after hominid processing include 20 complete tibiae, 16 complete femora, and 8 complete radio-cubiti, none of which were represented by articular ends in the faunal assemblage at the time of excavation (Bunn and Kroll 1986a:435, Table 3). Two additional types of skeletal parts, metapodials and humeri, were not removed by postulated scavenging hyenas because they are said to be "of relatively low nutritional value that would not have been particularly susceptible to selective removal by scavenging carnivores" (Bunn and Kroll 1986a:436). In this model of selective bone removal, hyenas are said to have removed both meat-yielding bones of the upper rear leg but only one bone from the upper front leg subsequent to extensive meat and marrow removal by hominids.

Our data certainly demonstrate selectivity but the removal bias is related to bone marrow; this is seen in the removal of complete bones (Table 24.1, 24.4, 24.6, and 24.7) and in the biased removal of broken bones, regardless of anatomical origin, that still contained marrow. Parts that offered neither meat nor marrow but only cancellous tissue were least often removed (Tables 24.6 and 24.7).

In Experiments 1A and 1B, where some meat remained on the bone units, proximal ends of both femora and humeri were recovered, with a strong recovery bias favoring those articular ends from which marrow had been removed (Table 24.10). Put in terms of hyena feeding strategy, when meat is minimally present, the bias in total bone unit removal is in favor of bones containing marrow, regardless of anatomical part. When greater amounts of meat were present, as was the case for all except one distal end in Experiments 1A and 1B, the bias shifts to favor meat, regardless of the presence or absence of marrow. Our results indicate that selection bias is not related to anatomical part per se (humerus versus femur) but appears to be determined by the state of the bones (with or without marrow, or with or without meat).

It is interesting to apply what we learned about the factors producing bias in hyena bone removal to the event sequence at the Zinj site outlined by Bunn and Kroll. They propose that femora were removed from the Zinj site in a biased way relative to

Table 24.10

Anatomical Part Recovery Involving Bone Units with Some Adhering Meat (Experiments 1A and 1B)

	Proximal ends		Distal ends	
	No marrow	With marrow	No marrow	With marrow
Originally present	8	7	8	7
Recovered	4 (50%)	1 (14%)	2 (25%)	2 (29%)

humeri because of their higher nutritional value. Given what we know about hyena bone removal bias, however, in order to accept a Bunn and Kroll scenario in which all humeri were ignored by hyena in favor of femora, we would have to imagine that all humeri had been fully processed by hominids for both meat and marrow, while a significant number of femora still containing marrow were abandoned by hominids and attracted scavenging hyena. Since Bunn and Kroll use the presence of femoral shaft splinters to indicate what they claim were originally whole femora processed by hominids for meat but not marrow, we must imagine (a) that hominids exploited only the humerus but not the femur for marrow and (b) that subsequently hyenas gnawed open all of the femoral shafts exactly where they found them on the Zinj site, ate the contained bone marrow, left the bone splinters, and carried off from the site the remaining articular end from each femur from which marrow had been consumed (hyenas partially destroy at least one articular end in the process of getting access to the marrow). We must also imagine that all *humeral* articular ends remaining from marrow processing by hominids were ignored by scavenging hyena.

An equally improbable alternative is that hominids processed all humeri and femora for both meat and bone marrow, abandoned the articular ends, and, subsequently, scavenging hyenas selectively removed all femoral articular ends, despite the absence of either meat or marrow, and ignored humeral parts in a similar state.

In either case, for Bunn and Kroll's arguments to be sustained, we have to propose that ancient hyenas did not approach the removal of parts from the Zinj floor in terms of nutritional potential but behaved in a more cultural fashion with a bias that is unrelated to food value but instead reflects what hyenas "like" to chew.

The scale at which hyenas remove bones is quite high: approximately 71% total removal in Isaac's experiment and 69% in our experiments for large bones. Assuming, as Bunn and Kroll do, that hyenas did scavenge the Zinj floor, and if the frequency of gnawed pieces can be regarded as some clue to the extent of this scavenging, then certainly more than half of the large bones would be missing from the site. With a scavenger "filter" operating at this level, there is no possible justification for treating the remnant bone deposit as an accurate or even a suggestive sample of hominid animal processing and consumption activities, much less as an example of hominid procurement activities. All of Bunn's arguments about the significance of the Zinj floor bone assemblage may be dismissed as mere wishful thinking if the presence of the carnivore filter is used to explain the animal-gnawed bone.

Other problems are apparent in the arguments about the behavior of the early hominids at the Zinj location. The work on site structure is problematic for those who insist on interpreting the summary data from the total excavation. Ohel's (1977) pattern recognition work reveals major differences between the faunal content of the clustered circular distributions relative to the remainder of the site, e.g., the area shown as diffuse scatter in Figure 24.12. Those familiar with the data have recognized the difference and have commented that large items tend to occur in the zones of diffuse scatter. In the earlier literature it was simply assumed that since the Zinj site was by definition a "living floor," the zones of diffuse scatter could be interpreted as the outer edges of the site. Binford (1981a) challenged this view after conducting a multivariate analysis of the faunal material from all of the reported Olduvai sites. That analysis indicated important differences in the composition of faunas occurring on the "floors" and suggested that these differences probably related to the operation of independent formation processes that contributed differentially to the summary composition of fauna on different "sites." This view has been consistently "doubted" (Isaac 1984a) or simply ignored.

If we review the data currently available on the site structure of the Zinj locality, some interesting and provocative facts appear that are germane to this controversy. In the distribution maps for artifactual material of different sizes published by Kroll and Isaac (1984:Fig. 12), one notes immediately that the distribution of small flakes and flake fragments (Figure 24.13A) defines nicely the nucleus of the bone distributions illustrated here in Figures 24.1C and 24.1D. Turning to the distribution of large lithic elements (greater than 40 mm), we note a totally independent distribution, with the greatest number of pieces occurring in areas other than those defined as the circular and elongate concentrations. The medium-size pieces exhibit a pattern that has some characteristics of both the large and the small plots. Any differences in the spatial distribution of bone in terms of size is unclear from the Kroll and Isaac (1984) distribution maps, but in the map prepared by Leakey (1971:Fig. 24) a scattered,

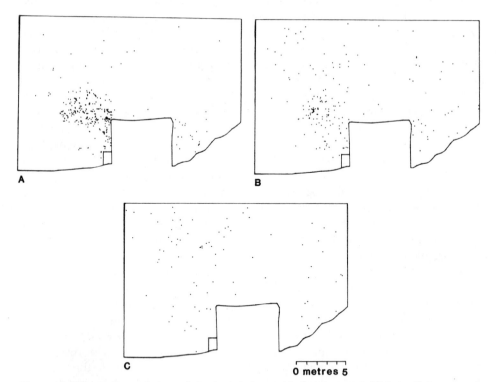

Figure 24.13. Dissected plans of FLK Zinj showing the distributions of (A) small (0–19 mm), (B) medium (20–39 mm), and (C) large (>40 mm) flakes and flake fragments. The plans include pieces plotted in situ as well as well as those recovered by screening and assigned random positions within their 1 × 1-m units of recovery (from Kroll and Isaac 1984: Fig. 12).

unclustered, "diffuse" distribution of large bone is evident across the site. Ohel (1977) also notes that large bone is distributed independently of the small, fragmented bone.

Based on a comparison with other locations, we strongly suspect that the diffuse scatters of large bones and large lithics result from a generalized, episodal accumulation on the landscape that is unrelated in any integrated fashion to the localized activities indicated by the circular and elongate clusters (Figure 24.12). If so, the summary of *all* the fauna from the Zinj excavations represents an aggregate of materials deposited in very different and, most likely, independent contexts. How can such an aggregate be used to argue about food-procurement proclivities of the hominids responsible for the circular and elongated clusters of tools and bones? Such a procedure only makes sense if the analyst has made up his mind—believes before analysis—that the diverse patterning demonstrable on the floor represents the structured consequences of differentiated hominid activities occurring in the context of a single occupation. Determining whether such a single occupation ever occurred is, of course, one reason why archaeologists conduct analysis of the data. Evaluating the likelihood of such a past condition is what research should be directed toward. Instead, Bunn and Kroll assume this condition prevailed in the past and they structure their data in these terms. Not only are Bunn and Kroll's (1986a) arguments internally inconsistent, but they present their conclusions as the justification for the form, presentation, and discussion of data.

We cannot overemphasize the fact that research does not advance by the simple restatement of uniformed suggestions and guesses about the dynamics of the past. Nor is our understanding advanced by arguments that are inherently self-contradictory. We must identify the knowledge we need to acquire in order to make interpretation possible, and then we must proceed with the necessary research. For instance, the relationship between animal gnawing behavior and diagnostic criteria for recognizing past processes is crucial, so more experiments of the kind reported here are planned.

Presently available information points to a recognizable and diagnostic gnawing pattern characteristic of bones gnawed by a single species at sites where whole carcasses are being consumed versus the situation in which a gnawing animal has access to already dismembered carcasses and broken bones. The gnawing pattern on the bones from the Zinj floor needs to be reported in detail before there is more speculation about the substantial consumption of "meaty" parts by the hominids who are also alleged to have had early access to "meaty" carcasses—a not so veiled allusion to hunting.

An example of research designed to reduce ignorance is the fieldwork of Robert Blumenschine, whose conclusions contribute to the interpretive perspective being argued here. Given our current knowledge of animal scavenging, if animals had gnawed the bones on the Zinj floor after the hominids had abandoned their site, there is no way the animal-gnawed bone could have maintained an isomorphic distribution with the stone tools and cut-marked bone. In light of the current evidence we have argued that the observed distributions could only have resulted from the bones having been gnawed prior to their introduction to the site by the hominids. This condition certainly identifies scavenging as the mode of procurement for animal products at the Zinj site.

Blumenschine's work supports this view. He notes that the summary data available on body sizes and anatomical parts "are consistent with . . . scavenged bone assemblages" (Blumenschine 1986:144). We expect that when the gnawing pattern is finally described for the tooth-marked bone from the Zinj floor it will be recognizable as a pattern inflicted by gnawing animals at a carcass. It is also imperative that the faunal material be described in subsets representing the clearly different structural areas on the Zinj floor. Only then will it be possible to evaluate whether these areas do or do not represent different and independent formation conditions. Continuing to discuss the "assemblage" of either tools or fauna as if it reliably referred to only a single hominid "occupation" with organizational integrity ensures that we will not be able to interpret accurately the total body of data available from this important location.

NOTES

1. At the same time that these arguments were being made, Binford (1984c) was researching the problem of how to recognize the sequence in which modifying agents might have had access to the faunal assemblages recovered at archaeological sites. Using data supplied by Richardson (1980a, 1980b). Binford noted that the patterns of tooth-inflicted destruction or marking on bones gnawed by carnivores at kill sites were distinctly different in terms of placement, frequency, and type of tooth-inflicted marks from the patterns of modification produced by gnawing animals either at dens or when presented with already disarticulated and processed bones. This patterning has direct implications for the data from the Zinj floor. If hominids were introducing to that site disarticulated body parts scavenged from carnivore-ravaged carcasses, the pattern of carnivore tooth marks would be expected to reflect the status of carnivores as first feeders. If, on the other hand, hominids were the initial feeders, and if carnivores had scavenged the debris from hominid processing and feeding, the patterns of carnivore-inflicted modifications would *not* resemble those produced at kill sites. Publication of a detailed description of the gnawing patterns observable on the faunal assemblages from the Zinj floor would make such a discrimination possible and is therefore encouraged. (In the study reported here, we describe the gnawing patterns we observed, but unfortunately their similarity to or difference from those on the Zinj floor materials cannot be assessed.)

2. This implication does not apply to Binford's results since he used multivariate analytical techniques that were designed to reveal multiple "causes" operating on the assemblage recovered by the excavators.

Chapter 25

Were There Elephant Hunters at Torralba?

In recent years there has been growing skepticism among some students of the pre-*sapiens sapiens* hominids that the earlier romantic views, which pictured early man as a mighty hunter, are an accurate construction of the past. In fact, the trend in much recent work has been to modify this view and to see as unwarranted much of the evidence previously cited in support of the "mighty hunter" view of the past. Some have begun the serious investigation of the distinct possibility that early man was more commonly a scavenger of animal carcasses than a successful predator. This view, while seriously discussed for the pre-*Homo erectus* hominids, has not been popularly adopted for the investigation of *Homo erectus* himself. In fact, many theorists consider *Homo erectus* to be the author of what is referred to as the "hunting way of life" and believe that this shift may in fact stand behind the species' successful radiation into new environmental zones (Shipman 1984b).

Recent analysis (Binford 1985b; Binford and Stone 1986) of the archaeological remains of Europe and Asia seeking to document the successful penetration of *Homo erectus,* or at least "*erectus*-grade" hominids, into the temperate zone yields ambiguous results suggesting that hominids were not successful hunters even as late as 200,000 years ago! Each time the results of the new investigations are discussed the conversation inevitably shifts to the site of Torralba (Figure 25.1), where the excavators and interpreters of the archaeological remains have certainly made the most known and generally accepted case for big-game hunting as basic to the early way of life for an *erectus*-grade hominid anywhere in the world.

Clearly, if any changed view of hominid life during the evolutionary era dominated by *erectus*-grade hominids is to be sustained, the data from Torralba must be faced. That has now been done, using only the published data. This analysis will make possible a new discussion of the meaning of Torralba in the assessment of the role of hunting in hominid evolution.

LOOKING BACK AT THE CLAIMS

During the early 1960s, when it was *assumed* by nearly all prehistorians that Lower Paleolithic hominids were hunters, the interpretation of the data from Torralba was

Originally appeared in *The Evolution of Human Hunting,* edited by M. H. Nitecki and D. V. Nitecki, published by Plenum Press, New York, pp. 47–105, © 1987.

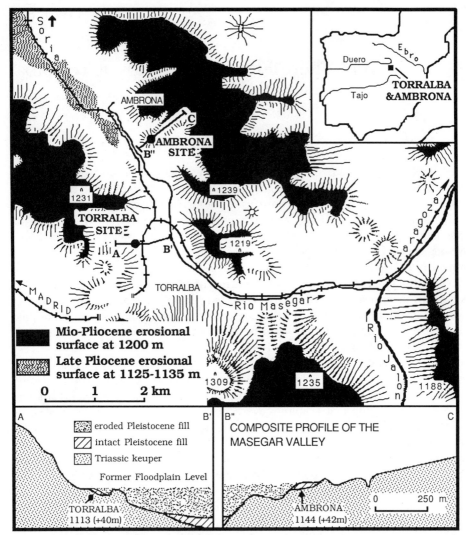

Figure 25.1. Approximate locations of Torralba and Ambrona. (From Klein 1987:13, Fig. 1).

presented in support of this assumption. Certainly the well-published pictures of *in situ* elephant bones and associated stone tools together with well-executed reconstructive drawings of what life was like at Torralba (Howell 1965) made this site the most visible evidence for Lower Paleolithic big-game hunting in the English language literature. Subsequent interpretive literature (Freeman 1975a, 1978b) regarding this site has reinforced and enlarged this picture of the past.

I am an archaeological methodologist. My concern is with how we as archaeologists warrant or justify our constructions of a past. The past is gone, and our constructions of the past are all based on inferences. The crucial task of inference justification is the linchpin of archaeological investigation. My concern in the following discussion is focused on this "linchpin." Can the argument for Lower Paleolithic big-game hunting survive a detailed evaluation from a methodological perspective?

The Early Days of "Self-Evident" Interpretation

During the early years of the excavations at Torralba I was a colleague of F. Clark Howell at the University of Chicago. I had the privilege of seeing the wonderful maps of bones and archaeological specimens as they were brought from the field to our busy laboratories at Chicago. I was as excited as most others by archaeological data collected in a detailed and well-documented manner from what in those days were called "living floors." Like most of my fellow researchers, I believed the traditional wisdom of our field, which claimed that early hominids were hunters. I also viewed the field maps and other data as self-evident testimony to the validity of our belief in early man as a hunter. Howell (1965) summarized the evidence in his extremely influential book, *Early Man:*

> What made the fossil sites at Torralba and Ambrona interesting was the enormous number of elephant bones that they contained. These belonged to a straight-tusked species now extinct and somewhat larger than the African elephant of today. They were far and away too numerous to be explained away as having gotten there by accident. Furthermore, their condition and their position in the ground were extremely unusual.
>
> Mixed in with the bones were many signs of ancient human presence. Stone tools, of a type associated with *Homo erectus* in Africa, were abundant. There were also bone tools and even pieces of wood, pointed or vaguely spatulate at one end.
>
> There was also a quantity of material that shows different degrees of burning, some of it charcoal, some of it carbon. These materials were not so concentrated in any one place as to suggest the presence of continuous fires over a long period of time. Rather they were thinly and very widely scattered. Whoever had been lighting these fires was apparently burning grass and brush over large areas. This evidence, plus that of the elephant bones concentrated in what was once a bog, suggests that the setting of those fires had been purposeful—to drive the unwieldy elephants into the mud.
>
> In general, *Homo erectus* may be labeled as a hunter, and an extremely successful one at that. (Howell 1965:84)

At the time, at least to judge from the number who cite the Torralba data in textbooks as evidence for big-game hunting (e.g., Bordes 1968; Gowlett 1984; Jolly and Plog 1976; Pfeiffer 1978), most archaeologists accepted the suggested construction of a past, a view created by the archaeologists for *Homo erectus*. It must be recalled that the early sixties was an intellectual era when two trends were present in archaeology. The first traditional trend was made consistent by a strict empiricist bias on the part of archaeologists who generally believed that if we looked harder and increased our skills for seeing through the use of computers, better excavation strategies, and better recording and recovery methods, we would surely succeed in "seeing" an accurate past. Linked with this approach was the belief that our knowledge grew primarily as a result of seeing new and previously unseen things. This "progress-through-discovery" approach is perhaps nowhere better illustrated than in the many news conferences held by the Leakeys and in the regular news accounts, which claimed that some new discovery completely changed our view of human evolution or of what the past was like. It was commonplace for adherents to this view to seek their professional fortune by finding new and previously unseen things. This attitude is at least partially responsible for the "instant" interpretations of the Torralba data and the emphasis given to alleged "previously unknown" bone and wooden tools recovered from the site.

At the same time another trend was developing that focused on the logic of inferences made from archaeological observations. It was suggested that the assumptions archaeologists made about the nature of evidence and its implication for past events and conditions were, in the long run, a greater obstacle to the achievement of accurate inferences as to the nature of the past than were our poor observational techniques. From this perspective it was argued that increasing our observational skills was in fact an idle endeavor if pursued in ignorance as to what constituted evidence indicative of past events and conditions! Even more important, claims for discovery of previously unseen things and conditions were generally considered to be "grandstand" behavior. If they were new and previously unseen, how would we immediately know what they mean or imply in terms of the past? This is the epistemologically oriented perspective that I have consistently presented and used over the course of my career. In turn, the "success through discovery" and the "truth through looking harder" approaches have commonly been the target of some critical essays.

Analytical Approaches to Seeing

Leslie Freeman, my student at the University of Chicago during the early 1960s, along with many others was engaged with me in exploring new ways of "seeing" or recognizing patterning in the archaeological record. As we explored pattern recognition techniques we were frequently made aware of incompatibilities between what we saw, using new techniques, and what earlier archaeologists had inferred from the same facts, as "seen" or summarized by them. One of our major research interests was the investigation of archaeological assemblages as potential compounds built up by the manufacture and use of different types of tools in different activity contexts (Binford and Binford 1966). We were fond of citing evidence from relatively modern hunter-gatherers to demonstrate that activities were spatially differentiated on sites. We argued that at least some variability in assemblage content not only reflected different activity regimens at different places but also was the consequence of an excavational strategy that sampled various activity-differentiated segments within a site instead of uncovering complete sites.

It is not surprising that having invested so much, both during excavation and later in descriptive analysis, Leslie Freeman should try to apply to the Torralba data some of the pattern recognition strategies with which we were experimenting during his student days at Chicago. Results of Freeman's endeavors in this direction are summarized in his later paper (Freeman 1978b), and some of his attempts to expand the kinds of inference archaeologists could make from archaeological facts (something else we were trying to do in those Chicago days) are seen in his earlier paper (1975a; also see Freeman 1975b, 1981). What new or expanded views of the past did these efforts facilitate?

In Freeman's (1975a) initial synthesis he accepts the arguments and assumptions made during those early years of Torralba interpretation:

> The Torralba/Ambrona site complex is a set of special purpose hunting and pre-liminary butchering stations along a valley favored by game animals. . . .

> Each utilization of the Torralba site seems to have been of extremely short dura-tion—one might almost say ephemeral. Each occupation could very well represent the results of a single hunt, to judge from the fact that parts of several individuals (sometimes from all the individuals represented) were subjected to simultaneous processing in the secondary butchering areas. (Freeman 1975a:679–680)

Here we see a restatement of the original assumptions, specifically that the remains at Torralba were the result of hominid activity and that the activity indicated is the killing of game facilitated by game drives. A new element has been introduced, however: the assumption of "activity" areas and the citation of their heterogeneous content as evidence for the "duration" of site use by man. Freeman concludes that we see at Torralba the results of essentially single-episode phenomena in each of the several levels at Torralba. The important role of the original interpretation, used here as a basic assumption, is clear. If multiple animals were killed by hominids in one hunting episode, then the presence of multiple individuals in a separately recognized spatial localization within a single level proves that there was only one episode of hunting!

Another assumption hidden in Freeman's interpretations is that spatial differentia-tion in the dispersion and content of localizations on a site directly indicates con-sistently localized activities differentiated within a single occupation. Clearly, if one believes these things about the archaeological record, then the conclusion is self-evident that given the demonstration of localized tool and bone concentrations, and the observation that multiple individual animals occurred in such areas, single-epi-sode occupations are demonstrated! This conclusion is of course a tautology since with most deductive reasoning strategies one cannot reason to a position that contra-dicts the original assumptions. Importantly, the assumptions used here were historical assumptions about what the past was like and not theoretical assumptions about the way the world works and hence about what causes patterning in the archaeological record.

How could we arrive at Freeman's interpretations if (a) the original assumption about game drives was wrong and (b) there were other formation contexts that could result in heterogeneous localizations? We could not. Freeman's interpretative argu-ments summarized thus far are dependent upon the truth of the original interpreta-tions of the site. In short, no middle-range research (Binford 1981a) or reasoning stands behind the Torralba interpretations.

Let's continue with other interpretations.

> In some levels, there are several spatially isolated concentrations of statistically indistinguishable materials, representing multiple synchronous performances of the same set of game processing activities. Often the same body parts of several individuals of different species will be recovered from each such concentration. This situation strongly suggests a relatively egalitarian sharing of the product of the hunt among a series of probably similarly constituted social units—perhaps different teams or individuals who cooperated in the drive. (Freeman 1975a:681)

Once again the assumptions of episodal game drives and synchronous activity areas are made. Given these assumptions, the conclusion is drawn that a recurrent pattern of body-part associations in spatially discrete locations means an internally differentiated work force. Once again we must ask (a) what if the original interpretation of game drives is wrong, and (b) what if there are other formation contexts for organizationally variable localizations? If either were suspected, then the interpretations would collapse. Nevertheless, Freeman continues:

> Since most of the meatier body parts were carried away from the site, presumably to some nearby living site, or base camp, it is possible, even likely, that those active in meat processing at the Torralba butchering site did not include the total personnel of a coresident group. (Freeman 1975a:681–682; earlier Freeman had estimated the number of workers in the "team"-based work force engaged in butchering meat at between 10 to 35 individuals.)

Here we see inferences drawn from inferences; each is increasingly dependent upon the accuracy of the initial inferences instead of being justified in terms of arguments about the nature of causal processes operative in the past that produced the patterning in the archaeological record. The propositions used as assumptions in the interpretative arguments are consistently unwarranted inferences as to what the past was like. For instance, how does Freeman justify the assumption that meat was removed from the site of Torralba? Simple. He assumes that all the parts were originally present because he assumes that the animals were hunted by hominids and killed in groups on the site. Given that such assumptions are unwarranted, it is clearly reasonable to consider the possibility that the parts present at Torralba were introduced to the location and that the missing parts had never been there! This possibility is never considered simply because the interpreters of Torralba assumed as factual both the hominid role in the accumulation of the deposit and the particulars of the character of that role—big-game hunting using game drives in which multiple prey individuals were killed on the spot in single episodes.

Clearly, the crucial arguments to address are the original interpretations. If they were unwarranted, all derivative arguments would fall like a house of cards. Before taking on this important task, it is important to discuss from a methodological perspective the observations and arguments thus far presented about "activity areas" since they will be important in my assessment of the original interpretation that hominids were big-game hunters using game drives.

In Freeman's second paper he makes his case for activity areas. He devotes some time to the history of activity area research and presents what he believes to be the assumptions underlying activity area recognition strategies (1978b:67). He states these as follows:

Assumption 1: Prehistoric men performed markedly different activities in different places whenever space permitted.

Assumption 2: The implements used together in a specific activity or its products and by-products (or both) were usually abandoned together in a restricted area (whether or not abandonment was intentional).

Assumption 3: Materials exclusively related to different activities were abandoned in different places.

Assumption 4: The place of abandonment of materials related to an activity tends generally to coincide with the place of activity performance.

Freeman notes that these assumptions have not been "proven valid," but he then concludes that "we must proceed as though they might be true" (Freeman 1978b:67). Here we have a classic example of the point that Schiffer (1976) has made in the critical literature, namely, questioning whether a given model of archaeological formation processes is *relevant* (see Binford 1983a:157–167) to the data to which it is applied for interpretive purposes. Even more important in the case of Freeman's use of a model is the question of the relevance of alternative models that might account for localizations on Paleolithic sites.

Freeman generates a list of classes to accommodate the contents at the Torralba site and seeks to defend his use of nonnormalized data (raw counts) in a multivariate analysis of the samples from Torralba. (The use of raw counts completely violates the assumptions of the statistical techniques used by Freeman—namely, that one is working with normally distributed data.) Freeman presents his results as if (a) they were valid pattern-recognition results, and (b) they were exclusively understandable in terms of the activity area "assumptions" cited above. He summarizes his pattern recognition endeavors as shown in Table 25.1. After presenting these results, Freeman restates his assumptions as follows:

> All evidence from the Torralba site suggests that it was the locus of a range of activities involving the killing of game animals, dressing out meat from the carcasses, some secondary stages in meat preparation, and probably, limited consumption on the spot. The clusters (factors) seem to reflect these activities. (Freeman 1978b:87)

Freeman then interprets the results of his factor analysis in these terms. The association among becs, perforators, and elephant skulls as well as denticulates (Factor III) and bovid skull fragments are interpreted as follows:

> The skulls of both wild oxen and elephants have features that are necessary to sustain long, heavy horns or much heavier tusks. Extraction of the edible material from these creatures' heads requires some means of smashing the structure apart and some device for getting at edible fragments in nooks and crannies. The perforator-becs at Torralba would be suitable sharp-edged pointed probes for the latter process, and denticulates unite a series of small-pointed projections (and a series of hollow notches) in a working edge, which might have served a similar

Table 25.1
Summary of Freeman's Pattern-Recognition Results

Factor content		Associated (nonexclusively determined) variables
Tools	Animal bones	
Factor I		
(1) perforators	(1) elephant skull fragments	(notches)
(2) becs		
Factor II		
(1) utilized flakes	(1) unworked equid limbs	
(2) flakes	(2) bovid foot bones	
Factor III		
(1) denticulates	(1) bovid skull fragments	
	(2) cervid limb fragments	
Factor IV		
(1) endscrapers	(1) elephant teeth	(1) cervid antlers
(2) sidescrapers	(2) unworked tusks	(2) worked elephant ribs
	(3) worked tusks	(3) equid teeth
	(4) elephant scapulae	
	(5) elephant pelves	
	(6) elephant vertebrae	
	(7) equid skull fragments	
	(8) equid scapulae	
	(9) equid vertebrae	
	(10) cervid scapulae	
Factor V		
		(1) equid pelves
Factor VI		
	(1) cervid foot bones	
Factor VII		
(1) burins		
(2) paraburins		

> purpose. The Factor I cluster contains nothing like a battering tool, but the cervid limb bones (including the metapodials) in the Factor III cluster would serve the purpose well enough. (Freeman 1978b:87–88)

This is a classic example of a post hoc accommodative argument: that is, the a priori assumption is invoked to give meaning to the recognized patterns. Further post hoc accommodative arguments are offered to tailor the patterns to fit the original assumptions. I do not need to go through all of Freeman's post hoc accommodations; needless to say, they all fit the data.

What Is Done with the Recognized Patterns?

Freeman correctly recognizes that his patterns were generated by virtue of inter-assemblage comparisons. That is, the summed data from different levels at Torralba were the units among which patterning was sought. Given his commitment to the position that such assemblages should be variable exclusively by virtue of spatial differentiations among activities *within single, short-term occupations of essentially the same type* (game drives and subsequent processing of big game for meat) he proceeds to "strengthen" his original assumptions by demonstrating that the defining variables for the factors isolated in his pattern recognition endeavors do in fact differentially distribute when single excavated levels are studied spatially.

Freeman chooses for his demonstrations Occupations 7 and 8 from Torralba (Figures 25.2 and 25.3). He reports the results of a chi-square test to strengthen his argument that the defining variables are differentially distributed within single excavation units. I doubt that anyone viewing these distributions would question that they are distributed differentially, but Freeman does not discuss the patterning itself. Certain questions might reasonably be asked about the illustrated patterns. For example, in Occupation 7 there are clearly two forms of patterning: (a) a linear pattern running diagonally from Square 9-F to square 24-J and (b) a circular, clustered distribution above the "L" line. What is in each? In the linear distribution are primarily diagnostics of Factor II. Above the L line are primarily diagnostics of Factor IV. And what are these diagnostics? Factor II is defined by small items, utilized flakes, unretouched flakes,

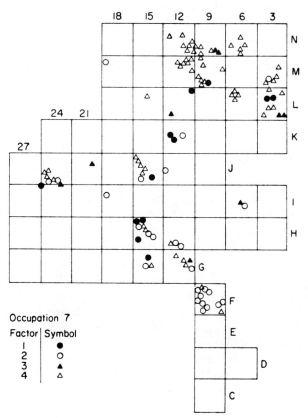

Figure 25.2. The distribution of factor-specific items in Occupation 7 at Torralba. Distance between grid lines = 3 m (from Freeman 1978b:90).

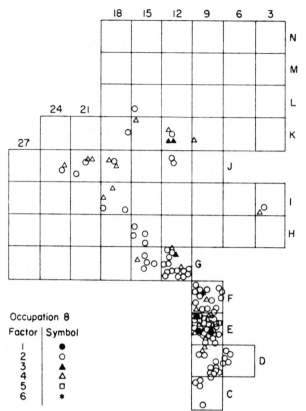

Figure 25.3. The distribution of factor-specific items in Occupation 8 at Torralba. Distance between grid lines = 3 m (from Freeman 1978b:91).

unworked equid limbs, and bovid foot bones. These are lineally arranged with apparently a greater concentration in the square 9-F area. What is diagnostic of Factor IV? Clearly the most abundant diagnostics are large or heavy items: elephant teeth, tusks, scapulae, pelves, and vertebrae, along with scapulae of both cervids and equids, and equid vertebrae. Is it not possible that what we are seeing is the structured result of differential erosion? Freeman never considered this possibility since he already assumed the hominid behavioral cause for his structured results.

A remarkable situation is apparent in the distributions summarized in Freeman's illustrations. Almost all of the remains in Occupation 8 form a linear distribution in exactly the same place as the linear distribution in Occupation 7 (Figures 25.2 and 25.3). Now, however, there is a greater concentration of diagnostics in the area of squares 9-F and E. Examination reveals that this "lower" distribution (which extends into squares 9-C through E) is similar to that found in Occupation 7, in that the small items of Factor II are more concentrated while the large items diagnostic of Factor IV are more common in the "upper" part of the distribution. In addition we note that the small item diagnostics of Factor I occur in the lower end of the linear distribution, which is not as evident in the Occupation 7 distribution.

What we see is a remarkable set of facts. If we are to be convinced by Freeman's arguments, we must imagine two groups of big-game hunters conducting independent big-game drives, separated in time by some unknown number of years, and placing analogous activities in exactly the same spot on the land surface. These separate activity areas yield analogous and similarly structured internal patterns—small items occur at the lower end of a linear pattern and large items are located at the upper end of this distribution. In addition, abruptly retouched pieces, items sometimes considered indicative of cryoturbation or analogous geological processes, are heavily loaded in Factor II in Freeman's results (Freeman 1978b:88). I see no evidence for "activity areas" in Freeman's results. I see suggestive evidence for the operation of natural processes as the major cause for the differential spatial distributions illustrated by Freeman.

I must conclude that all discussion, interpretation, and analysis thus far conducted has been carried out under the assumption that the site represents the structured remains of the activities of big-game hunters primarily taking game in game drives with an emphasis on elephants. This important interpretation was originally presented in the logical form of an argument from lack of evident alternatives. As Howell (1965) has described the archaeological evidence,

> What made the fossil sites of Torralba and Ambrona interesting was the enormous number of elephant bones that they contained. These belonged to a straight-tusked species now extinct and somewhat larger than the African elephant of today. They were far and away too numerous to be explained away as having gotten there by accident. Furthermore, their condition and their positions in the ground were extremely unusual. . . . Mixed in with the bones were many signs of ancient human presence. Stone tools . . . bone tools . . . and even pieces of wood. (Howell 1965:84)

Two alternative explanations were considered to account for the prevalence of elephant bones and their provocative distributions: (a) man was responsible for the archaeological patterning by virtue of the evidence of his presence—stone tools—or (b) the bone distributions were *accidental*. The latter alternative appeared to be improbable; therefore, the romantic view of "man the elephant hunter" was claimed. No alternative possibilities, such as natural deaths or geologically structured deposits, were investigated. The role of man appeared to be self-evident. In this reasoning process one quite literally assumes the truth of what should be the object of investigation.

It should be clear by now that the basic flaw in all the interpretative work thus far done at Torralba rests with the assumption that the remains are exclusively referable to the organized actions of hominids, and that these organized activities were multiple game drives. Given these initial interpretations, which served as the basis for all further interpretative arguments, we have an internally consistent construction of past conditions of life for the hominids who are assumed to have structured the remains.

Pattern Recognition: The Basis of our Knowledge of the Past

The first principle of successful inference as to the nature of the past must be the explanation of patterning made explicit by the interaction of our units of observation (our taxonomic summary of entities recovered and observed) viewed within a frame of reference. For the majority of practicing archaeologists, this frame of reference is most often formal, chronological, and/or spatial.

In the case of Torralba the chronological frame of reference is approximated by the stratigraphic sequence of levels or "occupation units" identified by the excavators. The spatial frame of reference is provided by the horizontal grid system in terms of which the site was excavated as well as the point-provenience maps generated during excavation. The formal frame of reference is provided by our strategies for observing the patterns of statistical interaction among our basic units of observation, our types or classes of phenomena. Patterning results when we use our observations to discover the statistical interaction between our classificatory units and our frames of reference. Patterning recognizable at this juncture is not imposed on the archaeological record by our conventions for observation. It is only this patterning, seen in terms of our frames of reference, that can directly inform us (in our own terms, of course) about the past. The task of archaeologists is to explain the resulting patterning, and insofar as we are successful, we will have constructed an accurate past. We cannot assume such explanation, nor can we use unjustified inferences as the assumptive basis for still further inference, as I have demonstrated has been done at Torralba.

Obviously the archaeologist can construct false frames of reference, date units of observation inaccurately, and lay out the grid incorrectly or record inaccurate provenience data for specific items. For our purposes, the most common source of error in many attempts to observe formal patterning (structure) in our data resides in using inappropriate analytical procedures when seeking the recognition of patterning. I have suggested that Freeman has committed such an error.

A NEW MULTIVARIATE ANALYSIS OF FREEMAN'S DATA

When one uses multivariate analytical techniques one seeks to discover patterning among the variables, which for archaeologists are commonly summary frequency counts for different recognized categories of things—e.g., tool "types" or anatomical and/or species classes of faunal remains. One is attempting to assess the common or shared variance among pair-wise comparisons for the variables being studied. The common variance of interest is not that which arises from the fact that some samples are large, having many items, while others are small, having few items. This variance may arise from numerous conditions that do not interest archaeologists at this stage of pattern recognition study. Some units may be small in terms of size of excavation, or variable in size as a result of differential placement of past occupations relative to the particular "grid squares" excavated through a stratified deposit. Such variance may well be a function of excavation strategy, and we do not want to confuse this patterning with patterning that might result from organized dynamics in the past. We want to see the latter clearly and unambiguously. For this reason, multivariate analysis *must* be carried out on normalized data, data that has been transformed in such a way as to eliminate variance arising from sample size differences.

In the early days of experimentation with multivariate techniques, several different normalizing conventions were used. Some of these include the calculation and study of percentages rather than raw counts, the calculation and study of ratio values rather than raw counts, and normalization with z-scores. The problem of normalization was essentially solved by using a chi-square calculation. That is, chi-square values were calculated for each raw cell count in a matrix. These values were then used as the data for analysis using multivariate techniques. This is a very elegant procedure, since what one looks at are the patterned and interactive suites of variables that consistently deviate from the summed character of all the cases. If all cases were identical there would be no result, even though they all shared an identical pattern. We are quite literally looking at the dimensionally summarized sets of variables that regularly deviate from the normative pattern described by the matrix as a whole. This approach allows us to see patterning that is structured not by our viewing techniques but by dynamic conditions in the past that structured our archaeological samples. Once data are normalized the matrix is processed using a singular value decomposition (Harpending and Rogers 1985) to produce a type of principal component multivariate result. I will consistently use this approach in the following analyses.

Contrasting my approach to those used by earlier analysts, I do not assume I know what the past was like and use such assumptions to guide my analysis. On the contrary, I assume that it is the *patterning* that is the source of information about the past, and the knowledge available to me for understanding patterning is the ultimate justification of any subsequent interpretations. In short, it is the middle-range knowledge of process and pattern that makes interpretation possible.

Analysis Step One: Looking at Classes of Remains

If we adopt Freeman's last three middle-range assumptions, which stipulate that implements used together are usually abandoned together, that different activities were generally conducted in·different places, and therefore that the place of abandoned materials generally coincides with the place of activity performance, what conclusions must be drawn from the following analysis?

I will begin the study of Torralba from a gross data perspective and then move to finer and finer resolution of observations. The first matrix was constructed using the ten stratigraphic levels as the cases (rows) and the seven classes of material remains at the variables (columns). Summed frequencies were calculated by level for each class of remains as reported by Freeman (1978b:72–73); these classes were (1) all tools, (2) all elephant anatomical units, (3) all equid remains, (4) all bovid remains, (5) all cervid remains, (6) all unworked unidentified bone, and (7) all worked unidentified bone. These data are presented in Table 25.2.

The previously outlined multidimensional analysis resulted in a three-component solution with the following eigenvalues: Dimension 1, 12.55 (38%); Dimension 2, 6.50 (20%); and Dimension 3, 5.08 (16%). This three-component solution (Table 25.3),

Table 25.2
Classes of Remains by Occupation

Occupation	Tools	Elephant	Equid	Bovid	Cervid	Unworked unidentified bones	Worked unidentified bones
1	97	182	80	15	28	85	64
2	30	3	6	5	2	10	2
3	56	42	32	2	13	21	26
4	107	99	54	24	19	66	60
5	45	31	33	9	18	26	10
6	29	13	8	5	5	25	9
7	30	17	12	5	8	10	11
8	19	12	9	2	2	7	3
9	88	140	44	6	8	31	25
10	124	25	57	9	17	42	24

which accounts for 74% of the variance in the data, exhibits some very provocative patterning. The most robust pattern occurs in Dimension 1, where tools are associated with all species *except* elephants. One can think of this situation as one in which tools and the non-elephant species are more common than in the matrix norm, while elephant remains and "worked" unidentified bone are less common. On the other hand, when elephant remains and worked bone are common, tools and the other species are less common than usual. This pattern documents the fact that the tools, when considered in a single group, covary with all the non-elephant material. In short, if we accept Freeman's assumptions, we would have to conclude that most of the events at Torralba indicated by faunal remains and tools were unrelated to events involving elephants!

Turning to Dimension 2 we see that all unidentified bone fragments tend to associate with bovids and cervids, while tools now covary with the greatly emphasized elephant bone, together with equids. Since Dimension 1 accounts for 38% of the total variance, clearly the deposition of tools was *greater* with the bovid and equid remains at the site than with the much discussed elephant remains. We must keep in mind that

Table 25.3
Analysis Step One: Three-Component Solution, Faunal Remains and Lithic Artifacts by Class

Dimension 1		Dimension 2		Dimension 3	
Tools	6.56	Unidentified unworked		Bovid remains	1.94
Bovid remains	2.23	bone	3.30	Tools	1.42
Cervid remains	1.91	Unidentified worked bone	2.87	Unidentified unworked	
Unidentified unworked		Bovid remains	2.33	bone	1.31
bone	1.57	Cervid remains	1.49	Elephant remains	0.68
Equid remains	1.27	----------------------------------		----------------------------------	
----------------------------------		Equid remains	−1.07	Unidentified worked bone	−0.48
Unidentified worked bone	−1.24	Elephant remains	−1.45	Equid remains	−2.85
Elephant remains	−10.01	Tools	−3.48	Cervid remains	−3.06

the two dimensions record independently varying patterns, and thus the episodes in which tools were structured in association with the bovid, cervid, and equid remains appear to be independent of the conditions that structured the association of tools with elephant remains. Based on these results alone we would have to conclude that the deposits at Torralba are palimpsests of independent depositional events. The most common situations are those in which bovid, cervid, and equid remains were deposited in regular ways *with* tools, while elephant remains were deposited independently and in a manner *unrelated* to tools.

The next most common situation is one in which elephant bones were deposited in association with tools independently of conditions that tended to result in breakage and modification of bones beyond recognition. In addition, bovid and cervid remains formed a separate suite that was unassociated with tools. The presence of these two suites suggest another set of depositional conditions, one in which bones get broken independently of hominid involvement (i.e., independent of tools). This is in marked contrast to the depositional situation in which elephant remains covary with tools. This pattern is consistent with some published observations (e.g., Freeman 1978b) that record the presence of elephant bones in "low" areas suggestive of ponds or marshes while other faunal remains are found "farther from the bog" on higher ground. In the latter context, bones could be exposed to more breakage, and the association of both "worked" and "unworked" bone in a context unrelated to tools suggests that what have been judged as worked bone are more likely to be remains exhibiting normal breakage unrelated to human activities.

Turning now to Dimension 3, which accounts for 16% of the variance, we see that tools again appear to be associated with bovids and so-called unworked unidentifiable bone fragments. These items vary independently of cervid and equid bone as well as "worked" bone. This dimension reinforces the earlier observation that most of the patterns of regular covariation between tools and bones are clearly with non-elephant species.

When we view all of the dimensions comparatively we note some interesting things. First, all species appear in covariant associations independent of or inversely related to tools (negative Dimension 1, positive Dimension 2, and negative Dimension 3). This can be seen as documenting the fact that all the species represented at the site were on occasion distributed independently of human activities (i.e., independent of tools). The most economical way of viewing this phenomenon is that the deposit is a palimpsest of both natural depositional events and hominid tool-using events. The vast majority of the latter involved bovids and cervids, with elephants being least important with regard to associated hominid activities. Second, elephant, bovid, and equid bones were regularly deposited independently of tools, while cervids tended to be deposited with both bovids and equids but not with elephants. So-called worked bone was exclusively associated with all these cases (negative Dimension 1, positive Dimension 2, and negative Dimension 3). On the other hand, in all cases of tool-associated suites of variables, only "unworked" unidentified bone was covariantly related. This highly consistent pattern strongly suggests that the properties of broken bone identified by the earlier analysts as being diagnostic of "worked" pieces were predominantly unrelated to hominid actions. This view is supported by my own observations of bones photographed by Aguirre (part of the unpublished Torralba site report) that are cited as evidence for human modification. These specimens appear to be hydrologically rolled, and the details of original modification are frequently obscured. In those cases where the modifications are preserved to some extent, they exhibit many properties of animal gnawing or natural abrasion and breakage. This view is further supported by a recent detailed study of alleged cutmarks on bones from Torralba (Shipman and Rose 1983). These researchers found few marks that could be identified as cutmarks and concluded that

> An obvious explanation for the paucity of cutmarks on these bones is that Acheulian people had little to do with the bones comprising these assemblages. An alternative explanation is that the ubiquitous sedimentary abrasion on the Torralba and Ambrona bones has obscured the diagnostic features of nearly all of the cutmarks that were once present on these bones. (Shipman and Rose 1983:472)

Even more important to the analysis being undertaken here was the recognition by Shipman and Rose of the nearly ubiquitous evidence for sedimentary abrasion:

> An important result of the entire study involves the extent of sedimentary abrasion observed on the specimens. Every one of the Ambrona specimens and all but three of the Torralba specimens showed microscopic evidence of abrasion. . . . This finding is remarkable considering that replicated specimens were intentionally selected to exclude those showing . . . visible signs of sedimentary abrasion. (Shipman and Rose 1983:468)

Additional work confirming the conclusions drawn from examining the photographs of alleged worked bone from Torralba has been produced by Klein and Cruz-Uribe (n.d.). These researchers found that 36–37% of the bones from Torralba exhibit gross sedimentary abrasion and rounding (many of the specimens have been characterized as "bone pebbles"). Thus, I think it can be confidently asserted that it is no longer feasible to defend either the earlier claims by the excavators (Freeman and Butzer 1966: Freeman 1975a, 1978b) or even the slightly more tempered claims (Freeman and Howell 1981, 1982) that Torralba was a high-integrity site of "living floors" on which the bones and tools were found roughly where they were dropped by ancient big-game hunters.

An additional claim illustrates the willingness of researchers to accept everything found at Torralba as resulting from hominid agencies. I am referring to the "worked" elephant tusk "artifacts" recovered at Torralba; I had the opportunity to examine these specimens in Berkeley in the spring of 1983. It is quite true that there is regularity in the pattern of breakage. In addition, the tusk tips frequently have scratch marks and other indications of abrasion. It must be recalled, however, that elephant tusks are in fact used as "tools" by elephants in removing bark from trees and in many other tasks, so that modified elephant tusks are not uncommon in nature. Although the breakage pattern at Torralba is quite distinctive, I have frequently observed the identical pattern on the ends of tusks from paleontologically excavated complete elephant carcasses. (A good example of this kind of breakage is found on the mammoth skeleton on display in the Natural History Museum at the University of Alaska, Fairbanks.)

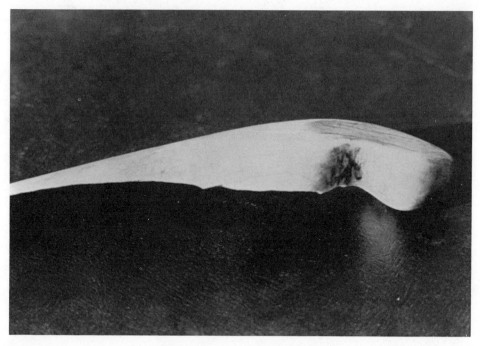

Figure 25.4. Worn and "worked" tip of a young elephant tusk (photograph by Binford).

Even more remarkable is the tusk tip shown in Figure 25.4, where the "distinctive" breakage pattern noted on the Torralba specimens is duplicated, but in addition an even more spectacular set of modifications characterizes the specimen. A deep groove has been worn into the tip of the tusk, which when seen in plan view looks very much like an abstract human figure. A side view of this specimen shows the remains of an earlier tip break still visible behind the "head" of the rounded area at the right. This specimen was recovered by Mike English, a game warden in Kruger National Park, South Africa. He found this tusk near a waterhole; Figure 25.5 illustrates typical behavior of the young male elephants he was studying.

As with many other claims for distinctive breakage, it is quite likely that this modification to elephant tusks occurs when the tips are knocked off while the animal is alive. I have been told that tusk breakage is common among young males during the time when they are beginning to compete among themselves and before they leave their mothers. And most of the alleged tusk "artifacts" at Torralba are from young elephants! I strongly doubt that hominids produced these "artifacts."

The skepticism expressed above regarding the integrity of the Torralba deposits is totally consistent with the results of the analysis thus far presented, specifically that the "worked" bone is consistently associated either with unidentified bone fragments indicative of natural breakage or with faunal groups that do not covary with hominid-produced tools. Further, the analysis clearly suggests that the depositional events at

Figure 25.5. Young male elephants sparring with one another at a waterhole (photograph by Binford).

Torralba are more complex than the single episodes of hominid hunting and butchering that are postulated by the excavators. The evidence for this conclusion is as follows:

1. There is strong and nearly ubiquitous evidence of sedimentary modification of the bones (Shipman and Rose 1983; Klein and Cruz-Uribe n.d.). The findings of these researchers are totally consistent with my own observations.

2. The different species present at Torralba segregate among themselves and independently associate with stone tools. This pattern is not consistent with the claims that different species were killed in single episodes and butchered in mass processing activities organized by multiple labor groups who performed different aspects of the butchering process in different places (Freeman and Butzer 1966; Freeman 1975a, 1978b).

3. The pattern revealed in this analysis shows that the stone tools only rarely covary with elephant remains, as opposed to their relatively frequent associations with bovid, equid, and cervid remains. This pattern contradicts the imaginatively presented picture of game drives at Torralba with elephants as a major food target.

Analysis Step Two: Looking at Stone Tools

Freeman has argued that the important unit for observation relevant to inferences about tool use is not the entity, the tool or item recovered, but the multiple utilized or modified edges on each item. He has therefore reported the frequencies not of tools but of edges. Thus, if a single item exhibits simple utilization on one edge and modification indicative of a scraper on another, this single item would be tabulated under two separate classes of variables—one tabulation for utilized pieces and another independent tabulation for scrapers. For instance, from the entire Torralba collection only 55 tools were classified as sidescrapers (extrapolated from Freeman 1975a:668; Howell 1966:135). Nevertheless, in the published "counts" (Freeman 1978b:72, Table 2), 73 sidescraper edges are tabulated among the levels reported. Clearly, if we are interested in the depositional context of the artifacts, which are, of course, the units lost or discarded by ancient hominids, Freeman's data do not report any units of relevance. His choice of variables is only useful if one is interested in tool histories—that is, when the artifacts as unit entities were components of a technologically aided set of activities. Put another way, it is artifacts that can be used and modified in different ways when they were part of a cultural system but it is entities that are discarded or lost.

Freeman's data-reporting techniques are not appropriate for investigations of the context of loss, abandonment, or natural reorganization of these items after they left the technological system. Properties of edges are relevant only in the dynamic context, not in the depositional context. Their study only makes sense if one assumes from the beginning that the depositional and subsequent archaeological contexts are one and the same and that both contexts are directly referable to the dynamic tool-use context of the past. Once we have good reason to doubt the validity of these assumptions, the study of edges makes little sense as a basis for "seeing" activity areas. Nevertheless, I have conducted an analysis on these data in search of patterning that might be relevant to the problems being considered here.

As in the previous analysis, I have used a chi-square normalization of the raw count data presented by Freeman (1978b). These normalized data were then subjected to a singular value decomposition resulting in a principal component multivariate view of the interaction among variables in the matrix. This solution accounts for 60% of the total variance, with Dimension 1 representing 30%, Dimension 2 representing 18%, and Dimension 3 representing 12%. The remaining 40% was distributed among many dimensions, all of which appeared to represent noise. This fact alone suggests that both the method of tabulation and the postdepositional history of the site have perhaps contributed to a rather unstructured set of relationships.

The results shown in Table 25.4 summarize some components of patterns that are well documented in the Paleolithic archaeological record and other characteristics that are difficult to understand. Perhaps the most noticeable pattern is the fact that lithic waste (positive Dimension 1) varies inversely with a very recognizable group of associated tools. The pattern of independent distribution of lithic waste is well known in the Paleolithic from the Oldowan through some Mousterian facies. Thus, this situation is familiar in one regard, but the particular group of tools with which waste is inversely correlated is atypical. Most students of the Paleolithic would recognize the group of tools mutually associated negatively in Dimension 1 as a variant of what is known from the Mousterian as a "denticulate" (Bordes 1963) assemblage, which

Table 25.4
Analysis Step Two: Three-Component Solution, Lithic Items Only

Dimension 1		Dimension 2		Dimension 3	
Lithic waste	7.48	Sidescrapers	3.38	Abrupt retouch	2.02
Utilized flakes	2.69	Endscrapers	2.81	Denticulates	1.27
Abrupt retouch	2.37	Cores	1.42	Burins	1.14
Choppers	0.29	Choppers	1.19	Cores	0.92
		Abrupt retouch	0.82	Utilized flakes	0.84
Burins	−0.24	Bifaces	0.46	Sidescrapers	0.80
Retouched edges	−0.57			Retouched edges	0.53
Endscrapers	−1.03	Retouched edges	−0.06		
Cores	−1.04	Lithic waste	−0.10	Perforators	−0.23
Perforators	−2.13	Notches	−0.45	Choppers	−0.40
Bifaces	−2.58	Burins	−0.45	Endscrapers	−0.45
Sidescrapers	−2.75	Utilized flakes	−1.44	Lithic waste	−1.42
Notches	−2.99	Denticulates	−2.52	Bifaces	−1.69
Denticulates	−3.99	Perforators	−2.64	Notches	−2.42

when accompanied by bifaces and some "Upper Paleolithic" tools may be known as "Mousterian of Acheulian tradition."

In my experience there is considerable lithic waste in denticulate-dominated assemblages, indicating that the tools generally seem to have been produced and discarded at the same place. This also characterizes the Mousterian of Acheulian tradition," but in these latter assemblages, denticulates may be associated with considerable quantities of nonlocal raw material, frequently in the form of hand-axes accompanied by flakes derived from retouching. Another earlier denticulate-dominated assemblage is from the site of Isernia, which dates from approximately 700,000 years ago. There, however, the frequencies of lithic waste are not reported, and the site is probably fluvially structured. Other "pre-Mousterian" assemblages dominated by denticulates and notches are reported. For instance, assemblages from the Evenosian "culture" (de Lumley 1975:790, 798), which was recognized by Bordes (1968:92) long ago as perhaps being ancestral to the "Denticulate Mousterian," are said to be characterized by much lithic waste. The assemblage from the roughly contemporaneous site of Cantalouette (Guichard 1965) is also dominated by denticulates and notches and has abundant lithic waste.

It is of course possible that at Torralba we are seeing some new "variant" of a denticulate-dominated assemblage (see Freeman's 1975a:670 summary of the Torralba assemblage) in which lithic debris is inversely related to denticulates and notches, especially since the excavators report that the majority of the raw materials used in tool production at Torralba were introduced from lithic sources located some distance from the site (Howell 1965:91). On the other hand, a significant proportion of the hand-axes were made of locally available limestone (Freeman 1975a:668), while the majority of the shaped tools, including denticulates, are said to be manufactured of flint and quartzite (materials not found at the site). This pattern is exactly opposite to that known from most Acheulian sites, where the large tools commonly are not associated with the debris of their manufacture and are made of materials exotic to the site, and where small tools are frequently associated with the debris of primary reduction. It is possible that the large numbers of composite tools, those noted by Freeman as having multiple types of edges, indicate that the archaeological remains at Torralba were actually used as a lithic source by groups of hominids who occasionally visited the site. The subsequent hominid modification of many of the tools would obscure their original form, and certainly cores would be greatly reduced by such reuse. This type of hominid behavior is suspected as early as the Oldowan, and if it can be substantiated for the Torralba materials, it would challenge the excavators' views that the deposits reflect the remains of well-planned, cooperative game drives. The presence of hand-axes of locally available limestone undermines the conclusion that at Torralba the hominids planned ahead and "geared up" for the hunt. During the Acheulian, bifaces appear to be one of the more regularly transported items, but this does not appear to be true at Torralba.

Still another possibility is that since the reported tool frequencies are not counts of items, but rather counts of edges on items, the first dimension in its negative aspect is primarily reporting the types of edges that in fact tend to occur on single items most frequently. That we are seeing some by-product of the classificatory procedure is a distinct possibility, since such covariation among edges on a single piece would always be associated with provenience and since the "counts" represent independently tabulated properties of single entities. It is the entities that have provenience. This possibility must not be dismissed since waste, utilized flakes, abruptly retouched pieces, and choppers are all classes for which it is hard to imagine multiple edge properties.

Turning now to Dimension 2, we note that sidescrapers, endscrapers, cores, choppers, abruptly retouched edges, and bifaces are grouped in opposition to perforators, denticulates, utilized flakes, burins, notches, and lithic waste. We see here the commonly occurring opposition of scrapers on the one hand and denticulates/notches on the other, which occurs most frequently in Mousterian and "pre-Mousterian" assemblages. This familiar pattern is demonstrated in these data both by the inversely varying pattern on Dimension 2 and by the independent distribution of scrapers and denticulate/notches (i.e., they appear on different dimensions). The association of scrapers with choppers (also known as core scrapers or core axes) and cores is a fairly well known pattern. In fact, this is one of the few patterns of tool-type association that correlates with a rather unambiguous faunal context. At the well excavated and documented Middle Stone Age elephant butchery site of Mwanganda's village in Malawi (Clark and Haynes 1970), stone tools were unambiguously associated with and clustered around three major segments of a single elephant carcass. One focus of artifact clustering was an elephant femur, and another was an upper thorax section represented by ribs, vertebrae, and the skull and mandible. A short distance away were the humerus and a distal radius shaft section. The assemblage was mainly composed of scrapers followed by roughly equal numbers of small core scrapers and notch/bec forms. Chopper/core scrapers were the most common large tools. By far the most numerous items were unmodified flakes (lithic waste), which amounted to 77% of the assemblage. It would be interesting to see the suite of edges isolated in positive

Dimension 2 as being similar to this well-documented context of tool use in elephant butchering. As in the case of the denticulate association, however, lithic waste is inversely correlated.

The functional association of shaped tools remains provocative. As has been noted by the excavators, most of the lithic materials appear to have been introduced, and only some large tools appear to be made of locally available materials. It must be emphasized that this pattern is the reverse of that known from most Acheulian sites, where the large tools are more commonly found at some distance from the sources of materials of which they were made. If subsequent work continues to sustain this emerging pattern, then it would appear that the tool users at Torralba were ill pre-pared to deal with the conditions they encountered on the site. They had to make large tools on the spot (these are the tools that the excavators assume were related to hominid hunting activities), and according to the reports of many composite tools, it may have been necessary to exploit archaeological specimens for recycling and fur-ther reduction and modification. Such a scenario does not fit well with the idea of planned game drives!

In its negative aspect Dimension 2 is quite provocative. If we view the "perforators" as reused or specialized denticulates, we thus see the negative aspect as a "denticu-late" manifestation without bifaces and scrapers but with utilized flakes, notches, and lithic waste. The distribution of this dimension throughout the levels may well indi-cate the location of archaeological remains that have some integrity.

Dimension 3 groups some edge forms that are not easily interpreted. Perhaps the most important feature is that notches dominate the negative aspect while denticulates appear on the positive aspect. Occurring with notches are the bifaces, lithic waste, endscrapers, choppers, and perforators, which represent a suite of artifacts that proba-bly do not normally exhibit multiple edge forms. Varying with the denticulates and inversely with the above group are abruptly retouched edges, burins, cores, utilized flakes, sidescrapers, and retouched edges. These types of edges are more easily imagined as perhaps occurring on a single piece with some other edge form. The question of whether the method of classification is responsible for this dimension is not easily solved since the combinations of edges and their frequencies on single pieces are not reported. Before venturing a "functional" interpretation of this dimen-sion I feel we must await a more detailed report of the site data.

Despite the analytical limitations imposed by the use of the published data catego-ries, we can make the following observations. (1) Notches and denticulates, followed by the majority of the other shaped pieces, tend to vary independently of lithic waste and utilized flakes. (2) Sidescrapers tend to vary inversely with denticulates, notches, and perforators when lithic waste is associated with the latter artifacts. (3) Side-scrapers and cores always occur in association with each other when lithic waste is absent. We have noted that the results of this analysis reflect well-known patterns from other sites, especially with regard to the generally inverse relationships between scrapers on one hand and denticulates/notches on the other. Torralba is one of the few sites where faunal material is apparently associated with these opposing patterns. The faunal data may provide some context for these patterns and thereby offer clues to their meaning.

Analysis Step Three: Faunal Remains

In addressing this material I have once again used the data presented by Freeman (1978b). In his original tabulation he independently listed parts considered "worked" and parts considered "unworked". Because the patterned relationships among animal parts may give some indication of site integrity, as well as of the possible differential distribution of animal parts caused by hominid movement and/or introduction of anatomical segments from elsewhere, I have summed the frequencies of worked and unworked classes for the same anatomical units. The modified data derived from Freeman's (1978a:72–73) tabulations and used in this analysis are summarized in Table 25.5.

As in previous cases I have normalized the data by calculating chi-square values for the cells in the matrix. These were then used as input for a singular value decomposition producing a principal component multivariate solution on completely normalized data. A four-component solution that accounts for 63% of the variance was accepted.

Table 25.5
Faunal Remains by Occupation

	Occupation									
Variables	1	2	3	4	5	6	7	8	9	10
Elephant teeth	16	0	5	8	4	2	0	1	10	5
Elephant limbs	42	2	9	24	4	0	4	0	23	3
Elephant ribs	29	1	12	17	5	4	3	7	27	4
Elephant skulls	4	0	2	10	4	2	1	2	12	0
Elephant tusks	30	0	6	14	4	2	5	2	18	6
Elephant feet	11	0	4	11	3	1	0	1	18	0
Elephant scapulae	8	0	1	2	0	0	0	0	5	0
Elephant pelves	9	0	1	1	1	1	1	0	5	2
Elephant vertebrae	33	1	2	11	6	1	3	0	22	6
Equid teeth	32	6	9	21	19	3	2	2	23	22
Equid skulls	5	0	3	2	3	1	1	1	4	2
Equid limbs	14	1	6	13	4	1	7	3	7	18
Equid scapulae	7	0	2	4	2	1	0	0	2	3
Equid feet	7	0	4	6	2	0	1	2	6	4
Equid vertebrae	11	0	2	3	1	0	0	0	2	4
Equid pelves	4	0	6	5	2	2	1	1	0	4
Bovid teeth	0	4	1	8	6	2	1	0	1	0
Bovid skulls	5	1	0	9	2	0	2	0	1	0
Bovid limbs	9	0	0	5	0	3	2	2	3	6
Bovid feet	1	0	1	2	1	5	5	2	1	3
Cervid antlers	15	0	5	3	3	0	5	1	5	8
Cervid skulls	2	0	2	2	1	0	1	0	1	2
Cervid limbs	2	1	0	7	1	2	0	0	1	4
Cervid scapulae	4	0	1	2	1	1	1	0	1	1
Cervid feet	2	1	3	4	10	2	1	0	0	2
Cervid vertebrae	3	0	2	1	2	0	0	1	0	0
Unidentified bones	149	14	47	126	36	34	21	10	56	66

The remaining 37% is distributed among a series of low-valued dimensions that appear to represent noise. Dimension 1 accounts for 21% of the total variance, Dimension 2 for 17%, Dimension 3 for 13%, and Dimension 4 for 12%. The results of these operations are summarized in Table 25.6.

The most striking feature of the above patterns of relationships is that Dimension 1, which accounts for 21% of the variance, tells us very clearly that elephant remains vary inversely with the remains of the other large animals (bovids, cervids, and equids). If we look primarily at the variables heavily loaded on Dimension 2, the positive aspect tells us that teeth and skulls of bovids, equids, and elephants are associated and are accompanied by cervid feet, elephant feet, and elephant limbs. These parts behave as a suite and vary inversely with the feet and limb bones of bovids and equids as well as cervid antlers and equid pelves. Keeping in mind that most of the tabulated items are fragmentary rather than complete anatomical units, we must consider the possibility that Dimension 2 represents the contrast between a lag deposit (positive aspect) and a transported bone assemblage (negative aspect). The former has large or dense bones, such as teeth, while the latter has the remains of small species and fragments of generally smaller bones. This conclusion is just a suggestion at this point; however, the associations of covariantly related parts make little sense as segregations related to butchering or other organized meat processing in light of recent research at elephant butchery locations (Frison and Todd 1986; Scott 1980).

Dimension 3 has some of the same properties as Dimension 2, in that its positive aspect has bovid feet associated with elephant skulls, ribs, and feet, followed by equid skull parts. Since we already know that most of the tabulated items are fragmentary, the absence of teeth could be due to the fact that small fragments are easily transported by natural agencies. The association varies inversely with equid vertebrae, equid teeth, unidentified bone, cervid antlers, equid scapulae, and elephant limbs. The negative aspect is dominantly an equid association of parts that might be expected to remain at the site of a carcass, with cervid antler (which I have been told is mostly shed red deer antler at Torralba; Howell, personal communication 1984) and fragments of elephant limbs in a palimpsest association.

Dimension 4 groups cervid feet and vertebrae with equid teeth, skulls, pelves, and feet, again joined by cervid antlers. These are small and light cervid bones and could easily represent materials naturally deposited into areas where perhaps equid carcasses once existed, since both equid teeth and axial skeletal parts are represented. In its negative aspect this dimension isolates unidentified bone and bovid skulls, limbs, teeth, and feet, along with elephant limbs and cervid limbs. This group has some properties of a bovid carcass associated with fragments of cervid and elephant limbs varying in a coordinated manner.

While this is a very "noisy" solution, several facts are clear. (a) Elephant remains vary inversely with bovids, equids, and cervids. (b) In several combinations what might be seen as bovid, equid, or cervid carcass associations occur independently, with carcass remnants of only equids and cervids occurring together. (c) In all dimensions except the first, some elements are always inversely related to other elements from the same type of animal. Clearly, this implies movement of parts of individual animals, if we imagine that complete carcasses on the site served as the sources of the

Table 25.6
Analysis Step Three: Four-Component Solution, Faunal Remains Only

Dimension 1		Dimension 2		Dimension 3		Dimension 4	
Bovid teeth	4.79	Bovid teeth	5.02	Bovid feet	3.98	Cervid feet	3.19
Cervid feet	4.35	Cervid feet	3.15	Elephant skulls	3.51	Cervid vertebrae	2.25
Bovid feet	3.59	Equid teeth	2.26	Elephant ribs	3.29	Equid teeth	2.05
Unidentifiable bones	3.14	Elephant feet	2.11	Elephant feet	2.14	Equid skulls	1.77
Cervid limbs	2.41	Elephant skulls	1.71	Equid skulls	1.00	Cervid antlers	1.77
Equid pelves	2.05	Bovid skulls	1.54	Bovid teeth	0.75	Equid pelves	1.34
Equid limbs	2.10	Elephant limbs	1.38	Cervid feet	0.47	Equid feet	1.19
Equid teeth	1.39	Elephant vertebrae	0.92	Bovid limbs	0.41	Cervid skulls	0.95
Bovid skulls	1.04	Cervid vertebrae	0.42	Equid pelves	0.29	Equid limbs	0.89
Bovid limbs	0.63	Elephant scapulae	0.41	-------		Elephant teeth	0.86
Cervid skulls	0.61	Cervid limbs	0.38	Cervid scapulae	−0.07	Elephant ribs	0.77
Cervid vertebrae	0.35	Elephant teeth	0.25	Elephant teeth	−0.14	Equid vertebrae	0.54
Cervid scapulae	0.34	-------		Elephant tusks	−0.29	Equid scapulae	0.41
Equid scapulae	0.09	Equid scapulae	−0.03	Bovid skulls	−0.31	Elephant pelves	0.18
-------		Elephant ribs	−0.09	Elephant scapulae	−0.39	-------	
Equid skulls	−0.01	Equid skulls	−0.11	Elephant pelves	−0.42	Elephant tusks	−0.13
Cervid antlers	−0.13	Cervid scapulae	−0.54	Cervid skulls	−0.50	Elephant vertebrae	−0.14
Equid feet	−0.72	Elephant pelves	−0.61	Cervid vertebrae	−0.63	Elephant feet	−0.16
Equid vertebrae	−1.05	Equid feet	−0.62	Cervid limbs	−0.68	Cervid scapulae	−0.17
Elephant skulls	−1.19	Cervid skulls	−0.68	Equid feet	−0.69	Elephant skulls	−0.20
Elephant teeth	−1.43	Unidentifiable bones	−0.71	Elephant vertebrae	−0.91	Elephant scapulae	−0.36
Elephant pelves	−1.73	Elephant tusks	−0.78	Equid limbs	−0.93	Bovid feet	−1.00
Elephant tusks	−2.64	Equid vertebrae	−0.82	Elephant limbs	−1.07	Bovid limbs	−1.16
Elephant ribs	−2.99	Equid pelves	−1.38	Equid scapulae	−1.10	Bovid teeth	−1.29
Elephant scapulae	−3.17	Cervid antlers	−2.63	Cervid antlers	−1.17	Elephant limbs	−1.31
Elephant feet	−3.57	Bovid limbs	−2.89	Unidentifiable bones	−1.26	Cervid limbs	−2.08
Elephant vertebrae	−3.61	Equid limbs	−3.31	Equid teeth	−1.59	Bovid skulls	−2.19
Elephant limbs	−3.81	Bovid feet	−4.08	Equid vertebrae	−2.46	Unidentifiable bones	−2.29

bones. Although these implications are certainly not conclusive, at least some of this movement is probably referable to modification of land surfaces by water, solifluction, and other natural processes. The inversely related patterns suggest that many bones could actually have been accumulated by hominids and introduced to the site as anatomical segments or bone sets. This possibility cannot be ruled out with positive evidence, and the noisy patterns seen here are consistent with such a possibility. The argument that all the bones derived from animals killed at the site is not demonstrable. This becomes a crucial point when it is recalled that stone tools predominantly associate with cervids, equids, and bovids, and not with elephants, which behave in this analysis more like carcass remnants.

This analysis was very frustrating. We know something about the transport probabilities of bones, and we have several pilot studies of elephants and other faunas to serve as guides for the recognition of fluvial transport and sorting under a variety of conditions (see Frison and Todd 1986). Unfortunately, we cannot use any of this knowledge because of the way in which the Torralba faunas are reported. We know that many bones are abraded and rolled, yet these important facts are not reported. We know that most bones are broken and fragmentary, yet the bones are summarized in terms of sets of anatomical parts as known in living animals without consideration of the problem of formation processes. The units in which bones occur in these deposits are not anatomical units per se but instead bone fragments, which must be studied in terms of properties that could have affected their sorted and restructured presence in these deposits. It is these data, summarized in classes that are not relevant for such analyses, that have served as the basis for all the published interpretations as well as the arguments forcefully put forth regarding big-game hunting at Torralba. This can only be described as unfortunate.

Analysis Step Four: Combined Tool and Faunal Variables

My original idea in doing a sequence of analyses was simply to enable recognition of patterning by looking at stone tools and bones independently that might not be as obvious when both types of remains were viewed together. My final step in pattern recognition was to study the total matrix of both bones and tools as originally presented and studied by Freeman (1978b:72–73).

In his original tabulations, Freeman independently listed faunal parts considered "worked" and parts considered "unworked." Because I am interested in the patterned covariation among the parts of animals as some indication of site integrity as well as the possible differential distribution of animal parts caused by hominid activity, I have retained Freeman's distinctions and have studied, using my own techniques, the identical matrix of data studied by Freeman in his analysis. As in previous cases I normalized the data by calculating chi-square values for the cells in the matrix. These were then used as input for a singular value decomposition producing a principal component multivariate solution. The six-component solution summarized in Table 25.7 accounts for 79% of the total variance, distributed as follows: Dimension 1, 19%; Dimension 2, 15%; Dimension 3, 13%; Dimension, 4 12%; Dimension 5, 10%; and Dimension 6, 10%.

In order to discuss the patterning revealed by the independent dimensions in the principal component solution I have prepared a different form of table, one that displays the patterning more graphically. Table 25.8 summarizes the Dimension 1 patterning in this manner.

Here we again see the pattern recognized when we studied both categories of remains (Table 25.3), namely that the elephant bone varies inversely with that from all other species. Those parts of other species loading along with elephant are small or light parts that might be expected to be readily transported by natural agencies. Covarying with the non-elephant species are a suite of tool classes that have consistently high loadings (see Table 25.7, Dimension 1). As we shall see, this is consistent with the earlier results, where tools were predominantly shown to covary with the non-elephant species (Table 25.3). Turning to the negative aspect of Dimension 1, we see a grouping of all the elephant bone and a much more weakly associated suite of tool classes (see Table 25.7, Dimension 1) headed by sidescrapers, bifaces, and endscrapers. Clearly we are being told two important facts. Elephant remains vary inversely with the other species, and sidescrapers and bifaces rather unambiguously go with elephants and are inversely related to the species/tool relationships indicated by the positive component. It cannot be overemphasized that both bifaces and sidescrapers are infrequent tool forms at Torralba relative to denticulates, notches, and retouched and utilized forms (see Freeman 1975a:670). If this were all we knew about the Torralba site, we would be forced to recognize two separate activities involving different species and different tool assemblages. One is the set of activities in which cervids, equids, and bovids were involved and the hominids were using a tool kit similar to that described earlier as being associated with an unambiguous butchering site at which the butchers seem mainly to have produced the tools at the carcasses. On the other hand, the association of the elephant remains with scraper edges (which are suspected as commonly being compound-edge tools) and bifaces (which are said to be made mainly of local materials) together with endscrapers, notches, denticulates, perforators, and cores—but in the absence of waste—is a strange association. If these elephant hunts were well planned, one wonders why the butchers were not equipped for the task ahead. They had to make their hand-axes on the spot of poor material, and they quite possibly made use of a variety of tools picked up on the site. (This suggestion will be clarified when the other dimensions are considered.) The normal Acheulian pattern of frequently transported hand-axes does not appear to apply at Torralba. Similarly, the common pattern of scrapers inversely related to notches and denticulates does not seem to apply when elephant remains are associated.

Dimension 2 reports an independent pattern present at Torralba (Table 25.9). There are several striking features to this component. Perhaps the most important is that there is generally an inverse relationship between the alleged worked bones and their unworked counterparts for both species and anatomical parts. In addition, all of the unidentified bones (both worked and unworked) go with the "worked" bones on the negative aspect of Dimension 2. The exceptions to this generalization are "worked" elephant tusks, which I have already suggested are the naturally broken tips of young elephant tusks, known to occur while the animals are still alive. The other exception is worked bovid limbs, which appear with the "unworked" bones. One way to view this

Table 25.7
Analysis Step Four: Master Loadings

Case	Variable	Dimension 1	Variables	Dimension 2	Variables	Dimension 3
1	−3.74	elephant feet	−4.98	bovid teeth	−3.64	worked unidentified bone
2	−3.69	unworked elephant limb	−4.94	denticulate	−3.43	worked elephant rib
3	−3.67	worked elephant limb	−3.08	cervid feet	−2.57	unworked unidentified bone
4	−3.42	elephant vertebra	−3.08	notch	−2.40	worked elephant tusk
5	−3.31	worked elephant rib	−2.10	bovid skull	−2.32	equid vertebra
6	−2.86	elephant scapula	−2.06	perforator	−1.96	worked equid teeth
7	−2.44	sidescraper	−1.89	equid pelvis	−1.88	equid pelvis
8	−2.40	elephant skull	−1.86	worked unidentified bone	−1.60	equid scapula
9	−2.35	unworked elephant rib	−1.56	cervid vertebra	−0.89	cervid scapula
10	−2.31	worked elephant tusk	−1.11	unworked unidentified bone	−0.84	endscraper
11	−2.30	unworked elephant tusk	−0.82	biface	−0.79	cervid vertebra
12	−1.47	elephant teeth	−0.74	cervid limb	−0.69	abrupt retouch
13	−1.34	bovid skull	−0.70	retouched edge	−0.65	elephant scapula
14	−1.29	biface	−0.67	worked equid limb	−0.61	cervid limb
15	−1.24	elephant pelvis	−0.60	core	−0.60	cervid antler
16	−1.22	worked unidentified bone	−0.47	cervid skull	−0.56	bovid skull
17	−0.98	endscraper	−0.36	worked equid teeth	−0.54	cervid skull
18	−0.80	notch	−0.30	elephant skull	−0.35	elephant pelvis
19	−0.59	equid feet	−0.25	equid feet	−0.32	unworked bovid limb
20	−0.40	equid vertebra	−0.24	worked elephant rib	−0.30	bovid feet
21	−0.32	cervid vertebra	−0.23	equid skull	−0.25	unworked equid limb
22	−0.12	cervid scapula	−0.11	worked elephant limb	−0.16	sidescraper
23	−0.11	denticulate	−0.05	burin	−0.10	elephant teeth
24	−0.11	perforator	0.05	cervid scapula	−0.06	core
25	−0.09	core	0.07	chopper	−0.05	chopper
26	−0.09	equid skull	0.09	utilized flake	0.06	worked bovid feet
27	0.12	equid scapula	0.22	unworked equid teeth	0.13	cervid feet
28	0.22	worked bovid limb	0.23	abrupt retouch	0.13	elephant vertebra
29	0.26	burin	0.28	bovid feet	0.28	equid feet
30	0.41	cervid antler	0.38	equid scapula	0.34	equid skull
31	0.65	worked equid teeth	0.59	elephant feet	0.60	worked equid limb
32	0.67	cervid skull	0.79	worked bovid limb	0.91	waste
33	0.69	chopper	0.90	endscraper	0.93	biface
34	0.76	unworked bovid limb	0.90	worked elephant tusk	0.99	burin
35	0.87	retouched edge	1.06	sidescraper	1.22	bovid teeth
36	0.95	unworked equid teeth	1.07	cervid antler	1.36	notch
37	1.08	worked equid limb	1.14	unworked bovid limb	1.43	elephant feet
38	1.21	bovid teeth	1.33	unworked equid limb	1.45	unworked elephant rib
39	1.44	unworked unidentified bone	1.49	equid vertebra	1.60	retouched edge
40	1.54	bovid feet	1.64	elephant scapula	1.60	denticulate
41	1.59	cervid limb	2.00	elephant pelvis	1.96	unworked elephant tusk
42	1.72	equid pelvis	2.01	elephant teeth	2.07	utilized flake
43	2.46	cervid feet	2.31	unworked elephant tusk	2.08	worked elephant rib
44	2.60	unworked equid limb	2.36	unworked elephant rib	2.24	unworked equid teeth
45	2.99	abrupt retouch	2.89	elephant vertebra	2.87	elephant skull
46	5.36	utilized flake	2.90	unworked elephant limb	2.94	unworked elephant limb
47	10.18	waste	5.17	waste	3.60	perforator

(*continued*)

pattern is that Dimension 2 separates the largely untrampled or geologically unmodified levels from the heavily trampled and/or geologically modified deposits. For those who wish to see the variability at Torralba as referable exclusively to hominid activity, a case could be made that the negative aspect of this component, upon which the majority of the tools with significant loadings are grouped, represents major hominid activities during which many bones were broken. This suggestion is found to be plausible when it is realized that it is skull parts and limb bones that are predominant

Table 25.7 (*Continued*)

Case	Variables	Dimension 4	Variables	Dimension 5	Variables	Dimension 6
1	−4.42	cervid feet	−3.84	worked elephant rib	−2.62	cervid limb
2	−3.40	unworked equid teeth	−2.72	worked bovid limb	−2.09	biface
3	−3.31	bovid teeth	−2.14	unworked equid limb	−1.81	bovid teeth
4	−1.71	unworked elephant rib	−2.00	sidescraper	−1.73	waste
5	−1.57	worked elephant tusk	−1.21	elephant teeth	−1.53	bovid skull
6	−1.47	abrupt retouch	−1.08	elephant skull	−1.41	worked elephant limb
7	−1.32	elephant vertebra	−1.04	unworked unidentified bone	−1.34	notch
8	−1.28	worked unidentified bone	−1.01	perforator	−1.04	core
9	−1.27	elephant teeth	−0.91	cervid vertebra	−0.94	retouched edge
10	−0.95	elephant skull	−0.89	cervid limb	−0.89	worked equid teeth
11	−0.77	chopper	−0.86	untilized flake	−0.85	unworked elephant rib
12	−0.69	retouched edge	−0.82	worked elephant limb	−0.70	worked unidentified bone
13	−0.66	core	−0.71	worked elephant tusk	−0.61	elephant skull
14	−0.61	worked elephant limb	−0.46	equid feet	−0.57	unworked bovid limb
15	−0.59	burin	−0.35	abrupt retouch	−0.45	sidescraper
16	−0.58	sidescraper	−0.28	notch	−0.37	endscraper
17	−0.55	equid scapula	−0.24	waste	−0.36	denticulate
18	−0.46	elephant pelvis	−0.16	unworked equid teeth	−0.29	chopper
19	−0.44	elephant feet	−0.11	worked equid teeth	−0.16	elephant teeth
20	−0.31	cervid limb	−0.11	equid scapula	−0.12	unworked elephant limb
21	−0.31	equid skull	−0.11	equid vertebra	−0.10	unworked elephant tusk
22	−0.29	cervid scapula	−0.04	denticulate	−0.05	worked bovid feet
23	−0.26	cervid vertebra	−0.03	endscraper	−0.03	worked unidentified bone
24	−0.22	bovid skull	−0.02	elephant feet	0.06	worked elephant tusk
25	−0.10	elephant scapula	−0.02	chopper	0.02	elephant feet
26	0.10	unworked elephant limb	0.05	bovid feet	0.15	abrupt retouch
27	0.17	utilized flake	0.16	elephant scapula	0.18	bovid feet
28	0.19	endscraper	0.25	equid skull	0.24	elephant scapula
29	0.23	equid vertebra	0.26	bovid teeth	0.26	elephant vertebra
30	0.33	bovid feet	0.37	equid pelvis	0.35	utilized flake
31	0.68	waste	0.43	core	0.37	worked equid limb
32	0.76	cervid skull	0.63	unworked elephant rib	0.38	cervid scapula
33	0.92	unworked bovid limb	0.67	elephant pelvis	0.49	equid scapula
34	0.94	worked equid teeth	0.69	unworked elephant tusk	0.61	elephant pelvis
35	0.98	unworked elephant tusk	0.75	cervid feet	0.84	equid vertebra
36	0.98	worked bovid limb	0.78	cervid scapula	0.89	perforator
37	1.20	bovid teeth	0.79	bovid skull	0.99	burin
38	1.25	biface	0.87	elephant vertebra	1.03	cervid skull
39	1.43	perforator	1.20	biface	1.24	unworked equid limb
40	1.44	unworked equid limb	1.23	unworked bovid limb	1.34	worked elephant rib
41	1.45	equid feet	1.36	cervid skull	1.59	equid feet
42	1.53	cervid antler	1.49	worked unidentified bone	1.81	unworked equid teeth
43	1.88	notch	1.73	retouched edge	1.94	equid pelvis
44	1.99	worked elephant rib	1.99	burin	2.09	equid skull
45	2.03	worked unidentified bone	2.11	cervid antler	2.49	cervid feet
46	2.39	denticulate	2.42	unworked elephant limb	2.53	cervid antler
47	2.51	worked equid limb	2.74	worked equid limb	3.01	cervid vertebra

for all species, including elephant. Clearly some bias in anatomical parts seems to be represented, and it is head parts that in other sites are frequently abundant when denticulates and notches dominate the tool assemblage. The activity-related interpretation is also consistent with patterns recognized earlier in which lithic waste tends to vary independently of most of the tools. The previously observed connection between sidescrapers, endscrapers, and elephants appears here again, with what clearly seem to be elephant carcass suites or death-site remains. The presence of waste and utilized

Table 25.8
Analysis Step Four: Dimension 1, Combined Tool and Faunal Analysis

Cervid	Equid	Bovid	Elephant	Tools
Positive				
feet	unworked limbs	feet		waste
limbs	pelves	teeth		utilized flakes
skulls	worked limbs	unworked limbs		abrupt
antlers	unworked teeth	worked limbs		retouch
	worked teeth			retouched
	scapulae			edges
				choppers
				burins
Negative				
vertebrae	feet	skulls	feet	sidescrapers
scapulae	vertebrae		unworked limbs	bifaces
	skulls		worked limbs	endscrapers
			vertebrae	notches
			worked ribs	denticulates
			scapulae	perforators
			skulls	cores
			unworked ribs	
			worked tusks	
			unworked tusks	
			teeth	
			pelves	

Table 25.9
Analysis Step Four: Dimension 2, Combined Tool and Faunal Analysis

Cervid	Equid	Bovid	Elephant	Tools
Positive				
antlers	vertebrae	unworked limbs	unworked limbs	waste
scapulae	unworked limbs	worked limbs	vertebrae	sidescrapers
	scapulae	feet	unworked ribs	endscrapers
	unworked teeth		unworked tusks	abrupt
			teeth	retouch
			pelves	utilized flakes
			scapulae	choppers
			worked tusks	
			feet	
Negative				
feet	pelves	teeth	skulls	denticulates
vertebrae	worked limbs	skulls	worked ribs	notches
limbs	worked teeth		worked limbs	perforators
skulls	feet			bifaces
	skulls			retouched
				edges
				cores
				burins

flakes makes it somewhat easier to see aspects of the positively associated variables as being related to carcass processing. No matter how we interpret the patterning, the case for "activity areas" is very hard to sustain. The elephant carcass material is inversely related to remains of other species, making it difficult to argue that the differences in tools represent tools appropriate to sequential processing steps in the butchering of a single animal. In addition, it must be kept in mind that we are studying different stratigraphic levels at Torralba. If these two sets of interrelated tools and body parts represented phases in a processing sequence, we would not expect them to be inversely related to one another among the various levels at Torralba.

Dimension 3 (Table 25.10) offers further insight into the suggestions made regarding Dimension 2. Here we see some very interesting associations. First, the positive aspect groups head and leg parts of both equids and bovids and a suite of elephant bones that have some of the properties of a skull and a leg association joined by ribs. The tools that are linked to this association are perforators and utilized flakes, along with retouched flakes and a heavy tool—in this case, bifaces—plus waste. These artifact forms are all "at home" with the notches and denticulates with which they are also associated. Perhaps a similar tool kit is associated with a similar processing task, regardless of the species being processed. This could then be seen as a similarly organized suite of tools, as was seen in negative Dimension 2. In the previous case, however, the main difference was that equids and cervids were the associated species. When we consider the negative aspect of Dimension 3, the occurrence of tool suites appears to be even more plausible. We see a clear carcass grouping of body parts from cervids and equids associated with a skull and a leg set from bovids and another carcass set—ribs, scapulae, pelves, and teeth—of elephants. As was the case in nega-

Table 25.10
Analysis Step Four: Dimension 3, Combined Tool and Faunal Analysis

Cervid	Equid	Bovid	Elephant	Tools
Positive				
feet	unworked teeth	teeth	unworked limbs	perforators
	worked limbs	worked teeth	skulls	utilized flakes
	skulls		worked ribs	denticulates
	feet		unworked tusks	retouched
			unworked ribs	edges
			feet	notches
			vertebrae	burins
				bifaces
				waste
Negative				
scapulae	vertebrae	skulls	worked ribs	endscrapers
vertebrae	worked teeth	unworked limbs	worked tusks	abrupt
limbs	pelves	feet	scapulae	retouch
antlers	scapulae		pelves	sidescrapers
skulls	unworked limbs		teeth	cores
				choppers

tive Dimension 1 and positive Dimension 2, sidescrapers and endscrapers seem to go with carcass indicators, also accompanied here by abruptly retouched edges, cores, and choppers. Choppers appear with the scraper forms in all previous suites in apparent association with carcass indicators, while cores and abruptly retouched edges have appeared in association in two of the three examples seen thus far. As in the case of Dimension 2, it must be kept in mind that these inversely related suites of tools and faunal associations occur independently across the different levels at the Torralba site.

We have begun to recognize a pattern, and the characteristics of Dimension 4 (Table 25.11) generally support what we have seen thus far—notches and denticulates varying inversely with choppers, cores, and sidescrapers. Similarly, we see that with the denticulate tool suite (positive aspect), head parts of cervids, teeth and limbs of equids, and teeth and limbs of bovids go together and only associate with worked elephant ribs, unworked tusks, and unworked elephant limbs. In addition, there is the provocative loading of "worked equid teeth" with denticulates. I have previously noted that in some Mousterian assemblages equid upper teeth may be "worked;" their crowns have been crushed and "flakes" have even been removed from their lateral surfaces. In both Mousterian assemblages (Binford 1984c:159–165) and the recently studied fauna from Zhoukoudian (Binford and Stone 1986) upper teeth of equids are sometimes burned, particularly the fourth premolars and first molars. I have suggested that this results from the roasting and subsequent impact breakage of skulls while they are resting on their teeth on a hard surface. The associations indicated by

Table 25.11
Analysis Step Four: Dimension 4, Combined Tool and Faunal Analysis

Cervid	Equid	Bovid	Elephant	Tools
Positive				
antlers	worked limbs	worked limbs	worked ribs	denticulates
skulls	feet	unworked limbs	unworked tusks	notches
	unworked limbs	feet	unworked limbs	perforators
	worked teeth			bifaces
	vertebrae			waste
	pelves			utilized flakes
				endscrapers
Negative				
feet	unworked teeth	teeth	unworked ribs	abrupt
limbs	scapulae	skulls	worked tusks	retouch
scapulae	skulls		vertebrae	choppers
vertebrae			teeth	retouched
			skulls	edges
			worked limbs	cores
			pelves	burins
			feet	sidescrapers
			scapulae	

positive Dimension 4 have strong analogies to other known hominid-processed faunas in which heads and lower legs were being accumulated and processed for "marginal food." In short, the denticulate/notch "tool kits" predominantly associate with non-elephant parts and, significantly, with parts of heads and limbs/feet (see Table 25.11). Various elephant parts may infrequently appear, but their presence varies inversely across independent levels with elephant carcass indicators.

Turning to the negative aspect of Dimension 4, elephant now dominates the associated species. This repeats the now established pattern in which elephant remains vary independently both of the other species and of the frequently occurring tool "edge" classes. Thus, elephant tends to vary inversely with tool frequencies in general (Tables 25.3 and 25.11). As in previous cases, when an elephant carcass assemblage of bones is indicated, cores, choppers, and sidescrapers, sometimes accompanied by abruptly retouched pieces, are related. We appear to have the repetition of a very robust and internally consistent pattern. Elephant remains vary independently of the other fauna as a group. Various combinations of the other species occur in different stratigraphic levels, and elephants may sometimes coincide with varying combinations of the other species. Elephant may occur with equids, but only rarely is there any interaction except independence noted between bovids and elephants. The vast majority of the animal/tool interactions involve the non-elephant species. Among these positive animal/tool associations, when denticulates and notches (sometimes accompanied by bifaces and other small tools) dominate the tool suite, the related anatomical parts are heads and limbs, with axial parts rare. On the other hand, when sidescrapers, endscrapers, cores, choppers, and abruptly retouched edges dominate the tool associations, the dominant anatomical part frequencies, regardless of species, are suggestive of the presence of carcasses. Since elephants generally vary independently of the other species, the latter tool group strongly associates with bone suites that appear to represent elephant carcass remains.

Dimensions 5 and 6 continue as variations on this theme. Summaries of these components are presented in Tables 25.12 and 25.13. Given the rather clear pattern demonstrated by the initial dimensions to be extracted (which account for most of the variance among the tool-yielding levels at Torralba), it is not surprising that these dimensions document situations in which these robust patterns are somewhat more confused. The last two meaningful dimensions can most likely be seen as some measure of the frequency with which independent events were compounded on single occupation surfaces at Torralba.

Positive Dimension 5 shows the rare situation in which all species are represented. When this situation occurs, the only tools related are low-count forms (burins) and large tools (bifaces and cores). One suspects that this pattern is perhaps related to postdepositional disturbance. The negative aspect of this dimension, however, exhibits a return to the robust pattern previously outlined. Carcasses seem indicated for the equids, and these relate to a suite of elephant parts that could represent naturally sorted carcass remnants, with the lighter parts having been removed by natural agents. With what is most likely naturally sorted carcass remains of equids and elephants we see the familiar group of tools—sidescrapers, perforators, utilized flakes, abruptly

Table 25.12
Analysis Step Four: Dimension 5, Combined Tool and Faunal Analysis

Cervid	Equid	Bovid	Elephant	Tools
Positive				
antlers	worked limbs	unworked limbs	unworked limbs	burins
skulls	pelves	skulls	vertebrae	retouched
scapulae	skulls	teeth	unworked tusks	edges
feet		feet	pelves	bifaces
			unworked ribs	cores
			scapulae	
Negative				
vertebrae	unworked limbs	worked limbs	worked ribs	sidescrapers
limbs	feet		teeth	perforators
	unworked teeth		skulls	utilized flakes
	worked teeth		worked limbs	abrupt
	scapulae		worked tusks	retouch
	vertebrae		feet	notches
				waste
				choppers
				endscrapers
				denticulates

Table 25.13
Analysis Step Four: Dimension 6, Combined Tool and Faunal Analysis

Cervid	Equid	Bovid	Elephant	Tools
Positive				
vertebrae	skulls	feet	worked ribs	burins
antlers	pelves		pelves	perforators
feet	unworked teeth		vertebrae	utilized flakes
skulls	feet		scapulae	abrupt
scapulae	unworked limbs		feet	retouch
	vertebrae		worked tusks	
	scapulae			
	worked limbs			
Negative				
limbs	worked teeth	teeth	worked limbs	bifaces
		skulls	unworked ribs	waste
		unworked limbs	skulls	notches
		worked feet	teeth	cores
			unworked limbs	retouched
			unworked tusks	edges
				sidescrapers
				endscrapers
				denticulates
				choppers

retouched edges, notches, and waste. Viewing this dimension as the above-described pattern of carcass-related anatomical parts and tools, with the added dimension of some natural sorting, makes a great deal of sense.

Dimension 6 seems to represent the other half of the pattern seen in negative Dimension 5, namely processing locations for skulls and limbs that have also been modified by natural sorting agents (Table 25.13). The positive dimension now loads primarily small and low-count tools and what appear to be carcass remains from cervids, equids, and elephants. This rare interaction of carcass indicators for multiple species must be viewed as carcasses with which hominids were rarely if ever involved since only small tools are related, and these have low loading values. They may represent tools easily transported by natural agents. In any event, the only pattern that could possibly be seen as a "mass kill" occurs in positive Dimension 6. Ironically, tools are only marginally involved, and these are small and hence could be naturally sorted forms.

The negative dimension associates elephants and bovids in a rare pattern of interaction in which both appear to represent head and limb associations. The elephant suite exhibits a clear bias for heavy and "lag" deposit remains, however, such as tusks and teeth. These could represent highly modified carcass remains (lag deposits) forming a background for bovid processing events carried out by hominids. This suggestion would render more understandable the rare association of both notches and denticulates with sidescrapers linked to cores, waste, and retouched flakes.

I consider the results of this pattern recognition study to be exciting and provocative. We have isolated some robust patterns in the Torralba data. The interaction between hominids and faunal remains seems clear. In fact, the results are not in conflict with the results that Freeman obtained (see Table 25.1); however, because of his procedures he could not see the detail observable here. His first three factors all linked skull and limb parts of a variable suite of largely non-elephant species to notches, denticulates, utilized flakes, lithic waste, perforators, and becs. These three factors accounted for the majority of the variance in his data. Factor IV then loaded what is clearly the elephant carcass suite of bones, and as we found, endscrapers and sidescrapers were strongly linked to the carcass indicators. Freeman had before him patterns demonstrating that one suite of the most abundant tools went with the non-elephant species, which were primarily represented by head and leg parts. Independent of the above relationships, elephant carcasses varied with scrapers. It is very hard to see how killing an elephant and initially processing it could result in a secondary processing area dominated by cervids, equids, and bovids. Freeman simply believed the earlier intuitive interpretations (Freeman and Butzer 1966) and accommodated his pattern-recognition results to these beliefs.

CONCLUSIONS

Much of the bone from Torralba has been heavily modified by natural agents; we strongly suspect that water and solifluction and other, biologically produced modifications have occurred, such as trampling, particularly by elephants. This means that the excavated surfaces, while probably variable in integrity (Binford 1981a:19), cannot rationally be assumed to represent high-integrity "living floor" surfaces where the total content can be directly referable to hominid actions. Instead, careful taphonomic studies and informed considerations of formation processes are required even for remains and tools unambiguously produced by hominids. Thus far such studies have not been conducted. In fact, the popularized interpretations of the Torralba data have essentially pretended that these problems were nonexistent. This situation immediately calls into question the interpretations made under bad assumptions.

Claims for high frequencies of cut marks (Howell et al. 1963; Howell and Freeman 1982), patterned breakage of bone by hominids for purposes of bone tool production (Biberson and Aguirre 1965; Howell 1965:84; Freeman 1975a:675), and the citation of special anatomical parts, such as the alleged tools manufactured from the tips of elephant tusks and thought to have been hafted (Freeman 1975a:675; Howell and Freeman 1982:12), are common. Recent middle-range research has cast grave doubt on the accuracy of such interpretations. As pointed out here, investigations by Shipman and Rose (1983) show that very few of the specimens selected specifically by the investigators as "good" examples of bones exhibiting cut marks could be accepted as such when modern identification techniques were used. During the course of these investigations much evidence indicative of abrasion and other natural modifications was noted on the bones. These findings strongly support Klein and Cruz-Uribe's (n.d.) work, which reports a high order of modification by natural agents and the observation that many bones are clearly rolled or modified by solifluction. My own taphonomic research supports these conclusions, particularly emphasizing that the "distinctive breakage" patterns are frequently observable on bones broken by natural agents or are a consequence of marrow bone breakage by hominids where no tool manufacture was intended or carried out. Finally, the "hafted elephant tusk" spear points have been noted to simply result from natural tip breakage among living elephants. Thus, most of the early and spectacular claims for unique and provocative actions by hominids using bone tools turn out to be enthusiastic arguments made with little knowledge of patterns in nature. In short, middle-range studies did not anchor such interpretations; instead, "what else could it be" arguments warranted romantic views of the Torralba hominids.

Other reconstructions of ancient life have also been based on Torralba data. For instance, manuports (natural but allegedly hominid-introduced stones) have been "identified" and interpreted at Torralba.

> Some manuport accumulations could be deliberate stockpiles of ammunition made for future eventualities; a social group sophisticated enough to conduct a drive like those suggested would probably have been capable of moving the prey quite precisely in a given direction, taking advantage of the terrain. Stockpiles of raw material for tool manufacture as well as ammunition caches might have been made at several suitable "natural abbatoirs" along the valley. (Freeman 1975a:680)

I had intended to add manuports to the list of "tools" presented by Freeman for study in this analysis. In fact, scattered in the literature are counts of manuports for all the levels used in this analysis. Nevertheless, still other reports give conflicting counts, so I concluded that I could not be sure that the reported counts that seemed to be consistent did in fact derive from the same years of excavation as those represented by Freeman's (1978b) tables. During the course of this study, however, I did analyze a matrix of tools and fauna with counts of manuports from similar proveniences. The results were striking. Manuports varied with no other variables and behaved inversely with both tools and fauna on the first component. This situation was mainly caused by the report of 1700+ manuports from Level I. Level I at Torralba is the only stratum described as being heavily disturbed, and it even yields "patterned ground" phenomena known to result from freeze/thaw conditions operating on deposits (Butzer 1965:1719). One wonders how one could identify manuports in what is described as a "coarse, subangular to subrounded gravel" deposit (Butzer 1965:1719). I think it is clear that the investigators have been overzealous in their identification of manuports. Secondary and low variance components did group manuports with tools of the denticulate/notch suite discussed in this report; however, much of the variance in the occurrence of manuports remained unaccounted for. It seems quite likely to me that manuports do exist at Torralba, but their indiscriminate identification has largely obscured this important fact. I think the identification of ammunition piles is unwarranted since the only levels where manuports appeared to vary with the tools were levels yielding less than fifty such items, and most contained between one and ten.

Another area of unwarranted interpretation concerns the evidence for fire at Torralba. Early in the history of the site's excavation the recognition of diffuse charcoal in the levels at Torralba was taken as evidence for purposeful fires used by the hominids "to drive unwieldy elephants into the mud" (Howell 1965:84, 94–95). There seems to be no realization here that fire is a natural and constant part of ecosystems. The presence of dispersed charcoal in a geological deposit does not demand "heroic" interpretation. This is particularly true in sediments collected in lakes and bogs, where floating carbon is concentrated and then deposited as the water level retreats.

The age structure of the elephants at Torralba was initially said to be biased in favor of young elephants, which were thought to be "most vulnerable to the hunt" (Biberson 1964:216). This view has more recently been revised and the claim has been made that "adult specimens make up 70% of recognizable individual elephants" (Freeman 1975a:677). If this is true, it would be hard to argue for a "catastrophic" death situation for the elephants involved. Nevertheless, the citation of age profiles of whatever accuracy as evidence for hunting is strange since I know of no data available at that time that described what a natural elephant death population might look like. Now such data is accumulating (Soffer 1985), and I have been informed by Gary Haynes (personal communication, 1986) that the Torralba elephants are similar to known natural elephant death populations. Arguments favoring hunting interpretations based on age profiles, particularly "catastrophic" game driving techniques, seem to be totally unwarranted for Torralba.

Freeman has advanced the interpretation of the Torralba data beyond the specific data-centered approach cited above. He has entered into the domain of pattern recognition studies and as a consequence has presented a much more elaborate picture of past life at Torralba than that presented in the early scenario of big-game hunters using game drives. His analytical goal was to warrant his claim that the vast quantities of meat obtained in the game drives were sequentially processed, leaving in the archaeological record structured and redundant patterns referable to "activity areas."

This report has been a restudy of the same data used by Freeman. While better data would certainly be desirable, it is these data which have been used in constructing a picture of past life at Torralba. I have been concerned with the methodological issue regarding the degree to which earlier interpretations are warranted.

Results of this Study

This study was conducted using analytical strategies to ensure that all the assumptions of the pattern recognition techniques used were in fact met. It was conducted in a step-wise fashion.

Preliminary analysis was conducted on a matrix of summed frequencies for the separate species represented at Torralba as well as the sum of tool counts, each tabulated by "occupation" level. This gross overview approach established certain patterns that were later found to permeate the results of all subsequent analyses. Most striking perhaps was the recognition that artifacts dominantly covary with the non-elephant species—cervids, equids, and bovids. This suite varies *inversely* with elephant remains. Independent of this dominant pattern was a second pattern in which elephant bones varied with equid remains and both covaried with tools. This suite was inversely related to bovid and cervid remains. In addition, bovids alone were linked to tools and bovids and tools together varied inversely with equids and cervids.

These patterns immediately alert us to several important implications. First, the differential distributions and associations of tools at Torralba are species-related. If Freeman's arguments regarding "activity areas" were correct, we would expect the tools to be partitioned differentially within species groups. This is definitely not the case. Second, the predominant interactions between tools and species are with the cervid, equid, and bovid group and only secondarily with elephant remains. Third, equid remains are the only ones that are associated with tools twice in the solution, and cervid remains are never independently associated with tools. This immediately suggests not only that the dominant hominid involvement was with the cervid, equid, and bovid groups but that, among these, equid remains were the most common companion of hominid presence at the site.

The two following analyses, which considered tools and fauna independently, illustrate important patterns within each class. Both, however, share some important properties. Perhaps the most noticeable feature was that both were rather "noisy" solutions. It should be recalled that in the faunal study the distinctions between "worked and unworked" bones were ignored and the classes were collapsed. In my experience, when one obtains "noisy" solutions the important variables underlying the structure in the materials being explored are not well represented among the variables chosen for study.

In the tool study we learned that lithic waste varies inversely with most of the tools. The next most important independent pattern is that sidescrapers, endscrapers, cores, choppers, abruptly retouched edges, and bifaces vary inversely with lithic waste, notches, burins, utilized flakes, denticulates, and perforators. This provocative pattern is well known in Europe; denticulates and notches tend to vary inversely with scraper forms in Mousterian assemblages. This pattern is inherent in the Torralba data, and viewing Torralba as a whole, it is the denticulate/notch suite of tools that dominates the numerical frequencies (see Freeman 1975a:670). We note a third independent pattern, one in which abruptly retouched pieces, denticulates, and burins (as dominant elements) vary inversely with notches, bifaces, and lithic waste. This is clearly a breakdown of the "denticulate/notch" pattern into a provocative subpattern. This result was encouraging in that a familiar pattern emerges, suggesting that some structural facts regarding the past organization of hominid technologies remain at Torralba.

In the faunal study the pattern seen in the gross study of fauna and tools was reinforced and elaborated. As in the early study, elephant remains varied *inversely* with the remains of cervids, equids, and bovids. Independent of this overriding pattern was an association of heads of bovids and elephants accompanied by elephant limb bones. This suite varied inversely with feet and limbs of bovids and equids and with some cervid parts. This relationship tells us that, while the inverse relationship between elephants and other species is continuing, there is some interaction between elephant skull parts and bovid skull parts. Although additional independent patterns continue to document the overall independence between elephants and other species, interspecies relationships are suggested. The nature of these interactions is unclear, however, since taphonomically ambiguous clues indicate that the interactions could be caused by either natural or hominid agents.

In the final analysis, an integrated matrix of both tool-edge frequencies and species categories broken down by anatomical units was searched for patterning. In this study the distinctions made by the excavators between "worked" and "unworked" bones was maintained. This study yielded a more robust solution than those previously obtained, suggesting immediately that there was significant structured interaction between fauna and tools and between "worked" and "unworked" bones. The patterns we had seen in earlier studies were clarified, and some really exciting results were obtained. There was repeated confirmation of the previously recognized pattern in which denticulates and notches dominate a suite of tools that varies quite independently of tool sets dominated by side- and endscrapers. We also noted that in a comparative environment of tools the faunal remains break out into a dichotomy of what appear to be carcass remnants versus aggregated head and limb parts from different species. *The scraper-dominated tool suite is regularly associated with the carcass indicators, regardless of species, while the denticulate/notch-dominated tool suite is consistently related with the head and limb pattern, regardless of species* (except elephant). These are truly exciting results, since never before have we seen the *context* of the pattern of independent variation between denticulated and notched tools versus the scraper class of tools so familiar to most European archaeologists.

Even more important for the interpretation of the Torralba site is the fact that carcass indicators vary independently among species, and inversely within species, with the head and limb associations. This has immediate implications for the validity of Freeman's argument that activity areas are the organizational framework standing behind the patterns noted at Torralba. Simply stated, no activity area differentiation is indicated. *The differentiations are independent of one another and commonly are inversely related within a species class, and as such they could only arise as independent episodes of hominid activity at the site.* It is also quite clear that no mass coincidences of carcasses ever occurred at the Torralba location. They vary independently of one another among the species and inversely among the differentiated activities indicated. *Game drives could not account for the accumulations at Torralba.*

Finally, *the dominant tool suite at Torralba, the denticulate/notch suite, is interactively related to non-carcass indicators.* The vast majority of episodes of hominid use at Torralba refer to the accumulation of marginal animal parts from carcasses, most of which were located elsewhere. Head and limb parts appear to have been aggregated and processed at Torralba. In fact, no anatomical parts indicative of bovid carcasses are reported from Torralba. The exploitation of carcasses using a scraper-dominated tool kit is rare, but when it occurs, primarily equids, fewer cervids, and minimal numbers of elephants appear to be involved. These tools are frequently "compound" tools made from the same suite of raw materials as the denticulate/notch tool suite. One can speculate that the hominids were opportunistically "surprised" by the presence of exploitable carcasses and reworked their tool kits into appropriate forms for butchering or, alternatively, scavenged tools from already present archaeological assemblages, occasionally manufacturing larger tools from poor but immediately available materials. *It cannot be overstressed that the involvement by hominids with carcass remnants at the site of Torralba is a very minor aspect of the overall behaviorally relevant materials found there.* In turn, the total artifact inventory from all ten occupations at Torralba amounts to only 785 pieces (Freeman 1975a); as I have suggested previously (Binford 1981a:15–18), hominids were not the major agents responsible for the presence of faunal remains at Torralba.

The exciting patterned interaction demonstrated here between tools and fauna is totally inconsistent with the heroic interpretations that have been popularized. Instead, the patterns are consistent with (a) minimal and episodically sporadic hominid presence; (b) accumulation of marginal parts of animal carcasses for processing, thus far repeatedly seen in the Lower Paleolithic and strongly suggestive of scavenging; and (c) occasional exploitation of carcasses of a variety of species independently distributed in the Torralba deposits. This ad hoc exploitation was performed by poorly equipped hominid groups. Judging from the extremely low frequencies of carcass-related tools, we cannot view this behavior as anything but expedient exploitation of resources that "present themselves," and it carries no positive evidence that is in anyway suggestive of planned hunting.

Chapter 26

Searching for Camps and Missing the Evidence? Another Look at the Lower Paleolithic

INTRODUCTION

One of the first premises of science is that the external world is knowable in terms of itself. For the scientist, however, reality is somewhat more complicated because we seek to know the world in our terms. We approach experience with both prior knowledge and conventions for interpreting experience. Given this situation, the task before us is to seek an understanding and evaluation of the intellectual tools with which we approach and interpret experience. Science should be viewed as a procedure for learning about the limitations of our prior knowledge and the conventions we use for interpreting experience. It is with this understanding of the scientist's challenge that a further discussion of the "data" from the early Pleistocene regarding the patterns of life practiced by our ancestors appears to be appropriate.

During the late 1950s and throughout the 1960s, a very productive shift in archaeological thinking occurred. It was reasoned that in order to know something of the character of life at the dawn of the tool-using era we had to examine the archaeological record in units relevant to past life. Previously, most archaeological investigation into Paleolithic deposits had used essentially a mining strategy. Strata cuts were made into deposits in search of temporal patterning in the clustered remains from the past. The shift to a search for "living floors" was in fact a search for units of observation more relevant to the question of how early humans lived. This in itself was reasonable, logical, and appropriate. In retrospect, however, we may ask if the realization of such an admirable goal was frustrated by our own ideas regarding the character of early hominid behavior. In short, our biases as to the nature of early lifeways provided operational definitions for recognizing new units of observation that we hoped would inform us about early hominid adaptations. At that point we had aborted the first principle of science—namely that the external world is knowable in terms of itself; instead, it became "knowable" only in terms of our biased use of prior knowledge.

Originally appeared in *The Pleistocene Old World,* edited by Olga Soffer, published by Plenum Press, New York, pp. 17–31, © 1987.

CULTURAL VERSUS NICHE GEOGRAPHY

In the preceding context of reasoning, a crucial assumption was made. We expected that early hominids, like modern humans, operated in their environments in such a way that their behavior was the interface between a technologically aided "cultural geography" and the properties of the natural environment in which they lived. Modern humans construct environments (residences, settlements, etc.) or modify their environments to serve their needs and then exploit their natural setting in ways that sustain both themselves and their cultural construct. In the search for "living floors," the presence of tools was implicitly taken as an indication that early humans had a cultural system through which they interfaced or articulated with the natural environment. The very idea of living places and "home bases" assumes the presence of a cultural geography. This view is consistent with studies of modern humans that focus on the relationships between the settlement system and the characteristics of resource distribution within the natural environment (see Binford 1982b for a discussion of the organized relationship between the cultural geography and the natural environment as it conditions the structure of the archaeological record). On the other hand, many animals do not "construct" an environment to serve their needs but instead move within their natural environment among the places where they may obtain the resources essential to their biological success. We commonly say that, although animal behavior is not organized culturally, nevertheless it is not random in an environment. It produces a pattern of differential placement, differentiation of behavior, and intensity of use within a habitat, resulting in a "niche geography." Such mobility-based behavior is a direct response to the structure of the natural environment with regard to differential locations of species-specific requirements. Given the same environment or the same geographic region, different species may behave in distinctive and patterned ways. We may reasonably ask, If this behavior was technologically aided so as to result in permanent "traces" or additions to the landscape, would we not see distinctive distribution patterns among such traces that would refer to the characteristic actions of different species?

Early hominid adaptations were clearly tool-assisted. Did hominids also adapt to their natural environment by the creation of a technologically aided cultural environment? This is certainly a question we would like to answer, one that demands of archaeological methodology a means of discriminating between a technologically aided adaptation and an adaptation that, in addition, may be operating out of a "created environment." This challenging question becomes even more interesting when we recognize that many species do in fact position themselves in their environment in service of their needs. For example, hyenas both dig dens and use natural features for denning activities. Bones that accumulate in such places are different from those remaining at kill sites (Binford 1984a).

We can imagine two very different types of organized land use. One articulates a cultural geography with an environmental geography; the other simply creates an archaeological landscape in direct response to the structure of the natural geography as it differentially offers "need servicing" and conditions the behavior of an animal species. In attempting to evaluate the organizational character of a Paleolithic archaeological landscape, the archaeologist is not only faced with the possibility of different and unimagined forms of organization. In addition, the archaeological landscape is not isomorphic with the dynamic functions of a past system. Dense aggregations of materials may be understood in several ways: They may be the result of a consistent use of a place for similar purposes over varying lengths of time; they may be the result of multiple and different episodes of use; or they may be aggregations of the traces of diffuse episodes caused by natural agencies, such as fluvial action. (And there are still other confusing possibilities.) Although some archaeologists may regard these conditions as "distorting" and hence in need of transformation into their specific "systemic contexts," I am convinced that the cumulative character of an archaeological landscape carries diagnostic information about the organizational properties of the systems of origin.

CONSEQUENTIAL WORKING ASSUMPTIONS

At the outset, living floors were considered to be places where hominids lived, and it was therefore assumed that hominids operated in terms of the interfacing type of organization we see among modern humans—namely a cultural geography. The model of modern hunter-gatherers served as the expected form of organization among early hominid social units, and therefore living places were envisioned as camps or residential locations at which early humans lived and maintained themselves and to which foods and materials for tool manufacture and use were introduced. These expectations had immediate and seemingly self-evident implications for the recognition of living sites in the archaeological record. In their own words, the early proponents of living floors were looking for

> concentrated occurrences of implements, restricted vertically as well as horizontally in their extent. (Howell *et al.* 1959:42)

> An occupation floor: an area of limited but variable extent on an occupation surface where artifacts in primary context are concentrated on what the distribution pattern of the aggregate suggests was a former camping place or workshop of prehistoric man. (Clark 1974:73)

> Living floors, in which occupational debris, including artefacts and food debris, is found on an old land surface or paleosol throughout a depth of only a few centimeters. (M.D. Leakey 1979:48)

The assumption that sites reflecting focused hominid behavior would resemble modern collector-forager camps provided archaeologists with a model with which any suspected "living floor" could be evaluated. At such a place, artifacts and food debris would be both vertically and horizontally concentrated (and Clark 1974 hints at additional facts of site structure). It is therefore not surprising that vertical and horizontal concentrations of tools, and sometimes associated fauna, were automatically interpreted as camps. After the first "discovery" of living floors in the deposits of the very ancient past, an elaborate literature grew up that focused on the importance of camp life to the adaptations of the early hominids. For instance, while discussing the famous "living floors" of Olduvai Gorge, Mary Leakey notes that

> there is, unfortunately, no means either of assessing the length of time during which any camp site was occupied or of estimating the number of resident hominids. Some light may be thrown on this problem when the study of Bushman sites now being undertaken by DeVore, Lee and Yellen has been completed, since the Bushman was undoubtedly one of the nearest modern parallels to the early hunter-gatherers of Africa. (M.D. Leakey 1971:259)

In the subsequent site report on Olorgesailie, Glynn Isaac repeatedly illustrates this tendency to assume the past to be like what we know of human adaptations in the present. For example,

> The function of the sites as centers of domestic life could best be attested by evidence of sleeping and feeding arrangements. However, there are no traces of bedding and only fragmentary evidence of food consumption. The circumstances make it seem likely that these gaps are due to imperfect preservation, and it seems reasonable to suppose that at least some of the artifact concentrations are the durable remnants of the shifting home bases of itinerant bands. (Isaac 1977a:87)

The willingness of Isaac and Richard Leakey, with the support and encouragement of *National Geographic* and Time-Life Books, to accommodate the data from the archaeological record to the researchers' prior beliefs regarding the character of early hominid life resulted in a decade of published material purporting to describe the character of culturally organized camp life among the early hominids (Isaac 1971, 1978a,b, 1983a,b; Leakey 1981; Leakey and Lewin 1977, 1978). It is not surprising that this elaborate view was a simple derivative of the assumptions that guided the arguments justifying the recognition of living floors in the first place. Isaac argued that, at the very dawn of the appearance of tool-using hominids, "men" were hunters living in social groups characterized by a male-female division of labor. The products of the hunt were returned to sleeping locations (home bases), where altruistic sharing took place among adults as well as with children. The women's role in provisioning was centered on gathering wild plant materials. Thus the social basis of later, more elaborate "culture" was thought to be in place at the inception of tool use. It was this view of "hunting and gathering" that both prompted the quest for and justified the identification of living floors, and in turn, living floors were then cited as evidence that this view was correct. Such a procedure is a methodological tautology. Its use guarantees that we are not investigating the external world in terms of itself, rather, we are accommodating the external world to what we believe to be true. Such a procedure rarely leads to learning.

This tendency was exacerbated by a general lack of appreciation for the fact that the static archaeological record cannot be interpreted as the simple reflection of uni-dimensional, event-related properties of a past system. The archaeological record must be understood in terms of a different temporal perspective than is characteristic of our own or of ethnographers' experience in cultural systems. The dynamics that change land surfaces and that differentially bury segments of an archaeological landscape are not isomorphic with the dynamics of either past systems or their internal differentiations (Binford 1982b). The archaeologist must realize that a buried deposit is not a preserved "moment of the past" but is in fact a buried surface collection. Modern archaeologists are becoming increasingly sophisticated in their understanding of some of the important dynamics that stand behind surface collections (Camilli 1985; Ebert et al. 1983) and are working out ways of understanding the systemic implications of these surficial associations.

If we seek to conduct investigations under the assumption that the external world is knowable in terms of itself, and at the same time acknowledge that we are the sources of ideas about the world, we must also acknowledge that the external world does not communicate with us directly. It does not render up its secrets unprompted by us. We must use our ideas and our conceptual tools to tease insight from our experiences. We can only operate in this way with the knowledge we have at the moment and with our culturally provided ideas and concepts for dealing with the world. How then do we avoid the methodological tautology as exemplified in the example of the identification of "living floors"? How do we succeed in knowing the external world in terms of itself, when we in fact interpret the external world in terms of our subjective knowledge and the culturally guided perspectives of our time? The answer must be that we do not approach the external world in search of verification for our ideas and slip into the trap of accommodating experiences to fit what we *believe* to be true. We must use our knowledge of the moment in as broad a fashion as possible and seek ambiguity between our various ideas about the world and our experiences in the world. It is only through the exposure of ambiguity that we are alerted to the fact that some of our ideas are limited or perhaps wrong.

The goal of understanding the nature of early hominid life in terms of itself can only be accomplished if we have strongly contrastive yet plausible alternatives. In this context, the intellectual challenge is then shifted to the methods of inference justification used by archaeologists rather than the skill with which archaeologists are capable of accommodating facts to their beliefs. In such a context, a simple operational definition that serves to identify what one wants to see in the external world cannot survive unevaluated. In the context of evaluation, we cannot help but learn. The presence of contrastive general arguments as to systems-wide significance immediately places in constructive perspective ambiguities in the ways in which we assign meanings to particular observations (unlike low-level arguments of relevance, which frequently pass for "multiple working hypotheses"; see Binford 1983c:157–167 and 1984c:255–264). We may gain even more constructive insights if the competing arguments are equally successful in accommodating the same basic facts. This situation results in the recognition of middle-range research problems that must be solved if evaluations between two competing arguments are to be made rationally.

BINARY VARIABILITY IN THE OLDOWAN AND ACHEULIAN

It is important to begin by reviewing some of the facts upon which most archaeologists would agree. One of the most robust and long-lasting patterns of variability thus far isolated is best described as the "binary" pattern of assemblage variability in the Lower Paleolithic. Although many archaeologists may disagree on the details of this pattern, most who know the data recognize that beginning with the important materials from Olduvai Gorge (1.8 million years ago), there are sites that predominantly yield large tools (choppers, chopping tools, and somewhat later, spheroids) and others that typically yield small tools of the scraper class. There are also sites in which these two independent components occur together. This binary pattern continues into the later Acheulian period. Kleindienst (1962) formalized the recognition that a significant pattern of correlated inverse variation exists between the "small-tool" and "large-tool" components of the Acheulian. Subsequent pattern-recognition work (Binford 1972b; Clark and Kurashina 1976; Isaac 1977a) has confirmed the inverse intralocational relationship between the hand ax-cleaver group of tools and the small-tool group, largely composed of scrapers.

In all studies of the Acheulian, a third grouping of tools appears, the so-called heavy-duty tools, with frequencies that vary independently of the other two groups but do not necessarily vary inversely with either group individually. Long ago I pointed out that the structure of variability in the Acheulian was vastly different from that generally known from the products of *Homo sapiens,* particularly in the lack of coincidence between associational patterning and co-variant patterning (Binford 1972b:285–292). What is found together does not regularly co-vary with other locational units. Instead, assemblage units represent coincident associations among artifact sets that co-vary strongly at the intralocational scale of analysis. This is not the structure of variability expected among ethnically differentiated social units, nor in my opinion is it the structure of variability expected if we were looking at "camps" or base camps that served as the hubs of exploitive activities. In the latter case, we should see some structural consequences of an integrated strategy. Such an integration should ensure that there would be some co-variant patterning of the intralocational level responsive to major geographical and environmental conditions, resulting in geographically differentiated patterning of both the co-variant and associational kind. The fact that this type of patterning is not demonstrable in the Oldowan or in the Acheulian should alert us to be skeptical when interpreting vertical and horizontal associations of artifacts as "camps."

There is a significant ambiguity between our organizational expectations and the robust patterning demonstrable for assemblages from the early time ranges. Associations at places do not appear organized; only behavior with respect to the environment per se seems to be organized. One can argue that this behavior looks much more like a tool-assisted direct adaptation to the environment than like a modern human strategy of constructing a cultural environment from which one exploits the natural environment. The latter strategy generally results in assemblages with a structure of interactive, co-variant relationships within the hubs of operation. No such associational structure is thus far demonstrable in the early time ranges. Put another way, the associations among artifacts at sites appear to be fortuitous responses to the organizational properties in the natural environment and not reflective of organizational properties within or variations among the adaptive systems themselves. Against this warrant for skepticism regarding the existence of camps, let us array the more detailed observations of excavators.

Kalambo Falls

In the context of early hominid studies, there is little question that the credit for shifting excavation procedures from a mining strategy to the exposure of broad horizontal areas in order to search for behaviorally relevant distributions must go to Desmond Clark (1954, 1962, 1965, 1969) with his work at Kalambo Falls and to F.C. Howell and his team at Isimila (Cole and Kleindienst 1974; Howell 1961; Howell et al. 1962; Howell et al. 1972). Several very interesting observations were made in these pioneering works. For instance, although it is clear that a modern analog of a hunter-gatherer camp was the "knowledge base" from which both Clark and Howell were working, they used the model judiciously and frequently pointed to facts of the "external world" that did not fit neatly with the model. At Kalambo Falls, for example:

[Excavation A1, Floor IV]: The uppermost of the Acheulian occupation floors within the White Sands Bed was a horizon of no thickness. . . . As with the lower horizons, this can have been an occupation of only very temporary duration. (Clark and Kleindienst 1969:105)

Floor IV . . . grid squares C and D 8 and 9 contained practically no artifacts. . . . Of particular interest are the two small concentrations of flakes in grid squares E and F 8 and 9 and in C and D 7, which are associated with anvils. (Clark and Kleindienst 1979:106)

[Excavation A1, Floor V]: The tools are associated with a number of large primary flakes in hard quartzite which were concentrated in a flaking area in squares D and E4 and 5. Two of these flakes were found to join and they had been obtained by breaking up boulders of quartzite by anvil technique. On the floor, hand-axes and cleavers were found in small groups as if discarded where they had been used. (Clark and Kleindienst 1969:106)

[Excavation A1, Floor Vb]: The scatter of tools and waste on this eastern half of what is believed to be the undisturbed part of Floor Vb is sparse. It comprises several hand-axes and cleavers but very few flakes, showing that the large cutting tools had been carried in from elsewhere. (Clark and Kleindienst 1969:107).

[Excavation A6, Floor V1]: At a depth of 4 feet 6 inches (1.37 m) occurred a pebble line containing a number of artifacts of Acheulian type. Together with the tools were angular and sub-angular rock fragments and cobbles. The artifacts comprised fifteen unmodified flakes including two hand-axe trimming flakes and thirteen flake fragments and chunks, one utilized piece, one small tool and one bevel-based core scraper. (Clark and Kleindienst 1969:120)

[Excavation B1, Floor V]: This floor was continuous over the whole area excavated and is preserved also under the unexcavated sections. . . . A magnificent Acheulian floor with quantities of tools but comparatively little waste . . . , tools lay in the greatest profusion (109 hand-axes and 93 cleavers) in an area 21 × 24.5 feet (6.4 × 7.4 m) in the southeast part of the floor. (Clark and Cole 1969:159)

[Excavation B2, Floor V]: This horizon was the southward continuation of the main Acheulian floor excavated in 1956 at B1 and lithologically it is the same. It had no thickness and the tools lay horizontally thickly scattered in "clusters" on the flat surface of a fine, white river sand. (Clark and Cole 1969:172)

[Excavation B2, Floor V1]: Floor V1 is . . . associated with the large log and patches of carbonized vegetation. The stone artifacts comprise some large cutting tools and a number of flakes. (Clark and Cole 1969:173)

Several points are of extreme importance in the above observations.

1. In situations where tool concentrations were low, there appears to be some behavioral integrity. Frequently these were flake associations with anvils (Excavation A1, Floor IV) or "flaking areas" where large primary flakes and associated debris were produced with an "on-anvil technique" (Excavation A1, Floor V).
2. Hand axes and cleavers were frequently scattered and unassociated with debris (Excavation A1, Floor V), prompting the excavators to comment that "the large tools had been carried in from elsewhere." This lack of association between large tools (hand axes and cleavers) and chipping debris was also noted in Excavation B1, Floor V.
3. The absence of hand axes and cleavers did not necessarily imply that they had not been present at the location because it was noted in Excavation A6 that hand-ax trimming flakes were found in an assemblage lacking hand axes or other large tools.

These observations are directly suggestive of certain conditions of site formation: (a) *there are localized and small episodes of raw material reduction common with an "on-anvil" technique;* (b) *some tools, particularly hand axes and cleavers, were commonly made elsewhere and transported to their final resting places in the deposits;* (c) *some situations where only flakes and relatively small tools occur also yield "hand-ax" trimming flakes, indicative of the former presence of hand axes at these locations;* and (d) *the hand-ax trimming flakes do not appear to have been produced by an "on-anvil" technique.* We might therefore suggest that at least two sets of tactics appear to be represented in the Acheulian deposits at Kalambo Falls. First, some tools seem to have been expediently manufactured, presumably at the place of use. The "on-anvil" technique is common, and this technique is frequently associated with modified tools of the "small-tool" category (scrapers and other small tools). Second, tools (generally hand axes and cleavers) may occur independently or in association with the smaller, expediently manufactured tools and may be either unassociated or associated with manufacturing debris. In this second set of tactics, some planning depth seems to be implied. Minimally, the hominids sometimes went to one place to manufacture their tools in presumed anticipation of use elsewhere. The depth of planning, however, does not appear to be great because many of these transported tools are not worn out or greatly reduced, and in fact many appear to be in "mint" condition.

Taking the Acheulian from Kalambo at face value, we seem to be seeing accumulations of tools representing at least two situations—disposal of tools made elsewhere, presumably in the context of their use, and expedient manufacturing of tools on the spot to deal with contingencies met in the environment. Neither of these conditions is what is expected to dominate assemblages at a base of operations—a camp or home base. The ambiguous character of the Acheulian pattern is further highlighted by the fact that some "sites" have high frequencies of transported tools and few expedient tools, whereas others have high frequencies of expediently produced tools and low frequencies of transported tools (Clark 1965). In most cases involving modern hunter-gatherers, the mix of various tactics related to tool manufacture and logistics of use observable within residential locations is fairly constant, whereas variability among residential sites is manifest in frequency differences among formally different tools produced using similar tactical strategies. Unlike residential sites of *Homo sapiens,* what seems to stand behind variability in assemblage composition from different "sites" in the Acheulian are varying mixes of technological tactics, not organizational differences in how tools are differentially used in activity sets. In modern situations, when tactical differences stand behind interassemblage variability, we are generally looking at functionally and formationally different types of sites, many of which are not residential in character.

Isimila

I turn now to one of the more important Paleolithic records—the site of Isimila. At this site there were two major geologically developed "members" or macrodeposits. The upper member was originally designated "Sands 1a', 1, and 2," whereas the lower member was designed "Sands 3-5." Into these different members of the Isimila formation a large number of excavations were made, each identified by a letter and a number.

> In the uppermost sands (1) there was dense and generally continuous occupation throughout. . . . Restricted implement concentrations were recognizable from the extensive natural exposures . . . and the various trenches. . . . These concentrations differ in their vertical occurrence within the sands.
>
> In all the main sand horizons there are examples where *these occurrences might be said to be both horizontally and vertically diffuse.*
>
> *There are other occurrences where the implements are horizontally concentrated but are vertically diffuse.*
>
> *Concentrated occurrences of implements, restricted vertically as well as horizontally in their extent, represent another pattern.* (Howell et al. 1959:40–42; emphasis added)

Here we have some very interesting observations. The archaeological record is not presenting us with neat little units of localized artifact concentrations. Scattered artifacts occur in both a vertical and a horizontal mode within the deposits; similarly, there are vertically diffuse horizontal locations, and in some cases both horizontal and vertical concentrations meet the operational definition of "living floors." We are getting a glimpse of what may simply be an archaeological landscape. It is quite true that during the 1950s and early 1960s we knew very little about such phenomena, but as a result of recent archaeological and ethnoarchaeological work we have learned much. For instance, pioneering work by Thomas (1975) demonstrated that the character of human use of different microenvironments varied within a single region; hence distinctive differences were apparent among the archaeological remains found in each. In more recent years, "off-site" archaeological approaches (Camilli 1983, 1985; Dunnell and Dancey 1983; Foley 1980, 1981a,b; Larralde 1985a,b; Wandsnider 1985) began to uncover many previously unsuspected complexities in the formation of archaeological remains on land surfaces. Similarly, my observations of the mobility and land-use patterns of hunter-gatherers (Binford 1976, 1978a,b, 1979, 1980a, 1982b, 1983c,d) lead us to expect archaeological landscapes that are differentiated in ways reflective of the organization of an adaptive strategy. If we use these new expectations and data to rethink some of the early materials, how is our view of the past modified?

Returning to a consideration of Isimila, one generalization is of extreme importance.

> These differences in vertical concentration might be considered to represent lag concentrations. However, a variety of evidence opposes this conclusion. The implements are generally fresh, sometimes even in mint condition. The sediments reveal no signs of torrential runoff or deltaic deposits which would indicate substantial water transport; linear alignment, suggestive of creep or gentle slope water action, was absent. *The more vertically diffuse distribution may represent cumulative occupation of an area during much of the period of accumulation of the sands in which the implements occur.* . . . At any rate, *this type of distribution does not seem to represent an occupation floor* comparable to the more vertically-restricted occurrences. (Howell et al. 1959:43–44; emphasis added)

The observers clearly see the diffuse occurrences of tools, whether recovered in a vertical or horizontal mode, as essentially in situ materials deposited by hominids. What is of extreme interest given this situation is simply the degree to which the composition of the diffuse deposits is any different from what occurs on "living floors." If we were seeing small localities of tool use and abandonment in the diffuse deposits, or perhaps short-duration camping spots, then we would generally expect them to be different from central bases, where the focus of all the different strategies of resource procurement and processing would be represented (see Binford 1978a: 483–497). In describing the largely horizontally diffuse deposits in "Sands 1," the excavators note that

> the variation in one horizon at Isimila is comparable to that recorded between stratigraphically distinct land surfaces at Olorgesailie. (Howell et al. 1962:70)

The binary pattern of the hand ax-cleaver group versus the small-tool group is as marked among the vertically diffuse deposits as it is among so-called living floors. Unit H9-J8 is described as vertically diffuse, yet the aggregate composition of the assemblage is not greatly different from that recovered from upper J6-J7, which is considered to be a living floor! Similarly, when the vertically dispersed materials from K18 are lumped, they are quite similar to the "living floor" assemblage from one of the high-density levels at lower J6-J7. In short, there is no assemblage differentiation between the so-called living floors and the summarized aggregates of tools from the diffuse deposits. The same binary pattern, hand axes and cleavers versus small tools, is observable. The behavioral conditions standing behind the scattered artifacts in the diffuse deposits appear to be the same as those that contributed to the aggregations on the so-called living floors. *The only phenomenon regularly correlated with the "living floors" appears to be a geologically stabilized land surface*—a paleosol.

Olduvai and Beyond

This point is particularly easy to demonstrate with the well-known assemblages from Olduvai Gorge. For instance, two locations—MNK, H13 and FLK North Levels 1-2— are described as vertically diffuse deposits. Both of these are very similar, and each differs only slightly from the assemblage at HWK East Level 1. All three are classified as Oldowan; each is dominated by choppers associated with low frequencies of poly-hedrons, discoids, and spheroids, and all have very low frequencies of light-duty scrapers. These deposits alternate chronologically with assemblages of differing con-tent, which are classified as "Developed Oldowan," and all postdate the famous "living floor" assemblage at the Zinjanthropus site (FLK 22) where there is a high frequency of small tools, dominated by light-duty scrapers. Similarly, other roughly contemporary locations of diffuse deposits also yield chopper-dominated assemblages and variable proportions of light-duty tools. As at Isimila, there seem to be no struc-tural differences in the composition of assemblages from living floors and from diffuse deposits. In the latter assemblage, it seems clear that the deposition of tools was episodal and the assemblage represents a temporally averaged aggregate of dis-crete and nonintegrated events of tool manufacture, use, and discard. On the other hand, at locations that have been designated "living floors," where land surfaces appear to have been relatively stable, more events are represented per unit of sedi-mentation; in addition, more discrete episodes are occasionally documented, as in the case of the fractured bone concentrations at FLK 1-2 and FLK 22. Such episodes are not necessarily unique to stable surfaces, but they are more likely to be found by archae-ologists on surfaces where traces of more events are aggregated. At Olduvai Gorge, as at Isimila, the only condition consistently associated with "living floors" is a geo-logically stable land surface, a feature that Mary Leakey (1971:258) included in her recognition criteria for "occupation floors." This characteristic, coupled with the similarity between the temporally collapsed assemblages from the diffuse deposits and the assemblages on the "living floors," leads one to conclude that a stable land surface was subject to the same episodal utilization as the many surfaces in the diffuse deposits. Both are the consequence of many discrete, nonintegrated events of tool manufacture, use, and discard, but on the stable land surfaces this palimpsest is vertically undifferentiated in the archaeological record. One can make the case that there are no camps in the Lower Paleolithic record—only archaeological landscapes varying in the frequency of episodal use at different magnet locations in the natural environment.

When viewed in this manner, the two basic tactics that were suggested as standing behind the Kalambo Falls assemblage variability—a transported and an in situ expedi-ent manufacturing component—become even more intriguing.

One of the most distinctive features of the tool aggregates recovered from the Olduvai Bed I deposits is that they tend to be dominated by choppers and chopping tools. These tools are often manufactured from basalt, yet debitage (when present) is generally quartzite—the material from which small flake tools were often manufactured. Apparently the vast majority of the choppers, spheroids, and subspheroids were not manufactured at the locations where they were found. In contrast, on-the-spot manufacture of the small-tool components of the Oldowan assemblages appears to be regularly indicated. At this earlier time, we are apparently seeing the cumulative effect of two distinct tactics of tool use. In the first tactic, tools are manufactured in one place and carried through an unknown series of situations until they are discarded at very different places. The second tactic relates to the conditions that prompt the need for small tools, which appear to be more appropriate for cutting and scraping tasks. Under such conditions, the small tools are manufactured and seemingly discarded on the spot.

Given these two tactical dimensions, a third situation is clearly implied—namely locations in the landscape where the large tools were manufactured. Both in the very early materials as well as throughout the duration of the Acheulian, such locations have been documented. For instance, the famous site of DK at Olduvai yields an association of large tools and debitage from the same raw material. Similarly, some of the well-investigated sites at Koobi Fora also exhibit large tools and associated debitage from the same raw materials. Comparable assemblages from a somewhat later period can be found at the Olorgesailie MFS location, and there are many examples from Acheulian contexts.

The suggestion that large tools were deliberately designed and differentially transported is at variance with the ideas recently advanced by Glynn Isaac (1983c) based on work by Nicholas Toth (Bunn et al. 1980; Toth 1982).

> I am suggesting that in spite of the diversity of forms the early assemblages were fundamentally simple. They display a good empirical knowledge of conchoidal fracture. This immediately yields two major classes of manufactured objects. That is, (1) the lump of stone from which flakes have been struck and (2) the flakes themselves. The first class can be regarded as "cores." However, in the early time ranges the lumps with flakes removed have been regarded as the principal tools with designations such as chopper, discoid, scraper, or polyhedron being added. The flakes, unless retouched, have conventionally been regarded as "waste" or "debitage." (Isaac 1983c:15)

Toth's and Isaac's view has the advantage of being economical, but its acceptance would ironically force the conclusion that the tool-yielding "sites" from Bed I at Olduvai were episodal aggregates and not "camps" in the sense that they were originally conceived by Isaac. As previously mentioned, the majority of the debitage and flake tools from the Bed I locations is quartz or quartzite, whereas the large "core" pieces (primarily choppers) from the same sites are made of basalt. If Isaac is correct in stating that these are "cores," then clearly they were discarded as such and were not reduced at those sites for the production of small tools. In short, the episodes standing behind the aggregates of material commonly considered camp assemblages were independent and nonintegrated. I obviously think this was true, but I also think the choppers, spheroids, and some of the other tool forms were items designed to be systematically carried around and that they represent a different set of tool supply and use tactics than those indicated by the small-tool components on these "sites."

The same basic organization seen in the Oldowan is observable in Acheulian assemblages—only the form of the regularly transported tools has changed. Hand axes and cleavers are now the forms habitually transported, whereas small tools and choppers appear to be expediently manufactured and used in single episodes. At many Acheulian locations, the large-tool component is accompanied by little debitage of the raw materials from which they were made. Similarly, in the Acheulian there are classic sites from internal drainages that yield hand axes and/or cleavers almost exclusively, and the absence of flake by-products cannot be explained by natural agencies. Kathu Pan in South Africa comes to mind, and those familiar with the literature could add many more. One particularly striking description is provided by Desmond Clark (1980:536–537):

> [In] the floor of the Karga Depression . . . , concentrated in the eye of one spring (K10) . . . were found many pointed handaxes in chert, often with unworked butts. Curiously, there were almost no other associated tools or waste. It is clear that these bifaces had not been made at the site.

CONCLUSIONS AND IMPLICATIONS

I think that a robust argument can be sustained to the effect that the organization of tool manufacture and use in the Oldowan and Acheulian periods was essentially the same. One set of tactics consisted of the manufacture of portable tools and their transport to locations where they were episodally discarded or lost, presumably in the context of use. The planning depth standing behind this strategy of equipping mobile persons does not appear very great because there is almost universal agreement that hand axes are rarely found "used" or battered (this is less true of some choppers in the Oldowan). This lack of extensive use wear and associated debitage suggests to me that the planning depth standing behind this equipping of mobile persons was very short indeed (Binford 1983c:74–75). It appears that this transported component had a very wide geographical distribution and is characteristic of "out-of-the-way" locations, such as the spring at Karga Oasis mentioned earlier. This could suggest that the "mobile" persons had a relatively large foraging area. On the other hand, the expedient manufacture of tools, such as small scraper forms, occurred episodally on the spot, and these tools were seemingly used on the spot as well. What is important is that they were not manufactured from the same materials as the transported tools.

These facts support the inference of two independent strategies. The transported tools were very seldom reduced to small tools. The persons carrying out small-tool production and use were not equipped with transported "cores." What is more important is that comparative quantitative studies demonstrate that these two components tend to vary inversely with one another, in both the Oldowan and the Acheulian. I strongly suspect that we are looking at independent feeding ranges for the segment of the tool-making population using the transported tools versus the segment of the population commonly producing expedient small tools. Are we seeing differences between feeding strategies of males and females? Or, one might suggest, are we seeing different strategies among different contemporary species of hominids? This latter proposition seems unlikely if the view developed here is correct—namely that there is a basic organizational stability from the Oldowan through the late Acheulian. There are no serious claims for the presence of sympatric species of hominids contemporary with the late Acheulian. In the absence of such claims, it would be hard to sustain the interpretation of different tactical behaviors (the same as in the late Acheulian) characteristic of sympatric species during the Lower Paleolithic.

Regardless, the major point to be made here is that we are probably looking at an archaeological landscape generated episodally and not the remains of a cultural geography wherein populations operated out of "camps" into an environment, as do modern human populations. The variability at locations commonly called sites by archaeologists is most likely the result of differential overall land-use patterns characteristic of the two segments of the tool-using population marked by the two sets of tactics outlined here. Differential "assemblage" compositions result from the differential geographical conditioning for the episodal events appropriate to the two sets of tactics, transported versus expediently produced tool-use events. It is most unlikely that we are seeing structured assemblages derived from organizationally integrated tool-assisted actions centered in camps. Early humans were probably not very much like us.

Chapter 27

Technology of Early Man: An Organizational Approach to the Oldowan

In recent years, the discovery of hominid skeletal remains applicable to the important question of the evolutionary appearance of the ancestral forms of the genus *Homo* has been truly staggering. Paralleling the discovery of relevant fossil materials has been the recognition that hominid evolution was not a simple lineal system of descent. Great variability exists among the hominid fossils, and consequently there has been controversy among the experts regarding the "proper" taxonomic and temporal arrangements of these specimens. It has become increasingly clear that in the interesting era prior to the widespread appearance of *Homo erectus* and the long-recognized Acheulian archaeological complex of Eurasia and Africa multiple hominid forms (some would say four) are thought to have lived during the time period spanned by the Bed I–II deposits at Olduvai Gorge.

One Australopithecine form, *A. boisei,* and two *Homo* forms, *H. habilis* and early *H. erectus,* could by chronological implication have contributed to the archaeological record as it is known from Beds I and II at Olduvai Gorge. At present, *Australopithecus boisei (Zinjanthropus; OH.5)* is well documented at FLK 22, which is in the middle of Lower Bed I. Two teeth from site DK, which represents the oldest deposits at Olduvai, have also been ascribed to this hominid (M. Leakey 1971:234). Another form championed by Louis Leakey, *H. habilis* (OH.7 and 8), was initially described on the basis of materials from the middle of Bed I at site FLK NN3, which dates between FLK 22 (the "Zinj" site) and the basal deposits at DK. Restudy in light of more recently discovered materials from the Lake Turkana area tends to confirm Louis Leakey's recognition of the FLK NN3 specimens as being distinct from *H. erectus,* although there is still disagreement as to whether this is a genus *Homo* specimen or an advanced example of the genus *Australopithecus.* Regardless, the materials from Bed I clearly point to the contemporaneity of two morphologically different types of hominids associated with archaeological materials typically called Oldowan.

The picture became even more complicated when a hominid specimen (OH.13) recovered from Bed II at MNK was assigned by Louis Leakey to his *H. habilis* taxon. MNK OH.13 is from deposits much more recent than the Bed I locations in which *H. habilis* is found, and it seems likely that this "small-brained *Homo*-like" creature is not *H. habilis.* Finally, a fourth hominid, *H. erectus* (represented by OH.9 from LLK), has

A paper prepared for the Anthropological Society of Washington, Washington, D.C., © Academic Press 1989.

been reported from Olduvai Bed II. (Originally OH.12 was identified as *H. erectus* and assigned to the top of Bed II, but more recent work places this material in deposits from Bed IV; Rightmire 1981:191.) Mary Leakey considers *H. erectus* to have been the likely author of the Acheulian (site EF-HR) as known from Bed II deposits at Olduvai Gorge.

Given this variety of hominid fossils and the inference that *H. erectus* was the author of the Acheulian, during Bed I and II times three types of hominids could conceivably have contributed to the archaeological remains known as the Oldowan, if the typological distinction between Developed Oldowan and Acheulian is sustained. If not, all four hominid forms could have been contributors. This possibility is further supported by the finds of *H. erectus* in the Lake Turkana area, which (if dated in the most conservative manner) would further confirm the presence of *H. erectus* in the region during the time that at least some of Bed II was deposited at Olduvai Gorge.

Regardless of how the experts resolve the problems of the biological relationships among these fossil hominids (given the fact that at least some of the species distinctions will remain), it seems unlikely that all would have behaved in the same manner or occupied the same "niche" in the behavioral and adaptive sense. Equally, we might expect that all of these closely related forms (or at least more than one of them) could have been experimenting with tool use. Nevertheless, the default posture among the archaeologists has been that only the "true" ancestor of man made and used tools. Thus the contemporary hominid forms were not seen as contributing to the archaeological record, and it could therefore be read as a document referable only to the behavior of our "real" ancestor. While this posture saves archaeologists from having to face the challenging problem of treating the archaeological record as potentially having been formed by differing hominids, it simply avoids the issue of what we would, in fact, like to learn—namely, which of these sympatric forms of hominids were tool users?

Unfortunately, the analytical approaches thus far utilized in discussing the Olduvai materials have generally adopted the default posture:

> The cultural material from Bed I and the base of Bed II can be referred to the Olduwan and remains virtually unchanged from the base of the Upper Member of Bed I to the lower part of Bed II. It is characterized by choppers of various forms, polyhedrons, discoids, scrapers, occasional subspheroids and burins, together with hammerstones, utilized cobbles and light-duty utilized flakes. (Leakey 1971:1)

Here we see the archaeologist summarizing the contents of the archaeological record rather than adopting an analytical approach. Regardless of the fact that the sites investigated in the Bed I deposits are not identical, or are not even very similar in some cases, they are considered to be "noisy" expressions of a single normatively conceived culture—the Oldowan. Turning to the somewhat more variable materials from Bed II, the archaeologist makes the following generalizations:

> In Bed II there is evidence for the existence of two industrial complexes whose contemporaneity, in the broad sense, has been confirmed at a number of different sites. One is clearly derived from the Oldowan and has been termed Developed Oldowan, while the second must be considered as primitive Acheulian. In the

Developed Oldowan A from the Lower Bed II Oldowan tool forms persist, but there is a marked increase in spheroids and subspheroids and in the number and variety of light-duty tools. In the upper part of Middle Bed II and in Upper Bed II a few bifaces are also found in Developed Oldowan assemblages, but they form such a negligible proportion of the tools that it has been considered unjustifiable to assign this industry to the Acheulian. It has, therefore, been termed Developed Oldowan B to distinguish it from the preceding phase (A) which does not include bifaces. Sites where bifaces amount to 40 percent or more of the tools have been classed as Acheulian. (Leakey 1971:1–2)

In this passage the archaeologist has astutely recognized some variability in the content of the archaeological record. Bed II assemblages are distinguishable from Bed I assemblages in the presence of spheroids, in an increase in modified small tools, and in the occasional presence of bifaces. The features that distinguish Bed II from Bed I materials are used as criteria for defining the Developed Oldowan. It is further noted that bifaces occur on some Developed Oldowan sites. Since bifaces are considered to be diagnostic of the Acheulian, the variability is noted terminologically by defining Developed Oldowan A as those assemblages without bifaces and Developed Oldowan B as those with bifaces. Bed II sites yielding assemblages containing 40% or more bifaces (handaxes) are designated as Acheulian. Two things are clear in this description. First, the archaeologist is making a judgment as to what is a significant difference among variable archaeological assemblages. Second, a further judgment is then made as to the *meaning* of these differences in historical terms.

For example, the interpretations are offered that *H. habilis* was the author of the Oldowan and the Developed Oldowan and that *H. erectus* was the likely author of the Acheulian. The accompanying arguments simply accommodate the variability in the archaeological record to the subjective postures of the author regarding the "real" ancestry of the genus *Homo* and the further belief that only members of this genus were tool makers. Such an approach is unacceptable. We must use *independent* lines of evidence, meaning that the analytical methods and the interpretive principles must be justified in ways independent of our biased views of the historical situation that is the target of our search for knowledge.

The failure to independently justify both the taxonomic assessments of variability and the meanings assigned to the recognized variants is further exacerbated by the Leakey position on the assumed *H. habilis* to *H. erectus* transition. For instance, there is thought to be a direct connection between *H. habilis* and the Oldowan materials, and further it is thought that *H. erectus* was the author of the Acheulian—yet these remains appear interstratified in Bed II at Olduvai Gorge. The argument is therefore made that there is no gradual transition, at least at Olduvai Gorge, between the Oldowan and the Acheulian; hence the Acheulian is intrusive in the Olduvai region (Leakey 1967:440–441, 1971:273).

Olduvai Gorge is generally recognized as one of the (if not the) most important sites in the world as far as information potential regarding the behavior of humankind's early forebears. Unlike many other important sites, Olduvai has been well published and continues to receive much research attention. In fact, the meaning and implications for understanding early hominid behavior of the materials collected by the Leakeys during the 1960s are still controversial 20 years later. Much of this debate has centered on faunal remains and their significance for understanding the diet of early hominids. Paralleling and embedded in many of these arguments are other issues, particularly the reality of the "home base" model of early hominid life and all that it implies for the organization of lifeways during the early eras of hominid tool use. During the course of these debates other models of early hominid life have been proposed (Binford 1981a, 1984c; Potts 1982:198) to account organizationally for the spectacular associations of tools and fauna recovered by the Leakeys at Olduvai. While these debates are of methodological interest and potential importance for altering our earlier views of hominid life, they remain *generic* arguments that do not face the important issue of the possibility that we may not be looking at the products of *Homo*-specific behavior. Can we say that the sympatric hominid forms did not use tools and hence leave some trace of their potentially differing behaviors? The answer must be a resounding no, since this problem has remained uninvestigated and has commonly been ignored in favor of scenarios that fit with the investigators' prior ideas of hominid evolution.

Problems such as those outlined above, dealing with the manner in which archaeological observations are used in argument, frequently derive from a lack of attention to archaeological methodology and particularly from a failure to pursue detailed pattern-recognition approaches and analytical procedures currently available to archaeologists. I have therefore conducted an extensive pattern-recognition study of the published data from Olduvai Gorge. The purposes of this study were to uncover the structure of variability among the various sites and levels recorded at Olduvai and to study the interaction among these units in the faunal data (both species and anatomical part frequencies), stone tools, and such characteristics of the deposits as their temporal sequence, composition, and thickness. This analysis resulted in the recognition of some fascinating patterns.

ANALYTICAL PROCEDURE

The approach I have taken to pattern recognition is somewhat new and has not been widely discussed in the analytical literature. I use a multivariate technique, but one which is for the first time reliable and meaningfully readable in my opinion. I began exploring the utility of multivariate techniques early in my career, and I have used them many times. The commonly available techniques were various forms of factor analysis that required certain critical assumptions about the data and its distribution, but these assumptions have rarely been met in practice. Most early multivariate studies used a matrix of correlation coefficients as the basis for analysis; however, autocorrelations frequently arise from differences in sample sizes among the cases one studies using such approaches. Various transformations have been tried in an effort to solve this problem (e.g., percentages or ratio values), but most of the time these measures also present some problems.

Henry Harpending of the University of Pennsylvania is experimenting with a new approach to multivariate study. He reasoned that the single transformation that would meet the assumptions of multivariate analysis was in fact a simple one. The matrix of raw data (counts) could simply be transformed by calculating chi-square values for all cells in the matrix. These normalized values would meet all the requirements of basic multivariate approaches. Chi-square values are measured deviations from the assumption that all cases are identical and only vary in size. Because row and column totals are used to obtain the chi-square values, the direction (plus or minus) and the magnitude of the value measures quite directly the differences among the cases as evaluated from these totals. What is even more elegant is that chi-square values are normally distributed, a typical assumption of multivariate techniques. Harpending and Rogers (1985) have written a series of programs for microcomputers using this approach. I have experimented with these programs on many data sets (several of which were control data sets in that I already understood the basis of the variations present) and have found that Harpending's approach to multivariate analysis is the cleanest and most informative I have ever seen. I have used these methods on the analysis of the published Oldowan data.

The steps are simple. One inputs raw count data into a matrix of cases and variables. These values are then transformed into a matrix of chi-square values, maintaining the original case and variable arrangement. This normalized matrix is then subjected to singular value decomposition, the basic multivariate strategy standing behind principal component analysis. The results are two sets of values presented as left and right values. The left values are the dimensional scores for the cases, and the right values are the dimensional scores for the variables. Because the chi-square values are presented as positive or negative values, the dimensions reported as a result of singular value decomposition are also scored in this manner. The results are directly readable as inversely related suites of variables. The plus or minus sign identifies the character of the content of a case relative to the dimensions among which the variables are distributed.

Table 27.1 summarizes the raw count data from nineteen Olduvai Bed I and Bed II localities for twenty-seven artifact classes as summarized in the various site descriptions (Leakey 1971). These data were subjected to the analytical procedures outlined above. Table 27.2 summarizes the results of the singular value decomposition (principal component solution) for the normalized data presented in Table 27.1. Table 27.3 summarizes the dimensional values for each of the three dimensions given in Table 27.2 as they are distributed across the nineteen sites. The first dimension, accounting for the majority of the variation from an identity model, exhibits no temporally clustered variation; that is, the plus and minus values appear scattered between Bed I and Bed II. On the other hand, Dimensions 2 and 3 definitely exhibit a biased distribution of plus and minus values corresponding with the distinctions between Bed I and Bed II. In fact, all the minus values for Dimension 2 (except MNK OH.13) are found among Bed I locations; conversely, all positive values (except MNK OH.13) are found among Bed II sites. We seem to have isolated an interesting pattern with chronological implications. When we examine Dimension 3 we note essentially the reverse pattern. All the Bed I sites (except DK) yield positive values, and all the Bed II sites (except MNK OH.13) yield negative values. This pattern basically reports two important facts. First, Dimension 3 varies independently of Dimension 2, and second,

Table 27.1

Raw Counts of Artifacts by Class at Nineteen Olduvai Localities

	Side choppers	End choppers	Two-edged choppers	Pointed choppers	Chisel choppers	Polyhedrons	Discs	Spheroids	Subspheroids	Heavy-duty scrapers	Light-duty scrapers	Burins	Misc. tools
BK	64	16	15	0	6	8	33	23	176	18	105	23	1
TK	22	8	5	0	0	4	12	44	60	20	102	15	0
FC Tuff	8	2	2	0	1	2	4	6	16	12	9	1	6
FC Floor	28	17	0	3	1	4	4	10	38	11	9	1	3
MNK Main	69	18	7	0	2	9	19	16	143	24	59	0	3
MNK OH.13	14	7	3	1	1	2	2	0	6	5	4	0	0
MNK 3–5	90	25	10	4	5	25	9	17	97	16	48	0	25
HWK 2	12	3	1	0	0	4	2	0	11	2	3	0	3
HWK 1	22	12	3	1	0	0	3	0	1	4	0	2	0
FLK 1–2	52	26	3	4	1	5	8	3	9	13	12	0	3
FLK 3	16	3	0	0	0	3	2	0	2	1	0	0	0
FLK 4	4	2	2	0	1	3	1	0	3	1	1	0	0
FLK 5	14	4	4	0	0	0	3	1	0	3	0	0	0
FLK 6	1	0	3	0	0	0	0	0	0	0	0	0	0
FLK 15	0	0	1	0	0	0	0	0	0	0	0	0	0
FLK 22	15	2	0	0	0	9	3	0	0	9	18	4	0
FLK NN1	3	0	0	0	0	0	0	0	0	1	0	0	0
FLK NN3	0	2	0	0	0	1	0	0	0	1	0	0	0
DK	30	7	4	5	1	32	27	7	0	10	20	3	8

	Awls	Utilized flakes	Anvils	Utilized nodules	Utilized cobbles	Hammerstones	Heavily utilized flakes	Whole flakes	Resharpening flakes	Broken flakes	Core fragments	Bifaces	Manuports	Modified nodules
BK	45	263	4	25	83	18	0	652	5	4403	627	38	418	93
TK	23	331	9	20	25	15	5	267	0	5117	1129	39	139	52
FC Tuff	0	22	2	0	22	8	0	39	1	417	75	3	107	15
FC Floor	2	39	7	0	59	23	0	99	3	607	159	5	251	53
MNK Main	7	139	24	9	136	64	0	0	0	0	0	9	754	63
MNK OH.13	0	4	3	11	43	15	0	31	3	484	50	0	67	0
MNK 3–5	14	158	19	0	113	27	0	169	0	818	187	14	1184	89
HWK 2	1	17	0	0	20	6	1	25	0	130	40	3	21	27
HWK 1	0	2	0	14	32	21	0	11	0	11	11	1	163	0
FLK 1–2	0	68	12	49	23	62	0	178	3	575	86	5	170	0
FLK 3	0	11	4	14	5	15	0	28	0	61	5	0	39	0
FLK 4	0	1	0	11	11	5	0	5	0	15	0	0	17	0
FLK 5	0	0	5	7	7	10	0	14	0	52	26	1	29	0
FLK 6	0	5	6	2	6	4	0	18	2	65	10	1	7	0
FLK 15	0	0	2	2	0	2	0	1	0	1	0	0	0	0
FLK 22	0	73	5	40	4	13	0	258	0	1862	155	0	96	0
FLK NN1	0	1	0	6	0	3	0	0	0	2	0	0	18	0
FLK NN3	0	2	0	5	0	1	0	7	0	21	8	0	24	0
DK	0	37	3	79	20	48	0	242	16	481	118	0	5	0

Table 27.2

Principal Component Solution for Normalized Data from Table 27.1

	Dimension 1	Dimension 2	Dimension 3
Side choppers	17.45	−8.71	2.96
End choppers	10.02	−5.84	4.64
Two-edged choppers	4.73	−4.42	3.38
Pointed choppers	2.20	−5.16	−1.12
Chisel choppers	2.73	−0.64	−1.14
Polyhedrons	4.87	−10.66	−7.23
Discs	4.32	−7.85	−4.79
Spheroids	2.43	2.31	−1.31
Subspheroids	18.29	9.02	−7.78
Heavy-duty scrapers	6.73	−2.75	0.97
Light-duty scrapers	4.72	3.01	−4.19
Burins	−2.84	−0.01	−0.58
Miscellaneous tools	6.21	−1.34	−4.80
Awls	0.23	3.89	−2.84
Utilized flakes	6.53	4.30	−2.98
Anvils	9.20	−4.34	4.42
Utilized nodules	3.14	−29.73	4.39
Utilized cobbles	24.67	−0.95	1.28
Hammerstones	15.40	−17.99	5.73
Heavily utilized flakes	−1.50	1.21	0.34
Whole flakes	−7.29	−20.83	−11.50
Resharpening flakes	−0.78	−10.54	−5.53
Broken flakes and chips	−46.56	7.35	4.29
Core fragments	−17.07	4.98	2.95
Bifaces	0.44	3.21	−0.61
Manuports	69.20	10.61	3.58
Modified nodules	12.52	8.83	−8.39

within each dimension the positive and negative aspects are inversely correlated with one another across the suite of sites represented in the matrix. This means that the sites in negative Dimension 2 are the same as those in positive Dimension 3 (and are from the early time period), but the variables these dimensions represent vary independently of one another. The same situation obtains for positive Dimension 2 and negative Dimension 3 with regard to sites from the late time period.

In summary, Dimension 1 accounts for the greatest amount of variance but shows no chronological distribution. Dimension 2 (negative) represents early, essentially Bed I phenomena, as does positive Dimension 3. In contrast, positive Dimension 2 and negative Dimension 3 represent late, Bed II phenomena. The appearance of contemporaneous aspects on different dimensions attests to the independent behavior of the derived suite of variables within each time period.

I turn now to the content of these dimensions and to explanation of their positive and negative aspects as presented in Table 27.2.

Table 27.3
Values for Each of Three Dimensions from Table 27.2 by Site

	Dimension 1	Dimension 2 (Transported)	Dimension 3 (Expedient)
Bed II			
BK	−20.99	5.49	−8.21
TK	−39.12	14.31	−7.58
FC Tuff	1.22	3.30	−0.30
FC Floor	9.42	3.04	−1.54
MNK Main	61.41	7.88	−2.39
MNK OH.13	−2.32	−2.87	6.17
MNK 3–5	45.62	10.89	−2.86
HWK 2	2.99	0.88	−5.82
Bed I			
HWK 1	26.32	−7.44	10.49
FLK 1–2	5.81	−18.47	4.12
FLK 3	7.44	−12.28	3.22
FLK 4	8.12	−10.74	2.60
FLK 5	5.78	−7.97	6.66
FLK 6	−0.66	−5.05	1.42
FLK 15	2.25	−8.08	5.10
FLK 22	−21.41	−4.52	2.23
FLK NN1	8.11	−6.50	4.81
FLK NN3	4.35	−3.36	1.99
DK	−4.82	−34.47	−11.21

SUMMARY OF THE PATTERN-RECOGNITION STUDY

Pattern A

Among all the assemblages, regardless of age or depositional condition, the greatest amount of systematic covariation is in the opposition between artifact classes indicative of lithic work (resharpening flakes, whole flakes, broken flakes and chips, heavy flakes, core fragments, and "burins") and the remaining suite of tool classes recognized at Olduvai (all the chopper forms, the modified and utilized nodules and blocks, manuports, modified tools, utilized flakes, light-duty scrapers, etc.). Put in very simple terms this means that, in the places where lithic work was carried out, shaped tools, choppers, utilized and modified artifacts, and "transported" or introduced manuports were generally not deposited in amounts proportionately related to those of lithic manufacturing tools and debris. This dimension may primarily represent autocorrelations of diversity with sample size on the positive aspect and a different "cause" of sample size on the negative (e.g., a behavioral or environmental cause; Binford 1986e). For some it may be hard to view this difference in the amount of manufacturing debris as reflecting different "cultures." After all, the tools had to have been manufactured *somewhere*, and it is in those locations of production that we would expect to find the greatest amounts of lithic reduction debris. Nevertheless, this simple correspondence between place and by-products of manufacture is by no means certain, since there is an acknowledged and provocative pattern of differential use of lithic raw materials at Olduvai, and differences in raw materials were not tabulated in the matrix being studied (Table 27.1).

Mary Leakey has previously noted that "flakes derived from the manufacture of heavy-duty tools are lacking or very scarce at most early living sites, where the tools appear to have been introduced in a finished or half-finished state" (Leakey 1971:273). The lithic debris on most Olduvai sites is from different raw materials (quartz or quartzite) than most of the larger tools (lava and other materials). Thus one could argue that one set of behaviors makes use of the large tools, commonly of lava but, in later times, of quartzite, which were transported from their locations of production to their locations of use or discard. These production locations for transported tools may exhibit evidence of repeated episodes of use (e.g., site DK). One could even imagine that these "transported tools" were not really produced at any one spot but were modified as they were carried around. The absence of recognizable production sites might then reflect a different tool trajectory than that which we expect in more modern contexts.

We could, for example, imagine one hominid moving across the landscape carrying few, if any, modified tools and occasionally encountering a situation in which tools are required. This hominid makes them on the spot, primarily by a technique of smashing up relatively small quartz and quartzite pebbles and chunks. After such an episode, the hominid would abandon both the location and the by-products of its tool-assisted behavior, moving again until another situation is encountered and tools produced in this crude manner are again appropriate. We might also imagine another hominid who is a habitual carrier of materials that may be modified for derivative elements, such as flakes, or used directly as tools (Toth 1982; Toth and Schick 1986:26–29). This second hominid disposes of these transported tools in various contexts of use or where mobility is interrupted. Over time an archaeological landscape is created by virtue of many acts of disposal or abandonment of these transported tools. In other words, we might imagine one species that is tool equipped and another that is an expedient tool maker and user and more often carries only manuports. Given the fact that we did not code raw materials, Dimension 1 may be picking up variability in both of the modes suggested or, more likely, primarily in only one. This latter possibility seems likely in that it is the side choppers, end choppers, spheroids, utilized cobbles, and nodules as well as manuports (all commonly acknowledged transported elements) that contrast most markedly with the unambiguous suite of lithic reduction classes loaded negatively on Dimension 1. If there is a bias, we can expect lithic reduction debris to appear on subsequently derived dimensions.

Let us examine the structure of the available data relative to the research designs used in its generation. In the original work at Olduvai Gorge the major organizational phenomena assumed to be standing behind variability noted in the archaeological record were the differences between "living sites" and ephemeral locations where the hominids did not live but where tool-assisted behavior nevertheless took place. In short, a model of modern hunter-gatherers' use of places was assumed to stand organizationally behind variability in the nature of deposits excavated at Olduvai Gorge (see Leakey 1971:252–262). Alternatively, much of the variability could be seen as a sampling bias arising from the chance location of excavations relative to the assumed site structure thought to be present at the Olduvai "living sites." For instance, when speaking of the materials recovered from FLK NN1, Mary Leakey comments as follows:

> It is clear that if an occupation floor ever existed at this level, then only a small part of the marginal zone has been preserved, comparable to the outskirts of the "Zinjanthropus" floor at FLK I. (Leakey 1971:44)

Given these assumed conditions in the past, the entire model of the past generated to accommodate the Olduvai data is not surprisingly couched in the "living site" context. We may reasonably ask if there is any support for this assumption of organized lifeways among the early hominids. As a result of my work with both the Olduvai data and Acheulian assemblages (see Binford 1985b), it can be said with great certainty that there is *no relationship* between the structure of variability recognizable within the data recovered archaeologically and the imposed model of past organization assumed in the interpretation of these same data. In short, there is no structural correlate with the "types" of sites seen by the excavators (Leakey 1971:258–262) or with those discussed as basic to hominid life (Isaac 1971, 1978a, 1978b, 1983a). The content of "diffuse" deposits exhibits the same range of structural variability as does the content of so-called living sites. I must make one minor qualification to this statement: there is a minor bias, but one which is statistically not meaningful, between so-called living floors and the evidence of considerable lithic reduction activity (Pattern A discussed above). This is not surprising, since lithic work was one of the major recognition criteria of "living sites" in the first place.

> Although the period of habitation certainly varied at each site, the usual criteria for living sites are always present, i.e., tools, debitage, utilized lithic material and also a variety of broken animal bones. (Leakey 1971:272)

It seems clear from the lack of any regular relationship between the assumed organizational units called base camps and the dispersed vertical and horizontal artifact scatters that the spatial structure of the archaeological landscape is not what was assumed and in fact stood as a guide to archaeological investigations. We must seek ways of discovering the nature of this landscape and the factors that conditioned the deposition of artifacts differentially within it. What seems clear from the pattern-recognition work described here is that we are dealing with an archaeological landscape that has been differentially preserved and also was characterized by magnet places at which hominids left clustered artifactual traces (many localizations are quite clear; see Kroll and Isaac 1984). We do not yet understand, however, what conditioned the production of the archaeological landscape or the social and subsistence-related behaviors that may have organizationally stood behind the structured patterns we can see at the present time.

Pattern B

The second structural pattern demonstrable among the Olduvai sites has important temporal implications. The structured patterning is expressed in two dimensions, which are summarized in Table 27.4. The best way to describe this pattern is in the form of a four-celled table in which the upper row represents the Bed II deposits (above HWK 1) and the lower row represents the deposits of Bed I (including and below HWK 1). On the right side are a group of tools that exhibit mutual patterns of covariation and behave independently of all other cells. Similarly, on the left are a group of tools that exhibit mutual patterns of covariation and behave independently of the other cells.

Several of the groupings are of extreme interest. First, both the early and the late suites of artifacts on the left side of the table lack lithic debris and manuports, while both suites on the right side of the table have these classes of items. Second, both suites to the left have whole flakes and resharpening flakes, while both suites to the right lack them. Third, the suites to the left have more classes of core tools as well as higher dimensional values on core tools than do the suites of tools on the right. These observations implicate the past in an interesting way. Although there were changes in the forms of tools used in the early and late periods, as well as perhaps some change in lithic techniques, it appears that these basic suites of tools remained *unchanged* through time. A similar structural character to the way in which tools were used and discarded is evident in both time periods.

In short, we can note that during both the early and late periods there was a dichotomy in the ways certain tool-assisted acts were performed across the archaeological landscape. When large numbers and classes of transported "core tools" were used, there was a corresponding and proportional presence of whole flakes and resharpening flakes. This situation regularly occurred in the context of using hammers to bruise and modify otherwise natural stones. In contrast, there was another context of tool use and modification in which many manuports (naturally occurring un-modified stones deposited out of place, geologically speaking) were introduced and in which fragmented cores, broken flakes, and chips were regularly produced. In addition, only limited types and numbers of "core tools" occur in this second context.

Crosscutting these two "organizational" contexts of tool deposition was change through time in assemblage content. Hammers and anvils were replaced by sub-spheroids and spheroids in both of the late structural contexts. Similarly, the bruised and battered nodules and blocks appear to have been more extensively modified from use in the late period than in the early period. There is also a marked increase in the kinds and forms of modified small tools that occur in both contexts in the late period. Finally, side choppers, two-edged choppers, and end choppers, which are common in the early period, decrease and are eventually replaced by bifaces and chisel choppers in the late period.

This overall pattern can be seen as a single, dichotomously organized, tool-assisted adaptive system changing through time while organization of the technology and the functional integration of tool-assisted activities remains unchanged. At the same time there is a change in the forms of some tools and perhaps in the techniques of tool

Table 27.4

Scores on Dimensions 2 and 3 in a Multidimensional Analysis of Variance Using a Chi-square Model

Late Material (Bed II)			
Negative dimension 3		Positive dimension 2	
		Manuports	10.63
Whole flakes	11.50		
Resharpening flakes	5.35		
Modified nodules and blocks	8.39	Modified nodules	8.83
		Core fragments	4.98
		Broken flakes	7.35
Subspheroids	7.78	Subspheroids	9.01
Spheroids	1.30	Spheroids	2.31
Polyhedrons	7.23		
Discs	4.79		
		Bifaces	3.21
Chisel/choppers	1.14		
Pointed choppers	1.12		
Bifaces	0.06		
Miscellaneous tools	4.80	Utilized flakes	4.29
Light-duty scrapers	4.18	Awls	3.89
Utilized flakes	2.97	Light-duty scrapers	3.01
Awls	2.86	Heavily utilized flakes	1.21
Burins	0.06		

Early Material (Bed I)			
Negative dimension 2		Positive dimension 3	
		Manuports	3.58
Whole flakes	20.83		
Resharpening flakes	10.54		
Utilized nodules	29.73	Utilized nodules	4.39
Utilized cobbles	0.09	Utilized cobbles	1.28
Hammers	17.99	Hammers	5.73
Anvils	4.33	Anvils	4.42
		Cores	2.95
		Broken flakes	4.29
Polyhedrons	10.66	Two-edged choppers	3.38
Side choppers	8.71	Side choppers	2.96
Discs	7.85		
End choppers	5.84		
Pointed choppers	5.16		
Two-edged choppers	4.42		
Heavy-duty scrapers	2.75	Heavy-duty scrapers	0.09
Miscellaneous tools	1.33	Heavily utilized flakes	0.03
Burins	0.001		

production or manipulation. One could argue, however, that there are two behavioral traditions—a "chopper–whole flake tradition" and a "manuport–expedient lithic production tradition." Both would have to have been undergoing roughly parallel changes in some technical design and technique phenomena. I should point out that my analysis yielded three additional dimensions of structured variance. While the participation of the chopper class and the modified small tool class varied, nevertheless the patterns apparent in these additional dimensions all paralleled the distinctions noted above between assemblages with proportionately varying frequencies of manuports, core fragments, broken flakes, and chips as opposed to those without manuports but with a major emphasis on hammers (both in the form of hammers themselves and in the form of used and/or modified nodules and blocks), all exhibiting a consistent association with whole and resharpening flakes. The presence of two aspects of tool deposition that exhibit consistent structural properties in both the early and late periods of the Oldowan is a very basic characteristic of the materials from Beds I and II at Olduvai Gorge.

I think it can be said that Mary Leakey correctly noted some of the major differences between the early and late materials, and her distinctions between Oldowan and Developed Oldowan are sustained (although specified in more detail) here. What she missed completely was the dichotomous character of both of these temporal complexes. In each there is a marked independence between two contexts of tool deposition. First is the context in which cores are reduced to lithic debris. Second, and even more provocative, is the fact that when lithic reduction is viewed in a more fine grained manner there are two types of assemblages: whole flakes and resharpening flakes regularly covary with the "core tools" and occur in proportional contexts in which hammers or "bashers," such as nodules and blocks, have inflated values, while "core fragments," broken flakes, and chips occur in proportional association with manuports and an impoverished presence of the chopper "core tool" class with an equally minimal presence of hammers and bashers.

Mary Leakey's distinction between Developed Oldowan A and B (without and with bifaces, respectively) is not maintained by my analysis. Bifaces can be shown to regularly covary with both subtypes of Developed Oldowan (whole flake vs. manuport-dominated expressions). The "fossile directeur" approach, which separated the Developed Oldowan into A and B types depending upon the presence of bifaces in specified quantities, is apparently deceiving. Bifaces in the Oldowan are relatively infrequent, and in small assemblages they can be expected to be absent much of the time. My normalized principal component analysis demonstrates, nevertheless, that they can be expected to occur in both recognized organizational contexts of the Developed Oldowan as explicated here (see Toth 1982:136–137 for a discussion of typological problems with the biface category). This recognition places the problem of the appearance of the Acheulian in a different light.

In recent years it has become generally recognized that the Acheulian is an internally varied technological complex. Some sites yield high frequencies of hand axes and cleavers and relatively few small tools, while others yield small tools in considerable quantities and hand axes are scarce or absent (Binford 1972b; Clark and Kurashina 1976; Isaac 1977a; Kleindienst 1961, 1962). It is believed by many that this is the result of organizational differences in the use contexts of tools within a single behavioral system. In addition, there appears to be a parallel condition in the later, "non-Olduvai" Acheulian in that hand axes and cleavers are not generally associated with lithic debris, while small tools are more commonly associated with lithic debris (e.g., at Broken Hill) and sometimes spheroids. This dichotomous pattern in the Acheulian seems to have analogies in the Oldowan. The increase in the use of hand axes could be seen as the simple development of a tool that is more useful and more easily transported than many of the "chopper" forms transported earlier in the Oldowan. Such a development would then simply parallel other changes in tool use occurring within a common organizational form, for example, the Oldowan itself. It is this strong analogy between the structural character of interassemblage variability in the Acheulian and that reported here for the Oldowan that leads me to suspect that the dichotomous structure of the Oldowan is *not* referable to different hominid species but instead represents the variable behavior of a single species. (It must be remembered that no one is arguing for sympatric species during the span of time covered by the Acheulian.) Nevertheless, while there is clearly an analogy between the organizational properties of the Oldowan and the Acheulian, they are not identical. We cannot simply assume that only one type of hominid made and used tools during the era that Beds I and II were deposited at Olduvai.

FAUNAL PATTERNING

Additional analysis was conducted on the fauna studied from both the standpoint of the species groups tabulated by Mary Leakey (1971) and in terms of the anatomical part frequencies for larger mammals as presented in *Bones* (Binford 1981a:264–265). The latter frequencies were count conversions made directly from Mary Leakey's (1971:276) percentage table.

When the data (counts—NISP for species) summarized by Mary Leakey (1971:257) were normalized by calculating chi-square values and studied with a singular value decomposition yielding a principal component solution, the results were as summarized in Table 27.5.

The analogous patterning in all the significant dimensions is clear. Let me exemplify with a discussion of Dimension 1. Here we see strong positive values for crocodiles and tortoises and a weak positive value for primates. The clue to the significance of this distribution rests with the crocodiles and tortoises. It is reported that most of the crocodile remains are shed crocodile teeth. These can hardly be considered to have been introduced by the hominids; they are much more likely to have accumulated as a natural background deposit unrelated to hominid activities. Similarly, the spatial patterning demonstrable at FLK NN3 (Kroll and Isaac 1984) strongly suggests that the tortoise remains are unrelated to the thin scattering of tools on the site. In short, the positive aspect of Dimension 1 seems to reliably report species whose presence represents the natural accumulation (i.e., an accumulation of in situ death or depositional events) on a land surface and is unrelated to the activities of hominids or other transport agents. Negative Dimension 2 has a similar character but adds carnivores to

Table 27.5

Principal Component Solution for Normalized Faunal Data

Dimension 1		Dimension 2		Dimension 3		Dimension 4		Dimension 5	
Crocodiles	67.7	Crocodiles	44.3	Elephants	70.0	Carnivores	22.9	Primates	9.15
Tortoises	43.0	Elephants	18.7	Tortoises	15.5	Bovids	14.0	Giraffes	6.43
Primates	1.2	Primates	3.21	Suids	5.7	Crocodiles	2.0	Rhinos	4.82
----		Rhinos	2.49	Rhinos	1.2	----		Bovids	3.81
Rhinos	−5.63	Hippos	2.17	----		Primates	−1.9	Equids	3.27
Hippos	−9.89	Giraffes	1.20	Primates	−2.7	Elephants	−2.3	Suids	2.49
Giraffes	−12.5	Suids	0.09	Giraffes	−5.7	Suids	−2.3	Tortoises	0.03
Suids	−18.2	Bovids	0.03	Hippos	−5.9	Tortoises	−3.6	----	
Elephants	−18.3	Equids	0.05	Crocodiles	−8.2	Rhinos	−9.2	Crocodiles	−1.31
Equids	−23.3	----		Carnivores	−9.2	Giraffes	−10.2	Elephants	−1.67
Carnivores	−23.9	Carnivores	−6.6	Equids	−10.8	Hippos	−30.2	Carnivores	−13.5
Bovids	−58.7	Tortoises	−63.3	Bovids	−11.5	Equids	−35.5	Hippos	−16.8

the natural background suite, and positive Dimension 3 adds elephants. We know of at least one nearly complete elephant carcass from FLK 6 that as such represents an in situ depositional event. These aspects of analytically isolated components (positive Dimension 1, negative Dimension 2, and positive Dimension 3) may be best interpreted as having isolated discrete background deaths or depositional events varying only with environmental context.

When the other sets of species are viewed as independently varying among dimensions or inversely varying on dimensions, we see that positive Dimension 2 as well as both positive and negative aspects of Dimension 5 might also represent background sets of species. Crocodiles, primates, or (in the case of negative Dimension 5) hippos have the highest scores in these aspects of the dimensions. Hippos, which have a low to moderate representation, are associated directly with carnivores, elephants, and crocodiles—all species suspected to represent background species in their own right. I provisionally refer to these sets as diverse background associations. It is relatively easy to imagine a land surface characterized by some duration of opportunity for deposition. This duration may well be monitored by the species discussed above as representing discrete background events. Correlated with these events would be other depositional events representing time-averaged depositions related to the duration of time in which this land surface was exposed. This is what seems to be implied by the species recognized here as generalized background phenomena.

Differing from the sets of species discussed above are species associations indicated by the negative aspect of Dimension 1. Here we see large-animal species (mostly terrestrial) that might be suspected as having been introduced to locations by hominids or otherwise aggregated by other agents (e.g., the species identified from the Zinjanthropus floor; Bunn and Kroll 1986a). This also seems to be the situation for negative Dimension 3 and negative Dimension 4, each representing perhaps differing environmental contexts. The negative aspects of both Dimensions 3 and 4 are the most likely candidates for containing faunas accumulated by hominids. When the results of the analysis are viewed in the above manner, the interpretations of the various dimensions are as follows:

	Aspect/Dimension
natural, *in situ,* discrete background events	$+1, -2, +4$
diverse-event background accumulations	$+2, +3, +5, -5$
possibly aggregated accumulations	$-1, -3, -4$

LINKING THE FAUNA AND THE TOOLS

It is certainly desirable to discover if there is any regular patterning that links the major aspects of the Oldowan technology, as discussed earlier, with the species indicators or depositional conditions suggested above and further with indicators of faunal composition considered in terms of skeletal properties. In order to accomplish this assessment, several sources of variation need to be eliminated from consideration. My major interest here is to eliminate variability among the species that might indicate environmental difference and consider only for the moment the indicators of depositional context that have been suggested above. Similarly, in terms of the organizational properties of the tool assemblages, I wish to eliminate the effects of the demonstrable changes through time in the dichotomous aspects of the Oldowan technology in order to see if there is a general set of relationships common to the two recognized aspects of the technology (transported vs. manuport/locally reduced raw material) regardless of change in each through time. Finally, it is my conviction that the anatomical composition of animal bones recovered from the various Olduvai sites are data that are crucial for the development of any understanding of the activities of hominids at locations yielding tools and bones.

Since my initial excursion into the domain of pattern-recognition work on the Olduvai fauna (Binford 1981a), there has been endless criticism (Bunn 1982:495; Bunn and Kroll 1986a; Freeman 1983; Isaac 1983a:417–419) of my use of the data on anatomical part frequencies presented by Mary Leakey (1971). I have answered some of this criticism (Binford 1983b, 1984c, 1987d), but many empiricists simply do not understand analysis and the role of assumptions and transformations necessary to ensure that data are meaningfully comparable. Perhaps more disturbing is the failure of most of my critics to understand the difference between a multivariate pattern-recognition search and empirical generalizations from the raw data as they like to see it. This failure is very clear in the recent attempts of Bunn and Kroll (1986a) to use data from a single site as presented in raw observational units to challenge the accuracy of patterning extracted from a matrix of interassemblage comparisons while at the same time ignoring the discussions of complexity that were presented regarding the site they used (see Binford 1981a:276). Bunn and Kroll examined the "Zinj" site as a case which in their view contradicts the generalizations made from a complete matrix of comparisons. This is analytical naivete. Since much of this debate derives in my opinion from a failure to understand both pattern-recognition work and data analysis, I seek in this analysis of skeletal part composition to use very simple measures.

I am once again going to use the data summarized by Mary Leakey (1971:276) for the Oldowan site faunas. Nevertheless, there are severe limitations to these data. For instance, isolated mandibular and maxillary teeth are not tabulated independently (this is also unfortunately true in Bunn 1982b). Similarly, tabulations of ribs and vertebrae appear to be counts of something similar to NISP (see Grayson 1984), while counts of limb segments seem to be close to MNEs (Binford 1984c). The lumping of podial elements renders these observations essentially useless as well. Many researchers will most likely once again point to these difficulties and argue that the "real world" is being violated. Their counsel is that we should wait until "good" data are available before proceeding with any analysis. I completely disagree with such Boasian suggestions. Analysis and the recognition of patterning, as well as arguments about patterning once it is recognized, are the tools that drive the search for relevant and potentially meaningful units of observation. The way we observe the world is not prescribed by the way the world presents itself to us; there are no self-evident natural units out there to be discovered as guides for the generation of data. These guides come from our arguments about data, and only in this context can we learn what is relevant to observe and in what way observations are to be made so as to render meaningful comparisons possible. Available data must be used so as to light the way to the more meaningful production of data in the future. I hope to demonstrate the value of this approach to learning here.

I use the following variables in this analysis (Table 27.6):

1. *the percentage of unidentified bone reported from each Olduvai site by Mary Leakey (1971:256, Table 3), rounded to the nearest whole percentage point*

Table 27.6
Summary of Values for the Variables Used in the Analysis

Site	1	2	3	4	5	6	7	8	9
BK	54	1.59	23	46	—	15.04	55.02	5.49	8.21
TK	35	0.75	33	32	—	1.34	37.24	14.31	7.58
FC tuff	59	1.0	0	24	—	8.25	25.74	3.29	0.29
FC floor	43	1.5	0	38	—	4.58	45.90	3.04	1.54
MNK main	50	1.2	31	43	—	12.24	62.64	7.87	2.39
MNK OH.13	36	0.59	25	41	13.97	3.44	2.20	6.17	2.87
MNK 3–5	16	1.47	06	55	0.25	0.47	19.20	10.89	2.86
HWK 2	04	0.88	49	40	—	27.34	16.08	0.88	5.82
HWK 1	11	1.50	41	57	—	5.41	34.18	10.49	7.44
FLK 1–2	39	1.39	27	56	19.49	2.89	48.64	4.12	18.46
FLK 3	26	1.44	25	46	13.58	2.80	34.03	3.21	12.28
FLK 4	24	1.18	20	50	16.83	7.41	32.89	2.60	10.73
FLK 5	47	1.09	39	55	16.63	1.82	36.73	6.66	7.97
FLK 6	14	1.16	67	46	—	86.67	23.10	1.42	5.05
FLK 15	43	1.43	34	77	2.21	3.80	13.50	5.10	8.07
FLK 22	69	1.74	19	40	7.76	10.67	24.27	2.23	4.51
FLK NN1	05	0.62	32	48	11.76	5.36	3.13	4.81	6.50
FLK NN3	05	2.69	29	38	96.10	0.79	17.26	1.99	3.36
DK	14	2.27	26	46	71.60	33.01	6.23	0.00	34.46

2. *the ratio of metapodials to other limb bones, exclusive of the scapula, as indicated by articular ends* This figure was calculated from the MNE values given in Binford (1981a:264). It should be noted that four errors were identified in this table as published; however, the errors were not present in the data used in the 1981 analysis. These errors are as follows: column 31, distal radiocubitus should be 1.10; column 31, distal metacarpal should be 2.52; column 33, distal metacarpal should be 2.93; and column 33, distal metatarsal should be 2.93. In order to obtain the ratio, the MNE values for metapodials (proximal and distal) were summed for each site. The MNE values from all other limb bones, exclusive of the scapula, were also summed. The total for metapodials was then divided into the total for all other limb bones. The expected ratio for a complete animal carcass is 2.0. Values lower than this indicate some bias in favor of preserved metapodial articular ends. The lower the values of the ratio, the less complete the representation of upper limb bones relative to metapodials.

3. *the percentage of articular ends remaining on complete limb bones relative to the total articular end estimate for the site* In Mary Leakey's Table 8 (1971:276), the percentages of the total tabulated fauna represented by complete limb bones are reported, along with the percentages represented by isolated articular ends for the homologous bone. These were converted to MNE counts using the total bone counts given in the table. These values have been summarized in Binford (1981a:285, Table 6.02, row 4) and are summarized again in Table 27.6, column 3, as percentages of the number of complete limb bones.

4. *the percentage of all bones (MNE) representing appendicular elements* These values were calculated by summing the MNE values for teeth, pelvis, ribs, and vertebrae and dividing by 4, yielding a mean value for the axial skeleton (summarized from Binford 1981a:264–265, Table 6.03). The same procedure was used to obtain the value for the appendicular skeleton, summing scapula, proximal and distal humerus, radiocubitus, metacarpal, femur, tibia, and metatarsal and dividing by 13 to obtain a mean MNE value for the appendicular skeleton. These two mean values were then summed and the value for the appendicular skeleton was divided by the total of the two values, yielding a percentage value for the representation of the appendicular skeleton. A complete carcass would yield a value of 50%; thus these values can be read as an indicator of bias for or against appendicular elements in the assemblage. It is well known that ravaged carcasses exhibit a bias in favor of axial skeletal parts.

5. *the sum of values indicative of discrete background events* The summed values for positive Dimension 1, negative Dimension 2, and positive Dimension 4 as presented in Table 27.5 for each site are taken as the value indicative of the total contribution made by discrete background events at each site.

6. *the sum of values indicative of general background events* The summed values for positive Dimensions 2, 3, and 5 as well as negative Dimension 5 (Table 27.5) are taken as the value indicative of the total contribution made by general background events at each site.

7. *the sum of values indicative of introduced fauna* The summed values for negative Dimensions 1, 3, and 4 (Table 27.5) are taken as the value indicative of the total contribution made by introduced fauna at each site.

8. *the value for the contribution of the manuport/expedient tool production technological component* The value treating negative signs as positive values for positive Dimension 2 and positive Dimension 3 of Table 27.3 is taken as the measure of this technological aspect, ignoring the changes occurring through time.

9. *the value for the contribution of the transported component of the technology* The value treating all signs as positive for negative Dimensions 2 and 3 of Table 27.3 is taken as the measure of this technological aspect, ignoring the changes occurring through time.

As in previous cases, the data in Table 27.6 were normalized by the calculation of chi-square values for each cell. These normalized chi-square values were then subjected to singular value decomposition, yielding a principal component multivariate summary of the data. This solution is quite robust, accounting for 68% of all the variance (Dimension 1 = 29.2%, Dimension 2 = 23.7%, and Dimension 3 = 14.81%). The results are summarized in Table 27.7.

It seems clear that the transported component of the tool technology is associated with both discrete and generalized background fauna and high indicators of complete bones (positive Dimensions 1 and 2). The very high loadings for discrete background events (Dimension 1) strongly suggests that the transported assemblage is accumulated on surfaces in a manner that is related to the duration of exposure of that surface. This is consistent with a formation process composed of a series of discrete depositional events resulting in a time-averaged accumulation or an archaeological palimpsest of a coarse-grained type at sites dominated by the transported component. On the other hand, the negative aspects of both Dimensions 1 and 2 consistently associate the expedient tool component—manuports and lithic debris—with introduced bone (i.e., bone suspected as having been transported by hominids), unidentified bone (suggestive of considerable bone breakage, perhaps effected by the hominids), and more important, high percentages of bones from the appendicular skeleton. The inverse relationship characterizing this suite of associations relative to *all indicators of background faunal accumulations* for Dimension 1 and only to discrete background fauna for negative Dimension 2 suggests that the behavioral context of site formation for the manuport and in situ lithic reduction is quite different from that for the transported component. We can understand this relationship when we remember that lithic reduction results in many items derived from relatively few acts of lithic processing. Thus the quantity of such items localized in one place is apt to be a function of the amount of material processed per event and not necessarily of the number of such events represented. Under such conditions we would not expect a strong set of relationships between the amount of debris and the length of time the surface was exposed (as indicated here by background fauna). This general lack of relationship probably reflects still another provocative aspect of the spatial organization of Oldowan technology—namely, the acts of lithic reduction and the frequently associated abandonment of manuports are (a) less common than acts of discard of transported tools and (b) not likely to occur in the same place for any extended period of time. That the latter is true seems supported by the tightly clustered distributions known thus far for Oldowan assemblages—for example, the strongly clustered distribution of

Table 27.7

Principal Component Solution for Normalized Data from Table 27.6

Dimension 1		Dimension 2		Dimension 3	
discrete breakage	25.33	general breakage	18.89	unidentified bone	7.69
transported tools	4.37	complete bone	7.89	general breakage	6.34
complete bone	1.07	transported tools	0.39	discrete breakage	2.94
long bones/metapodials	0.75			introduced bone	2.29
generalized breakage	0.66	long bone/metapodial	−0.73	long bones/metapodials	0.22
		% appendicular	−1.54		
% appendicular	−1.73	expedient tools	−2.66	transported tools	−1.09
expedient tools	−3.54	introduced bone	−4.62	expedient tools	−4.65
introduced bone	−7.79	discrete breakage	−5.93	% appendicular	−6.13
unidentified bone	−9.94	unidentified bone	−8.05	complete bone	−6.40

small items demonstrable on the Zinj floor (FLK 22; Kroll and Isaac 1984:24, Fig. 12) as well as at Koobi Fora FxJj50.

The relationships isolated in this analysis point to another very important property of the technological organization. When transported tools are discarded, there is little evidence of aggregations of transported faunal remains; for example, at FLK 4 (Leakey 1971:Fig. 34), FLK NN1 (Leakey 1971:43–44), and FLK NN3 (Leakey 1971:Fig. 20), as well as DK (Leakey 1971:Fig. 7). In general there is a very diffuse horizontal distribution to both tools and faunal remains with many independently distributed patterns of fauna and tools (see FLK NN1 and HWK 2). Much of the fauna could in fact be natural background, as is suggested in this analysis. On the other hand, when the manuport/expedient lithic reduction aspect of the assemblage is represented, there does appear to have been transport and aggradation of faunal remains on the site—the Zinj floor being a good example, with FLK 1–2, 3, FC-floor, and MNK Main supporting this generalization. Put another way, when hominids carried and disposed of modified "core" tools or produced derivative flakes from these tools they did so in the absence of any transport or aggregation of animal products. When tools were transported, animal parts were not aggregated, at least not in any highly clustered sense.

In marked contrast, when hominids were processing lithic raw materials and using and disposing of tools in expedient production contexts, they were transporting and aggregating parts of animals at the same spot (see the distributions on the Zinj floor; Kroll and Isaac 1984:10, Fig. 2a). Simply put, when tools were transported and discarded, animal parts were not transported and aggregated; on the other hand, when (expediently produced) tools were manufactured on the spot, animal parts were transported to and aggregated at the same places as the lithic reduction events. The hominids *either* transported tools and did not aggregate animal parts, *or* they did transport animals parts and processed them with tools expediently produced on the spot. The latter events appear to represent discrete tool- and bone-processing activities of short duration.

Turning now to the results obtained in Dimension 3 in the analysis of the relationships between fauna and stone tools, we obtain an expected separation among fauna in general, unidentified bone, general background fauna, discrete background fauna, introduced bone, and greater than normal presence of upper limb bones. This can be seen as representing sites where natural faunal accumulations are well represented and where faunal preservation is good. On the negative aspect of this dimension are all the tools plus inflated values for the percentage of appendicular skeletal elements as well as complete bones, both features already seen to exhibit a structured relationship with tools. I think it should be clear that this dimension reflects the differential preservation of bone versus stone tools. It therefore provides a good indicator of preservational differences among the sites studied.

CONCLUSIONS

How do these patterns inform us about hominid life in the Lower Paleolithic? Several things seem clear.

1. The planning depth standing behind the use of stone tools seems very shallow indeed. Tools are produced and transported and then discarded across the landscape when they still have much potential for use. The planning appears to be episodal in character and not in any way similar to the planning strategies known from the archaeology of fully modern man. Modern tools are commonly designed for long-term roles and are frequently maintained in the technological system for considerable periods of time. The lack of planning depth described for the earlier hominids is seemingly indicated by the remains at the "processing locations" (e.g., the Zinj floor), where transported and aggregated parts of animals occur. In this context, the tools were expediently produced, used, and discarded in the immediate context of processing animal products.

2. The archaeological remains at the locations where animal products were aggregated and processed do not exhibit properties commonly associated with base camps as known from modern human systems. In the latter, base camps are the hubs or focal points of subsistence activities as well as the activities centered around replacement, repair, and maintenance of the technology. In the locations where animal products are aggregated, the tools for their processing are manufactured on the spot and the lithic assemblages exhibit none of the properties indicative of locations where the transported tools were manufactured or where activities occurred in which transported tools originated or were being returned to. The sites appear to be simple processing locations and not hubs of technological or subsistence activities.

3. The sites where transported animal products were aggregated and processed do not appear to be internally differentiated spatially in any way. There are localized bone-processing and tool-manufacturing and -use clusters on these sites, but tool manufacturing does not distribute independently of the bone-processing activities, and no other recognizable localizations of tools are indicated. In thick or "diffuse" deposits, such as MNK Main, some multiple localizations are recognizable, but the nature of the deposit strongly supports the view that these were not contemporary localizations but palimpsest accumulations of separate episodes over considerable periods of time.

4. The distribution of fauna and tools at the sites thus far studied does not support the position that the local group was composed of multiple families, nor that there was food sharing among segments of the feeding group represented. Among modern humans, organized in family groups, consumption is almost always done in base camps, where the families are partitioned spatially. This results in multiple and redundant localizations of both food-processing and -consumption areas on such sites. Thus far, no such internal partitioning of multiple processing and consumer locations is demonstrable on Oldowan sites where there is reason to suspect rough contemporaneity among localizations. Under the hunting and sharing argument we would not expect to find the patterning indicated in this analysis, in which a fairly consistent suite of animal products covaries with a single tool suite. It has been shown that when interfamilial sharing occurs, the anatomical part frequencies vary among the localizations of similar family-centered functions (see Binford 1984d). If excavation has not been extensive enough to reveal multiple consumer locations, then the chance encounter of single ones at different sites or in different levels would not yield a

consistent pattern of anatomical part bias as suggested in the study done here. The localizations appear to be processing locations. I see no data currently available that would warrant a further inference that these represent central place consumer locations, or home bases.

5. There has been much discussion of hunting versus scavenging of animal products as well as repeated suggestions that the early hominids were consuming considerable quantities of meat (Bunn et al. 1980; Bunn 1981, 1982a, 1982b; Bunn and Kroll 1986a). I consider these arguments unjustified and ill-founded. As currently presented, they rest on (a) the aggregation of animal parts at discrete localizations isomorphic with tool distributions, as at the Zinj site, a point not in dispute; and (b) a reported high frequency of tool-inflicted cutmarks on the bones (Bunn 1982b; Bunn and Kroll 1986a).

I also find the reported frequencies of cutmarks at these sites higher than those thus far documented from other studied localities, and I do not dispute the patterned presence of cutmarks, including those indicative of dismemberment. There is, then, no dispute as to the nature of the data as thus far reported. The question is about the meaning of these observations and how such meanings are justified. Bunn has consistently maintained that

> some ancient hominids were using stone tools to systematically butcher the meaty carcasses of a range of smaller and larger animals and that substantial quantities of meat and marrow were probably being consumed by hominids. We believe the data are consistent with a subsistence strategy combining hunting of at least small animals, hunting or aggressive scavenging of large animals, and transporting of portions of carcasses to favored locations in the . . . landscape. Given the large quantities of meat and marrow available during hominid feeding events, it is likely that cooperative food sharing . . . occurred nearly two million years ago. (Bunn and Kroll 1986a:442)

How do we go from aggregated tools and bones, and tool-inflicted cutmarks, to the above inferences? Are the data self-evident? Do the high frequencies of cutmarks really tell us about quantities of meat available? Do the aggregations of animal parts really tell us about food sharing? Is hunting really implicated by the data as summarized by Bunn and Kroll (1986a)? I think not. In fact, I see no justification for the inferences drawn by Bunn and Kroll. They certainly cannot appeal to the argument that there are no other alternatives, and they have in no way addressed these alternative interpretations, as any good scientist must do when interpretive ambiguity exists (see Binford 1986f).

6. Is Olduvai also the Oldowan? Many of the current discussions of the early eras of tool use make reference to data not only from Olduvai Gorge but from several other important locations. Prominent is the work done by Glynn Isaac and his team (Bunn et al. 1980; Harris 1978; Isaac 1976; Isaac et al. 1976) at Koobi Fora, but there are other locations as well (e.g., Chavillon 1982; Chavillon et al. 1978, 1979; Clark and Kurashina 1979a, 1979b; Howell 1976, 1978a, 1978b; Williams et al. 1979). Given the understanding of variability notable among the Olduvai locations or sites, one could see the Shungura formation artifacts (Chavillon 1970, 1976; Chavillon and Boisaubert 1977;

Merrick 1976; Merrick and Merrick 1976) as anticipated by the manuport/expedient lithic reduction aspect of the Olduvai materials. The strong manuport component seems absent in the Shungura materials, however. The Gombore site of Melka Kunture, Ethiopia (Chavillon 1982), seems at home with the transported component as recognized among the Olduvai sites. On the other hand, the material from Garba IV (Chavillon 1982) seems more analogous to the manuport/expedient lithic reduction aspects of the Oldowan assemblages at Olduvai (see Piperno and Piperno 1974). At Gadeb, particularly Level 2E, the transported component seems indicated, but it alternates with recognizable Acheulian materials, possibly suggesting a shift in function for the typologically recognizable Oldowan materials as discussed in this chapter in the context of Acheulian developments. The above comparisons are somewhat unsatisfactory, unfortunately, since the materials are not reported in comparable detail to those from Olduvai Gorge.

By far the best documented and most important comparisons thus far drawn are between the materials from Koobi Fora and those from Olduvai. Isaac (1984b:49) has summarized some of the interesting differences between Koobi Fora and Olduvai as follows:

1. There is a larger proportion of large stones of all kinds in the Olduvai assemblages (i.e., manuports, choppers, polyhedrons, hammerstones, battered nodules, etc.).
2. Spheroids and subspheroids become prominent components of most Olduvai assemblages from Upper Bed I onward. These particular forms do not occur at Koobi Fora for any stratigraphic level, and battered, pounded pieces in general are much rarer at Koobi Fora.
3. For any given category at any site at Olduvai, be it chopper, discoid, polyhedron, or plain flakes, the mean size is notably larger than the mean for almost any site at Koobi Fora. Only the values for channel bed assemblages at Koobi Fora overlap at all the range of values for Olduvai assemblages.
4. Smaller flake scrapers and other retouched flakes are relatively rare at Koobi Fora whereas they are fairly well represented at the Olduvai Bed I assemblages and become even more so in Beds II, III and IV.

These very important observations represent the beginnings of important comparative pattern-recognition work that must be carried out in ever-increasing scales if an understanding of the behavioral basis of the Lower Paleolithic is to be achieved. For instance, it is my impression that most of the materials thus far reported from Koobi Fora appear representative of the pattern I have called the "transported component" as represented at Olduvai Gorge. Certainly the provocative work of Toth seems to support the strong analogy to the transported component recognized here. This is also true for the comparative statements given above by Isaac. Unfortunately, the faunal assemblages reported thus far from Koobi Fora appear to have suffered considerable attrition (most are primarily composed of teeth and long-bone splinters—anatomical elements expected to be most resistant to attritional processes both mechanical and chemical).

There are three exceptions to this generalization as reported by Bunn (1982b:340):

FxJj38SE, FxJj50, and FxJj64. FxJj38SE is viewed as exceptional in the Koobi Fora data suite and is currently being interpreted as owing its uniqueness primarily to the operation of nonhominid agents, particularly fluvial deposition (Bunn 1982b:101). In marked contrast is the faunal assemblage from the important site of FxJj50. There appears to be unambiguous evidence for hominid involvement with at least some of the fauna (see Bunn et al. 1980; Bunn 1982b:103–108), in spite of evidence for fluvial alternation of the deposit. What is most interesting is the common presence of bones from relatively large animals and the high relative frequencies of ribs and vertebrae, while skull parts are low in frequency relative to other assemblages. This frequency patterning is consistent with the patterning extracted in this analysis for the trans- ported component of the Olduvai assemblages, namely, that transported tools more commonly associate with higher frequencies of bones from the axial skeleton. Equally interesting in this regard are the remains from FxJj64, where the tools are reported to be in association with fauna strongly represented by elephant ribs (see Bunn 1982b:109–112). While not conclusive, the latter two sites are consistent with the patterning isolated among the Olduvai assemblages, where axial skeletal parts more commonly associate with the transported component.

What makes the Koobi Fora data so fascinating is the seeming representation of only the transported component and the general absence of manuports and modified and battered nodules. This could be interpreted in at least two ways. First, the transported component is found over a much wider geographic range than is the expediently produced tool component, and Koobi Fora represents an area near the edges of the wider range. Second, the transported component represents a different hominid adaptation exclusively represented at Koobi Fora, while two distinct hominid adapta- tions are represented at Olduvai. If one takes the view that the two artifact components isolated in this study represent different tool-assisted feeding strategies, then the data from Koobi Fora can be seen as supporting the view that the transported component represents the feeding strategy that is more spatially extensive.

7. How can we use the patterning thus far isolated to solve the problem with which this essay began—which hominids made which tools? Isaac and his team have made provocative observations at Koobi Fora, noting that the sites yielding stone tools tend to be clustered along stream channels while the fossils of *Homo* tend to be clustered in lake margin contexts (Isaac 1984b:58–62). In contrast, *Australopithecus boisei* is found primarily at Koobi Fora (a small sample) in channel contexts where the tools are also localized. On the other hand, based on an extremely small sample from Olduvai Beds I and II, *Homo* and *A. boisei* are found in lakeside deposits in roughly equal frequency. Compounding the possible associations of types of tool assemblage and environmental setting is the fact that at Koobi Fora essentially all of the tool-using sites are in upland channel contexts, while all the sites at Olduvai Beds I and II are in lake margin or fluvial- lacustrine contexts and none are known from fluvial contexts in uplands away from the lake. In order to assess the patterns of assemblage variability thus far recognizable, we desperately need either tool-yielding sites at Koobi Fora in a lake margin context or upland fluvial contexts for early (Bed I and II) period sites at Olduvai Gorge. In addition we need to understand much more about the ecology of death for the various forms of early hominids. Thus far we can recognize some fascinating patterning, some hints to

systematic ecological relationships, but we lack control comparative material from comparable time periods for the range of ecological settings thus far sampled in different places. I strongly suspect that we are seeing the archaeological consequences of a single tool-assisted adaptation, but this unfortunately remains an impression. Understanding the roles of technology and the patterned use of the landscape by tool-assisted hominids is a critical research goal that must be achieved before there can be much meaningful discussion of niche or niches occupied and the type of organization standing behind the archaeological landscapes being "sampled" through excavations. It is certainly my impression both from published materials (Isaac 1984b:61–62; personal communication, 1985) and conversations shortly before his shocking and untimely death that Glynn Isaac was moving closer and closer to the postures I have been advocating (Binford 1985b, 1987d) and spending less and less time trying to defend his earlier ideas of home bases and a modern human settlement system. We need to obtain environmentally controlled samples from comparable time periods before we can begin to see the nature of the tool-assisted adaptations of the Lower Paleolithic. I am confident that, the more we learn, the less they will look like us.

Chapter 28

Isolating the Transition to Cultural Adaptations:
An Organizational Approach

Writing in the early 1920s, A. L. Kroeber commented on the "transition" to fully modern humankind[1] as follows:

> The Lower Paleolithic culture, at least in its latest form, was carried by Neanderthal man; Upper Paleolithic culture is in great part associated with Cro-Magnon man, whose anatomy was nearer our own. Did not this relatively modern structure involve also a relatively modern set of mental faculties, and these in turn, by their own sheer worth, produce the richer culture? (Kroeber 1923:396)

Early textbooks in American anthropology almost without exception noted the marked contrast between the Upper Paleolithic and what preceded it. The Old Paleolithic, as it was sometimes called, was appreciated as having been produced by creatures different from us in perhaps fundamental ways. Since early anthropological thought was essentially an idealist's view both of modern man's distinctiveness and of his predecessors' "deficiencies," it is not surprising that Kroeber chose to contrast early man with modern man in terms of mental faculties:

> Patience and forethought of a rather high order are thus involved in the making of implements of the Neolithic type. . . . By comparison, the earliest man lacked these traits. They would not sit down to-day to commence something that would not be available for use until a month later. What they wanted they wanted quickly. To think ahead, to sacrifice present convenience to future advantage, must have been foreign to their way of life. (Kroeber 1923:144)

There may be some advantage to a return, at least in part, to this point of view. Focusing on the behavioral consequences of planning and on the organization of early hominid use of tools may be among the most productive avenues of research on the transition between the archaeological remains deposited before and after the appearance of *Homo sapiens sapiens.*

PLANNING DEPTH, TACTICAL DEPTH, AND CURATION

Modern populations commonly take actions that will make possible further action at a much later time, indeed often initiating the sequence long before the anticipated

Originally appeared in *The Emergence of Modern Humans: Biocultural Adaptations in the Later Pleistocene,* edited by Eric Trinkaus, published by Cambridge University Press, Cambridge, © 1989.

conditions are observable in the environment. A move to a fish camp along a salmon stream, for example, is generally made before salmon appear in the stream (O'Leary 1985) on the basis of stored and analyzed knowledge of the environment and of the behavior of fish. The group may well engage in the manufacture and repair of fishing gear long before any direct indication that salmon are present, will be present, or might be exploited. When the salmon arrive, heavy labor investments are made in obtaining fish, which are then processed for stores that may serve as food for the group over a six- to eight-month period. In this example we clearly have an instance of planning. The potentially variable length of time between anticipatory actions and the actions they facilitate, amount of investment in anticipatory actions, and proportion of activities so facilitated may be conceived as *planning depth,* and the technologies of modern populations exhibit this depth to a high degree.

A second characteristic of technological systems designed and maintained by *H. sapiens sapiens* is a high degree of what I shall call *tactical depth*—the variable capacity, based on stored knowledge of mechanical principles, environmental characteristics, and hence opportunities, to find more than one way to skin a cat. Although people may plan the manufacture, maintenance, and replacement of technological elements, their ability to anticipate future conditions is not always perfect. A hunting party equipped with well-designed weapons may be unsuccessful and shift its food-procurement endeavors to fishing. Under these conditions it may find its hunting gear inappropriate and use it as a source of raw materials for manufacturing fishing gear on the spot. Again, the members of the party may lose their gear, for example, while crossing a swollen river, and look around in their immediate environment (which they generally know quite well) for raw materials with which to manufacture replacements. This equipment is designed to play a very different role from that of the lost gear—a short-term, expedient role—and may be formally unlike it.

For the archaeologist, this capacity for technological adjustment to the immediate circumstances results in interesting and complicated patterns. The archaeological remains of fully modern humankind exhibit great variation arising from the frequent combination of tactical options conditioned by immediate circumstances. When this flexibility is combined with considerable planning depth, the variation may be bewildering. Assemblages are reticulated compounds of differentiated components, and rarely is any strong set of "categorical" differences recognizable among "types" of places occupied by a single system. Likewise, when independent measures of the conditions being coped with at the time of archaeological deposition (e.g., environmental indicators and faunal remains) can be monitored at different places and different times, there is rarely any categorical patterning of association between particular tools and given species or activities. The ability to shift tactics to accommodate unanticipated conditions precludes such robust and simple patterning (see, e.g., Straus 1987).

Another aspect of modern mankind's behavior that is variable and interesting is the degree to which technology is *maintained*—the amount of labor investment in the design and production of tools so as to ensure them a long use life. I have called this maintenance behavior *curation* (Binford 1979). While planning depth may be present without curation, it is difficult to imagine curation without planning depth.

Curation may be signaled in the archaeological record by the differential selection of raw materials. Again, items playing long-term roles may be transported many times to many places and therefore they may be expected to occur only rarely with the debris from their manufacture. Such items may also have major investments made in their maintenance along the way. Curation may be most obvious in complicated tool designs yielding both great durability and easy maintenance, such as a modular one; parts that are more subject to breakage (such as projectile points) may be designed for ease of manufacture and replacement.

As planning depth increases, so do the number of manufacturing steps and the variety of tools used to produce the final product—a tool designed for use in directly coping with the environment. The larger the inventory of tools performing interjacent roles relative to these instrumental end products, the more reticulate and "non-categorical" the patterning among tool forms when different sites are compared. For instance, where an instrumental technology is primarily manufactured from nonlithic raw materials, with lithics being used interjacently, the lithics may in comparison appear impoverished and crude. We may be further led astray by comparing the interjacent tools of one system with the crude and poorly designed instrumental tools of an earlier system.[2] Very different planning depths underlie these two situations. To avoid these kinds of errors, we need an organizational understanding of the contexts of the tools. Tools designed to facilitate repair or maintenance of other tools are direct clues to planning depth, as also is independence between the disposition of tools used to make tools and that of the tools designed to be used in directly coping with the environment.

The techno-adaptive strategies of modern hunter-gatherers are extremely variable in planning depth, tactical depth, and curation. Technological features reflecting differences in these components scale remarkably well with environmental variables in the near-modern world (Binford 1980a; Kelly 1983). In addition, this patterning has been strongly linked to regularly varying patterns of mobility (also responsive to environmental variables) and has been elaborated and explicated by further research (Torrence 1983) regarding time scheduling of labor inputs for both production and maintenance of technologies. The work done to date clearly supports the view that planning depth, tactical depth, and curation differentially contribute to adaptive success in different environments.

The relatively fine-tuned relationships between technological characteristics, viewed in these terms, and environmental variables document the fact that culturally organized technologies are modern humans' extrasomatic means of adaptation. Woodburn (1980) recognizes an analogous distinction in speaking of immediate- and delayed-return strategies with regard to labor investments, but he fails to take the next step in seeking to understand the contrasts he recognizes. Marshack (1972:14) points to some of these same properties in identifying "time-factored" processes and behavior. He notes correctly that "sciences . . . are themselves 'time-factored,' since the processes of cognition and recognition, of planning, research, analysis, comparison, and interpretation are also sequential, interrelated, developmental and cumulative."

Despite the geographic (Binford 1983d) and sequential (Binford 1980a) patterning in their adaptations, it is primarily the scheduling variations in both space and time in the accessibility of resources, coupled with the incongruent patterns of availability for needed suites of resources, that condition the degree of planning depth, tactical depth, and curation among modern hunter-gatherers (Binford 1980a). There is a global pattern of variation that is understandable largely in ecological terms.

First, "technological areas" or "culture areas" correspond nicely to environments of differing forms and dynamics. Studies of the material products of modern preindustrial peoples (e.g., Kroeber 1939; Wissler 1914) have long since demonstrated this, but the causal implications have not been pursued. Second, more planning depth, tactical depth, and curation seem to characterize technologies in relatively inhospitable environments, those that are most variable in terms of seasonal productivity. This pattern betrays a very consistent evolutionary set of responses to the earth's environments, presumably the consequence of the interactions between the structure of the environments and the "capacity" of modern human populations to solve problems in nearly identical ways.

Consideration of the transition from earlier forms to fully modern man often takes the form of citing the earliest evidence for certain categorical forms of behavior recognized as characteristic of the latter—the earliest evidence for symbolism, for an aesthetic sense, for a "human" form of social organization. There is, I think, a kind of chauvinism, ethnocentrism, or even racism associated with this approach. It is not uncommon to hear that the properties we consider most admirable in our behavior are those to be differentially investigated. This tends to place many researchers on the defensive with reference, for example, to the seeming lack of technological achievement of even relatively modern peoples living in equatorial and subequatorial settings (e.g., Hutterer 1977a, 1977b; Watanabe 1979, 1985). The criteria for identifying fully modern human behaviors must be developed in the context of a firm understanding of what conditions variation among modern populations in the way our "human nature" is expressed in different environments. The global patterning just mentioned is only now being recognized. Much of the variation among modern hunter-gatherer societies is not yet understood. Nevertheless, I do not consider it premature to seek an understanding of the transition in terms of our budding appreciation for such patterning.[3]

The earliest evidence for technologically aided adaptations is largely restricted to the subequatorial zones. Thus any assessment of the role of technology and the organizational basis for adaptations among the early hominids must be made in the context of our understanding of the adaptations of mobile hunter-gatherers in such settings. A striking difference between modern hunter-gatherer adaptations in subequatorial zones and in equatorial forests has to do with mobility. In the forest, residential mobility is high and "logistical" mobility low, as is the extent of foraging coverage relative to a "base camp" (Kelly 1983). Technology may be curated, and much of the instrumental technology is manufactured of light materials, such as bamboo and wood and combinations thereof. While the inventory of tools may be small, their designs tend to be ingenious, facilitating a wide range of specific activities. The deeper in the forest, generally the smaller the package size of the foods exploited. Scavenging is rarely reported, consumption of animal products seems to be immediate, and no storage of such products is indicated.

Table 28.1 summarizes the contemporary ethnographic data on productivity of habitat and types of weapons used in obtaining animal foods in equatorial settings. These patterns seem to put to rest the notion of a Garden of Eden, the claim that humans should respond only to the quantity of potential food available (e.g., Foley 1982). It is very clear that the technology varies with the character of the environment. In high biomass tropical settings, blowguns and relatively small poisoned arrows permit the hunter to gain access to the generally small animals of the canopy and may be used in conjunction with nets for taking the very small animals of the forest floor. As productivity goes down (in this setting an indication of drier conditions), larger shock weapons (bow and arrow, lance, spear) become more important. In the relatively dry tropical forests and forest savannah margins, a wide variety of relatively small terrestrial animals can be effectively hunted with strong shock weapons. Groups living in environments with both small and large animals (e.g., the Hadza) use poison when taking larger prey. The body sizes of the animals regularly taken with shock weapons commonly range from about 15 kg up to 65 kg, with the latter size being rather rare. Animals in the larger body-size range are almost invariably taken with poisoned projectiles. It is in these settings that groups are most commonly described as regularly scavenging meat from natural animal deaths as well as kills by nonhuman

Table 28.1

Productivity of the Environment, Diet, and Hunting Equipment of Modern Equatorial and Subequatorial Hunter-Gatherers

Group	NAAP (per m²)[a]	Dependence on plants (%)[b]	Hunting equipment	Reference
Walbiri	174	60	Spear thrower and spear	Meggitt (1962)
G/wi	252	87	Bow and poisoned arrow	Silberbauer (1972:288–290)
!Kung	329	80	Bow and poisoned arrow	Lee (1979:116–157)
Hadza	666	65	Bow and poisoned arrow	Woodburn (1968:52)
Dorobo	1144	40	Bow and poisoned arrow, poisoned spear or lance	Huntingford (1955:620)
Aweikomo	1623	40	Bow and arrow, lance	Henry (1964:166–168)
Guayaki	1715	40	Bow and arrow	Clastres (1972:145–147)
Agta	2073	35	Bow and arrow, dogs, net (drives)	Griffin (1984:47)
Siriono	2115	70	Bow and arrow	Holmberg (1969:14–16)
Mbuti	2200	60	Bow and arrow, net (drives), poisoned arrow for monkeys	Putnam (1963:330)
Semang	2814	65–70	Bow and poisoned arrow, blowgun with poisoned darts	Murdock (1934:89)
Punan	3535	80	Blowgun with poisoned darts, dogs	Urquhart (1951:256)

[a] NAAP = net above-ground annual productivity, or the amount of new (nonroot) plant cell production each year, calculated by this author. This estimate is derived from rainfall and temperature data available in contemporary world weather records. The estimate is the result of a three-step inferential sequence using Bailey (1960), Rosenzweig (1974), and additional information from Chang (1968) on the natural history of runoff. The procedure will be explained in detail in a forthcoming publication by this author on hunting and gathering adaptations.

[b] Dependence on plants as a percentage of total diet calculated by Murdock and Morrow (1970).

predators. In still less productive environments, poison is incorporated into weapons designed for hunting in the tropical forest canopy to weapons designed for use against the larger animals of the forest margins and the savannah, and shock weapons drop out of the primary technology.

The technologies of these modern hunter-gatherers vary in design and principle with variations in the environments in which the technologies are employed. Quite literally, the technology is basic to the subsistence adaptations worked out relative to each environment.

In high-biomass equatorial forests, residential mobility is quite high and duration of occupancy of any one place short (Kelly 1983). In addition, there is less spatial differentiation in the organization of the technology. Mobility and flexibility in group size are the means by which hunter-gatherers adjust to the varying availability of subsistence resources in their habitats.

Finally, although modern hunter-gatherer technologies vary in planning and tactical depth and in the role of curation, they all have planning-based adaptations. We therefore find patterned contrasts between the places occupied by groups, where artifacts are discarded during the course of the production, repair, and maintenance of the technology, and the places in which instrumental tools are lost or abandoned while they are being used to obtain subsistence or other products from the environment.

In the light of all this, what can be said about the organization of technology in the pre-*H. sapiens sapiens* adaptations?

THE ORGANIZATION OF ADAPTATIONS IN THE LOWER PALEOLITHIC

The periods prior to the Mousterian of the Rissian era are characterized by a lack of evidence for planned occupation of locations. Whereas modern humans occupying a given place produce a structured set of spatial relationships among the components of the occupied surface that indicates planning (see Binford 1978b, 1983c; Hayden 1979; Kent and Vierich in press; Yellen 1972, 1977a), early hominid sites exhibit differential patterns of tool or debris density (Isaac 1981b), but the organization of space relative to events anticipated to occur in it is not clearly indicated. Identifications of base camps and other organized aspects of a settlement system in the Lower Paleolithic (Harris 1978; Isaac 1971) are an artifact of the researchers' views of the archaeological record (Binford 1987b). For instance, the criterion for a "living floor" in the Lower and Middle Paleolithic is usually the vertical and horizontal concentration of artifacts and fauna, but the contents of so-called living floors do not differ from clear aggregates of tools derived from so-called diffuse deposits (Binford 1987b). This seems to me to indicate that adaptation was not achieved technologically; rather, technology was an aid to adaptations organized in other terms.

Early tool-assisted systems of behavior show a robust pattern of division into expediently produced and used and transported components.[4] This pattern is now demonstrable in the Oldowan (Binford 1986c) and continues throughout the Acheulean (Clark and Kurashina 1976; Isaac 1977a). In Oldowan assemblages there is a component of minimally modified small tools accompanied by lithic debris of the same raw material, with tool production (pebble smashing) and use occurring in the same place. The other side of the technological coin is the modification of pebble "cores" to produce choppers, chopping tools, and polyhedrons. The raw materials used are different from those found in the expedient, "small tool" component, and manufacture does not normally appear to have taken place where the tools are found. When this does occur, a very different type of lithic-reduction procedure—hammerstone or anvil flaking of hand-held items as opposed to impacting of pebbles resting on a surface—seems to be indicated. Finally, items that appear to have been recycled or used for a long time and "miscellaneous" or unique tool forms regularly covary with this transported component.

Although the forms of the tools are somewhat different, the same basic pattern is demonstrable in the Acheulean; there is a transported aspect to the technology (here in the form of hand axes and sometimes cleavers) that is not commonly associated with the debris from their manufacture or with many (or many varieties of) small tools and an expedient small-tool aspect that is commonly associated with lithic debris.[5]

These two aspects of the technology vary inversely with one another in interassemblage comparisons and are associated with different kinds of faunal assemblages. The expedient component covaries with faunas composed primarily of lower limbs and head parts, primarily mandibles; the transported component is associated with faunas composed of more axial skeletal parts and indicators of carcasses or carcass parts. The total amount of bone is generally less with the transported component, and indicators of naturally accumulated "background" faunas occur with these assemblages, with fewer artifacts being deposited per episode of "occupation." All of the early sites dominated by the transported component appear to be palimpsests of episodic events.

The early time ranges present a picture of tool-assisted behavior that is episodic and "individual" in focus. Among modern hunter-gatherers, as we have seen, technologies tend to include curation that normally takes place in a camp. Many (if not most) of the places in which tools are used to procure food are thought by some researchers to be largely below the visibility threshold of the archaeologist (see, e.g., Yellen 1977a). The patterning seen in the early time ranges seems to represent a nearly opposite type of organization and role for technology. The highly visible archaeological "sites" seem to be the places where the technology is used in coping with the environment. For instance, the battered "hammers" known particularly from the early levels at Olduvai Gorge seem to relate to the immediate lakeside setting, and phytoliths derived from aquatic tuberous plants, "cattails" in American terms, have been recovered from these tools (Glynn Isaac, personal communication 1985). The frequencies of these tools seem to vary with the presence in the environment of this type of plant, and they are found in the spots where the plants occurred. Hammers of the Olduvai Gorge type are rare or absent at Koobi Fora (Bunn 1982b; Bunn et al. 1980), and the microenvironment there has not been described as supporting large numbers of such plants; the same applies to the essentially streamside locations known from Bed II at Olduvai Gorge. On the other hand, lakeside sites from Ethiopia are more analogous to the situations of Bed I at Olduvai, and the hammers reappear in them even though they are considered later than the Bed II deposits at Olduvai (Clark and Kurashina 1976). This same situation seems to apply to other aspects of the Oldowan technology. Tools are concentrated where they were used, not where persons employing a planned technological exploitation of the environment resided and returned with both products of their technology and the means to maintain it.

Another contrast with modern technology is the fact that, whereas modern tools that are regularly transported are also frequently among the most curated, the early transported tools commonly do not show much evidence of use and may accumulate in large numbers in certain places. It is hard to imagine a planned strategy in which large tools are considered essential that might produce either of these conditions. If transport of tools was backed by much planning depth, one would expect a tool to be used until its functioning was impaired by damage. Again, if someone was anticipating work in a place in which he had performed it many times before, it is hard to imagine that he would not know that there were many appropriate tools already there. It is therefore unlikely that the concentrations of transported tools represent base camps. The depositional contexts are consistent with an episodic accumulative process rather than a planned, integrated strategy of land use. Once again one can argue that the artifacts accumulated on the landscape where the hominids were engaging nature, not where they were living and planning subsistence activities.

In one of the few intensive regional studies of the Acheulean as well as later remains, the distribution of Acheulean hand axes is strongly tethered to the raw materials from which they were made (C. G. Sampson, personal communication 1987). There is a very steep falloff curve in hand ax frequency as one moves away from the raw material sources. This small-scale spatial distribution does not support a view of substantial planning depth or curation; rather, it reflects only very small-scale mobility relative to very short periods during which the tool was functioning in the technological system. This same pattern seems to characterize the distributions of hand axes in the Hunsgi Valley of India (K. Paddayya, personal communication 1987).

The Acheulean provides us with another important and puzzling contrast to the technologically based adaptations of modern nonagricultural humans; we have Acheulean materials from many different environments in Africa, western Europe, the Near East, and India, and, except for possible minor variations that can be understood in terms of the types of raw materials available for artifact production and distribution (Villa 1978), no patterned differentiations convincingly covary with grossly different environments. Given what we know of the modern situation, and leaving aside the question of ethnicity and the sociology of a culture-based human world, this lack of correspondence between technology and environment is surprising. Once again, it suggests that technology is not the means of adaptation but an aid to adaptation, with very little variation in the social organization or the contexts of tool use standing behind the archaeological record over this vast span of space and time.

The remarkable similarity in early hominid technology over vast areas calls to mind what we see in other species of animals, namely, a generic organizational basis of behavior that is common to the species. There is nothing in the data of the Oldowan or the Acheulean to suggest in any way a cultural or extrasomatic mechanism of inheritance serving to make possible the occupation of varying niches by subpopulations of a single species. We are not looking at rudimentary or nascent cultural systems (Binford 1973; Binford and Ho 1985); instead we have a technologically aided, biologically based panspecific form of adaptation.[6]

Because early stone tools were frequently found in association with animal bones, for years it was assumed that the makers of the tools had been hunters. Around 1980, some researchers began to question this simple interpretation (see Binford 1985b). Isaac and his team, working at Koobi Fora, noted that, while most of the sites referable to the Plio-Pleistocene boundary were characterized by clear associations of bones and stone tools, the composition of the fauna was hard to reconcile with a hunting model. Because species and individual animals were often represented by a single bone, scavenging seemed a reasonable alternative to consider (Bunn et al. 1980).

Working at about the same time on tabulations of the bones recovered from Olduvai Gorge, I found many of the patterned associations among skeletal parts strikingly similar to those among bones either abandoned by or transported by non-hominid scavenger-predator animals such as lions or hyenas. I also found a different pattern of skeletal part association at natural death and kill sites, where the bones were largely lower leg and head parts of ungulates, than at sites left by hominid hunters (Binford 1981a). Because these are both the parts that generally yield the least food (Binford 1978a) and the ones commonly abandoned by predator-scavenger animals at the sites of their kills, I suggested that the pattern in the Olduvai data was more consistent with scavenging than with hunting. In the same year, another research team (Potts and Shipman 1981) reported animal toothmarks, sometimes overprinted by tool-inflicted cutmarks, on some of the bones recovered by the Leakeys from Olduvai Gorge—exactly what one would expect if the hominids accumulated bones scavenged from carcasses previously ravaged by animals. A striking new view of early hominid diet and the context for site formation was emerging (see Shipman 1983, 1984a, 1984b; Binford 1985b, 1986f; Binford et al. 1988; Bunn and Kroll 1986a). If we had been wrong about the occurrence of hunting at the time of the earliest visible archaeological sites, then finding out when hunting did begin became a fascinating challenge.

At Klasies River Mouth, a site on the southern coast of Africa that spans the important time period just preceding and including the appearance of forms of fully modern humans, I attempted to distinguish between hunting and scavenging primarily on the basis of data on skeletal part frequencies and patterned frequencies of animal gnawing on bones (Binford 1984c). The occupants of the cave at Klasies River Mouth appear to have regularly scavenged marginal parts of medium-size to large animals, and there was a foreshadowing increase in the hunting of small animals and the young of large species.[7]

To see whether this pattern was unique or represented a first glimpse of a previously unsuspected late shift to hunting, I examined data from Swanscombe and Hoxne in England, dating between 200,000 and 350,000 years ago, and Abri Vaufrey, spanning the period from 300,000 to 90,000 years ago (Binford 1987c). All three sites yielded evidence indicative of scavenging, with Abri Vaufrey and to some extent

Hoxne showing a bias toward meat-yielding parts. Study of Zhoukoudian, which dates from about 450,000 to 220,000 years ago, further supported the view that hunting, although assumed, was not demonstrable, and that early man may have been a scavenger (Binford and Ho 1985; Binford and Stone 1986). Restudy of data collected earlier from the French site of Combe Grenal suggested that during very cold periods some 30,000 years before the appearance of fully modern man there may have been some systematic hunting of medium-size animals, particularly young individuals, but as at Klasies River Mouth larger animals (horses and cattle) were most likely scavenged throughout the sequence. The surprising pattern seemed to be consistently telling us that our ancestors turned to hunting just prior to the appearance of humankind. Like the other characteristics that first appeared in this time period (see Binford 1982c; Gilman 1984; Mellars 1973; Pfeiffer 1982; Straus 1977; White 1982, 1985), hunting may simply have been part of the transition.

Although these studies were provocative, there remained the impressive claims for the organized hunting of big game at Torralba, a site at least 250,000 and perhaps as much as 450,000 years old, by men of *H. erectus* grade (see Freeman 1978b; Howell 1965). A restudy of the Torralba data (Binford 1987d) revealed some fascinating patterning. The majority of the stone tools at Torralba covary positively with the faunal remains of bovids, equids, and cervids, and this entire group varies inversely with remains of elephants. Denticulates, notches, perforators, bifaces, cores, and retouched flakes covary with the heads and lower limbs of all species, while sidescrapers, endscrapers, utilized flakes, and choppers covary with carcass parts of all species. At the same time, the carcass parts and heads and lower limbs vary independently of each other. Such patterning could only have arisen as independent episodes of hominid activity at the site (Binford 1987d:52). There were no mass kills at Torralba, no game drives, no activity areas in which large quantities of meat were processed by socially differentiated "labor" units. Perhaps equally surprising, the tool suite associated with bones from lower limbs and heads, an association recognized from earlier sites as a tentative indication of scavenging, is the dominant one. It seems likely that, as elsewhere, these bones were accumulated by the hominids rather than representing animals killed there. Finally, although there is a distinctive suite of tools that covaries with carcass indicators, there is no indication that hominids hunted or caused the deaths of the animals. In fact, the pattern of raw-material use characteristic of this suite suggests that the hominids encountered carcasses unexpectedly and were forced to produce the tools needed to deal with them using local sources and already present lithic remains. This behavior too is consistent with scavenging, and little planning depth stands behind it.

Two major conclusions may be drawn from the recent studies. First, given our current understanding of faunal remains as recognizably referable to scavenging versus hunting, all the arguments that presuppose hunting appear to be unwarranted.[8] Second, the contention that many sites represent the remains of pre-*Homo sapiens* home bases also appears to be unwarranted. This issue is perhaps best discussed with reference to patterning in tool assemblages and inferences regarding the organization of subsistence practices.

PATTERNING IN THE MIDDLE PALEOLITHIC

The independent variation noted at Torralba between tool suites dominated by denticulates and notches and scraper-dominated assemblages is perhaps the most robust and repetitive pattern in the assemblages roughly dated to the early Riss in western Europe and synchronous climatic events around the world.[9] In addition, the Middle Paleolithic is characterized by an increase in the complexity of patterning within assemblages (Bordes 1953, 1961). As Bosinski (1982:165) summarizes the situation,

> the spectrums of stone-artifacts are more differentiated and the assemblages can be grouped to different industries . . . , which represent space-time units. An important role is played by the appearance of Levallois technique . . . resulting in a greater variability of flake types, as well as of retouched tools.

Rather than seeing the beginnings of macroregional patterning as the emergence of culture in the sense of self-conscious ethnic groups, I view it as heralding a shift in the role technology played in hominid adaptations. In the earlier part of this period hominids appear to radiate into northern latitudes during phases of relative warmth and then are regularly wiped out or retreat south with shifting floral zones in some areas as warm climate is replaced by colder conditions (see Bosinski 1982; Freund 1982; Roe 1982; Tuffreau 1982). Roughly coincident with these radical shifts in range is the regionalization just mentioned.

This shift is not unique to the margins of the hominid range; regional patterning also occurs within the African continent (Clark 1982) beginning around 200,000 years ago. While the situation in the Near East is similar, the picture there is clouded by the attempts of Jelinek (1982a) to force this variation into the period after 130,000 years ago.[10] I feel quite confident that the Near East will be found to fall more in line with the trends seen in the Middle Paleolithic elsewhere as more work is done, particularly at the important site of Kebara (Bar-Yosef et al. 1986). The situation is also clouded in central Europe by a conservative adherence to culture-historical approaches (see Lyubin 1977; Valoch 1982) and a consequent failure to seek an understanding of the patterning documented in the archaeological record.

Very little can be said about India and China, although progress is being made in unraveling the temporal and typological jumble that the archaeological record there presents (see Misra and Bellwood 1985; Paddayya 1982). The patterns of assemblage variability seen elsewhere for the Middle Paleolithic are, however, not yet documented there (Ghosh 1982). In China I found it difficult to distinguish stone tools said to date to the very early time ranges from tools recovered from sites said to date as recent as 120,000 years ago or even from sites geologically dated to as recent as 30,000 years ago. While the summary articles treating the area speak of a Middle Paleolithic (Qui 1985), this period is not defined or described in a manner that would permit comparison between the Chinese materials and materials from the West.[11] Since quantitative summaries are not generally reported from the Chinese sites, discussion of assemblage variability in this important time period is impossible. Nevertheless, there is a clear regional distinctiveness to the material, and there are indications of considerable variation among the sites of this time period.

Middle Paleolithic regionalism is coupled with some increase in the hominid range, and one can see these two as the first glimmerings of evidence for a new role for technology. Technology may be increasingly serving as the basis for hominid adaptations in diverse environments.

In the Middle Paleolithic of western Europe, there is a fascinating pattern of "alternation of industries" at sites yielding long temporal sequences (see Bordes 1961; Laville et al. 1980) that is unlike anything known from the archaeological record of modern man. There are also repetitive patterns over time regardless of assemblage form. Long ago Bordes noted a correlation between denticulate-dominated assemblages and inflated frequencies of horse bones at Combe Grenal. This pattern has been measured, and Bordes's general impressions have been confirmed (Chase 1986). At Torralba a similar denticulate-dominated suite of tools was strongly associated with equids as well as bovids and cervids, and the bones, like those linked with denticulates at Combe Grenal, were predominantly parts yielding marginal food returns. This long-term association between a suite of tools and a very particular faunal context would be difficult if not impossible to duplicate in the archaeological remains of fully modern groups.

Even more striking is the discovery in the French Mousterian (Geneste 1985) of a strong dichotomy between assemblages manufactured on high-quality raw material using the Levallois technique, representing movement of raw material away from its sources, and rich in Mousterian points, scrapers, and bifaces and assemblages made of local raw material using non-Levallois methods of reduction and characterized by high frequencies of notches and denticulates as well as abruptly retouched pieces and pieces with irregular retouch. These two types of assemblages clearly imply a technology that is certainly transported and perhaps minimally planned and an expedient tool kit largely produced on the spot—the old pattern seen initially in the Oldowan.

In addition, many researchers conclude that mobility was high, group size was small, and planning depth, even with regard to the transported material, was limited. There is a general falloff in the size and degree of utilization of material with distance from known sources that suggests that the technology was being carried along rather than made and repaired in a central place. Middle Paleolithic sites are palimpsests of many episodes of use and not planned occupations of any substantial duration. In further contrast to sites produced under modern human conditions, they do not display the variation in sequentially accumulated remains that results from tactical exploitation of their environments in terms of planned strategies. In thick deposits that are similar overall from bottom to top, arbitrary levels separating the deposits into subunits do not exhibit statistically meaningful variation (Binford 1982b). I view this as evidence that there is no organized integration between the social domain and its "needs" and the tactical flexibility in the technology.

Another clue to organizational differences between fully modern humans and hominids of the Middle Paleolithic relates to the relationship between bones and artifacts. Although variable with site function, among modern groups the "turnover rate" in the technology is commonly much slower than the consumer rate for foods. Among groups heavily dependent upon hunting, this generally results in there being many more bones in sites than there are tools. In the archaeological remains dating prior to 40,000 years ago, this pattern seems to be reversed. For instance, at the Mousterian site of Combe Grenal, which spans approximately 80,000 years, there are 17,389 tools and only 6,932 bone fragments. There is little evidence that this ratio is affected by preservation. What seems to be suggested is that animal foods played less of a role in the diet, at least in places selected for use as shelters, and tools did not stay in the system very long—another clue to a lack of planning depth.

Some researchers, including myself, suspect that the western Mousterian includes tools for making tools, which may mean that there were several planning steps in the technology. Thus far, however, planning steps are not easy to relate to a spatial organization of technologically integrated behaviors. Tool manufacture seems to be subordinated to the movements of the hominids. Interjacent tools appear incidental rather than regularly differentiated and planned as such. The planning alternatives that seem to stand behind the major axes of technological differentiation, at least as far as lithics are concerned, continue to be limited to whether or not to carry tools.

Early tool assemblages, including those of the Middle Paleolithic, appear very wasteful. What appears to be "recycling" has been suggested for some of the Torralba tools and is strongly suspected for many forms of Mousterian ones—limaces, some Quina scrapers, cores.[12] Rather than being an indicator of greater planning depth and even curation, this may simply be the result of palimpsest accumulations at "magnet" locations in the habitat that were regularly used as lithic sources by poorly equipped groups or by groups not arriving with tools. Such an interpretation is consistent with the strong indication that the mobile groups commonly manufactured tools from local materials on the spot. This interpretation is well illustrated by one of the few sites in the world where the extensive exploitation of an elephant carcass during the Middle Paleolithic time range seems clearly indicated, Mwanganda's Village (Clark and Haynes 1970). Here the tools were manufactured of local material on the spot and then used and discarded in direct association with the body parts exploited. This suggests that the hominids were not equipped with tools when they discovered the elephant carcass and had not planned to hunt elephants. Similarly, the limited exploitation of the elephant carcass at Lehringen (Adam 1951), carried out with what appear to be transported tools, suggests that the carcass was a chance encounter rather than a result of planned hunting. We simply do not yet understand the organizational contexts in which tools were transported versus those in which groups were not tool-equipped during the Middle or the Lower Paleolithic. One thing is certain, however: these dichotomous patterns are unlike anything thus far known from the archaeology of fully cultural systems of the past 25,000–35,000 years.

Perhaps the greatest contrast between the Mousterian and the culturally organized systems of modern hunter-gatherers is in the relationships among mobility, environment, and technological organization. Modern hunter-gatherer adaptations achieve their stability and security by highly flexible patterns of movement within their environments and flexible group size and composition. In turn, mobility and flexibility in social unit composition are strongly correlated with the manner in which the technology is organized. All indications are that groups in the Middle Paleolithic were uniformly small and their mobility very high whatever the environmental form or dynamics (Clark 1985; Geneste 1985). Related to this lack of mobility and group-size flexibility is the minimal organization of the technology, its quick turnover rate, and the lack of planning depth.

THE TRANSITION

Among the remarkable changes in the content of the archaeological record across the threshold represented by the appearance of fully modern groups in many regions are the elaboration of burial; art; personal ornaments; new materials, such as bone, antler, and soft stone; long-distance movement and circulation of goods; and increased variation in site size, duration, and content (L. Binford 1982c; S. Binford 1968b; Conkey 1978; Gilman 1984; Harrold 1980; Isaac 1983d; Marshack 1972; Mellars 1973; Orquera 1984; Pfeiffer 1982; White 1982, 1985, to mention only a few). Many of these new archaeological features directly inform us about something organizationally quite new: the presence of language (see White 1985 for an excellent review and Pfeiffer 1982). In short, they signal the appearance of culture.

How are we to understand the process of transition? It is well documented that we have examples of anatomically modern humans with what appear to be full Mousterian assemblages (Jelinek 1982b); similarly, we have Neanderthals with what had previously been judged to be distinctively Upper Paleolithic assemblages (Vandermeersch 1984). To further complicate the picture, there appear to be areas of the world where the transition closely coincides chronologically with the appearance of *H. sapiens sapiens* and areas, such as northern Asia, in which the appearance of fully modern humankind seems to be roughly coincident with its occurrence in other areas, but the transition in terms of symbolic indicators appears delayed until around 22,000 years ago. In marked contrast have been the claims for very early fully modern humans in southern Africa (Beaumont et al. 1978) and equally early claims for stone tool industries that have properties suggestive of exceptional planning depth by Middle Paleolithic standards (Beaumont et al. 1978; Singer and Wymer 1982).

Although I suspect that language is the basis of culture as we know it, I am quite sure that culture develops in response to evolutionary processes. It does not simply bloom in response to somatically based behavioral potentials or realities. Indicators of language need not signal fully culturally organized systems of adaptation as we know them among modern populations. Many researchers have seen the transition as a "punctuated" event or a kind of Rubicon, and in one way of thinking this view has some merit. The long, tedious, and relatively unchanging patterns of the Middle and particularly the Lower Paleolithic contrast so dramatically with more recent remains that a disjunction is indicated when one looks ahead from the past. Looking back from the present, however, we have generally failed to seek a processual understanding of this transitional event. If culture is subject to evolutionary conditioning, then surely the early days of populations possessing a cultural capacity must have been importantly different from later times. For example, while the early Aurignacian remains from Germany have a very modern feel (Hahn and Owen 1985), the contemporary and even more recent "Aurignacian" of central France, which sometimes alternates in a "Mousterian" fashion with the Chatelperronian (Roc de Combe; see Bordes 1967b), does not.

Archaeologists are making great strides in unraveling the picture of the Upper Paleolithic in western Europe (see Bailey 1983; Price and Brown 1985), but a nagging problem remains: the conditions and selective contexts that favor the origin of culturally organized systems as such are apt to be different from those that favor diversification and increase in complexity of those systems. Once evidence for symbolic behavior is apparent, the general approach has been one that seeks to understand variation and change as if selection were operating on systems fully organized culturally; the interesting era of the restructuring of hominid adaptations into human adaptations is ignored. Evolution is lost to view.

Only in cultural evolution can an easy transition occur in the character of the behaviors subjected to selection. We need to see this latter transition as distinct from the evolutionary events that occurred when the populations being modified were not fully cultural in their organization. Addressing this problem demands an understanding of the organizational basis for the hominid adaptations predating the transition. Models and projections from the present to the ancient past have misguided interpretation for far too many years. Clive Gamble has aptly commented that "it is during this period that a change occurred in the dominant relations between social and ecological systems" (1986:382). As archaeologists we will not grasp the transition unless we begin to worry about how to measure variables such as planning depth, mobility, group size, and compositional variability and then proceed to see how these properties vary with environmental conditions as a clue to the ecology of ancient populations. A shift from describing the consequences of dynamics, artifacts, to seeking methods that permit us to use the artifacts to illuminate the dynamics within which they were once participants is crucial for productive work.

One of our greatest challenges as archaeologists is to explore the limits of relevance of our theories and our knowledge of "mankind" and "culture." The transition probably represents a major boundary of relevance for both. Only recently have archaeologists suspected this; hence most interpretation of the ancient past is made by analogy with what we think we know about modern humans and modern hunter-gatherers. Such an approach ensures that we will never understand either the transition or the ancient past. In a conference discussion at the School of American Research in 1986, for example, Wolpoff maintained that language and culture must have been present in the Lower and Middle Paleolithic, arguing first that only selection operating on a cultural capacity could explain the demonstrable increase in brain size during the period between roughly 2,000,000 and 40,000 years ago and second that the stability in tool assemblages can be understood only in terms of learning rooted in language and culture. I agree that we can accommodate our data from the past to such a model; this has clearly been done by most archaeologists. I disagree that such accommodative argument demonstrates the accuracy of the model. The best approach is to adopt the null hypothesis, thus putting the burden on the archaeologist to demonstrate that other possibilities are untenable or that the preferred method is unambiguously the best. Only with this strategy will we be in a learning posture relative to the ideas and beliefs we use in interpreting the archaeological record. Only with such a skeptical attitude toward the traditional wisdom that has guided our interpretations will we ever learn about the actual conditions characteristic of the past.

The conference discussion among the physical anthropologists was largely a debate between those who saw the biological changes at the transition as continuous relative to earlier populations in the same region and those who saw discontinuity, implying population replacements or changes in patterns of gene flow. Waiting in the wings was discussion of perhaps a far more important set of issues, namely, what the changes and the various regional morphological patterns implied in terms of *behavior* and its ecological context. While I find the historical questions interesting, I return to the question, How do we explain history? There was little discussion of *how* and *why* a hominid population should have radiated, the type of discussion that is crucial for guiding good research by archaeologists. This seems to me to be the contemporary situation in all treatments of the transition, and therefore the central issue is how we are to gain the knowledge we need. I have suggested that we need different approaches; we need to use our knowledge of modern humankind in different ways than those that have characterized most previous work, and we need to rethink some of the properties commonly ascribed to the past.

NOTES

1. Throughout this chapter I refer to *Homo sapiens sapiens* as fully modern man, humans, or humankind. The terms "hominid" or "early man" indicate *H. sapiens neanderthalensis* and earlier groups.

2. This is the error that was made by Hayden (1979) in his study of Australian lithic tools.

3. There is a very vocal group of contemporary researchers who endlessly seek to justify the position that we cannot generalize from near modern hunter-gatherers. It is claimed that they are not "pristine" because they exist in the complicated modern world. History is frequently cited as the cause of both their presence and their ethnographic characteristics; therefore, it is claimed, comparative study and generalization are unwarranted and misguided endeavors. We are asked instead to return to the sterility of historical particularism and cultural relativism (Schrire 1984). These postures are central to those who adhere to such archaic views as "free will" and human choice as the causes of cultural variability (e.g., Sackett 1982). These idealists decry comparative study and demand that both comparative and scientific approaches are wrong and inappropriate by virtue of the uniqueness of the human condition, suggesting that all we can do is essentially become moral philosophers (e.g., Hodder 1982c; Saitta 1983). I consider such postures misguided and embarrassing to our science, and while acknowledging their existence, I do not consider them worthy of serious discussion here.

4. It is the latter characteristic that has led some (e.g., Toth 1985) to infer curation for these systems.

5. Certain areas yield artifact suites during the Acheulean that are strictly speaking not Acheulean in form, apparently lacking the major diagnostic, hand axes. In many places these assemblages are called by different names: the Clactonian (Collins 1969; Ohel 1979), the Sohan in India (Sankalia 1974), and variants of the "chopper-chopping tool tradition" in

China and northern Asia (Movius 1944). In the former two cases it is unclear whether these are "non-hand ax variants" of the dichotomous "Acheulean" as known in the West or are "true" regional variants differing from the Acheulean. Most researchers have been persuaded, however, that the "chopper-chopping tool tradition" of Asia is non-Acheulean in the hand axe sense of the term, although what I consider to be unconvincing challenges to this view appear from time to time (Bae 1980; Kim and Chung 1978).

The types of analysis that led to the recognition of a dichotomy in Acheulean assemblages have generally not been employed in the analysis of the Asian material, but my analysis of the stone tool assemblages from Zhoukoudian (Pei and Chang 1985) reveals a very similar dichotomous pattern. What are generally called choppers and chopping tools covary with whole flakes and flakes struck off the choppers, although these latter artifacts occur only in small numbers. This set of tools is positively associated with bolas (spheroids, in African terms) and reflects hand-held lithic reduction technique. Retouched tools (small tools, in an Africanist's sense) are not generally associated. The raw materials are very diverse, and most were brought to the site from elsewhere. This is unmistakably the transported component recognizable in the Oldowan and the Acheulean. Varying independently of and inversely with this component is a component consisting of small retouched tools, mostly of local materials and almost exclusively produced by a bipolar technique, and much lithic debitage.

6. When researchers first began to recognize the surprising patterning of the Lower and Middle Paleolithic, it was originally interpreted in cultural historical terms. This interpretation was challenged as unrealistic during the 1960s (see Binford and Binford 1966; Binford 1972b, 1973). As was the general procedure at the time, this challenge was offered in terms of expectations derived from comparative considerations of modern hunter-gatherer behavior. It was suggested that the emerging patterning of the Middle and Lower Paleolithic reflected organized activity variants, as were then becoming demonstrable for the archaeological remains of modern hunter-gatherers. Subsequently I learned more about the types of patterning seen among modern hunter-gatherers (Binford 1975b, 1976, 1978a, 1978b, 1979, 1980a, 1981a, 1982b, 1983a, 1983c, 1984b, 1984c, 1986a, 1987a; Binford and O'Connell 1984), and instead of clarifying our understanding of Middle and Lower Paleolithic patterns of assemblage variability, the Middle and Lower Paleolithic began to appear more and more distinct from anything we could see or understand about the culturally based adaptations of fully modern populations. This apparent contrast led me to be more and more skeptical of interpretative techniques used on early materials, that is, interpretation by simple reference to seeming analogies between the archaeological remains of early man and piecemeal knowledge of modern man. One of the more controversial areas of research that my skepticism led me to consider was diet.

7. This conclusion has been controversial (e.g., Deacon 1985; Scott 1986; Singer and Wymer 1986), but see Binford 1986g for a response to most of these objections.

8. The supposed sexual division of labor between (male) hunting and (female) gathering—regarded as the structural or evolutionary context for our long period of juvenile dependence, food sharing, and parenting support during the postweaning, prepubescent period—and the patterns of sexual dimorphism seen among fully modern humans are not historically sustained at this point. This does not mean that food sharing, particularly between adult females and their juvenile offspring, did not occur, only that hunting does not appear to be its basis.

9. The "fit" between the Torralba lithic patterning and that known from other Riss and more

recent European sites makes me skeptical of the earlier dating for this site that has been suggested in many publications.

10. Jelinek (1982a) has argued that there is a normative directional temporal trend in flake size throughout the Near Eastern Middle Paleolithic. Since one can expect lithic reduction strategy to be responsive to technological needs in differing resource environments, I strongly doubt that this pattern will be confirmed by future research.

11. "Parallel traditions" have been suggested for the Chinese material (see Jia et al. 1972). While I certainly agree that forms of assemblage differ widely, I do not think that "cultural tradition" is the way to interpret this variation.

12. Some researchers have noted differences in ratios of flakes to cores and have inferred "economizing" behavior on the part of Middle Paleolithic hominids (e.g., Munday 1977, 1979).

Part V

Conclusions

Chapter 29

Coping with Culture

Is debate worth all the effort? As we have seen, it is very difficult to pursue in archaeology, and antagonists rarely perform at very admirable levels. Why not "clean up" our journals and acknowledge that Guppies are correct? Debate is really rather unpleasant and a behavior appropriate only, if at all, to the youth eager to make names for themselves. I have touched upon the other side of the coin with regard to the characteristics of various participants in debate. Is this not really an admission that Hodder's characterizations of individuals is really accurate, that their motives explain their actions, that we are endlessly engaged in power negotiations, that we live in a world of charlatans of self-interest, that objectivity is a myth, that science is a facade?

Patterning in our literature could be viewed in a motivational (intentionality) context. To be sure, that does occur and is certainly one side of the reality coin that is archaeology. Is that all there is? The Yippie admonition to "become aware" is good advice to our field. I have previously addressed the issue of paradigm and tried to point out its awesome power (see Binford and Sabloff 1982). All through my discussions of debate I have sought to cast the arguments of many as understandable (not simply as little polemical ploys of self-serving behavior in the ongoing power negotiations of our time). My clear suggestion is that their paradigmatic underpinnings render the arguments of many internally logical and their behavior (their "action") rational given such codes of thought.

The utility of the concept of culture is not questioned here, nor is the existence of the culture of science, to which the term "paradigm" refers, being questioned.[1] In fact, it was the recognition of this cultural phenomenon that was basic to the criticisms frequently referred to as the "new archaeology." My concern, then and now, is how we learn in the midst of all this "reality." For instance, the Yippies suggest that we abandon science in the face of these realities. The Yuppies suggest that we engage in labored self-examination in order to uncover the power of paradigms and of our culture itself. I have found that it is very difficult to achieve the nirvana of introspective self-examination. Even with a debate partner pointing out characteristics of one's paradigm, these guides to self-examination are commonly rejected, diverted into irrelevant issues, and otherwise deflected. The other position, that we should give up, abandon science, and adopt common-sense perceptions of the social "reality" in which we participate as the only guide to true understanding, also seems naive and unworkable given what we know of the world beyond the everyday social life we experience.

485

We can point to much cultural variability in our modern world, and more important we can document many long-term patterns from our studies of the archaeological record. Similarly, we can point to regularities in these patterns, both in the tempo and sequence of differentiations as well as in parallel and sequentially similar trajectories known from historically different traditions. These large-scale patterns beckon us to learn. They suggest that determinant or, if you wish, conditioning processes are at work, operating at scales not visible to the participants in those systems. Attempting to understand such long-term patterns by reference to the petty negotiations of volitional man can be construed as a demand for the recognition of goal-directed assumptions and an understanding of process on the part of mortal participants that certainly must have exceeded our powers of the present time. Another view is that such understanding is unnecessary, that the large-scale patterning archaeologists are able to see is simply the cumulative result of all the little, short-term volitional acts merging to produce a dialectical process responsible for the patterning. Understanding therefore rests in recognizing all the little volitional acts. The patterning does not have reference to the operation of large-scale processes; the results of all the little volitional acts are seen as simply painted at a scale inaccessible to the normal participant.

These conflicting paradigmatic suggestions regarding what the world is like include some built-in theoretical suggestions as to how it might work. How do we learn more? How do we use these suggestions to increase our knowledge? Certainly, becoming aware of our own paradigm as a conditioner of our thoughts and actions would be useful. I find the suggestion that we look inside ourselves to be unsatisfactory. In order to recognize the power of our own paradigms we must have some external frame of reference with respect to which we can appreciate its content. Another paradigm is a good frame of reference, an alternative view, a different base from which to view experience. I view debate as one of the major means through which one may gain "self knowledge." If one is truly paradigm-bound, however, other paradigms appear as strange, misguided, false views of the world that need to be corrected. They are useless, and one is continually adopting the posture that advocates of such senseless views must be senseless themselves. This is empiricism, an epistemological paradigm that is common to the advocates of most of the other paradigmatic views mentioned here. This paradigmatic posture ensures that empiricists will never use opposing paradigms for purposes of examining their own thought, since advocates securely believe that they see nature clearly. This is one reason why I have chosen debate as a medium to make others aware of their own uncritical acceptance of an unevaluated set of assumptive views about the world.

It should be clear from a reading of the literature that the defender of a paradigm rarely changes his or her mind as a result of debate. To me this indicates that the hidden paradigm, the epistemological paradigm, insulates debaters and ensures that most debate will deteriorate into name calling. Nevertheless, debate is still one major avenue for change in that the student, the reader of debate, the uncommitted, may see issues more clearly, at least the issues that are placed in the public domain. This is one reason that we have a responsibility to debate—that responsibility is aimed at the next generation of participants. Unfortunately, such intentions frequently are subverted by partisans who are charged with teaching our field to students. Many professionals do not see as their task the guiding of students into fruitful participation within the field; instead, students are seen as Puppies who should pass on the intellectual genes of the parent into the gene pool of the next generation. They are simply enculturated into the paradigm of the teacher, and reading or exploring other alleles is viewed as a waste of time and perhaps even a mark of unreliability with regard to the expected role as intellectual gene bearer. Under these conditions we do not have a science; we have a normal ethnocentric process of enculturation rather than education designed to expand our knowledge and reduce our "disciplinocentric" view of knowledge.

I have consistently, over many years, hammered away at unevaluated assumptions and basic "self-evident" positions. I clearly think that empiricism protects ignorance, protects special interest groups, and fosters that wonderful feeling of righteousness that is so commonly expressed in public debate. As I have tried to illustrate, this paradigmatic view of learning influences the behavior of individuals as participants in our field—Guppie monopolies, Puppie behavior, and so on. Thus I do not deny some of the Yippies' descriptive claims about our world—the world of participation in quick-time events. The issue is not whether we have culture (read "paradigms"), not whether our actions are the combined consequence of our "codes" and our volitional goals, not whether we have motives or engage in power negotiations. We do all these things in life, even on the pages of our journals. We can even decide our goals. Some choose the goal of being right; I choose the goal of learning. Given the description of our field presented in Chapter 1, we have more specific goals—we seek to learn about the past in an accurate manner.

One of the first situations of which archaeologists must become aware is simply that the past is gone. This has a great effect on how we proceed with the pursuit of our learning goals. While addressing the claims of structuralists, Ernest Gellner (1982) made a very important observation. Simply put, he noted that words are cheap. They cost us nothing. The success of science is rooted in the search for a way to change that situation. The successful sciences have made great progress in developing ways to ensure that words are not cheap. In many natural sciences, where arguments among participants advocating opposing views of causation may exist, there is an assumption of accountability. It is standard practice to seek in experience an arbiter for opposing views. Experiments are designed, the world of dynamics is investigated. When a claim about nature is made, the research task is clearly to design ways to evaluate it. In addition there are even more practical consequences for the sciences who have companion applied fields. Words are not cheap if a bridge designed from the perspective of a faulty understanding of physics and mechanics collapses and many persons are killed. Such a fall directly implicates the knowledge and understanding used in its construction. There is a feedback between words, ideas, positions, and experience. The result is that learning occurs. In such disciplines where there is accountability, the concern is with our ignorance, since that is where there is clear risk. Speaking from ignorance can be very costly. The goal of researchers is not to be right relative to alleged knowledge already available, but instead to use every available means to recognize their ignorance, since ignorance represents risk and high costs to those who mistake ignorance for knowledge, fantasy for understanding, unevaluated paradigmatic common sense for truth. In fact, skillful scientists are those who are able to isolate and recognize their own ignorance, so they are the very ones most capable of telling others how to prove them wrong. If their advice proves correct, their colleagues hail them as stellar practitioners of science, and we have learned something.

As I see the situation in archaeology, words are still cheap and the challenge to us is to make our ideas accountable to experience. In spite of the fact that the past is gone and therefore only knowable through statics, our challenge if we are to be engaged in productive learning is to develop and make use of established ways to ensure that we are accountable to experience and that our focus is on our ignorance, not our righteous complacency and satisfaction with our alleged knowledge and understanding. I have frequently tried to point out the dead end of accommodative arguments. Accommodative arguments are really only possible in a field that is not held accountable by experience. Accommodative arguments in archaeology take the following form: observations are made on the archaeological record, and then someone proceeds to suggest that the observations are evidence for certain conditions in the past that are consistent with what they already believe about the past. I have repeatedly called for hardheaded inference justification. I have argued that the transformation of observations into evidence must be done for each class of observations independently. Each pattern or formal characteristic must be investigated as an isolated problem, a domain for which causal understanding must be built up so that inferences are justified. These justifications must be grounded in research-based learning on the phenomena under investigation, not as is common practice in archaeology on the raising of observations to the status of evidence by an act of argumentative will on the part of the investigator. We are all capable of imagining some set of conditions that, if true, would account for what we see. We can in turn accommodate anything we see to what we want to believe. These tactics are well demonstrated in my criticisms of and arguments with the interpretations of the Lower Paleolithic sites. It is the basis for my dismissal of most Yippie interpretations of the past, and it is the basis of my skepticism that well-meaning self-evaluation is adequate to move us to the goal of learning. In the absence of methodology and a hardheaded concern for the very difficult question of how we learn, words remain cheap, experience can simply be molded to our self-centered views, and there is no call for accountability in experience. More tragically, the reader of our literature is left without guidelines for evaluating our products and falls back on that age-old criterion of plausibility or, more commonly, the simple acceptance of authorities' views. Plausibility is only a veiled word standing for what we thought we already knew. Acceptance by plausibility criteria results in adherence to folk knowledge and to one's unrecognized paradigm. This does not mean that we cannot develop a better basis for plausibility evaluations—that capability certainly exists in the developed sciences. Sadly, however, this criteria remains largely undeveloped in our field.

In the absence of attention to the issue of how experience can be used as an arbiter of our ideas, words remain cheap. In fact, with reference to the fallen bridge mentioned above, most of the time there is no way of recognizing when one of our "constructions" falls down. A critic may seek to point out that such a fall has occurred, but the defender is generally able to present an argument to the effect that no fall has occurred (see Binford 1983a:157–209). We may then spend many years arguing over whether a collapse has even occurred. In the world of dynamics, falls are events, facts are properties of events, and commonly there is little debate over the failure of a prediction or a bridge. But in the world of statics there are no facts of history, only facts of observation here in the present (see Chapter 5). Claims for failure of fit between words, ideas, and experience are subject to debate regarding the meaning to be assigned to observations. If one is not seeking failures as clues to ignorance, even true failures will be passed over as simple differences of opinion as to the meaning imparted to observations. Tests of ideas are difficult to force and difficult to recognize in our field. As Gellner has pointed out, words, ideas, theories, constructions are cheap. As the old saying goes, You get what you pay for.

Empiricists are blindly willing to interpret observations as having self-evident meaning to the past. What is a scientist to do when faced on the one hand with the empiricists' "quick fix" notion of understanding and on the other with their willingness to interpret the past when only ignorance and lack of research stand behind their "bright ideas"? Under these conditions all one can do is use the information available to suggest that there might be more to the world than the empiricist is considering (my strategy on cutmarks in Chapter 23 or the "embedded" procurement suggestions made in Chapters 9–11); thus it might be prudent to think twice before accepting the empiricists' knowledge claims. Such a conservative posture is sure to infuriate empiricists, since they think they can simply see the world truly and that advance in the field should proceed rapidly and as a result of blinding flashes of insight. Science actually proceeds slowly, deliberately, and with great care if it is to be successful. It can only succeed if there is a hardheaded consideration of where knowledge comes from coupled with great care in the use of alleged prior knowledge. Citing patterning in the archaeological record as the justification for the interpretive devices used for explaining the patterning seen seems to me to be the ultimate accommodative argument. That this has been done is not questioned; that it is inevitable is, however, not true. The only option available seems to me to be a search for prior knowledge where it is accessible in the present, given the general absence of a germane body of prior knowledge to the discoveries we might make while pursuing pattern-recognition goals. As Albert Spaulding (1953b) pointed out way back in the 1950s, what I have called second- or third-order derivative patterning is likely to have reference to some organizing process in the past. Finding out what that organizing process was is the challenge we face. Archaeology is the science of the archaeological record; our task is simply learning how to conduct our studies so that we are not led to construct a false past. Since the beginnings of pattern-recognition approaches to discovery, there have in fact been major changes in our field. Studies of all types of formation processes increasingly fill our journals; field studies specifically designed to provide control conditions as regards the relationships between statics and dynamics are now commonplace. Experimental work, ethnoarchaeological work, ethnohistorical work are acknowledged avenues to learning.

The science of archaeology is growing. Nevertheless, we are a far cry from the claims made earlier for our field by Michael Schiffer (1976:1): "The 'new' or 'processual' archaeology finally has reached maturity. . . . A period of normal science . . . has emerged in archaeology." To my way of thinking, Kuhn's (1970) concept of "normal science" may be descriptively accurate of the historical trajectories of some sciences, but Kuhn's description is a long way from a law carrying the implication of necessary condition as the term is used in science. If a science views its goals as primarily learning, with all that implies as regards searching out our own ignorance and complacency with received knowledge, it is hard to imagine a science engaged in mere puzzle solving. Although I accept the Kuhnian description regarding paradigm dependence as accurate for many fields, including our own, I do not accept it as an explanation, only a historical description. As Spaulding (1968) has noted (quoting Brodbeck 1962), "there is no such thing as 'historical' explanation, only the explanation of historical events." Thus I do not accept the arguments derived from this historical description (the red herring of paradigm dependence) as implying that there is a fatal flaw in all scientific method, nor do I believe that it is of any importance whatsoever as a statement on intellectual limitations to our learning goals. A learning science is a changing science. It is difficult to imagine that change within a learning science does not arise as a consequence of the cumulative research carried out by the participating scientists. Only when one has a discipline dedicated to protecting as adequate the received knowledge of the discipline does one have true paradigm dependence, and hence stagnation, which can be manifested as puzzle solving. I think that that was the condition in traditional archaeology. I do not see it as the pervasive condition today, although there is much progress to be made, particularly in purging ourselves of nonproductive empiricst ideas. In spite of real progress, the other side of our coin—the volitional acts of individuals who almost yearly proclaim a new paradigm—betrays to me an unfortunate acceptance of the Kuhnian description as a processual law. It is not. Those vocal claims frequently argue against the goal of learning, and they do so with unfounded beliefs regarding alleged limitations on such goals or alternatively they appear as defenders of traditional archaeology with all its empiricist underpinnings. Debating such positions needs to be done, but not at the expense of our primary job, learning about the archaeological record and what it implies about the past.

NOTE

1. When I first read Kunn (1970), my initial response was simply that it was nice that after all these years practitioners of another discipline had discovered the anthropological message about the power of culture. Later, when Hodder began his push for doing away with science, I felt a bit embarrassed that a participant in the field of anthropology should just have discovered anthropology's central concept—culture.

References

Adam, K.

1951   Der Waldelefant von Lehringen, eine Jagdbeute des Diluvialen Menschen. *Quartär* 5:75–92.

Akerman, K.

1979   Heat and Lithic Technology in the Kimberleys, W. A. *Oceania* 14(2):144–151.

Albrecht, Gerd, Hubert Berke, and Francois Poplin (editors)

1983   *Naturwissenschaftliche Untersuchungen an Magdalenien-Inventaren vom Petersfels, Grabungen 1975–1976.* Tübinger Monographien zur Urgeschichte. Institute für Urgeschichte der Universität Tbingen. Federal Republic of Germany: Verlag Archaeologica Venatoria.

Allchin, B.

1957   Australian Stone Industries, Past and Present. *Journal of the Royal Anthropological Institute of Great Britain and Ireland* 87(1):115–136.

Ascher, R.

1968   Time's Arrow and the Archaeology of a Contemporary Community. In *Settlement Archaeology,* edited by K. C. Chang, pp. 43–52. Palo Alto, California: National Press Book.

Bae, K. T.

1980   Chon'gong-ni Paleolithic Site Excavation Report. In *Archaeology in Korea, 1979,* Vol. 7, edited by Kim Won-Yong, pp. 27–39. Seoul, Korea: University Museum, Seoul National University.

Bailey, G.

1983   *Pleistocene Hunters and Gatherers in Europe.* New York: Cambridge University Press.

Bailey, Harry P.

1960   A Method of Determining the Warmth and Temperateness of Climate. *Geografiska Annaler* 43(1):1–16.

Bamforth, D. B., and A. C. Spaulding

1982   Human Behavior, Explanation, Archaeology, History, and Science. *Journal of Anthropological Archaeology* 1:179–195.

Barbieri, J. A.

1937   Technique of the Implements from Lake Mohave. In *The Archaeology of Pleistocene Lake Mohave: A Symposium,* edited by Elizabeth W. Crozer Campbell and William H. Campbell. *Southwest Museum Papers* 11:99–107.

Bar-Yosef, O., B. Vandermeersch, B. Arensburg, P. Goldberg, H. Laville, L. Meignen, Y. Rak, E. Tchernov, and A.-M. Tillier

1986   New Data on the Origin of Modern Man in the Levant. *Current Anthropology* 27:63–64.

Beaumont, P. B., H. R. de Villiers, and J. C. Vogel

1978   Modern Man in Sub-Saharan Africa prior to 49,000 Years B.P.: A Review and Evaluation with Particular Reference to Border Cave. *South African Journal of Science* 74:409–419.

Behrensmeyer, Anna K.

1986   Comment on Binford and Stone. *Current Anthropology* 27:469.

Behrensmeyer, A. K., and D. E. Dechant Boaz

1980   The Recent Bones of Amboseli National Park, Kenya, in Relation to East African Paleoecology. In *Fossils in the Making: Vertebrate Taphonomy and Paleoecology,* edited by A. K. Behrensmeyer and A. P. Hill, pp. 72–93. Chicago: University of Chicago Press.

Benedict, Ruth

1934   *Patterns of Culture.* New York: Houghton-Mifflin.

Biberson, P.

1964   Torralba et Ambrona. Notes sur Deux Stations Acheuleénnes de Chasseurs d'Elephants de la Vielle Castille. *Diputación Provincial de Barcelona, Instituto de Prehistoria y Arqueología, Monografías* 6:201–248.

Biberson, P., and E. Aquirre

1965   Experiénces de Taille d'Outils Préhistoriques dans ses Os d'Elephant. *Quaternaria* 7:165–183.

Binford, Lewis R.

1962   Galley Pond Mound. In *Archaeological Investigations in the Carlyle Reservoir, Clinton County, Illinois,* by Lewis R. Binford. *Southern Illinois University Museum Archaeological Salvage Report* 17:58–109.

1963a   Red Ocher Caches from the Michigan Area: A Possible Case of Cultural Drift. *Southwestern Journal of Anthropology* 19:89–109.

1963b   The Hodges Site: A Late Archaic Burial Station. *Anthropological Papers, Museum of Anthropology, University of Michigan* 19:124–148.

1963c   The Pomranky Site: A Late Archaic Burial Station. *Anthropological Papers, Museum of Anthropology, University of Michigan* 19:149–192.

1963d   A Proposed Attribute List for the Description and Classification of Projectile Points. *Anthropological Papers, Museum of Anthropology, University of Michigan* 19:193–221.

1964   A Consideration of Archaeological Research Design. *American Antiquity* 29:425–441.

1965   Archaeological Systematics and the Study of Cultural Process. *American Antiquity* 31:203–210.

1967   Smudge Pits and Hide Smoking: The Use of Analogy in Archaeological Reasoning. *American Antiquity* 32:1–12.

1968   Archaeological Perspectives. In *New Perspectives in Archaeology,* edited by S. R. Binford and L. R. Binford, pp. 5–32. Chicago: Aldine.

1971   Mortuary Practices: Their Study and Their Potential. In *Approaches to the Social Dimension of Mortuary Practices,* edited by James A. Brown. *Memoirs of the Society of American Archaeology* 25:6–29.

1972a   *An Archaeological Perspective.* New York: Seminar Press.

1972b   Contemporary Model Building: Paradigms and the Current State of Paleolithic Research. In *Models in Archaeology,* edited by D. Clarke, pp. 109–166. London: Methuen.

1973   Interassemblage Variability—The Mousterian and the "Functional Argument." In *The Explanation of Culture Change: Models in Prehistory,* edited by C. Renfrew, pp. 227–254. London: Duckworth.

1975a   Sampling, Judgment, and the Archaeological Record. In *Sampling in Archaeology*, edited by James W. Mueller, pp. 251–257. Tucson: University of Arizona Press.

1975b   Historical Archaeology: Is It Historical or Archaeological? *Popular Archaeology* 4(3–4):11–30.

1976   Forty-Seven Trips: A Case Study in the Character of Some Formation Processes of the Archaeological Record. In *Contributions to Anthropology: The Interior Peoples of Northern Alaska*, edited by Edwin S. Hall. *Ottawa, National Museum of Man, Mercury Series* 49:299–351.

1977a   General Introduction. In *For Theory Building in Archaeology: Essays on Faunal Remains, Aquatic Resources, and Systemic Modeling*, edited by Lewis R. Binford, pp. 1–13. New York: Academic Press.

1977b   Forty-Seven Trips: A Case Study in the Character of Archaeological Formation Processes. In *Stone Tools and Cultural Markers: Change, Evolution, and Complexity*, edited by R. V. S. Wright, pp. 24–36. Canberra: Australian Institute of Aboriginal Studies.

1977c   Olorgesailie Deserves More Than the Normal Book Review. *Journal of Anthropological Research* 33:493–502.

1978a   *Nunamiut Ethnoarchaeology*. New York: Academic Press.

1978b   Dimensional Analysis of Behavior and Site Structure: Learning from an Eskimo Hunting Stand. *American Antiquity* 43:330–361.

1979   Organization and Formation Processes: Looking at Curated Technologies. *Journal of Anthropological Research* 35:255–273.

1980a   Willow Smoke and Dogs' Tails: Hunter–Gatherer Settlement Systems and Archaeological Site Formation. *American Antiquity* 45:4–20.

1980b   Review of *Living Archaeology* by R. Gould. *American Scientist* 68:704–705.

1981a   *Bones: Ancient Men and Modern Myths*. New York: Academic Press.

1981b   Behavioral Archaeology and the "Pompeii Premise." *Journal of Anthropological Research* 37:195–208.

1982a   Objectivity–Explanation–Archaeology 1981. In *Theory and Explanation in Archaeology*, edited in Colin Renfrew, M. J. Rowlands, and B. Abbott-Segraves, pp. 125–138. London: Academic Press.

1982b   The Archaeology of Place. *Journal of Anthropological Archaeology* 1:5–31.

1982c   Reply to "Rethinking the Middle/Upper Paleolithic Transition" by R. White. *Current Anthropology* 23:177–181.

1983a   *Working at Archaeology*. New York: Academic Press.

1983b   Reply to "More on the Mousterian: Flaked Bone from Cueva Morín" by L. Freeman. *Current Anthropology* 24:372–377.

1983c   *In Pursuit of the Past: Decoding the Archaeological Record*. London: Thames and Hudson.

1983d   Long Term Land Use Patterns: Some Implications for Archaeology. In *Working at Archaeology*, by L. R. Binford, pp. 379–386. New York: Academic Press.

1984a   Bones of Contention: A Reply to Glynn Isaac. *American Antiquity* 49:164–167.

1984b   An Alyawara Day: Flour, Spinifex Gum, and Shifting Perspectives. *Journal of Anthropological Research* 40:157–182.

1984c   *Faunal Remains from Klasies River Mouth*. New York: Academic Press.

1984d   Butchering, Sharing, and the Archaeological Record. *Journal of Anthropological Archaeology* 3:235–257.

1985a   Brand "X" Versus the Recommended Product. *American Antiquity* 50:580–590.

1985b   Human Ancestors: Changing Views of Their Behavior. *Journal of Anthropological Archaeology* 4:292–327.

1985c   Hominid Evolution: The Problem of Behavior and Niche. Proposal submitted to the National Science Foundation. Ms. on file, Department of Anthropology, University of New Mexico, Albuquerque.

1986a   An Alyawara Day: Making Men's Knives and Beyond. *American Antiquity* 51:547–562.

1986b   Isolating the Transition to Cultural Adaptations: An Organizational Approach. In *Patterns and Processes in Later Pleistocene Hominid Evolution,* edited by Erik Trinkaus. Cambridge, England: Cambridge University Press.

1986c   Technology of Early Man—An Organizational Approach to the Olduwan. To appear in a book edited by Alison Brooks. Washington, D.C.: Anthropological Society of Washington.

1986d   In Pursuit of the Future. In *American Archaeology Past and Future: Papers Presented at the Special Anniversary Session for the 50th Annual Meeting of the Society for American Archaeology, Denver,* edited by David J. Meltzer *et al.,* pp. 459–479. Washington, D.C.: Smithsonian Institution Press.

1986e   Reply to Thackery. *Current Anthropology* 27:511–515.

1986f   Comment on "Systematic Butchery by Plio/Pleistocene Hominids at Olduvai Gorge" by Henry T. Bunn and Ellen M. Kroll. *Current Anthropology* 27:444–446.

1986g   Reply to Singer and Wymer. *Current Anthropology* 27:57–62.

1987a   Researching Ambiguity: Frames of Reference and Site Structure. In *Method and Theory for Activity Area Research: An Ethnoarchaeological Approach,* edited by Susan Kent, pp. 449–512. New York: Columbia University Press.

1987b   Searching for Camps and Missing the Evidence? Another Look at the Lower Paleolithic. In *The Pleistocene Old World: Regional Perspectives,* edited by Olga Soffer, pp. 17–31. New York: Plenum Press.

1987c   A Taphonomic Study of the Fauna from the Abri Vaufrey. In *La Grotte Vaufrey à Cenac-et-Saint-Julien (Dordogne): Paléoenvironnements, Chronologie et Activités Humaines,* edited by J.-P. Rigaud. *Memoire de la Société Préhistoric Française* 19.

1987d   Were There Elephant Hunters at Torralba? In *The Evolution of Human Hunting,* edited by M. H. Nitecki and D. V. Nitecki, pp. 47–105. New York: Plenum Press.

Binford, Lewis R., and Jack Bertram

1977   Bone Frequencies and Attritional Processes. In *For Theory Building in Archaeology: Essays on Faunal Remains, Aquatic Resources, and Systemic Modeling,* edited by Lewis R. Binford, pp. 77–153. New York: Academic Press.

Binford, Lewis R., and Sally R. Binford

1966   A Preliminary Analysis of Functional Variability in the Mousterian of Levallois Facies. In *Recent Studies in Paleoanthropology,* edited by J. D. Clark and F. C. Howell. *American Anthropologist* 68:238–295.
        Binford, Lewis R., and W. J. Chasko

1976   Nunamiut Demographic History: A Provocative Case. In *Demographic Anthropology,* edited by B. W. Zubrow, pp. 63–144. Albuquerque: University of New Mexico Press.

Binford, Lewis R., and C. K. Ho

1985   Taphonomy at a Distance: Zhoukoudian, "The Cave Home of Beijing Man"? *Current Anthropology* 26:413–442.

Binford, Lewis R., and James F. O'Connell

1984   An Alyawara Day: The Stone Quarry. *Journal of Anthropological Research* 3:406–432.

Binford, Lewis R., and M. L. Papworth

1963   The Eastport Site, Antrim County, Michigan. *Anthropological Papers, Museum of Anthropology, University of Michigan* 19:71–123.

Binford, Lewis R., and George I. Quimby

1963   Indian Sites and Chipped Stone Materials in the Northern Lake Michigan Area. *Fieldiana: Anthropology* 36:277–307.

Binford, Lewis R., and Jeremy A. Sabloff

1982   Paradigms, Systematics, and Archaeology. *Journal of Anthropological Research* 38:137–153.

Binford, Lewis R., and Nancy M. Stone

1985   "Righteous Rocks" and Richard Gould: Some Observations on Misguided "Debate." *American Antiquity* 50:151–153.

1986   Zhoukoudian: A Closer Look. *Current Anthropology* 27:453–476.

Binford, Lewis R., and Lawrence Todd

1982   On Arguments for the "Butchering" of Giant Geladas. *Current Anthropology* 23:108–110.

Binford, Lewis R., M. G. L. Mills, and Nancy M. Stone

1988   Hyena Scavenging Behavior and Its Implications for the Interpretation of Faunal Assemblages from FLK 22 (The Zinj Floor) at Olduvai Gorge. *Journal of Anthropological Archaeology* 7:99–135.

Binford, Lewis R., Sally R. Binford, Robert Whallon, and M. A. Hardin

1966   Archaeology at Hatchery West. *Society for American Archaeology Memoir* 24.

Binford, Sally R.

1968a   Ethnographic Data and Understanding the Pleistocene. In *Man the Hunter,* edited by Richard Lee and Irven DeVore, pp. 274–275. Chicago: Aldine.

1986b   A Structural Comparison of Disposal of the Dead in the Mousterian and Upper Paleolithic. *Southwestern Journal of Anthropology* 24:139–154.

Binford, Sally R. and Lewis R. Binford

1969   Stone Tools and Human Behavior. *Scientific American* 220:70–82.

Binford, Sally R., and Lewis R. Binford (editors)

1968   *New Perspectives in Archaeology.* Chicago: Aldine.

Blumenschine, R. J.

1986   Early Hominid Scavenging Opportunities. *British Archaeological Reports, International Series* 283.

Blumenschine, R. J., and T. M. Caro

1986   Unit Weights of Some East African Bovids. *African Journal of Ecology* 24:273–286.

Boas, Franz

1938   Introduction. In *General Anthropology,* edited by Franz Boas. *War Department Education Manual* EM 226:1–6.

1943   *Race, Language and Culture.* New York: Free Press.

Bordes, François

1953   Essai de Classification des Industries "Mousteriennes." *Bulletin de la Société Préhistorique Française* 50(7–8):457–466.

1961   Mousterian Cultures in France. *Science* 134:803–810.

1963   Le Mousterien à Denticules. *Archeoloski Vestnik: Acta Archaeologica* XIII–XIV:43–49.

1967a   Considérations sur la Typologie et les Techniques dans le Paléolithique. *Quartär* 18:25–55.

1967b   La Stratigraphie du Gisement du Roc de Combe (Lot) et ses Implications, by François Bordes with J. Labrot. *Bulletin de la Société Préhistorique Française* 64(1):15–28.

1968   *The Old Stone Age.* New York: McGraw-Hill.

1978   Comment. *Current Anthropology* 19:359–360.

1980   Le Debitage Levallois et ses Variants. *Bulletin de la Société Préhistorique Française* 77(2):45–49.

Bordes, François, and Donald Crabtree

1969   The Corbiac Blade Techniques and Other Experiments. *Tebiwa* 12(2):1–21.

Bordes, F., and C. Dortch

1977   Blade and Levallois Technology in Western Australia. *Quartär* 27/28:1–19.

Bordes, Francois, and Denise de Sonneville-Bordes

1970   The Significance of Variability in Paleolithic Assemblages. *World Archaeology* 2(1):61–73.

Bosinski, Gerhard

1982   The Transition Lower/Middle Paleolithic in Northwestern Germany. In *The Transition from Lower to Middle Paleolithic and the Origin of Modern Man,* edited by Avraham Ronen. *British Archaeological Reports, International Series* 151:165–175.

Bradley, B.

1975   Lithic Reduction Sequences: A Glossary and Discussion. In *Lithic Technology,* edited by E. H. Swanson, Jr., pp. 5–14. The Hague, The Netherlands: Mouton.

Brain, C. K.

1981   *The Hunters or the Hunted? An Introduction to African Cave Taphonomy.* Chicago: University of Chicago Press.

Brokensha, P.

1975   *The Pitjantjatjara and Their Crafts.* Sydney: Aboriginal Arts Board, Australian Council.

Bunn, H. T.

1981   Archaeological Evidence for Meat-Eating by Plio–Pleistocene Hominids from Koobi Fora and Olduvai Gorge. *Nature (London)* 291:574–577.

1982a   Animal Bones and Archaeological Inference. *Science* 215:494–495.

1982b   *Meat-Eating and Human Evolution: Studies on the Diet and Subsistence Patterns of Plio–Pleistocene Hominids in East Africa.* Ph.D. dissertation, Department of Anthropology, University of California, Berkeley.

1983a   Evidence on the Diet and Subsistence Patterns of Plio–Pleistocene Hominids at Koobi Fora, Kenya, and Olduvai Gorge, Tanzania. In *Animals and Archaeology: Hunters and Their Prey,* edited by J. Clutton-Brock and C. Grigson. *British Archaeological Reports* 163:21–30.

1983b   Comparative Analysis of Modern Bone Assemblages from a San Hunter–Gatherer Camp in the Kalahari Desert, Botswana, and from a Spotted Hyena Den near Nairobi, Kenya. In *Animals and Archaeology: Hunters and Their Prey,* edited by J. Clutton-Brock and C. Grigson. *British Archaeological Reports* 163:143–148.

Bunn, H. T., and E. Kroll

1986a   Systematic Butchery by Plio/Pleistocene Hominids at Olduvai Gorge, Tanzania. *Current Anthropology* 27:431–452.

1986b   Reply to Binford. *Current Anthropology* 27:448–451.

Bunn, H. T., J. W. K. Harris, G. Isaac, Z. Kaufulu, E. Kroll, K. Schick, N. Toth, and A. K. Behrensmeyer

1980   FxJj50: An Early Pleistocene Site in Northern Kenya. *World Archaeology* 12:109–136.

Burkett, M. C.

1933   *The Old Stone Age: A Study of Paleolithic Times.* Cambridge, England: Cambridge University Press.

Butzer, K. W.

1965   Acheulian Occupation Sites at Torralba and Ambrona, Spain: Their Geology. *Science* 150:1718–1722.

Callahan, E.

1979   The Basics of Biface Knapping in the Eastern Fluted Point Tradition: A Manual for Flint-Knappers and Lithic Analysts. *Archaeology of Eastern North America* 7(1):1–180.

Camilli, Eileen L.

1983   *Site Occupational History and Lithic Assemblage Structure: An Example from South-eastern Utah.* Ph.D. dissertation, Department of Anthropology, University of New Mexico, Albuquerque.

1985   Prehistoric Use of Landscapes and the Archaeological Surface Distribution. Paper presented at the 50th Annual Meeting of the Society for American Archaeology, Denver.

Carr, C.

1984   The Nature and Organization of Intrasite Archaeological Records and Spatial Analytic Approaches to Their Investigation. In *Advances in Archaeological Method and Theory,* Vol. 7, edited by M. B. Schiffer, pp. 103–222. New York: Academic Press.

Chang, Jen-Hu

1968   *Climate and Agriculture: An Ecological Survey.* Chicago: Aldine.

Chang, K. C.

1967a   Major Aspects of the Interrelationship of Archaeology and Ethnology. *Current Anthropology* 8:227–243.

1967b   *Rethinking Archaeology.* New York: Random House.

Chase, Philip G.

1986   Relationships between Mousterian Lithic and Faunal Assemblages at Combe Grenal. *Current Anthropology* 27:69–71.

Chavaillon, J.

1970   Decouverte d'un Niveau Oldowayen dans la Basse Vallée de l'Omo (Ethiopie). *Bulletin de la Société Préhistorique Française* 67:7–11.

1976   Evidence for the Technical Practices of Early Pleistocene Hominids. In *Earliest Man and Environments in the Lake Rudolf Basin: Stratigraphy, Paleoecology and Evolution,* edited by Yves Coppens *et al.,* pp. 565–573. Chicago: University of Chicago Press.

1982   Position Chronologique des Hominids Fossiles d'Ethiopie. *Congrès Internationale de Paléontologie Humaine* 1:766–797.

Chavaillon, J., and J. Boisaubert

1977   Prospection Archéologique dans le Gemu-Gofa et la Basse Vallée de l'Omo. *Documents Histoire Civilisation Ethiopienne* RCP 230, *CNRS Fascicule* 8:3–10.

Chavaillon, J., N. Chavaillon, F. Hours, and M. Piperno

1978   Le Debut et la Fin de l'Acheuléen à Melka-Kunture: Methodologie pour l'Etude des Changements de Civilisations. *Bulletin de la Société Préhistorique Française* 75:105–115.

1979   From the Oldowan to the Middle Stone Age at Melka-Kunture (Ethiopia): Understanding Cultural Changes. *Quaternaria* 21:87–114.

Christenson, A. L., and D. W. Read

1977   Numerical Taxonomy, R-Mode Factor Analysis, and Archaeological Classification. *American Antiquity* 42:163–179.

Clark, J. D.

1954   An Early Upper Pleistocene Site at the Kalambo Falls on the Northern Rhodesian/Tanganika Border. *South African Archaeological Bulletin* 9(34):51–56.

1962   The Kalambo Falls Prehistoric Site: An Interim Report. In *Actes du IVe Congrès Panafri-cain de Préhistoire et de l'Etude du Quaternaire: Section III. Pré- et Protohistoire,* edited by G. Mortelmans and J. Nenquin. *Annales Series IN-8, Science Humaines* 40:195–201.

1965   The Influence of Environment in Inducing Culture Change at the Kalambo Falls Pre-historic Site. *South African Archaeological Bulletin* 20(75):93–101.

1980   Human Populations and Cultural Adaptations in the Sahara and Nile during Prehistoric Times. In *The Sahara and the Nile,* edited by M. Williams and H. Faure, pp. 527–586. Rotterdam: A. A. Balkema.

1982   The Transition from Lower to Middle Palaeolithic in the African Continent. In *The Transition from Lower to Middle Paleolithic and the Origin of Modern Man,* edited by Avraham Ronen. *British Archaeological Reports, International Series* 151:235–255.

1985   Leaving No Stone Unturned: Archaeological Advances and Behavioral Adaptation. In *Hominid Evolution: Past, Present, and Future,* edited by Phillip V. Tobias, pp. 65–68. New York: Alan R. Liss.

Clark, J. D. (editor)
1969   *Kalambo Falls Prehistoric Site,* Vol. 1. Cambridge, England: Cambridge University Press.
1974   *Kalambo Falls Prehistoric Site,* Vol. 2 Cambridge, England: Cambridge University Press.

Clark, J. D., and G. Cole
1969   The Excavations: Sites B, C, and D. In *Kalambo Falls Prehistoric Site,* Vol. 1, edited by J. D. Clark, pp. 153–189. Cambridge, England: Cambridge University Press.

Clark, J. D., and C. V. Haynes
1970   An Elephant Butchery Site at Mwanganda's Village, Karonga, Malawi, and Its Relevance for Paleolithic Archaeology. *World Archaeology* 1:390–411.

Clark, J. D., and M. R. Kleindienst
1969   The Excavations: Site A. *Kalambo Falls Prehistoric Site,* Vol. 1, edited by J. D. Clark, pp. 85–152. Cambridge, England: Cambridge University Press.

Clark, J. D., and H. Kurashina
1976   New Plio–Pleistocene Archaeological Occurrences from the Plain of Gadeb, Upper Webi Shebele Basin, Ethiopia, and a Statistical Comparison of the Gadeb Sites with Other Early Stone Age Assemblages. In *Proceedings of the Union Internationale des Sciences Préhistoriques et Protohistoriques, IXe Congrès,* pp. 158–216. Nice, France: University of Nice.

1979a   Hominid Occupation of the East-Central Highlands of Ethiopia in the Plio–Pleistocene. *Nature (London)* 282:33–39.

1979b   An Analysis of Earlier Stone Age Bifaces from Gadeb (Locality 8E), Northern Bale Highlands, Ethiopia. *South African Archaeological Bulletin* 34:39–109.

Clarke, D. L.
1973   Archaeology: The Loss of Innocence. *Antiquity* 47(1):6–18.

Clarke, R.
1935   The Flint Knapping Industry at Brandon. *Antiquity* 9(31):38–56.

Clastres, Pierre
1972   The Guayaki. In *Hunters and Gatherers Today,* edited by M. G. Bicchieri, pp. 138–174. New York: Holt, Rinehart and Winston.

Clutton-Brock, J., and C. Grigson (editors)
1983   *Animals and Archaeology: Hunters and Their Prey. British Archaeological Report* 163.

Cole, G. H., and M. R. Kleindienst

1974   Further Reflections on the Isimila Acheulian. *Quaternary Research* 4:346–355.

Collingwood, R. G.

1956   *The Idea of History.* New York: Oxford University Press. (Originally published in 1946 by Clarendon Press, London.)

Collins, D.

1969   Cultural Traditions and Environment of Early Man. *Current Anthropology* 10:267–316.

Commins, Saxe, and Robert N. Linscott

1947   *Man and the Universe: The Philosophers of Science.* New York: Random House.

Conkey, Margaret, W.

1978   Style and Information in Cultural Evolution: Toward a Predictive Model for the Paleolithic. In *Social Archaeology,* edited by Charles L. Redman, Mary Jane Berman, Edward V. Curtin, William T. Langhorne, Jr., Nina M. Versaggi, and Jeffrey C. Wanser, pp. 61–85. New York: Academic Press.

Courbin, Paul

1981   *Qu'est-ce que l'Archéologie?* Paris: Payot.

Coutier, L.

1929   Experiences de Taille pour Rechercher les Anciennes Techniques Paléolithiques. *Bulletin de la Société Préhistorique Française* 26:172–174.

Crabtree, D. E.

1972   An Introduction to Flintworking. *Occasional Papers of the Idaho State University Museum* 28.

Crabtree, D. E., and B. R. Butler

1964   Notes on Experiments in Flint-Knapping: I. Heat Treatment of Silica Materials. *Tebiwa* 7:1–6.

Cushing, F. H.

1895   The Arrow. *American Anthropologist* 8:307–349.

Deacon, J. H.

1985   Review of L. R. Binford, *Faunal Remains from Klasies River Mouth. The South African Archaeological Bulletin* 40:59–60.

Deetz, James F.

1967   *Invitation to Archaeology.* Garden City, New York: Natural History Press.

1982   Households: A Structural Key to Archaeological Explanation. *American Behavioral Scientist* 25(6):717–724.

de Lumley, H.

1975   Cultural Evolution in France in Its Paleoecological Setting during the Middle Pleistocene. In *After the Australopithicines: Stratigraphy, Ecology and Culture Change in the Middle Pleistocene,* edited by K. W. Butzer and G. L. Isaac, pp. 745–808. The Hague, The Netherlands: Mouton.

Denham, W.

1975   Population Properties of Physical Groups among the Alyawara Tribe of Central Australia. *Oceania* 10:114–151.

de Sonneville-Bordes, D.

1967   *La Préhistoire Moderne.* Perigeux, France: Pierre Fanlac.

Dibble, Harold L.

1984   Interpreting Typological Variation of Middle Paleolithic Scrapers: Function, Style, or Sequence of Reduction. *Journal of Field Archaeology* 11:431–436.

1987   The Interpretation of Middle Paleothic Scraper Morphology. *American Antiquity* 52:109–117.

Dortch, C. E.

1977   Early and Late Stone Industrial Phases in Western Australia. In *Stone Tools as Cultural Markers: Change, Evolution and Complexity,* edited by R. V. S. Wright, pp. 104–132. Atlantic Highlands, New Jersey: Humanities Press.

Dunnell, Robert C.

1971   *Systematics in Prehistory.* New York: Free Press.

Dunnell, Robert C., and William S. Dancey

1983   The Siteless Survey: A Regional Scale Data Collection Strategy. In *Advances in Archaeology Method and Theory,* Vol. 6, edited by Michael B. Schiffer, pp. 267–287. New York: Academic Press.

Ebert, J. I., S. Larralde, and L. Wandsnider

1983   Distributional Archaeology: Survey, Mapping, and Analysis of Surface Archaeological Materials in the Green River Basin, Wyoming. Paper presented at the 41st Plains Conference, Rapid City, South Dakota.

Edwards, R. (editor)

1973   *Australian Aboriginal Culture* (2nd ed.). Canberra: Australian National Commission for UNESCO.

Elkin, A. P.

1948   Pressure Flaking in the Northern Kimberley, Australia. *Man* 130:110–113.

Ellis, H. H.

1940   Flint-Working Techniques of the American Indians: An Experimental Study. *Ohio Historical Society Publication* 72.

Evans, J. C.

1872   *The Ancient Stone Implements, Weapons and Ornaments of Great Britain.* London: Longmans.

Fischer, A., B. Bronnow, J. H. Jonsson, F. O. Neilsen, and C. Petersen

1979   Stone Age Experiments in Lejre: Internal Organization of Settlements. *National Museum of Denmark, Working Papers* 8.

Flannery, K. V.

1982   The Golden Marshalltown: A Parable for the Archaeology of the 1980s. *American Anthropologist* 84:265–278.

Foley, R. A.

1980   The Spatial Component of Archaeological Data: Off-Site Methods and Some Preliminary Results from the Amboseli Basin, Southern Kenya. *Proceedings of the VIII Pan-African Congress in Prehistory and Quaternary Studies,* pp. 39–40.

1981a   Off Site Archaeology: An Alternative Approach for the Short-Sited. In *Pattern of the Past: Studies in Honour of David L. Clarke,* edited by I. Hodder, G. Isaac, and N. Hammond, pp. 157–183. Cambridge, England: Cambridge University Press.

1981b   Off Site Archaeology and Human Adaptation in Eastern Africa: An Analysis of Regional Artefact Density in the Amboseli, Southern Kenya. *British Archaeological Reports, International Series* 97.

1982   A Reconsideration of the Role of Predation on Large Mammals in Tropical Hunter–Gatherer Adaptation. *Man* 17:393–402.

Ford, James A.

1954   On the Concept of Types: The Type Concept Revisited. *American Anthropologist* 56:42–54.

1962   *A Quantitative Method for Deriving Cultural Chronology.* Technical Manual 1. Washington, D.C.: Pan American Union, General Secretariat, Organization of American States.

Fowke, G.

1891   Stone Art. *Bureau of American Ethnology Annual Report* 13:47–178.

1892   Stone Art. *Bureau of American Ethnology Annual Report* 14:139–405.

Freeman, L. G., Jr.

1968   A Theoretical Framework for Interpreting Archaeological Materials. In *Man the Hunter,* edited by R. Lee and I. DeVore, pp. 262–267. Chicago: Aldine.

1971   El Hueso Trabajado Musteriense de Cueva Morín. In *Cueva Morín: Excavaciones 1966–1968,* edited by J. González Echegaray, K. W. Butzer, Arlette Leroi-Gourhan, J. Altuna, B. Madariaga, and J. M. Appelániz, pp. 135–161. Santander, Spain: Patronato de las Cuevas Prehistóricas.

1975a   Acheulian Sites and Stratigraphy in Iberia and the Maghreb. In *After the Australopithecines: Stratigraphy, Ecology and Culture Change in the Middle Pleistocene,* edited by K. W. Butzer and G. L. Isaac, pp. 661–743. The Hague, The Netherlands: Mouton.

1975b   By Their Works You Shall Know Them: Cultural Developments in the Paleolithic. In *Hominisation und Verhalten,* edited by Kurth Eibl-Eibesfeld, pp. 234–251. Stuttgart, Federal Republic of Germany: Gustav Fischer.

1978a   Mousterian Worked Bone from Cueva Morín (Santander, Spain): A Preliminary Description. In *Views of the Past: Essays in Old World Prehistory and Paleoanthropology,* edited by L. G. Freeman, Jr., pp. 29–51. The Hague, The Netherlands: Mouton.

1978b   The Analysis of Some Occupation Floor Distributions from Earlier and Middle Paleolithic Sites in Spain. In *Views of the Past: Essays in Old World Prehistory and Paleoanthropology,* edited by L. G. Freeman, Jr., pp. 57–115. The Hague, The Netherlands: Mouton.

1981   The Fat of the Land: Notes on Paleolithic Diet in Iberia. In *Omnivorous Primates: Gathering and Hunting in Human Evolution,* edited by Robert S. O. Harding and Geza Teleki, pp. 104–165. New York: Columbia University Press.

1983   More on the Mousterian: Flaked Bone from Cueva Morín. *Current Anthropology* 24:366–372.

Freeman, L. G., Jr., and K. W. Butzer

1966   The Acheulaan Station of Torralba (Spain): A Progress Report *Quaternaria* 8:9–21.

Freeman, L. G., Sr., and F. C. Howell

1981   Acheulian Occupation at Ambrona (Spain). Paper presented at the 46th Annual Meeting of the Society for American Archaeology, San Diego.

1982   Acheulian Hunters on the Spanish Meseta: Torralba and Ambrona Reconsidered. Paper presented at the 81st Annual Meeting of the American Anthropological Association, Washington, D.C.

Freund, Gisela

1982   Der Übergang von Alt- zum Mittelpaläolithikum in Süd-Deutschland. In *The Transition from Lower to Middle Paleolithic and the Origin of Modern Man,* edited by Avraham Ronen. *British Archaeological Reports, International Series* 151:151–163.

Frison, George C., and Lawrence C. Todd

1986   *The Colby Mammoth Site: Taphonomy and Archaeology of a Clovis Kill in Northern Wyoming.* Albuquerque: University of New Mexico Press.

Fritz, John M., and Fred T. Plog

1970   The Nature of Archaeological Explanation. *American Antiquity* 35:405–412.

Gamble, Clive

1986   The Palaeolithic Settlement of Europe. Cambridge, England: Cambridge University Press.

Geertz, Clifford

1973   *The Interpretation of Cultures.* New York: Basic Books.

Gellner, Ernest

1974   *Legitimation of Belief.* Cambridge, England: Cambridge University Press.

1982   What Is Structuralism? In *Theory and Explanation in Archaeology,* edited by Colin Renfrew, M. J. Rowlands, and B. Abbott-Segraves, pp. 97–123. London: Academic Press.

1985   *Relativism and the Social Sciences.* Cambridge, England: Cambridge University Press.

Geneste, J. M.

1985   *Analyse Lithique d'Industries Mousteriennes du Périgord: Une Approche Technologique du Compontement des Groups Humains au Paléolithique Moyen.* Ph.D. dissertation, University of Bordeaux, France.

Gentry, A. W., and A. Gentry

1978   Fossil Bovidae (Mammalia) of Olduvai Gorge. *Bulletin of the British Museum of Natural History* 29(4), 30(1).

Ghosh, A. K.

1982   Pebble-Core and Flake Elements: Process of Transmutation and the Factors Thereof. A Case Study of the Transition from Lower to Middle Palaeolithic in India. In *The Transition from Lower to Middle Paleolithic and the Origin of Modern Man,* edited by Avraham Ronen. *British Archaeological Reports, International Series* 151:265–282.

Gifford, Diane, Glynn L. Isaac, and C. M. Nelson

1981   Evidence for Predation and Pastoralism at Prolonged Drift: A Pastoral Neolithic Site in Kenya. *Azania* 15:57–108.

Gilman, Antonio

1984   Explaining the Upper Palaeolithic Revolution. In *Marxist Perspectives in Archaeology,* edited by M. Spriggs, pp. 115–126. Cambridge, England: Cambridge University Press.

Glassie, H.

1975   *Folk Housing in Middle Virginia.* Knoxville: University of Tennessee Press.

Gould, Richard A.

1967   Notes on Hunting, Butchering, and Sharing of Game among the Ngatatjara and Their Neighbors in the West Australian Desert. *Kroeber Anthropological Society Papers* 36:41–66.

1968   Living Archaeology: The Ngatatjara of Western Australia. *Southwestern Journal of Anthropology* 24:101–122.

1971   The Archaeologist as Ethnographer: A Case from the Western Desert Aborigines of Australia. *World Archaeology* 3(2):143–177.

1974   Some Current Problems in Ethnoarchaeology. In Ethnoarchaeology, edited by C. B. Donnan and C. W. Clewlow. *Institute of Archaeology Monograph* IV:29–48.

1977   Ethno-archaeology, or Where Do Models Come from? In *Stone Tools as Cultural Markers,* edited by R. V. S. Wright, pp. 162–168. Canberra: Australian Institute of Aboriginal Studies.

1978a   From Tasmania to Tucson. In *New Directions in Ethnoarchaeology,* edited by Richard A. Gould, pp. 1–10. Albuquerque: University of New Mexico Press.

1978b   Beyond Analogy in Ethnoarchaeology. In *Explorations in Ethnoarchaeology,* edited by Richard A. Gould, pp. 249–293. Albuquerque: University of New Mexico Press.

1978c   The Anthropology of Human Residues. *American Anthropologist* 80:815–835.

1979 Caribou Hunters—Review of *Nunamiut Ethnoarchaeology* by L. R. Binford. *Science* 20(4394):737–739.

1980a *Living Archaeology.* New York: Cambridge University Press.

1980b Review of *Ethnoarchaeology* by C. Kramer. *Archaeology* 33:737–739.

1981 Brandon Revisited: A New Look at an Old Technology. In *Modern Material Culture: The Archaeology of Us,* edited by Richard A. Gould and Michael B. Schiffer, pp. 269–281. New York: Academic Press.

1985 The Empiricist Strikes Back: A Reply to Binford. *American Antiquity* 50:638–644.

Gould, Richard A., and S. Saggers

1985 Lithic Procurement in Central Australia: A Closer Look at Binford's Idea of Embeddedness in Archaeology. *American Antiquity* 50:117–136.

Gould, Richard A., and Patty Jo Watson

1982 A Dialogue on the Meaning and Use of Analogy in Ethnoarchaeological Reasoning. *Journal of Anthropological Archaeology* 1:355–381.

Gowlett, J.

1984 *Ascent to Civilization: The Archaeology of Early Man.* New York: Knopf.

Grayson, Donald K.

1984 *Quantitative Zooarchaeology: Topics in the Analysis of Archaeology Faunas.* New York: Academic Press.

Greenway, J.

1972 *Down among the Wild Men.* Boston: Atlantic–Little, Brown.

Griffin, James B.

1943 *The Fort Ancient Aspect: Its Cultural and Chronological Position in Mississippi Valley Archaeology.* Ann Arbor: University of Michigan Press.

Griffin, P. Bion

1984 Forager Resource and Land Use in the Humid Tropics: The Agta of Northeastern Luzon, the Philippines. In *Past and Present in Hunter Gatherer Studies,* edited by Carmel Schrire, pp. 95–121. New York: Academic Press.

Gubser, N. J.

1965 *The Nunamiut Eskimos: Hunters of Caribou.* New Haven, Connecticut: Yale University Press.

Guichard, J.

1965 Un Facies Original de l'Acheuleen: Cantalouette (Commune de Creysse). *l'Anthropologie* 69:413–464.

Hahn, Joachim, and Linda R. Owen

1985 Blade Technology in the Aurignacian and Gravettian of Geissenklosterle Cave, Southwest Germany. *World Archaeology* 17:61–75.

Harpending, Henry, and Alan Rogers

1985 Antana: A Package for Multivariate Data Analysis. Ms. on file, Department of Anthropology, Pennsylvania State University, State College, Pennsylvania.

Harris, J. W. K.

1978 *Karari Industry: Its Place in African Prehistory.* Ph.D. dissertation, Department of Anthropology, University of California, Berkeley.

Harris, Marvin

1979 *Cultural Materialism: The Struggle for a Science of Culture.* New York: Random House.

Harrold, F.

1980 A Comparative Analysis of Eurasian Paleolithic Burials. *World Archaeology* 12:195–210.

Hawkes, K., and James F. O'Connell

1981   Affluent Hunters? Some Comments in Light of the Alyawara Case. *American An-thropologist* 83:622–626.

Hayden, Brian

1976   Curation: Old and New. In *Primitive Art and Technology,* edited by J. S. Raymond, pp. 47–59. Calgary, Alberta, Canada: University of Calgary Archaeological Association.

1978   Snarks in Archaeology, or Inter-Assemblage Variability in Lithics (A View from the Antipodes). In *Lithics and Subsistence: The Analysis of Stone Tool Use in Prehistoric Economies,* edited by D. D. Davis. *Vanderbilt University Publications in Anthropology* 20:179–198.

1979   *Paleolithic Reflections: Lithic Technology and Ethnographic Excavations among Australian Aborigines.* Atlantic Highlands, New Jersey: Humanities Press.

Haynes, G.

1982   Utilization and Skeletal Disturbances of North American Prey Carcasses. *Arctic* 35(2): 266–281.

Hempel, C. G.

1966   *The Philosophy of Natural Science.* Englewood Cliffs, New Jersey: Prentice-Hall.

Henry, J.

1964   *Jungle People.* New York: Vintage Books–Random House.

Hesse, M. B.

1974   *The Structure of Scientific Inference.* London: Macmillan.

Hill, Andrew

1975   *Taphonomy of Contemporary and Late Cenozoic East African Vertebrates.* Ph.D. dissertation, University of London.

1976   On Carnivore and Weathering Damage to Bone. *Current Anthropology* 17:335–336.

1979   Butchery and Natural Disarticulation: An Investigatory Technique. *American Antiquity* 44:739–744.

Hill, James N.

1965   *Broken K: A Prehistoric Society in Eastern Arizona.* Ph.D. dissertation, Department of Anthropology, University of Chicago.

Hodder, Ian

1981   Towards a Mature Archaeology. In *Pattern of the Past: Studies in Honour of David L. Clarke,* edited by Ian Hodder, Glynn L. Isaac, and N. Hammond, pp. 1–13. Cambridge, England: Cambridge University Press.

1982a   *Symbols in Action: Ethnoarchaeological Studies of Material Culture.* Cambridge, England: Cambridge University Press.

1982b   *The Present Past—An Introduction to Anthropology for Archaeologists.* New York: Pica Press.

1982c   Theoretical Archaeology: A Reactionary View. In *Symbolic and Structural Archaeology,* edited by Ian Hodder, pp. 1–16. Cambridge, England: Cambridge University Press.

1984a   Archaeology in 1984. *Antiquity* 58:25–32.

1984b   History vs Science: No Contest. Review of L. R. Binford (1983) *In Pursuit of the Past* (Thames and Hudson) and J. G. D. Clark (1983) *The Identity of Man* (Methuen). *Scottish Archaeological Review* 3(1):66–68.

1985   Postprocessual Archaeology. In *Advances in Archaeological Method and Theory,* Vol. 8, edited by Michael B. Schiffer, pp. 1–26. New York: Academic Press.

1986   *Reading the Past: Current Approaches to Interpretation in Archaeology.* Cambridge, England: Cambridge University Press.

Holmberg, A. R.

1969   *Nomads of the Long Bow.* Garden City, New York: Natural History Press.

Holmes, W. H.

1894   Natural History of Flaked Stone Implements. In *Memoirs of the International Congress of Anthropology,* edited by C. S. Wake. pp. 120–139. Chicago: International Congress of Anthropology.

1919   Handbook of Aboriginal American Antiquities: Part I. The Lithic Industries. *Bureau of American Ethnology Bulletin* 60.

Howell, F. Clark

1961   Isimila: A Paleolithic Site in Africa. *Scientific American* 205:118–129.

1965   *Early Man.* New York: Time–Life Books.

1966   Observations on the Earlier Phases of the European Lower Paleolithic. *American Anthropologist* 68:88–201.

1968   The Use of Ethnography in Reconstructing the Past. In *Man the Hunter,* edited by Richard Lee and Irven DeVore. pp. 287–288. Chicago: Aldine.

1976   Overview of the Pliocene and Earlier Pleistocene of the Lower Omo Basin, Southern Ethiopia. In *Human Origins: Louis Leakey and the East African Evidence,* edited by Glynn L. Isaac and E. R. McCown, pp. 226–268. Menlo Park, California: W. A. Benjamin.

Howell, F. Clark, and L. G. Freeman, Jr.

1982   Ambrona: An Early Stone Age Site on Spanish Meseta. *The L.S.B. Leakey Foundation News* 22:11–13.

Howell, F. Clark, K. W. Butzer, and E. Aguirre

1963   Noticia Preliminar sobre el Emplazamiento Acheulense de Torralba (Soria). *Excavaciónes Arqueologicas en España* 10:1–38.

Howell, F. Clark, G. Cole, and M. R. Kleindienst

1959   Isimila, An Acheulian Occupation Site in the Iringa Highlands, Southern Highlands Province, Tanganika. Paper presented at the IVth Pan-African Congress on Prehistory, August 22–29, Leopoldville, Belgian Congo.

1962   Isimila, An Acheulean Occupation Site in the Iringa Highlands, Southern Highlands Province, Tanganika. In *Actes du IVe Congrès Panafricain de Préhistoire et de l'Etude du Quaternaire: Section III. Pré- et Protohistoire,* edited by G. Mortelmans and J. Nenquin. *Annales Series* IN-8, *Science Humaines* 40:43–80.

Howell, F. C., G. Cole, M. R. Kleindienst, M. R. Szabo, and K. P. Oakley

1972   Uranium-Series Dating of Bone from the Isimila Prehistoric Site, Tanzania. *Nature (London)* 237:51–52.

Huntingford, W.

1955   The Economic Life of the Dorobo. *Anthropos* 50:602–631.

Hutterer, Karl L.

1977a   Reinterpreting the Southeast Asian Paleolithic. In *Cultural–Ecological Perspectives on Southeast Asia,* edited by W. Wood, pp. 9–28. Athens, Ohio: Ohio University Center for International Studies.

1977b   Reinterpreting the Southeast Asian Palaeolithic. In *Sundra and Sahul: Prehistoric Studies in Southeast Asia, Melanesia and Australia,* edited by J. Allen, J. Golson, and R. Jones, pp. 31–71. New York: Academic Press.

Ingold, T.

1983   The Significance of Storage in Hunting Societies. *Man* 18:553–571.

Isaac, Glynn L.

1971   The Diet of Early Man: Aspects of Archaeological Evidence from Lower and Middle Pleistocene Sites in Africa. *World Archaeology* 2:278–298.

1976 Stages of Cultural Elaboration in the Pleistocene: Possible Archaeological Indications of the Development of Language Capabilities. In *Origins and Evolutions of Language and Speech,* edited by S. R. Harnad, H. D. Steklis, and J. Lancaster. *Annals of the New York Academy of Science* 280:275–288.

1977a *Oloroesailie: Archaeological Studies of a Middle Pleistocene Lake Basin in Kenya.* Chicago: University of Chicago Press.

1977b Squeezing Blood from Stones. In *Stone Tools as Cultural Markers,* edited by R. V. S. Wright, pp. 5–12. Atlantic Highlands, New Jersey: Humanities Press.

1978a The Food Sharing Behavior of Protohuman Hominids. *Scientific American* 238(4):90–106.

1978b Food Sharing and Human Evolution: Archaeological Evidence from the Plio–Pleistocene of East Africa. *Journal of Anthropological Research* 34:311–325.

1980 Casting the Net Wide: A Review of Archaeological Evidence for Early Hominid Land-Use and Ecological Relations. In *Current Argument on Early Man,* edited by L. K. Konigsson, pp. 226–253. Oxford, England: Pergamon.

1981a Archaeological Tests of Alternative Models of Early Hominid Behavior: Excavation and Experiments. *Philosophical Transactions of the Royal Society of London B* 292:177–188.

1981b Stone Age Visiting Cards: Approaches to the Study of Early Land Use Patterns. In *Pattern of the Past: Studies in Honour of David L. Clarke,* edited by Ian Hodder, Glynn L. Isaac, and N. Hammond, pp. 131–155. Cambridge, England: Cambridge University Press.

1982 Bones in Contention: Competing Explanations for the Juxtaposition of Early Pleistocene Artifacts and Faunal Remains. Paper presented to the 4th International Archaeozoology Congress, April, London.

1983a Bones in Contention: Competing Explanations for the Juxtaposition of Early Pleistocene Artifacts and Faunal Remains. In *Animals and Archaeology: Hunters and Their Prey,* edited by J. Clutton-Brock and C. Grigson. *British Archaeological Reports* 163:3–19.

1983b Review of *Bones: Ancient Men and Modern Myths. American Antiquity* 48:416–419.

1983c Aspects of Human Evolution. In *Evolution from Molecules to Men,* edited by D. S. Bendall, pp. 509–543. Cambridge, England: Cambridge University Press.

1983d Aspects of the Evolution of Human Behavior: An Archaeological Perspective. *Canadian Journal of Anthropology* 3:233–243.

1984a Picking Bones: A Reply to Lewis Binford. *American Antiquity* 49:167–168.

1984b The Archaeology of Human Origins: Studies of the Lower Pleistocene in East Africa, 1971–1981. In *Advances in World Archaeology,* Vol. 3, edited by Fred Wendorf and Angela E. Close, pp. 1–87. New York: Academic Press.

Isaac, Glynn L., and D. Crader

1981 To What Extent Were Early Hominids Carnivorous? An Archaeological Perspective. In *Omnivorous Primates: Gathering and Hunting in Human Evolution,* edited by Robert S. O. Harding and Geza Teleki, pp. 37–103. New York: Columbia University Press.

Isaac, Glynn L., J. W. K. Harris, and D. Crader

1976 Archaeological Evidence from the Koobi Fora Formation. In *Earliest Man and Environments in the Lake Rudolf Basin: Stratigraphy. Paleoecology and Evolution,* edited by Y. Coppens *et al.,* pp. 533–551. Chicago: University of Chicago Press.

Jia Lanpo, Gai Pei, and You W.

1972 Excavation Report of the Paleolithic Site of Shiyu, Shanxi (in Chinese). *Kaogu Xuebao* 1:39–58.

Jelinek, Arthur J.

1965 Lithic Technology Conference, Les Eyzies, France. *American Antiquity* 31:277–278.

1982a The Tabun Cave and the Paleolithic Man in the Levant. *Science* 216:1369–1375.

1982b   The Middle Paleolithic in the Southern Levant, with Comments on the Appearance of Modern *Homo sapiens.* In *The Transition from Lower to Middle Paleolithic and the Origin of Modern Man,* edited by Avraham Ronen. *British Archaeological Reports, International Series* 151:57–101.

Johanson, Donald, and M. Edey

1981   *Lucy: The Beginnings of Mankind.* New York: Simon & Schuster.

Johnson, L. L.

1978   A History of Flint-Knapping Experimentation, 1838–1976. *Current Anthropology* 19:337–372.

Jolly, C. J., and Fred Plog

1976   *Physical Anthropology and Archaeology.* New York: Knopf.

Jones, K. T.

1984   *Hunting and Scavenging by Early Hominids: A Study in Archaeological Method and Theory.* Ph.D. dissertation, Department of Anthropology, University of Utah, Salt Lake City.

Jullien, R., and B. Pillard

1969   Les Lagomorphes Découverts sur le Sol de la Cabane Acheuleénne du Lazaret. In *Une Cabane Acheuleénne dans la Grotte du Lazaret (Nice),* edited by H. de Lumley. *Memoires de la Société Préhistorique Française* 7.

Karlin, C., and M. Newcomer

1982   Interpreting Flake Scatters: An Example from Pincevent. *Studia Praehistorica Belgica* 2:159–165.

Kelly, Robert L.

1983   Hunter–Gatherer Mobility Strategies. *Journal of Anthropological Research* 39:277–306.

Kent, Susan

1984   *Analyzing Activity Areas: An Ethnoarchaeological Study of the Use of Space.* Albuquerque: University of New Mexico Press.

Kent, Susan, and Helga Vierich

in   The Myth of Ethnic and Economic Determinism—Anticipated Mobility and Site Organi-
press   zation of Space. In *Farmers as Hunters—The Implications of Sedentism,* edited by Susan Kent. Cambridge, England: Cambridge University Press.

Kim, W. Y., and Y. W. Chung

1978   A Preliminary Report of Chon-Gok-Ni Acheulean Biface Culture (in Korean). *Jindan Kakbo* 46–47.

Klein, Richard G.

1980   The Interpretation of Mammalian Faunas from Stone Age Archaeological Sites, with Special Reference to Sites in the Southern Cape Province, South Africa. In *Fossils in the Making,* edited by Anna K. Behrensmeyer and Andrew P. Hill, pp. 223–246. Chicago: University of Chicago Press.

Klein, Richard G.

1987   Reconstructing How Early People Exploited Animals: Problems and Prospects. In *The Evolution of Human Hunting,* edited by Matthew H. Nitecki and Doris V. Nitecki, pp. 11–45. Plenum, New York.

Klein, Richard G., and Kathryn Cruz-Uribe

n.d.   An Overview of the Torralba Fauna. In *Torralba: An Acheulian Butchering Site on the Spanish Meseta,* edited by L. G. Freeman, Jr., and F. C. Howell. Ms. in authors' possession, University of Chicago.

Kleindienst, M.

1961   Variability within the Late Acheulian Assemblage in Eastern Africa. *South African Archaeological Bulletin* 16(62):35–52.

1962   Components of the East African Acheulian Assemblage: An Analytic Approach. In *Actes du IVe Congrés Panafricain de Préhistoire et de l'Etude du Quaternaire: Section III. Pré- et Protohistoire,* edited by G. Mortelmans and J. Nenquin. *Annales Series* IN-8, *Science Humaines* 40:81–105.

Knowles, F. H. S.
1944   The Manufacture of a Flint Arrowhead by Quartzite Hammerstone. *Pitt–Rivers Museum, Occasional Papers on Technology* 1.

Knowles, F. H. S., and A. S. Barnes
1937   Manufacture of Gunflints. *Antiquity* 11(42):201–207.

Kramer, C. (editor)
1979   *Ethnoarchaeology: Implications of Ethnography for Archaeology.* New York: Columbia University Press.

Krieger, A. D.
1944   The Typological Concept. *American Antiquity* 9:271–288.

Kroeber, A. L.
1923   *Anthropology.* London: George G. Harrap.
1939   *Cultural and Natural Areas of Native North America.* Berkeley: University of California Press.

Kroll, E., and Glynn L. Isaac
1984   Configurations of Artifacts and Bones at Early Pleistocene Sites in East Africa. In *Intersite Spatial Analysis in Archaeology,* edited by H. Hietala, pp. 4–31. Cambridge, England: Cambridge University Press.

Kuhn, Thomas
1970   *The Structure of Scientific Revolutions* (2nd Ed.). Chicago: University of Chicago Press.

Lancaster, Jane
1978   Carrying and Sharing in Human Evolution. *Human Nature* 1:82–89.

Landau, M.
1981   *The Anthropogenic: Paleoanthropological Writing as a Genre of Literature.* Ph.D. dissertation, Department of Anthropology, Yale University, New Haven, Connecticut.

Larralde, Signa L.
1985a   Previous Work in the Navajo-Hopi Land Exchange Area. In The Navajo-Hopi Land Exchange Project Phase I Interim Report, edited by Eileen Camilli. Ms. on file, Bureau of Land Management, Las Cruces District Office, Las Cruces, New Mexico.
1985b   Surface Distributions and Chronological Control. Paper presented at the 50th Annual Meeting of the Society for American Archaeology, Denver.

Laville, H., J-P. Rigaud, and J. Sackett
1980   *Rock Shelters of the Perigord: Geological Stratigraphy and Archaeological Succession.* New York: Academic Press.

Leach, Edmond
1973   Concluding Address. In *The Explanation of Culture Change: Models in Prehistory,* edited by Colin Renfrew, pp. 761–771. London: Duckworth.

Leaf, M.
1979   *Man, Mind, and Science.* New York: Columbia University Press.

Leakey, Mary D.
1967   Preliminary Survey of the Cultural Material from Beds I and II, Olduvai Gorge, Tanzania. In *Background to Evolution in Africa,* edited by W. W. Bishop and J. D. Clark, pp. 417–446. Chicago: University of Chicago Press.

1971   *Olduvai Gorge: Vol. 3. Excavations in Beds I and II, 1960–1963.* Cambridge, England: Cambridge University Press.

1979   *Olduvai Gorge: My Search for Early Man.* London: Collins.

Leakey, Richard

1981   *The Making of Mankind.* New York: Dutton.

Leakey, Richard, and Roger Lewin

1977   *Origins.* New York: Dutton.

1978   *People of the Lake: Mankind and Its Beginnings.* Garden City, New York: Anchor Press/Doubleday.

Leakey, Richard, and Alan Walker

1985   *Homo erectus* Unearthed. *National Geographic* 168:624–629.

Lee, Richard B.

1968   What Hunters Do for a Living, or How to Make out on Scarce Resources. In *Man the Hunter,* edited by Richard B. Lee and Irven DeVore, pp. 30–48. Chicago: Aldine.

Lee, Richard B.

1979   *The !Kung San.* New York: Cambridge University Press.

Legge, A. J., and P. A. Rowley-Conwy

1985   Starr Carr Revisited: A Re-Analysis of the Faunal Remains. Ms. on file, Department of Continuing Education, University of London.

Leone, M. P.

1982   Some Opinions about Recovering Mind. *American Antiquity* 47:742–760.

Leone, M. P., and A. M. Palkovich

1985   Ethnographic Inference and Analogy in Analyzing Prehistoric Diets. In *The Analysis of Prehistoric Diets,* edited by R. I. Gilbert and J. H. Mielke, pp. 423–431. New York: Academic Press.

Leroi-Gourhan, A., and M. Brézillon

1972   *Fouilles de Pincevent: Essai d'Analysis Ethnographique d'un Habitat Magdalenien (la Section 36).* Paris: Centre National de la Recherche Scientifique.

Lewin, Roger

1981a   Mount St. Helens and a Climate Quandry (Research News Section). *Science* 211:371–373.

1981b   Protohuman Activity Etched in Fossil Bones. *Science* 213:123–124.

1984   Man the Scavenger. *Science* 224:861–862.

Linton, Ralph

1936   *The Study of Man.* New York: Appleton.

Longacre, William A.

1963   *Archaeology as Anthropology: A Case Study.* Ph.D. dissertation, Department of Anthropology, University of Chicago.

1981   Kalinga Pottery: An Ethnoarchaeological Study. In *Pattern of the Past: Studies in Honour of David Clarke,* edited by Ian Hodder, Glynn L. Isaac, and N. Hammond, pp. 49–66. London: Cambridge University Press.

Lovejoy, C. O.

1981   The Origin of Man. *Science* 211:341–350.

Lovett, E.

1877   Notice of the Gun Flint Manufactory at Brandon, with Reference to the Bearing of Its Processes upon the Modes of Flint-Working Practiced in Prehistoric Times. *Proceedings of the Society of Antiqueries of Scotland* 21:206–212.

Lyubin, V. P.

1977   *Must'erskie Kultury Kavkaza* (in Russian). Leningrad, U.S.S.R.: Academy of Sciences.

Marshack, Alexander

1972   *The Roots of Civilisation.* London: Weidenfeld & Nicolson.

McBurney, C. B. M., and P. Callow

1971   The Cambridge Excavations at La Cotte de Saint-Berlalade, Jersey. *Proceedings of the British Prehistoric Society* 37:167–207.

McIntosh, R. J.

1980   Review of *Living Archaeology* by R. A. Gould. *Science* 210:1117–1118.

Mech, L. D.

1966   *The Wolves of Isle Royale.* Fauna of the National Parks of the United States, Fauna Series 7. Washington, D.C.: U.S. Government Printing Office.

Meggitt, M.

1962   *Desert People.* Sydney, Australia: Angus and Robertson.

Meillassoux, C.

1973   On the Mode of Production of the Hunting Band. In *French Perspectives in African Studies,* edited by P. Alexandre, pp. 187–204. Oxford, England: Oxford University Press.

Mellars, P.

1973   The Character of the Middle–Upper Paleolithic Transition in Southwest France. In *The Explanation of Culture Change: Models in Prehistory,* edited by Colin Renfrew, pp. 255–276. London: Duckworth.

Mellor, D. H.

1982   Probabilities for Explanation. In *Theory and Explanation in Archaeology,* edited by Colin Renfrew, M. J. Rowlands, and B. Abbott-Segraves, pp. 57–63. London: Academic Press.

Merrick, H. V.

1976   Recent Archaeological Research in the Plio–Pleistocene Deposits of the Lower Omo Valley, Southwestern Ethiopia. In *Human Origins: Louis Leakey and the East African Evidence,* edited by Glynn L. Isaac and E. R. McCown, pp. 461–482. Menlo Park, California: W. A. Benjamin.

Merrick, H. V., and J. P. S. Merrick

1976   Archaeological Occurrences of Earlier Pleistocene Age from the Shungura Formation. In *Earliest Man and Environments in the Lake Rudolf Basin: Stratigraphy, Paleoecology, and Evolution,* edited by Yves Coppens *et al.,* pp. 574–584. Chicago: University of Chicago Press.

Miller, D., and C. Tilley

1984   *Ideology, Power and Prehistory.* Cambridge, England: Cambridge University Press.

Mills, M. G. L.

1978   Foraging Behavior of the Brown Hyaena (*Hyaena brunnea* Thunberg, 1820) in the Southern Kalahari. *Zeitschrift Tierpsychologie* 48:113–141.

1984a   The Comparative Behavioural Ecology of the Brown Hyaena *Hyaena brunnea* and the Spotted Hyena *Crocuta crocuta* in the Southern Kalahari. *Koedoe Supplement* 237–247.

1984b   Prey Selection and the Feeding Habits of the Large Carnivores in the Southern Kalahari. *Koedoe Supplement* 281–294.

1985   Related Spotted Hyaenas Forage Together but Do Not Cooperate in Rearing Young. *Nature (London)* 316:61–62.

Mills, M. G. L., and M. E. J. Mills

1977   An Analysis of Bones Collected at Hyaena Breeding Dens in the Gemsbok National Parks (Mammalia: Carnivora). *Annals of the Transvaal Museum* 30(14):145–157.

1978   The Diet of the Brown Hyaena *Hyaena brunnea* in the Southern Kalahari. *Koedoe* 21:125–149.

Misra, V. N., and P. Bellwood (editors)

1985   *Recent Advances in Indo–Pacific Prehistory.* New Delhi: Oxford–IBH.

Moore, J. A., and A. S. Keene

1983   Archaeology and the Law of the Hammer. In *Archaeological Hammers and Theories,* edited by J. A. Moore and A. S. Keene, pp. 3–13. New York: Academic Press.

Morris, B.

1982   The Family, Group Structuring and Trade Among South Indian Hunter–Gatherers. In *Politics and History in Band Societies,* edited by E. Leacock and R. Lee, pp. 171–187. Cambridge, England: Cambridge University Press.

Movius, Hallam L., Jr.

1944   Early Man and Pleistocene Stratigraphy in Southern and Eastern Asia. *Papers of the Peabody Museum of American Archaeology and Ethnology* 19(3).

Mulvaney, D. J.

1969   *The Prehistory of Australia.* New York: Praeger.

Munday, Frederick C.

1977   *The Mousterian in the Negev: A Description and Explication of Intersite Variability.* Ph.D. dissertation, Southern Methodist University. Ann Arbor: University Microfilms.

1979   Levantine Mousterian Technological Variability: A Perspective from the Negev. *Paleorient* 5:87–104.

Murdock, George Peter

1934   *Our Primitive Contemporaries.* New York: Macmillan.

Murdock, George Peter, and Diana O. Morrow

1970   Subsistence Economy and Supportive Practices: Cross-Cultural Codes 1. *Ethnology* 9:302–330.

Muto, G. R.

1971   A Stage Analysis of the Manufacture of Chipped Stone Implements. In *Great Britain Anthropological Conference 1970: Selected Papers,* edited by C. Melvin Aikens. *University of Oregon Anthropological Papers* 1:109–118.

Newcomer, M. H.

1970   Conjoined Flakes from the Lower Loam, Barnfield Pit, Swanscombe. *Proceedings of the Royal Anthropological Institute, 1970* 51–59.

1971   Some Quantitative Experiments in Handaxe Manufacture. *World Archaeology* 3(1):85–95.

1979   Comment on "The Clactonian: An Independent Complex or an Integral Part of the Acheulean?" by M. Y. Ohel. *Current Anthropology* 20:717.

Newcomer, M. H., and G. de Sieveking

1980   Experimental Flake Scatter Patterns: A New Interpretative Technique. *Journal of Field Archaeology* 7(3):345–352.

O'Connell, James F.

1974   Spoons, Knives, and Scrapers: The Function of Yilugwa in Central Australia. *Mankind* 9:189–194.

1977   Room to Move: Contemporary Alyawara Settlement Patterns and Their Implications for Aboriginal Housing Policy. *Mankind* 11:119–131.

1979   Room to Move: Contemporary Alyawara Settlement Patterns and Their Implications for Aboriginal Housing Policy. In *A Black Reality: Aboriginal Camps and Housing in Remote Australia,* edited by M. Heppell, pp. 97–120. Canberra: Australian Institute of Aboriginal Studies.

1980   Notes on the Manufacture and Use of a Kangaroo Skin Waterbag. *Australian Institute of Aboriginal Studies Newsletter* 13:26–29.

O'Connell, James F., and K. Hawkes

1981   Alyawara Plant Use and Optimal Foraging Theory. In *Hunter–Gatherer Foraging Strategies,* edited by B. Winterhalder and E. A. Smith, pp. 99–125. Chicago: University of Chicago Press.

O'Connell, James F., P. K. Latz, and P. Barnett

1983   Traditional and Modern Plant Use among the Alyawara of Central Australia. *Economic Botany* 37(1):80–109.

Ohel, Milla Y.

1977   Patterned Concentrations on Living Floors at Olduvai, Beds I and II: Experimental Study. *Journal of Field Archaeology* 4:423–433.

1979   The Clactonian: An Independent Complex or an Integral Part of the Acheulean? *Current Anthropology* 20:685–726.

O'Leary, Beth

1985   *Salmon and Storage: Southern Tutchone Use of an "Abundant" Resource.* Ph.D. dissertation, Department of Anthropology, University of New Mexico, Albuquerque.

Orquera, L.

1984   Specialization and the Middle/Upper Paleolithic Transition. *Current Anthropology* 25:73–98.

Oswalt, W. H.

1974   Ethnoarchaeology. In *Ethnoarchaeology,* edited by C. B. Donnan and C. W. Clewlow, Monograph IV, pp. 3–14. Los Angeles: Institute of Archaeology, University of California.

Paddayya, Katradagga

1982   The Lower/Middle Palaeolithic Transition in the Hunsgi Valley, Peninsular India. In *The Transition from Lower to Middle Paleolithic and the Origin of Modern Man,* edited by Avraham Ronen. *British Archaeological Reports, International Series* 151: 257–264.

Patrik, L. E.

1985   Is There an Archaeological Record? In *Advances in Archaeological Method and Theory,* Vol. 8, edited by Michael B. Schiffer, pp. 27–62. New York: Academic Press.

Pearson, Michael Parker

1982   Mortuary Practices, Society and Ideology: An Ethnoarchaeological Approach. In *Symbolic and Structural Archaeology,* edited by Ian Hodder, pp. 99–113. Cambridge, England: Cambridge University Press.

Pei, Wen Chung, and Senshui Chang

1985   *A Study on the Lithic Artifacts of Sinanthropus* (in Chinese). *Palaeontologia Sinica* 168D(12).

Perkins, D., and P. Daly

1968   A Hunters' Village in Neolithic Turkey. *Scientific American* 219(5):97–106.

Perper, T., and Carmel Schrire

1977   The Nimrod Connection: Myth and Science in the Hunting Model. In *The Chemical Senses and Nutrition,* edited by M. Kare and O. Maller, pp. 447–459. New York: Academic Press.

Pfeiffer, John E.

1978   *The Emergence of Man* (3rd Ed.). New York: Harper & Row.

1982 *The Creative Explosion.* New York: Harper & Row.

Piperno, M., and G. M. Piperno

1974 First Approach to the Ecological and Cultural Significances of the Early Palaeolithic Occupation Site of Garba IV at Melka Kunture (Ethiopia). *Quarternaria* 18:347–382.

Pond, A. W.

1930 Primitive Methods of Working Stone, Based on Experiments of Halvor L. Skavliem. Logan Museum, Beloit College, Bulletin 2(1).

Popper, K.

1959 *The Logic of Scientific Discovery.* New York: Harper & Row.

1972 *Objective Knowledge: An Evolutionary Approach.* Oxford, England: Oxford University Press.

Potts, Richard B.

1982 *Lower Pleistocene Site Formation and Hominid Activities at Olduvai Gorge, Tanzania.* Ph.D. dissertation, Department of Anthropology, Harvard University, Cambridge, Massachusetts.

1983 Foraging for Faunal Resources by Early Hominids at Olduvai Gorge, Tanzania. In *Animals and Archaeology: Hunters and Their Prey,* edited by J. Clutton-Brock and C. Grigson. *British Archaeological Reports* 163:51–62.

1984a Home Bases and Early Hominids. *American Scientist* 72:338–347.

1984b Hominid Hunters? Problems of Identifying the Earliest Hunter/Gatherers. In *Hominid Evolution and Community Ecology,* edited by Robert Foley, pp. 128–166. New York: Academic Press.

Potts, Richard B., and P. Shipman

1981 Cutmarks Made by Stone Tools on Bones from Olduvai Gorge, Tanzania *Nature (London)* 291:577–580

Price, T. Douglas and James A Brown (editors)

1985 *Prehistoric Hunter–Gatherers: The Emergence of Cultural Complexity.* New York: Academic Press.

Purdy, B. A.

1981a *Pyrotechnology: Prehistoric Applications to Chert Materials in North America. Early Pyrotechnology.* Washington, D.C.: Smithsonian Institution.

1981b *Florida's Prehistoric Stone Technology.* Gainesville: University Presses of Florida.

Putnam, Patrick

1963 The Pygmies of the Ituri Forest. In *A Reader in General Anthropology,* edited by Carleton S. Coon, pp. 322–342. New York: Holt, Rinehart & Winston.

Qui, Zhonglang

1985 The Middle Palaeolithic of China. In *Palaeoanthropology and Palaeolithic Archaeology in the People's Republic of China,* edited by Wu Rukang and John W. Olsen, pp. 187–210. New York: Academic Press.

Raab, L. M., and A. C. Goodyear

1984 Middle Range Theory in Archaeology: A Critical Review of Origins and Applications. *American Antiquity* 49:255–268.

Radcliffe-Brown, A. R.

1930 The Social Organisation of Australian Tribes. *Oceania* 1:34–63.

1956 On Australian Local Organization. *American Anthropologist* 58:363–367.

1965 *Structure and Function in Primitive Society.* New York: Free Press.

Rathje, William A., and Michael B. Schiffer

1982 *Archaeology.* New York: Harcourt Brace Jovanovich.

Richardson, P. R. K.

1980a   Carnivore Damage on Antelope Bones and Its Archaeological Implications. *Paleontologica Africana* 23:109–125.

1980b   *The Natural Removal of Ungulate Carcasses, and the Adaptive Features of the Scavengers Involved.* M.S. thesis, Faculty of Science, University of Pretoria, South Africa.

Rigaud, J.-P.

1982   *Le Paléolithique en Périgord: Les Données du Sud-Ouest Sarladais et Leur Implications.* Ph.D. dissertation, University of Bordeaux, France.

Rightmire, G. P.

1981   *Homo erectus* at Olduvai Gorge, Tanzania. In *Homo erectus: Papers in Honor of Davidson Black,* edited by B. A. Sigmon and J. S. Cybulski, pp. 189–192. Toronto: University of Toronto Press.

Rivers, W. H. R.

1912   The Disappearance of Useful Arts. In *Festskrift Tillägnad Edvard Westermarck,* pp. 109–130. Helsingfors, Finland. (Reprinted in 1931 in *Source Book in Anthropology,* edited by A. L. Kroeber and T. T. Waterman, pp. 524–534. New York: Harcourt Brace.

Roe, Derek A.

1981   *The Lower and Middle Paleolithic Periods in Britain.* London: Routledge & Kegan Paul.

1982   The Transition from Lower to Middle Palaeolithic, with Particular Reference to Britain. In *The Transition from Lower to Middle Paleolithic and the Origin of Modern Man,* edited by Avraham Ronen. *British Archaeological Reports, International Series* 151:177–190.

Rosenzweig, Michael L.

1974   *And Replenish the Earth: The Evolution, Consequences, and Prevention of Overpopulation.* New York: Harper & Row.

Rouse, Irving

1939   Prehistory in Haiti: A Study in Method. Yale University Publications in Anthropology 21.

1960   The Classification of Artifacts in Archaeology. *American Antiquity* 25:313–323.

Runes, Dagobert D.

1979   *Dictionary of Philosophy* (reprint of 1962 edition). Totawa, New Jersey: Littlefield, Adams.

Sackett, James R.

1977   The Meaning of Style in Archaeology: A General Model. *American Antiquity* 42:369–380.

1982   Approaches to Style in Lithic Archaeology. *Journal of Anthropological Archaeology* 1:59–112.

1985   Style and Ethnicity in the Kalahari: A Reply to Wiesnner. *American Antiquity* 50:154–159.

1986a   Style, Function and Assemblage Variability: A Reply to Binford. *American Antiquity* 51:628–634.

1986b   Isochrestism and Style. *Journal of Anthropological Archaeology* 5:266–277.

Saitta, D. J.

1983   The Poverty of Philosophy in Archaeology. In *Archaeological Hammers and Theories,* edited by J. A. Moore and A. S. Keene, pp. 299–304. New York: Academic Press.

Salmon, M. H.

1982a   Models of Explanation: Two Views. In *Theory and Explanation in Archaeology,* edited by Colin Renfrew, M. J. Rowlands, and B. Abbott-Segraves, pp. 35–44. London: Academic Press.

1982b   *Philosophy and Archaeology.* New York: Academic Press.

Sampson, C. G.

1974   *The Stone Age Archaeology of Southern Africa.* New York: Academic Press.

Sankalia, H. D.

1974   *Prehistory and Protohistory of India and Pakistan* (2nd Ed.). Poona, India: Deccan College Press.

Schiffer, Michael B.

1975   Factors and Tool Kits: Evaluating Multivariate Analysis in Archaeology. *Plains Anthropologist* 20(67):61–70.

1976   *Behavioral Archaeology.* New York: Academic Press.

1981   Some Issues in the Philosophy of Archaeology. *American Antiquity* 46:899–908.

1985   Review of *Working at Archaeology* by L. R. Binford. *American Antiquity* 50:191–193.

Schleicher, C.

1927   Un Industrie Qui Disparaît: La Taille des Silex Modernes. *L'Homme Préhistorique* 14(5):113–133.

Schrire, Carmel (editor)

1984   *Past and Present in Hunter Gatherer Studies.* New York: Academic Press.

Science News

1981   The Giant Gelada Murder Mystery . . . and Possible Evidence for Meat Eating (Anthropology Section). *Science News* 120:15.

Scott, Katharine

1980   Two Hunting Episodes of Middle Paleolithic Age at la Cotte de Saint-Berlade, Jersey. *World Archaeology* 12:137–152.

1986   Review of *Faunal Remains from Klasies River Mouth* by L. R. Binford. *Journal of Archaeological Science* 13:89–100.

Service, Elmer

1962   *Primitive Social Organization: An Evolutionary Perspective.* New York: Random House.

Shipman, P.

1981a   Applications of Scanning Electron Microscopy to Taphonomic Problems. *Annals of the New York Academy of Sciences* 276:357–385.

1981b   *Life History of a Fossil: An Introduction to Vertebrate Taphonomy and Paleoecology.* Cambridge, Massachusetts: Harvard University Press.

1983   Early Hominid Lifestyle: Hunting and Gathering or Foraging and Scavenging? In *Animals and Archaeology: Hunters and Their Prey,* edited by J. Clutton-Brock and C. Grigson. *British Archaeological Reports* 163:31–49.

1984a   Early Hominid Lifestyle: The Scavenging Hypothesis. *AnthroQuest* 28:9–10.

1984b   Ancestors: Scavenger Hunt. *Natural History* 93(4):20–27.

1986   Scavenging or Hunting in Early Hominids Theoretical Framework and Tests. *American Anthropologist* 88:27–43.

Shipman, P., and J. Rose

1983   Evidence of Butchery and Hominid Activities at Torralba and Ambrona: An Evaluation Using Microscopic Techniques. *Journal of Archaeological Science* 10:465–474.

Shipman, P., W. Bosler, and K. L. Davis

1981   Butchering of Giant Geladas at an Acheulian Site. *Current Anthropology* 22:257–268.

1982   Reply to Binford and Todd, "On Arguments for the 'Butchering' of Giant Geladas." *Current Anthropology* 23:110–111.

Silberbauer, George B.

1972   The G/wi Bushmen. In *Hunters and Gatherers Today,* edited by M. G. Bicchieri, pp. 271–326. New York: Holt, Rinehart & Winston.

Simek, Jan F.

1984   A K-Means Approach to the Analysis of Spatial Structure in Upper Paleolithic Habitation Sites. *British Archaeological Report* 205.

Singer, R., and J. Wymer

1982   *The Middle Stone Age at Klasies River Mouth in South Africa.* Chicago: University of Chicago Press.

1986   On Binford on Klasies River Mouth: Response of the Excavators. *Current Anthropology* 27:56–57.

Smith, B.

1982   Explanation in Archaeology. In *Theory and Explanation in Archaeology,* edited by Colin Renfrew, M. J. Rowlands, and B. Abbott-Segraves, pp. 73–82. London: Academic Press.

Soffer, Olga

1985   *The Upper Paleolithic of the Central Russian Plain.* New York: Academic Press.

Spaulding, Albert C.

1953a   Review of "Measurements of Some Prehistoric Design Developments in the South-eastern States" by James A. Ford. *American Anthropologist* 55:588–591.

1953b   Statistical Techniques for the Discovery of Artifact Types. *American Antiquity* 18:305–313.

1954a   Reply to Ford. *American Antiquity* 19:391–393.

1954b   Reply to Ford. *American Anthropologist* 56:112–114.

1960   The Dimensions of Archaeology. In *Essays in the Science of Culture: In Honor of Leslie A. White,* edited by Gertrude E. Dole and Robert L. Carneiro, pp. 437–456. New York: Crowell.

Spencer, B., and F. J. Gillen

1899   *The Native Tribes of Central Australia.* London: Macmillan.

1912   *Across Australia,* Vol. 2. London: Macmillan.

Speth, John D.

1983   *Bison Kills and Bone Counts: Decision-Making by Ancient Hunters.* Chicago: University of Chicago Press.

Speth, John D., and G. A. Johnson

1976   Problems in the Use of Correlation for the Investigation of Tool Kits and Activity Areas. In *Culture Change and Continuity: Essays in Honor of James Bennett Griffin,* edited by C. E. Cleland, pp. 35–57. New York: Academic Press.

Speth, John D., and Katherine A. Spielmann

1983   Energy Source, Protein Metabolism, and Hunter–Gatherer Subsistence Strategies. *Journal of Anthropological Archaeology* 2:1–31.

Stanislawski, Michael B.

1975   What You See Is What You Get: Ethnoarchaeology and Scientific Model Building. Paper presented at the 40th Annual Meeting of the Society for American Archaeology, Dallas.

Stanner, W.

1965   Aboriginal Territorial Organization: Estate, Range, Domain, and Regime. *Oceania* 35:1–26.

Stocking, G. W.

1974   *A Franz Boas Reader: The Shaping of American Anthropology, 1883–1911.* Chicago: University of Chicago Press.

Straus, Lawrence

1977   Of Deerslayers and Mountain Men: Paleolithic Faunal Exploitation in Cantabrian Spain. In *For Theory Building in Archaeology: Essays on Faunal Remains, Aquatic Resources, and Systemic Modeling,* edited by Lewis R. Binford, pp. 41–76. New York: Academic Press.

1987   Upper Paleolithic Ibex Hunting in Southwest Europe. *Journal of Archaeological Science* 14:163–178.

Tanner, N.

1981   *On Becoming Human.* Cambridge, England: Cambridge University Press.

Tanner, N., and A. Zihlman

1976   Women in Evolution: Part I. Innovation and Selection in Human Origins. *Signs* 1:585–608.

Taylor, Walter W.

1948   A Study of Archaeology. Memoir of the American Anthropological Association No. 69. *American Anthropologist* 50(3), Part 2.

Testart, A.

1982   The Significance of Food Storage among Hunter–Gatherers: Residence Patterns, Population Densities, and Social Inequalities. *Current Anthropology* 23:523–537.

Thomas, David Hurst

1975   Nonsite Sampling in Archaeology: Up the Creek Without a Site? In *Sampling in Archaeology,* edited by James W. Mueller, pp. 61–81. Tucson: University of Arizona Press.

1983   The Archaeology of Monitor Valley: 2. Gatecliff Shelter. *Anthropological Papers of the American Museum of Natural History* 59 (Part 1).

Thompson, R. H.

1956   The Subjective Element in Archaeological Inference. *Southwestern Journal of Anthropology* 12:327–332.

Tilley, C.

1982   Social Formation, Social Structures, and Social Change. In *Symbolic and Structural Archaeology,* edited by Ian Hodder, pp. 26–38. Cambridge, England: Cambridge University Press.

Tindale, N. B.

1965   Stone Implement Making Among the Nakako, Ngadadjara and Pitjandjara of the Great Western Desert. *South Australian Museum Records* 15(1):131–164.

1974   *Aboriginal Tribes of Australia.* Canberra: Australia National University Press.

Tixier, J., M. L. Inizan, and H. Roche

1980   *Préhistoire de la Pierre Taillée: I. Terminologie et Technologie.* Paris: Cercle de Recherches de d'Etudes Préhistoriques.

Todd, Lawrence C., Jr.

1983   *The Horner Site: Taphonomy of an Early Holocene Bison Bonebed.* Ph.D. dissertation, University of New Mexico. Ann Arbor: University Microfilms.

Todd, Lawrence C., and David J. Rapson

1987   Preliminary Summary of Bugas-Holding Site Butchery Patterns. Ms. on file, Department of Anthropology, University of Wyoming, Laramie.

Tonkinson, R.

1978   *The Mardudjara Aborigines: Living the Dream in Australia's Desert.* New York: Holt, Rinehart & Winston.

Tooby, J., and Irven DeVore

1987   The Reconstruction of Hominid Behavioral Evolution through Strategic Modeling. In *The Evolution of Human Behavior: Primate Models,* edited by Warren G. Kinzey, pp. 183–237. Albany: State University of New York Press.

Torrence, Robin

1983   Time Budgeting and Hunter–Gatherer Technology. In *Pleistocene Hunters and Gatherers in Europe,* edited by G. Bailey, pp. 11–22. New York: Cambridge University Press.

Toth, Nicholas

1982   *The Stone Technologies of Early Hominids at Koobi Fora, Kenya: An Experimental Approach.* Ph.D. dissertation, Department of Anthropology, University of California, Berkeley.

1983   Review of *Bones: Ancient Men and Modern Myths. Appetite: Journal of Intake Research* 4(1):51–56.

1985   The Oldowan Reassessed: A Close Look at Early Stone Artifacts. *Journal of Archaeological Science* 12:101–120.

Toth, Nicholas, and Kathy D. Schick

1986   The First Million Years: The Archaeology of Protohuman Culture. In *Advances in Archaeological Method and Theory,* Vol. 9, edited by Michael B. Schiffer, pp. 1–96. New York: Academic Press.

Tribe, D. E., and L. Peel

1963   Body Composition of the Kangaroo (*Macropus* sp.). *Australian Journal of Zoology* 11(2):273–289.

Trigger, Bruce

1978   *Time and Tradition: Essays in Archaeological Interpretation.* New York: Columbia University Press.

Trinkaus, Erik

1975   Squatting Among the Neanderthals: A Problem in the Behavioral Interpretation of Skeletal Morphology. *Journal of Archaeological Science* 2:327–351.

Tuffreau, Alain

1982   The Transition Lower/Middle Palaeolithic in Northern France. In *The Transition from Lower to Middle Paleolithic and the Origin of Modern Man,* edited by Avraham Ronen. *British Archaeological Reports, International Series* 151:137–149.

Tylor, E. B.

1881   *Anthropology: An Introduction to the Study of Man and Civilization.* New York: Appleton.

Urquhart, I. A. N.

1951   Some Notes on Jungle Punans in Kapit District. *The Savawak Museum Journal* 5(3):495–523.

Valoch, Karel

1982   The Lower/Middle Palaeolithic Transition in Czechoslovakia. In *The Transition from Lower to Middle Paleolithic and the Origin of Modern Man,* edited by Avraham Ronen. *British Archaeological Reports, International Series* 151:193–201.

Vandermeersch, B.

1984   A Propos de la Decouverte du Squelette Neandertalien de Saint Cesaire. *Bulletin et Memoire de la Société d'Anthropologie de Paris* 14(1):191–196.

Villa, Paola d'Amelio

1978   *The Stone Artifact Assemblage from Terra Amata: A Contribution to the Comparative Study of Acheulian Industries in Southwestern Europe.* Ph.D. dissertation, University of California, Berkeley. Ann Arbor: University Microfilms.

Walker, A.

1981   Koobi Fora Hominids and Their Bearing on the Origins of the Genus *Homo.* In *Homo erectus: Papers in Honor of Davidson Black,* edited by B. A. Sigmon and J. S. Cybulski, pp. 193–215. Toronto: University of Toronto Press.

Wandsnider, LuAnn

1985   Geomorphological Processes and the Integrity of Archaeological Remains in Dune Fields. Paper presented at the 50th Annual Meeting of the Society for American Archaeology, Denver.

Washburn, S. L., and C. S. Lancaster

1968   The Evolution of Hunting. In *Man the Hunter,* edited by Richard B. Lee and Irven DeVore, pp. 293–303. Chicago: Aldine.

Watanabe, Hitoshi

1969   Neanderthalers vs *Homo sapiens:* Behavioral Adaptability to Arctic Winter. *Proceedings of the 8th International Congress of Anthropological and Ethnological Sciences, Tokyo/Kyoto (1968)* 3:280–283.

1985   The Chopper–Chopping Tool Complex of Eastern Asia: An Ethnoarchaeological–Ecological Reexamination. *Journal of Anthropological Archaeology* 4:1–18.

Watson, P. J.

1979   The Idea of Ethnoarchaeology: Notes and Comments. In *Ethnoarchaeology: Implications of Ethnography for Archaeology,* edited by Carol Kramer, pp. 277–287. New York: Columbia University Press.

1982   Review of *Living Archaeology* by Richard Gould. *American Antiquity* 47:445–448.

1986   An Archaeological Odyssey. *Reviews in Anthropology* 13(4):263–270.

Watson, P. J., S. LeBlanc, and C. L. Redman

1971   *Explanations in Archaeology: An Explicitly Scientific Approach.* New York, Columbia University Press.

Weaver, K. F.

1985   The Search for Our Ancestors. *National Geographic* 168:560–623.

Wendt, H.

1956   *In Search of Adam.* Boston: Houghton Mifflin.

Whallon, Robert, Jr.

1973   Spatial Analysis of Occupation Floors I: Applications of Dimensional Analysis of Variance. *American Antiquity* 38:266–278.

White, E., and D. M. Brown

1973   *The First Men.* The Emergence of Man Series. New York: Time–Life Books.

White, Leslie A.

1949   *The Science of Culture: A Study of Man and Civilization.* New York: Farrar, Straus & Giroux.

White, Randall

1982   Rethinking the Middle/Upper Paleolithic Transition. *Current Anthropology* 23:169–192.

1985   Thoughts on Social Relationships and Language in Hominid Evolution. *Journal of Social and Personal Relationships* 2(1):95–115.

Wiessner, Polly

1982   Beyond Willow Smoke and Dogs' Tails: A Comment on Binford's Analysis of the Hunter–Gatherer Settlement Systems. *American Antiquity* 47:171–178.

1983   Style and Social Information in Kalahari San Projectile Points. *American Antiquity* 48:253–276.

1985   Style or Isochrestic Variation? A Reply to Sackett. *American Antiquity* 50:160–165.

Will, R. T.

1984   *Nineteenth-Century Copper Inuit Subsistence Practices on Banks Island, Northwest Territory.* Ph.D. dissertation, University of Alberta, Calgary.

Williams, M. A. J., F. M. Williams, F. Gasse, G. H. Curtis, and D. A. Adamson

1979   Post-Pleistocene Environments at Gadeb Prehistoric Site, Ethiopia. *Nature (London)* 282:29–39.

Wissler, C.

1914   Material Cultures of the North American Indians. *American Anthropologist* 16:447–505.

Woodburn, J.

1968   An Introduction to Hadza Ecology. In *Man the Hunter,* edited by Richard B. Lee and Irven DeVore, pp. 49–55. Chicago: Aldine.

1980   Hunters and Gatherers Today and Reconstruction of the Past. In *Soviet and Western Anthropology,* edited by Ernest Gellner, pp. 95–117. London: Duckworth.

1982   Egalitarian Societies. *Man* 17:431–451.

Wright, J. V.

1977   Trends and Consequences in Canadian Prehistory. *Canadian Journal of Archaeology* 1:1–14.

Wylie, M. Alison

1982a   Epistemological Issues Raised by a Structuralist Archaeology. In *Symbolic and Structural Archaeology,* edited by Ian Hodder, pp. 39–46. Cambridge, England: Cambridge University Press.

1982b   An Analogy by Any Other Name Is Just as Analogical: A Commentary on the Gould–Watson Dialogue. *Journal of Anthropological Archaeology* 1:382–401.

1985   The Reaction against Analogy. In *Advances in Archaeological Method and Theory,* Vol. 8, edited by Michael B. Schiffer, pp. 63–111. New York: Academic Press.

Wymer, John

1968   *Lower Paleolithic Archaeology in Britain as Represented by the Thames Valley.* London: Baker.

1983   The Lower Paleolithic Site at Hoxne. *Proceedings of the Suffolk Institute of Archaeology and History* 35:168–189.

Yallop, C.

1969   The Alyawara and Their Territory. *Oceania* 39:187–197.

Yellen, John E.

1972   Trip V Itinerary, May 24–June 9, 1968. In *The Exploring Human Nature Educational Series.* Cambridge, Massachusetts: Educational Development Center.

1977a   *Archaeological Approaches to the Present: Models for Reconstructing the Past.* New York: Academic Press.

1977b   Cultural Patterning in Faunal Remains: Evidence from the !Kung Bushmen. In *Experimental Archaeology,* edited by D. Ingersoll, John E. Yellen, and W. MacDonald, pp. 271–331. New York: Columbia University Press.

Zihlman, A.

1981   Women as Shapers of the Human Adaptation. In *Woman the Gatherer,* edited by F. Dahlberg, pp. 75–120. New Haven, Connecticut: Yale University Press.

Index